THE SUPER SUMMARY OF WORLD HISTORY

REVISED

THE SUPER SUMMARY OF WORLD HISTORY

REVISED

WITH A STRONG EMPHASIS ON WESTERN EUROPEAN AND AMERICAN HISTORY

COMPLETELY REWRITTEN AND UPDATED
BY

ALAN DALE DANIEL, BA, MBA, JD

Library of Congress Control Number: 2008904529
ISBN: Hardcover 978-1-4363-4326-8
Softcover 978-1-4363-4325-1
Ebook 978-1-4500-6251-0

This book was printed in the United States of America.

To order additional copies of this book, contact:
Xlibris Corporation
1-888-795-4274
www.Xlibris.com
Orders@Xlibris.com
49740

Contents

Time Line of World History

3.7 Million BC *Australopithecus* in Africa (dates in dispute). Modern human type footprints dated to 3.7m yrs? Hummm . . . . *Based on latest theories of anthropology (2010, but these too are disputed).* Translation: this too will change.

1.8 Million BC *Homo erectus* (dates in dispute), another proto human

350,000 BC Proto-Neanderthals Appear in Europe

130,000 BC Prehistory Starts—Africa—*Homo sapiens* appear.

45,000 BC *Homo sapiens* Appear in Europe

30,000 BC Cave Paintings—First Art *Lascaux*, France

20,000 BC Ice Age (latest) at its height

15,000 BC Coldest Era of the Ice Age Ends. General warming trend starts

10,000 BC Ice Age (latest) *interglacial* begins.

16,000 BC Homo Sapiens appear in North America (dates in dispute) Some in 20,000 BC?

Neolithic Revolution 8500 BC Agriculture and Animal Husbandry—The most important event in history

8000 BC Pottery In China

5000 BC Copper In Wide Use

3500 BC Writing Begins in Sumer—Middle East on Euphrates River.

3200 BC Bronze In Use—Middle East

3100 BC Egypt United by Menes—First Pharaoh (King actually)

2500 BC Yao Dynasty Founded in China

2371 BC Sargon of Agade Invades Sumer—First conqueror.

2000 BC Abraham Leaves Ur for Canaan (dates not certain)

1250 BC City of Troy destroyed by Greeks (Trojan War)

1250 BC Massive eruption of island of Thira. Destroys Crete civilization

1206 BC Collapse of Bronze Age Culture All around Mediterranean.

600 BC Mayan Civilization in Mexico

753 BC Rome Founded on Tiber River

600 BC Lao Tzu Founds Taoism In China

563 BC Birth of Gautama Buddha. Dies 483 (dates at issue). Start of Buddhist Religion.

549 BC Confucius Teaches In China

490 BC Battle of Marathon—Persia's first invasion in Greece

480 BC Warring States Period In China

480 BC Xerxes Invades Greece—Second Persian invasion

334 BC Alexander the Great Conquers Persia (Dies 323 BC)

264-146 BC Punic Wars Rome fights Carthage for rule of Med

206 BC Han Dynasty—China Beginning of Civil Service

116 BC Rome at Its Height—Emperor Trajan

44 BC Caesar Murdered

2-4 BC Jesus Christ Born (Dies about AD 36?) (Dates in dispute)

All dates AD from here on . . .

AD 33-36 Jesus Was Crucified—Followers proclaim Resurrection (dates in dispute). Start of Christian Religion.

400 Japan United Under Yamato Clan

452 Plagues Start Sweeping Across Europe

455 Fall of the Western Roman Empire—Date is somewhat arbitrary. Start of the Dark Ages

570 Birth of Muhammad. (Dies 632) Start of Muslim Religion.

670 Silla Clan Unites Korea

700 Muslims Ban Use of Greek Language

711 Muslim Invasion of Spain

732 Charles Martel Wins Battle of Tours—Muslims turned back, Europe saved

793 Viking Raids on Europe Begin

1066 Normans Invade England—Last successful invasion of England

1095 Crusades Begin

1150 Little Ice Age Begins

1206 Genghis Khan Made Ruler of Mongols

1240 Mongols Sack Kiev in Russia

1241 Mongol Invasions of Europe—Mongols win at Legnica

1241 Mongols at the Gates of Vienna—Death of Odegei Khan saves Europe

1279 Mongol Empire at Its Height—Control Silk Road to China

1279 Kublai Khan (Mongol) Conquers South China—Southern Song Dynasty falls
1291 Crusades End

1300 The Renaissance Starts in Italy and spreads through Europe

1341 Black Death in China—1348 Black Death strikes Egypt

1350 Black Death in Europe—Last of the plagues sweep Europe

1368 Ming Dynasty—China

1430 Printing Press Invented Gutenberg

1440 Aztecs in Mexico

1451 Durer Born (Dies 1528)—Artist

1453 Fall of Constantinople—Ottoman Turks then invade Europe

1475 Michelangelo Was Born (Dies 1654)

1492 Columbus Discovers America—Thought he had reached India
Columbus: he started out not knowing where he was going, when he got there he didn't know where he was, when he got back he didn't know where he had been, and he did it all on borrowed money. Now there's a great man!
1500 Start of the Age of Empires

1508 Battle of Du—Vasco de Gama defeats Muslims at Sea

1517 Martin Luther Rebels against Catholic Church—Nails ninety-five theses to church door—Start of Protestant Reformation

1518 Conquistadores in Mexico—Cortez: Pazarro in Peru 1531

1519 Magellan Sets Sail to Circumnavigate the Globe

1522 Magellan's Expedition Returns to Europe—but Magellan Died in the Philippines

1533 Henry VIII (England) Adopts Protestant Religion

1553 Shakespeare Born in England

1588 Spanish Armada Sails for England—ships do not return

1600 Battle of Sekigaharea Japan Establishes Tokugawa Shogunate

1606 Rembrandt Was Born (Dies 1669)

1611 King James Bible Printed

1618 Thirty Years War Begins—Ends in 1648 (fought in Europe)

1642 English Civil Wars Begins—Ends in 1649 (fought in England)

1661 Louis XIV Born—King of France The "Sun King" dies 1715.

1756 Seven Years War in Europe (French and Indian War in United States)—France and UK in world war.

1775 Battles at Lexington and Concord—American Revolution starts

1776 US Declaration of Independence
Official separation from Britain—human rights derived from God, not government

1777 Battle of Saratoga—French decided to support United States in Revolutionary war

1783 Simon Bolivar Was Born—Frees Latin America. Dies 1830

1788 US Constitution Ratified—1789 Washington elected first president

1789 French Revolution Begins

1793-94 Reign of Terror in France

1799 Napoleon Bonaparte—Establishes military dictatorship—end of the French Revolution

1812 Napoleon Invades Russia—Defeated & loses his vast army & his Empire.

1812 War of 1812 US v Great Britain

1814 First Steam Locomotive—England Industrial Revolution well underway

1815 Battle of Waterloo—Napoleon defeated for last time. (Dies 1821)

1815 Congress of Vienna—Establish European peace for ninety-nine years (WWI ends the peace)

1819 Simon Bolivar Begins Liberation of Latin America

1825 Erie Canal Opens—Connects NY to Great Lakes

1837 Telegraph Invented 1844—Morse patents telegraph in United States

1839 Photography Invented In France—Daguerreotype.

1846 Mexican-American War Ends in 1848—Mexico cedes southwest to US

1848 Marks & Engle Publish *Communist Manifesto*

1850 **Little Ice Age Ends**

1861 US Civil War Begins—Ends April 1865

1869 Transcontinental RR Complete (United States of America)

1874 Impressionists' First Exhibit In Paris, France.

1871 Bismarck Declares German Empire

1883 Hiram Maxim Invents Machine Gun

1885 Daimler Invents Internal Combustion Engine In Germany

1893 New Zealand Gives Women the Vote. Why?—1st nation to allow women to vote

1898 Spanish-American War—Philippines to United States

1900 Max Plank's Quantum Theory—The subatomic world's "laws"

1900 Freud Publishes *The Interpretation of Dreams*

1903 Wright Bro's First Powered Aircraft Flight—Kitty Hawk, North Carolina

1905 Einstein's Theory of Relativity—New "laws" of the universe

1910 Cubism (painting) Picasso and Braque—Artists

1913 Stravinsky's "The Rites of Spring" Symphony causes riots

1914 Archduke Ferdinand Assassinated—The Black Hand's murder starts WWI

1914 August, World War I Begins—2,250 die each day on Western Front

1917 Communist Revolution in Russia—USSR

1917 USSR Sues for Peace with Germany—Lenin first leader in USSR

1917 United States Enters WWI on Allied Side—Zimmerman telegram, code breakers

1918 Germany Sues for Peace—Ending WWI

1919 Versailles Treaty Ends WWI—US Senate disapproves. U. S. signs separate peace with Germany

1919 Influenza Pandemic—Worldwide 50,000,000 to 100,000,000 deaths

1920 US Women Get the Vote. France gives women vote. Why?

1920 Radio Broadcasting Begins

1927 First Talking Movies

1929 Great Depression—US stock market crash

1933 Adolf Hitler Elected Chancellor in Germany

1933 Roosevelt Elected President of USA—In office until death in 1945

1939 September, World War II Begins—Hitler orders invasion of Poland

1940 June, France Falls

1941 June, Hitler Invades USSR*—Dooms Nazi Germany*

1941 December 7, Japan Attacks USA at Pearl Harbor

1942 June, Battle of **Midway.** Japan loses 4 aircraft carriers.

1943 German Sixth Army Surrenders at Stalingrad—Initiative to USSR in the East

1943 May, German U-boats Defeated in Battle of Atlantic

1944 June 6, Allied forces Land in France D-Day—Nazi's now in an Allied vice

1945 February, USMC Lands on Iwo Jima.—Raise US Flag on Mount Suribachi

1945 May, Germany Surrenders—Hitler kills himself and wife in bunker

1945 August, Atomic Bombs Dropped on Japan—Hiroshima, Nagasaki, destroyed

1945 Japan Surrenders—World War II ends

1945 Cold War Begins

1948 State of Israel Established

1949 China Falls to Mao and Communists—Major cold war defeat for USA

1950 Korean War Begins—UN reacts and sends troops

1951 Red China Enters Korean War—US intelligence failure

1953 Korean War Cease-fire—War technically never ended

1954 French Defeat at Dien Bien Phu

1955 US Civil Rights Movement Underway—*Brown vs. Board of Education* (May, 1954)

1957 First Satellite in Orbit—USSR launches *Sputnik*

1960 Senator John Kennedy Elected as US President—Defeats Vice President Nixon

1962 Kennedy Commits US Troops to Vietnam

1963 November, Kennedy Assassinated—L. B. Johnson becomes US President.

1964 Johnson Wins US President—Increases troop levels in Vietnam

1964 Civil Rights Act Passes US Congress—First of several Civil Rights Acts

1967 Antiwar Protests in United States Growing—Johnson states he will not run in 1968

1968 January, Tet Offensive, So Vietnam—***United States wins battle, press reports defeat***

1968 Nixon Wins US Presidential Election—H. Humphrey loses (Dem)

1969 US Moon Landing: Armstrong & Aldrin First men on another world

1973 United States Out of Vietnam—North Vietnam signs peace treaty

1973 Nixon Resigns Office of President—Watergate Scandal

1974 Internet Protocol Suite Invented—*Start of the Internet (TCP/IP)*

1975 North Vietnam Invades South Vietnam—The South falls.—Massacres by North.

1979 USSR Invades Afghanistan—Fights until 1989 (end USSR and cold war) then leaves

1980 Ronald Reagan Elected President—Defeats USSR in cold war (ends in 1989)

1981 Reagan Begins Arms Race with USSR. Goal: destroy USSR economically (it worked)

1987 World Population Reaches *5 Billion* (that's a lot of people!)

1989 Soviet Union (USSR) Falls—End of cold war

1992 Internet Goes from Near 0 usage to 350 million in 2006

2000 George Bush (Second) Elect President—Florida vote count disputed

2001 Terrorist Attack World Trade Center—How important in world history? Too soon to tell.

2008 B. Obama elected. 1st Black President of USA—Triples US national debt

---

Not all events in this time line are covered in the text.

Taking the Long View

After about 1980, it is difficult to say what we are studying is "history" because it is still within the lifetimes of most people, and in such cases the **"long view"** of history is lost. In fact, I would have to say that anything occurring after 1950 is probably not history. It is best that "history" is written by people who were not alive at the time of the events and not affected by the emotions of the time including emotions passed down from their parents or their friends. My writings herein on Vietnam suffer from the prejudices of my age and my political positions both at the time of the war and now in the aftermath of the war and its perceived impact on the war in Iraq and the War on Terror. Even writing about the Great Depression is somewhat hard because my dad was alive during the Depression and told me a lot about his experiences during that time; thus, my view is colored by those remembrances. However, no one is ever free of prejudices and history has a lot to do with forming those prejudices. Nonetheless, I have written this history to include the Cold War up to its end in 1989 but very little thereafter. So, readers, beware of what anyone says about events within their lifetime. The long view will sort it all out. For now, be aware that like it or not my prejudices will come through no matter how much I try to suppress them. This is true of everyone, although some may be better at avoiding the pitfalls than others. The key is to be aware that no one is without a point of view, and most people who want to write about anything have very strong points of view. Awareness is the key. Have fun!

AD^2

Introduction

We are going to do an extreme summary of world history with a heavy concentration on Western Europe and the United States of America. Using this method, we will first lay a foundation so the pieces of history will have a place to fit as we study them. It is like looking at the picture before you build a puzzle; it makes it easier. After reading this summary you should be able to pick up any detailed history book and quickly understand where the era fits into the total stream of history.

A little background on your author will help you understand his point of view. I was born in 1947 in Bakersfield, California, my dad died just after I graduated from High School, I earned a BA in history from San Fernando Valley State College (California State Northridge now) by working my way through, and then, from 1970 to 1975, I served as a helicopter pilot for the United States Marine Corps. While in the marines, I went to night school and earned my MBA from Pepperdine University. After the marines, I attended law school, obtained a JD from Pepperdine University School of Law in 1978, and passed the California bar that same year. I was a California attorney for over twenty-five years in both private and public practice. The City Attorney's Office for the city of Bakersfield hired me in 1984 and I spent twenty years as their water law attorney (among many other things) leaving the city in 2004.

My thesis study for my history degree was Herodotus, probably the greatest historian ever, even though Thucydides was probably just as good. Both Greeks, both fun to read, and both about as impartial as a person can get while still breathing.

In this work I attempt to be impartial, as all historians should; however, I am prejudiced as all of us are, and by knowing that I am a staunch conservative Republican and a Christian will aid you in processing my writings, helping you know why I think some things are very important and others not so much. I like to compare events. How were the priesthoods in Egypt and the Dark Ages alike? Why didn't China fall, as Rome did, into a complete collapse after conquest from outside invaders? Art in Europe seems to predict the future, but art in the East does not. Why is this? And so on.

By comparing cultures and trying to notice similarities and differences between them, we can learn at a deeper level than simply memorizing bare sets of facts.

The history of our world can be divided into sections, and here are the ones we will use:

Prehistory (before the written word—150,000 BC to about 8000 BC in the near east)

> The most important events in human history occur here: agriculture, writing, societal organization

Ancient history (8000 BC to about AD 455 or the fall of Rome)

> The rise of cities and complex administrative organizations

The Dark Ages (AD 455 to AD 1300)

> The failure and disintegration of Roman Western civilization and societal organization in Europe.

Renaissance (AD 1300 to AD 1500)

> Rediscovering ancient wisdom and moving beyond, with the help of science and the printing press

Age of Discovery to World War I (1500 to 1914)

> Europe finds out that the world is a large place, and then devours it while building a golden age of progress

World War I (1914 to 1918)

> WWI cracks the Western world, then the Great Depression shatters it as the West totters on the brink of total economic and social collapse

Interwar Years and World War II (1918 to 1945)

> The entire world tumbles into another total war, and then crawls over broken landscapes into the future

Cold War (1945 to 1989)

> As the world rebuilds and rearranges itself, a twilight war rages menacing all, and after it fades the future darkens yet again with new threats of religious wars without end

Postmodern History (End of the cold war in 1989 and beyond . . . well, a little beyond)

> Technology makes breathtaking advances while humanity's thoughts grow cold and dark. New wars erupt with new methods of killing. What will rule the future, destruction or progress? Does progress really exist?

The invention of agriculture and animal husbandry was THE most important event in secular history. The invention of writing and the invention of the printing press were some of the next most important events, but nearly every historian will agree that without agriculture and animal husbandry the world would be a far different place. Religious folks will say the advent of their religious leader, such as Jesus Christ, Mohammad, or Buddha for example, was by far the most important event in history; however, that leads to a decision based solely on religion and a religious leader's impact. A Christian is not going to say the birth of Buddha was more important than the birth of Jesus. Because of this, I will stay away from proclaiming the start of a religion as the most important event in history although the start of the great religions truly was of immense importance.

Just for fun, let's guess at the top twenty events in world history (based on how they influence our present world), in order of importance (religion excluded). Here is my list. Does your list match?

TOP 20 EVENTS IN HISTORY (MY OPINION)

1. *The Invention of Agriculture and Animal Husbandry (8,500 BC). The Neolithic Revolution.* This will also include the invention of spoken language, the wheel, metallurgy, social order (government), and the idea of god and an afterlife (maybe), to name a few other "minor" items that go along with 8500 BC. *As far as importance, nothing else comes close.*
2. *The invention of writing (5,000 BC).*
3. *The invention of the Printing Press (AD 1430).*

4. *The Discovery of the Scientific Method (AD 1469,* Natural History *published).*
5. *Tesla & Electricity Generation (AD 1881, first US Electrical power plant).*
6. *World War I, and World War II (AD 1914-1945).*
7. *World Population explosion (AD 1800 on).*
8. *The Start of the Latest Interglacial Period (15,000 BC).*
9. *The Fall of the Western (AD 455) and the Eastern Roman Empire (AD 1453).*
10. *The Discovery of the New World (AD 1492).*
11. *The Industrial Revolution (AD 1804, first locomotive)*.
12. *The Black Plague (AD 1341 China, 1347 Europe).*
13. *Pasteur's theory of germs (AD 1864).* Start of medical advances.
14. *The Invention of Flight (AD 1903).* Leads to satellites, moon landing, jet aircraft etc.
15. *The rise of Megacities (AD 1950).*
16. *The Invention of the Microprocessor (AD 1971, first types).*
17. *The Invention of the telephone (AD 1876).* Leads to radio, TV, cell phones, etc.
18. *Plato, Aristotle (429 BC).* Philosophy begins.
19. *The Theory of Relativity and Quantum Mechanics (AD 1905).* Start of modern science.
20. *The Invention of the Internet (AD 1974).*

---

21. *The philosophic/religious Wars of Communism (1917)*

Some of these items, such as the telephone, represent the start of a tremendous advance covering many areas. Religious events are excluded. Which was more important, the birth of Christ, Mohammad, Buddha, or Lao Zi? All this will depend upon one's religious beliefs, so all of them are excluded.

In this study of history, I conclude that **people are both rational and irrational.** In matters of science, engineering, and basic economic decisions people are at least 80 percent rational; however, in matters of politics, religion, social interaction, philosophy, and law people are at least 80 percent irrational. This dualistic nature of humankind is the source of many problems, and it is seemingly part of our genes. In this case, rational means the actions (or events, or results) can be understood on many levels by most people, can be copied for the betterment of all (or the vast majority), and can be built upon for advancement. Irrational is the opposite in that the actions cannot be understood on any level by most people, and if copied or built upon would bring immense harm.

Throughout this history I have sacrificed exactness for readability. Many statements are "slam dunk," such as, in the reign of Augustus, the Pax Romana ushered in two hundred years of peace. Well, in fact, it did not because there was at least one civil war within the empire and other minor wars on the boarders, but to go into all the detail would destroy the readability of the text and ruin the super summary concept.

I apologize for the quality of the maps herein. Please use the Internet references to see the maps (and photographs) in full color, and in a size that is easy to read. The Internet, especially Wikipedia and Olga's Gallery (http://www.abcgallery.com), is a wonderful source for viewing historical art in full color.

Good reading!

AD^2

Dedications

To: My Wife, ***Lori***, who puts up with all this history stuff, and her grandson Zimri (Z-man) for all the joy he brings into our lives.

To: *Clarice Young*, who read over endless amounts of text looking for errors, and was good-natured about it. How do people do that? And to Charlie Young, whose thoughts helped me delve deeper into history.

To: Dr. *Sally A. Schumacher*, my high school history teacher who taught me to love history, and *Mrs. Grey* my grade school teacher who saved my academic life when she had the South High School counselors put me into college prep classes—over their objections.

To: *Sam McCall*, of Bakersfield Jr. College who taught me to look at the big picture in history, and to the *entire staff of Bakersfield Jr. College* who were nonpareil in their instruction of this struggling and starving student.

To: Rita Rowland, Gary Lack, Allen Shaw, Gary Fachin, Tim Otto, Trudy Slater, Debbie Lund (faithful secretary and proof reader), Christopher Noyes, the Gifford family who saved me from starving while I was in college, especially Gail, Glen Spickler who looked after me in times of need, the Honorable Richard Oberholzer, Milo Hall, Dennis Sherman, a Bible teaching pastor, Ralph Kahlen and his dad who told me about the Eastern Front in WWII, Connie L. Daniel (mother), James R. Daniel (father), James K. Daniel (son), Cristin Daniel (daughter), Charlie Daniel (brother), and other friends too numerous to mention who have supported my fascination with history—or at least put up with it.

Thank You, thank you, one and all.

AD2

CHAPTER 1

PREHISTORY 150,000 BC TO 3,500 BC (APPROXIMATE)

Going back to the very beginning of time we discover the **Big Bang** started the entire universe off about 13 to 15 billion years ago. Currently accepted theories (Einstein's Theories of Relativity for example) hold that our entire universe started out as a point far smaller than the period at the end of this sentence—in fact, smaller than an atom. Before the Big Bang space, time, and matter did not exist—at least as we know them. Then, for unknown reasons, the small point began to expand rapidly. An "explosion," of sorts took place and the entire universe began to expand from that infinitesimal point. Researchers studying space are discovering leftovers from the big bang; for example, the cosmic radiation present everywhere we look in space. Scientists are finding numerous other proofs of this long past mysterious event; thus, the Big Bang theory enjoys wide scientific support. It is difficult to imagine stuffing all the matter from over 200 billion galaxies into an area much smaller than a pinpoint. Nonetheless, that is where our theories and our mathematics leave us. Thus, the mystery lingers.

While many interesting things go on in the first few billionths of a second after the Big Bang occurred one phenomenon is especially intriguing—**inflation.** As originally proposed, the Big Bang theory could not explain the universe as it exists now. Explaining the present nature of our universe required something more, for example, why does the universe have a uniform temperature, how could atoms come into existence, and the how did the basic forces controlling matter come about? Mr. Alan Guth, a physicist, came up with an explanation now termed "inflation." Mr. Guth theorized that at 10^{-36} (that means a 10 with 36 zeros after it) of a second after the Big Bang the universe accelerated its speed of expansion, and this speed was incredibly different from

the normal speed of the expansion—*faster than the speed of light.* At 10^{-34} of a second this acceleration (inflation) stopped. Thus, for something like three times less than a trillionth of a second the universe expanded at a rate more than 100 times greater than normal, then it went back to its normal rate of expansion. Without this inflationary period our universe would not exist. Alternatively, if the inflation took place for a different length of time our universe would not exist. Fundamentally, any change in the time of inflation destroys the ability of matter and atoms to come into existence. Brian Greene has a good explanation of this phenomenon for the non-scientist in *The Elegant Universe,* Greene, Vintage Books, 2003, page 355 et seq.

Our universe contains mysteries so deep that we earthlings may not solve them. As we have seen, the Big Bang theory states the universe started with a massive "explosion" of sorts; then, as the universe sailed off creating space, time, matter, and whatnot it cooled off and began to form atoms. From those atoms the universe, and our small blue world, were constructed—we think. What we measure and study here on earth is the framework for exploring the known universe; however, recent discoveries call into question the assumption that the universe works the same in deep space as it does here on earth. Astronomers discovered that the galaxies we observe are not slowing down as they travel away from one another—they are speeding up! As we know from watching explosions here on earth, gravity slows down the flying debris and soon the explosion is over. If gravity acts the same way in deep space the galaxies should be slowing down, but they are not. Astronomers say this acceleration is a function of "dark energy," an unexplained force in the universe. In another problem, astronomers found that atoms make up only four percent (4%) of the universe. The rest of the universe is some kind of "dark matter." As dark matter and dark energy are concepts without foundations here on earth they are beyond scientific explanation at this point in time. In fact, they are little more than names. These mysteries may defy solution if we fail to reach beyond our solar system.

Here we may note the vastness of the universe. One light year is about six trillion miles, and it takes 100,000 light years to cross the **Milky Way**—our galaxy. The Milky Way may contain as many as 3 trillion stars (suns). From our sun it would take about 26,000 light years to reach the center of our galaxy. Our sun, which is at the end of one of several arms spiraling out from the center of our galaxy, revolves around the center of the Milky Way about once every *220 million years.* The size of the universe is tough to determine, but the observable matter is about *93 billion light years across.* Even our solar system is large. Neptune, the most distant planet from the sun in our system, is 2.8 billion miles away. No matter how one slices it the universe is a **big** place.

As the universe formed our solar system fell into place with its planets circling a medium sized yellow sun. Our earth circles in the diminutive life zone at the perfect distance from our sun. The moon, one of the largest and closest orbiting objects anywhere in the solar system, probably formed after a collision between earth and some other earth-sized planet. As the two planets blasted into one another the moon tore away, and by some means the earth managed to acquire more iron from the striking planet thereby creating an especially large iron core. This outsized iron core produces unusually strong magnetic fields which shield the earth from deadly cosmic rays. Without this large iron core no life would exist on this planet. This scenario is not fact, it is one of several theories trying to explain the uniqueness of our water-covered planet. After everything had formed up and the surface of the earth cooled enough the march to life began . . . somehow. It is extremely hard to say how. No one knows how life first formed or how it came to be so complex so quickly. The theory of evolution tries to explain the development of life after it began; however, it has no application to the question of how life started.

History deals with people and not the physical events described above, but knowing the earth is a rocky planet with water—lots of water—at the exact position in the solar system it needs to be, and with many exceptional features that sustain life, helps us understand the uniqueness of our planet and thus ourselves. Even our universe is exceptional. For life to exist anywhere in the universe several of its most fundamental properties must be present at pinpoint exactness. To illustrate: the relationship between the strong nuclear force and the electromagnetic force[1] could not vary by even one part in 10 to the 16th power (10^{16}), otherwise life would not exist on our planet or anywhere else. Commentators and scientists remark that perhaps the most amazing thing about the universe is that it is understandable. Somehow, mere people—less than a flea speck in the universe—figured out how the universe works. These patterns ordering our universe are dense and intricate beyond all imagination, nevertheless, on both the subatomic and universal level the patterns are there. Because our species discovered these breathtaking patterns *we know chaos does not rule our universe or our world. Why* our world and the universe are so well ordered on so many levels cannot be explained by science.

---

[1] The four fundamental forces in the universe: gravity, the strong and weak nuclear forces, and the electromagnetic force.

Now, on to people, their decisions, and history.

For our purposes, prehistory starts about 150,000 BC when modern man comes onto the scene, and ends about 3,500 BC when writing makes its appearance in Sumeria—according to widely accepted current theories. By definition, *history must revolve around the written word.* Without the written word history, as we will use the term in this study, does not exist. When we say writings we mean text by someone who lived at or near in time to the events, and who witnessed or participated in the events or at least talked with those who did. In this way we can attempt to reach back into the past and pull up the thoughts, sights, emotions, and actions of those who were there. We cannot understand the ancient mind very well even with these writings, because their lives were so different from ours. Can we really know what is was like to live in a hut covered with animal hides, hunt for our food, drink from mud holes, and live in fear of the noises of the night? Until people start writing down their thoughts we must simply guess at what went on inside their heads.

Please be acutely aware of *how inaccurate most dates are in prehistory and ancient history.* Even though the dates seem to be precise numbers (2071 BC for example) most of them are rough educated guesses. Kings lists are good points to pin past events on *if* you know when at least one of the kings lived, but often we do not. A chronicler may say King Joe lived 50 years, but this may be an estimate by the ancient writer based on hearsay rather than personal knowledge.

From the writings of our forefathers we have proof that one thing never seems to change, at least from the time that writing began, and that one thing is **human nature**. From the earliest written legends to our latest 3D movies the nature of people remains a constant. What it was like at the very beginning of human existence is speculation, but once writing begins it is apparent that human nature remains unchanged throughout history. The mind of humanity remains remarkably consistent (or is that inconsistent . . .); accordingly, the fundamental thoughts and emotional processes of our ancient brethren are the same as ours today.

Before proceeding to the arrival of *Homo sapiens sapiens*[2] into Europe we should mention one proto human type that existed, more or less unchanged, for over *one million years—Homo erectus* (upright man). This

2 The repeated word *sapiens*—meaning wise—is correct, but hereinafter we will stick to one *sapiens* after *Homo.*

archaic human type spread throughout the old world including China (Peking man, 600,000 BC), but did not manage the trek to the Americas. *Home erectus* was a fire user[3], built dwellings (some of impressive size up to fifty feet in length), carved wood into spears and bowls, used stone hand axes, and lived in groups. The ability to use fire is a big deal.[4] With fire *Home erectus* could ward off the cold, keep dangerous animals away, and light the night . . . at least a little bit. Art, at least sophisticated art, is missing from the evidence of *Homo erectus.* Modern humans alone seem to have the ability or desire to create detailed and refined art. One amazing fact about this ancestor (latest theory) is he lasted so long. *Homo erectus* is thought to have been around for over 1 million years and may have overlapped modern man by 50 or 60 thousand years or more. *Homo sapiens* have been around for about 150,000 years. Compared to the one million plus years for *Homo erectus* modern man has barely started.

Another interesting proto human was the **Neanderthal**. Neanderthals had, on average, a brain as large as *Homo sapiens.* Neanderthals inhabited Europe and areas as far east as Palestine by about 200,000 BC. After modern humans arrived in Europe about 50,000 BC Neanderthals went extinct, although some claim they intermingled with *Homo sapiens* making Neanderthals part of the modern human genome. If modern man and Neanderthals interbred this would mean they were the same species and should all be identified as *Homo sapiens.* Interbreeding is difficult to prove, nevertheless, modern DNA research is showing there are genetic similarities. Both *Homo sapiens* and Neanderthals are said to have the gene for speech, and a few researchers think that intermingling caused the gene sharing; however, all this is speculation and other investigators can cite evidence pointing to extinction.

Researchers using modern methods to image the human brain have recorded areas that are more active than others when the brain is involved in certain tasks. The doctors conclude the brain's pre-frontal cortex (front part of the brain) is the center for generating long-term goals and analyzing

---

3 There are some indications in Java that Homo erectus was still around forth to fifty thousand years ago. For a completely different take on ancient man and the case for different time frames for human existence, see *Bones of Contention,* Lebenow, Baker Books, 2004 or *Icons of Evolution: Science or Myth, Why Much of What We Teach About Evolution Is Wrong,* Wells, Regnery Publishing, 2002. Another alternate explanation is *Darwin's Black Box, The Biochemical Challenge to Evolution,* Behe, Free Press, 2006.

4 Used fire, but they did not make fire. It seems the art of creating fire from scratch was not mastered.

how to achieve them. This area also manages the ability to learn from the past. It is also one of the most modern areas of the brain; that is, the newest or most recently evolved (*Change Your Brain, Change Your Life*, Dr. Amen, 1998, Three Rivers Press). If this is so, we can speculate that *Homo erectus* may have lacked a developed pre-frontal cortex, thus lacking the ability to set goals far into the future and work toward achieving them as easily as *Homo sapiens.* Because of the developed pre-frontal cortex, *Homo sapiens* may have learned from previous errors far easier than *Homo erectus.* These two traits alone may account for the dominance of modern man over this successful but now obsolete predecessor.

The first true "humans" were the *Homo sapiens* and they developed in Africa (says the latest theory) by around 150,000 BC, then spread to Europe about 50,000 BC. We classify this period as the Old Stone Age or the **Paleolithic** because of the type of tools used and the houses *Homo sapiens* lived in. As the human race advanced and the tools and houses became more sophisticated humanity moved into the Middle Stone Age or **Mesolithic**. The final era of the stone ages is the **Neolithic** or New Stone Age, again classified by the tools used and houses lived in. The chart below may help the reader understand the three stone ages.

Paleolithic	2.5 million years BC to 80,000 BC	Types of Tools: Pebble tools to Acheulian hand axe
Mesolithic	80,000 to 10.000 BC	Types of Tools: blade tools, micro-lithe blades formed
	15,000 BC	Coldest period of Ice Age ends
	10,000 BC	Interglacial begins
Neolithic	10,000 to 5000 BC	Types of Tools: obsidians and flint blades well made pottery, and **agriculture**.

(All dates approximate)

Note, the New Stone Age brings in agriculture; and this was the greatest advance in the long history of humanity.

In prehistory there is no writing, and this makes investigating the era especially hard. We do have bits of physical evidence left by prehistoric peoples and it tells us a lot. People lived in groups, learned to build houses with hearths and shelves, and often buried their dead in cemeteries. Some graves contained bodies along with jewelry and clothing. Other burials involved cremating the body and placing the ashes into urns, followed by a burial of the urn (the Urnfield culture). Artistry included brightly colored realistic pictures inside caves, impressive carvings, and pottery. Our ancestors constructed very simple to very sophisticated stone tools, consumed a large variety of animals, grains, nuts, fish, and fowl from the areas they inhabited, and they eventually developed trade with other sets of people outside their area. Archeologist have found woven and died clothing dating from 26,000 BC, and clay cooking pots from 12,500 BC. These assertions are based on solid physical evidence from archeological sites, accordingly, there is little speculation about the fundamental facts; however, some books and articles on prehistory are based on the surmises of those studying the period, and this guesswork is *not* fact.

FIGURE 1 NEOLITHIC CAVE PAINTING 30,000 BC
(SEE FRONT COVER FOR COLOR)

Let us discuss an illustration of speculation. Beautiful cave paintings found in France (Lascaux) and Spain date from **30,000 BC**. The paintings are far inside the caves in all but inaccessible places. Animals and animal life are the main subjects, and some are painted with what appear to be spears or arrows in the animals. The infrequently depicted people are poorly drawn stick figures. Nearly everyone writing about the paintings classify them as high art or art with a ritual purpose. The best paintings are beautiful, containing well-executed color usage and lifelike qualities for the animals; however, are they the Rembrandts of their era? Could the paintings be graffiti placed there by wayward youths? After all, graffiti in large cities is often well executed, colorful, and generally pleasing except for its location.

Most textbooks explain that the paintings were spiritual in purpose, and played a vital part in tribal customs; however, ***without writing we do not know why*** these paintings came to be, and explanations telling us why are speculation.[5] Thus, student of history, beware of those telling you what no one can possibly know.

The history of the human race is short in comparison to its prehistory. If we start with *Homo erectus* there are well over one million years in prehistory, and about five thousand years for history. In addition, the world's most important inventions and discoveries take place in prehistory. The invention of agriculture, animal husbandry, the wheel, the discovery of how to make and use fire, how to mine and refine metals, the invention of language, and the invention of writing all take place in prehistory. It was in the prehistoric era that humans began burying their dead, establishing early cities, and developing new ways of living together. Every foundational theme underlying the human race began in prehistory.

During the prehistoric era humans must have engaged in mass migrations that eventually led to *Homo sapiens* covering the globe by about 9,000 BC. Anthropologist theorize that modern humans originally migrated out of Africa into the Middle East and Europe, thereafter into Russia, India, China, Indochina, the Pacific Ocean area, including Australia, and finally across the Bering Sea to North and then South America[6]. Great disagreements exist over the timing of the crossing to North America with the old theories

---

5 Prior to this, art in any form is nearly nonexistent. It seems proto-humans were not able to create art or what they did create was lost. Note this art is a form of communication and can tell us a lot about the world at the date it was made. These wonderful cave paintings, in full color, are at http://www.wikipedia.org/wiki/History_of_painting.

6 Current theory (AGAIN). Please note that the current theory means the *current widely accepted theory*. There are always many other theories around, but one is generally the current accepted theory (meaning widely accepted). EVERYTHING is open to better theories, but most never make it because they cannot overcome the current widely accepted theory. I now theorize this is getting dull . . .

claiming a 10,000 BC crossing, but newer theories putting the migration at 16,000 BC or earlier. No one is certain what happened because time covers up a lot of evidence; thus, the activities and movements of the earliest humans are largely unknown. Another set of facts lost to time is how humans developed into three races. As early humans are so few it seems they had to start as one race, separating out thereafter; however, all our explorations have failed to find a widely accepted explanation for racial differences in humans.

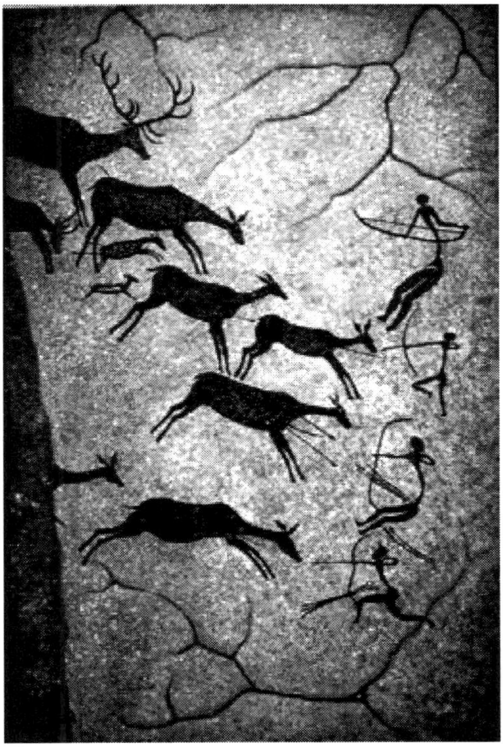

FIGURE 2 CAVE PAINTING 30,000 BC, VALTORTA CAVE

There are certain fundamental processes that identify the human race. Wherever *Homo sapiens* have wandered we find important fundamental traits—here is a list of 10 important ones:

TEN HUMAN TRAITS

1. Art—*Homo sapiens* constantly create beautiful things. Rock carvings and paintings, statuettes, antler carvings, flutes, bead necklaces,

and rope adornments of all kinds. This is not an exhaustive list, but art is a common commodity with modern humans. Not so with proto humans as we find almost no art from their era, and the few samples we do find are not sophisticated.

2. Buildings—Humans like to construct shelters. Some of the most impressive structures were the mammoth bone houses put together by early hunters. As time went forward the buildings became more elaborate. Some proto-humans managed to construct long houses and huts, but only modern humans construct monuments like the Mayan pyramids in Meso-America or the skyscrapers of Chicago.
3. Machines—mankind has moved forward using machines. Some machines are very simple like the bow and other extremely complex like a moon rocket, but only machines allowed people to advance from the caves to the stars. The invention and use of ever more impressive machines is *the* hallmark of human kind. There are *six basic machines*: the wheel and axial, the lever, inclined plane, wedge, pulley, and screw. From these seemingly easy ideas men reached the moon and sent machines beyond our solar system.
4. Governments—wherever humans go, at least since the advent of writing, we find governance. For good or evil people organize. Groups form and leaders emerge. Then the leaders assume the task of making sure the group prospers. Once government is in place it never goes away, unless by annihilation through disease, disaster, or enemy action—after which it soon returns.
5. Communication—people not only organize they communicate with one another in various ways. The spoken word for communication purposes (language) starts about 250,000 BC. The fact that humans organized into groups leads to speculation that language was required; however, it is nearly impossible to know when true language use started. What is clear is that the development of language with its ability to transfer exacting ideas between people was a key turning point in human development (Hey, that's my chicken!). Homo sapiens would have problems moving beyond the caves without language because ideas would remain locked away in the individual's head. Sharing knowledge and ideas moves us forward.
6. Social Organizations—before written history people grouped themselves together by kinship, family and tribe, at least as far as anyone can tell from ancient indications of kinship. The earliest humans and proto humans buried their dead, often in cemeteries and sometimes placing more than one individual into a grave. This

might indicate kinship. After writing developed we see that clans, tribes, and kin are the basic organizational units of society. From what we can tell, this has been true for 50,000 years or more.

7. Warfare—From the start killing other humans was common. Early on the fights were most likely small, but as soon as large civilizations came about large wars became common. The more organized the civilization the larger the wars.
8. Religion—is a constant with *Homo sapiens.* Even proto humans buried their dead with what appears to be personal items. As soon as writing begins we read references to gods. Strangely, from many early human societies we find that the gods demand blood sacrifice. In some cases the preferred blood was human. Even in Meso-America, far away in time and distance from Europe and Mesopotamia, blood was necessary to appease the gods. Why this is part of early religion remains a mystery.
9. Desire for more—this is another constant with *Homo sapiens.* Somehow, what is there is never enough. Humans were always going forward to the next horizon both physically and mentally. Of course, not all fit into this category, but it is a most common human trait. Only people seem to have this kind of desire. Ants and bees build and they search for other locations for their habitation; however, they simply reproduce what has gone before. Humans want to make what has gone before obsolete, just like the computer you bought yesterday.
10. Time—it seems humans have always recognized the concept of time. Early monuments tract the sun and calendars are early inventions of many civilizations. The knowledge that time moves, things change, and people die has a profound effect on human thinking, and human thinking is the key stuff of history.

NEOLITHIC REVOLUTION—AGRICULTURE 8,500 BC

After modern humans established themselves the world over they were still hunters and gatherers. In Europe during the Neolithic Age, bands of people were settling into at least semi-permanent dwellings, using bones and hides of the woolly mammoth to cover living areas that contained fire pits and storage. Graveyards start appearing near the ancient villages. In some burials all the heads are facing in the same direction, beads often cover the body, and the corpse often had personal items such as hairbrushes, shoes, bows, spears and the like, buried with it.

In Europe farming was slow to develop, however, in the warmer regions of the world a new farming lifestyle was starting about 8,000 BC on the Tigris and Euphrates Rivers in the Middle East, the Nile River in Egypt, and the Indus River on the Indian subcontinent. People began founding permanent living places with cultivated crops grown in the rich soils of these river valleys, and they acquired herd animals for meat, hides and milk. The crops might have been growing wild in these areas and humans developed the idea of planting the seeds of these wild plants so they could control their growth. By planting the seeds at a certain time of year they would all come to ripeness at the same time thereby allowing the people to harvest them all at once, and giving the farmers a great surplus of food. By somehow storing the extra grain (maybe in clay pots) they could survive the winter (non-growing) season. With goats or cattle for milk, meat, and hides the stationary folks could build a nice life without the necessity of following the herds as a hunter-gatherer society must. By abandoning the nomadic life people could build permanent structures to live in, accumulate more goods, and have a lot more to eat. By constructing irrigation systems the sedentary types could increase their crop yields and the amount of land under cultivation. Their biggest problems may have involved how to store the surplus so it would not spoil. Much of this is speculation because it all happened in prehistory; accordingly, we cannot know the true sequence of events. What we do know is these permanent communities grew in size to become the first cities.

Around 8,500 BC at the walled city of **Jericho**, in the Jordan Valley of modern day Israel, domesticated cereals made their appearance. Jericho was a 10 acre walled citadel where we find the first evidence of settled farming based on domesticated corps.

The most important event in the existence of humanity was the invention of agriculture and animal husbandry, which started about 8,500 BC. I cannot emphasize this enough. Food was and is the underpinning of every human activity. Western society is currently awash in food, and we do not think of it as the foundation for all we see around us. The discovery of agriculture made an abundance of food possible. Before farming, people in hunter-gatherer groups spent their time hunting or preparing to hunt. Meat is hard to store for long periods without refrigeration (or even with it), thus, tribes had to follow the herds if one wanted to stay near the grocery store, so to speak.

With agriculture and animal husbandry creating a food surplus people could sit out harsh times and survive. A surplus of food allowed the *specialization of work,* as some people could do work unrelated to hunting or farming.

Now the person who excelled at making shoes could do that and the farmer could use his surplus to purchase the shoes. The net result was the farmer had food and very good shoes, and the shoemaker had food, very good shoes, and could spend his time doing what he did best. Others could use their time to trade with far away peoples who had resources, such as metal, the locals did not have. **Refining metal ore** into copper, bronze, or iron was a time-consuming task and required a lot of skill. People busy hunting all day would have problems mining the ore and refining it, not to mention the movement from area to area would prevent the investment in tools or skills needed to mine and refine the ore. Once people acquired permanent homes a few people could invest their time in *mining* and developing the skills to make copper or bronze objects because the metal items would sell at a high price, thus giving the metalworker a good return on his time and resource investment. In fact, the development of metallurgy was vital to the advance of stationary civilizations. The foundations of a modern specialized economy started prior to written history with the growth of cities and specialization of work.

The growing towns soon had permanent structures, specialists in many crafts, and built-in incentives to invent new ways of working and living. One of the new ideas involved **writing**, and that was the start of history because people began keeping track of what was going on around them. People may have tried putting things in writing as far back as 6,000 BC, but the real development took place in the Middle East in the Euphrates River area about **3,500 BC in Sumer**. It was a big step toward the modern world.

Meanwhile, in Europe, prehistory went on except with a twist. Even though Europe seemed to lag behind in many skills of civilization—including writing—they managed to build massive stone structures about the same time as Mesopotamia and Egypt were constructing enormous structures. Erecting stone circle **megaliths**, such as Stonehenge, took place about 2,600 BC. The first signs of construction at Stonehenge are from nearly 8,000 BC. There are thousands of these stone structures with a geographic range from the Mediterranean through France, Spain, Denmark, England and Scandinavia. Discovering the purposes for these massive stone works has proved elusive, but they resemble nothing else from that period found anywhere else on earth. It is clear, or as clear as prehistory can be, that the idea for these stone monuments arose from inside Europe. Europe

remained in the non-writing, or prehistoric, stage for many centuries after writing developed in the Middle East, the Mediterranean, China, and India. Why Europe beyond the Mediterranean took so long to enter the historic era is hard to explain, especially when the European tribes had shown themselves capable of constructing the colossal megaliths.

These large stone circles may have had ritual purposes or may have been solar calendars; however, it is very hard to discern the reasons for the construction because of the lack of written records. There is a wide "road" connecting Stonehenge to a nearby site; thus, these two sites may have a complex ritualistic connection. It is fair to say that whatever the purpose for the construction the effort involved was gigantic, and required an organization of community talent and creativity that was remarkable for the time.

Africa spent nearly all of its existence in the pre-writing or prehistoric "era," with the notable exceptions of Egypt and Carthage in North Africa. This is difficult to imagine, since humanity itself is said to have originated in Africa. Sub-Saharan Africa seems locked in the moment without the need to develop writing. Our history will largely ignore Africa, South America, the Pacific Ocean areas, and Central Asia (Siberia and the lands east of the Ural Mountains). No one recorded what happened in these vast areas; thus, there is no "history." The final analysis involves *impact on history,* and the high civilizations developed in the Middle East, Egypt, India, China, Greece, Rome, and the nearby surrounding areas had the real historic impact. Africa, northern Europe, the interior of Asia from Mongolia to the Urals, the Pacific Ocean areas, and all of the Americas have little or no impact on history before AD 1000, and many of these areas (Africa, South America, the Pacific) had little impact right up to the modern era.

DIFFERING VIEWS OF HISTORY

Before we get too far in our story, we need to point out that we can view history in at least three fundamentally different ways. We will start with the **cyclic view**. Modern historians and many great civilizations, such as India, support this idea. In the cyclic view history moves like a great wheel, constantly repeating itself. The cycles are not exactly the same each time, but much like the seasons they repeat consistently even though the details may differ. The second great idea is history moves like an **ascending line**. In this view history is advancing somewhere, even though that somewhere may be unknown. Thus, history has a purpose. Christian theology sees history this way, as do the Jews, Muslims, and several philosophers such as Karl Marx. Under this way of thinking, history will reach a climactic moment after which all will stabilize or completely end. The Mayans of Central America also saw history this way, and thought it would all end in disaster in December of 2012. Many of these concepts about history purposefully advancing somewhere revolve around an end of the world scenario, such as the return of Jesus Christ or a cataclysmic end of everything like the Maya. Under the theories of Marx, the world was advancing to a worker's utopia. Of course, there is also the Chaos (**Post-modern**) view shared by overburdened, coerced, history students and the indefatigable Homer Simpson who imagine history as a stack of irrelevant, unconnected, and meaningless events unworthy of notice—much less a grade. To quote Homer Simpson, "It's just a bunch of stuff that happened." While Homer is making it sound funny, in fact the Post-modern view is quite prevalent. In this view, history has no turning points, shows no purpose, displays no repeating patterns, and there is really no such thing as progress. This is the Post-modernist view of no mega-narratives, that is, no over arching pattern or theme. History is a series of "fractured narratives" (*The Times History of the World,* Overy, page xvii).

Arguing any of these theories presents little challenge. History, as we know it in 2010, fits none of the categories perfectly. Those claiming repetition have an endless number of past civilizations as proof, and those saying history is advancing to an end must await that event because there is no other way to know if they are right. Saying history is a bunch of stuff that happened, without patterns or themes, is another idea that will have to wait for a non-end. Hard to do.

Let Us Learn From History

What can we learn from Pre-history? Remember that unknown and unrecorded events have large impacts on history, thus your actions, even if unrecorded, will have an influence on the future for good or evil. Someone had to be the first farmer. Thank goodness for that ancestor. Because of that person we have enough food to avoid hunting every day of our lives. Be thankful for nice living accommodations. By nice, I mean anything better than a hole with dry grass for a floor. Even very small things in our lives, such as indoor running water and flushing toilets, would be magical to our prehistoric ancestors. Think upon how great we have it, and it is all because those unknown guys and gals so long ago never gave up trying to do better. (What did the gals do? Naturally, they nagged the guys for more stuff.)

BOOKS AND REFERENCES:

http://www.txstate.edu/anthropology/cas/cas_projects.html—or for photos of Acheulian hand axes and other Paleolithic artifacts.

Or see *http://www.txstate.edu/anthropology/cas/cas_projects.html* for similar stone age objects.

The New Penguin History of the World, Roberts, J. M, Penguin Books, 2007. Foundational.

The National Geographic Almanac of World History, Daniels and Hyslop, National Geographic, Washington, DC.

The Times Complete History of the World, Richard Overy, Barnes and Noble, New York, 2007.

The Outline of History, the Whole Story of Man, Vol. 1 & 2, by H.G. Wells, Doubleday and Company, 1956. These volumes have been brought up to date, at least to 1956, by Raymond Postgate. Even though dated, this is a wonderful read.

The Oxford Atlas of World History, Concise Edition, O'Brien, Institute of Historical Research, University of London, 2007.

The Oxford Desk Encyclopedia of World History, Oxford University Press, 2006.

National Geographic Almanac of World History, by P.S. Daniels and S.G. Hyslop, National Geographic, 2003.

The Penguin Atlas of World History, Vol 1 and 2, by Kinder & Hilgemann, Penguin Books, 1964, 2003. *This is the BEST two volume atlas on World History. Fantastically illustrated; this is a must read for anyone interested in history. These two volumes cover every important event that can be mapped up to the year 2002. The volumes are small, but well worth the trouble of getting a magnifying glass to look at them. AD2*

The World, An Illustrated History, Edited by Geoffrey Parker, Harper and Row, New York, 1986.

Bones of Contention, Lebenow, Baker Books, 2004

Icons of Evolution: Science or Myth, Why Much of What We Teach About Evolution Is Wrong, Wells, Regnery Publishing, 2002.

Darwin's Black Box, The Biochemical Challenge to Evolution, Behe, Free Press, 2006

The Times History of the World, Overy, 2008, Times Books.

CHAPTER 2

ANCIENT HISTORY 8000 BC TO AD 455

From **8000 BC to 4000 BC,** anatomically modern humans began an **agricultural revolution** in the Middle East that spread throughout the globe setting the foundation for cities and city-states. Eventually, these city states evolved into larger political entities which then developed ruling classes (elites—can't get away from 'em), armies, priests, and bureaucrats (such as the ever present tax collectors). Along the way, the invention of writing led to what we now identify as history. In our short historical survey the terms Stone Age, Bronze Age, Iron Age, advanced civilizations and whatnot are often used. Please understand that while ancient Greece may be in the Bronze Age (using products made of Bronze, which is a metal made out of a mixture of tin and copper), Europe may still be in the Neolithic Stone Age and Central Asia in the Paleolithic Stone Age. The world did not develop in a uniform manner. For most of ancient history nearly the entire world was in the Stone Age era. Only a few places managed to achieve a written language and the other trappings of urban civilization. While many things were happening elsewhere, we will only concentrate on the most advanced areas of civilization.

GEOGRAPHY

Geography's impact on the ancient world and its people was massive. The affect of land features goes unappreciated today because our modern world greatly reduces their impact. Ancient people lived in mud huts, caves, or just a hole in the ground with a grass roof. Imagine the smell of the village they occupied, especially with the trash piled a stone's throw away (fish heads included). Fire was the only heat or light they enjoyed. Even today, the wilderness possesses a remarkable weight during its deepest nights.

What our primeval friends did have was wind, rain, snow, and sun hammering them 24/7. Geography determines how much, and what kind, of natural conditions people have to tackle each day. After all, when all that stands between you and an ice storm is a mammoth hide weather becomes extremely important. The first needs for a settled agricultural based community were water, open land to grow crops, and grass to feed the domesticated animals. When choosing a site people took patterns of weather into account, building materials, and probably thought about other tribes or clans lurking about. After evaluating an area, the folks might decide to settle down (or not) and then start to build houses, canals, corrals, and maybe a wall to keep out unwanted strangers. Once a good area was located and heavily invested in the residents wanted to keep others out. And why not? A good location, and the investment of time and labor, made it important to protect for themselves and their descendants.

By way of illustration, from 1000 BC until about AD 1500 whoever controlled the area between China and Europe, astride the "silk road", became fabulously wealthy. Empire after empire grew rich in this region by acting as middlemen between the riches of Asia and European consumers. These well positioned empires included Persia, Parthia, Kushana, the Mongols, Ottoman Turks, and the Caliphates of Islam. The overland route was necessary because a geographic feature stood in the way of an ocean route: Africa. After the Muslim defeat at the sea Battle of Du in 1508 the land route fell out of use. European seafarers captured the trade since ships moved cargo long distances at less risk and expense than land travel. Nonetheless, the merchants of Asia, and the middlemen, enjoyed a virtual monopoly on silk, spices, jade, and other oriental luxuries for about 2,500 years because of geography.[7] Thus, we ascertain the significance of geography.

SECURITY

Prior to settlement and farming, it appears people were relatively peaceful. Of course, it is hard to tell with few archeological sites, no written history, and immense expanses of time between the prehistoric era and ourselves. That much time erases a lot of evidence; nevertheless, we find no evidence of large battles. Even cave paintings only depict people hunting. After building large settlements, and investing time and resources enhancing the land with irrigation systems and permanent structures, people would

---

[7] China's ability to keep secret how silk was made for 2,000 years also contributed to the monopoly.

naturally resist efforts to seize their improved territory. Because of this inherent problem of investment into land and permanence, **war**, which is fighting between organized groups of armed combatants, appeared in spades. It seems the creation of villages and cities led to warfare.

Throughout history we find groups of people coveting the property of others, especially if they believe they are tougher than the ones owning the prized possessions (that human nature thing). As groups organized into cities it seems some leaders decided taking the land, property, and women of their neighbors was a good thing—especially if they had a larger army. Villages or clans with small armies faced critical problems if a large army appeared; consequently, very early on, communities built protective enclosures such as stone walls or wooden stockades. Good walls can even the odds against a larger army. The city of **Jericho** near the Dead Sea was founded by 8500 BC, and its construction included a surrounding stone wall over twelve feet high with towers thirty feet tall. In front of the wall the inhabitants constructed a ditch cut out of solid rock. Whoever erected this citadel spent a lot of time, labor, and resources protecting themselves. Throughout history we will find that walls define good times or bad times. Many sturdy walls around every town in a region shouts danger, but open cities without walls whisper safety. Today we find people putting iron bars on the doors and windows of their homes. These are essentially walls, and tell us life is dangerous. Others have gone so far as to live in so-called gated (read walled) communities within our great modern cities. The walled communities are constructed because security is failing, and people feel a need for additional protection. Just like people ten thousand years ago, people today build walls when security is uncertain.

Of course, security needs go far beyond walls, and these needs consume countless resources. Good protection requires an army; thus, men of military age must be trained and be equipped for war. Walls, ditches, armaments, and time for the men to train are all necessary for resisting outside conquest—or internal trouble. Towns fearing a siege would allocate additional resources for the storage of extra food and water so the city could withstand these attacks. A considerable effort had to go into protection for an urban area to survive 8,500 years ago. Another form of protection is the gods. If the gods (or the god—singular) were on your side then your army would succeed. If the gods were against you then all your armies, weapons, walls, and storehouses would be useless; therefore, appeasing the gods and shamans was a major concern. During pre-history some of this is guesswork, but after writing allowed us to read the ancient's thoughts we know security concerns were high.

SUMER AND UR

The first civilization of note was located at the outlet to the sea of the Tigris and Euphrates rivers near the Persian Gulf. A group of folks started to farm the very fertile land eventually establishing several large and well maintained cities on the alluvial plain by about **5000 BC**. These cities came together to form the civilization of **Sumer** about **3500 BC**. The city-states of Sumer, twelve in number, were involved in irrigating their abundant crops and needed a way to record the yields of the land. Thus, about **3300 BC,** Sumer developed what were probably the **first written records**, and they are (drum roll)—*receipts and tallies of crops.* (Huh?) In **Cuneiform writing** the records were wedged shaped marks pressed into wet clay which became permanent upon drying. Why were records of grain deposits or land yields so important? Crops were the foundation of Sumer's economy; accordingly, they probably decided to record the data because memories have a way of differing from year to year, or hour to hour for that matter. It is also probable that it had something to do with taxation (where there is government there is taxation). The why is lost to us but the records are there—warehouses full of them. From such monotonous undertakings our written language (and history) was inaugurated. Peculiarly, the language of Sumer was confined to the small area of the twelve cities, never expanding beyond them; however, the idea of writing spread swiftly throughout the world.

The Sumerians also made a beverage that is still popular today, **beer**. Moreover, they had many varieties of beer, most of them made from barley. The beer trade was important to the ancient Middle East, and went as far east as India. Egypt appears to be the ancient capital of beer brewing. The Egyptians processed something like 50 varieties of beer, ranging from red or white to premium. No wonder this area needed language and writing. How else can you order the right kind of beer all the way from India?

Sumer gave the world another item easily recognizable today, a numbering system based on 60, the sexagesimal system (!!—are they kidding?). Never heard of it? Recall that our time base is 60—sixty seconds to a minute, 60 minutes to an hour. The number of degrees in a circle (360) is also from the base of 60. Therefore, the basis of modern time and writing came from the long ago land of Sumer.

The Bronze Age replaced the Stone Age about 3500 BC in Mesopotamia. Metallurgy made remarkable advances and became a mainstay of urban civilization. Bronze is a mixture of copper and tin, which makes bronze much harder than copper alone. Bronze Age tools were superior to Stone or copper tools. Craftsmen turned out better plows, needles, tools for tending crops, and weapons. Such useful knowledge and materials quickly reached other areas. Bronze weapons gave the city folks an edge over nomads persistently battering at their gates. In China, the Bronze Age began earlier than the Middle East, and it seems each area independently developed its metalworking expertise. How is it that two widely separated civilizations both discovered that tin mixed with copper produced a harder metal? Can it be that humans think along similar lines no matter where they are located?

FIGURE 3 SARGON OF AGADE—FIRST CONQUER

Human beings are endlessly competitive it seems, and that bit of human nature immediately caused trouble. As originally constituted, the cities of Sumer comprised twelve independent city-states. Then a fellow named *Sargon of Agade* invaded and conquered the cities in 2334 BC, thereby establishing himself as the ruler of them all. It is said that Sargon was the world's first conquer, although Menes of Egypt seems to have been ahead of him. He expanded his empire, but it did not last, and the city-state system returned with the city of **Ur** being the big dog of the pack for a few hundred years. Ur fell around 2000 BC to other invaders, and the story of the Middle East—and the world—has not changed since. One empire after another conquered the area of Sumer, or part of it, only to be overthrown by another in due time. The Middle East is a key starting point for urban civilization, and war and conquest emerged instantly thereafter. It seems civilization got off to a bad start and never recovered.

These early wars were horrible. Imagine you live in a walled "city" of 8,000 people (men, women, and children), meaning you can field an army of less than 2,000 maximum. The normal figure for fighting men would be twenty percent of the population, or about 1,600 men in this instance. Assume an army of 5,000 well-armed invaders appear demanding that your city send out wagonloads of copper and grain, plus all the girls between the ages of ten and fourteen. Your choices are: (1) give them what they want, knowing a similar bounty will be required every year, moreover, your girls will suffer rape and slavery in a faraway land; or (2) fight, knowing defeat means burning your city, slavery for your young men, slaughter for the older citizens, and rape and slavery for your all your girls. These were the hard choices faced by the city's leaders. The city's army was like a college football team; the biggest, strongest, and most athletic young men the city can muster will fight the invader, probably within sight of the city.[8] If your young men lose, you get to watch them butchered as you contemplate your own demise. A "win" still requires the death and wounding of many of the city's young men; however, you keep your independence and your property. Nevertheless, the invaders may regroup and return. As one can see the choices were anything but good.

Abraham

Around 2000 BC a man left Ur with his wife and traveled west, eventually settling in the land of Canaan which we now call Israel or Palestine. *This one man was to be the father of the world's three great monotheistic religions.* Abraham would begin the Jewish religion, and through the Jews the Christian religion. By his handmaiden he was to father of the Islamic religion. As you know from our present-day headlines it was also the start of a LOT of trouble. The amazing thing about the religions Abraham originated is that many other religions, with abundant adherents, were around at the same time; however, they all faded away. Thousands followed the religions of Egypt, Babylonia, Assyria, Greece, and many others, while those following the one God of Abraham were very few. Yet, 4,000 years later, it is the

---

8 Another choice is to defend behind your walls, but that means a siege during which the population faces starvation and numerous assaults from the invader attempting to breach the walls. If your city was well prepared with lots of stored food and ample water it would be wise to try and hold out inside the walls. What would you do if you led the city?

religions spawned by Abraham that enjoy billions of adherents, while the other religions from his time are extinct.

When Abraham moved to the land of Canaan no one would claim this was a supernova event in history; and, at his death, no one would have thought this man had forever changed the world. As students of history we should note that events so breathlessly watched and reported on today will be meaningless in a hundred years, and perfectly erased in five hundred. Yet, events are taking place at this moment that will substantially impact the world one thousand years hence, but they will go unnoticed during our time. Ask your friends what they know about World War I. If they know anything it would be surprising, and that conflict was only 96 years ago. The current "newsworthy" happenings are actually very un-newsworthy. Who would have thought, at the time, the American Revolution would change the world, or a few men guarding a bridge against a small unit of English troops would trigger that change? Who knew in 1960 that computers would shrink to tabletop and then pinhead size and take over our world so completely? The birth and death of Jesus Christ went utterly unnoticed. That is why history must take the ***long view*** as I call it, because what seems important today will most likely be nothing at all in one hundred years.

EGYPT

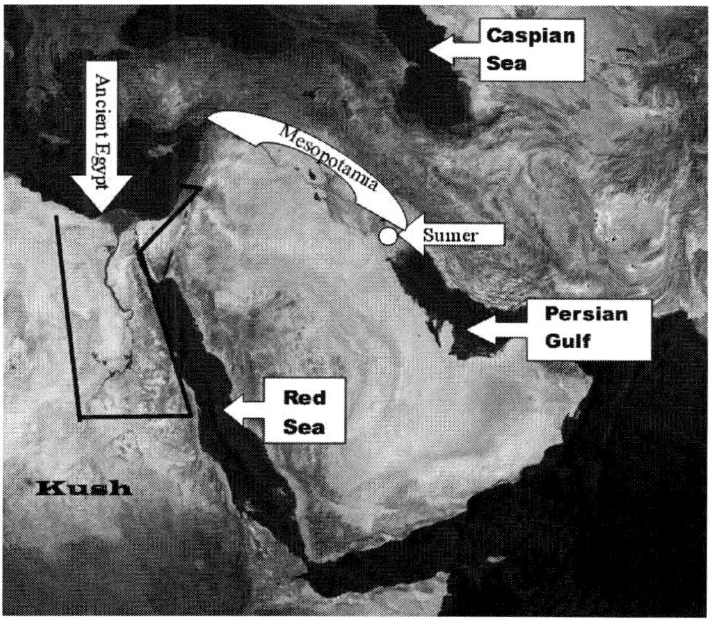

FIGURE 4 EGYPT & THE MIDDLE EAST

Egypt played an important role in ancient history, as it is one of the earliest highly developed civilizations. Egypt was an isolated area with harsh deserts to the west and east, the Mediterranean Sea to the north, and the wilds of Africa to the south (here we note the importance of geography again). From about 4500 BC, the civilization along the Nile developed from farming communities to the empires of Upper and Lower Egypt. Around 3100 BC, an almost mythical ruler known as **Menes** conquered Upper and Lower Egypt founding the first of twenty-two dynasties to rule over Upper and Lower Egypt for *over 2,500 years.* The United States of America has been around about two hundred fifty years. An eye blink to the ancient Egyptians. The Egyptian rulers were **Pharaohs**, and the people considered the Pharaoh a god on earth.[9]

Egyptian history is divided into three eras: **The Old Kingdom** (3000 to 2150 BC)**, the Middle Kingdom** (1975 to1630 BC), and the **New Kingdom** (1550 to 1070 BC). After each of these kingdoms came a phase of unrest, or conquests, termed "**intermediate periods**" after which the Egyptians restored their old way of life.

Great buildings recall the era of ancient Egypt. During the Old Kingdom the Pharaoh Khufu ordered the Great Pyramid[10] at Giza constructed around 2550 BC.[11] Even after the end of the New Kingdom in 1070 BC Egypt went on, although its power was significantly reduced. Still, Egypt's great building projects continued. Pharaoh Necho II (610 to 595 BC) built a canal between the Nile and the Red Sea to improve trade with the east. Actually, the "canal" had a few high and dry spots that required towing the boats across land (how would you like the job of pulling boats overland). Nonetheless, it was a great time saver, otherwise the circumnavigation of Africa was required to reach the Persian Gulf.

The Egyptians maintained a **stable society** for thousands of years, and this stability was the hallmark of their culture. As the sky and the Nile were

---

9 The term Pharaoh comes from the New Kingdom. In earlier times Egyptian rulers were just kings. I will use the term Pharaoh for all the Egyptian rulers.

10 The architect, Imhotep, is one of the few names of lesser officials surviving into our time.

11 We should note the stone part of Stonehenge in England was constructed about 2900 BC, nearly 400 years before the Great Pyramid. 400 years is nearly twice as long as the USA has been a nation. One of our greatest challenges is understanding Stonehenge. What makes it so hard is its complexity, as it is tied into the surrounding countryside and other local ceremonial monuments.

stable so was life in Egypt. The dynasties did change, and periodically invaders came from outside their land to harass and overcome them, but the Egyptians quickly (in historical terms) re-established their control and continued their old ways of life. Their art forms reflect this stability. The Egyptians established rather unique artistic methods, and painting or carving these highly stylized depictions of people and animals resisted change for over two thousand years. This kind of stability is remarkable, and it is what allowed such a grand culture to develop and sustain itself for thousands of years.

The Egyptians enjoyed a perfect setup in the Nile River Valley. The Nile River flooded dependably, and those yearly floods deposited rich silt upon a level floodplain on which the Egyptians planted their crops yielding wonderful amounts of grain that all but guaranteed a surplus year after year. The Egyptians developed extensive canal and irrigation systems off the Nile River. In addition, the isolation protected them from invaders, and consequently allowed them to avoid a standing army (during the Old Kingdom), thereby saving funds normally spent on military protection. Instead, they spent their surpluses on civic projects. For many years the only consistent threat to Egypt's way of life came from the south—the kingdom of Nubia(also known as Kush). The Egyptians pushed south, past the great waterfalls of the upper Nile (cataracts), and established a series of impressive forts to protect their southern borders. For thousands of years these prevented incursions that would otherwise threaten the peace of the Nile Valley. The Nile River Valley and its surrounding area offered up riches beyond farming. From the area of Syene (Assuan) came gold, granite, sandstone, and copper; from Heliopolis limestone; from Hermopolis alabaster; from the Red Sea's western coast granite, gold and emeralds; and from Sinai copper, garnet, and turquoise. These riches (and beer) allowed Egypt to build a large trading empire.

The Egyptians liked to study the world around them, especially the sky (well, it is a desert—what else can you look at after dark?). From these studies they developed sophisticated astronomical data and ideas about the afterlife that would deeply influence their civilization and others that would follow. Christian and Hebrew sacred texts feature Egypt prominently. These sources tell us how the Hebrews became slaves in Egypt, and then—around 1200 or 1300 BC—how the prophet Moses led them east, out of Egypt to Palestine.**12** During the journey to their new homeland, Yahweh (God)

---

[12] In ancient Egypt, the east was associated with life and the west with death. This was because the sun rose from the east giving life, and set in the west bringing darkness

presented the Hebrews with the Ten Commandants at Mount Sinai. God later gave the Torah to the Hebrews. These writings found their way into the Christian Bible as the first five books of the Old Testament. These five books help form the religious foundations of the Western World.

The Egyptians developed hieroglyphics, a form of writing using pictures and symbols for whole ideas rather than individual words or letters; thus, no alphabet was developed. Since each symbol or picture stood for an idea this made hieroglyphics exceptionally difficult to decipher (much like the written Chinese language).[13] The Egyptians also invented a simpler, faster way to write for everyday use, and that writing style eventually traveled to the land of **Phoenicia** transforming itself into an *alphabet*. To write upon something besides stone the Egyptians invented *papyrus*, an early form of paper. A lot of their records and day-to-day events were recorded on this medium which, unfortunately for us, deteriorates rapidly. As a result, countless Egyptian records were lost over time.

The gigantic pyramids and complex burial practices leave the impression that Egypt was a land seemingly living for the dead, but this is not the entire story. The Pyramids at Giza are immense stone monuments built to house dead Pharaohs (current theory). The Pharaohs wanted their tombs' built out of exactly cut limestone stone blocks. Within the mountainous structures the ancient architects constructed passages leading to various chambers, one of which held the Pharaoh's sarcophagus. The pyramids, along with the colossal and mysterious underground tombs in the **Valley of the Kings,** tell us of a society focused on the afterlife, and willing to expend enormous resources to ensure safe passage of the Pharaoh into the heavens; however, this safe passage into the heavens had an earthly impact.[14] Ancient Egyptians believed in a balance between earth and heaven, and the tombs of their Pharaohs were designed to help maintain that balance in both realms. The Pharaoh's passage to the stars helped maintain the critical heaven-earth balance that guarded against chaos. The old reborn Pharaoh

---

and death. By going east, the Hebrews were symbolically traveling toward life. Dr. Richard Buehrer's concepts.

13 The Rosetta Stone, a slab of stone with Egyptian hieroglyphics and two other later known languages carrying the same message, enabled the hieroglyphics to be deciphered.

14 The sarcophagi in all three great pyramids are gone, apparently stolen by grave robbers in the distant past. In the Great Pyramid everything is gone except the lower stone shell of the sarcophagus. The Valley of the Kings is the burial place of over 60 Pharaohs.

in the heavens would continue the divine order there (or "maat"), and the new Pharaoh would maintain maat on earth. In times of chaos the Egyptians thought the heaven-earth maat was disturbed.

The pyramids of the Old and New Worlds had different construction methods and vastly different functions. The **Aztec pyramids** in the New World were massive but rubble-filled construction, and only the structure's exterior surface had cut stone. Atop the Aztec structures were temples where bloody sacrifices took place to honor and appease the gods; thus, the Meso-American pyramids were not tombs, rather they were places of slaughter where the living encountered a horrifying end to life. Aztec society required the victim's heart be cut out, and while still beating, held up to the sun. The Aztecs thought blood alone fed the gods and prevented them from ruining the earth. The Aztecs seem to have inherited these beliefs from their predecessors.

In Mesopotamia, the pyramids were stepped structures constructed of sun-dried brick. Called **ziggurats**, the stepped construction method allowed tall and stable structures to ascend skyward, toward the desert sun. On top of their man-made mountains the priests of Mesopotamia performed rituals to appease and honor their somewhat fickle gods, trying to keep the gods tranquil and generous toward their people. Since the ziggurats were substitute mountains for ritual purposes there was no reason to bury people in them. Strangely enough, over time the bricks melted into the desert and today they look like small mountains. Along the Tigris and Euphrates rivers the inhabitants stuck with the ziggurat structure and the mountaintop idea, but the stepped construction's influence on early Egypt may have been important because the first Egyptian temple structures were also stepped.

Egypt's pyramids eschewed mountain top rituals; rather, they were both a tomb for their god on earth and a passageway for the Pharaoh to the heavens. For the Egyptians the pyramid connected earth and heaven. In Egyptian pyramids the stones inside and out were closely cut—so closely cut a playing card could not be slid between them. The outside surfaces of the three great pyramids at Giza were originally smooth and faced with white limestone so each would brilliantly reflect the desert sun. Inside the pyramid the Pharaoh rested in safety until securing passage to the sky and the world beyond, thereby ensuring a tranquil life to those remaining behind in Egypt. In a sense, while the Egyptian tombs focused on the afterlife they also focused on the present, because as order was maintained among the stars so order would be maintained on earth. Some commentators say the pyramid was an eternal life machine guiding Pharaoh's journey to the stars.

Egyptians believed in life after death and judgment after death for one's actions in life. Nonetheless, not everyone bought off on the Pharaohs being gods or on judgment after death, because the riches of the tombs were plundered on a regular basis. The problem was so severe a new underground burial location was constructed in the Valley of the Kings. Here the Egyptians created elaborate underground tombs rivaling the pyramids for spectacular construction. The Pharaohs entombed in this valley received extra protection from patrolling guards. In the end even this failed, and pillaging of the splendid underground tombs went on. Even so, the tombs in the Valley of the Kings are every bit as amazing as the oft-visited Great Pyramids. It was here that Carter found the now famous King Tut of Egypt.

The Egyptians may have constructed the Great Pyramids to conform to the stars in Orion's belt, and they may have seen the Nile itself mirrored in the sky by the Milky Way's band of stars crossing near the constellation of Orion. The ancient Egyptians still veil their secrets about why they placed the Giza Pyramids as they did. Strangely, the great pyramids on the Giza plateau contain no hieroglyphics or other writings inside. In addition, large boats are buried right beside the pyramids. Written records of how and why the great burial chambers were created are nowhere to be found. Modern scholars speculate on the methods of construction, and the experimenter's mud ramps show practical ways to accomplish the task, but such experiments are not definitive. Much smaller pyramids contain pictures of pyramid building, but they show only small pyramids under construction. We cannot be certain of anything; not how, when, or even why Egyptians' built the Giza pyramids leaving all our "facts" in the realm of speculation.[15] It is human nature to brag about deeds that stun the world. The missing writings deepen the Egyptian riddles, but the finely

15 Inside the Great Pyramid, there is a kind of graffiti above the vault in the kings' chamber saying a certain group of workers built it for Khufu; however, the discovery of these markings is in question. Originally, the markings were in candle smoke

cut stone mountains stand with us still reminding us of Egypt's remarkable stability.

Note that Egypt overcame at least two outside invasions during the intermediate periods, and then re-established their former way of life. Compare this to the fall of Rome where the Roman world totally disappeared. Why did Egypt eventually prevail over the invaders while the Romans did not?

MESOPOTAMIA

Mesopotamia, the land between two rivers, was the location of many a mighty empire. Mesopotamia was the centerpiece of the **Fertile Crescent** area of the ancient world. The Fertile Crescent began at the Persian Gulf, continued up the Tigris and Euphrates Rivers, then turned south down the coast of the eastern Mediterranean and thence to the border of Egypt, thus forming a kind of crescent (Well, it does sound better than "the fertile upside down U"). In Mesopotamia the rivers flooded irregularly so life was a bit unsettled in the food category. In addition, the area is open for invasion from all sides, again showing the importance of geography. Perhaps the gods were thought to be capricious because of the unsettled nature of existence along the narrow corridor of urbanization. Nonetheless, great empires were common on the Tigris and Euphrates rivers because the soil was fertile and previous occupants constructed sophisticated irrigation systems.[16]

Another reason Mesopotamia prospered was trade. The two mighty rivers were freeways to the ocean, then India, Egypt and beyond. The copper trade was so busy on the Euphrates River that the ancients called it the Copper River.[17] From the north came lapis lazuli (precious stones), from the west stone and wood, from the south copper, and from the east the luxuries of India all flowing into the Tigris and Euphrates River valley. Through all of history trade will mean prosperity to those who have it, and privation for those who do not. In addition, trade escorted the spread of another astounding concept, the **alphabet**.

---

that may have been made by the workers on the expedition finding the markings, but this too is speculation.

16 Tigris and Euphrates—Tigris being the upper river (T = top). The irrigation systems lasted until the Mongols murdered everyone in the area about AD 1200, then they silted up never to be repaired. (See the Mongols in the Dark Ages section)

17 p. 21, Bauer, *The History of the Ancient World,* 2007, WW Norton & Co

On the western edge of the Upside Down U . . . oops . . . Fertile Crescent, assembled a group of seafaring traders known as the **Phoenicians.** They established their trading cities on the eastern coast of the Mediterranean Sea at Tyre, Sidon, and other locations, about 1100 BC. The Phoenicians established spin-off trading towns throughout the Mediterranean world, including Carthage which was one of the ancient world's most remarkable cities. Even though their sailing ships went west with trade goods the cargo itself was coming from inland; that is, the Fertile Crescent and its attendant trading partners. The Phoenicians developed the **alphabet** (theirs was only 22 letters) from informal Egyptian script. With an alphabet, a few letters are easily assembled into millions of words because *the letters stand for sounds* rather than ideas. The assembled words are the ideas, and when the words represented by the letters are spoken out loud they sound like the spoken language. Thus, one does not have to commit thousands of picture ideas to memory. All that is necessary is to sound out the word from the letters. This connection between the spoken word and the written word was a brilliant stroke, and from the Phoenicians' central Mediterranean trading location this idea quickly spread east and west (never made it to China). This Phoenician alphabet leads to Aramaic and Greek scripts, and eventually Latin which was the foundation of many modern western languages (English, French, Spanish . . .).

Walled cities were common in Mesopotamia, and the larger the city the higher the wall. The open nature of the area and its nearness to the Caspian Sea, either side of which was a common incursion route from the plains of southern Russia, caused it to endure constant raids and outright invasions. Picture this roll call of changing kingdoms: the old Babylonian empire (1792 BC) was overthrown by Hittites (1595 BC), the Hittites departed after being vanquished by the Peoples of the Sea (1200), the Assyrians (694 BC) eventually filled the void left by the Hittites; the Assyrians were overthrown by the Chaldeans (neo-Babylonians or Medes) (626 BC), which were replaced by the Persians (539 BC), who were conquered by the Greeks (331 BC). And we have not listed all the empires, just the major ones. The Romans came later, then the empire of Parthia, and on and on. It never really ends. More than a little of this turmoil came from nomads around the Caspian and Black Sea.

For about three hundred years, Assyria was the dominant military and political power in the Middle Eastern region. Assyria began to expand in 911 BC and held on to an empire reaching from the northern Tigris River (Turkey) to the Persian Gulf (Mesopotamia), including Egypt, until its defeat by Babylonian Nabopolassar in 626 BC. The Assyrian capitol at

Nineveh fell in 612 BC. The Assyrians used iron weapons, much harder than bronze, and excelled at siege warfare and the use of cavalry. The Assyrians were ruthless beyond compare. An area refusing their demands for subjugation had their cities razed and every inhabitant butchered. For example, the Assyrian king Ashurnasirpal boasted he overthrew a city, skinned some leaders alive, walled some of them up alive, impaled others, beheaded some and had their heads hung from tree branches around the city, burned the young men and women alive, and the rest, he bragged, were driven into the desert to die of thirst. Not the kind of fellow one chooses to have over for tea. Walled cities often refused demands by invaders because sieges commonly failed; however, the Assyrians invented siege machines that breached the walls and brought cities down quickly. Nevertheless, all the empires, whether benign or ruthless fell one after the other. Whether Babylonian, Egyptian, Hittite, Persian, or Greek, no one could gain power and hold it indefinitely.

FIGURE 5 BABYLON, THE HANGING GARDENS

In Babylonia, King Hammurabi (1792-1750 BC) set forth a code of 282 laws governing his empire. His were not the first laws, nor were they the first written down; however, they are the most complete set of laws found from this era. Most of the laws would make sense in the twenty-first century because they deal with common problems and have common-sense solutions. For example, if a person injured another's property, restitution was in order; or if a builder constructed a house that fell down, he was to pay the homeowner for damages. Obviously, people in the ancient world had problems similar to ours, and their solutions were exactly like ours, in that the governing body took steps to reach equity in disputes. In our modern world law continues to play a critical part in our societies, showing some things never change. Hammurabi's Code, chiseled into stone and placed in a prominent public place, gave notice to all what the laws were so his subjects knew the rules and the punishment for breaching the rules. It might show that the king would settle all similar problems in a similar way, no matter who was involved. Enforcing laws in such a manner would be a new way of thinking for eastern rulers. Oriental kings normally exercised the power of life and death over their subjects, and they could be as fickle as they wished.

Thus, in Mesopotamia, we have the rise and fall of numerous empires. King after king, and empire after empire, conquered, grew wealthy, and then grew weak, eventually becoming the conquered. This cycle continues even today, on both a local and worldwide scale. Will governments always continue in this fashion?

The Bronze Age Collapse

In approximately **1200 BC,** there was a widespread collapse of eastern Mediterranean Bronze Age civilizations. This collapse threw the eastern Mediterranean world into a Dark Age, and it took hundreds of years to recover. The shattered empires include the Minoan civilization on Crete, cities around the coast of Turkey, the Hittites of inland Turkey, and civilizations along the Palestinian coast. Their protective walls fell, the interior structures collapsed and burned, plus the population of the area decreased rather substantially. Egypt repelled a mighty invasion; however, the conflict substantially weakened the kingdom. Some scholars believe a physical disaster struck the area and destroyed these sophisticated civilizations. The massive super-eruption of the island of Thira may have caused the destruction of the Minoan civilization on the island of Crete about 1450 BC; although others think the Dark Age came due to invasions launched in 1200 BC by a mysterious *Iron Age* group named the "***Peoples of the Sea.***" Warriors with iron weapons could have easily defeated opponents wielding bronze weapons. The evidence for invasion comes from the extension and heightening of walls protecting cities in the area almost simultaneously with the rise of problems. The cities fell after the walls were improved, which implies some warning of an invasion and an attempt to prepare. In Egypt, the Pharaoh and his advisors decided to meet the invader at sea. This change in strategy may have saved the Egyptians, who won a significant naval victory by destroying the invading force before it landed. Whether or not these invaders were the same "Peoples of the Sea" or "Sea Peoples" described by others is unknown; however, the Egyptians repelled the invaders after cities around the Mediterranean fell in sequence from Crete, to Turkey, and then Palestine, leading to speculation the invaders proceeded around the northern and eastern Mediterranean before descending on Egypt. In addition, after the Egyptian victory the Peoples of the Sea disappear from history.

Apparently, the marauders did not care to settle in or near the cities they sacked.[18] The invaders appeared, destroyed, and then disappeared. It is possible that natural disasters contributed to the fall of the ancient Bronze Age cities, but the extension and heightening of the city walls indicates the disasters were manmade. More research may turn up better evidence, but for now, this inexplicable collapse of the high Bronze Age civilizations of the eastern Mediterranean remains a tantalizing enigma. Some authors hold the "invasion" was actually a great migration from the Black Sea and Caspian Sea area, rather than an invasion coming from the west to the east.[19]

Here we should note the importance of **great migrations of peoples**. The mystifying Bronze Age collapse could be the result of mass migrations from central Europe, most of which were Indo-European stock carrying iron weapons. We cannot know for certain. About 1300 BC, Iron Age peoples of the "Urnfield Culture"[20] were expanding out of their original territory in central Europe, leading some scholars to think this migration resulted in the Mediterranean problems. Dates can be most uncertain in ancient history. Other great migrations taking place throughout history influenced civilization in remarkable ways. In fact, there is an ongoing

---

18 One exception may be the Philistines who are spoken of in the Bible and whom the Israelites engaged in constant warfare.

19 P. 276 et seq, Bauer, *The History of the Ancient World*, 2007, WW Norton. Ms Bauer calls them "Sea Peoples". The problem with a migration is the people in a mass migration normally settle down in the conquered areas. No settlement took place after the Sea Peoples came through.

20 The Urnfield culture cremated their dead and placed the ashes into urns. These urns (clay) were buried in cemeteries (fields); thus, the Urnfield culture. (*urn* in a *field*? Now do you get it? Come on, wake up! Swill down some coffee.) *The Penguin Atlas of World History*, Vol 1, p18.

debate about which has more historical importance, the rise of large cities and empires, or the mass migrations of peoples. The cities gave us culture, agriculture, social organization, and specialization. Mass migrations, such as the Franks and Goths moving into Europe and toppling the Western Roman Empire, overthrew entire civilizations, changed social structures across entire regions, and often represent turning points in history. These mass migrations of entire populations from one area to another, usually for reasons unknown, are so numerous they are hard to list. Here are just a few: Asiatic peoples from the area of Mongolia pushing the Germanic people into Europe from about 200 to 1000 AD (sometimes called the Age of Great Migrations), the Sarmatians and Scythians marching into the Black Sea area after 2000 BC and fighting everyone in sight, the movements of Dorian peoples into Greece about 1100 BC pushing out the Mycenaeans, the Bantus moving from Central Africa to the eastern and southern areas of Africa after 2000 BC, and the Vikings moving out of Scandinavia for raids and settlement from 800 to 1100 AD. Such migrations are not elements of the ancient past. Movements such as the Europeans across North America in the 1700's, or the movements of Latin Americans to North America today (2010) are examples of massive and disruptive movements changing the course of history.

HARAPPAN CIVILIZATIONS—INDUS VALLEY

3300 to 1700 BC

In the Indus Valley about 3300 BC, a magnificent Bronze Age farming civilization arose that we call Harappan for the city of Harappa. Within the Indus Valley there were over 70 cities, but two stand out: **Harappa** and **Mohenjo-Daro**. The Harappans laid out their cities in perfect north-south grids, with fired brick buildings, brick gutters, excellent drainage, and access to water in every house. Hygiene was a major concern of the inhabitants. Each house had a room set aside for bathing, complete with a drainage system to carry the water away. The society developed exacting weights and measures for common use. These may account for the expert grid layout of the cities, and the sophisticated sanitation systems. What makes both these cities even more fascinating is the lack of monumental structures. There were no large structures or extra large houses, plus large temple complexes and ceremonial centers are missing. All the houses were close to the same size, and all their baked mud bricks were exactly the same size. The size was, in centimeters, 17.5 x 13 x 30. How weird is that? Some of these facts, like no large houses, point to an egalitarian society.

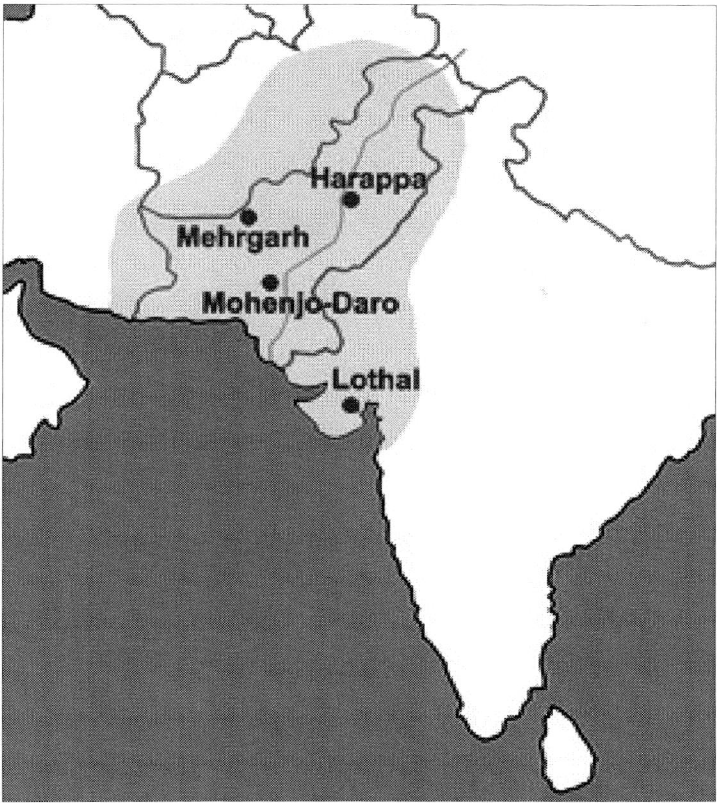

FIGURE 6 HARAPPAN CIVILIZATION

Thirty years ago archeologist thought the cities in the Indus River plain were constructed without walls; however, recent work shows the cities did have walls—thick *double walls* complete with ramparts and watchtowers. Inside the two walls was an imposing citadel to further increase protection.[21] Normally, protection like this means the people are frightened, but we have no idea why they needed such expensive and extensive protection. Our problem with the Indus civilizations is a lack of written records. Archeologists found cylinder seals in abundance, and recorded about four hundred symbols from the seals; thus, it is thought the society was literate, but no books or written records can be located. The lack of records severely hampers the hunt for facts about this civilization. The mere fact that the houses are the same size, wholly different from other ancient cultures, leaves us wondering what kind of society existed in the Bronze Age Indus Valley.

---

[21] p. 106-107, Bauer, The History of the Ancient World, WW Norton publisher

The Indus Valley pre-Aryan peoples created excellent pottery, flint blades, and copper wares. This manufacture was widely used in trade, and it found its way westward to the Fertile Crescent, and eastward to the Indian subcontinent. Indus Valley civilizations began to decline about 1800 BC. Why is unclear. Aryan invaders carrying iron weapons enter the area in 1700 BC, but it seems the civilization was already on a downward spiral. After the Aryan arrival, Harappan civilization soon vanishes completely.

THE ARYANS AND IRON AGE CIVILIZATIONS IN INDIA

1700 to 500 BC

The Aryans came to the Indus Valley sweeping all before them; however, they were not the cultural equal of the preceding Harappan civilization. As a result, India and the Indus Valley fell into a dark age from which we can gather very little information. The Aryan language forms a cluster of languages that include German, English, and Sanskrit. These nomadic Aryan people probably arrived from Turkistan, and their arrival completely changed the language and culture of India, ushering in the Vedic period that followed the ancient Harappan. The Aryans brought an Iron Age culture into the valley, but it lacked a written language—at least initially. This Aryan culture dominated India through its religious underpinnings, the Upanishads, eventually developing into the complex religious and social caste system still seen today. What we do have from this era are the literary epics of Hinduism (the Vedas): Ramayana and Mahabharata. Hinduism was formed from early Aryan beliefs and prospered in India. It prevailed over Buddhism which spread from India to the rest of Asia and became a dominant force in these areas.[22] The Mahabharata is a key myth in Indian culture. In this story of an epic heroic war, the Krishna, its hero, finally manages to defeat his enemies in an enormous final battle (what else?). From this myth materializes many stories that dictate how one should live his life and perform his duties to society. The story was composed between 400 BC and 400 AD (current theory), and it is here the ancient gods of pre-history are established forever in India's story. The myth blurs itself into history, and it is as real in India today as it was in ancient times. Even in 2010, India's people dance to the gods of pre-history and their society continues as prescribed so many thousands of years ago in the ancient texts. In the countryside, away from the large cities, the rural people live the same as their ancient ancestors. The houses are the same, they tell the

---

[22] See: **China** for a more complete discussion of Buddhism.

same stories, and live the same religion. The Aryan impact on India has been enduring.

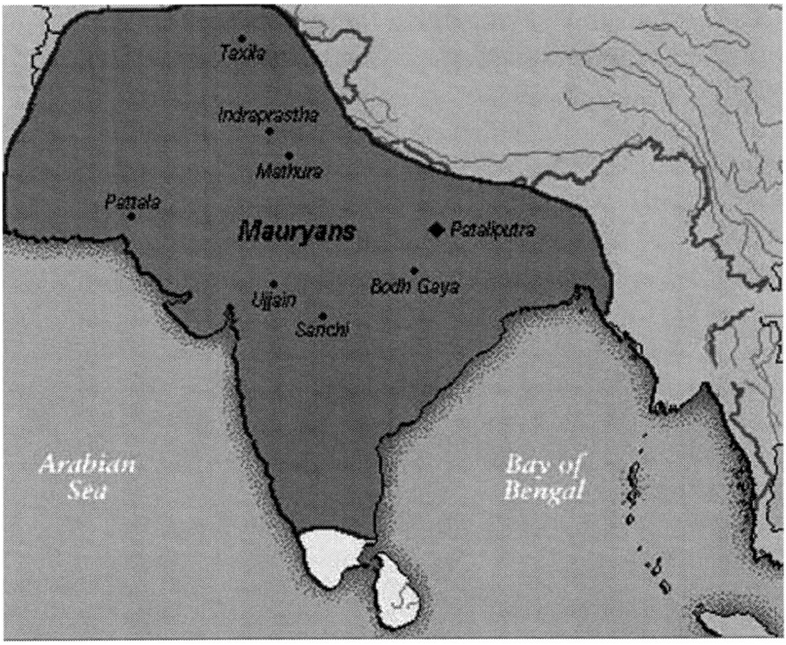

FIGURE 7 MAURYA EMPIRE

The Maurya dynasty united India in 321 BC. This was the first time the subcontinent enjoyed one ruler, as the Aryan clans had practiced constant warfare since their arrival. Following the fall of the Maurya dynasty, the Gupta dynasty unified the northern areas of India in the fifth century, bringing about what most scholars believe was a golden age. This dynasty was ruined when the Huns arrived in the fourth century. There was a resurgence of the northern dynasties in the seventh century, and this allowed a flowering of Indian culture. The Mongols were to arrive again in AD 1526 and unite the subcontinent under an Islamic dynasty; however, Hinduism would survive even under Islamic rule in India proper. The area of modern day Pakistan converted to Islam during the Mongol period, and this division still troubles the subcontinent, and the world, today.

GREECE AND ROME

Greece and then Rome dominated European, Mediterranean, and Near East history from *1200 BC to AD 1453.* Greece, a mountainous area in the northeastern Mediterranean, was comprised of city-states, with each small area being self-governing and each adopting vastly different ways of governance. Rome was a city that grew to govern the entire Mediterranean area, Western Europe (Gaul, Spain, Portugal, parts of Germany and England), Turkey, North Africa, Egypt, and some of Mesopotamia. If one counts the Eastern Roman Empire, Rome lasted from 753 BC to AD 1453 when the capitol of the Eastern Roman Empire, Constantinople, fell to the Turks. The fall of the Western and Eastern Roman Empires, about AD 455 and 1453 respectively, are among the most significant events in world history.

THE GREEKS

800 BC to 338 BC

We will start with the amazing Greeks. Of all the cities in ancient Greece, Athens is the best known. The main Greek city-states were up and running by 800 BC. From about 750 BC, when Homer wrote the *Iliad* and the *Odyssey,* to 404 BC, when the Peloponnesian War between Sparta and Athens ended, Greek civilization exploded with grandeur. The Greeks, who began with almost nothing, perfected Art, poetry, literature, political values, science, philosophy, warfare, and other areas of Western culture. Greek sculpture is copied even today; modern philosophers still argue with Socrates, Aristotle, and Plato; Herodotus and Thucydides founded the study of history; Homer's writings about the history of the Trojan War founded epic poetry; the Greek heavily armored civilian soldiers (hoplites) founded the military principles with which Alexander the Great would conquer the East. Athens laid the foundations of democracy, which were eventually passed down to Europe and America. Greece was the foundation for the Western world we know today. And even today, in philosophy, sculpture, history, political thought, poetry, and literature the Greeks remain unsurpassed.

INDIVIDUAL GREATER THAN THE STATE

Most of these new ideas came from Athens. Athens was a democracy where, for much of its history, every male citizen could vote on critical issues of the day in a public assembly. This reflected a new idea, an idea foreign to rulers in the East. The idea, which spread to the Western world from Greece, was **the individual is greater than the state.** From the point of view of Western democracy this was *the greatest political idea ever discovered.* It is still the defining factor in governments, both East and West.

A much older idea ruled the East, where the great rulers of Babylonia, Persia, Egypt, and many others always held on to the opposite**: the state is greater than the individual.** In Athens, a person could oppose the city (read "the government") and demand satisfaction from the group of gathered Athenian citizens rather than give in to an order from a ruler. Greek citizens considered themselves *free men,* and they participated in the governance of their cities. One man's word was not the law. In the East, the old idea of rule by one person maintained its sway. An oriental king could have anyone, one man or an entire army, put to death on his word alone.

If we stop to think about our world in 2010, we see the concept of one person (or perhaps a small group) autocratic rule is still paramount in China, Southeast Asia, North Korea, Russia, the Middle East, Africa, and many places in South and Central America including Cuba. The idea that the individual is more important than the state took hold in England, France (to some extent), Germany (finally), Italy, Greece, Austria, Spain (well, kind of . . . at least since Franco died), some areas of the Balkans, some parts of Eastern Europe (Poland, Latvia, etc), India, Canada, Australia, New Zealand, and the United States. The reader will note that the *English* colonies are the primary nations that practice democracy and believe the individual is more important than the collective (United States of America, Canada, Australia, New Zealand, India, and England itself). This idea divides the world even now.

Of Gods and Governments

The linkup of god and government is a powerful combination for controlling individuals.[23] We do not know when this amalgamation first occurred; however, once the linkup was secure, making *god and the state one,* any decision became impossible to challenge. Anyone opposing the government was both a traitor and a heretic. This is the pattern for most of history. The oriental dictators of Egypt, Babylonia, Persia, and so many others, coupled religion and leadership of the state; thus, the ruler was

23 Normally, I will use the term "god" for "the gods" or "gods" interchangeably. So when reading the word *god,* understand that it means gods or the gods as well, because most societies in the ancient world were polytheist Poly = many, thus many gods. Pantheist were also about. Pan = all; thus a god in everything, including the person.

anointed by the gods, guided by the gods, and in touch with the gods so his decisions were also anointed by the gods. The priesthood confirmed, on behalf of the ruler, that god (or the gods) agreed, and the common person lacked any power to challenge this powerful duet.[24]

The Greeks broke this pattern. Greek government leaders were not considered gods, or god's appointees, so their decisions could be openly questioned. It took more than mere opposition to the government to make a person a traitor or a heretic. A person could question the wisdom of the leaders without fearing reprisals; well . . . most of the time . . . err . . . maybe every now and then . . . with carefully chosen words. The west eventually adopted this viewpoint, separating church and state. The kings of the Orient disagreed then, and modern despots disagree now. Hitler, Stalin, Mao, fascism, and communism all agree governments are not ordained by god (in fact, they think there is no god); and they agree the individual is nothing, as only the state gives an individual meaning. Thus, *the government becomes god,* as Hobbes opined in *The Leviathan,* published in AD 1651. When the government is separate from god but *does* recognize god's existence, its actions can be limited by god's pronouncements (sometimes called natural law); however, if the government *does not* believe in or acknowledge god, then there are **no limits, moral or otherwise, on government action**. Such governments are the most dangerous of all.[25] Greek city-states were having problems with governance, until an outside force came to oppress them.

THE PERSIANS INVADE GREECE

From at least 750 BC to about 490 BC, Greece was a disunited land, as the city-states spent a bunch of time warring with one another. In fact, Greece enjoyed diversity through three separate peoples: the Mycenaeans (also called Arcadians), Ionians, and Dorians. (And you thought diversity was a good thing.)The Dorians, arriving last, about 800 BC, threw the Greek peninsula into turmoil, on top of creating a hundred year dark age;. It seems the only uniting elements were a common language and culture. The Greeks habitually divided the world into two parts, those who spoke

---

24 In Egypt the Pharaoh was considered a god on earth, plus he was backed by a powerful priesthood.

25 As shown by godless Communist governments that have destroyed well over 94 million lives in their short history (*The Black Book of Communism: Crimes, Terror, Repression,* by Stephan Courtois, 1999).

Greek and the barbarians who did not. The Greeks also established colonies—many colonies, all around the Aegean Sea. Later they expanded to the Black Sea, Italy, Sicily, and Lebanon and beyond. Still, Greece was an area of small kingdoms and internecine warfare, where unity was unattainable (so much for the benefits of "diversity").

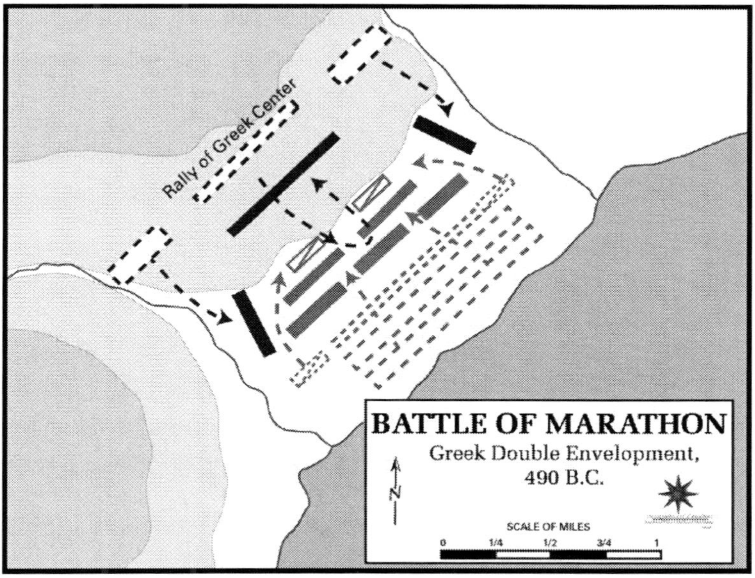

FIGURE 8 BATTLE OF MARATHON

Persia's expansion took them to Anatolia in Western Turkey, and contact with Ionian Greek colonies. These Greeks were a tough bunch to govern, and a revolt against Persia was soon underway (the Ionian Revolt—there's a creative name). The Ionian Greeks requested help, and Athens sent aid to their fellow Greeks. Persia crushed the revolt, but mighty King Darius, ruler of Persia, fumed about diminutive Athens giving aid to the uprising. Darius decided on a strong raid to teach Athens a lesson. The result: a most important battle, and the start of many unanticipated events.

The great battle took place at **Marathon** on the eastern shores of Greece in 490 BC. The Persians chose the place of battle, but they chose poorly. Sailing from Persia, the army headed west and decided to land at a beach near the town of Marathon, which was a relatively confined area; soon, an Athenian hoplite army opposed them. The Persians were accustomed to battling their foes on the open plains of the Middle East where swiftly moving cavalry could decide battles; but now, in this confined battlefield, cavalry maneuver was not possible. In addition, a Greek force of heavily armored men faced them with huge sturdy shields arranged like a wall in front of them, and this formation could repel Persian arrows that were a significant part of Persian tactics. The type of battle that developed was one in which the strengths of the Persians (maneuver and speed) were of little use. Instead, the strengths of the Greeks, the use of heavy infantry in defense and attack, were favored. The Greeks funneled the Persian attack into a narrow field and then quickly closed in on their flanks. After the Persians broke, the Greeks pursued the fleeing men, slaughtering many before they could regain their ships. It was a considerable victory by a very small force over a much larger one. After the victory, a runner named *Pheidippides* (these Greek names are tough!) ran from Marathon to Athens and declared, as he dropped dead from exhaustion, "Athens is victorious." We still celebrate this run today in the Marathon—only the runners do not drop dead at the end (even though they may feel like it). This victory was significant in many ways, but most importantly, *it saved the idea of democracy from extinction*. Free men defeated the Persian army seeking to enslave them and crush their beliefs.[26]

What the Greeks could not know was the affair was beginning, not ending. Another king of Persia waited in the wings, with plans to overturn Greek miscalculations. **Xerxes**, son of Darius, eventually assembled an army and designed a powerful invasion to subjugate the Greeks. It turns out that angering people such as the Persians, possessing huge armies and vast resources, is a bad idea.

In 480 BC, Xerxes marched against the Greeks. This time the Persian king assembled a huge army, so vast the chroniclers of the day said it was immeasurable.[27] With such a large army, a sea invasion was out of the question. The Persians crossed the Hellespont using a road constructed over a fantastic pontoon boat bridge, an engineering feat for all time,

---

26 OK, this is somewhat overstated since the raid was designed to kick Athens sideways and then leave. It was a punishment raid to teach the Greek snobs a lesson to stay out of Persian affairs; instead, it made them even more confident. We must still consider the idea that a successful raid may have encouraged the Persians to continue the conquest, one cannot know. In addition, other historians give an entirely different account of the battle (See p. 72, *With Arrow, Sword and Spear . . .* Bradford, 2001, Fall River Press). All these millennia later, it is tough to know exactly how it happened.

27 So, naturally, we try to measure it even though we were not there. The general consensus is Xerxes fielded about 250,000 to 300,000 men, a truly vast army for 480 BC.

afterward marching around the Aegean Sea toward Athens alerting the Greeks that all of Asia was coming their way.

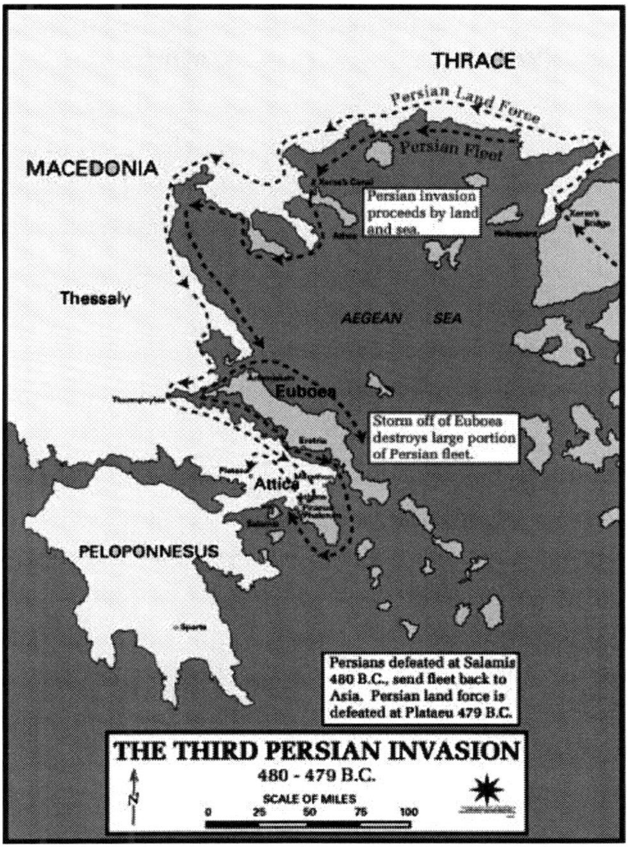

FIGURE 9 PERSIAN WARS—XERXES ATTACKS

The Greeks decided to unite against this invader from the east.[28] To impede the Persian's progress, the Greeks sent a small force north to the narrow pass at **Thermopylae** (hell's gate—thermo meaning hot, and pylae meaning gate) because this area was very tight, with the sea to one side and sharply ascending mountain cliffs to the other, and a small warrior group could buy their fellow Greeks time.

---

28 They had united during the first invasion by Darius, but the Athenians won the victory before the Spartans, or other city states, could arrive. The Spartans were also consulting soothsayers about the timing of battle (they always did), and they did what these magicians ordered.

The resulting three-day stand comes down to us as one of the most noble and enduring clashes of arms in history. At Thermopylae, six thousand Greeks, including men from Athens and Thebes, accompanied three hundred Spartans in the defense of the pass. The Spartans certainly bore the brunt of the fighting, but to say they were alone is simply inaccurate.

The immense Persian army came upon the Greeks holding the narrow pass and began their assault. Because of the nature of the terrain, the fighting favored the Greeks. As at Marathon, maneuver here was impossible. Persian horses and archers were useless, and the heavily armored Greeks with their ponderous shields, stabbing spears, and cleaving swords were in their element. By necessity, the Persians attacked the Greek wall of shields and men head-on, and a slaughter resulted as the lightly protected Persians failed to penetrate the Greek line. The Persian shields were (probably) wicker, their swords light, and they wore little armor in keeping with their philosophy of speed and maneuver to win battles. Like the German Army at Stalingrad in 1942, the Persian army was committed to a battle it was not designed to fight; consequently, the Persians failed to breach the Greek line. Even after two days of hard fighting, the Spartans and their allies held against the gargantuan eastern army. The Persians needed a new approach or they would likely spend a long time, and lose men unnecessarily, fighting for the pass.

Then the Persians got a break. A Greek who knew the area came to Xerxes telling him of a sinuous mountain trail around the pass that would allow the Persians to surround the Greeks and defeat them quickly. Xerxes sent his troops by night through the mountains, but the Greeks discovered the move and most fled the trap. The Spartans, and about one thousand men from Thebes, stayed and prepared for death. The Persians surrounded the remaining Greeks demanding surrender, but the Spartans and their allies refused. Xerxes ordered his men forward. All the Greeks died, fighting to the last man. Legend claims the Spartans fought until their swords and spears were broken, finally dying while scratching and clawing at their assailants. No man surrendered, so he would die free rather than suffer slavery for even a moment. And so it ended after three days. Xerxes and his prodigious army marched on leaving the blood-soaked ground behind. The Greeks erected a marker at the pass, reading, *"O traveler, go tell the Spartans that here we lie in obedience to their commands."*

Movies and legends ignore the reality of historical situations. Xerxes was dependent on his navy to supply his army and keep him safe from sea raiders. The navy Xerxes brought was huge, in keeping with the way mighty eastern monarchs of the day liked to do things. He was trying to show the small and disjoined Greek states they were powerless against him. The Athenians seemed to agree, since they abandoned their city and fled to nearby islands—but things are not always as they appear.

The **Oracle at Delphi** played a large role in Greek society. This famous Oracle had the ability, it seemed, to foresee events and give advice about them. The city of Athens sent emissaries to the Oracle asking what to do about the Persian invasion. The answer was mystifying (as usual), "You will be saved only by the wooden wall." What was that supposed to mean?

Themistocles (another arduous Greek name), a brilliant Athenian commander, thought he knew—the *wooden wall was ships.* He lobbied for an expansion of the Athenian navy. After a lot of haggling, common in democracies to this day, it was agreed and Themistocles set about preparing for the unequal battle. As the Persian army advanced on vacant Athens and burned it, the new and larger Athenian navy was setting a trap. In a narrow straight between the island of **Salamis** and the mainland, the Greeks awaited the Persians. The Greeks, under the command of Themistocles, managed to sucker the Persians into attacking into the narrow straight, where the faster and easier-to-handle Greek triremes destroyed a large part of the Persian fleet.[29]

Salamis was THE victory of the Persian wars, more important than Thermopylae or the later victory at Plataea. Without his navy, Xerxes' supply lines and lines of communication back to Persia were in danger of disruption by naval raids. Very large armies require very large amounts of supply, and cut supply lines were a grave danger to the Persian force. So, Xerxes quickly determined he had won the war. After all, he marched his army into the center of Greece, burned Athens, and beat up many other Greek city-states around the Aegean Sea. Athens, as the chief offender among Greek cities aiding the Ionian Revolt, and the victor at Marathon, was reduced to ashes and therefore suitably punished. Why wait around for the surrender of a bunch of individual cities?

Xerxes declared victory and went home with his huge army, but left a smaller army behind to hold the ground won. The next year, the Greeks

---

[29] The trireme was the principle warship of the ancient world at this time, being made up of three decks of rowers and a metal ram to the front which would sink or heavily damage ships when it was driven into their sides. The crew was about two hundred.

assembled in concert against the reduced Persian army, smashing them at the **Battle of Plataea** in 479 BC. The Persian defeat freed the Greeks from Persian tyranny, and the individual remained greater than the state.

After the Persians—The Peloponnesian War

The Greeks would celebrate their victory over the Persians for centuries to come, but unity and cooperation dissolved with Persia's retreat. Soon after the Persian threat departed, Athens decided to build an empire and formed the *Delian League*. This league encompassed Greek cities around the Aegean, and involved trading partnerships and agreements for mutual defense. Athens was the three-hundred-pound gorilla in the organization, and it soon began to show. Athens raised taxes on their "partners" and generally started acting as if they owned the other city-states. Since Athens' main rival was Sparta, some of the cities threatened to join with Sparta to escape from the "voluntary" league. Soon, Athens and Sparta were engaged in a long and especially brutal war for control of Greece and its many colonies.

The terrible **Peloponnesian War** was fought between **431 and 404 BC**. Athens foresaw the war (well, they should have since they started it), and knew they could not defeat the Spartan Army in a straight up battle. To counter the Spartan Army, they constructed a walled corridor between Athens and their port of Piraeus (the long walls). When the Spartans invaded, the Athenians withdrew behind their walls and waited the Spartan Army out. The Spartans could not successfully storm the long walls; subsequently, the war degenerated into Athenian naval raids on the Peloponnesian peninsula (the area controlled by Sparta) and Spartan attacks into Athenian territory to burn crops and hold the Athenians inside the long walls.

Athens survived a ghastly plague and the Spartan raids, but they could not survive the death of their war leader, **Pericles**. A new leader, **Alcibiades**, advocated increasing aggressive action, eventually convincing Athens to launch an expedition to conquer the city of Syracuse on the island of Sicily. The Athenians put together a massive fleet and an impressive army; nevertheless, distance, mismanagement from the outset, a spirited defense by the citizens of Syracuse, and significant help from Sparta destroyed the imposing Athenian fleet and army.[30] After the debacle, Athens was

---

30 Alcibiades was not there for the defeat in Sicily. Athens wanted him back to stand trial for desecrating the gods. He fled to Sparta and gave them good advice about

without reserves or money. Ultimately, she surrendered to the Spartans, dropping the curtain on the magnificent intellectual and artistic pageant of ancient Greece.

Several items are worth noting about the Peloponnesian War. Guess who sponsored the Spartans financially? The Persians financed the Spartans in a brilliant diplomatic move that destroyed their rivals by pitting the Greeks against one another. Only one Greek historian, Herodotus, wrote about the Persian Wars, and only one Greek historian, Thucydides, wrote about the Peloponnesian War. Finally, there was the short-lived Spartan victory. Shortly after Sparta "won" the war with Athens, other city-states defeated the Spartans (Thebes mainly); and, once more, Greece fell back into the warring city-states fiasco. The wars went on until **Phillip of Macedonia**[31] conquered Greece at the battle of Chaeronea in 338 BC, and placed it under the rule of an eastern-style king.

The splendor of Greece comes from its many accomplishments in art, literature, philosophy, science, democracy, and more. Its tragedy stems from an inability to unite and quell their desire for more. Athens fed its ambition; and Sparta, though it wanted to be left alone, bowed to its predestined clash with Athens. The failure was diplomatic as well as military. Like the start of World War I, the parties could not put away their human nature, their distrust of one another, their craving for power, their ambitions, the desire to control, and the fear that if they were not in control, others would control them. In Athens, charismatic orators captured the crowds' attention, convincing them to vote for really dumb ideas. This chapter in Athenian history should convince anyone of the dangers in democratic governments. The divided Greeks could not avoid war any more than a divided world can. Plato, a famous Greek philosopher, wrote, *"Only the dead have seen the end of war."* Thus far, over 2,000 years of history—and human nature—prove him correct.

---

how to defeat Athens. Then, after being caught with the wife of a Spartan King, he fled to Persia, and gave them good advice about how to defeat the Greeks. After all of this, he returned to Athens where he was again given a command (!!), and suffered an immediate defeat. He fled again to Persia, eventually being killed in Persian Phrygia after Lysander (a Spartan) asked that he be killed. Guess the Persians owed Lysander a favor. This fellow Alcibiades was the mother of all traitors. How dumb were the Athenians to take him back? Sounds like Eva Peron in Argentina(oops, we don't cover that. You'll have to look it up elsewhere—Wikipedia maybe).

[31] Father of Alexander the Great

ALEXANDER THE GREAT

334 to 323 BC

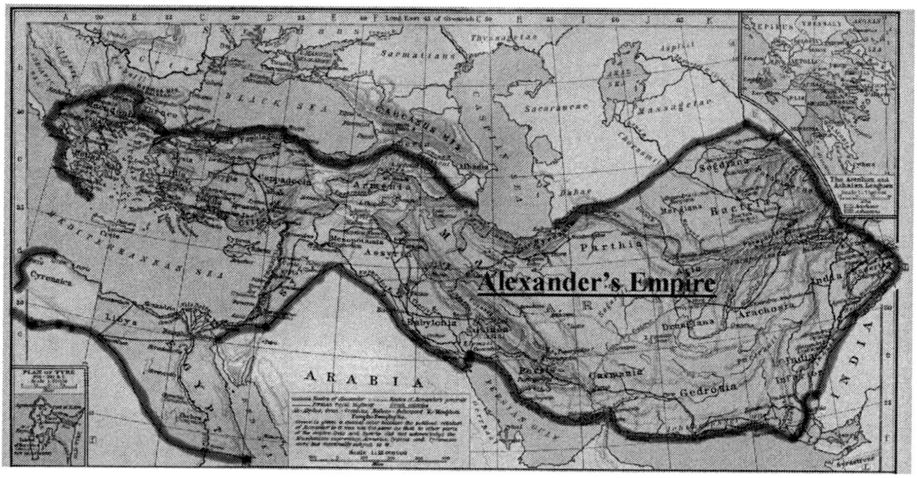

FIGURE 10 ALEXANDER'S EMPIRE

We must mention one more small item before we move on to Rome, and that "small item" is **Alexander the Great**. Alexander was the son of Phillip, who died by assassination about 334 BC making Alexander king; thereafter, Alexander set out to conquer Persia. **In 334 BC,** he landed in Asia Minor, present-day Turkey, and began a conquest that many say is unequalled to this day. He defeated the coastal cities along the eastern Mediterranean to establish a base for supplies, vanquished Egypt, and then turned on the Persian Empire. In a series of engagements the Greeks under Alexander defeated huge, but poorly led, armies of the Persians.

His main victories were at Issus in 333 BC and Gaugamela in 331 BC. At Gaugamela, Alexander went forward even though outnumbered, and on a battlefield chosen by Darius III, ruler of the Persian Empire. During the battle, Alexander moved his cavalry to the right, while he was riding at its head. Darius moved his lines to match, and this caused an opening in the Persian line, near the center, into which Alexander promptly charged. This was the key moment in the action, and Darius, recognizing defeat was upon him, left the field. Alexander decided not to pursue the Great King immediately, because his left flank was in trouble, and he returned to aid his comrades. Darius' own commander murdered him, but Alexander in turn executed the commander for his actions. Even with Persia at his feet, Alexander was unfulfilled; so he drove on to India. Alexander was primed to go further, but his tired and lonely army wanted to go home. Though undefeated, they had been away from home for years; and the Greek geographers told Alexander the end of the world was right over the next hill. Alexander and his Greeks turned back.

Alexander soon died (323 BC), and his empire was split into four areas (Macedon, Egypt, Syria, and Pergamum) each ruled by one of his chief commanders. What to do with the memory of Alexander? A fantastic general, a good administrator, and a man who wanted to bring the Greek and Asian world together; however, he died soon after his conquest, so his dream of unity failed. The great general died young. Had he lived, he might have been able to do more than any person after him to unite the East with the West. When Alexander died, he may have taken the best chance for a unity of ideas and culture between East and West with him to the grave.

ROME

753BC to AD 1453

Rome was THE CITY ruling the Mediterranean and Western Europe for over a thousand years. Its history is long, and complex; thus, we will break Rome into two eras, The Republic and The Empire. Rome started as a Repubic about 753 BC, and grew to rule Western Europe, and the Mediterranean Sea, before morphing into the Empire era after Caesar's death in 44 BC. The huge empire was difficult to govern; consequently, the Romans divided it into eastern and western regions in AD 284 with an emperor in charge of each. Pressure from nomads invading from central Asia destroyed the Western Roman Empire about AD 455, but the Eastern Roman Empire lived on and prospered until finally conquered by the Turks in 1453. After the split, the city of Rome remained the center of governance in the west; while in the east, Constantinople became the empire's center, growing to enormous wealth and power. Under Justinian the Eastern Roman Empire (Byzantium) nearly equaled the size of Rome, and its wealth was vast.

How to describe Rome? Given only one word, it would be grandeur. The Romans lived large. Roman engineers were the best in the world, and those skills were on display throughout the realm. Roman cities boasted wonderful heated public baths, running water at public fountains, paved roads, magnificent buildings, theaters, and sports arenas. The Coliseum at

Rome was incomparable. The Romans constructed numerous underground passageways in the Coliseum where people and animals could pass under the stadium, popping up inside the arena to amaze the crowds. The Romans even staged naval battles there by filling the arena with water. Built outside the Coliseum were shops and offices, much like our modern malls. Even underground Rome was a wonder, where excellent outsized sewers carried away the waste products of urban life. Everywhere the Romans constructed a city these amenities were common. Another Roman invention was cement. Not just any cement, but a kind made with volcanic ash that was much harder than cement in common use today and much longer lasting.

Very well constructed Roman roads, running in straight lines for miles, were crowned so water would run off, surfaced with stone, and had distance markers at regular intervals. These roads allowed swift, safe travel. The numerous roads tied the empire together as nothing else could. Along their roads the Roman legions traveled 20 miles per day, if necessary, to reach trouble spots throughout the Roman world. Trade, a bulwark of civilization, moved safely throughout Rome on these same roads.

Roman skill and vision were simply beyond compare in the ancient world. Still standing today, and in use in the twentieth century, are Roman aqueducts that brought fresh water down from the mountains to refresh the citizens of Rome 2,000 years ago. Such aqueducts were common throughout Rome, as well as open-air theaters, ostentatious villas, and arenas for sport and entertainment. At Caesura in Palestine, (modern day Israel) what was probably the world's first artificial harbor was constructed, and it was huge. All over the Rome, brilliant feats of engineering were commonplace; thus, the incredible became the feasible.

These engineering feats differed from those in other ancient civilizations. In Mesopotamia, Egypt, Babylon, Assyria, and Meso-America, royalty and religion reserved the massive building projects. In Rome, the massive construction was for the people. The Coliseum, aqueducts, Trajan's Forum, fountains, roads, and the wonderful baths were constructed for the citizens of Rome. There were glorious temples to the gods, but the majority of Roman construction was to benefit the people and not kings, queens, priests, or the gods—at least not at first.

Rome established the law as a key component of Western life, a concept still deeply rooted in Western thought. The idea of codified law came to Europe from Rome. Perhaps no other concept transferred from Rome to the West was as important as the way Romans thought about law and its central position in society. Around 451 BC the *decemvirs,* a board of ten lawmakers, set out the first written laws of Rome, which were then debated, amended, and passed by an assembly of all the people. The laws were written down on Twelve Tables and set in the Forum for all to read. The Roman Forum was a gathering place for the populace where matters of state were debated. The decisions of the Roman Republic were made in public, for all to hear. Open debate, freedom of speech, open government, and voting for who would run Rome were the hallmarks of the Republic of Rome.

The need for written laws was to ease the strife between the *patricians, and plebeians. Patricians* were the old landholding families; thus, "fathers" of Rome—patrician means father—while the *plebeians* were the non-fathers, or everyone who was not a patrician, usually the non-landholding masses including slaves. For years these written laws quelled the problems between the antagonistic groups. With the added institution of the *Tribune,* or person protecting the plebs from injustice, the system markedly improved. Only a plebe could hold the office of Tribune. Through the scheme of reducing laws to writing and plebe protection through the Tribune, Rome achieved societal peace for hundreds of years while waging relentless war on their frontiers.

Rome grew slowly and by conquest.[32] Its first major rival outside of Italy was the city-state of **Carthage**, located on the coast of North Africa. Carthage was in the way of Roman expansion because it controlled the island of Sicily, the southern coast of Spain, and a large portion of the northern coast of Africa. War was inevitable, and it came in the form of three wars, all of which Carthage lost. The three **Punic Wars** determined who would rule the Mediterranean.

The Punic Wars

Carthage was founded by a group of seafarers from the eastern coast of the Mediterranean, the Phoenicians (Punic is a form of the word *Phoenician*). The Phoenicians were expert sailors, and legend has it that they sailed

---

[32] Not every opponent was smashed. The Gauls (Celts) sacked and burned Rome around 390 BC. Rome had been engaged in a brutal war with two cities near the city of Rome, Fidenae and Veii, and the arrival of the Gauls simply overwhelmed their exhausted and depleted legions. Rome often lost, but the Romans were amazingly tenacious. 10 year wars were nothing to them. And they were willing to replace losses by bearing higher taxes almost endlessly as well. Could we do that? Nah . . .

around the continent of Africa. They founded many cities to secure their trading routes since they were traders and good executives above all else. The colonies and cities they founded were footholds in the local areas, expanding their ability to trade with local inhabitants. Carthage became a great city because of its excellent harbor, access to the interior of Africa where gold, ivory, pottery, and many other valuable goods were located, and its site near the center of the Mediterranean. As it accumulated power, Carthage founded colonies in Spain, Sicily, and key locations around the western Mediterranean which were eventually in the path of Roman expansion. The first Punic War began over Sicily. This developed into a naval war,[33] but Carthage and its splendid navy managed to lose it. As the war started Carthage was winning, since its navy was superior to Rome's. Then the Romans got an idea. Their strength was their ideal land army, so they simply had to get their army into the naval fight and they could prevail. The Romans accomplished this by using grappling hooks to hook the Carthaginian vessels and pull them over to the Roman ships, and then the Romans dropped planks (called ravens) across to the enemy ship. Their army units (waiting on the Roman ship) stormed across and easily defeated the Carthaginian crews. Quite a trick, and one Carthage never managed to counter. The net result was a total Roman victory over Carthage's naval power. After a twenty-three-year war, Carthage lost Sicily and gained an implacable enemy.

The Second Punic War is synonymous with **Hannibal**, a brave and resourceful Carthaginian general, who won numerous victories but lost the war. In an unexpected move in the year **218 BC**, Hannibal moved north through Spain and France and crossed the Alps into Rome (Italy) with an army of about thirty thousand men. The Romans were stunned by the move, but responded promptly. Several battles were fought which were all significant Carthaginian victories. Fabian, elected consul of Rome after these enemy victories, managed to avoid losing to Hannibal by simply refusing battle. Fabian would keep to the hills where Hannibal's cavalry was ineffective and then attack the Carthaginian troops where they were weak. The Roman Senate quickly tired of this strategy and relieved Fabian after he failed to stop Hannibal from reaching winter quarters; nevertheless, Fabian did keep the vital local tribes loyal to Rome. After Fabian's dismissal the Senate decided to take the Carthaginian straight on. The legions finally pulled Hannibal into a decisive battle outside the village of **Cannae** in Southern

---

[33] The main ship of this war was the quinquereme which had *five* banks of oars. This ship was larger than the trireme which had three banks of oars and had been the mainstay of the Persian Wars.

Italy in **216 BC**. As the Roman legions approached it appeared Hannibal was at last going to be overthrown. He was outnumbered, and the Romans were very certain of their legions' ability to fight.

In the Republic era of Rome two consuls ruled, which allowed one to go to war while the other stayed to rule in the capitol of Rome. Normally, a consul would have two legions with him, however, in the previous battles Hannibal had destroyed the two legions and its consul. This had never happened before; hence, the Romans decided to respond with a maximum effort. At Cannae, the Romans had assembled *both consuls and four legions.*

CANNAE

Cannae was one of the great military encounters of all time. Hannibal's outnumbered army annihilated a much larger Roman army through arranging his forces in a shallow crescent formation and allowing the center to give way as the Roman legions advanced. Using his superb cavalry and strong flanks that had not given ground, Hannibal then pushed in both the Roman flanks and surrounded the legions. In the densely packed center, the Romans could not fight, retreat, or maneuver. The resulting victory was total. Out of approximately fifty thousand legionaries, thirty-five thousand found their graves, while Hannibal lost about 5,700. (Some reports say seventy thousand legionaries fought, and fifty thousand died).[34]

[34] These figures are difficult to compute. A legion was six thousand men, so four legions would be twenty-four thousand troops; however, the Romans also had auxiliary troops to assist the legions, and they may have numbered another twenty-four thousand plus supply units. At any rate, a lot of people died.

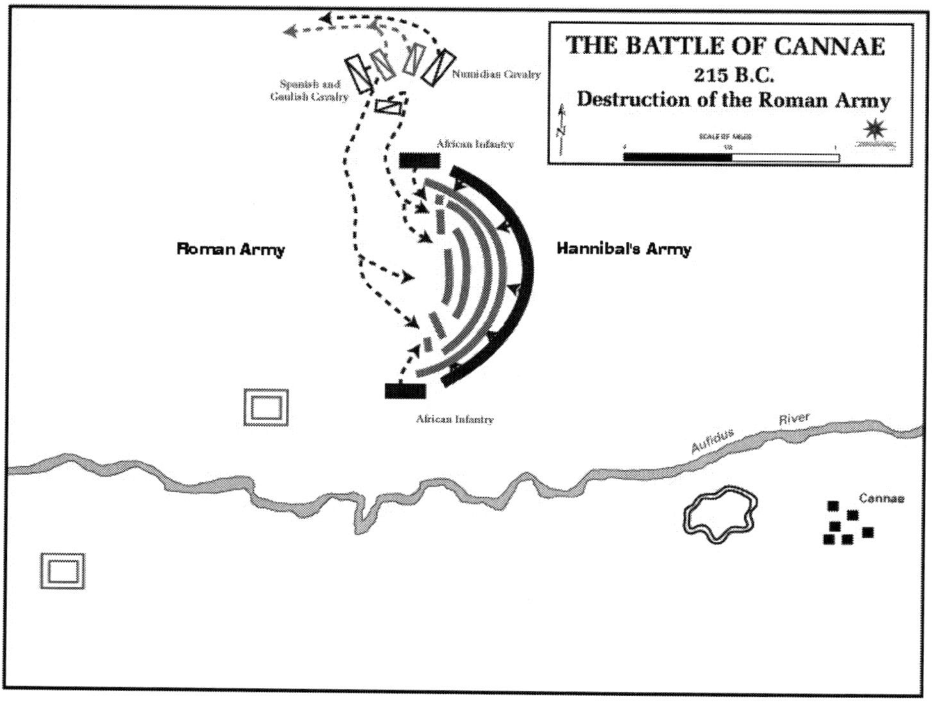

FIGURE 11 HANNIBAL AT CANNAE

Hannibal now controlled Central Italy, but he could not take the city of Rome because of its stout walls. Hannibal did pillage the countryside for *sixteen years,* causing widespread economic problems in central and southern Rome, but his main objective, persuading the numerous tribes in Italy allied with Rome to change sides, eluded him. Since Hannibal now controlled Central Italy, he sent for reinforcements from Carthage to replace his losses and put even more pressure on Rome; but reinforcements did not appear. Enemies of Hannibal in Carthage blocked sending high-quality troops to Italy and this effectively eliminated the brilliant general's chances of beating Rome.

One Roman general decided he could conquer Hannibal by not attacking him, at least, he would not directly attack right away. **Scipio Africanus** assaulted Hannibal's base in Spain thus depriving the Carthaginian of reinforcements and other support. Scipio had hit and hurt the army of Carthage in Italy through his conquests in Spain, and Hannibal's strength faded even as he continued to engage Roman armies in Southern Italy. Scipio then landed in North Africa thereby causing Carthage to recall Hannibal. In this way Scipio at last extracted Hannibal from Italy by *not* confronting him. This was a brilliant move, forever placing Scipio among the world's best generals. Hannibal met General Scipio not far from Carthage at the battle of **Zama** in **202 BC**, where Rome won the final battle of the Second Punic War. Reduced to little more than a small city-state on the Southern Mediterranean, Carthage would slowly grow prospers one last time. To his credit, Scipio did not burn Carthage to the ground or otherwise unwisely harm her citizens. His peace treaty did strip Carthage of its lands and its treasury, but considering what the Romans had done to other enemies, this was a peace long on generosity. Scipio thus *won both the war and the peace.* This has seldom been accomplished. Through his masterful victories and his thoughtful peace Scipio Africanus placed himself among the greatest men in antiquity. Eliminated as a threat, Carthage remained a semi-prosperous city at the edge of the empire, thus benefiting Rome through trade and taxes. Other Roman leaders destroyed the efforts of the gifted Scipio for reasons of pride and little else.

"Carthage must die" was the dull refrain of Cato, a Roman senator, who ended every speech in the Roman Senate with that slogan. Rome got its chance for another war with Carthage in 149 BC by siding with Numidia (an African state) against their old enemy. Carthage was a shadow of its former self and was quickly defeated by 146 BC, succumbing after a short siege. Rome razed the city, sowing salt on the land (thereby preventing crops being grown there) and declaring northern Africa a Roman colony. The inhabitants of Carthage were either murdered or taken away as slaves. Hannibal fled the city, but the emissaries of Rome followed. Discovered by Rome's agents in the eastern Mediterranean, Hannibal died by his own hand far away from his beloved Carthage.

The Punic wars gave Rome control of the western Mediterranean and set Rome on the road to a massive empire. *The key to its growth was its professional army that was rigorously trained, superbly disciplined, well armed, and well led.* The Roman legions worked together and fought as a united entity. Often faced with enemies who outnumbered them dramatically, the Roman legions managed to outgeneral and outfight the less-disciplined throngs that defied them.

THE ARMY, THE REPUBLIC, AND THE EMPIRE

The Roman Army after 107 BC centered on the legion, consisting of six thousand men divided into ten cohorts of six hundred men. Each cohort then divided into six "centuries" of one hundred men lead by a *centurion.*

Support troops normally accompanied the legions, such as archers, slingers, cavalry, and skirmishers that may have numbered up to an additional six thousand per legion. The legion in formation had remarkable flexibility, and in the hands of generals like **Julius Caesar, Marius**, and **Sulla,** it proved to be nearly unbeatable. With these formations Rome conquered Greece, Palestine, Lebanon, Syria, Egypt, North Africa, Spain, Portugal, Gaul (present-day France), part of England and Germany, the Balkans, Turkey, and for a time Mesopotamia.

As Rome expanded, its armies patrolled the empire, protected trade, and enforced Roman law. Whatever else Rome was, it was also an empire of trade. Numerous ships sailed the Mediterranean Sea, many with tons of cargo in their holds bound for the various ports around the empire. For trade the Romans constructed wooden super ships, some over 200 feet long, that could carry up to 2000 *tons* (that's right—TONS) of cargo.[35] Obviously, the Romans were serious about trade. Roman conquests around the coast of Turkey, and its access to the Black Sea, permitted Rome's traders to receive goods from the orient, central Asia, and other faraway places, spreading it about the empire on its fine roads and Mediterranean waterways. Observe that the Mediterranean Sea was at the very center of the Roman Empire; thus, one could travel by boat to almost any important point in the Empire (note the importance of geography . . . again). This successful economy helped made Rome rich, although plunder from its conquests was an important addition. As time went on, Rome ceased to expand and encountered economic troubles beyond its capacity to solve. Splendor has its price.

Rome did not start out as an empire; rather it started as a republic with representatives from the tribes that made up Roman culture having a vote on the management of the state. The elites governed the Roman Republic, and gave the lower classes few rights. Landed nobles (Patricians) ran the Roman Senate, numbering about three hundred men, although it grew larger in the twilight years of the republic (as many as six hundred or more).[36] During the Republic the Romans appointed two men as head of state, both known as consuls. Each man had to agree on any action taken. The Romans wanted to avoid giving too much power to one man; thus,

---

35 One ship was purported to be 400 feet long. Such large construction requires great expertise in ship building.

36 Originally, the head of each clan making up the Roman Republic would comprise the Senate. As time went on, the power of the person was as important as the clan he or she came from.

they adopted a system of dual representation at the top post. The Romans rotated the consuls annually. By this method they were trying to keep the consuls' popularity low, forestalling a mob installed dictator. This fear of a charismatic personality controlling "the mob" in democratic governments remains today. The framers of the US Constitution were well aware of Rome's problems. During the Republic the Senate adopted the laws, and the citizens elected the Senate anew each year. Not everyone was a citizen, but it was an electoral process where the citizens decided who made the laws. This grossly oversimplifies Rome's way of government during the Republic, but the keys were *a division of power,* so no one could win perpetual rule, *the vote* by Rome's citizens to decide their leaders, and an *open government* where decisions were openly debated and openly made. However, away from the forum trouble was brewing.

The real problem was the army. Landowners serving for part of each year originally made up the Roman army; however, as the years rolled on the army became professional and answered to their commanders rather than the Roman Senate. The change came about after a rather minor event in North Africa, where an ally of Rome, Numidia, had a succession problem. After Numidia's king died in 118 BC, his nephew Jugurtha seized the crown. The new usurper king turned out to be murdering slime and was soon at war with Rome; however, the Romans did not do well in the long and expensive campaigns. **Gaius Marius** then appeared on the scene and completely reorganized the Roman Army. The early legions used the "maniple" of 60 men, usually arranged in 4 to 5 rows of 15 columns. Each row carried different weapons. During the wars of the later Republic, the number of rows decreased and weapons improved, but by the time of the war with Numidia fundamental changes were necessary. Long campaigns far from native soil were not possible for a citizen army needing to go home and tend to farms and families; thus, Marius introduced a **professional army** that could stay at war indefinitely. He allowed non-land owners to join which attracted numerous recruits of homeless farmers to fill the ranks. The weapons standardized, the standard formation was reduced to three rows, and Marius reorganized the keystone unit from the maniple to the **cohort** which consisted of 3 maniples or 120 men. [37] This army brought Jugurtha to defeat, and won the rest of the Roman Empire; however, it also welded the men to their

---

[37] Another widely used unit, a **century,** consisted of 100 men led by a centurion. Note that every centurion Jesus encountered in the Bible was an upright man of great personal character. Maybe that is the fundamental reason Rome lasted so long.

commander. As a professional army they followed where the commander led, even if that road led to Rome itself.[38]

The Roman and Latin tribes were unrelated, and Roman arrogance finally drove the Latin people into revolt. This was one of intense rivalry, only ending after a Roman compromise proposed by Lucius Caesar (father of one Julius Caesar) was accepted. Under laws proposed by Lucius, the Latins would at last be citizens of Rome. One war ending and another one starting was typical for this age. As the Latin war raged, Mithridates, a king in Asia Minor, revolted. Mithridates' revolt was defeated, but along the way to victory Marius and one of his former generals, **Cornelius Sulla**, started a Roman civil war with one another. Sulla won and then *marched on Rome*. The Roman constitution forbade such a move, but Sulla had an excellent army and simply entered the city and took charge. He murdered his opponents (a common Roman theme), reformed Roman law, and then left again to finish off the rebels in Asia Minor. Sulla established the precedent of a general at the head of his army entering the city of Rome to establish order. Of course, "order" is in the eye of the beholder.

After Sulla left the city, Marius returned to Rome and purged anyone associated with Sulla (that murder thing again). Marius swiftly expanded the purges which spread fear throughout the city of Rome. Sulla, victoriously finished with rebellions in Asia Minor and Greece, then returned to Rome and once more defeated the followers of Marius. As might be expected, he then purged those aligned with his opponent and became dictator. He retired in 80 BC after a successful rule as dictator. Two of Sulla's most competent officers were **Pompey** and **Crassus**, who would play a role in future Roman political and military intrigue. It was Crassus and Pompey who finally crushed the rebellion of the slave and gladiator Spartacus.

In Rome, as the Republic gave way to popular generals such as Caesar and the establishment of an empire, the crowd (or mob as some would say) gained additional influence. The generals who wanted to expand their clout promised the crowds of Rome great benefits for backing them. A bidding war of sorts began with each popular general promising more if the mobs would back him instead of a rival. [39] In Rome itself, a kind of class warfare

---

38 p. 200, *With Arrow, Sword, and Spear . . .* , Bradford, 2001, Fall River Press.

39 In the city of Rome, the poor constituted a huge percentage of the population. Politicians had given patronage to these poor for years in return for their votes; thus, from the start, the wealthy had gained and maintained power through

prevailed with the *Plebes* clashing with the *Patricians* for wealth and power. Later Roman emperors simply bribed the crowds with "***bread*** and ***circuses,***" which was free entertainment in the arena and free bread for the public. The mobs in the city of Rome grew so dangerous that a legion was posted there to protect the emperor from his public. This legion, the Praetorian Guard, became ever more powerful because they could kill the emperor as easily as protect him; however, we are not yet at the death of the Republic and the establishment of emperors. Back to history.

Pompey went on to kick Rome's enemies sideways from Greece to Egypt, while back in Rome Crassus had joined with Julius Caesar[40] in a financial partnership making them both wealthier. Caesar became consul for one year and began to redistribute land to the poor of Rome, making him the champion of the masses. After serving as consul he took over the governorship of Gaul (France today), and demonstrated that he was a man of outstanding military talents by conquering the whole place. He wrote a book on his brilliant conquests thereby showing himself to be a master propaganda artist as well. Crassus felt he needed to prove himself a general as well, so he invaded Parthia. Parthia was a large empire on the eastern edge of Rome. These Parthian's had repelled Roman incursions before and were skilled warriors. They were especially good with the bow and arrow. Crassus, the wealthiest man in Rome but no general, died like a ensnared rat in Mesopotamia near the city of Carrhae, along with 70,000 Roman legionnaires doing porcupine imitations because of all the Parthian arrows sticking out of them. The Parthian army had brought up caravans of arrows for the fight. Ouch! After this encounter Rome stayed away from Parthia . . . of course, no Roman general had wanted to invade in the first place.

Caesar, seeing that the informal triumvirate of himself, Pompey, and Crassus, had been undone by Parthia, wanted to march on Rome from

---

buying votes from the poor. The net result was Rome was ruled by a few wealthy families who could pay the patronage. Hannibal added to the problems, because as he ravaged the countryside the rich bought up the land of the destitute farmers sending them into the city to join the poor while the rich grew ever richer. After the defeat of Hannibal, the rich used slaves to work the farmland on their massive estates thus increasing their wealth further and driving up the number of poor in Rome itself. Caesar had made a name for himself redistributing land to the poor, so he was one up in the bidding war as crossed the Rubicon.

[40] Caesar lived from 100 BC to 44 BC. His life was ended by murder in the Roman Forum.

Gaul with his victorious army and establish himself as dictator; however, under Roman law a general had to abandon the position of commander upon re-entry into Italy (at the Rubicon River). Caesar marched up to the Rubicon, the boundary no general could legally pass with his legions. Pompey, who was in Rome, convinced the Senate to remind Caesar he must not enter Rome with his army. The Republic was at the brink. The legions were now loyal to their commanders, whom they had served under for years and enjoyed scores of victories. *This made the legions servants of their commanders and not the Republic and its Senate. This divided loyalty doomed the Roman Republic.*

Caesar, against the orders of the Senate, crossed the Rubicon (a river in Northern Italy)[41] and entered Rome to the triumphant roar of the greedy citizens. Caesar was loved by the masses of Rome, and by distributing money and land to the *plebes* he increased his popularity. What followed was a series of civil wars between Caesar and his rivals (Pompey, Crassus, Anthony and their allies) which Caesar won. Caesar returned to Rome triumphant. The mobs of Rome adored him. After his return he was made perpetual dictator; however, not everyone wanted Rome under a dictatorship, no matter how wise the dictator.[42] A few members of the Senate formed a conspiracy to eliminate Caesar, thus regaining the republic. This group murdered Caesar in the Forum on the ides of March (the fifteenth) in 44 BC.

Before going on, we need to discuss a smallish fire. No, not a fire destroying a city, or a fleet, or a forest—just one building. This fire destroyed the **Library at Alexandria**, the largest library in the ancient world and the depository of all the knowledge of the time. Plutarch said Caesar started the fire accidently while burning enemy boats in 48 BC, but what really caused the conflagration is unclear. The books of the ancient world were scrolls, normally just rolled up and placed in wooden holders like wine racks. The fire easily burned the library and all its contents, depriving our

---

41 Modernly, someone who has crossed the Rubicon has committed himself to an unalterable course of action.

42 **Cleopatra** VII, Queen of Egypt, last of the Ptolemies, played a role in this part of the drama. She was impregnated by Caesar, had his child by caesarean section (note the name), and returned to Rome with him. None of this endeared him to members of the Senate. After Caesar's death she returned to Egypt, became the lover of another famous Roman general, Mark Anthony, had twins by him, and committed suicide after her armies were defeated by Octavian in 31 BC. Who could make this stuff up?

world of the knowledge of their world. When the library burned thousands of years of history and learning burned as well. This was a disaster beyond measure. If I could reverse one event in the ancient world the burning of the Library at Alexandria would be it.

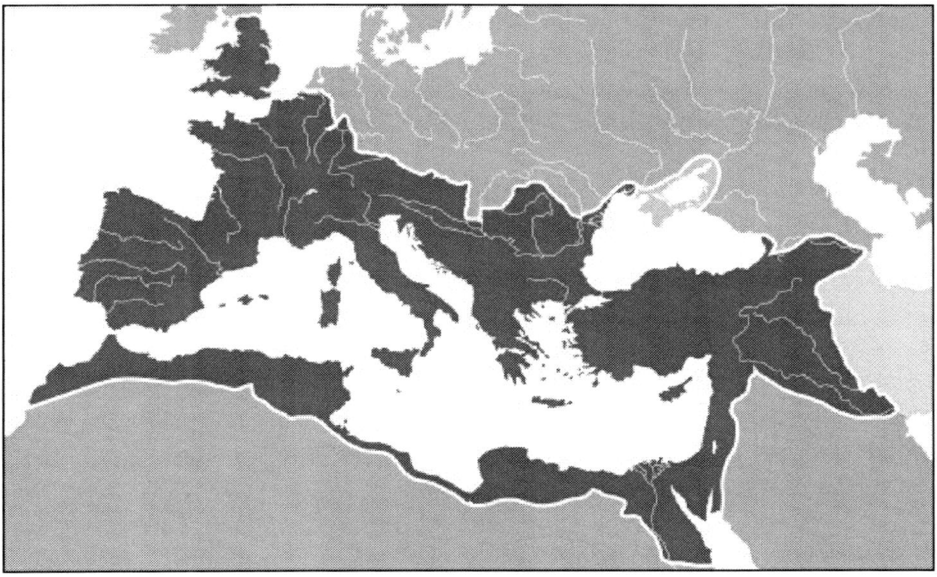

FIGURE 12 ROMAN EMPIRE AT ITS HEIGHT UNDER TRAJAN—115 AD

In spite of the elimination of Caesar, the republic failed to reassert itself and another period of civil war began with Octavian battling the conspirators. Eventually, **Gaius Octavian** (later Augustus) won the wars against those who plotted the assassination of Caesar, and he took over as **Caesar Augustus**.[43] Under Augustus, the office of dictator would transmute into Roman Emperor. Augustus was one of Rome's greatest leaders. Under his rule, the Pax Romana (Roman peace) initiated two hundred years of peace within the empire, the poor were fed, land was given to the soldiers and numerous building projects were undertaken increasing the opulence of the city. Unfortunately, the civil wars had undermined the Roman Legions, and upon those legions the safety of the Empire rested.

While all these earth-shaking events were transpiring, a small event took place in a remote and grimy province on the very fringe of the Roman Empire. It was an event gathering no notice at the time, but it was a

[43] Caesar began to mean prince or king, and the words *Kaiser* (German) and *Czar*(Russian) came from the word *Caesar*.

world-changing moment. **Jesus the Christ was crucified** outside the gates of Jerusalem in **AD 33**. Jesus had claimed to be the Son of God (Messiah of the Jews) during his 3 year ministry, but the Jews rejected him and demanded the Romans crucify him as a blasphemer. The Roman governor, Pontius Pilate, gave Jesus over for scourging and crucifixion with two criminals that same day. Three days later, his infinitesimal group of followers, who fled and hid on his arrest, began to claim Jesus had risen from the dead, ascended into heaven, and truly was the Son of God. From this insignificant event in an insignificant place the **Christian religion** was born.[44]

Caesar had adopted Octavian as his son (Caesar was Octavian's great uncle) in his will. After Caesar's murder Octavian became emperor; thus, Caesar found a way to keep the empire intact through a novel method of transferring the power of governance. The death of a dictator often causes problems with the transfer of power. Normally, an heir takes over, however, if there are many heirs wars start endangering the existence of the state. Under Caesar's concept, as an emperor neared the end of his rule he adopted a person as his son who would then go on to rule in his place after his death. Gaius Julius Caesar Octavian Augustus (maybe those Greek names were not so bad after all), for example, chose the best man he could find to rule the empire after his death, in this case Tiberius, and adopted him as his son; thus, the power transfer problem was solved. If Emperors following Augustus followed his example the result would be a kingship based on **merit** instead of heredity—at least as long as each emperor followed the plan.

Childless Augustus died in AD 14 choosing Tiberius as his successor. Not a great choice, but Tiberius made an even worse choice for his successor, Caligula. Caligula spawned horrendous crimes, including killing his grandmother and engaging in sex with his three sisters. He also dissolved the Senate, making everyone angry in the process. Somehow, through it all, the Roman bureaucracy held on and held the empire together. After Caligula decided he was divine the Praetorian Guard decided to test that out and killed him, showing that being divine is not easy; thereafter, Claudius became emperor. After yet another round of murders and conquests, mostly in Britain, Claudius adopted Nero as his heir. Nero was 16 when Claudius died, and he was a poor leader. Nero drank, ran around with women endlessly, and raised taxes (sounds like most modern politicians).

---

[44] This the only major religion started by a penniless dead man, with no children, and zero followers remaining out of only twelve to begin with, one of which had sold him out to the authorities.

He also engaged in a hideous persecution of Christians.[45] After a life of killing people for no reason, including kicking his pregnant wife to death, the Praetorian Guard put Nero to death. Rome rejoiced.

Their followed a series of emperors rejecting rejoicing, but they held things together: Galba (AD 68), Vespasian (AD 69), Titus (AD 79), Domitian (AD 81), Nerva (AD 96), **Trajan** (AD 98), and Hadrian (AD 117). In AD 138 Hadrian's successor, Antoninus Pius took over, ran a good administration, and then, adhering to Roman tradition, named **Marcus Aurelius** as his heir. Too bad, because Marcus Aurelius broke the long tradition of awarding power to the most worthy man. Marcus gave the empire to his son **Commodus**, a worthless man who murdered one of his sisters and slept with another. Commodus, his mind filled with filth from the start, was terminated by a conspiracy of his personal whores in AD 192. Civil War followed, and a rapid succession of emperors that were unworthy of the post.

A group of very poor leaders was at the helm as the empire declined.[46] The empire was not able to hold on to its far-flung territories. Just as before, in the early empires of the Middle East, barbarians from the east and north began to pound the frontiers of the western Roman world. Slowly at first, the empire pulled back, still trying to defend on the boundaries of the great rivers the Rhine and the Danube. Nothing the Western Empire could do stopped the invasions of the barbarians; thus, Western Rome disappeared from history.

Diocletian, who became emperor in **AD 284**, **split the empire** into two parts, east and west, to better govern the whole. However, the real economic strength of the Roman Empire was in the east. In my opinion, the Eastern Empire was stronger because it enjoyed a connection to Asia through the Silk Road, and was better able to trade and build its wealth through these contacts. When **Constantine** became emperor, he moved the capital to Byzantium and renamed the city after himself—Constantinople (is this typical of a politician or what?). Slowly, the two halves of the empire stopped supporting one another, and the west grew ever weaker until it could no

---

45 Nero liked to burn Christians lashed to poles along the streets at night as street lights. Imagine the smell. If no one complained the city must have smelled pretty bad beforehand.

46 It was under the Emperor Trajan in AD 117 that the empire reached its greatest geographic extent. After Hadrian took over he began to reconsolidate the empire and went over to the defense.

longer defend its boarders from the barbarian tribes attacking from the east. As the Western Roman Empire fell, the invaders settled into Gaul, Spain, and Italy itself. Constantinople and the Eastern Roman Empire would last until defeat by the Turks in AD 1453. The west fell in about **AD 455** after numerous sacks of the city of Rome.

It was during the Western Empire's decline that the Christian religion began to be accepted, and eventually became the mainstay of European culture after Rome's demise. The emperor Constantine granted Christianity legal status in AD 313 through the **Edict of Milan**, thus preventing further persecution of Christians. In 380 it became the official religion of the empire, and by AD 392, Christianity was the empire's only legal religion. Through a series of church counsels beginning in the 300s, the church settled on which books would comprise the Bible, and settled various questions concerning key elements of the faith (**Apostles' Creed**—2d century, **Nicene Creed**—AD 325). **St Jerome** (AD 374-420) and **St. Augustine** (354-430) were major contributors to church doctrine. By the time the Western Roman Empire was at its end in AD 455, the Catholic Church has taken up its position as the philosophical and religious center of Western Europe. In addition, the importance of Rome's preserving and transferring classical Greek culture and learning to the West cannot be overstated. The ability of Western Christianity to absorb these classics was a key factor in the Renaissance.

The fall of the Western Roman Empire centered on the following problems—in order of importance:

1) Major Economic Weakness. After the empire split into the eastern and western halves the Western Empire became weaker by the year. After losing the oriental trade, and the food supplies from Egypt, the Western Empire degraded incessantly.
2) Total Corruption of the Government in Rome. By the end of the empire in the West, the Roman emperors, the senators, and the administrators were scoundrels of the first order. The great leaders who had built Rome had long since left the government and the army.
3) The Roman Army Failed to Adapt to Changing Warfare. The Roman legions, which emphasized infantry formations, were becoming obsolete because of improvements in heavy cavalry formations. Leadership was also wanting, and strategic thinking was not the forte of the legions and their leaders as the end neared.

4) Rome Always on the Defense. After AD 117, Rome was always on the Strategic and Tactical defensive. Clausewitz in his classic book *On War* stated that the purpose of a defensive strategy was to hold on until the time came for offensive action, because on the defense one possesses no ability to control the ultimate decision. Rome, somewhat like the USA in the Vietnam War, could not effectively take offensive action against the barbarian tribes accumulating beyond their frontiers. The enemy's center of gravity was beyond the Rhine and Danube Rivers, in their temporary homelands, and beyond these mighty rivers the German tribes were out of Rome's reach. The distance and the physical barriers destroyed Rome's ability to strike at their enemy's center of gravity. The barbarians could build their strength to strike when and where they wanted. Against this kind of problem, Rome had no effective answer.

Was holding Gaul an overextension of Roman power? The riches of the empire came from Spain, North Africa (Egypt), and the east—not Gaul (my opinion). Defending the Rhine took many legions. Could the Romans continue winning by creating a buffer zone in a small area north of Italy, and fortifying the passes through the Alps and the Pyrenees? By water born trade Rome could maintain prosperous contact with all its major provinces in Spain, the Levant, Turkey, Greece, North Africa and thence the Far East. By not overextending themselves into Gaul, perhaps the Roman Empire had a chance to survive into the medieval era.

The fall of the Western Rome took generations. After about AD 200, the population consistently fell all over the Western Empire. Land once cultivated fell into disuse. The size of towns shrank. Trade, as measured by shipping, fell over one-half. In addition, a rather-bad plague hit the Roman world about 169 to AD 170. The population decline continued until the seventh century. Under Diocletian, the value of Roman coinage fell endangering the finances of the empire; however, Constantine saved the day by instituting gold coinage that held its value because the empire kept the content pure and correctly weighted. However, the Western Empire's power was waning, and after the Eastern Empire removed Egyptian grain from the city of Rome, the end was near. By AD 500, barbarian tribes settled where they pleased, and Rome's legions no longer patrolled the roads or kept the peace. Rome slowly became only a ghostly image in the minds of those few once knowing its glory. Soon, even that remembrance faded as history pulled its dark cloak over the Roman West.

Discussion of the Fall of the Western Roman Empire

Let us digress for a moment and discuss an overview of history to this point: the fall of the Western Roman Empire about AD 455.[47] The fall of the Western Roman Empire ushered in a new age in Europe. Rome (in the west) was obliterated, and what took its place was a new society in which the learning and unity of the Romans was utterly lost, replaced by disunity, chaos, and a distinct lack of quality in every aspect of life. *Seldom has the world experienced such a complete loss of knowledge.* How do people forget how to build frame and panel doors, how to read and write, or how to make light wheels with spokes? In a relatively short period, memories of Roman quality, accomplishments, and innovation faded. Mud huts sprang up under the great Roman aqueducts, and rubble rapidly replaced wonder.

Comparing this total cultural collapse to conquests in Asia, we note that China suffered invasions as brutal as those invasions suffered by Rome (the Mongols for example); nevertheless, China continued as a culture and a people. The invader's language, dress, and cultural identity were absorbed into China, never to return. Rome fell and its culture, dress, language, heritage, and learning were totally lost for centuries; however, by contrast, China endured the invasions and fundamentally remained the same. It may be that the vastness of both the geography and the populace of China just swallowed the invaders whole. The invaders normally brought a somewhat crude culture into China, so the more sophisticated culture of the Chinese may have been so attractive to the conquerors they were ready to copy and adopt it as their own.

Egypt also survived at least two outside invasions, and their population was much smaller than China's; still, they managed to retain their ancient traditions, dress, and culture, and in due course, toss the invaders out. Why did Rome fail to do the same?

These questions are impossible to answer, because after the fall of Rome the area fell back into a prehistory of sorts, in that few remaining inhabitants of Western Europe could read or write. The Roman population declined for decades before the conquests, and the invader's numbers were large; thus, perhaps the more numerous invaders—after killing off many more Romans—simply overpowered the remaining Roman population. We may

---

47 The fall of the Western Roman Empire took decades, so the date of 455 is somewhat arbitrary, but by this date the governmental protections (army) and bureaucracy (administration) were gone forever.

speculate that since Rome fell slowly, and inhabitants of the West knew of safer areas in the empire, they escaped the descending carnage using the Roman roads; thus, the Romans left and the invaders were all that remained. In the other instances, such as China, the population stayed and eventually overcame the invaders along with reestablishing their culture. In Egypt, their sophisticated society may have kept them apart from a set of crude invaders, or they may have simply felt their gods would eventually bring them through. All this is conjecture, but by making comparisons we can obtain a deeper understanding of history.

This view of the Western world becoming a big heap of debris after the Western Roman Empire fell is somewhat dated as many historians now say the period we once called the "Dark Ages" were nothing of the kind. They say a new vigor was put in place eventually giving the world the Renaissance, the printing press, science, and the flowering of the modern world. In my mind, "eventually" is the key word, because that "eventually" took centuries and a lot of luck. *There was no guarantee the world following Rome would produce anything.* In fact, the world after Rome looked very much like the one Rome had conquered. Before Rome, Europe was a mass of warring tribes without large well-constructed cities, roads, administrative organization, trade, or safety—all of which came by way of Rome. After Rome, the landscape reverted to the past: a disarray of unconnected crumbling towns, a shrinking population, constant war between local warlords, rampant disease, falling farm production, no protection from lawless bands roaming the countryside, and little or no trade. Thus, the term "Dark Ages" is well applied to Western Europe after the fall of Rome.

Whatever view we take, the collapse of the Western Roman Empire is a watershed in history, as what came after Rome was far different than Rome was or ever would have been. Now is a good time to review the past many thousands of years and see if we can discover some unity in the story of humankind.[48]

The Need for Protection

From the earliest writings of the Bible in Genesis, we find that murder was one of the first acts of humanity. After God expels Adam and Eve from the Garden of Eden, they have two sons, and soon thereafter one son,

---

[48] Some philosophers say the world outside our brain cavity is nothing but chaos, and we mentally impose order on a disordered world.

Cain, murders the other, Abel.[49] The Bible gives no definitive reason for the murder of Abel. Of course, many view these biblical stories as fables; however, the story illustrates one undeniable truth—people kill one another on a regular basis for no reason.

From the dawn of history, in heroic stories of Gilgamesh, Isis and Osiris, the Iliad, Beowulf, and others we find that bloody conflict is a major theme. It seems men were slaughtering each other as soon as they became *Homo sapiens,* and the abundance of walled cities is the proof. Since large walls are such an early development, we can assume war developed early on as well. In most areas walls were the rule, and they went up early on, and they were made very strong. **Jericho,** a very ancient city, built a massive wall by 8000 BC. In the Iliad, Homer describes the walls of Troy as so immense the Greeks failed to breach them after a ten-year war. The Greeks got into the city through a trick (the Trojan horse). Walls, especially very hefty walls, take a lot of time, serious labor, and skill to construct. Such undertakings require major resources in terms of time, food, labor, talent, and materials—precious commodities in ancient times. At the Bronze Age collapse in 1200 BC, archeologists note that several major cities extended and strengthened their walls before the advent of a disaster overwhelming the people behind those walls. The obvious conclusion is they feared an invader, and spent the time and effort required to strengthen their chief defense against attack—the wall. A government that cannot protect its citizens cannot govern. In the final analysis, protection from war, chaos, and starvation is the first order of business for any government. Therefore, security is at the center of governance. People often chose a dictatorial government and security over a democratic government and uncertainty. This is a common thread throughout history.

Murder and war seem to be a permanent part of humanity's story. Is such vile behavior ensconced in our genes? What does all this say about us as human beings? Why have we consistently conquered, murdered, raped, and pillaged our neighbors—and anyone else we could find? Why this must be so is a root that grows deep in our history and our psyche, but it is logically impossible to explain.[50] It seems people such as Stalin, Hitler, Mao, Genghis Khan, Caesar, and Sargon, who were willing to kill anyone to obtain supremacy, are always around. Even at an individual level, Jack the Ripper's ilk still walks among us, ever so willing to take the lives of others

---

[49] Genesis 4: 1-16

[50] Freud would say human beings were irrational, and this may prove it. See Sigmund Freud under 1900: The Dividing Line to the Modern World in this tome.

for pleasure. So it was 4,500 years ago, and so it is today. Just as protection was vital 4,500 years ago, it is still indispensable today. When a government ceases to protect, it ceases to govern.

INVADERS FROM THE CENTER OF THE WORLD

Observe that ancient civilized areas favored building on great rivers with access to coastlines. This may be so because of the need for trade to build a great city. The traders could travel down these rivers to reach the ocean which is the leading platform for trade. Boats can carry a lot of cargo a long way much easier than people using animals can cross great distances. Until the advent of railroads, boats were by far the preferred choice for moving cargo. Thus, from the Middle East to China we find the first civilizations along great rivers leading to the coast.[51]

From the land mass at the center of the Old World, east of the Urals and west of Mongolia north of the Caspian and Black Seas, came raiders steadily battering the civilizations along the great rivers of the ancient world. These threats came from nomadic peoples living deep in the Eurasian land mass, and apparently living without large permanent cities. The nomadic invaders toppled or weakened empire after empire. We do not know why the invaders kept appearing from the same general location. Experts theorize that a "sea of grass," stretching from China to Europe, allowed the nomads to travel from one end of the Eurasian land mass to the other while raiding all the way. The **sea of grass** was essentially non-broken grassland where nomads grazed horses and moved freely from the border of China to Eastern Europe. Still, miles of unbroken grassland cannot explain everything. Certainly, the region of the Black Sea and beyond was vast, and could maintain large numbers of inhabitants, but why move south repeatedly? In addition, why were these invaders so effective in overcoming the civilized people in Mesopotamia, Greece, Italy, Turkey, India, and China? When these clans moved south, they had effective leaders, an excellent military organization, and sometimes superior arms. So far, archeologists have not discovered numerous significant ancient cities to the north of the Fertile Crescent or agricultural societies with great irrigation systems, large buildings, permanent roads, libraries, or other trappings of

---

51 Not so in Meso-America. The Mayan, Aztecs, and Incas—just to name three—did not establish their great cities on major rivers. As time went on in the ancient world many cities would be established away from great rivers (Hattus, the Hittite capitol, and Nineveh, the Assyrian capitol for example).

organized power; thus, the origin of these invaders is tough to establish with certainty.

Recent discoveries (2007-09) of new civilizations in the region of Turkistan dating from 2000 BC by Russian archeologists may explain where the nomadic invaders came from. These cities are large and well organized urban environments that possibly sustained sizeable populations, probably five to ten thousand or more. To date only a few cities are under excavation, but the Russian archeologists are only scratching the surface. Unfortunately, written languages are not part of the present discoveries. Note the climate in the area of discovery is wet, and this kind of climate quickly dispatches evidence of civilization. Pottery that was painted grey is the most common find (painted grey ware). Pottery may be the longest lasting product of civilization because it does not decay easily, although normally found in a shattered condition. The painted grey ware is not located in Mesopotamia or Egypt, but India has numerous examples; thus, we assume the pottery came to India by trade or possibly the people creating the painted grey ware were the Aryan clans who invaded India.

We should note that in areas with significant rainfall ancient civilizations are hard to find. The climate has a marked influence on the remains of civilizations in such areas. Decay, flooding, effects of vegetation growing amongst the ruins, and other climatic impacts, destroys evidence quickly. Numerous insects also have a detrimental impact on artifacts, and such creeping life is most prevalent in wet areas. Dry areas, such as we have in Egypt and Mesopotamia, help preserve the ancient ruins and artifacts; thus, we have a lot more information about civilizations of these desert areas than we do from northern climates.[52]

Accordingly, we do not know why the invaders came, how they developed advanced warfare methods, or even where they lived beforehand. Recall these same types of nomadic invaders eventually conquered the Western Roman Empire. It seems the center of the world incubated warriors capable of conquering well-established built-up civilizations living near the mighty rivers of the Old World. History holds countless mysteries, but it shields its secrets extremely well.

---

52 Here is an example: assume a civilization grew up before 15,000 BC in the area of present day Moscow. Then the latest ice-age hit and the massive mile thick glaciers scraped the area clean. How could such a civilization be found? The moraines in front of the glaciers might contain some evidence, but it would be shattered & pulverized evidence, to say the least.

GREEK PHILOSOPHY

The Greeks invented **Western philosophy**. Philosophy is a search for truth, but this quest avoids involving the gods. Once god is involved, it is religion or theology. Typical of the Greeks, they usually left god out of philosophy. Philosophy is often summed up as a battle between **Plato and Aristotle**, but the numerous Greek philosophers in Athens and Greece covered every basic philosophic idea.

Plato thought we lived in a world *separated from reality*. He believed we were as men chained inside a cave watching shadows on a wall. Since the shadows are all we could know we would think they were reality, but reality exists outside the cave. Reality, according to Plato, is impossible for humans to experience because we are trapped in our existence—we cannot walk out of the cave. Plato also believed that an object in the world, say a chair, was an expression of a perfect concept existing somewhere else; thus, there may be many different concepts of "chair" here in our sensory world, but somewhere there is the perfect "chair" from which all our ideas of "chair" originate. **Aristotle** thought the world we live in *is reality,* and what we see, hear, taste, and feel are facts. "A is A," Aristotle might say. Thus the great divide: is our sensory world real or not? Can we trust what our senses tell us? Aristotle says yes, Plato says no. These two views sum up Western philosophy. The argument is "what is reality?" If we fail to agree on what is real, advancing to a discussion of what is truth fails as well.

Western philosophy bogged down in this problem of what is reality and entered into definitional arguments (**epistemology**) that went nowhere. **Hume** even destroyed the concept of knowledge from experience. Many Western philosophers tried to meet these challenges. **Descartes, Kant**, and many other brilliant men gave plausible answers, but other philosophers would punch holes in their concepts and on it would go with no real progress in the search for truth. In the end, Western philosophy has not advanced much past "what is reality" and that is just where Aristotle and Plato left us. Can humans, with human limitations, ever agree on reality or truth? History thinks not. We will take up modern philosophy in the postmodern chapter of our story.

SOPHISTS

Before leaving Greek philosophy, we must address the **Sophists**. Sophists were teachers of rhetoric and were renowned in 5th century Greece for their ability to win any argument using clever words and logic. The key element was their disdain for the truth, because winning the argument was the goal, and not the truth of any issue. Their methods made a mockery of the idea of truth. The Sophist are still with us today (2010) in the form of "spin doctors" and other consultants and speakers normally working for politicians. Their job is to turn any issue to the benefit of their client. Truth or facts are nothing to these neo Sophist, whose power is multiplied by the visual and print media as the more than willing agents of these modern day truth manipulators. Note that Sophism is a major part of modern day propaganda and big lie techniques, which are used consistently on the pubic of every nation throughout our world (and you thought the past was different . . .).

OF GODS AND MEN

In the ancient world, the impact of beliefs in a god, or the gods, had an enormous effect on the peoples of the time. In pre-history, even as far back as Neanderthals, humans (or archaic human types) were *burying their dead.* Often the burials contain common items such as bowls, shoes, jewelry, or weapons. It appears odd that even archaic humans would bury their dead in a common area (cemetery as we say), arrange them in a particular way, such as the fetal position with the legs curled up and the head down, leave personal objects in the grave, and often point all of the dead in the same direction. What does it mean? What were these archaic humans thinking?

Actually, knowing what it means is impossible, because in pre-history folks simply had no written records. Written records can tell us why, but physical evidence can only vaguely point to why. What we learn from physical evidence is mostly how, since without written records of their thoughts the human reasons for the why are impossible to ascertain. Thus, in pre-history we must guess. We can *guess* that burials and the afterlife had a connection. Common objects placed in the grave, such as jewelry, may indicate the dead would use them in another life. Of course, we bury people today in suits and ties with no concept that these are useful in an afterlife. We do this because it is customary for the dead person to look good at the funeral. In ancient times, perhaps the jewelry and the adornments were simply there to help the body look good for the relatives and clan members. Placing the body in a fetal position may indicate that death was another form of birth. This sounds like a good argument; however, it may be that in the fetal position it took less time to dig the grave. In the final analysis, it is impossible to know.

Prehistory fog spreads everywhere when it comes to believing in a god or gods. Once history begins, we find that people are deeply "religious" since they believed gods controlled nearly every aspect of nature and their lives. This strengthens the argument that prehistoric peoples believed in gods, but it cannot be conclusive. What is conclusive is at the very dawn of written history atheists are hard to find, at least among the kings, queens, and scribes who wrote the manuscripts we read to discover their thoughts. *Kings or queens allude to their power coming from the gods* and this is nearly universal in the ancient world. Thus, we find the earliest civilizations with gods, usually a lot of them, and normally the kings or queens claimed that the gods placed them in authority. Even the Greeks, who often ran secular governments, believed in the gods.

Our modern world consistently challenges the belief in a god or gods. Science explains the world through naturally occurring phenomena eliminating the need for gods—say the naysayers. Explaining everything through natural processes is possible, well . . . almost everything . . . and atheists expound endlessly on how worthless and harmful religion can be.[53] Yet, we have a worldwide fact that everywhere and at every time in history people believed in god. Of course, the ancients thought about gods much differently than we currently think about god. Inscriptions by ancient kings show that the image of the god WAS the god. The Babylonians lost their statute of Marduk, a famous god of Babylonia, when the Assyrians ripped it off after winning a war. The Babylonians spoke of Marduk being in Assyria rather than Babylonia. Obviously, believing that god is the stone image changes as history goes on, but we need to try and think on how that belief would change one's perception of god.

Is religion another example of something programmed into our genes? History seems to say yes, because it is *a universal human attribute* to believe the gods can somehow guide life or affect events. Another explanation for believing in gods is people realize they must die. Animals do not seem to know they will die, but people do. This necessity to face death, because of humanity's ability to reason forward to the future, might dictate a belief in something

---

53 Science has not explained how life can come from dead matter, or how human consciousness developed, or where races of people came from. to name a few items. Plus, science does not answer *why*, it answers *how*.

beyond this life; consequently, dying need not be the final moment. Is life hopeless without an afterlife? Why do human minds think up the notion that anything exists after death? How do ideas of god come into our minds? Is it a natural consequence of being human? No one can say, because the human brain hides its operational secrets, but since every identified society with a written history believes in the gods, we must appreciate the notion is a compelling one.

People also confront the **problem of good and evil**. Greek philosophers endlessly explored these matters, evolving numerous ideas about the nature of man and how good and evil relates to human existence. Other early societies, such as the Hebrews, also evolved such knowledge; however, they claim their knowledge came directly from Yahweh. In the book of Genesis, the serpent tells Eve that if she eats the forbidden fruit ". . . God knows that in the day you eat of it your eyes will be opened, and *you will be like God, knowing good and evil*" (emphasis added) (Genesis 3:5). This is a key moment in the Bible, because it turns people into conscience beings knowing right from wrong. Such consciousness brings awareness of life, and a unambiguous future death. This, of course, sets people apart from animals in a dreadfully significant way, as the knowledge of good and evil remains hidden from animals—only humans can know good and evil. Inevitably, the gods played a role in matters of morality. In ancient societies the gods determined what humans faced after death; thus, to gain a pleasant future in the hereafter, one must obey the gods in the here and now. Therefore, the gods' requirements for entry into the afterlife, or for avoiding a painful now, became virtue in this life.[54] How did people know what the gods' desired? The priest, shaman, sage, or seer told them.

Now the circle is complete. If the gods tell the shaman to slaughter the neighbors, it must be a good thing. It comes down to *who contacts the gods and reveals God's truth* to the poor humans denied contact with the immortals. Somehow, a trusted priestly class developed and gained exceptional power. *Trust* is the key word, because believing a particular mortal divines the thoughts of god requires trust. Must the priest be obeyed? In society after society, the answer was *yes*, the priest—god's representative—must be obeyed.

---

[54] God's truth is "revealed" to man; that is, the gods tell man what is good or evil as man cannot discover the god's truth on their own. Note how virtue differs: in Norse society killing the enemy is a large virtue, in Christian society one is encouraged to love ones enemies.

It often happened that the priest and king were in full agreement about god's commands, so the king ordered the population to obey god's demands. A powerful permutation results when the priest and king, often one in the same person, agree. To disobey makes a person a traitor and a heretic. The Hebrews despised their neighbors because they obeyed gods (priest) ordering them to throw babies into the divine fire to appease them. How could a person throw their tiny new child into a roaring fire? The priest and king gave the command, and the people obeyed. Based on this, I opine that the combination of king and priest is the most tyrannical power combination of all time.

Achieving a lasting world peace is a dream reaching back millenniums; however, overcoming ancient human traits to achieve lasting world peace has proven impossible. History tells us these human traits are deep set and unchanging. Today neighboring nations aim powerful weapons at one another because their gods tell them the other nation, with false gods, is evil, fit only for destruction.[55] From 8,000 BC to AD 2010, the fundamentals remain the same.

The Role of Food, Disease, and Administration in Ancient Times

Agriculture, coupled with animal husbandry, was the most important invention in secular history, and this was accomplished in the prehistoric era. After the development of agriculture, good land for growing crops and building irrigation systems became more important. As these lands were discovered and developed, people had to protect them from interlopers who would damage, destroy, and steal what had been built-up. When the world began to move to this stay-in-one-place "urban" lifestyle, a lot changed. The direct result of these changes were relatively large cities, trade with other parts of the world, the wheel, sailing boats, writing, and a growing dependence of people upon one another as **specialization** became common.

Trade and the compact nature of urban living made **disease** a common threat. Goods coming in from Asia to the Middle East might carry diseases that the people in the Middle East had never confronted. In addition, living around herd animals, and probably using their waste products to fertilize crops and whatnot, meant more contact with the diseases spread by herd animals and their by-products. There is little doubt that the centuries

[55] Israel, Syria; India, Pakistan; Iran, Iraq . . . etc.

required for building up urban civilization in the Middle East bought the human race, or at least some of the human race, immunity from herd animal diseases, and maybe disease in general as foreign trade goods and travelers spread viruses and germs around the Old World. In the New World, where herd animals did not exist, the people were not immune to these Old World diseases; thus, millions upon millions of Native Americans died just from contact with the Europeans.

Bureaucrats, a hated word in the modern world, were at the center of early progress. Large and dependable food and water supplies were the foundation for the high civilizations in China, India, Egypt, Mesopotamia, Greece, and Rome. As men became free to imagine, and then build, they proved exceptionally good at restructuring the world around them for additional comfort and protection. It might be difficult to believe, but the development of **administrative capacity** (bureaucrats and bureaucracy) in these early civilizations was another key to their survival and growth. We often underestimate the importance of administrative competence. If the city of Rome failed to bring in food and water in abundance, and remove trash and human waste, it could not have grown to any size at all. Administrative organization was required for the competent construction of roads, sewers, and aqueducts. In Rome, efficient bureaucrats were able to discern the need for aqueducts, systems for trash removal, roads for food transport, and sewers to move away the after products of humankind so the city could endure. A lack of water or sewage disposal alone could have doomed the city of Rome, or any other large city of antiquity. As these cities grew, and the need for all these additional improvements became obvious, a system for taxation developed so the administration could afford to construct the public facilities necessary to keep the city alive. All these problems are with us today, and our solutions are the same. Whoever these unknown and unnoticed people were, they were extremely important for the foundation and expansion of urban civilization. Once again, what is not reported is often more important than what is reported. The same is true in modern civilizations. If the bureaucracy fails the entire civilization suffers, but when the bureaucracy succeeds the results are little noticed. If the educational system, the sewers, roads, water infrastructure and whatnot works, no one notices. Let them fail, even a little bit, and everyone notices.

However, what happens if these little noticed things and people somehow fail? What if the competent administrators, tax collectors, artisans, laborers, and farmers leave or die? We are about to discover the answer to this question. After Rome collapsed in the west the competent administrators disappeared, and the resulting world went very dark. We will now travel to the eve of the modern world, as the **Dark Ages** build the foundation for a colossal leap forward in human thought and technology—after a few bad centuries.

Let Us Learn

What can we learn, for our personal lives, from the ancients? Rome teaches us to be tenacious. Rome lost many battles, but Rome never quit, and that is something for each of us to internalize. Rome also over extended itself; thus, we need to learn to analyze our finances and energy reserves to see if we are overextending ourselves. Can you really work, go to school, and run a home? Some can, but can you? Have you spent too much? Financial over extension can be deadly. Greece teaches us to unite. Squabbles over matters, significant or not, weakens the unit. Find a way to come together and multiply your strengths. Greece did, for a moment, and defeated the greatest empire on earth. India teaches the value of continuity. Being consistent in philosophy and tradition brings stability and progress. Egypt can teach us the same thing. Stability is very important for survival. Egypt also avoided unnecessary wars for centuries which enriched it financially and culturally. Limit your activities to what is reasonable for your situation, and reap the financial rewards of stability. The Fertile Crescent teaches us the importance of trade. Commerce is vital, so try to get involved in trade of some kind. It brings many financial rewards. The era also shows us the importance of protection. When necessary, build good walls (emotional, physical, financial etc), they will protect you from outside problems not of your making.

The ancients knew the sophists spewed evil. Learn to recognize "spin," and political lies affording the listener nothing in the way of accurate information. In Athens, the sophist led people astray by great oratory. Demand substance, not great oratory. The ancient Greeks taught us the significance of the individual, and the tyranny of the collective. The greatest political ideal ever espoused is: **the individual is greater than the state**. Never let that ideal die. Object if people say the government must substitute its collective decisions in place of individuals' decisions. Whenever a government substitutes its thinking for your thinking, its decisions for your decisions, it is saying the government is greater than you are. Object in every way possible! Economic freedom, capitalism, private property, and political freedom brings more prosperity and happiness to the average person than any other system. Trusting the government brings tyranny, regulation of everyday life, and restrictions on private property. Taxes are another way government controls individuals. *Money is power*, and when the government takes your money, it takes your power to decide. As taxes increase, tyranny increases. Write letters and speak out in public, challenge people pushing the collective viewpoint, run for office, and vote against all saying the individual must bow to the state. The Greeks knew the importance of the individual; now, 2500 years after Marathon, it is your turn to step up and stand against any person or entity claiming the government is superior to you. Tell all who will listen that you are superior to any government. Remember Marathon, Thermopylae, and Salamis where vastly outnumbered men said no to tyranny. They sacrificed all, you can at least sacrifice a few moments of your time to add your voice to freedom's call.

BOOKS AND RESOURCES:

The History of the Ancient World, From the Earliest Accounts to the Fall of Rome, Bauer, Susan Wise, 2007, WW Norton & Company. Great book, easy reading, fun stories.

With Arrow, Sword, and Spear, A History of Warfare in the Ancient World, Bradford, Alfrred, 2001, Fall River Press. Excellent accounts of ancient world, and goes far beyond warfare.

The NIV Study Bible, Zondervan Press, 2002. Good historical information.

The New Penguin History of the World, Roberts, 2007 Penguin Books. One of the best histories around. You can't go wrong with Roberts.

The Outline of History, The Whole Story of Man, Wells, H.G., revised by Raymond Postgate, 1956, Doubleday & Company. Great maps and illustrations.

The War Chronicles, From Chariots to Flintlocks, Cummins, J., 2008, Fair Winds Press.

The Decline and Fall of the Roman Empire, Gibbon, Edward, 2005, Phoenix Press (Abridged Edition). Hard to read, but a classic none-the-less.

Guns, Germs, and Steel, The Fates of Human Societies, Diamond, Jarad, 20005, WW Norton.

BOOKS AND REFERENCES ON PHILOSOPHY

The Essential Philosophy, Everything You need to Understand the World's Great Thinkers, Mannion, 2006, Adams Media Corporation. (The title is overdone, but the book is excellent)

Philosophy For Beginners, Osborne, 1992, Writers and Readers Publishing. (Philosophy in cartoon form, a lot of fun and one can actually learn a thing or two).

CHAPTER 3

THE DARK AGES 455 TO 1400

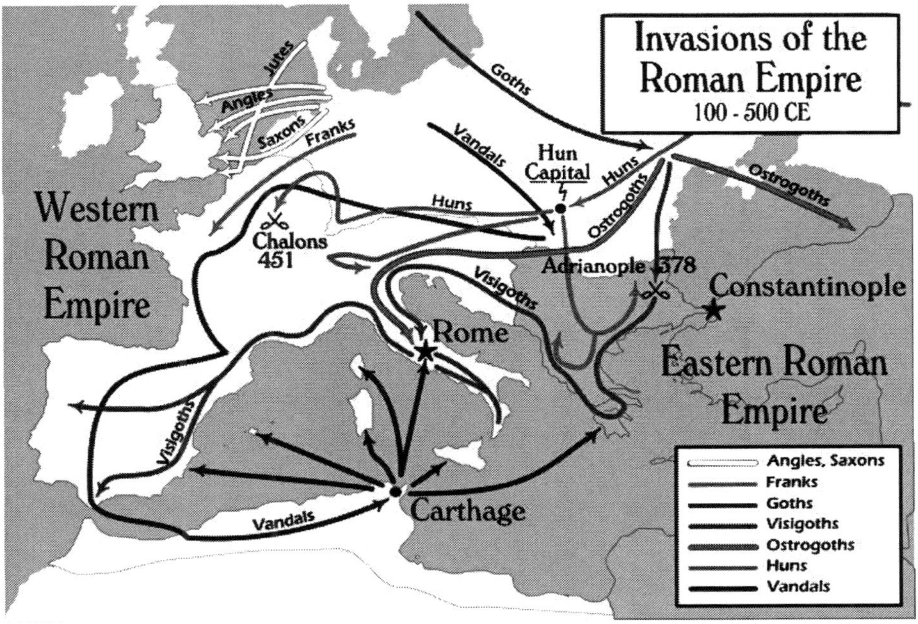

FIGURE 13 BARBARIAN INVASIONS OF ROME 100-500 AD

Ancient history has reached its end. This is the start of a new era. As pointed out above, most scholars think these times, between the fall of the Western Roman Empire (about AD 455) and the Renaissance (about AD 1400 to 1500) should not receive a pejorative moniker.[56] The Middle Ages is a neutral term resulting in a non-judgment of the times. Medieval is another term we apply to this epoch, but I think we should stick with

56 From this point forward, dates will be rendered with the year only, unless we specifically are referring to BC dates; thus, a date with no AD or BC is assumed to be AD.

the term *Dark Ages*; and you will see why after discovering what was going on. In this section, we will consider only Western Europe. The Dark Ages can be easily divided into two parts: the early Middle Ages, and the High Middle Ages. About 1000 AD is the turning point from the early to the High Middle Ages. The High Middle Ages began with a population gain, and new agricultural techniques that increased crop yields. The population increase led to growing towns and a new class of people—the city businessman or **burgher**. This new merchant class gained power as the High Middle Ages moved on and brought prosperity to the townsfolk. By 1200 the future looked bright, and then a triple whammy brought the good times to an end. The Black Plague (1346), the Little Ice Age (1300), and the Hundred Years War (1346) hit and effectively destroyed the future. The Mongol invasions (1241) did not help Eastern Europe either because they also denuded the area of people. The Mongols really liked killing.

TOTAL LOSS OF ROMAN CULTURE

The fall of the Western Roman Empire shattered Europe. Unity evaporated, and isolation of the various towns and villages returned. Cities disappeared, trade collapsed, the population decreased, culture was gone, quality in the crafts vanished, language changed (Latin was no longer universal), thus, people from different areas could not understand each other), and safe travel was a distant memory. **Walls** started going up around the towns and villages because the regional government's protection buckled. **Isolation**, economic and social, had returned to the land. The need for **Protection** became a vital problem.

Another feature of the Dark Ages was the *loss of knowledge*. In the ancient world, the Romans, Egyptians, Hittites, and others, knew how to make frame and panel doors, light wheels with spokes, and other rather simple but effective craft works. After the fall of Rome, these methods of construction were lost. This is especially hard to understand because this kind of knowledge commonly passes from father to son, or one can learn from looking at the construction itself. This knowledge could only be lost if all the people knowing these crafts were dead or had left the area. For example, if only one craftsman knew how to construct a frame and panel door, the usefulness of the technique was so obvious it would rapidly spread to others in the same line of work. Instead, we have the baffling total loss of these craft skills. To speculate on almost no information, the craftsmen probably left for the Eastern Roman Empire on those wonderful Roman roads. The result of this loss of knowledge was slab doors, solid wood wheels, and a lack of medical techniques, illiteracy and other problems for Europe.

Knowing how to administer urban environments was also lost, resulting in many urban centers heading for nonexistence due to terrible living conditions. Civilization was collapsing. Cities of the Dark Ages were profoundly different from the cities of Rome. With no efficient removal of trash and human waste, disease was common. The inability to bring fresh water and food into large urban areas, such as the city of Rome, resulted in the collapse of urban populations as people moved to the rural areas to find food and work. As cities disintegrated, trade fell apart completely changing everything. Until the return of cities Europe was stuck fast in the doldrums. Some good news seemed to appear about AD 800, when a warming period began in Europe, and more cereal crops sprouted in northern climates; thus, for a while the population expanded. Even in the best of times, the peasant lived on the edge of starvation, but abundant food crops at least allowed healthier living. Then the climate changed bringing disaster. The cold of the **Little Ice Age** set in about 1300, dramatically cutting food production, and leading to widespread famines throughout Europe.

The shattering of the Western Roman Empire was forever. Today the effects are obvious. Germans cannot speak to Frenchmen, Italians, Englishmen, etc., without an interpreter. You get the picture. The tribes overrunning Europe could not speak to one another, and eventually nations developed that could not speak to one another. The money, cultures, traditions, and languages became different all over Western Europe.[57] All this was a direct result of the cataclysmic fall of Rome in the West.

EVENTS OF THE DARK AGES

Worse yet, between the fall of the Western Roman Empire and the year 1453 (or so), the following events fell upon Europe in addition to the problems of dissolution and economic collapse:

- o *The Black Death*: Numerous plagues swept over Europe starting first in about 452 and ending with the last plague (named the Black Death) which began in about **1346.** The Black Death ended around

57 Note that in spite of the Mongol invasion and conquest of China, its culture, language, and administration remained nearly the same right into modern times.

1350. These plagues killed about 25,000,000 to 100,000,000 people by some estimates. (Figures from this time are very rough). Some experts think about fifty percent of the population died during the last great plague; others put the death toll at one third. The huge variations in death figures stems from the lack of reliable statistics from the era. What we do know is enormous numbers of people died.

- *The Little Ice Age*: The Little Ice Age was a 500 year period of cold and rainy weather that descended on the world about 1300 AD and stayed until 1800. Prior to the Little Ice Age there was a 400 year medieval warming period in Europe starting about AD 800 and lasting until about AD 1200, during which crops fared much better because of healthier growing conditions. Grapes were being grown as far north as England, and Viking explorers settled Greenland. A climatic reversal set in by **1300**, and in 10 years the average temperatures dropped by 4 degrees. This cold hit Europe especially hard, and was responsible for numerous crop failures, famines, and hardships killing millions because of the extreme cold. In 1315, unusually heavy rains began, lasting until 1320, destroying the cereal crops that were the foundation of medieval society. The ice age drove the Vikings out of Greenland as well as putting end to grape growing in England. Famine caused 1.5 million deaths by 1320. The worst cold hit between 1605 and 1680 when the temperature averaged 7 degrees cooler.

- *The Muslim Invasion of Spain:* Beginning about AD **711** when the Muslims entered Iberia and involving constant warfare until 1492 when the Muslim expulsion was complete.

- *The Mongol Invasions*: The Mongols devastated Hungary and Poland in **1241**, and the threat went on for decades as the Mongols kept returning. The Mongols slaughtered people by the hundreds of thousands as they turned cities into empty villages, murdering, raping, and plundering their way across the globe.

- *The Viking (Northman) Raids*: Starting about **793** and continuing for centuries, the raids grew in size and consequence until the raiders became settlers. The result was regular warfare between the Vikings and the peoples already on the land. The Viking raids were so fierce they kicked Europe back into the Dark Ages for many extra decades.

- *The Crusades*: From **1095 to 1291**, Christian Europe waged a series of campaigns to win back the Holy Land from the forces of Islam. Islam conquered Jerusalem in 638, going on to conquer vast areas in North Africa and Spain annihilating Christians throughout their areas of conquest. Eventually, the Eastern Roman Empire fell to Islam after Constantinople fell in 1453. These were religious wars of astonishing brutality. After these wars ended, Europe was unable to regain Christian territory except for Spain, but it gained knowledge of the ancient Roman and Greek world that had been lost for centuries. This knowledge was essential for the future growth of Europe as it led to the European Renaissance.

- *The Hundred Years War*: Commencing in **1346** and lasting through 1453, France and England engaged in endless battles for control of France (the war was in France) and destroyed a large part of the French countryside and its economy. Peasants suffered needlessly as armies trampled and burned crops, destroyed villages, and battered the peasant's meager existence decade after decade.

- *The Fall of Byzantium and the Muslim Invasions of Europe*: After the fall of the Eastern Roman Empire in **1453** (the Byzantine Empire with its capitol at Constantinople), the Muslims pushed into Eastern Europe threatening to overrun Vienna. These were religious offensives that resulted in massive casualty tolls. The Fall of Byzantium is often used as a milestone to mark the end of the Dark Ages.

- *The Growth of Cities* finally pulled Europe out of the morass of feudalism, disunity, economic isolation, and local tyranny. After the Black Plague finished killing off nearly everyone in 1350, the population began to recover, the discovery of better farming techniques made farming more productive, new foods arrived from the New World to supplement the Old World's crops, and competence began to return to city administration. As the trade routes opened up, the cities began to increase in size and power. It was this slow but steady improvement in urban development, coupled with the ideas of the Renaissance, which was pulling Europe out of its perpetual darkness.

This is NOT an exhaustive list, but displays how especially rough life was for common people in this era. Life during this period was awful due to appalling weather after 1300, numerous crop failures, constant hunger, warring armies trampling fields of crops, plagues and sickness everywhere, and foreign raiders killing everyone in sight (Muslims, Vikings, Mongols and others). In the late medieval period groups of clerics traveled around accusing people of being witches or warlocks, [58] killing them if they failed certain ridiculous tests (like being boiled alive). Life was austere, to put it gently. This justifies the Dark Ages label for this era because the common person suffered a terrible hammering for centuries.

Of course, not everything was bad. The age saw important agricultural advances such as the iron-tipped plow, three field crop rotation, and other "delights" making farming much more productive; however, remember who would get almost all the additional crop production—everyone but the peasant growing the crops.

The Catholic Church

Very few institutions can directly trace its dress, organization, rituals, and a lot more to the age of knights, castles, and courtly ladies. Nevertheless, when men were still hacking away with swords while puffing around in armor, the Catholic Church was fully formed and a key part of the feudal world. It is still with us in 2010, and still running very much as it ran in AD 1,000. Some details changed, but when attending Catholic Church services one is experiencing a tiny slice of medieval culture firsthand.

The Catholic (meaning universal) Church, centered at Rome, developed as the Western Roman Empire fell becoming a mainstay of life in the Dark Ages. The **Roman Catholic Church** grew from the ashes of the Western Roman Empire, and its boundaries approximated those of the Western Empire. The Church held together the various cultures growing in Europe, it was the repository of learning, and it was uniform in its language (Latin—the same as the Roman Empire). Often its monasteries were centers of commerce. The Church alone set forth a moral code embodied in Christian teachings. The Catholic Church tried to limit the impact of the constant fighting between the various warlords in Europe.

---

58 "**Witch hunters**" as they styled themselves. One stated that his book on how to detect witches was covered with the skin of a witch. The killing began about 1250 and lasted until 1712 (the last witch trial in England). In 1487, the height of the witch hunts, a book was published describing witches' habits and how to detect them named *Malleus Maleficarum* (Hammer of Witches). Thousands died from these inquisitions across Europe, and men were often killed as well as women, but women seemed to have borne the brunt of the mania.

The knights serving the lords were often hired thugs who galloped about oppressing the peasants and clergy as well as attacking other knights. Many of these heavily armed men were recruited to battle the Vikings; but as the raids subsided, the warlords went back to local skirmishing. The Catholic Church tried to establish the "Truce of God," where the knights vowed to avoid killing the innocent (peasants, clergy, and townsfolk for example), and the "Peace of God", where knights promised to refrain from waging war during certain times of the year (Christmas for example). How well this worked is unknown, but at least the Catholic Church was trying to bring a moral order into people's lives.

The Church built immense cathedrals, monuments dedicated to the worship of the Christian God. These shrines of the High Middle Ages (1400 to 1500) became wondrous examples of architecture's response to the age. Early cathedrals were of the **Romanesque** style, with thick walls and smallish windows; however, they remain imposing monuments. Later cathedrals, termed **Gothic**, were taller with very detailed carved stone interior decorations, and flying buttresses that allowed thinner walls with stain glass windows. At the very top of these impressive structures, in places unseen, are stone gargoyles fabricated with great skill, even though cloistered. The mindset was one of creating for God, who could see all, and not man, who would probably never see them.

The Christian Church split in half in AD 1054, after the Western and Eastern churches had enough of one another and formally diverged onto their own paths. The Eastern Church (Orthodox—or true) maintained control in Byzantium, Eastern Europe, Russia, the Ukraine, and Greece. The Western Church (Roman Catholicism—or universal) maintained sway in Western Europe. The split centered on cultural and political considerations, although doctrine was different. The sack of Constantinople by the Fourth Crusade in 1204 was key to widening the split. The Eastern Church saw Latin Christians destroy their beautiful city and slaughter its inhabitants. Meanwhile, the West thought the East was recalcitrant in not recognizing the primacy of Rome. The failure of the West to help defend Constantinople in 1453 during the Ottoman Turk attacks made the split even worse. Just to make things even on all sides, the leaders of each church, the pope in the west and the Patriarch of Constantinople in the east, excommunicated the followers of the other. Thus, at least one-half of Christianity will burn in hell—according to the other half. Interestingly, a similar thing happened in Islam. After the death of Mohammad, their spiritual founder, Islam split in two (Shea and Sunni sects), each side saying the other was bound for hell. (It seems many people are hell bound, according to people claiming to be heaven bound . . .)

Feudalism

A foundation point for the age was the institution of feudalism, a system of governance that included economic relationships as well as social and legal undertakings. The local king (normally the top warlord in the area) owned all the land, but the warlord needed people to farm the land. Therefore, the warlord allowed the serfs to farm his land for a portion of the crops. In times of war, the serfs could form part of the army protecting their warlord's land. As time progressed, some of the warlords gave their land to the Catholic Church, thereby establishing the Catholic Church as a major power in economic and spiritual realms.

How all this came about is guesswork, because when the Western Roman Empire fell learning was lost and little was written down. What we can discern are the results, warlords—often called kings—ruling over small areas coming under their protection. (Sounds like modern Los Angeles gangs) Warlords built large castles for protection (walls again) and for internecine warfare, each trying to better his lot by battering his neighbors.

The Guild System

The important institution of **guilds** grew up during the Dark Ages. Under the guild system, a craftsman applied to join a group of skilled workers doing his type of work (building with bricks or stone for example), and if accepted, he would agree to keep the methods taught confidential and otherwise obey the guild's rules. Guilds were social as well as professional organizations. The guild would test and assign certain categories of work skill to their members and set payment guidelines for that level of skill. The category of apprentice might be the entry-level skill group, then journeyman, and finally master. The guilds would impart knowledge regarding the craft to their members and encourage study to advance the group's knowledge; however, this knowledge was secret. The guilds were powerful and important groups. It is said that in Paris even the prostitutes had a guild.

The problem was guilds imparted additional rigidity to the economic system hindering trade and industry growth. Some people might be able to do the job for less, but the guilds were powerful; thus, those with money (the ones doing the construction or buying the goods) wanted to maintain good relations. As bad as the plagues were in Europe, they did accomplish one important economic benefit, *they created a real labor shortage* and in those conditions the guild's power to limit commerce diminished.

GOVERNMENT DURING THE DARK AGES

During the early Dark Ages (453-1000), Europe shattered into little governments. The Roman imperial governmental system crashed, and the governments that remained were local in nature and thoroughly inept. Nation states, empires, and other regional governments simply did not exist immediately after Rome's demise. Not until cities began to grow in size, wealth, and power did competent government begin to reassert itself.

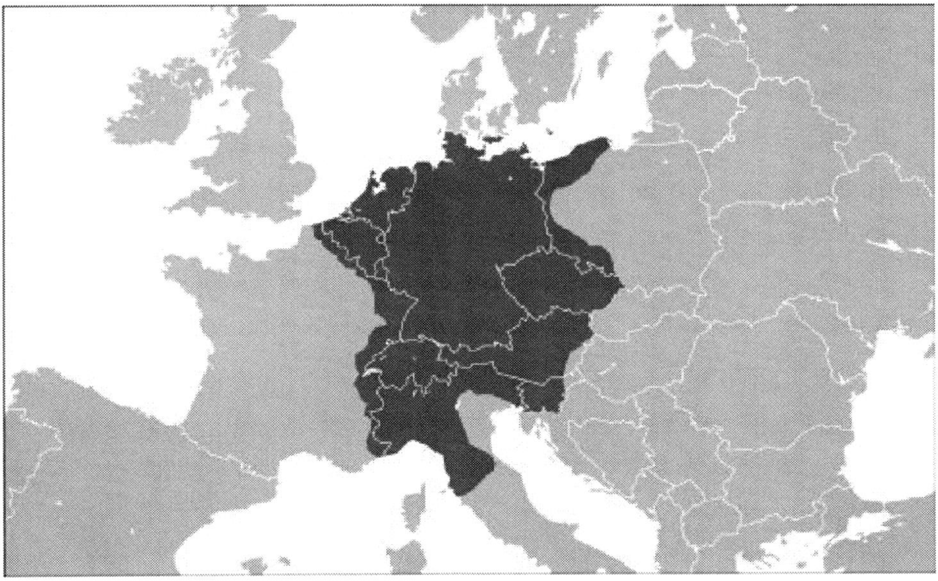

FIGURE 14 HOLY ROMAN EMPIRE.

Cities favored the central government of a king over local warlords because the king could subdue a larger area, thus helping trade flow. Kings looked to the growing wealth of cities to fill their coffers. Slowly, central governments grew until kings controlled large areas forming states. The first areas advancing to the European nation state concept were France and England.

THE FRANKS—FRANCE

In AD 496 the King of the Franks, Clovis, converted to Christianity. This was the start of the **Merovingian dynasty.** By the time of his death in AD 530, he conquered the area we now call France, and formed it into a state. None of the regional "kings" of the era governed like a national government today. Many of the local warlords still ran local areas, but they were allied with the king of the region and owed him feudal duties. It was nothing like our unified nation states in 2010. The **Carolingian Empire** arose in 751 in Gaul (France) when Pepin the Third deposed the last Merovingian ruler becoming the king. Thereafter, he expanded his rule to include an area nearly as large as the old Western Roman Empire. After the death of Pepin III in 768, his son **Charlemagne** (786 to 814) continued to expand the empire. He was a truly great ruler. For over forty-six years Charlemagne ruled his lands, termed the **Holy Roman Empire**, by constantly traveling and waging war. He refused to sit about his castle letting others tell him what was going on (smart guy), he went out and saw for himself. He established special schools and began pulling Central Europe out of its Dark Age.

On Christmas Day, in the year AD 800, the Pope Leo III crowned Charlemagne Roman Emperor. If this sounds odd, it should. The Roman Empire was gone, so how was this fellow being crowned emperor? To many Germanic tribes, Rome, as a central government, was all they knew. Anyone who controlled Gaul (the West) had to be a Roman emperor. Accordingly, the empire continued in the minds of people even though gone for hundreds of years. Such was the impact of Rome. In the East at Constantinople, the Emperor (a woman named Irene who had killed her son to reach the position) did not like the pope crowning someone Roman Emperor. After all, the Eastern Empire of Byzantium considered themselves the real Roman Empire, while the pope controlled a backwater group of near barbarians. By giving the crown of Rome the pope implied the true crown of Rome was his alone to give. Charlemagne did not like the pope crowing him either. If the pope had the power to give the position he also had the power to take it away. The clear implication was the Church was greater than the state. The great king said nothing and went away not realizing what the pope had started.

Charlemagne kept governing and ignoring the Roman crown. Through his efforts alone he put many Dark Ages scourges to flight. The Holy Roman Emperor Charlemagne died in 814, but the Dark Ages, which seemed to be ending with his rule, resumed with a sudden vengeance. The cause was bloodthirsty raiders from the north.

The *Viking raids* on Europe and England started about 800 and continued unabated for decades. These raids, along with intense plagues, crammed Europe back into the putrid pit of the Dark Ages. One ongoing theme did mark the tenure of the Holy Roman Empire. This empire, and its successors the Hapsburg dynasty, stood between the Muslims and the conquest of Europe for centuries after the fall of the Byzantine Empire and Constantinople in 1453.

The disintegration of Charlemagne's large empire came quickly after his death. His grandsons divided the empire into three parts with **Henry the Fowler** establishing the Saxon dynasty of *German* kings and **Hugh Capet** starting the Capetian dynasty of *France.* **Lothair** got the ***center*** between the kingdoms of the east (Germany in modern times) and the west (France of modern times). One side or the other was forever overrunning the land of King Lothair between the two great peoples of France and Germany. *Alsace—Loraine* lies in this area, and Germany and France have contested the region for generations.

France was having trouble enough when the English King Edward III claimed the throne of France in 1337 and invaded in 1346. This was the start of the **Hundred Years War** between France and England to determine who would rule the country. The English won tremendous bloody victories at Crecy (1346), Poitiers (1356), and Agincourt (1415), crippling France for a generation. Incompetent French leadership was the main cause for the unmitigated series of disasters. By 1422 Charles, the dauphin (crown prince) of France, was holed up in a dingy castle in Touraine and ruled almost nothing. To become king he had to be consecrated in the cathedral of Reims, but the cathedral and the surrounding area was held by hostile forces. Out of nowhere, a 16 year old girl who had heard voices telling her to save France arrived and told the dauphin she would raise the English siege of Orleans on the Loire River. Her name was **Joan of Arc**. The illiterate gal led the royal army to the attack on a ring of English forts surrounding the city of Orleans. She decisively defeated the English and broke the siege. The voices then told Joan to get the dauphin to Reims so he could be anointed. Her army fought its way through to the cathedral and the dauphin was consecrated on July 17, 1429. France now had a legit king.

Joan's life did not end well. Eventually captured in battle she was tried and burned as a witch by the English. This was a large error. By burning Joan the English really ticked off the French populace and ensured their own defeat in the Hundred Years War. By dying a martyr Joan had won the war for France. The French king made a deal with his local enemies and then turned on the English. In a series of victories he drove the English off the continent. In 1453 the war was at last over with the French king in control of France.

Thus, an illiterate 16 year old farm girl saved France. Guess the voices knew what they were doing.

ENGLAND

Early on, the Anglo Saxons ruled England, but the Viking raids (Danes to the English) and settlements were putting pressure on them. Alfred the Great (849-899) managed to drive them out from most of their conquests and established the Anglo Saxons as the undisputed rulers. The Anglo Saxons had few noblemen but a good sized class of land owning men (thanes), both governed by the unwritten laws of tribal customs as much as anything else. It was during this era that the epic tale of Beowulf was created (the Danish and Scandinavian connections are strong in this story). In 1066, Harold Godwinson was the most powerful man in England, but he had problems with the succession to the throne which led to a few bigger problems.

William, leader of the Normans, had a claim to the English throne but Harold had the title. William decided to mount an invasion, and assembled 700 transport vessels to move on isle of England. The **Normans** invaded in **1066** and managed to defeat the Anglos and Saxons at the **Battle of Hastings** after an arrow killed Harold Godwinson. The Normans now became the rulers of England and the last successful invaders of the island. **William the Conqueror**, leader of the Normans, created a new society in England. They created a written survey, named the Doomsday Book, in 1086 listing all the assets William controlled—for tax purposes of course. The tally was precise down to the last sheep. This was the most comprehensive survey undertaken in the middle ages. William constructed large castles and handed out land to his loyal servants who fought by him in battle. Thereafter, William engaged in constant warfare keeping his kingdom secure and trying to expand it in France (Normandy) by warring against France's King Philip I. Wounded in battle while in France, William died in 1087. The Norman conquest brought England, which had been tending toward Scandinavian ties, into the culture of Western Europe.

Henry II took over in 1154 and brought great prosperity to the kingdom. He laid the foundations of common law and the jury system. Richard the Lion Hearted followed Henry II but spent most of his time fighting in the Holy Land and France. He died in battle and was replaced by King John. John's reign was an unhappy one, and he ended up being forced to sign the Magna Carta at Runnymede in June of 1215. The Magna Carta

(Great Charter) gave rights to various noblemen, the church, merchants and more, and it established that the king could not imprison or deprive a free man of land without a legal judgment ". . . of his peers or by the law of the land." Thus, the king was put below the law and forced to recognize the rights of others. The Magna Carta was a big deal in the history of democracy. At last, the king was brought under control of the law. John's son, Henry III, took the throne in 1216 and went even further by allowing Parliament's powers to increase. By the time Edward I took power in 1272 Parliament was growing more powerful, and Edward fully cooperated with the representative body. The Model Parliament of 1295 gained control of the nation's finances, eventually developing into the House of Commons. At this point England was well on its way to its modern form.

THE VIKING RAIDS

Bold raids by Scandinavian Vikings began around 793 when Lindisfarne in eastern England was stormed, and increased in severity throughout the next 200 years. Because of their shallow draft boats, which were eminently seaworthy, the raiders not only invaded coastal areas they could foray up large rivers and plunder deep inland. Paris and Poitiers, in France, suffered plundering in 843 and 864 respectively. England, France, Germany, Spain, Italy, and others experienced large Viking strikes. England was a favorite target and, in 866, an enormous landing force captured the city of York and then stayed. Over the next 40 years a constant state of warfare existed in the area of York, as the Vikings—called the Great Heathen Army by their opponents—sought to expand their territory while seizing loot and women. **Alfred the Great** of England realized the Vikings were fierce but lightly armed hit and run raiders seeking gold and other valuables; hence, not a stable long-term army. Alfred calculated they were not equipped mechanically or mentally to sit out long sieges; accordingly, he constructed sturdy forts around the Viking areas. When incursions came, people just ran into the fort and then waited for the raiders to leave. As the Vikings had no ability to storm robust forts, their era of expansion in England collapsed. The Great Heathen Army was at last defeated.

Vikings were efficient traders and bold colonist. They ventured as far as Moscow and Kiev, and founded the kingdom of the Rus. (and you thought Russian's were Mongols) They traveled down the great rivers to Novgorod and set up trade links to Byzantium (Constantinople) by AD 907. As seafarers and raiders, the Vikings have never been surpassed.

Even as the Viking raids battered Europe, another invader began gathering power in the Middle East. After AD 600, **Islam** became an aggressive force in the eastern Mediterranean, conquering the Middle East, North Africa, eastern Europe, Constantinople, and even Spain for a time. Islam's ruthless warriors murdered Christian in the hundreds of thousands, demanding conversion to Islam or death. Only Spain was re-conquered, and that did not occur until 1492. In essence, Christianity inherited the Western Roman Empire and Islam the Eastern Roman Empire (and a lot more).

THE MONGOLS

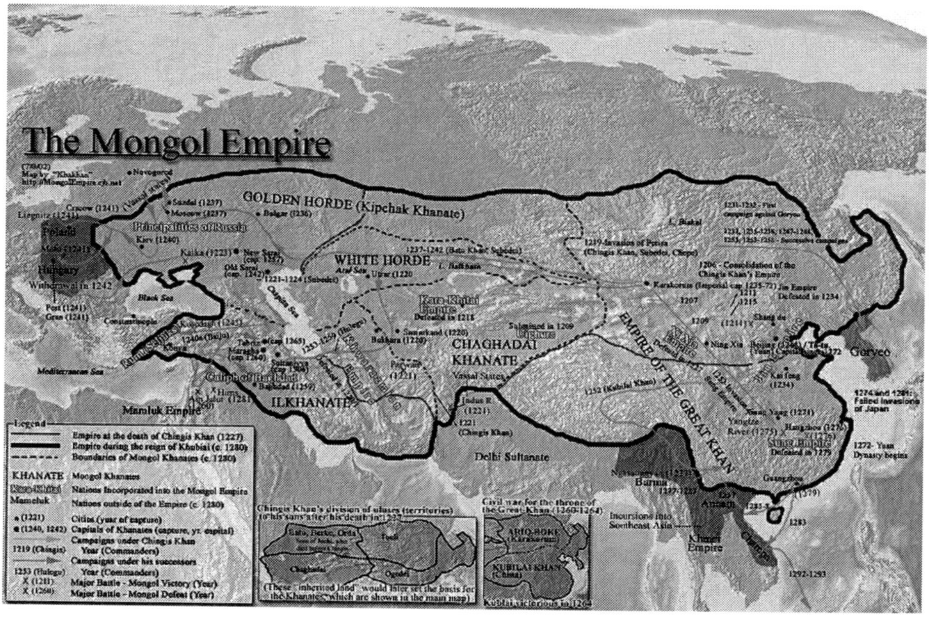

FIGURE 15 THE MONGOL EMPIRE ABOUT 1253

The **Mongols** of central and eastern Asia united under **Genghis Khan in 1206** (ruling from1206 to 1227). The Great Khan eventually conquered China, Persia, Rus (Russia), and Eastern Europe, never knowing defeat. In 1211, Genghis devastated the Chin Empire in China then moved west destroying the Khorezm Empire in campaigns lasting from 1215 to 1245. (Genghis was replaced by his heirs after his death, and the campaigns went on) The Mongol conquest spread from *northern China to the Black Sea.* Sacking Kiev in Russia in 1240, the Mongols reduced the once great city to ashes and slaughtered everyone in the place. Genghis Khan died in 1227, splitting the empire between four of his sons. **Batu,** Genghis Khan's grandson, fell on Europe in 1241, riding to the gates of Vienna while defeating and butchering the Poles, Templars, and Teutonic Knights at the battle of **Legnica**. Batu then defeated the Hungarian army in 1241 at the battle of the Sajo River again taking a tremendous toll on his enemies. The Mongols were prepared to march on Central Europe when Batu died, and the Mongols retreated to bury Batu and choose a new leader. With the death of the Great Khan Batu in 1241 the Mongol pressure on Europe eased somewhat; nevertheless, they held Rus (western area of Russia) until the late 1400s. In 1279 the Mongol Empire reached its zenith as *the largest land empire in history*. By controlling the 5000 mile "Silk Road" between China and Europe, they derived enormous wealth. The trading centers of Central Asia began declining as trade shifted to sea routes away from the land-bound caravans passing through Mongol territory. Around 1260 the Mongol Empire split into four large units with Kublai Khan ruling Mongolia and China, the Golden Horde ruling Russia and some of Eastern Europe, and Il-Khan ruling the Middle East. (and converting to Islam) The fourth Mongol state was the Jagadai Khanate that continued to rule over central Asia until the 1400s. In the late 1300's, **Timur**, yet another great Mongol conquer, set out to repeat the conquests of Genghis, and he did quite well. He took central Asia, Northern India, Persia, parts of Russia, and the Middle East. Timur died in 1405, his conquests remaining in Mongol hands until the 1500's.

Like all empires, the immense Mongol Empire did not last. **Ivan the III** of Rus refused tribute to the Khans and re-conquered Moscow in 1480; thereafter, he married the niece of the last emperor of Byzantium and claimed for himself the title of **Czar** (Caesar). Ivan conquered a large area to the east of Poland and established himself as a monarch rightfully demanding respect. He began the myth that Moscow was the Third Rome and the center of the true faith (note the references to Rome once again). This was to be Russia, land of the Rus, destined for great power and wealth. With Ivan's conquests, the Mongol's time had passed.

EUROPE BATTLES TOWARD THE RENAISSANCE

In Western Europe growth was slow until about AD 1000. The Christian religion managed to convert the Scandinavians, Poles, and Magyars from around 950 to 1050. As some order emerged around the year 1000, trade began to pick up, towns began to grow, and artisans expanded their wares. In growing towns such as Paris, Salerno, Oxford, and Bologna, **universities** were established and started work on the theological, scientific, legal, and philosophic underpinnings of modern Western society. Great names in philosophy and modern thought emerge from this era such as **Thomas Aquinas**, Roger Bacon, and Duns Scotus. Aquinas would accept the translations of Aristotle and develop a philosophy that brought science (Aristotle) religion and philosophy to the same conclusion; God did exist. Commercially and intellectually Europe was growing.

Europe was moving ahead politically as well. Monarchs began to call on members of the local town for advice. Then the towns assigned representatives to see the sovereign. *Eventually, elections chose these town representatives.* The monarchs clearly saw the power of the towns as they grew into powerful cities and dared not ignore them. These elected representative bodies slowly became **parliaments**, and their power grew as time moved on. The crowned heads trying to build power were able to call on the city and its rich merchants for additional taxes, and money was power (things never change). These funds enabled the national kings to establish their superiority over the local warlords partially through the purchase of powerful artillery to batter down castle walls. This new money helped the monarchs carve out national boundaries ultimately leading to nation states. Of course, all this brought so much power to the parliaments they could challenge the king for ultimate authority over the nation—and in some cases, they won. Overall, things were looking up for Europe in the early 1200s, but numerous new tribulations were approaching that would quell the happy times.

In **1347,** an ultra deadly executioner called on Europe by way of ships from the east bringing a merciless assailant—***the Black Death***. This eastern marauder exterminated over **25 million** lives possibly cutting the population of Europe by about **one-third to one-half**. It was total ruin. No one knew fleas that had bitten infected rats carried the disease. Rats were commonplace at the time, and fleas were everywhere just like all the other bugs. No one had invented bug killer, and bugs enjoyed eating on humans regularly. To the people of the age the disease just spread. Had God flung hell to earth punishing humanity for wrongs beyond comprehension? The Black Death of 1347 was the last of the great plagues to strike Europe in this era. The march of death by plague *started as early as 452* and continued to hit Europe in waves until the Black Death finally ended the disease cycle. The Byzantine Empire was on the rise under Justinian when the plague hit and destroyed about one-third to one-half of the people in the empire. It is thought that well over one hundred million (100,000,000) people died in the plagues that swept over Europe from 452 to 1347. These plagues helped destroy commerce and unity in Europe for a thousand years—just about the same amount of time assigned to the Dark Ages.

The Little Ice Age began in 1200, but hit in force by 1300 causing temperatures to drop precipitously and putting an end to high crop yields. The plague, the Little Ice Age, and the wars throttled any chance of recovery after 1200.

Chronic feudal wars, the **Hundred Years War** between England and France (fought in France), the **War of the Roses** in England, and other local wars too numerous to account continued while people died in throngs from the plague. The Hundred Years War between France and England coupled with the Black Death and the falling temperatures all but wiped out the population of France and central Europe. The bad times had returned in spades.

While all this was going on, the Catholic Church began arguing over who was the rightful pope. In the **Great Schism** (1378 to 1417) there were two popes, and each pope *excommunicated* the other as well as all his followers. They also mounted crusades against one another. This caused great problems for the Catholic Church. The Church decided to call a council to decide who the real pope would be. It couldn't make things any worse, right? The council of Pisa in 1409 elected a third pope who promptly excommunicated the other two, who then excommunicated him. The Council of Constance (1417) eventually named the one and only rightful pope, and said he must reside in Rome. The concept of a council of Church leaders solving a crisis of such magnitude put some Catholics on edge. Was a council's authority above that of the pope? The question still goes unanswered.

This was all very confusing for the common person. The mainstays of their world, the Catholic Church and the feudal system, were coming undone. The church bowed before the Black Death; there were popes aplenty; and the wars were destroying crops, towns, and livelihoods. The local feudal lords argued with the kings who wanted ever-increasing amounts of money and loyalty. The king and his army increased in power. Local towns were growing into cities with a lot of economic power, and they rejected feudal lords telling them what to do. They did not need the lords any longer. The townspeople were amassing power and wealth all their own, and it was enough to match any feudal lord. In Italy, the trading towns of *Venice and Florence* grew so powerful they were fielding large armies and navies.

Continuous wars diminished the feudal lords' powers while destroying the feudal system. If a government cannot provide protection it is worthless, and the feudal lords could no longer raise the money and manpower to protect the people. As a result, the powerful new cities began to protect themselves, and rural folks began to turn to the king for protection. The **nation state** was being born in Europe.

Change was in the air by the fourteenth and fifteenth centuries (the **years 1301 to 1500**), and today we call this sweeping period of change the **Renaissance**. *It started in Italy,* but quickly spread to Europe and then the world.

Let Us Learn

Can the Dark Ages tell us anything of worth for our daily lives? Recall that hard times do come into the best of worlds, and people can survive them. Governments come and go, but the foundations of life come from the individual's struggle to carry on and overcome all obstacles. Understand how religion can hold people together in bad times. Remember that progress, no matter how slow, is still progress. One small step forward (the iron plow) leads to others. So keep going forward, no matter how slowly, and the Renaissance will arrive. The Dark Ages also teach us the importance of unity. Disunity made the age so much worse. Stay unified in your home, workplace, church, school, or whatever. Say and do things that add to unity, not disunity.

Books and Resources

Great Rivals in History, When Politics Gets Personal, Cummins, J., 2008, Metro Books. P 50 starts William the Conquer and Harold Godwineson—the conquest by the Normans of England.

The Middle Ages, Bishop, M., 2001, Mariner Books. Probably the most readable short history of the Middle Ages.

The New Penguin Atlas of Medieval History, Revised Ed, McEvedy, C., 1992, Penguin Books. I love Penguin Atlases. Of course, ***The Penguin Atlas of World History Volume 1, From Prehistory to the Eve of the French Revolution,*** Kinder & Hilgemann, 1978, Penguin Books, contains chapters on the Middle Ages, and EVERYTHING in this book is wonderful. Kinder & Hilgemann's Atlas starts the Medieval period on page 111, "Early Middle Ages, the Slavs," and ends on page 211, "Late Middle Ages/China (1264-1368, India (999-1526). Super small print, great coverage.

Lost to the West, The Forgotten Byzantine Empire that Rescued Western Civilization, Brownworth, Lars, 2009, Crown Publishers. Wonderful book on the Eastern Roman Empire at Constantinople. Easy to read and full of good stories.

CHAPTER 4

THE RENAISSANCE 1300 TO 1500

As the Dark Ages were stumbling along their plague-ridden way, the Renaissance (means rebirth) finally put an end to them. After all the problems of the Dark Ages, light began to pour into the Western world. *A flowering of human knowledge and inventiveness began in Italy in 1300 or so, and it never stopped.* Historians like to end things; so for the purposes of history, the Renaissance ended about 1500. *In reality, it did not end* because the ideas and attitudes of the Renaissance never die in the Western world. The mind-set of the Dark Ages (Medieval mind-set—whatever) focused on the afterlife and the worship of God as the center of life. After the Renaissance, the **mind-set** looked to this life and what a person could accomplish here on earth as the center of life. Man began to imagine he could improve the world, and he could start without God's permission. The here and now became more important than the life beyond this world.

NEW THOUGHTS AND NEW ASSUMPTIONS

The mind-set of the Renaissance never changed in the West once it was established. In the Middle East, with Islam, the medieval mind-set remained; along with hard results for the modern world. *This clash of worlds is a clash of thought processes.* In Islam, their medieval mental outlook places the worship of their god (Allah) over everything of this world. This mind-set encourages young men to detonate their explosive-laden selves in crowded market places. *Islam never experienced a Renaissance,* and the resulting ancient view of life is at odds with the post-Renaissance Western world. The West might have directed the Renaissance to Islam, but Islam's swift and permanent Renaissance rejection blocked the acceptance of Europe's new mindset forever.

In the Far East, China, Japan, and Korea also failed to enjoy a Renaissance, but the continuity of their civilizations and flexibility of their philosophies allowed them to grow and change anyway. Nonetheless, without the arrival of the West, the Far East may never have entertained the thought processes of the modern world. The Renaissance came to the Far East via the West where it enjoyed at least partial acceptance.

Do theologians arguing about God matter? Yes, student of history, they do. As the here and now moved to center stage, the importance of man increased, and the things man could produce increased in importance. **Science and the scientific method** (much misunderstood) began to pry open the secrets of the universe. Advances in machines, art, writing, printing, building, and many more areas became common. The idea that life could get better, people could reduce pain, control crops, and do better than the ancients took hold. Once the idea of progress was established, the West never looked back. It is not that Western Europe rejected God; it was that Western Europe saw God in a new way. God was not against progress or science or thinking for oneself. The Bible was not intended to control every situation in life. Believe in God, but work for the here and now, was the new mind-set in Europe. Using these beliefs, the secular and spiritual worlds separated in Europe with tremendous implications for the world. Because Islam missed the shock of Renaissance, it failed to scrutinize its religious teachings, failing to acknowledge man might have more importance than believed.

Europe discovered the giants of antiquity.[59] The discovery of Aristotle, Cicero, Plato and other great writers and thinkers of Rome and Greece, fueled an explosion of new ideas in Europe. Painters discovered oil paint, canvas, and perspective with stunning results that left the ancients behind them. Masterpieces of sculpture and painting turned out by Michelangelo, Raphael, Donatello, Leonardo da Vinci, and others are beyond compare. Most of these artistic giants were contemporaries which makes all this even more amazing. Not since the glory days of ancient Athens had the world witnessed such an outpouring of talent, inventiveness, and creativity.

The advance to the modern world had just begun, but the **speed of progress** accelerated beyond all measure. From 1300 to 1500, the world of the peasant saw little change; but from these foundations, the world would witness amazing developments. A person alive in 1910, for example, could watch the world go from horses to motor cars to landing on the moon in

[59] Through Islam, oddly enough. Islam never took these ancient ideas into their philosophy. In the West they caused a revolution, in the Islamic world, nothing.

about sixty years. Look around your world and remember it all started in Italy about seven hundred years ago.

The key was a new outlook for the human mind. Once released, the avalanche of progress was unstoppable. The dazzling accomplishments of the Western world are unequaled anywhere so far, but these advances upset the remainder of the planet. A backlash is underway in the twenty-first century challenging the quantum leap forward brought about by the Renaissance and the scientific method (empirical method). The challenge comes from the Middle and Far East, and people not gaining (or perhaps *adopting* is a better word) the Renaissance mind and its empirical outlook. Those who challenge the Western mind-set have lost out on history. Without the challenge of fundamentally new ideas spawned by the Renaissance, old ideas and assumptions naturally stay in place. Areas of missing the Renaissance, or something like it, remain mired in thought processes traceable to ancient ways of reasoning.[60] This rebuff of new ideas is traceable to deflecting challenges to religious or traditional dominance in society. It is the ultimate rejection of the Renaissance.

How did Europe, of all places, manage to embrace such volatile new concepts? Why did Europe in 1300 begin to accept radical new perceptions of life, while other parts of the world rejected them? Islam preserved the books of Plato, Aristotle, and other Greek and Roman classics, eventually transferring them to Europe where they were studied in the developing universities. Islam rejected the ideas contained in the classics from Greece and Rome. One rejection explanation is the **Koran** (the Muslim sacred book) is believed to be the perfect book (literally, no flaws), and anything remotely contradicting the holy book is abruptly discarded.[61]

In Europe, theologians read the translations of the classic works (Thomas Aquinas, for example), but they accepted these classics as indispensable. Thomas Aquinas thought the books added to his understanding of the Bible. Western Christian theologians believed God created a discoverable world of order; thus, rather than reject ancient thinking, Aquinas sought to incorporate it into Christian theology. Instead of rejecting the thoughts of Greece and Rome, they embraced them with enthusiasm. *Christianity*

---

60 Ancient Egypt stayed as it was for four thousand years for a reason; new ideas were avoided to maintain the status quo.

61 Devout Muslims say the original language of the Koran is pure, and even translations to another language corrupt the book. *The Politically Incorrect Guide to Islam and the Crusades,* Spencer, 2005, Regnery Publishing, Inc

was able to accept this challenge, although not without struggle, and grafted the new thinking onto the Christian worldview. For example, Thomas Aquinas reached the conclusion that science, religion, and philosophy all reached the same conclusion of proving God's existence. Aquinas' conclusions are often termed **Scholasticism**—the reconciliation of logic, reason, and faith.

This acceptance was possible because Christianity told the theologians the world was an orderly place, and governed by a rational God. Thus, they could expect to find rational explanations for the world around them. Science gave them those explanations, and it did not conflict with the Bible or their view of God. This difference in thinking is the key to the all-important Renaissance in Europe. Those thoughts began a revolution of human ingenuity. Of all the differences made in painting and the arts, *the real change came with science and the printing press.* Science started looking at the world in an **empirical way** and fashioning man's products after these observations.

SCIENCE AND PSEUDOSCIENCE

The word "science," as used today, carries a tone implying "proven" or no dispute is possible. This thinking is erroneous. To make progress, scientific discoveries must be able to withstand a challenge, and when they fail, people start searching for better answers. *All scientific theories are always open to challenge.* New data is always coming in, so theories are always under suspicion. Even the raw data itself is open to challenge through additional experiments.

In science, theories are ALWAYS temporary. Modernly, cosmology theorizes how the universe started, and the predictions from these theories have proven correct thus far. "Proven correct," meaning the data collected from experiments and measurements agree with the theories. For illustration, the Big Bang would leave its "fingerprints" behind, that is, some evidence showing a stupendous explosion. We have found that data. This marks cosmology as a true science, even though one cannot go back and recreate the universe. This is so because the underlying math is repeatable, and experiments on cosmological theories show they conform with reality as we measure it. To understand the impact of science since the Renaissance, one must try to understand the method of "science." The "scientific method" requires research, careful observation, recording, and publishing. Why the recording and publishing? Recording and publication gives others the chance to test the results for themselves. Theories in science come from data. The data comes from careful observation and measurement of results during an experiment. The experiment is an attempt to isolate a few (hopefully one) pieces of data that can be measured. *Controlled* experimentation is critical.

Many fields claim to be scientific, but they do not predict; and their "experiments" are not repeatable. History is not a science because a repeatable experiment is impossible in this field. The *hard sciences* (chemistry, physics et al) do allow repeatable experiments; however, in **pseudoscience**, nothing is repeatable. In science, contradictory data is acceptable, even if unexplained. In pseudoscience, contradictory data sinks out of sight so the theories remain intact.

Presented as science, evolution's defenders claim the theory is proven; however, a theory is never proven, and the theories' data cannot be subjected to repeatable experiments. Darwin admitted in his book (1859, *The Origin of Species*) the fossil proof of his theory was missing, but he said it would be found. Many critics say those fossils were never found, but supporters of the theory assert otherwise. Some argue the Theory of Evolution is merely a pathway to **naturalism's** acceptance. Naturalism is the philosophy of explaining everything through nature; thus, eliminating a need for God. Those supporting Darwin object that it is science, not philosophy; nonetheless, few argue the impact of the theory on philosophy or the impact of naturalism on post-modernism.

The problem is fossil discovery is not a repeatable experiment. We must simply take the expert's word for the meaning of the fossil. There are finds or discoveries in anthropology, but nothing comparable to a repeatable experiment with controlled samples. The data is subject to an enormous number of explanations, but experts in the field only allow explanations fitting the theory. Challenging or validating a theory is impossible if the data remains open to widely varying interpretations. This was all worked out during the Renaissance. Men who began the scientific movement clearly understood the *repeatability of the experiments* was the key to progress. With this insight, the world began to move forward with **empirical knowledge,** and set the foundation for the inestimable progress to come.

THE ART OF OIL PAINTING

FIGURE 16 JAN VAN EYCK, THE ANCOLFINI PORTRAIT, MID 1400S

Art soared during the Renaissance. Discovering how to place **perspective** into paintings, making them especially lifelike, resulted in artwork never imagined before this era. The invention of **oil paints** and the perfection of painting on canvas, turned the art world onto new paths never before contemplated. Oil painting revolutionized color, enabling the artists to impart a stained-glass look to the painting. By applying color in thin glazes, the artists could achieve a glow from within the painting as the light passed through the various layers and bounced back through those same layers to the viewer's eye. The names of the giants of Renaissance art: **Jan van Eyck (1383 to 1440, Hans Holbein the Elder (1460 to 1524), Hans Holbein the Younger (1497 to 1543), Leonardo da Vinci (1452 to 1519), Albrecht Durer (1471 to 1528), Michelangelo (1475 to 1564),** and many others, launched Western art on an unparalleled journey to excellence. For the rest of the time, all paintings will be measured against the masters of the Renaissance.

Music also began to become more complex and beautiful during the Renaissance. From about 1410 through 1600, music began to press forward. At least part of this advance was using the printing press to print sheet music. From 1470 on, the printing press was turning out sheet music. During this period, famous makers of musical instruments began to arise, for example: **Stradivarius** (violins) and Meuschel (trumpets). **Baroque** music began about 1600, and this eventually led to the Classical age. Composers such as **Vivaldi, Handel,** and **Bach** were popular during the Baroque era. It was during the Baroque period that composers began to use more complex and elaborate musical themes, and changes were made in musical notation that were important in conveying the ideas of the composers to the performers of the piece. Baroque expanded the complexity of playing styles and forced the performers to become more proficient in their playing skills.

The Renaissance musical styles would lead to Baroque (1600 to 1760), the **Classical** musical era (1730 to 1820), and the **Romantic** era (1815 to 1910).

Let Us Learn

From the Renaissance era, we learn hope. A few fundamental changes, mostly in thought processes, changed the world. If the world changes for the better on such small things as thoughts, so can we. By adopting a mindset of progress, viewing the process of our lives positively, and seeing that a little knowledge goes a long way we can change ourselves. One good event or experience can trigger a mass of others. The history of the Renaissance shows us this is a fact.

We must learn to observe what is actually happening, rather than assuming we know or taking another's word for what is going on. The scientific method changed the European world, and by using the same idea of close observation, we can change our own world. See for yourself, if possible, what is actually occurring. In addition, learn to question what you are told. Is it a fact that the continents move over time? Ask what evidence that proves movement. Find out if something else might explain the evidence cited. Great authorities may say it is right, but great authorities (Aristotle, etc.) have been wrong before. The only way to know is to investigate and ask fundamental questions of those espousing the idea. The Renaissance taught us to rely on facts, not long held opinions.

FIGURE 17 VERMEER, GIRL WITH A PEARL EARRING, 1665-1675

BOOKS AND RESOURCES:

The Renaissance, A Short History, Johnson, P., 2002, Modern Library.

P 570 et seq, *The New Penguin History of the World,* Roberts, J., 2007, Penguin Books. Great on the large changes sweeping over Europe.

The Politically Incorrect Guide to Islam and the Crusades, Spencer, 2005, Regnery Publishing, Inc

CHAPTER 5

THE AGE OF DISCOVERY 1463 TO 1522

FIGURE 18 DRAWING OF RENAISSANCE SHIP

Another set of great events took place during the age of the Renaissance, the discoveries of new worlds outside Europe. (New to the Europeans. Folks living there thought the Europeans were "new"). This was part of the **Age of Discovery.** European monarchs wanted to reach the riches of China without using the overland route (the Silk Road) through the Muslim world because Muslims charged a lot for the privilege of crossing their territory, and the trips were long and dangerous. Prior to railroads, ships were the fastest and cheapest ways to move cargo long distances, so European nations wanted to reach the Orient by sea and avoid the Islamic tolls. One of the first monarchs to commit substantial resources to the quest for a sea route to India and China was **Henry the Navigator** of Portugal.

Under Henry, the Portuguese decided to find a route around the continent of Africa by a series of steps. Each voyage would go farther down the western coast of Africa mapping the area as they went. Year by year, each expedition would make more headway in trying to find a way around the continent. The Europeans had no idea how large Africa was so the Portuguese method was the safest. Along the way they established trading partnerships with the natives to get something out of the voyages, and that eventually led to slave trading. The Portuguese started acquiring settlements on the African coast in 1463. The **Cape of Good Hope** was reached in **1487** and so named because at last the coast was turning east.[62] The cape was aptly named for, in fact, they had turned the corner opening the sea route to India. By **1498** the Portuguese were in India and soon established a lucrative spice trade.

The Muslim world was not pleased with this new development because it destroyed their monopoly on trade with the East; thus, they declared a holy war on the Portuguese, built a large fleet, and confronted **Vasco de Gama** and his Portuguese fleet at **Du in 1508**.[63] The Portuguese won a total victory and drove the Muslims from the Indian Ocean. Soon afterward, Portugal established a series of forts along the route to India and monopolized the spice trade. The costs of sending out the explorers had been high so Portugal decided the trade route should be theirs alone. Portugal would eventually lose its spice empire to the Dutch and English one small piece at a time; but for decades, Portugal was the ruler of the Indian Ocean and its lucrative trade.

We should also note that Portugal became an empire. Thus, a small state on the edge of Europe ended up dominating the Indian trade routes for years. Other European nation states took notice and began a series of explorations that ended up claiming land and establishing empires. This is no small matter in history. *From about 1600, when the explorations began in earnest, to 1950 (350 years), the empires of European nation states dominated the world.* The Age of Discovery led directly to the Age of Empires. All these empires were European, at least at the start. This is so because only Europe had an age of exploration followed by an age of land grabbing. Most previous empires,

---

62 Note this was 5 years before Columbus sailed for India in 1492. All of Europe knew the Portuguese had turned the south coast of Africa, and everyone figured the way to India around Africa was now a Portuguese monopoly.

63 This was one of the most important naval engagements in history. Vasco de Gama was brilliant in the handling of his fleet, and the victory ended Muslim dominance of the Indian Ocean till this day (2010).

such as Rome, grew by warfare and seizing neighboring regions. Only Carthage, by comparison, grew somewhat like the empires of the 1600s and 1700s. The Phoenicians built an empire of trade and established the city of Carthage which grew to an empire itself by establishing trading posts that grew into cities answering to Carthage. The European empires started as empires of trade, slowly began to dominate the areas they traded with, and finally subjugated the peoples with superior technology and began to rule them.

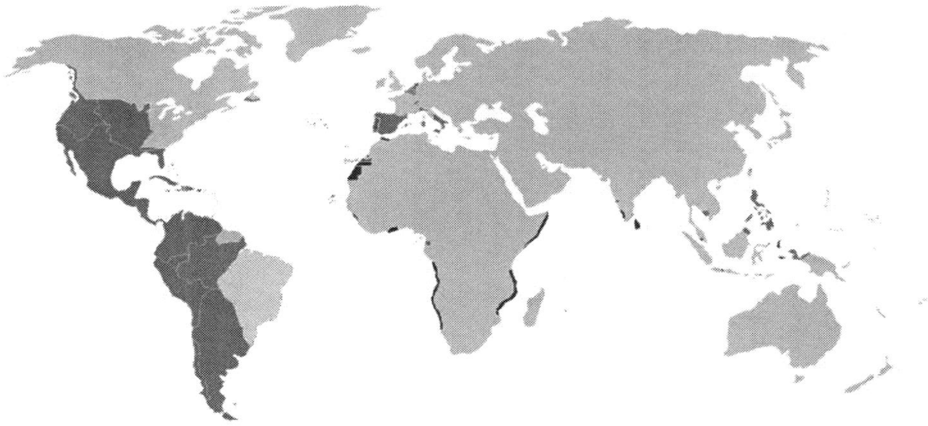

FIGURE 19 SPANISH AND PORTUGUESE EMPIRES BLACK EQUALS PORTUGAL

World War I ended at least four empires: the Austria-Hungarian Empire (all European), the Ottoman Empire (Middle East), the Russian Empire, which was replaced by the USSR—another Empire, and the German Empire (Africa and Pacific Ocean Islands). The Great War also added to the empires of France and England in Africa and the Middle East, and helped expand a new empire—Japan, which received "mandates" of Germany's Pacific islands. By 1939, the major empires were England, France, Holland (Dutch), Portugal, Japan, and the USSR. With the exceptions of Japan and the USSR, none of these empires remaining after World War I would have been established without the explorers.[64]

[64] ***The Discoverers: a History of Man's Search to Know His World and Himself*** by Boorstin, Daniel J. 2001, is one of the best books on this subject.

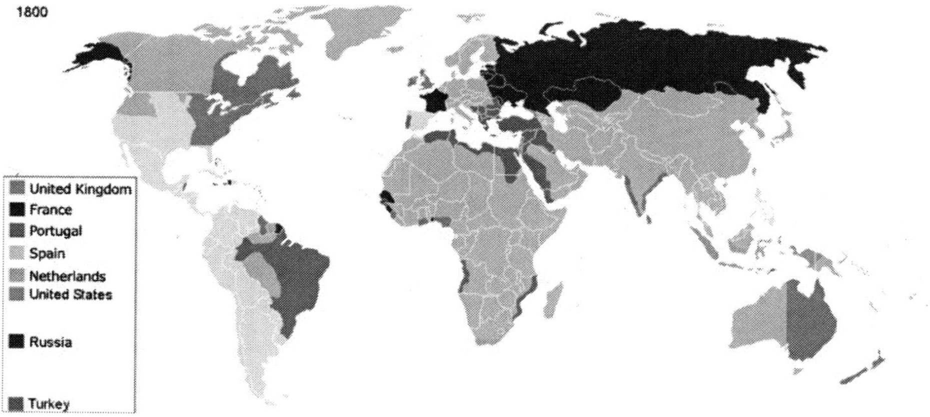

FIGURE 20 COLONIAL EMPIRES 1800

Christopher Columbus was probably history's most important discoverer because he found the "New World" of the North and South American continents, which were unknown in Europe. Europe knew about the Orient because they had been trading with the East for centuries, but they did not know about this new land that was only sparsely inhabited by people they called Indians.[65] The Europeans thought it was too good to be true—lots of land and no one of importance in the way. For the Europeans, nothing could have been better. For the Native Americans, nothing could have been worse. The Spanish were in a fix when Columbus approached them with his idea of getting to the Orient by going west. Portugal was making its way around the African continent, and was in no mood to allow others to assume their role. Spain, England, France, Holland, and other European monarchs, faced disruption of the lucrative trade with the Far East. Columbus at least offered them a chance to reach the Indies and gain another way to compete with Portugal. **Queen Isabella** of Spain decided to take the risk of backing Columbus and his idea of reaching the east by sailing west; but like many risk takers, she got something far beyond the assumed bargain. That something was even more incredible than a route to the Indies; it was an unknown world of vast potential and enormous mineral wealth. Columbus found something new and wonderful. Europe was ready to see what else the world held that was new and wonderful.

Now that the world was suddenly round someone needed to circumnavigate it. Magellan, a Portuguese turned Spaniard, accomplished the feat by setting

---

65 They were called Indians because Columbus thought he had reached India, or the Indies. The inappropriate name stuck.

out from Spain in 1519 and returning in 1522. Well, *he* didn't sail around the world, his crew did. He gets the credit for making the entire trip since he was in charge when the five ship fleet set out. The voyage made by Magellan and his crews was terribly hard. Out of 237 men only 18 managed to circle the globe; many died, some turned back. Magellan's real test came at Cape Horn at the tip of South America. As they sailed south along the eastern edge of South America toward the Cape, the rigging froze; and no food was available along the shores they passed. It was a barren and windswept land, offering them nothing they needed for continuing the voyage. Still, on he pressed. The nearer the small fleet got to the Antarctic the worse the storms became. He sailed through the Straits of Magellan (not the Straits of Magellan then of course) that were racked with violent storms, and somehow made it to the Pacific Ocean, which he so named because of the lack of storms encountered. Of course, after the straits and its storms almost anything would look passive. Then they started across the Pacific and found it to be almost endless. Magellan claimed everything he discovered for Spain. After surviving all the previous troubles, Magellan died in the Philippines fighting the natives. Before he made the passage around South America, part of his fleet turned back to Spain and told the Spanish authorities Magellan's fleet had perished. They were still in Spain when the sole surviving ship from Magellan's fleet sailed in and put the lie to their story. Those who turned back were executed for mutiny. So, only one ship returned to Spain, but it was enough to claim the Philippines and most of South America (Portugal got Brazil) for the sponsors of the voyage—Spain.

Spanish thugs . . . oops . . . troops under various vicious . . . oops . . . bold leaders conquered Mexico (the Aztecs)[66] and Peru (the Incas). The **Conquistadors**, the name for the Spanish troops—meaning conqueror—were brave and brazen beyond all imagination. Tiny groups of men fought enormous armies of natives and won. These men were courageous, and how they managed to conquer these native kingdoms is a story in itself, but the result of these conquests was the decimation and subjugation of the American natives.

---

66 Cortez conquered the Aztecs in 1521, and Pizarro conquered the Incas in 1532.

NATIVE EMPIRES IN THE AMERICAS

FIGURE 21 AZTEC CAPITOL OF TENOCHTITLAN

The native empires of the **Aztecs** and the **Incas** were large and powerful entities with absolute rulers, majestic cities, astounding temples of worship that resembled the pyramids of Mesopotamia, significant wealth, an understanding of astronomy, written language, large trading areas, and blood sacrifice to their gods. In other words, these were major civilizations. These noteworthy societies were preceded by other important Meso-American civilizations with all the fundamental attributes of cities found in the Fertile Crescent of the Middle East. These organized empires believed in gods, sacrificed to those gods, and had armies that conquered and oppressed other tribes in their areas. Cities grew up that were large, well organized, well administered, and were fed by farmers using complex irrigation systems to assist them in growing their crops, consisting of maize (corn) and potatoes. Sound familiar? It should, because these civilizations were very much like those in the Middle East, although they grew up in isolation from other empires. We *know* these civilizations grew up in isolation because upon contact with Europeans they died by the hundreds of thousands from diseases carried by the white invaders. Small pox was so deadly that it alone took millions of lives. If there had been contact between the regions these diseases could not have extracted such a deadly toll because the natives would have experienced them already and built up immunities. The crops of the Americas, maize and potatoes, were probably cultivated from at least 5000 BC. Europe had no idea these crops existed; thus, it is apparent no contact occurred after that time.

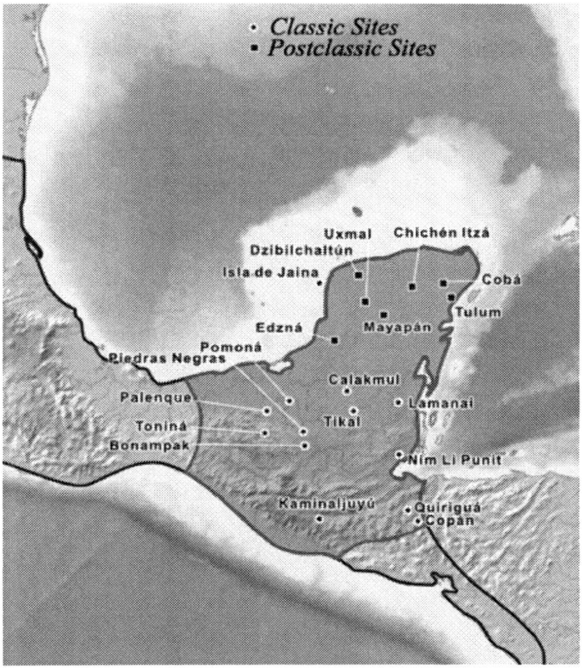

FIGURE 22 MESO-AMERICAN CULTURAL SITES (MAYA)

What these civilizations did *not* have in common with the Middle East, Europe, and Asia was **herd animal** husbandry. Unlike all the Middle Eastern civilizations, they did not have herd animals such as cows, horses, and sheep. In addition, their crops were corn based. Wheat and barley crops were unknown to them. The largest omission from their civilizations, in terms of inventions, was the wheel. None of the Native American cultures had invented the wheel even though they had round calendars, and some of their toys had wheels. They also did not have gunpowder, cannons, or rifles. In Europe, rifles were in use by 1520, and they were using cannons in 1320. These weapons were the difference between victory and defeat for the Native Americans in the Aztec and Inca Empires.

As these cultures grew up in isolation from cultures in the Middle East, but ended up much like them, it may be an indication of the universal underpinnings of human thought. Their gods were multiple, and they demanded sacrifices of blood. This was common in Mesopotamia even though the practice of human sacrifice was not so widely used. In

Mesopotamia and Egypt, the inhabitants constructed pyramids with steps,[67] which were a lot like those constructed in Meso-America. How is it that at least two widely separated cultures developed the pyramid as a shape for worshiping their gods?[68] Contact between these cultures is improbable, and they did not jointly emerge from a common civilization. Instead, I think inbred human personality traits are the common point of origin for a belief in gods, the geometric structures constructed to worship these gods, the warfare and sacrifice desired by the gods, the drive for domination over others, and many other things. If widely separated cultures develop much the same way with beliefs in conquest, war, gods, sacrifice to the gods, and massive buildings for ceremonial centers, it seems what was inside the people drove them to these beliefs and actions. We should note that cultures in China, Japan, Southeast Asia, and many other locals developed similar beliefs, even if their buildings were not the same.

These native empires started in Mexico, north of the Yucatan Peninsula on the Gulf Coast about **1200 BC**. The first were the **Olmecs,** who existed from about 1200 BC to 400 BC. Some doubt the Olmecs were an empire at all because their artifacts are restricted to a rather small region; however, they did construct substantial ceremonial centers with what seems to be an astronomical alignment, and these had pyramids and large plazas. The most conspicuous artifact left behind were gigantic stone heads with African facial features. This may indicate the culture was not of Native American origins; however, this is highly speculative. This culture vanished by 300 BC; why is open to speculation. Here we should note this is one of the few major civilizations growing up apart from a major river. The same is true of other Meso-American civilizations such as the Aztec, and the Inca in South America. In the Middle East, Turkey, India, and China the large empires grew up along major river systems.

About 300 BC, early **Mayan** civilization was starting in the area of Guatemala with intensive agriculture that included hillside terracing and canals. Composed complex hieroglyphics, the Mayan script was the most advanced system of writing in the Americas. Mayan math and astronomical skill enabled the invention of a highly accurate circular calendar that divided time into finite periods. It is said this legendary calendar predicts the end of

---

67 Atlantis is the most commonly referred to point of origin for cultures that are thousands of miles apart but manage to think and build much the same. Plato aside, there is no physical or other proof for the existence of Atlantis as a continent or a culture. Too bad, because it would be a lot of fun if such a place had existed.

68 Although in Egypt they advanced to a smooth-sided pyramid.

the world in 2012. The Mayans, and probably the Olmecs, were involved in blood sacrifice, a tradition enduring through all the major Meso-American civilizations. Blood, it seems, was necessary to nourish the gods. As with subsequent civilizations in Meso-America, it was the king's job to obtain sacrificial victims for the gods, and this involved the conquest, enslavement, and murder (sacrifice) of conquered peoples. These ideas lived on in the societies following the Olmec and the Maya, because these kinds of sacrifices were in vogue until the European invasion in the sixteenth century.

Around AD 800, the Mayan civilization suffered a mystifying collapse, and the population fell dramatically in the Yucatan area. This breakdown caused the fall of **Chichen Itza**, their magnificent city dominating the cities of the northern Yucatan Peninsula for centuries. The collapse led to a dispersion of the surviving population into smaller kingdoms. There was a re-emergence of the culture in about AD 1180, when the Mayan cities thrived once more. This relatively decentralized new Mayan culture thrived until the Spanish incursions of 1519.

The mysterious **Toltecs** civilization was ruling central Mexico about AD 850. Their society esteemed war and conquest. The Aztec rulers claimed descent from this legendary culture centered in the city of Tula. The discovery of this city led archeologists to believe it was at its height about AD 900, and destroyed about AD 1160. The city had large monuments, and the people practiced the same blood sacrifice as future cultures in the region.

The empire of the **Aztecs**, which probably replaced the Toltecs, centered on their capital super city of **Tenochtitlan**, constructed on a lake in the Valley of Mexico and home to about 250,000 people. Organized as an imperial structure under an absolute king, this impressive realm began its rise about AD 1400, eventually stretching from the Pacific Coast of Mexico to the Atlantic Gulf Coast. Although the Aztec Empire lacked an extensive road system, interconnecting trade routes were well established. The Aztecs practiced the blood sacrifice of their forbearers, and carried the ritual to extremes.[69] The Aztec Empire fell when Cortez conquered Tenochtitlan in 1521.

The **Inca Empire** in Peru centered on its capital city **Cuzco**, the religious, cultural, and political core of their Andes Empire. **Machu Picchu**, their

---

[69] Understand that this blood sacrifice entailed cutting the heart out of a living human victim and holding it up to the sun while the organ was still beating. Now that's a blood sacrifice!

temple complex, is surrounded by fortress walls and perched high on a peak for extra protection. This mountainous realm enjoyed well-constructed roads which assisted in keeping the rather-narrow 2,600-mile-long strip (from Ecuador southern Chile) along the Pacific coast of Peru unified as a kingdom. Apparently, an absolute emperor controlled all aspects of life and the economy. The conquistador Pizarro and his small army destroyed the Inca in 1532.

One great problem with the Spanish conquest was their destruction of the Aztec and Inca artifacts upon which they recorded their history, thereby leaving historians guessing about Mexico and South America's past. The Spanish viewed these items as tools of Satan as they thought the Native Americans were worshiping the devil. Many of these records were on gold objects that the Spanish were all too happy to melt down and send back to Spain.

SPANISH AND ENGLISH EMPIRES IN THE AMERICAS

After the Spanish won their American empire, they established a hierarchy over the population with the Spanish on top, then the Catholic Church, the Native Americans, and last the children of Indian and Spanish blood. Native Americans found themselves digging up gold for shipment back to Spain. Used as slaves they gained no benefit from their subjugation.

Using South America as place of exploitation, Spain took away all the gold they could find while turning the natives into vassals. [70] From California to the tip of South America (except for Brazil), the Spanish ruled it all as totalitarian overseers. South American gold made Spain rich beyond all belief and the most powerful nation in Europe. The challengers, England, France, Holland, and the city states of Italy, simply could not dig up endless amounts of gold to finance their every whim. Nonetheless, Spain soon fell from the great power ranks by unwisely spending its wealth.

Meanwhile, the English laid claim to the coast of North America and parts of Canada. The French were in North America as well and claiming

[70] The Catholic Church demanded the natives not be enslaved, so the Spanish just called it by a different name and did the same thing.

Louisiana, the Mississippi River Valley, and parts of Canada. In the 1600s, North America did not have tons of gold to dig up and haul off, and the natives were a mixture of friendly and very unfriendly, depending on the tribe; however, it was a good place to settle. Soon Europeans were coming and trying to make a home along the Atlantic coast of North America, on the Hudson Bay, and the coast of Canada. These were not hit-and-run adventurers. The folks arriving in North America were tough, resourceful people, looking to work hard and build a life of their own away from the old country. They came to stay and had no reason to enslave anyone; however, once they were ashore the lives of the natives in North America changed for the worst.

The newcomers shattered the lives of the Native Americans (Indians), ending their cultures and their very existence. The most deadly impact was unintended as the Europeans brought **diseases** the natives had never been exposed to, with devastating results. Germs that had little or no impact on the Europeans killed the Native Americans by the multiple thousands. Why the natives did not carry diseases that would do the same to the Europeans is a subject of study, but it is a fact that the natives died of Europeans' diseases by the millions; but the Europeans did not die in large numbers from native diseases.[71] This depopulation of the already-existing peoples simply made the conquest of North America that much easier for the newcomers. As the natives melted away, the Europeans took their place.

Because of the two different kinds of newcomers to South and North America the continents developed in very different ways. In South America, subjugation was the way of life with the Spanish ruling the natives. As such, only a few Spanish settled and stayed, usually as overseers of the natives. Those that stayed ran huge estates and lived as royalty. Here too the natives died of diseases in large numbers, but the Spanish were mostly concerned that enough of them remained to work the land or dig the gold. The Catholic Church looked after many natives and converted them to Christianity; however, it was a Christianity mixed with native ways.

In North America, independence was the way of life, with the newcomers establishing themselves on the land and pushing out the natives. The "Indian Wars" on the frontier were unremitting affairs. The fighting went on year after year as colonists moved west to gain more farmland. In the end, diseases, the crushing numbers of Europeans, and Europe's advanced technology overwhelmed the natives. The Native Americans in the North

---

71 *Guns, Germs, and Steel: the Fates of Human Societies,* by Jared Diamond, 2005.

lost their lives, their land, their culture, and their future every bit as surely as those Native Americans in South America had.

The Age of Discovery went on for decades as men sought new places to explore. For our purposes, the Age of Discovery will end with the voyage of Magellan in 1522 because it is a good date to hang our hat on, it found the extent of the South American continent, and "proved" the world was round—and very big.

Let Us Learn

From the Age of Discovery we find out that expectations are often wrong. Spending a lot of money on an adventure (project) involves unstated assumptions. Sure, the world is round and Isabella's advisors knew it, but the Europeans assumed nothing but ocean stood between them and Asia if they sailed west. So, beware of unstated assumptions and unproven expectations. Also, learn that scouting ahead can make a big difference. We must also learn that killing and oppressing people will ruin those doing the oppressing. Spain failed to benefit from its oppression in the New World. From settlers in New England and the North American colonies we learn the value of hard work. By staying put, working hard, saving, and protecting their profit, they set the foundations for a great nation. Keeping it simple, working hard and setting aside for the future pays off. We must note the importance of technology. Falling behind in technology doomed the Native Americans. Same for disease. Disease is a big deal, and disease alone changed the course of history more than once. Keep up with changing technology, and try to stay healthy.

BOOKS AND RESOURCES:

The Discoverers, Boorstin, D.J., 1985, Vintage. Outstanding book.

The New Penguin History of the World, Roberts, J., 2007, Penguin Books, Starting at page 546.

Chapter 6

The EAST

China

The history of China is a thorny subject. The names are strange and hard to spell, plus what was going on in China did not seem to affect Europe (although we know it did). *China's largest impact on the West was the result of Europe knowing about China and expending a lot of energy trying to get there for trading purposes.* The silks and spices of the Orient drew such good prices in Europe that it made sense for traders to get there however they could and bring back these most profitable items.

What seems odd is *China was not trying to get to Europe.* Chinese traders did not venture very far west or east. What did go west, with the armies of the Mongols and others, was disease and war. Of course, the wars imposed on the West from the East did not come from China proper; they came from the nomads living in the area west of China. The diseases that swept over Europe probably started in China, it is often hard to say, but this was not a purposeful export[72]

China's impacts on Europe were actually profound. Anything that kills off about one-third of the population of an area, such as the Black Death did in Europe, is important. The area of trade involved men taking action to get to China. The great explorers sailed west to reach the east (Columbus for example), and their tales of high adventure on the seas caused a lot of attention to be cast onto them. The opening of sea routes to Asia had an enormous impact on Europe, and helped to make Europe the dominant region of the world after they had secured the sea lanes to the orient. On the way to Asia, the explorers discovered other lands and claimed them

---

72 The Black Death is reported in China about 1341; and by 1347, it had reached Europe. This was the last of several plagues to sweep over Europe.

for their own. Such claimed areas often became colonies of the "mother country" and once again increased the wealth of Europe.

Thus, China, through its mere existence, had a massive impact on European history (and therefore world history) even though it is seldom mentioned in that light.

Why did China keep to herself and not venture out and try to gain knowledge and trade from the rest of the world? At one time, China did just that, reaching India and perhaps beyond; however, later emperors thought China was the center of the earth and that it had no need for exploration. Like any nation with a very long history it is not uniform from start to finish. What we have to look at is the larger trends, and China's trend for centuries was isolation. The Chinese called themselves the middle kingdom, or the center of all the earth—or at least the part that mattered. The Chinese had everything they needed so why venture out to the barbarian world? Aggressors came from Mongolia and conquered the Chinese; however, China prevailed because the newcomers did not change China, rather, China changed the newcomers. The invaders were few compared to the Chinese, eventually adopted Chinese ways, and gradually merged into the population until China was once more China—and the former conquerors were now Chinese.

A great Chinese asset is the continuity and stability of their ancient civilization. Ancient Egypt had a solid continuity for over 2000 years, but ancient Egypt is with us no longer while China is. Chinese continuity goes back to the Shang and Chou Dynasties.[73] These two dynasties gave China the structural organization that continued for centuries. After laying these foundations, China remained basically the same until the 20th Century. A strong centralized government, the basic land divisions, and the fundamental classes of society began during the reign of the Shang and Chou. The people of the land (peasants) and the ruling class (nobles and emperors) were set up as distinct groups, becoming nearly unchanging categories of people that formed the basis of Chinese life from these early dynasties until the modern world interposed itself. Thus, Chinese society resisted change and achieved a remarkable stability for about 3,500 years.

---

[73] The Shang dynasty was founded in 1600 BC, and the Chou was founded about 1050 BC. All dates in this section must be considered approximate; thus, when it says the dynasty lasted 200 years please be aware that means it lasted *approximately* 200 years.

The Chinese always thought their greatest asset was "the Chinese mind." As they scrutinized other cultures the Chinese noticed foreigners saw life quite differently, failing to understand the qualities of thought separating them from the Chinese. For example, the first legendary Chinese Emperor, Fu Xi, was famous for establishing a connection between the individual and nature (philosophy & keen insight), unlike western leaders such as Sargon famed for slaughter and conquest (war & killing). Unlike the West, Chinese philosophers avoided arguments about definitions (epistemology) or what was real and what was not, and stuck with practical subjects. Most Chinese philosophers were concerned with how to live now, what makes a superior person, and how one could grow to be a superior person. **Lao Tzu** founded Taoism in 600 BC, **Confucius** taught morality in 549 BC, and **Buddhism** started to infiltrate China in 200 BC from India. These eastern philosophies avoided conflicts about the afterlife. Life here on earth was stressed, and the afterlife was something no one could know.

Taoism concentrated on telling the adherent to flow with events as water flows down a stream, and concentrate on becoming a superior man. One key to Taoism was conformity with facts found in life. To struggle against the tides of the time was not the sign of a superior person. The Tao is "the way" or the principle governing an ordered universe.[74] **Confucius** was an ethics teacher stressing right living, honor, and obedience. He was especially concerned with governments, and wanted governments to be operated honestly and for the benefit of all, including the peasants. During his life his impact was not great; however, after his death his philosophies became widely accepted, and the model for government officials in China. **Buddhism** taught that one might achieve enlightenment by living right (right work, etc.) and trying to reach out to the universal "one" into which everything must someday merge. Buddhism taught the Eightfold Path to living and enlightenment. Named for **Buddha**, who was rich as a boy, but as a man he quit worldly things and began to contemplate what made people miserable. One day, while sitting under a tree, he was hit with the thought that "*wanting things*" is what makes men miserable. If people could get rid of this desire for more, they would be happy. Buddha did not write anything down himself, but his disciples wrote down his thoughts after he died, thus starting a movement that would sweep the East with his ideas. Buddhism requires one to focus on the ability to accept what is while turning aside the cares of the world. As a person's thoughts reach perfection, then enlightenment draws near. This enlightenment is to feel and experience

---

74 P. 41, *The Penguin Atlas of World History, Vol 1*, Kinder & Hilgemann, 1978, Penguin Books.

oneness with the universe[75] (Nirvana). Buddhism was originally simplistic and without ritual. In India, where it arose, it remained a minority religion; however, it spread to the whole of Asia and gained a massive following in China, Japan, and the rest of the world.

China's language was another unifying factor. The Chinese way of writing, in characters that identified an entire thought rather than an alphabet, shows another way the Chinese mind was, and is, different from the Western mind. Many of the concepts found in eastern writing (Chinese and Japanese) cannot be translated into English. As such, it is difficult to understand the thinking process since it remains hidden behind a language others cannot know unless they learn it and live it.

The Dynasties (this can get very dull)

Pottery found in China dates from 6000 BC, showing the ancient age settlers began farming the areas of the Yangtze and Huang river valleys in China. The earliest settlements were farming villages that grew into small towns. Rice farming was taken up at a very early time as well (about 6000 BC), and rice proved to be an excellent food source which facilitated the Chinese **population** leap. Evidence from these early eras show China's population growing rapidly; thus, China probably gained the population edge from the start of human history. China was working iron by 500 BC and making iron casts from 400 BC—over nine hundred years before casting became available in the Western world. By 1000 BC, China was making by far the finest pottery in the world along with using extreme temperatures to fire the pottery. About 1000 BC Chinese ink painting began.

From 2500 BC, large parts of China were unified under various dynasties starting with the **Yao**, which lasted two hundred years. Approximately 1994 BC, the **Xia** clan managed to gain control of enough of China to qualify as

---

75 Christians may argue this is "self-salvation." In Christian theology, Jesus Christ alone can save a person's soul, and one must confess Jesus is the Son of God and that Jesus Christ died on the cross to pay for their sins. A Buddhist (or Hindu) would see this as somewhat foolish, in large part because it avoids the question of conforming one's mind to the necessary attitude to reach the oneness of the universe. Hindus think there are many paths to truth so they accept Jesus as one way to the truth; however, Christians argue there is only one way, Jesus. In both Buddhism and Hinduism there are many complexities that go far beyond the ability of this text to explain them.

a dynasty. Xia's dynastic reign ended by 1600 BC with the inception of the **Shang** dynasty. The Shang lasted six hundred years before its overthrow by the **Chou** (also Zhou) in 1050 BC.

Together, the Shang and Chow dynasties established the fundamental patterns of Chinese life that would prove to be so enduring. The institutions established by the Shang and continued by the Chou would become the same institutions used by Imperial China for two thousand years. *The Chou established a strong unified central government* that was able, by using clans and the family unit, to run the nation. This strong central governmental control continues in China until this very day. *The Chou divided the country into landowning nobility and a peasant underclass.* One had to be a recognized member of a clan to be a noble. The peasants could not be members of a clan; thus, welding the peasants in place as workers of the land—and nothing else.

After the fall of the Chou dynasty in 480 BC, China entered into the **Warring States Period** until **221 BC**. During the Warring States Period, philosophy, technology, and the arts flowered. It was during this time of disarray that **Sun Tzu** wrote the famous *Art of War* that is still widely read today. Sun Tzu thought the greatest victories came without fighting. The goal was to bend your adversary to your will, and if accomplished without loss of life, then one had shown himself to be the greatest of generals (note the difference in the Chinese mind, very different from the west). Nevertheless, it was a period of extensive warfare and chaos failing to advance the overall society.

In 221 BC the **Qin** (also **Chin**, for which the nation was named) dynasty began after this clan was able to conquer and again reunite China under one ruler. The Qin had been fighting the nomads in the northern areas of China for years, and they put this knowledge of warfare to use in conquering the feudal states of the Warring States Period. After the conquest, the Qin dynasty started construction on The Great Wall to keep the nomads from the north out of China.[76] The Qin established a total dictatorship, created

[76] These "nomads" from the center of the Asian land mass were a problem for everyone. They attacked, under various names, China, Europe, the Middle East, and India. Their ability to use cavalry to defeat the civilized world on all sides of them is amazing. As historians, we have a problem understanding their background because they left very little written information about themselves. No writing, no history. The Huns were the great problem for the Han and constant wars were fought between the two "civilizations". The Great Wall was constructed to keep the Huns out more than anyone else.

one language for the entire nation, and required one system for weights and measures. Using harsh laws, the Qin oppressed the people. By murdering intellectuals with different ideas they instilled fear to maintain their rule. This harsh treatment led to discontent and rebellion.

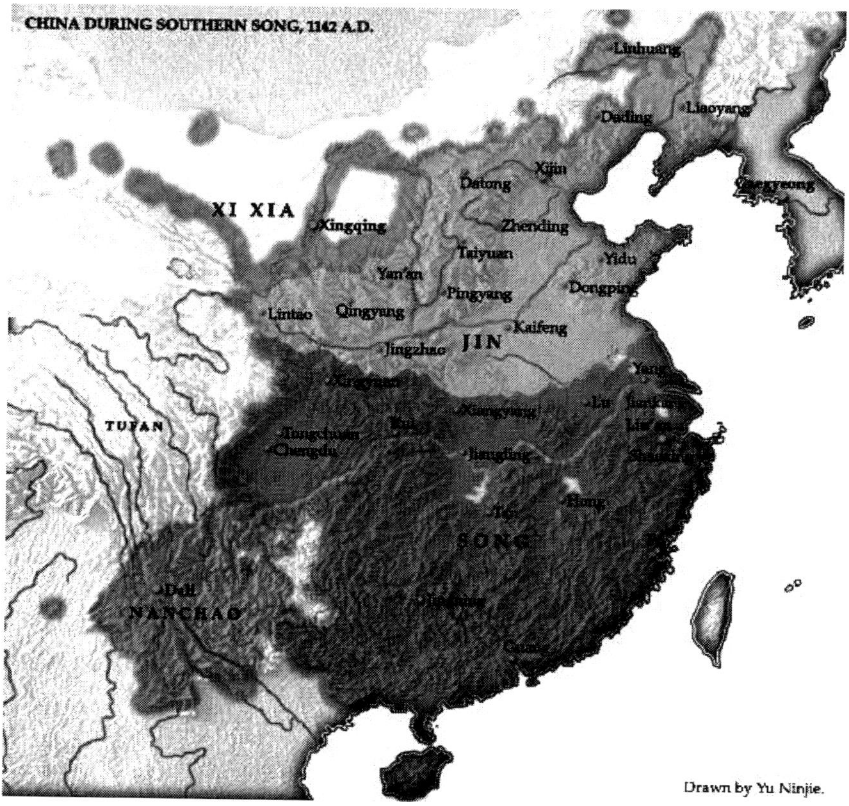

FIGURE 23 JIN (NORTH) AND SONG (SOUTH) DYNASTIES 1142 AD

In 206 BC the prosperous **Han dynasty** began and lasted four centuries until AD 220. The greatest ruler of the Han, **Emperor Wu**, started **the civil service system** in China wherein individuals were chosen for government jobs by testing rather than heredity. This fundamental change ensured a quality bureaucracy for China. The civil service system was part of a centralized government that was the norm in China since the Qin. The Confucius system and the civil service fit together well, as Confucius had taught that each person had his place in a great web of relationships and obligations. This web of relationships started in the home where each individual had a place with specific obligations, such as children to parents, and wives to husbands; then on to the larger world of peasants to local officials, local officials to regional officials, and so on, which then expanded out to the emperor and the entire world. As a part of this web of relationships and obligations, the civil servant had his place. The civil servant was to be an upright official and lead by example. The Confucius' system tempered the particularly harsh legalism in China and thereby assisted in holding the nation together.

Emperor Wu expanded the empire by conquering Northern Korea, Vietnam, and Thailand in Southeast Asia. Between 9 BC to AD 25, the Han dynasty was overthrown and then restored, thus showing a great resiliency. In the year 2 AD, a census taken by the Han dynasty recorded a population of **57 million**. This was a huge number for the time. China was in the population lead and never relinquished it. The West was starting to reach China during this period, and about AD 80 the great **Silk Road** trading route was established from Rome from China. [77] China managed to keep a complete monopoly on the riches of the East for centuries; thus, the Silk Road became a highway of wealth for European merchants if they could reach the portals of commerce in the East. Control of or access to this trade route would determine the economic viability of many empires.

In AD 220, China fell into a severe civil war that divided China into **Three Kingdoms** (Wei, Wu, and Shu). It was during this 300 year period (longer than the USA has been around) of war and unrest that Buddhism began to establish itself as a major religion in China. The wars continued and eventually the **Sui** dynasty, in AD 581, reunited China into one country. The Sui did not last long, and in AD 618 the **Tang dynasty** emerged. The Tang conquered territory well beyond previous Chinese borders, and they benefited from an excellent road and canal infrastructure. Trading silk—which the Chinese held a monopoly on by keeping its mode of production a secret—along the Silk Road and with the Indian Ocean trade network increased the nation's wealth. Civil war broke out once again in AD 755 when a great Tang general, An Lushan, rebelled against the throne. His rebellion was defeated, but it cost the empire so much blood and treasure the Tang never recovered. By 907 the Tang dynasty, one of the most brilliant in Chinese history, had disintegrated. From 907 to 960 is the time of the **Five Dynasties and Ten Kingdoms** where multiple states rose and fell rather quickly, leaving China searching for stability.

Note how closely this follows the basic outline of European and Middle Eastern civilization. Empire after empire arose, only to be conquered by

---

[77] This date is highly variable.

another empire. Some lasted longer than others, but the pattern is the same.

The Five Dynasties and Ten Kingdoms period ended in northern China when the Liao dynasty, as part of the non-Chinese **Khitan Empire**, gained control. The **Jin** conquered the Khitan in 1127 when they took over northern China. The European **Marco Polo** was traveling around China during the Jin period, and upon returning home told wondrous tales of the Far East, hence increasing western curiosity about Asia. Beginning in 960 and lasting until 1279 AD, **the Song dynasty** ruled much of southern China. Song emperors survived by retreating south, under pressure from the Jin and later the Mongols, and establishing a new capital at Hangzhou. They managed to create a competent government made up largely of the civil servants recruited from prosperous rural-area families. The Song dynasty was the first to use **gunpowder** weapons extensively in battles, some of them at sea. After the Mongol conquest of the Jin, the Song warred with the northern invaders for sixty-five years which considerably sapped their strength, but they managed to protect southern China from a Mongol conquest for many years.

The Mongol successors of Genghis Khan conquered northern China and the Jin by 1234. Commencing in 1231 they conquered Korea by 1236, then turned in earnest on southern China (the Song). **Kublai Khan** conquered the southern Song dynasty in 1279, establishing the **Yang** dynasty. Twice Kublai Khan tried to invade Japan only to have his fleets swept away by huge storms named *Kamikaze* (Divine Winds) by the Japanese. Once again weather and geography changed history.

In the early 1300's China suffered a great population loss due to the impact of the **Black Plague** (bubonic plague), which later moved on to the Middle East and Europe devastating the populace there. Historians estimate the Black Death killed 30 to 40 percent of China's inhabitants. Percentage wise, this is very close to the population losses in Europe from the plague. As a total number however, many more were lost in China. This massive population loss led to economic problems and then civil war in 1368.

In 1368, the Chinese rebelled against the Mongols and expelled them. So began the famous **Ming Dynasty** that reunited China. In 1420, the Ming moved their capital to Beijing and rebuilt the Great Wall. The Ming emperors also sent expeditions out to India and the coast of Africa. These expeditions concluded in 1433 because many thought the high cost was not worth the gain. It was during the Ming rule that Vietnam broke away and established an independent kingdom (again). During the Ming Dynasty China regained control of the Silk Road, linked its cities together by new canals and roads, developed additional agricultural land in southern China, produced fine pottery, and experienced a national economic and cultural resurgence placing China at the head of all oriental cultures of the era.

The Ming Dynasty lasted until 1644 when the **Qing Dynasty**, established by the **Manchu** as descendents of the Jin, overthrew the Ming. The Qing managed to conquer Mongolia then overran Korea in 1627. However, in the late stages of the Ming Empire Europeans began to arrive and establish themselves in traditional Chinese territory for trade. The Qin inherited this ominous trend. In 1683 the Qing annexed Taiwan, and in 1750 Tibet came under Manchu control. It was the emperor **Kang Xi** that accomplished these feats, and managed to expand Chinese influence into Central Asia. The expansion continued under Manchu Emperor **Qian Long** who forced Nepal, Burma, and Vietnam to acknowledge Chinese hegemony once again.

Trade with the West grew exponentially, but the Manchu limited the ports through which European trade could flow. The Manchu government also insulted Europeans with their shoddy treatment, and thus incensed the proud men who had trampled the rest of the world. Then, in a move that was boundless in audacity and malevolence, the British started importing **opium** from India, where it was cheap and plentiful, into China, and by 1830 Britain controlled *80 percent* of the lucrative drug trade. As England made enormous wealth the Chinese population began to suffer significantly. Millions of Chinese were addicted to the drug, and it wounded the Chinese homeland deeply as enormous amounts of cash began to leave China (Compare to the drug trade in the US from Mexico in 2010). As the trade was illegal in China, the Chinese government began taking steps to stop the trade of opium. This infuriated the British, and they declared war in 1839 after the Chinese blockaded their own port city of Canton to prevent the British from using the port for opium importation. By 1842 the British had prevailed in the **Opium Wars**, and China ceded Hong Kong to them as part of the settlement. By now the Chinese emperors were rulers in name only as the Western powers began dividing China up among themselves. Through it all the Chinese had little interest in the outside world. The barbarians, as they called Westerners, were at the gates; but China retained its inward gaze. The Opium Wars many have been the first international drug war.

In 1911 an army revolt against the Manchu, who had refused to consider any kind of reforms, spread throughout China. By 1912 the two thousand year old imperial system was crumbling, and young revolutionary reformers set out to change traditional China. These revolts led to years of chaos and internal warfare. Because of this domestic weakness Japan was able to annex Korea in 1910, and acquire large spheres of influence in Manchuria and Shantung province in 1918. The Western World complained about the Japanese land grabs, but the League of Nations proved ineffective, and the rest of the West did nothing substantial to stop the aggression.

During all this long history China remained one unified culture. Although the transitions were not smooth, it was often the case that Chinese were conquering Chinese until the arrival of the Europeans, when Chinese history changed radically for a few years. After the communist victory in **1949** that finally ended decades of civil war, China once more withdrew into itself, and for some time rejected foreign influences.[78] Today, in 2010, China is opening up and has a powerful worldwide economic, military, and political influence. One will quickly note this is unreservedly new in the history of China. China's communist leaders may have opened China for trade to protect themselves from rebellions, because the economic situation in China after the 1976 death of the murdering dictator **Mao** was extremely poor. In 2010, China has established itself as a world leader in trade and manufacturing. How long this will go on is difficult to say. Perhaps China has emerged from its long, inward-looking past to become part of a world now challenged by technology, cultural upheaval, economic interdependence, and strife as never before. One wonders if the Chinese mind can solve these problems.

JAPAN

This is another inward-looking nation believing it was the center of the universe, and blessed by its gods as the best place on earth with a perfect people. About 300 BC, invasions by clans from Asia bringing Bronze Age culture with them overran Japan. The island shattered into several small feudal states controlled by continually feuding warlords. During this time influences from China made their way to Japan via Korea. By AD 645 Buddhism was becoming a widely held belief replacing the ancient religion of ancestor worship. The mythological first emperor of Japan was Jimmu (660 BC to 585 BC), said to be the direct descendant of the sun goddess Amaterasu, and the sea god Ryujin. He is the claimed founder of the Yamato

[78] It can be argued that China's entry into the Korean War and the Vietnam War was for the purpose of keeping foreigners out of its sphere of influence.

Dynasty. The **Yamato clan** united Japan under a central government in AD 400. The Imperial Throne was later seized by **the Soga clan** that continued the Japanese traditions of rule by heredity. Eventually, the **Fujiwara clan** gained control of the throne by ensuring every emperor married a Fujiwara woman. (They must have been good looking gals). By this method, the head of the Fujiwara clan was always the father-in-law of the emperor.

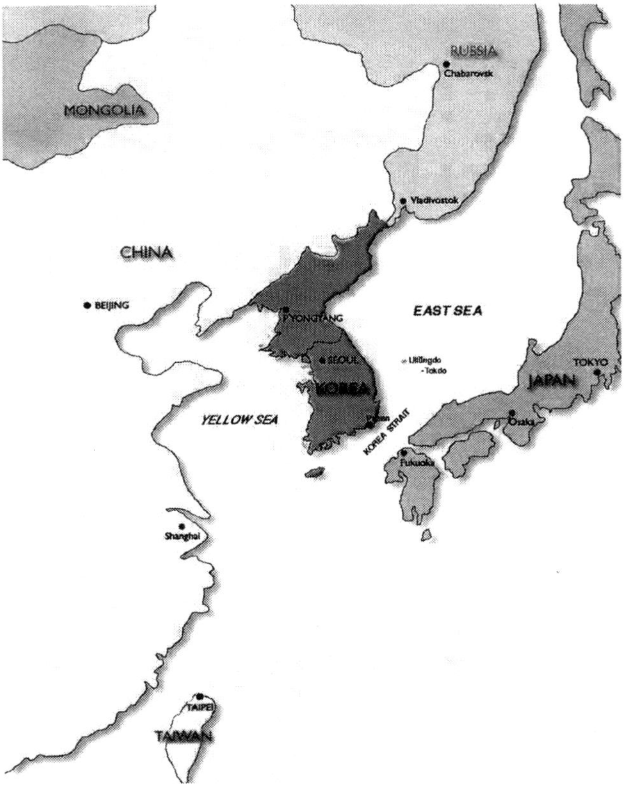

FIGURE 24 JAPAN, KOREA AREA MAP

In 1467, Japan fell back into a feudal period of war and division. This continued until about 1600 when a Japanese general named Tokugawa Ieyasu defeated Hideyoshi's army in the Battle of Sekigahara and established the **Tokugawa shogunate.** (Shogun means great general) This set up military rule in Japan until 1868. From 1543 to 1600, Japan accepted foreign influences including Christianity; however, this came to an abrupt end as the Tokugawa clan gained control of the nation. The Japanese began slaughtering Christians in 1600, and by 1638 the Tokugawa clan barred foreigners from its soil. Japan went into a period of complete isolation led by the Tokugawa. This in turn led to a blossoming of a pure Japanese culture entirely separate from Chinese, Korean, and Western influence for about two hundred years. The Tokugawa's competitor for control of Japan was the emperor; thus, the powerful clan made it a point to maintain strict control of the imperial court. The emperor became a puppet only serving to give legitimacy to the rule of the Tokugawa shogunate.

In 1853 the American Matthew Perry forced the opening of Japan to Western trade, although this led Japan to increasing hostility toward foreigners. Because of the intrusion of Westerners and the extraction of trade agreements, the Tokugawa clan weakened and was overthrown in 1858. In 1867 the resentment of foreign influence resulted in an overthrow of the shogunate and a restoration of imperial control (the **Meiji Restoration**). From 1867 until 1912, Japan absorbed Western ideas of manufacturing and warfare, adapting these ideas so well that they easily beat China in an Asian area conflict in 1895. In the **Russo-Japanese war** Japan easily defeated Russia in 1905 *becoming the first Asian nation to defeat a modern European power,* and thereby expanding their territorial control of areas near Japan. From 1858 onward Japan made tremendous strides in industrialization, trade, and territorial acquisitions.

Japan tried to use the Western model of a parliament by creating a **Japanese Diet in 1889**; however, the experiment failed as in **1926 militarists** factions gained control of the government. The militarist set the nation on the path of conquest starting with the annexation of Manchuria in 1931, quickly followed by a war with China, and the takeover of French Indochina in 1941. Japan entered World War II on the Axis side in December of 1941 with the attack on the US fleet at Pearl Harbor; thereby starting a war with China, the United States, Britain, Holland, Australia, New Zealand, and other US Allies. Japan suffered a complete defeat in August 1945 after the US dropped two atomic bombs on the island nation; one on the city of **Hiroshima** and the other on the city of **Nagasaki** (see World War II). Japan experienced occupation by US forces until September of 1951. Thereafter, *Japan grew into the second most powerful economy in the world* by 1980. This remarkable economic recovery, assisted massively by the Americans, displayed the resilience of the Japanese culture. In 2010, Japan continues to excel at trade and manufacturing, and she is poised to lead the way into the twenty-first century.

Through it all, Japan remained thoroughly Japanese. In spite of accepting the infusion of Western technology, and science it did not allow these influences to change Japanese culture. This is not an easy task, as normally accepting Western technological advancements leads to an idea that Western culture must be superior. The Japanese did not think this way, and rejected Western cultural ideology while accepting its technology.

KOREA

Korea is the third area of the East that completes a kind of triumvirate of nations around which the fate of Asia has swung. Korea is a small peninsula jutting out of the Asian mainland near Japan. Korea managed to establish a separate identity from China and Japan, and maintained that separate identity through centuries of pressure, warfare, and conquest. About AD 313 Korea had **Three Kingdoms** that were indigenous to the peninsula. These independent states lasted until about AD 668. By 670, the clan of **Silla** managed to unite Korea with Chinese support. The Silla clan endured defeat by the **Koryo** in 935, allowing the Koryo to rule the Korean peninsula until 1392. The Mongols supported the Koryo (no wonder they won). In 1388 the Koryo sent an army to invade China and overthrow the Ming dynasty; however, that army turned on the Koryo and defeated them thereby establishing the **Chosen Kingdom** that ruled until 1910; although, from 1627 until about 1910 it was subservient to the Manchu of China. During the period of the Chosen Koreans built an observatory in Seoul, and they invented moveable *metal* type for printing.

Overall, Korea was always a land in the middle. Japan or China normally dominated the peninsula; nonetheless, the Korean people maintained their identity as a separate populace. Today, Korea remains separated between north and south because of the Second World War and the Korean War. (See the Korean War)

INDIA

After years of battering at India's frontiers, Turkish Muslim invaders finally captured the northern city of Delhi in 1206 and established the Delhi Sultanate (1206 to 1520).[79] Under Muhammad Tughlug the Sultanate managed to bring most of India under its rule by 1335. This conquest put the Muslim faith in charge of India; however, it did not manage to overcome either Hinduism or Buddhism. In 1398 **Tamerlane**, the Mongol

79 Please see the previous chapters on India and the Aryans.

conqueror, destroyed the city of Delhi and set the stage for the destruction of the Delhi Sultanate in 1526 by **Babur**, another Muslim.

Before 1500 India's merchants helped establish the prosperous *Indian Ocean trade network* stretching from East Africa to Europe and Japan. This massive trading region brought affluence throughout the area. The regional trade connected the Mediterranean Sea to the Red Sea via trade routes across the Suez isthmus. It was this Indian Ocean trade the Portuguese began disrupting when they circumnavigated Africa on their way to India. They succeeded in reaching India in 1508 and began taking control of the sea routes in the area. Within 100 years the Portuguese began to lose out to the English, and the English Empire took control of the formerly Portuguese trading areas.

In 1526, Babur, a descendant of Tamerlane and Genghis Khan, established the **Mughal Empire** in India that lasted two hundred years. **Akbar the Great** (1556 to 1605) finished the conquest of India that his grandfather Babur started. Under Akbar, a Muslim, Hindus could hold office in the state bureaucracy, and Akbar himself married a Hindu princess. The Mughal Empire controlled most of the Indian subcontinent by 1600, going into a rather slow decline after 1700. Since Babur and his progeny were Muslim the Hindu majority were enduring the control of an outside religion. Under Islam, non-Muslims could be murdered if they refused to accept Islam or they could be left alive as second-class citizens paying extra taxes and otherwise being subservient to Muslims. Hinduism survived in spite of this oppression on the subcontinent; although, in the western regions of the Indus River, just off the subcontinent, Islam made good strides and converted many people. When India became independent in 1947 this western region, now called **Pakistan**, broke away and formed its own nation.

Gradually, the Mughal Empire gave way to the English Empire, mainly because of the efforts of the East India Company which was a private company chartered by the British Government. The **British East India Company** (East India Company) arrived in India in **1617**, and began trading in the province of Bengal by way of permits issued by the Mughal rulers in 1717. The officials governing the province of Bengal objected and entered into hostilities with the East India Company. At the Battle of Plassey in 1757, an army of the East India Company led by **Robert Clive**, defeated the forces of Bengal. Note that a private company had the resources to defeat a sitting government. Eventually, Robert Clive became the governor of Bengal. The East India Company expanded its control until the **Indian Rebellion of 1857**, also called the Sepoy Mutiny or the First War of Indian

Independence. This rebellion ended the Mughal dynasty and put the English crown in control of India. (The English government absorbed the Company) This English control would last until India and Pakistan gained their independence in 1947. India was the crown jewel of the English Empire, and protecting India and the sea routes to the sub-continent became a major part of English foreign policy.

The transition to independence for India and Pakistan was not smooth. After gaining independence in 1947, the partition of India from Pakistan began, and a huge movement of peoples, some 12 million, took place as individuals in the "wrong country" (Wrong religion in the wrong country actually) tried to reach the right one. Fighting began between Sikhs, Hindus, and Muslims leaving about 500,000 dead. It seems freedom does not come easily to lands divided by religion and history.

Today (2010), India is one of the world's most prosperous and populated nations. A leader in heavy industry, electronics, motion pictures, computers, and science India now thrives as a market based democracy. India has strong population growth, and its **population** is over **1.17 billion** with a median age of 24.9. India has the world's 12th most powerful economy as of 2010. Turns out that India is also an advertisement for the power of capitalism. From 1950 through the 1980s India was a socialist nation, and its governmental system and economy experienced slow growth because of corruption coupled with socialist inefficiency. In 1991, India *changed to a market based economy* and has achieved a GDP growth of 5.8 percent for 20 years making it the fastest growing economy in the world. Some estimates predict India will overtake the USA in GDP by 2043 (Since the US is going socialist after 2008 election of President Obama one can understand why). Meanwhile, Pakistan, the Muslim nation to India's west, has not fared so well. Economically stagnant for over 10 years its main economic products remain services and agriculture. Pakistan's poverty rate is at least 23 percent. Its population is nearly 175,000,000 and growing quickly. Political turmoil haunts Pakistan because of rogue Muslim fundamentalists, such as the Taliban, battling government troops while controlling large regions of the nation. Unfortunately, both India and Pakistan have acquired nuclear weapons and first-rate missile delivery systems, adding a dangerous edge to centuries old feuds.

Let Us Learn

The East teaches us the value of steady progress, and the dangers of pride. By progressing at a steady rate, China, India, and Japan stayed well ahead of the world century after century. Their pride, and their mistreatment of the European newcomers, led to a rather rude awakening when the Europeans flexed their muscle. China, Japan, and India needed to stay in touch with the rest of the world because their isolation eventually let them fall behind the advances taking place in the land of the barbarians. We learn that keeping up with new ideas and advancing technology is critical. So, do not isolate yourself and keep learning.

Books and Resources

The New Penguin History of the World, Roberts, J, 2007, Penguin Books

Roberts divides Eastern history as follows: (all page numbers correspond to the starting page of the section in Robert's book):

Roberts on China:

Ancient: p. 132
Classical: p. 444
Manchu Empire: p. 461
Republic and European Imperialism: p. 857
People's Republic: p. 985

Roberts on India:

Ancient: p. 120
Medieval: 338
British Rule: p. 638
Self Government: p. 975

Roberts on Japan:

Early: p. 36
Medieval: p. 466
Modern to 1945: p. 635
Post—1945: p. 1062

Chapter 7

Africa

A Very Modest "History"

Written history is not the stuff of Africa. What we have is oral traditions and some archeological evidence from which we can build up a slight traditional style history of sub-Saharan Africa. Modern African historians normally rely on oral traditions above other methods. The northern coastal regions of Africa were settled and urbanized by people with high cultures that included writing; thus, history. In this case we know a lot about Carthage and Egypt. If we set out south, beyond the desert wastes, we hit a region where virtually nothing was written down, and the climate and building materials are such that physical evidence does not last. In this section we will briefly discuss sub-Saharan Africa.

One of the earliest significant southern (tropical) African civilizations was the kingdom of **Kush,** in the area of Nubia on the "upper" Nile River.[80] Kush existed in the area where the White and Blue Nile join. Egypt either controlled or heavily influenced the area up to the Nile's 5th cataract for centuries; however, after the fall of the Egyptian New Kingdom in about 1070 BC, the area of Kush re-asserted itself and built a substantial empire with its capitol at Meroe. The main reason Egypt wanted to control the upper Nile was the gold fields found in this region, and after the reduction of Egypt's power, the state of Meroe (Kush) traded the precious metal far and wide from 900 BC until its fall in 350 AD. Meroe fell after the nearby kingdom of Axum invaded and overthrew the ailing empire. Once again, trade was the commonality that leads to prosperity. And once again, the Middle Eastern pattern of the rise and fall of empires was repeated all over Africa, albeit on a smaller scale.

---

[80] "upper" here means southern. Egypt considered the mouth of the Nile at the Mediterranean Sea the "lower" Nile.

Fundamentally, settlements in sub-Saharan Africa were small and usually limited to small scale agriculture, cattle raising, and hunter-gatherer societies. Major trading centers grew up in the north, including **Timbuktu** in the state of Mali, but none grew to a great size. Perhaps the most famous exception to the lack of substantial buildings was the important trading center at Great Zimbabwe that reached its peak about 1200 AD. This regional center was on the Zimbabwe Plateau, and its major trade was in gold and cattle. The granite stone blocks used for their expertly constructed walls and towers remained impressive decades after Great Zimbabwe disappeared from history.

Islam made inroads in Northern Africa—above the Congo basin—after AD 1000, and they began trading in gold, ivory, and **slaves** from AD 600 onward. Some northern areas of Africa became totally Muslim, but the southern areas managed to retain their own religious structures. Muslim traders first began trading slaves from Africa to the Muslim world in the Middle East. Muslims were by far the world's greatest slave traders. European slavers arrived in 1441 (**Portuguese**). By the time the European slavers arrived African tribes were already familiar with raiding other tribes to capture slaves for outsiders. It was a very lucrative operation for the African tribes and for the Muslim and European entrepreneurs engaging in the practice. By the 1500s, the Ottoman Turks held Northern Africa and the trading routes across the Sahara, thus controlling important trading centers and trade routes.

On the eastern coast of Africa an excellent trade system evolved into the *Indian Ocean trade network.* This trading area brought in, and disbursed all over Africa, goods from far away China, India, and the Mediterranean world. Areas all along the eastern coast of Africa prospered from this trading arrangement. The Europeans would spoil this trading system in the 1500s when Portuguese explorers looking for a way to the orient interrupted the sea routes used by the network. Soon the Europeans dominated the oceans off eastern Africa and determined what sea trade passed between various regions. In essence, Europeans began taking the trade to Europe and destroyed the lucrative trading system in the Indian Ocean.

The African slave trade went on with Europe and the Americas until *banned by England in 1808* in a unilateral act of conscience. It was England's sea power that allowed the nation to embark on the scheme that challenged much of Europe and the Middle East. In 1815, at the **Congress of Vienna**, Britain convinced nearly all of Europe to sign off on banning slavery. By the 1820's, both the British and French were trying to end the slave trade; however, the African tribes and states that made large profits from slavery were resisting this change. After all, the slave trade was extremely profitable for the African businessmen. The British even bombarded the coastal fortresses of the African slave traders who opposed the Euorpean attempt to limit their power. By **1880** the combined efforts of England, Europe, and America ended the African slave trade; however, this in turn caused economic problems in Africa causing a general financial collapse. The African economic problems led European colonial powers into opportunistically absorbing the entire continent into their empires by 1914 in the notorious "Scramble for Africa." When the European powers completed the scramble only two nations, Liberia and Ethiopia, remained free of colonial control. After World War I the victors redrew the lines of demarcation for African "nations" because Germany lost their colonial empire, most of which was in Africa, and the English and French seized these colonies. These lines of control only displayed European concerns, not African realities.

The colonial collapse after World War II led to African states gaining their freedom rather quickly. Unfortunately, they proved unable to effectively govern themselves. England was careful to develop its colonies so they could handle independence, but most other European nations, such as Belgium, just left, thereby allowing everything to fall apart behind them. The poorly drawn lines of nationhood left over from the Treaty of Versailles resulted in wars and relocation problems killing millions of innocents in Africa. Brutal dictators arose from the chaos, gaining control of wide areas, and brutalizing the population to maintain control. These dictators often obtained the blessing and financial support of the United Nations. The international organization was trying to alleviate suffering but achieved just the opposite. The dictators used the money to buy weapons to maintain their power. The problems of genocide, tribal warfare, religious warfare, disease, poor farming conditions, discrimination between tribes, poor leadership, dictatorships, exhausted economies, and a lack of management skills persist into 2010. The suffering in Africa since the end of colonial rule was, and is, appalling.

Let Us Learn

From Africa, we learn outsiders never have your best interest at heart.

BOOKS AND RESOURCES

A Short History of Africa, Oliver and Fage, 1990 Penguin 6th Edition. I really like this book. Easy and excellent reading, especially for a newcomer to African history.

Chapter 8

The Middle East and the Fall of Byzantium (The Eastern Roman Empire) 500 to 1453

Now we must again retreat in time, visit the Middle East, and review what happened when Islam expanded across Africa, conquered Spain, invaded France, and later invaded and destroyed the Eastern Roman Empire (called Byzantium). Once again, odd as it may seem, when Byzantium fell its Roman culture disappeared. The **Ottoman Turks** had no use for heathen Christian ways and obliterated the remains of Rome in the east.

In AD 640, out of the deserts of Arabia, came a new monotheistic religion firing its adherents to conquer in the name of their god Allah. Long before the fall of Constantinople, the Muslim warriors had swept out of Arabia, through Egypt, and across North Africa to the straits of Gibraltar. After crossing the Mediterranean to Iberia (Spain and Portugal) the Muslims destroyed the disunited forces of Christianity, conquering Iberia for Allah. Now that Spain was Muslim, the armies of Islam looked to the conquest of France as the next logical step to winning the world for their god.

Islam Turned Back at Tours

732

A powerful Muslim force crossed the Pyrenees Mountains and moved into Southern France where they shattered the Christian forces of Aquitaine before moving north and falling into battle with **Charles Martel** (the Hammer) at the **Battle of Tours in 732.** Accounts of the battle are somewhat terse and extremely scarce, but both Arab and Christian writers tell of the clash. The Muslims had never known defeat, and they outnumbered Charles and his men. After the battle began, Charles positioned his men in squares where fierce Muslim charges failed to dislodge them. It is said that it was the force of Martel's personality that held his men together as they withstood charge after ferocious charge. Although losing a large number of men in the clashes with Martel the Muslims were prepared to fight on. Then the Muslim army discovered a few of Martel's men had infiltrated into their camp, where they were releasing European prisoners and pillaging loot seized in previous battles. Many Muslims turned their horses around and hurried back to the rear trying to save their riches. Martel surrounded the remaining Muslim force and totally destroyed them, including killing their commander. Martel gathered his far-flung army and organized to renew the fight the next day, but the Muslim forces were gone ***never to return***.

Historians debate the significance of the victory at Tours; nonetheless, there is no doubt Charles Martel won one of the world's most important victories. Like the victory of Vasco De Gamma at Du, which destroyed an Arab fleet in the Indian Ocean securing the waterway forever for the West, the victory at Tours by Charles Martel and his men denied the Muslims entry into Europe for the rest of time (at least up until 2010), and saved Christian Europe. If Martel had lost, Europe could have suffered Islamic conquest. If Islam had won Europe we could forget about the Renaissance, the Age of Discovery, the flowering of literature, science, math, art, and all the rest that defines the Western world. Every person enjoying Western Civilization owes an immense debt to Charles Martel and his men who desperately fought and won against the Moors at Tours so long ago.

Although turned back at tours in the West, in **1453** the forces of Islam, under the Ottoman Turks, toppled the last of the Eastern Roman Empire when the city of Constantinople (Byzantium) fell. Byzantium was a Greek-speaking Christian empire, and all that remained of the once mighty Roman Empire in the east. The Byzantine Empire was quite large at one point, stretching from Turkey to Spain by AD 585; however, numerous defeats and poor rulers shrank it to a small size around its capital of Constantinople by 1300. The city of Byzantium's name was changed to Constantinople by Constantine the First (AD 306 to 337) who made the glorious city the center of the Eastern Roman Empire. Constantine was the first Roman emperor who converted to Christianity; thus, Byzantium became a Christian empire. Now, a little Byzantium background.

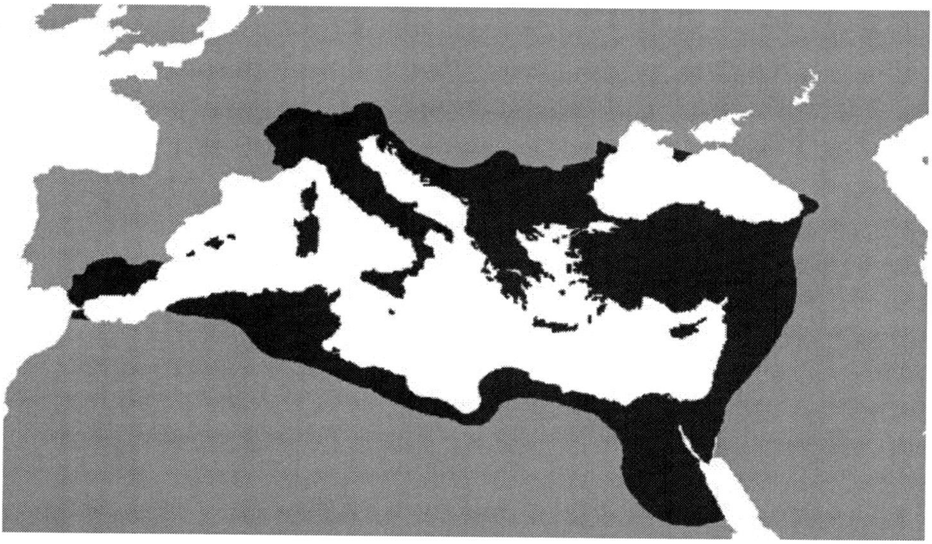

FIGURE 25 JUSTINIAN'S EMPIRE (BYZANTIUM) 527-585 AD

BYZANTIUM

The Roman Emperor Diocletian had split the Roman Empire into western and eastern parts in 285 with the goal of better governing each half; however, after the split, the economic power remained in the east, and thereafter the west declined as the east prospered. The city of Constantinople was founded on May 11, 330 by the Roman Emperor Constantine, who was out to found *Nova Roma* (New Rome). He chose a site with seven hills to mimic the old Rome, but his new city would be far more magnificent. The citizens of Constantinople called themselves Roman at the dedication of the city, and 1,123 years later when the city at last fell to the Turks, they still called themselves Romans. It was Constantine who called the counsel that set forth the Nicene Creed, which defined what it meant to be a follower of Christ and a Christian. When Constantine died he was laid to rest in his *Nova Roma* city at the Church of the Holy Apostles that he had previously ordered constructed.

The Byzantine Empire would be blessed with great, and not so great, rulers; however, through it all the riches of the East kept the empire alive. At the crossroads of east and west, commerce was the boon of the Byzantines. By keeping the area around the Mediterranean peaceful they encourage trade. The Roman roads and safe sea routes all contributed to Constantinople's commercial success.

At the **Battle of Adrianople** in AD 378 the Goths killed the Roman Emperor Valens and destroyed his legions. This defeat, and the threats from other barbarians, caused Theodosius II of Constantinople to build triple walls around the city some sixty feet high. It was these walls that defined and protected the marvelous city for over 1,000 years. **Justinian I** (527-585) became emperor of Byzantium and was successful in expanding the empire by constant battle. He managed the re-conquest of Italy and North Africa by about 527; nevertheless, the strain on the empire was great in economic terms. During his reign he had improved the system of taxation and tried to kill off corruption, but with the riches of east pouring in corruption was immortal. With his partner and famous queen **Theodora** (an unusual mix of whore and genius),[81] and his gifted general **Belisarius**, Justinian was successfully pushing the reunification of the old Roman Empire when disaster struck. Belisarius had returned Italy and North Africa to Imperial control when the bubonic plague infected the empire, the city of Constantinople, and his stunning Queen Theodora in 541. After Justinian lost his beautiful consort Theodora to the plague he was never the same, and the expansion of the empire stopped. AD 541 was the high point of the Byzantine Empire.

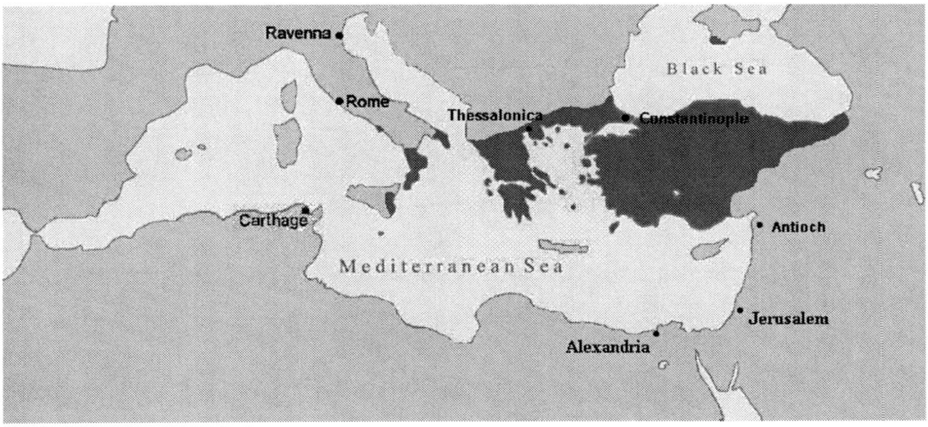

FIGURE 26 BYZANTINE EMPIRE 867 AD

Byzantium faced the same problem that Rome had faced: scheming aristocrats. Merchants, small manufacturing concerns, and small farmers began to disappear as wars, natural disasters, taxes, and corruption drove

---

[81] The History of the Decline and Fall of the Roman Empire, Edward Gibbon, Penguin Classics, ISBN 0140433945, p.563; http://en.wikipedia.org/wiki/Theodora_(6th_century)

them under. The wealthy aristocrats were waiting to buy up the land being sold by the small farmers. The middle class began to evaporate, and with it the strength of the empire.

The strength of Persia continued to grow, and by 619 they were threatening to topple Constantinople. Heraclius became emperor in 610 and he was already in deep trouble. He turned to the Church for money, and the patriarch gave it to him to save the city and the empire. This was a fusion of church and state unknown in the West. It took ten years to construct a winning army, but Heraclius did it and completely vanquished the Persians. All seemed well for the moment, but the moment soon passed with the coming of Islam.

The threat of Islam arose with a new religious prophet born after the death of Justinian. The prophet **Muhammad** founded his new religion (Islam) on a monotheistic belief in the one true god, Allah. The one true god chose to speak with his ultimate prophet secretly in a cave for some years before Muhammad reveled Allah to the world. These teachings were written down in the **Koran** the Muslim holy book. Muhammad prophesized all believers must submit to Allah, warning that Allah demanded control of every aspect of their lives. The new religion set forth an exacting series of requirements resulting in the government, all social life, law, worship, and even eating habits being controlled by the rules of the Koran, the perfect example of Muhammad's life, and pronouncements of Muhammad apart from the Koran. The religion condemned all non-believers, and death awaited those who failed to convert. The Muslims preferred dealing death to all heathens, although exceptions existed for "people of the book," meaning Christians and Jews, who could choose to live in total subjugation to Islam in lieu of death. Muhammad managed to conquer Mecca in 630, thereby ensuring his new religion a strong base of operations. He died in 632; nevertheless, his followers were determined to spread the word of Allah, and in 640 they began a series of fantastic conquests that swept the Middle East, North Africa, Iraq, Persia, Spain, and beyond by 1500.

Muslims believed the "umma," a religious and social community concept uniting all believers, was to have only one leader—a caliph. The caliph was a *religious and political leader*, thereby uniting the church and the state. The first caliph was **Abu Bakr.** Under the first three caliphs Islam expanded exponentially. There were two very successful caliphates (Islamic states): the **Umayyad Caliphate** (661-750) concentrated in Damascus, and the **Abbasid**

Caliphate (750-1258) focused at Baghdad.[82] Under the Caliphate's expert leadership the Muslim armies swept all before them.

Meanwhile, the empire of Byzantium was constantly under attack from all sides. Constantinople held out against two Islamic assaults from the south, one lasting four years between 674 and 678, and another in 717. However, to the north and west the Bulgars and Avars seized nearly all of the Balkans and reduced the empire substantially. Things were looking grim for the empire as it was subjected to simultaneous assaults from different directions.

A general recovery began for the city and the empire after 717, and Byzantium was once more able to recover lost territory in Greece, Macedonia, and Thrace. Following this period of expansion the Komnenoi (also Comneni) dynasty came to power in 1085 and managed to hold the empire together and expand its economic prosperity. Under great pressure, Emperor Alexius I Comnenus invited the Church of Rome to help save the Byzantine Empire. The pope understood the importance of the empire as a bulwark against Islam and responded. Pope Urban II delivered his sermon requesting men to save the Holy Land on November 18, 1095 and he received an overwhelming response. Unfortunately, the Crusaders refused to take advice from Alexius and suffered defeat after defeat. Then a total disaster. Disobeying the orders of the pope and his threat of excommunication, the Fourth Crusade sacked the great city of Constantinople in 1204, breaking its ability to resist further Muslim incursions. After the fall of the Komnenoi dynasty the empire entered a steep decline that eventually resulted in the fall of its capitol and the complete destruction of the Byzantine Empire. The fall of the great city opened up Christian eastern Europe to Muslim conquest.

In 1180 the great city at Constantinople protected about 400,000 inhabitants, in 1204 about 150,000, and by 1453 (the date of its fall) about 50,000. It was during the Fourth Crusade in April of 1204, that Constantinople was

---

82 None-the-less, this success was marred by civil war, in which split the Muslim world into two sects: **Sunni**, the majority of Muslims, perhaps 80 percent belong to this sect, believing the Muslim leader does not have to be a descendent of Muhammad, and the **Shiites** who believe Muhammad's son in law Ali should have been the leader of the Muslims. This division in the Islamic world continues today, and the consequences have been chaotic and bloody. Each sect believes the other is reprobate and in need of extermination. This led to conflicts of the most violent character which continue into 2010.

sacked by "Christian" troops originally on their way to fight the Muslims. A scheming duke (doge) of Venice, Enrico Dandolo, was seeking revenge for financial losses suffered to the emperor at Constantinople, and he managed to turn the crusade against the great city rather than the Muslims. The Christian crusaders slaughtered the inhabits, looting and burning the city for three days and stealing everything of value. The crusaders even dug up graves and pried open crypts containing the jeweled garments of past emperors, which they promptly stole. Ancient manuscripts with gold inlaid covers were hacked apart for the precious metal. The city failed to recover from this plundering by Latin Christians, and the weakening of the city greatly hastened its decline. The fact that Christian Crusaders attacked and pillaged the strongest Christian bastion in the east against Islam was incredible. Once Constantinople fell the entirety of Eastern Europe was open to Muslim invasion. The duke of Venice had opened the door to an incredible slaughter because of a personal vendetta. The pope was stunned. The call for help from Christian brothers had turned into an orgy of violence against those who had pleaded for aid.

By 1453 Constantinople was isolated in a sea of Islamic controlled territory. Knowing no help was coming from the West, or anywhere else, the 7,000 soldiers of Christ prepared to meet the 80,000 Turks of Allah. The Ottomans were able to capture the city by attacking from land and sea simultaneously, and by pounding the walls down with a massive cannon throwing stones (cannonballs) weighing 1500 pounds. The defenders of the city were few during 1453, but they held out for nearly two months providing yet another testament to the strength of the triple walls that protected the city for so many centuries. Even after the walls were opened up by the huge stone cannonballs, assault after assault was thrown back. The Ottoman Turks used their powerful cannon to batter the city again before their final assault, punching additional large openings in the walls and demoralizing the defenders. The last emperor, **Constantine XI**, refused to become a vassal of the Muslims, preferring to die in battle. He positioned himself at the weakest point of the wall, and as the enemy swarm stormed through the breach he charged forward. His body was never found. Cannons had overcome the old static defenses that turned back so many previous invaders. After the fall of the mighty city, and an immense slaughter of its citizens where the streets became slick with blood, Islam moved on by invading Eastern Europe and continuing their string of conquests. Byzantium was gone and Constantinople became the capitol of the Ottoman Turks. They renamed it Istanbul. It never regained its former glory or wealth. Rome was at last a distant memory.

As Constantinople was falling its citizens were leaving. They went west to Italy and France, bringing with them the classics of Greek and Roman literature. In addition, they brought the learning of the East where, for example, Arabic numerals (they were actually Hindu) and the concept of zero as a mathematical place holder proved far better than Roman numerals in calculations. The West had long been held back by the inability of the Roman numeral system to make complex calculations. Many other concepts in medicine and philosophy entered Europe from Constantinople. Thus, the fall of Constantinople was a kind of boon to Europe, and kick started the era we call the Renaissance.

THE CRUSADES

1095 to 1291

As we know from the above commentary, in 1095 **Pope Urban II** set off a religious war to regain the Holy Land of Palestine, and the city of Jerusalem, then under Islamic control. This was a natural response to the slaughter of Christians throughout the conquered area, and there was the threat to Christian Constantinople that had requested aid from the west. As European knights formed armies for the liberation of Jerusalem and Palestine, the name **Crusaders** attached itself to the men and the venture. Even though the Crusaders managed to retake Jerusalem in 1099 (the First Crusade), the Muslims counterattacked and re-conquered the city in a few years. In spite of four more Crusades the forces of Christianity failed to defeat Islam. The number of crusades is hard to count because a lot depends on what one defines as a crusade, however, most historians count five.

The Fourth Crusade sacked Constantinople and never attacked Muslim forces in the Holy Land; nevertheless, they did manage to destroy the last best bastion against Islamic invasion of eastern Europe. The final Crusade was the Fifth (1217 to 1221), and it also managed to accomplish nothing. Four Crusader states were established in Islamic territory during the Crusades, but these were small embattled kingdoms that failed to spread the Christian faith or expand their conquests. The forces of Islam destroyed all these Crusader states; however, Muslim armies lost so many men in battles at the Islands of Rhodes and Malta that it damaged Islam's ability to continue attacking Europe. Even though unsuccessful in holding the Holy Land, the Crusades did turn the tide of conquest against Islam.[83] The constant wars with the European Crusaders and the Mongols attacking from the east eventually wore down the Muslims reducing the wars between the Europeans and Islam. The Muslim advance into eastern Europe stopped at the gates of Vienna, and the advance into Western Europe had failed at Tours in 732; nonetheless, the conquests of Islam were vast, and they represent a continuing challenge to the West and Christianity.

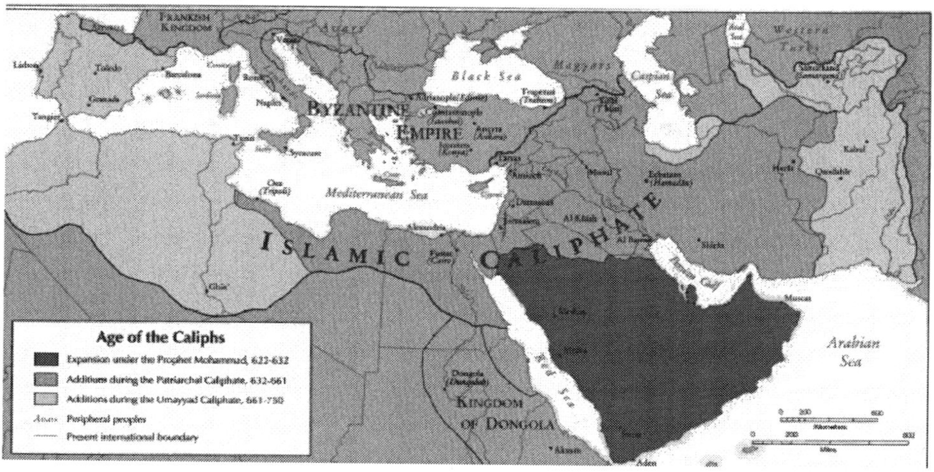

FIGURE 27 ISLAMIC CALIPHATE TO 750 AD

The Crusades influenced Europe far more than Islam. To Islam they brought only hate, but through their contact with the Muslims, Europeans brought back knowledge of the classical Roman and Greek world that started the European Renaissance.

Most of this section relies on the book *Lost to the West, the Forgotten Byzantine Empire That Rescued Western Civilization*, Brownworth, Lars, 2009, Crown Publishers.

Let Us Learn

From this complex era in the Middle East, and the political, social, and religious clashes of the Crusades we learn not to bite off more than we can

---

83 Acre fell in 1291, and this was the last of the major Levant Crusader strongholds; however, the island of Rhodes held on until 1522 and the island of Malta until 1798.

chew. Islam over extended itself, then broke up into factions over details thus sacrificing unity. Moreover, their treatment of other religions led to a backlash out of Europe, the Crusades, that punished everyone involved including the Europeans. The Crusades taught us to plan well before any significant undertaking, and if you cannot get everyone on the same page before the project starts then start over or abandoned the project. In essence the pope said, Go get 'em without any plan, and the segmented nature of the response displayed a disunity of ideals, goals, and actions on a broad scale. In addition, no one thought about the end game. Even if Jerusalem was taken, what then? How many people wanted to go there and stay? Not many. Failure to think through significant undertakings, ***especially the end game***, can turn worthwhile projects into disasters.

The forces of Islam failed to think through what caused the Christian backlash. It turns out that mistreating people, including killing and degrading them over religion, gets folks kind of riled up. In your own life remember the lesson of treatment of others. Treating folks poorly may result in them treating you poorly. Many a politician managed to discover that rule. Smart people give and command respect; however, respect for others comes before getting respect. Learn to admire others and respect their beliefs and accomplishments. Condemnation on a broad scale seldom achieves a necessary objective; rather, it normally ends up impeding the ability to gain any objective. Stay unified, stay respectful, plan well, define objectives closely and clearly, and prepare thoroughly for the task. Finally, think about the end game. What achievement is sought, at what cost, and what are the consequences of failure? Also, think about other ways to gain the same objective. This era taught us all this and more.

BOOKS AND RESOURCES:

The New Penguin History of the World, Roberts, J, 2007, Penguin. p. 358 et al fall of Byzantium; p. 342 et al Crusades.

Crusader Castles in the Holy Land 1192-1302, Nicolle, David, 2005, Osprey. Excellent maps and illustrations by Adam Hook.

A History of the Byzantium State and Society, Treadgold, Warren, 1997, Standard University Press.

Lost to the West, the Forgotten Byzantine Empire That Rescued Western Civilization, Brownworth, Lars, 2009, Crown Publishers. The best short book on Byzantium.

Chapter 9

The New World and the Rise of America

Columbus and 1492

The Age of Discovery led to the European discovery of the Americas in 1492 when Columbus ran into the land mass and thought it was Asia (actually he stumbled onto Cuba, but that's another story).[84] Spain sponsored the voyage, and Queen Isabella herself paid for the undertaking. Columbus returned with Native Americans that he called Indians because he thought he had found India or a set of islands near India. After a bit of additional exploring it was soon determined he had not reached Asia but a new land unknown in Europe. Of course, Spain claimed the new land, but the Spaniards were not so much interested in North America. The gold of Mexico and South America attracted them. Some areas of North America were claimed by Spain (Florida, parts of Southwest America), but Spain's real efforts went to gathering the South American gold and in turning the Native Americans into slaves . . . err . . . Christians.

Disease decimated the Native Americans. Some estimates say 70 percent of the population was destroyed by 1700, mostly from disease. The empires of the Inca and Aztecs fell to the Spanish Conquistadores and opened the way for the complete domination of the South American native societies. The Spanish simply placed themselves at the top of the social scale where

[84] This was the discovery of America because it was *publicized.* The Vikings and others may have arrived first, but they did nothing with the knowledge. Columbus came back and let everyone know how great he was; unfortunately, he failed to understand where he had been. Nonetheless, everyone in Europe knew that new lands had been found; thus, it was Columbus who discovered America because one who discovers something and keeps it secret has discovered nothing—except for himself.

the old rulers had been causing the population to follow their orders—or else. The new rulers were exploiters and used the natives as virtual slaves to mine the gold or grow the crops that would bring in money. Spain did well and prospered throughout the sixteenth century. England and Holland, plus other upstart nations, spent their time raiding Spanish possessions in the Caribbean and otherwise working to diminish Spanish power. For all the wealth flowing into Spain from the New World little was spent on improving the economy or the daily life of the peasants in Spain. The aristocracy made most of the money and depleted it on projects only benefiting them. Spain spent a lot of wealth on its army and on the wars it had to fight expanding or protecting its empire. Thus, the benefit to Spain for all the gold and wealth that came its way was brief.

After a few failures, the English finally established a North American colony in **1607** at **Jamestown, Virginia**. This colony, founded 115 years after Columbus' voyage, just managed to hang on in the face of disease (the colony was in a swamp), starvation, recalcitrant lazy colonists, and some hostile Native Americans. Other colonies placed farther north encountered fewer problems with disease and angry natives—at least at first. In 1664 the English took New Amsterdam from the Dutch and renamed it **New York**. This was a thriving port in 1664, showing how well the New World was treating people who came for hard work rather than exploitation.

This was the key difference between the colonies of North America and South America. Where Spain came to take and leave, the colonists of the north came to work and stay. The Spaniards looked to Spain as the homeland that they would eventually return to. In the north the colonists wanted to stay because the New World was their home. These men and women would live, work, and die in the new land. Their children would come of age in America while farming and working in the colonies, because for them the future was the New World not England or Holland or Germany where they came from. The Spaniards looked east toward home; the English colonists[85] looked west toward the new land.

---

85 OK, OK . . . . So they were not ALL English colonist, but I just can't type English, German, Irish, Dutch, French, Russian, Danish, Norwegian, Swedish, Finnish, Belgian, Italian, Sicilian, Swiss, Portuguese, Scottish, Welsh, and Lord knows how many others every time I type "colonist" . . . so . . . *English* colonist it is. They were the majority after all.

NATIVE AMERICANS

The Native Americans were in a conundrum. What were they to do now that the white men had arrived? In South America they were enslaved, and in North America they were driven out. The colonists of the north did not want to enslave them, they wanted them to go away. In the north farming was all important, so the settlers wanted to clear the land used for hunting by the Native Americans and plant crops. The northern colonists cut down the trees and built homes and farms everywhere. Eventually, cities arose on areas once roamed by Native Americans. Frequent wars broke out between the Natives and the colonists. Often the Natives would kill a rather large number of the white men, but the colonists always struck back. With disease killing millions of them the Native Americans could not effectively combat the white settlers. As more ships arrived with ever more Europeans, the Native Americans could only despair. Construction started on massive cities, the likes of which no Native American had ever seen or imagined. White settlers brought guns and technology as well as increasing numbers. All the natives could do was retreat, but they knew there was no end to this surge of people coming to use the land in new ways. The Native Americans had no place in this kind of world.

The Native Americans failed to unite against the white man. Some settled in and bartered with the newcomers trying to fit into the new milieu. Others, usually in piecemeal fashion, warred with the settlers in a losing attempt to change the flow of history. The warriors lost, as did the traders who were trying to fit in. The warriors lost their lives, their villages, and their families. The passive lost their culture and their identity. They became the Indians, or red men; people who were lost in a new age and unwelcome by those who occupied the land. Some Native Americans attended college, received degrees, and otherwise "made good" in the new white settlers' world; nevertheless, they failed to be accepted as full equal partners in the new society transplanted from Europe. Europeans had many prejudiced ideas, and these did not leave their minds because they crossed an ocean.

The Native Americans did not do much to endear themselves to the Europeans. Several of the tribes were at least part time cannibals. Needless to say, cannibalism enraged the colonist and was, to some, more proof the Indians were worth nothing but extermination. The natives also were fierce in battle. It was common for Iroquois warriors to bite chunks of flesh off the men they were fighting in hand-to-hand combat. So called Indian massacres stories were told and re-told all over the colonies. Europeans feared these warriors who moved like shadows and ambushed parties of white men in the dense forest of the eastern seaboard. Many Europeans came to hate the Native Americans as godless heathens asking for destruction. This is the common result of unremitting warfare such as the kind waged on the colonial frontier. (Or in modern Israel/Palestine)

As the Native Americans endured obliteration new problems arose for the settlers. French colonization of Canada and sections of America triggered a large war. In 1682, France claimed Louisiana and the Mississippi River lands. (All lands drained by the Mississippi River) Then in 1718, the French founded the city of New Orleans at the mouth of the Mississippi River, effectively gaining control of the waterway. In fact, all over the world the French and English were having problems with one another, and in **1756** they went to war. (Note the date, 20 years before the American Revolution) The war was termed the **Seven Years War** in Europe, but in America it was called the **French and Indian War** because the French took several Indian tribes as allies. This was a world war, with France and England battling over colonies and the seas connecting them. England won a decisive series of victories outside of Europe. In Europe the Seven Years War ended in a draw with England and Prussia fighting France, Austria, and Russia to a standstill. In the New World, England won in Canada and the frontiers of the American colonies. America and Canada became fully English possessions, with France's last bastion being Louisiana. The war ended in 1763 with the Treaty of Paris which gave England control of much of the world.

The American colonists were not "American" so much as they were English. At least that was what everyone thought at the end of the French and Indian War in 1763; however, back in England the Parliament believed the American colonists should pay their fair share of the war's cost. After all, the French and Indian war won the colonists a lot in terms of western land and safety from further French attacks. With the French gone, the Indian problems would abate because no outside force remained to unite them against the colonists. As a result, the English Parliament passed a series of acts **taxing** the colonists in America for the war. Some New England colonists objected to the taxes and started stirring up problems for the Crown (the English king and Parliament). These rabble-rousers felt America and England were different and the colonies should govern themselves separately. Early on, most people in the colonies did not want a break with England, although they did want respect. Unfortunately for the Crown, Parliament handled the growing crisis dreadfully, and more and more formerly English colonists became Americans by rejecting the idea of English rule.

THE AMERICAN REVOLUTION 1775 TO 1782

BACKGROUND

How did it happen that Englishmen in the colonies became Americans who wanted to rule themselves? This is one of those all important questions that is impossible to answer. How people separate from one government and decide to tie themselves to another is a critical study, but little useful information is around on which to test the theories.

A few items probably played a large role in the changeover. 1) *From the start Americans ruled themselves.* The home country was far away, and they simply could not wait for decisions from England to govern their lives. From the **Mayflower Compact in 1620** to the **Articles of Confederation** (and later the Constitution), the Americans had written their own rules and had put together institutions to enforce these rules. Once a group of people start governing themselves it is hard to put up with someone coming in and overriding local decisions. 2) Another factor might be that the *colonists had built their lives around the New World, not the old.* By 1776 they had lived in America for generations, and many of those people living in the New World had never seen the home country. England, as a place, meant little to them. 3) Note that *many wealthy men in the colonies were self-made,* and they balked at being told what to do.[86] The mother country deserved respect, but who gave them the right to order people about like servants? Successful colonists thought Parliament was out to skin them (financially) for a war the colonists did not ask for but fought to a successful conclusion with their own blood and money. Now the Crown wanted more. This aroused the ire of self-made men who wanted to control their own destiny.

Other English colonies such as Canada, Australia, New Zealand, India, and many others stayed with England until about 1950. What was the difference? England gave her colonies protection and prosperity through trade with the mother country. Protection is crucial, and without trade

---

[86] Self-made meaning they had earned their money themselves and did not inherit it. Many in England enjoyed wealth by inheritance, and they also enjoyed power and position by inheritance. In the New World, they didn't like people showing up acting as if they deserved something because of their birth. The New World expected people to earn their money and position, and not inherit it from an ancient ancestor. Many men in Parliament were there because of an inheritance of one kind or another.

the faraway colonies would struggle to survive. The non-rebelling colonies saw England's protection and trade as more important than self-rule. The Americans seemed to feel these were not critical items. France was a threat to the west of the American colonies, and Canada would be a threat to the north if the rebellion were successful. How could the Americans be sure of protecting themselves and maintaining their trading relationships? In fact, they could not have been certain of maintaining their freedom or their trade, but freedom was more important than potential problems. Perhaps it came down to good propaganda from American radicals who wanted to be free from England. The distinction between the attitude in America and the other colonies is the critical part. Why the attitudes were so different is hard to say.

With extremists in the American colonies making trouble and some moderates joining in, England decided to get tough and suppress these rumblings of discontent. The English Parliament did not do well in deciding how to handle the problem. *Soon, the Parliament turned a problem into a crisis and then a crisis into a shooting war.* Propaganda turned out by a rather well-to-do group of men in America made each English move a hammer blow against liberty and another insult to the colonists. In 1774, Britain passed the "Intolerable Acts"[87] to punish American colonists for the Boston Tea Party.[88] Soon thereafter British troops occupied Boston. The mood in the American colonies grew incredibly sour, and as the British Army stepped up its efforts to make sure no revolution occurred it accomplished the opposite.[89]

LEXINGTON AND CONCORD—THE WAR BEGINS

1775

The American Revolution became a shooting war on April 19, 1775, when a group of British soldiers set out to capture and destroy rebel rifles and

[87] This name, the Intolerable Acts, came from the American propagandist. The Adams cousins were especially good at this kind of thing.

[88] December 16, 1773. A group of men dressed like Indians boarded an English ship loaded with tea and threw the cargo overboard. This was a protest against English taxes on tea. Americans then began drinking coffee as a replacement for tea (tax avoidance) and never stopped. When you drink coffee, you are drinking to tax avoidance and revolution.

[89] p. 720, *The New Penguin History of the World*, Roberts, J., 2007, Penguin books.

gunpowder stored at Concord, Massachusetts. As the British advanced on **Lexington**, a small village along the way to Concord, a group of farmers turned riflemen entitled "**Minute Men**" barred the way at a small bridge. The English commander called for the men to disperse, but they stayed. Someone, no one knows who, fired off a rifle and the Red Coats then leveled a blast at the Minute Men.[90] Those who gathered to stop the English advance suffered several casualties, and the unharmed English marched on to Concord. The word of the confrontation spread across the countryside, and the surrounding farmers grabbed their rifles and ran to fight the British troops who had shot down their neighbors.

As the English were returning from Concord through the rolling hills and lightly forested area making up the countryside, the Americans gathered in small concealed groups and began to shoot the British column to pieces. Britain's troops had learned to fight on the broad plains of Europe, where armies smartly lined up about one hundred yards from each other and fired away. As the British troops in their red coats marched in line back to Boston the Americans used low stone walls, trees, and bushes to hide behind while they fired at the soldiers. The British tried to handle the incoming rifle fire by turning squads toward the Americans and firing off a large volley, but the Americans were behind faraway barriers making the English musket fire ineffective. As long as the attackers stayed away from the English column, and behind walls, they could inflict casualties while losing almost none of their own.[91] The British march back to base was a nightmare for the troops, and even though they arrived back at the city of Boston intact they lost many men. The American Revolution had commenced.

The **Continental Congress** assembled and appointed **General George Washington** to lead the American cause. ***George Washington was the indispensable man*** for America and the Revolution. Washington was the heart and soul of the revolution. Without George Washington there would be no United States of America and no worthwhile constitution. He was a man who did not obsess over power or glory. When offered the office

---

[90] The "shot heard round the world." Note that the British troops, who wore bright red coats, were called the Red Coats the world over.

[91] A **musket** is a long gun with no grooves in the barrel to spin the projectile. A **rifle** has grooves in the barrel to spin the projectile (a ball of lead in this case), and it makes the projectile more accurate over a longer distance. A musket had a hard time hitting something the size of a man at one hundred yards; a rifle could do that easily, and in experienced hands could hit such a target at two hundred yards or more.

of king after the revolution he turned it down, and he left the office of president after two terms when he could have stayed for 10 if he wanted. Washington was a giant of virtue among men. With all this said, he was human. He made errors, and his army paid dearly for them; however, no better man ever lived, and his honor and courage were the keys to victory as much as his leadership in the field. In terms of his impact on history, it is every bit as great as Julius Caesar or Napoleon.

Washington's men had managed to surround a British army in Boston, and they had taken the critical high ground of **Bunker Hill** overlooking the harbor, thus endangering the ability of English warships to stay and support the troops.[92] Overnight, it seemed to the astonished British commanders, the American "rebels" on the hill erected dug-in positions with trenches and earthworks. **General Howe**, the British commander, decided to assault the hill after a crucial maneuver to cut off and isolate the Americans was botched. The English "won" the battle of Bunker Hill, but the cost was very high. It took three assaults to take the bastion, and even the last assault was facing destruction when the rebels ran out of bullets. Most of the Americans got away. The position endangering the harbor was taken, but the English remained surrounded in the town. Howe decided to depart by sea for New York, thus escaping the siege and achieving better accommodations. This left Boston to the American patriots.

The Declaration of Independence

1776

The Continental Congress argued about independence from England. Even though a shooting war was underway many colonists wanted to stay with England. After the revolution was over, **John Adams** estimated that no more than one-third of Americans actively supported a break with the British Empire. As the debate in Congress droned on, a fellow named **Thomas Payne** published a pamphlet entitled ***Common Sense*** arguing to the vacillating public that Americans should be free. Should an island rule a continent, he asked? Public opinion then shifted strongly toward independence. Congress responded and on **July 4, 1776, adopted the Declaration of Independence,** expertly penned by **Thomas Jefferson**. The break with England was complete, and now the Americans had to make the dream a reality. All those signing the declaration were traitors,

---

92 It was actually Breeds Hill, but who cares at this point.

and England would be overjoyed to hang them. Each pledged their lives, fortunes, and sacred honor to the cause of freedom, and almost to a man they would sacrifice all three in the war for independence. Some died in action, many suffered bankruptcy, and all were stressed to the limit by the needs of the cause. These were the men who not only signed the charter of freedom but *put everything they had on the line* in a bid for success. Modern critics call them "dead white men." But they were among the greatest men that ever lived. They signed a document declaring war on the mightiest empire of the time—the British Empire—and the chances of success were meager. England had fleets of ships while the Americans possessed none; England benefited from massive numbers of well-trained men while the Americans mustered farmers who never fought in an all-out war; England had money, and lots of it, while the Americans had little money to pay and feed an army. And these were only a few of the problems. The disparity in national strength was profound.

Early Defeats and Trenton—the Last Chance

These disadvantages were on display at once as the British inflicted a terrible series of defeats on Washington and his small army in the summer of 1776. New York and New Jersey easily fell to the British. Washington nearly lost his entire army, and the war, in these contests. In battle after battle he was outmaneuvered, and the English regulars and their German mercenaries, the Hessians, outfought his army. Washington's men fought well enough for a relatively untried army, but they were consistently out flanked, outmaneuvered, or outnumbered so defeat followed defeat. By the winter of 1776, the men in the Continental Army were in rags, starving, and unpaid. Washington's army had been 20,000 men, but the size had shriveled dramatically as defeat followed defeat. Many of the one year enlistments ended on January 1, 1777, when the army would dwindle to 3,000 men. Without money for food, clothing, and pay for the soldiers how could the revolution survive? The Continental Congress was better at debating than obtaining funds. As the British and the Hessians settled in for the winter, General George Washington determined to risk the Revolution on one gamble. He needed a victory to keep the cause alive, and now he decided to get that victory or lose the cause trying.[93]

---

[93] 1776, David McCullough, 2006, Simon and Schuster

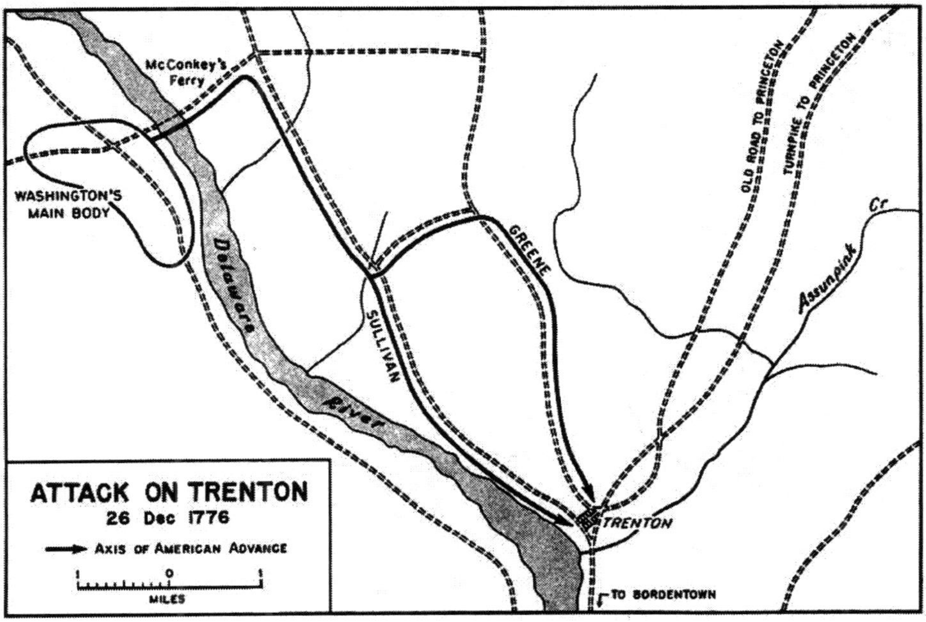

FIGURE 28 TRENTON 1776

On the frozen Christmas night of **December 25, 1776,** General Washington roused his tiny army to begin its march to the Hessian-controlled town of **Trenton,** New Jersey. There was no global warming[94] in 1776, and the Delaware River was all but frozen; however, Washington had to get his men, horses, and cannons across. The boat handlers transferred the entire army across the ice choked river without the loss of a man, horse, or cannon (few as they were). Onward through the night, through snow and sleet they marched, some dying along the way from cold, hunger, and exhaustion. Washington and his officers were there with the men encouraging them forward, knowing this was the final chance. Many colonial troops hurrying toward Trenton wore rags for clothes and marched barefoot with their feet bleeding into the snow-covered roads. Rushing through the night while fighting the awful weather, they drove painfully on trying desperately to reach Trenton before the sun was up. Surprise was all.

[94] In fact, the world was still in the so-called Little Ice Age.

FIGURE 29 1776 WASHINGTON CROSSING THE DELAWARE

The surprise was total, and Washington's troops won a stunning victory over the professional German mercenaries. Only Three Continental officers received wounds—one of them was James Monroe who would later serve as president. Over 900 Hessians entered captivity, and their commander lay dying. A few days later, at **Princeton**, Washington's men won another victory over a regiment of British regulars just outside the town. Word of the victories at Trenton and Princeton spread fast, the Continental Congress took hope, and the Revolution was alive once more. A victory, a very small victory, had saved the fledgling nation. The triumph also helped re-enlistments. After Trenton a few brave souls, still freezing and starving, came forward to fight on at Washington's urging. Thus, solitary freezing men, dressed in rags, ribs showing, feet unclad, stepped forward for freedom. We sit in our warm houses today protected by our Constitution because of these few unheralded heroes. These men were as brave as the Greeks at Marathon, but seldom remembered in that way.

Of course, it was far from being over. The British almost failed to notice the American "victory" and continued with their plans to put down the rebellion. Washington was not fighting a guerrilla war. He was building an army that could stand and fight the English and their mercenaries' straight up and win. He retreated to keep his army from total defeat, and his generals did engage in hit-and-run raids; but his goal was always to field an army that could stand toe-to-toe with the British. By winning set piece battles with the British Empire other nations might be convinced to aid the Americans, because the Americans could not win without significant outside help.

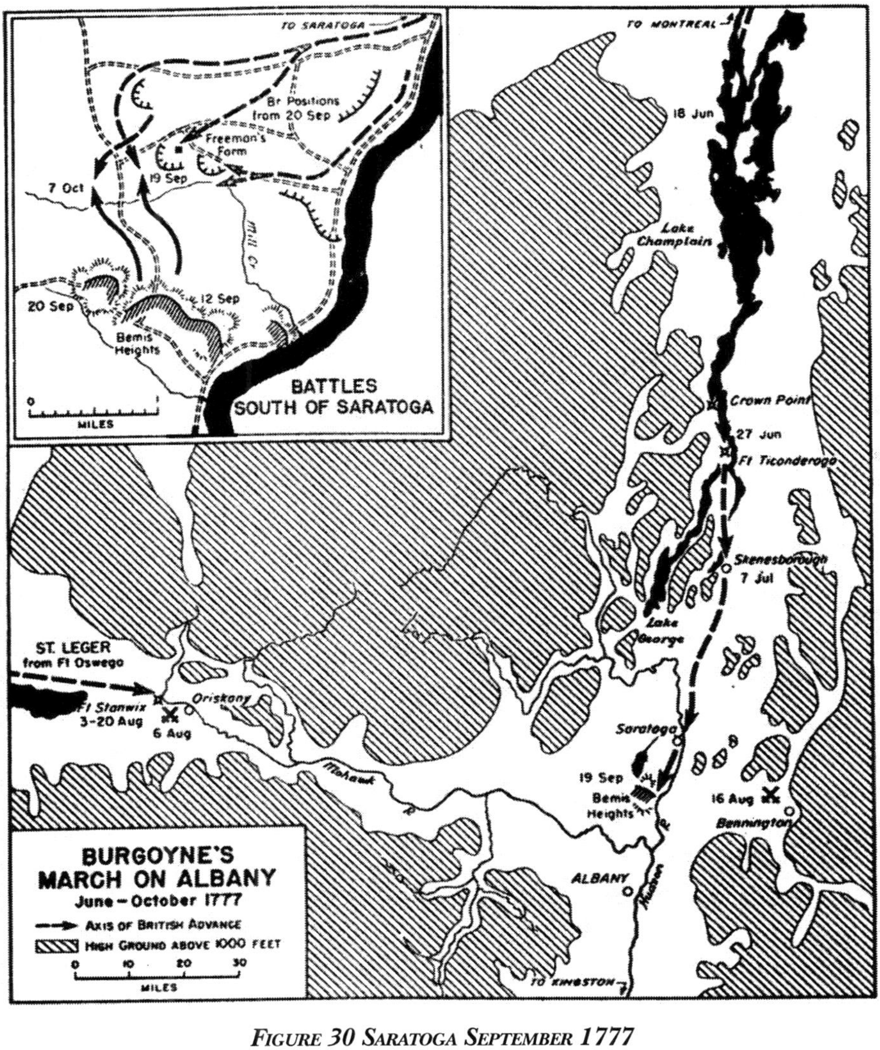

FIGURE 30 SARATOGA SEPTEMBER 1777

SARATOGA

1777

The English decided to cut American's northeast in half by invading through the Hudson River Valley thereby isolating New England, the hotbed of patriotism. Once accomplished, mutual support from adjoining regions would be stifled, and then each region could be defeated in detail. So it was that in 1777, **General Burgoyne**, a stuffed shirt of sorts, could be found leading an army down from Canada through the deeply wooded Hudson River Valley bound for Albany, New York, where General Howe had promised to meet him. This route is thick with shadowy forest, so Burgoyne hired Native American scouts to guide his brilliantly attired army. He also took along fine accommodations; after all, he was a gentleman and a general. At first the expedition went well, but before long the near impenetrable forest, and an undersized American delaying force, began taking a heavy toll.

By clogging narrow forest trails with felled trees and clever ambushes, the American woodsmen slowed the English advance to a crawl. Perhaps sensing disaster, the Native American scouts disappeared. Then word came that Howe refused to follow the plan and would not come up from Albany to meet Burgoyne's army. Nonetheless, the always tenacious British pressed on. Meanwhile, Washington assembled an army to confront the invasion, but he chose its leader poorly. Command of the American army at Saratoga went to the incompetent General Gates. Fortunately, for the Americans, a competent general was with the army, and he would make a real difference—**General Benedict Arnold.95**

As the fatigued British emerged from their forest nightmare, they found a spirited Americans army waiting at Freeman's Farm near **Saratoga**. Although weary, with their numbers diminished by their horrid march, the British could now confront the enemy and win control of the Hudson River. Across the field, disarray over tactics consumed the American command. Gates wanted to wait atop a fortified hill, but Arnold pressed to assault the redcoats at once. He pressed too hard. Gates was in command and he banished Arnold to his quarters. Good thing he was too proud to stay there. During the opening stages of battle Burgoyne's regulars overpowered

---

[95] p. 148 et seq *Great Rivals in History, When Politics Gets Personal*, Cummins, J, 2008, Metro Books. The chapter is entitled "Benedict Arnold and Horatio Gates, A Clash for Control." And the title says it all.

the colonials causing General Gates to flee to his tent. All appeared lost when Benedict Arnold rode into action accompanied by General Morgan. Arnold and Morgan rallied the faltering troops and charged off to a history changing victory. Under Arnold's leadership, the rag tag farmers of America won at Saratoga. General Burgoyne found himself surrendering his army of over 6,000 men to Gates, along with his military career. At last, an American army facing British regulars won in a toe-to-toe fight. In Europe, few knew how exhausted and demoralized Burgoyne's army had been. All they saw was an American victory, and Gentleman Johnny Burgoyne surrendering a large force of British regulars. Suddenly, the world had turned upside down.

PYLE, THE NATION MAKERS

Saratoga is a top battle in history because it changed the mind of the French monarch, Louis XVI, who decided to join the Americans against the English. **Benjamin Franklin,** America's ambassador in France, was working overtime to bring France to the American side. France had every incentive since England bested them in the Seven Years War, and France wanted some measure of revenge for their losses. However, backing a losing proposition did not interest France. The Americans had to convince the King they could win if helped, and Saratoga persuaded the King the war was worth the risk. France began sending significant aid, and in 1778 executed a formal alliance with the Americans while *declaring war on England.* Now the American Revolution was a world war. France's **naval power** was the key. The English had been operating at will along the colonial seacoast. Now their problems would multiply because a French fleet set sail to assist the Americans.

Although Saratoga was a great victory for the American Revolution, the general who had won the battle and probably saved the cause was disgruntled. Gates took total credit for the victory leaving General Arnold little recognition for his heroic labors. Moreover, he was shot in the leg and suffered rather badly after the engagement, adding to his disgust when few accolades came his way. Benedict Arnold knew Washington depended upon him, and that held his loyalty to the cause for a long while, but not until the end. Arnold's love for a Tory woman (a Tory supported the Crown) and his dislike for his rival American generals caused him to sell out the Revolution by agreeing to secretly transfer the fortress at West Point to the English. His plot came to light, and he fled with his lover to England where he continued to be ignored. Through the entire episode, and the remainder of his life, Arnold's Tory gal stuck by him as his nation came to despise him, and the name Benedict Arnold [96]still refers to a blackheart who stabs his friends in the back.

It was still a long haul, but in 1781 a French fleet bottled up an English army at **Yorktown** where American and French forces already had them surrounded on land. After a siege of some weeks the English surrendered, losing yet another army, this time under General Cornwallis. Still it did not end. Negotiations in Paris drug on until **1782** when Parliament at last voted for peace with the new United States of America (US, USA, or America).

THE AMERICAN FRONTIER

The United States of America eventually developed into a world power, but in the beginning it was just a few sparsely populated colonies on the eastern seaboard of the great North American continent. On the

---

[96] It would seem that after two hundred plus years calling someone a "Benedict Arnold" wouldn't be such a mighty insult, but it is. Arnold now has the recognition he craved, but recognition of the wrong kind.

frontier, the Native Americans were trying to hold up the advance of the Europeans (now Americans). During the nearly seven years of the American Revolutionary War, more colonists were killed on the frontier in the ceaseless "Indian Wars" than were killed fighting the Revolution. This frontier of scattered settlements and lone men tracking through the wilderness was an important part of the American mystique. Those fitting in nowhere else could travel west for land or some other opportunity. Those arriving with nothing could go west to clear land and establish ownership of something. The frontier was a way to let off society's steam because those without hope could go west and obtain, through hard work and unending danger, something of their own. There was little law in the west, and that is how those in the west liked it. Those born in the west often hated the impositions of civilization and continued west when civilization started creeping in. On the western frontier the same family names appear repeatedly. This was near total freedom from the law or the obligations of society. A person could do what he wanted when he wanted, and that developed into a way of life and thought still coveted by many in the United States. ***"Leave me alone"*** are extremely important words in the United States of America.

THE CONSTITUTION OF THE UNITED STATES OF AMERICA

1789

America had finally won its freedom. Each state had its charter or constitution providing for governance. The American states had been jointly governing themselves under the **Articles of Confederation** since 1775, but this weak document failed to pull the nation together. Now facing the task of coming up with their own national governmental system, the Americans carried a few powerful ideas into the process that we should remember:

1. Each state wanted to keep its individual identity. States were set up as separate colonies, and grew up very differently because of American geography. No colony wanted another colony telling them how to govern in their jurisdiction. This was an unstated assumption in the Constitutional debates seldom talked about, but it underlies many disagreements between Revolutionary era Americans.
2. Fear of a powerful central government was fervent. This is another given, although expressed in many different ways. One of the Constitutional Convention's main goals was to prevent the central

government from overpowering state governments and individual citizens. In this central task the convention failed.

3. The colonials believed revolting against an oppressive government was a God given right. The Declaration of Independence says so. This is a key reason for the Second Amendment to the US Constitution (the right to keep and bear arms) and the Bill of Rights (first 10 Amendments to the Constitution). The Bill of Rights entered the Constitution as an additional measure to keep the central government in check by giving rights directly to individuals; however, the ultimate weapon was always rebellion. In the 21st[st] Century, we may forget that revolutionaries who overthrew a powerful central government by force of arms founded our nation. The US Constitution reflects this fact.
4. Protecting private property was considered a key element to economic and political freedom.
5. Colonist did not want taxes levied on everything that moved. They wanted to be left alone.
6. The most important idea embodied in the US Constitution is: *the individual is greater than the state.* The original idea of the ancient Greeks found a new home in the Constitution of the United States of America.

The Continental Congress used the Articles of Confederation [97] until it proved a poor authority for governing the colonies. The entire American Revolution threw off the yoke of a too-powerful central government, therefore, the Articles of Confederation kept the central government's power minimal. Nonetheless, the power was so slight the colonies failed to function together as a team. For example, they had no central money supply or common roads, and some colonies were trying to impose import duties on other colonies. The net result was chaos.

In **1787, a Constitutional Convention** convened in Philadelphia to write a new document for operating the new nation. The gathering, as authorized by the various legislatures, was for the sole purpose of amending the Articles of Confederation; however, the delegates threw out the Articles of Confederation at once and began working on an entirely new instrument for governance. In this respect, their actions went far beyond their authority. George Washington agreed to head the convention, and through the

---

97 The Articles of Confederation were adopted by the Continental Congress in 1777, and were used throughout the Revolutionary War. They were used after the war (1782) until the adoption of the Constitution in 1789.

summer the delegates from the various colonies worked out the details of the document in secret. The framers of the Constitution decided they must find ways to limit the powers of the central government while giving it enough authority to unify the nation. To accomplish this they set forth each power of the president and each house of Congress separately.[98] In this way, they formed a federal government where the states retained the powers not specifically given to the federal entity (they thought). It was a new way of thinking, in that it established a representative government on two levels—one local (the state) and the other general (the federal or central). Another vital difference had to be resolved. Rural states wanted representation by state, but the more populous states wanted representation by population. The great compromise allowing the Constitution to be adopted was the creation of *two houses of Congress,* one established by population which the populous states would undoubtedly control (the House of Representatives), and another established by geographic area wherein two representatives from each state would serve (the Senate) and the rural states would probably control. There were other mighty problems such as slavery, but each one was solved by some sort of compromise that left everyone quite unhappy. But that is the nature of true compromise.

By these improvisations and compromises the Constitution of the United States evolved into a final document. The delegates to the Constitutional Convention were exhausted, but one last task remained—selling the document to the nation.

Many people not at the convention wanted more protection from a powerful central government, so *Ten Amendments* were added to the document *guaranteeing a set of individual rights to the people themselves* and further restricting government action. Without the promise of these amendments the Constitution might have failed adoption by the states. Each of these amendments guarantees the individual rights that the government cannot interfere with, such as freedom of speech, press, religion, assembly, freedom to petition the government, security of homes from unreasonable searches and seizures, freedom to own guns, freedom from unlawful arrest or multiple prosecutions, the right to a jury trial in criminal cases and civil lawsuits, the right to remain silent if charged with a crime, right to a lawyer in a criminal case, and the right to a reasonable bail among *many* others. Perhaps the ultimate expression of the individual being greater than the state was the Second Amendment which gave

---

[98] And later said in the Tenth Amendment that any power not specifically named in the document was given to the states, or the people.

citizens the right to own firearms. In dictatorial states firearm ownership is absolutely forbidden. These Ten Amendments are collectively referred to as the **Bill of Rights**.

The **Tenth Amendment** is often overlooked, but it is clearly a further attempt to restrict the power of the federal government, "*The powers not delegated to the United States by the Constitution, nor prohibited by it to the States, are reserved to the States respectively, or to the people.*" The men who worked out the powers of the federal government were unusually concerned about its potential power. They recognized that if central government wanted to the federal institutions could join together and simply take whatever power they desired. The delegates tried to divide the power and put the federal government in competition with itself, thus limiting its power; however, if all the federal institutions agreed to increase the power of the Federal Government nothing could stop them except new representation.

The framers wanted to limit Constitutional changes, but little did they realize the Constitution itself would provide the federal government with the power to change it with *no participation* from the people or the states. One result of this oversight was a tremendous growth in the power of the federal government.

The Constitution was submitted for ratification in 1787, and in 1788 New Hampshire voted to ratify making it the ninth and final state needed to approve the document. Eventually, all thirteen colonies ratified the Constitution. The Constitution took effect on March 4, 1789, and shortly thereafter the Bill of Rights was passed by Congress and ratified by the states as the first ten amendments to the Constitution. The indispensible George Washington became the first president of the United States under the new Constitution.

PROBLEMS—DISCUSSING THE CONSTITUTION

We often forget how much of this was an experiment with an unknown and unknowable outcome. The leadership of George Washington, the genius of Hamilton in running the treasury, low taxes, a hard working public, good luck, and a lot more were all necessary to bring about the new nation's success. After a few years the men who led the Revolution, signed the Declaration of Independence, put together the Constitution, and established the new government were gone. These men and their writings took on a mythical status. The Constitution became a document for the ages, something sacred. The convention in Philadelphia was believed to be a miracle of Divine Intervention for a nation blessed by God. Looking back all these years later[99] it still seems the American Revolution was the result of a series of battlefield miracles, and miraculous documents written by geniuses, all under the guidance of Eternal Providence.

The foundation of the Constitution was a representative government established in the **legislative branch** by two houses of Congress, the Senate and the House of Representatives (the House), and the **executive branch** operated by the president. The specific powers of each house in Congress and the president were set forth with exactness. Powers not specifically listed were not given. The Senate has two representatives from each state; thus, Wyoming, a state with a small population, has as much power in the Senate as the mega-population state of California. The House of Representatives establishes representation by the population of each state; thus, the more populous states like New York have more representatives than small population states like Maine. Each state is guaranteed at least one representative no matter how small its population. Both houses of Congress must approve a bill before it can become law. The president has the ability to veto bills he disagrees with, but Congress can over-ride his veto with a super majority 2/3 vote. The president cannot submit legislation; however, he enjoys many specifically enumerated powers. Members of the House are elected every two years and members of the Senate every six years; however, only one third of the Senate is elected every two years making the turnover much slower. In theory, every member of the House could be replaced every two years, but only one-third of the Senate could be completely replaced every two years. The president is elected every four years. Each house has a few special powers. The Senate, for example, must approve treaties by a 2/3 vote, and it sits as the judging body in the case of presidential impeachment. The House is the legislative body that all bills for raising revenue must originate in, and it is the body from which articles for impeachment of the president must be issued. The Constitution also established a judicial body, the Supreme Court, but it did not set forth the powers of the court. Justices appointed to the Supreme Court hold their office for life on good behavior. A simplistic Constitutional overview can be found in the rather ancient but easy to understand book, *Your Rugged Constitution* by Bruce and Esther Findlay, Stanford University Press, 1969.

The Constitution is a wonderful document; however, it was not and is not perfect. For example, it failed to say what happens if a state wants to leave

---

99 Two hundred plus years now, just a blink in time from a historical perspective.

the union. Can it just up and go without consequences? This omission led to the most terrible war in American history. The Constitution also failed to list the powers of the **Supreme Court**. As a result, the Supreme Court defined its own powers, and constantly expanded its sway and the dominance of the federal government. In effect, the Supreme Court wrote the Tenth Amendment out of the Constitution. Meanwhile, it wrote in unstated rights by resorting to rather-farfetched arguments about penumbras surrounding the rights given in the Constitution. If the Constitution tried to do anything it was to limit the rights and powers conferred upon the federal government to those written down in the document itself. The Constitution was not supposed to be a flexible "living" document through some weird interpretation of its language. The only flexibility given was the power to amend the Constitution through the stated amendment process. Instead, few amendments are passed; however, the words themselves are given meanings beyond all rational reasoning by the federal courts.

By assigning itself its own powers, the Supreme Court made itself the most dominant institution in the land because it can add to or take away rights and duties listed in the Constitution. No matter how outrageous the decisions nothing can be done about the federal judges. The Constitution places them in office for life on "good behavior." If a legislator acts irrationally the voters can oust that person from office. Then new lawmakers can change the laws improperly enacted. Not so for the federal judges. No matter how poor their decision there is no recourse for the people to overturn the decision or kick the judge out of office. Can a Constitutional Amendment overturn the decisions? Yes, but that process is all but impossible to complete even against minimal opposition. The powers taken by the federal courts, especially the US Supreme Court, have dramatically altered the balance of power between the government and the people toward the side of the government.

These and other flaws in the Constitution haunt the present day. The framers could not imagine our modern society. We try to bend the words of the Constitution to fit modern times rather than amend the document to deal with contemporary challenges. These results come from revering the document and believing the words came from on high. This delivers unlimited power to the federal courts because the courts step into the power vacuum and tell the millions of people in the United States what the Constitution means, thereby controlling how the United States operates its government. One striking example of this power is the Supreme Court decision changing the way states govern themselves. In the 1964 case of ***Reynolds v. Sims***, the US Supreme Court required every state in the union to *abolish its Senate100, which was elected by area* (county) and replace it with a body elected by *population.* The one-man-one-vote rule adopted by the court destroyed the constitutional compromise which allowed the government to come together initially. As a result, all states are now governed by population only, which delivers all the power into the hands of liberal urban areas. This horrific result remains (no Constitutional Amendment was passed) because once the population centers gained the power they were going to keep it. The ONLY way rural areas can get voting protection is before the Constitution is adopted. Thereafter, they can never bring enough political pressure to obtain fairness from dominating urban areas. The Supreme Court has set itself up as the arbitrator of how we can govern ourselves at the most basic level. All this happened because the framers of the Constitution failed to specifically list and limit the court's power, and "We the people . . ." refuse to amend the great document.

Now the American Revolution is over, and it is 1790 in the United States of America, but we have skipped a lot of history in Europe. So we will venture back to1600 in Europe and bring that story forward to about 1800.

Let Us Learn

The story of the American Revolution displays the futility of holding onto far away resources, the results of mistreating loyal people, and the importance of flexibility. Spain lost its colonies in the Americas through inflexibility and disrespect for the populace. Britain made similar errors. Neither took the time to figure out what the colonies needed or wanted. Both made false assumptions about the areas and peoples they controlled. Gathering accurate information, and evaluating that information coldly (no emotion) is vital to holding on to people and resources. Try not to assume. Set out to understand who and what you are dealing with, and then take the time to analyze the entire situation. What was the best "end game" for England once the American Revolution started? How about letting the colonies go politically and keeping a preferred trading relationship? Spain's end game might have included a special political relationship giving Spain extraordinary privileges in their former lands. By strongly opposing any change, both lost all.

---

[100] Two states had unicameral legislatures, meaning they had only one house, and that house was elected by population.

The Native American experience shows one must somehow radically adapt to radical change. How we handle massive, unplanned, fundamental, and shocking change can make all the difference in our lives. Unintended consequences, like millions of deaths from disease, can alter the ability to cope; however, one cannot simply cling to the old ways while losing everything. In addition, we must acknowledge, as shown by the Native Americans, some problems have no solution. If radical change invades your life recall how important allies are and rally your support group to help. If defeat is inevitable face it stoically. We all suffer ultimate defeat in the final analysis.

Native Americans effectively unifying against white rule could have altered history. If all the Native tribes in Mexico had aggressively opposed Cortez he could not have won. The Aztecs mistreated their vassal states; thus, these states joined the Conquistadores in crushing the Aztecs. Loyal vassal states fighting beside the Aztecs may have handed the Spaniards defeat. If Native Americans in North America had united against the newcomer's first landings, numerous defeats for the settlers would have followed, probably prohibiting settlement until European armies arrived to destroy the heathen opposition. Of course, the real defeat came from European diseases killing the populace, and as a result defeat for the Natives seems inevitable once contact occurred. We must learn that some problems are beyond solution. Whether individuals or entire populations some problems will vex us. Those types of problems exist everywhere; as all Native Americans well know.

BOOKS AND RESOURCES:

Great Rivals in History, When Politics Gets Personal, Cummins, J, 2008, Metro Books.

1776, David McCullough, 2006, Simon and Schuster

Common Sense, The Rights of Man and Other Essential Writings of Thomas Paine, Sidney Hook, 2003, Signet Classics

The Essential Federalist and Anti-Federalist Papers, Wootton, 2003, Hackett Publishing

Revolution 1776, Preston, 1933, Harcourt, Brace and Company (great book if you can find a copy).

Miracle at Philadelphia, The Story of the Constitutional Convention May to September 1787, Bowen, C., 1986, Little Brown Publishers (in paperback: ISBN: 0316103985) The classic on the Constitutional Convention.

Chapter 10

Europe from the Renaissance to 1900

Nation States, Religion, War, and The Armada

From about 1480 onward, the concept of "**nation states**" began to arise. The sentiment was new, in that ancient empires such as Persia and Babylonia were normally a collage of peoples, languages, and customs reaching over a vast area with the veneer of the empire's rulers settling over the indigenous peoples. The Spanish Empire, the British Empire, the Russian Empire, and the Austria-Hungarian Empire from the 1700s on, fit the same mold; however, the nation states' roots go much deeper. It was a large area such as France, inhabited by generally similar peoples speaking the same language and all answering to a powerful central government. The key is all the people in the nation state considered everyone in the nation as one united entity—that is, one people. Like the people of the ancient city state, everyone was in the same boat and would advance or decline together. Similar religions, customs, languages, and history all combined to convince these rather large groups to people to think of themselves as one unit. Nearly all modern Western European nations and their progeny fit this category. Here was a momentous change in human thought, and these new inclinations would lead to both good and evil consequences.

The new nations would dramatically improve the national infrastructure of roads, banks, general staffs for the army, and bureaucracies for the monarch. Parliament would dramatically improve its position in England. In 1688, as part of the Glorious Revolution restoring the English monarchy, the **incoming king accepted the English Bill of Rights**.[101] This bill of rights

[101] Note this is nearly 100 years before the American Revolution, showing the idea of fundamental rights was already an established part of the English thought process. Also, this document establishes individual rights against the government. The Greek ideal of the individual being above the state lived on.

gave Parliament the edge in the political relationship, and in due time Parliament became the controlling government body.

The discovery of the "New World" excited all of Europe. Part of the excitement involved exchanges of new foods. Corn (maize) and potatoes came to Europe, and wheat, barley, horses, and other herd animals went to the Americas. These new foods, along with an agricultural revolution in the 1700s, allowed an increase in the food production in Europe, helped ease some of the starvation prevalent in previous years, and contributed to a worldwide population upsurge from 1400 to 1700 (*world population increased from about 350 million in 1400 to 610 million by 1700*). These new foods also had some drawbacks, as the Irish found out in the potato famine of 1845 to 1852, where 30 percent of Ireland's population died because of an over dependency on potatoes. A fungus hit the potatoes destroying copious amounts of the crop. In spite of a tremendous death toll, England's Parliament acted slowly and ineptly. Nevertheless, the new foods helped the agricultural economies of Europe and the New World quite a bit.

As the explorers set out to find new worlds, inside Europe new religious rivalries were coming to the surface. From outside Europe Islam was hammering at the Balkans, while inside Europe the Roman Catholic Church suffered from increasing corruption. Several movements were trying to reform the Church, such as the monastic movement,[102] and humanist influences from philosophers like Sir Thomas Moore (1478 to1535), and Erasmus (1466 to1536) talked against corruption; however, no endeavor brought real change within the Church. A Church led by wealthy popes leading depraved lives was not going to change through its leadership. Some reformers paid with their lives for challenging Church doctrines, so many who desired restructuring stayed quiet.

All this changed with the advent of **Martin Luther** (1483 to 1546), an Augustinian monk who, in **1517,** nailed his ninety-five theses to a church door at Wittenberg, Germany, demanding the Catholic Church end corrupt practices, change its doctrines, and recognize *salvation by faith alone.* Luther took a big chance with his life, and he might have lost both his life and his spiritual battle if not for the protection of German princes who wanted to break from the pope and his long tradition of extracting money from them. With this protection, he survived several attempts on his life by the

[102] An attempt to build monasteries in nearly inaccessible places and live apart from the world

supporters of the pope, wrote a Bible that a common person could read,[103] and *printed* several tracts defending his position on the Bible. Marrying a defrocked nun only confirmed to all Catholics Luther was in league with Satan. Eventually, the **Protestant Reformation** spread across northern Germany, Scandinavia, and England (kinda sorta). From the city of Geneva, Switzerland, which became a religious state, John **Calvin** (1509 to 1564) spread his form of the Protestant faith (a belief in predestination, hard work, and thrift) to France and Holland. Calvin's Protestant sect had an outsized worldwide influence that lingers until this day. The Protestant Reformation generated many sects of Christianity, and many wars, causing millions of deaths across Europe. Like all religious wars, they were brutal.

The Catholic leaders of Europe had numerous problems. Under escalating attacks from the Muslim east they needed the German princes to help repel the threat; accordingly, they could not destroy them to get to Martin Luther. The problem of defending Catholic empires (like Spain) from upstart nations (like England) took men and money, adding to their woes and wreaking their ability to crush the Protestants. As the Protestant religion spread, the Catholic response became more violent as France and other nations began killing their own. In Spain, Phillip wanted to end the Protestant rebellion in the Netherlands that England was supporting. This small fact would lead to a famous sea battle and then the demise of a great Catholic worldwide empire, followed by the foundation of a new and even greater Protestant worldwide empire.

Henry VIII of England really threw a wrench into the religious works when he decided to replace his queen with a much younger woman. In times past the monarch could just buy the pope off, but this time the pope refused, thereby turning King Henry VIII into a fat vat of smoldering anger.[104] He decided the King of England could darn well head his own church, so he decided to go Protestant and reject the Catholic Church

---

103 Bibles of the day were written in Latin which only the priests could read. The Catholic Church wanted biblical interpretation in the hands of the church alone, because they feared a fragmentation of Christianity if everyone could read and interpret the scriptures. They were right. Note the bibles were printed. The printing press had a major impact on the Protestant Reformation.

104 The pope was under the power of the first wife's nephew, Emperor Charles V. Charles had sacked Rome and held the pope as a virtual prisoner. The first wife was Catherine of Aragon, next was Ann Boleyn, then Jane Seymour, Ann of Cleves, Katherine Howard, and, finally, Catherine Parr.

in **1533.**[105] Soon he had put his old queen away and married a much younger one—and then decided to marry another, and another, and, well, the whole thing just went nuts. King Henry ended up with six (6) wives, most going to their deaths to make way for the next woman in the king's bed. After King Henry's death, **Elizabeth I** of England, the daughter of Ann Boleyn (the second wife), eventually became queen; and she was a Protestant.

Henry VIII did more than just argue with Catholics over women and power. He set the foundations for the future might of England when *he decided to build the most advanced navy in the world.* His ships had the best cannons and the best designs. This decision, continued by his successors, was foundational and eventually made England the most powerful nation on earth for over 350 years.

Phillip, King of Spain and ruler of the Netherlands (at least he thought so), sent his army to fight the Dutch Protestants over their claim of independence (Holland, et al). It would be a war lasting eighty years. This was a tough war, fought over what amounted to salt marshes by troops wearing heavy armor pounding away with crude and inaccurate guns, long pikes, and heavy swords. The fighting gained little for Spain, and Phillip thought the so-called virgin queen of England (Elizabeth) was helping the rebels. So, following the custom of the day, Phillip sent diplomats to diplomatically tell the virgin queen to back off assisting the rebels. Elizabeth, following the custom of the day, gently replied she could do nothing of the sort, while lying and denying England was sending aid.—also part of the customs of the day. Naturally, this upset the Spanish king, but he still wanted a better reason to go to war, and Elizabeth gave it to him. There was another heir to the English throne, **Mary Queen of Scots,** a Catholic enjoying wide support in England. She was, however, Elizabeth's prisoner making it hard to push a claim. Mary made a few poor decisions and ended up charged with conspiring to kill Elizabeth (all true) which got her condemned to death. Soon her head was bouncing away from her otherwise gorgeous body, and the King of Spain had what he needed, a righteous reason to war with England.

---

105 Sort of Protestant. The Church of England retained much from Catholic teachings. Note the year. This is about 500 years after William the Conquer carried a flag into battle against the Saxons and Britons which had been blessed by the pope. 500 years is a LONG time. The US has been around less than 250. Thus, Henry was really running against a long tradition of Catholicism in England. This was a *world changing* event.

King Phillip constructed the **Spanish Armada**, a fleet consisting of numerous exceptionally outsized ships, to invade England. King Phillip planned to sail his fleet to Holland, load his waiting infantry aboard the massive ships, and thence sail to England and debark for conquest. Realizing he needed a lot of men to invade England, the Spanish king thought many large ships were necessary to haul the men and equipment. Phillip may have been right about the need for large ships, but did all of them have to be so large? Believing the Catholic God was on his side, King Phillip put the Armada to sea in **1588** with orders to sail for Holland.

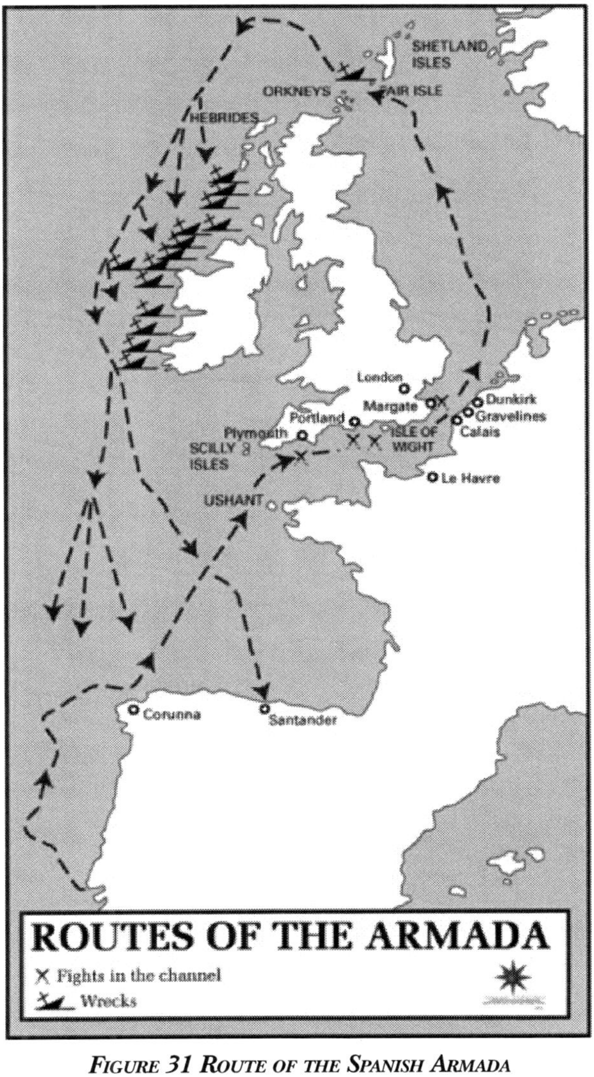

FIGURE 31 ROUTE OF THE SPANISH ARMADA

Things immediately began to go wrong for the Armada. Many of the ships were not seaworthy, and the men had little training in sailing, firing cannons, or otherwise surviving at sea. When the Armada appeared on the British horizon the English sea dogs set out in their small, but very maneuverable, ships to meet the challenge. Elizabeth was ashore with her army, all decked out in gleaming armor and ready to fight, but armies were unnecessary in this battle. The highly experienced English seamen vigorously attacked the Armada, but the grand ships sailed on with little noticeable damage. The Armanda successfully sailed to Holland, but unfortunately for the Spanish *the troops were not ready to board.* Somehow, no one informed them when the Armada would arrive. Seeing this was a mess, the Spanish dropped anchor, waiting for the morrow while trying to figure out what to do.

The English had other plans. Seeing the Spanish at anchor, the English unleashed several fire ships, burning from stem to stern, at the stationary Spanish Galleons when the wind was right. The fire ships caused a general Spanish panic, and a few of their ships were lost, but mainly the Spanish were unnerved. With things deteriorating and no troops appearing for the invasion, the Spanish admiral made a bad decision. He decided to return to Spain, but *not down the channel*—the way they came—but around Scotland and Ireland, and then back to Spain. The Spanish sailed north to their doom. On the way home tremendous storms struck the Armada tearing the vessels apart. The ships were not all that seaworthy anyway, and the massive storms simply gave them no chance. Nearly the entire Armada was lost at sea or driven onto the rocky Irish coast where plundering and murder awaited the warships and men courtesy of the area's unruly inhabitants.

The loss of the Armada, by whatever means, was a huge blow to the Spanish war effort. Building the Armada drained the treasury, always bad news in a war, and the loss of men hurt as well. This began the loss of the worldwide Catholic empire. Meanwhile, England celebrated a miraculous victory. Elizabeth I became a legendary leader by way of the defeat of the Armada, and England would go on to secure its place as the world's predominant sea power for 350 plus years (until the end of World War II in 1945). This was the start of the worldwide Protestant empire.

EUROPE UNDERGOES VAST CHANGE

The Catholic Church was undergoing a new beginning because of groups like the **Jesuit order** founded in 1540 by **Ignatius Loyola**. This spawned the **Counter-reformation** against the Protestants. Eventually, the **Council of Trent** (1545 to 1563) managed to stop the worst church offenses. None of this prevented the two warring Christian sides from murdering one another in the name of God. The Thirty Years War (1618 to 1648) devastated huge tracts of Europe, and the English civil wars (1642 to 1649) managed to do the same in England. The Puritans won in England, thereby allowing Oliver Cromwell to establish a virtual military dictatorship as "lord protector" (after beheading Charles I in 1649). These wars and beheadings failed to endear Catholics and Protestants to one another, so the fighting just went endlessly on. Cromwell died in 1658, followed in 1660 by the Restoration of the monarchy when Charles II became King of England. His son, James II, after losing a war with the Parliamentarians, lost his kingship which was assumed by the Protestant William of Orange, who became King in 1688. It was after this so-called Glorious Revolution that he took the crown as William III of England. Unknown to James II, he was the last Catholic monarch of England.

Another subtle, but extremely powerful, change was spreading in Europe. *Land*, the measure of wealth for probably 5,000 years, was becoming something less. *Money*—cash that is—created by trade and commerce was becoming the something more. Quickly, it seems from the record, the people at the pinnacle now longer held land. They had cash in the bank, ships for commerce, storehouses of goods, and other trappings of **capitalist** wealth. Landholders typically hold little cash. In feudal times land equaled power because people with land controlled commerce. Commerce was now flowing from fast growing cities where landholders had no say. As the merchants accumulated money and expanded their power, land was less valuable. Hard money was the language of the new era. This decreased the power of the landholding nobility somewhat, and it caused the monarchs pause, because their power was land based; after all, taxes came from land. Monarchs and parliaments learned to tax commerce to increase their wealth, but the nobility lacked that taxing power, so the landholders watched their power melt away into the cities of a new epoch.

While religious wars snuffed people out at a fantastic rate, something else was having a profound influence on religion and human endeavors of all types. **Science** was coming of age, and with the invention of the **printing press** the spread of experimentally confirmed knowledge was assured.

SCIENCE AND THE PRINTING PRESS (THE ROAD TO TOMORROW)

1430

One of the greatest inventions since the advent of language and agriculture, the **PRINTING PRESS** *is a key reason the modern world exists as it does today.*

Our modern world exists because of the printing press. In about **1430**, **Johann Gutenberg**, a goldsmith in Germany, invented a method of printing using movable type, the precursor of the modern printing press. His press was so good it spread all over Europe and the world very quickly. At the same time the printing press was producing books and pamphlets in large numbers, the Protestant Reformation, the rise of science, and new political ideas were emerging and changing the world. Without the printing press such ideas may not have spread as quickly or might fail to spread at all. The printing press was so powerful that Muslim countries banned it in 1515 because it might spread Western learning.

Large numbers of people began reading as books and tracts became widely available. They included: the Bible as translated by Luther, the King James Bible (1611), the tracts on science by Copernicus, Tycho Brahe, Kepler, Galileo, the political thoughts of Moore (*Utopia* 1516), Machiavelli (*The Prince* 1513), philosophers like John Locke, and literature by Shakespeare (1553 to1616). Once these ideas moved off the press their power was limitless. Efforts by churches and traditionalist to thwart the growth of new ideas about the earth, the universe, and mankind were condemned to failure once the concepts hit the printing presses and a literate public.[106]

The first book off the new printing press was the ***Gutenberg Bible* in 1455**. This book held the words of a man scourged and crucified in about AD 33 in the backwater Roman province of Palestine (modern day Israel). This poor fellow died crucified between two criminals, was not of noble birth or any kind of government official. His burial place was a cave with a rock rolled over the front. No one chiseled his words into stone like emperors or Pharaohs. He lived before the printing press, newspapers, tape recorders, radio, TV, or any modern method of keeping records of the spoken word. When he died, his friends said they did not know him, and his death went unrecorded in any official record we know about. It seems

---

[106] How did the public become literate so fast? Almost overnight, huge numbers of people in Europe learned to read.

the only thing owned when he died was the clothes on his back which were filthy, blood-soaked rags after his scourging and crucifixion. He died alone, childless, no wife, without money, without worldly power or position on the dusty outskirts of Roman civilization. Before his crucifixion, he made a strange statement: "*Heaven and earth shall pass away, but my words shall not pass away*" (Matt: 24:35). His statement was confirmed, at least in the short run, when Gutenberg published the Gutenberg Bible, because the man who spoke those words was Jesus Christ. The most printed book on planet earth is the Bible carrying the words of Jesus Christ who suffered scourging and crucifixion outside the gates of the city of Jerusalem so long ago.[107]

Yet, the printing press did not seem to be a friend of religion so long as it printed the words of men scouring the earth and the heavens for answers to the mysteries of life. The acceptance of the **scientific method** was the key to advancing empirical knowledge, and the advance of mankind's empirical knowledge grew spectacularly in Europe. This was the scientific revolution that was throwing out old ideas of an earth-centered universe through the work of **Copernicus, Brahe,** and **Kepler**. By explaining the movement of the planets in the sky they were able to prove that the sun was the center of the solar system. It was the start of a new way of thinking. Before, people looked to the past or the books of Aristotle or Ptolemy to explain the world, but now people would not read the classics to see what was fact or fiction. Now people *tested it for themselves,* and if the classic view failed the test, rejection was the result. New ideas based on **tested facts** became the accepted view, and any new empirically proven "facts" survived only so long as they withstood testing. This brave new empirical world started during the Renaissance and zoomed ahead during the 1600s and 1700s in Europe. **And its growth never stopped accelerating.**

The new scientific and practical advances were astounding: Peter Heinlein invented the first pocket watch in 1500; in 1515 the first rifles were developed; **Isaac Newton** described the laws of gravity in 1665 and in his publication of *Principia Mathematica* (1687) united gravity, inertia, and centrifugal force; William Harvey discovered how blood circulated in the human body by 1628; Fermat put forth the statistical theory of probability in 1659; John Kay invented the flying shuttle loom in 1733; and so on. After

---

[107] His words are now beamed into space, which could mean they will survive until the end of time as we know it, although the SETI project has stated radio beams disintegrate after a few years of traveling through space and become static. So why are they still looking for signals from space? The government must be paying.

laying the foundations of science, more discovery and invention followed until a tidal wave of progress swept the Western World.

THE ARTS—PAINTING

During this period, painting began to advance as never before. **Michelangel**o (1475 to 1654), **Titian, Durer, Raphael, Jan van Eyck, El Greco, Velasquez, Rubens, Rembrandt** (1606 to 1669), **Holbein,** and many others brought painting away from the stiff and unrealistic styles of the Middle Ages to the vibrant, realistic, and almost-animated paintings of 1400 to 1600. The artists were using new colors based on oil paints invented in 1400, and painting on new material (canvas) with new techniques founded on perspective drawing (perspective discovered about 1434) that brought the paintings alive. There was still an enormous amount of symbolism, but the depiction of the world became very real. Oils allowed new techniques of paint application including the layering of color where very thin coats of multiple colors were laid on over a long period. This allowed light to enter through the layers of thin paint and then bounce back to the viewer's eye, imparting a glow to the paintings that made the colors iridescent. Nothing like this had ever been seen before.

SPEED OF CHANGE

Due to the printing press new ideas now spread with astonishing speed and clarity. Ideas spread by word of mouth can warp quickly, but once written down the idea remains the same no matter how many people read the book or pamphlet. This foretells the pace of change in the modern world. Today, 2010, the pace of change is so fast that most of it goes unreported and almost unnoticed. A publication called *Science News* comes out once *per week* filled with summaries of new discoveries which most people will never hear of directly. The flow of information has been increasing since 1455, and it is now so great (with the Internet, TV, radio, computers, newspapers, etc.) it is impossible to sort through it all. In ancient Persia, the fastest way to get information around was by pony express (not their name for it). Until the telegraph in 1837, pony express was the quickest way possible to transmit detailed information. Now, the push of a button electronically transports a hundred pages of text to Japan from America in seconds. Hence, from 1837 to 2010, the speed of information transfer has increased from a running horse to the speed of light. From before 5000 BC to 1837, it had not increased at all.

THE FRENCH REVOLUTION 1789 TO 1799

The French Revolution is so significant it is difficult to exaggerate its importance. Yet, it is a very complex revolt changing France and Europe a lot, but then changing them very little. The Revolution started in 1789 when starving people in Paris, France, decided to do something about it. Riots and confrontations shook the government, escalating until the king and queen were captured and then beheaded by the unleashed forces of change. Shortly thereafter, suspicious radicals commenced beheading anyone they could lay their hands on calling them enemies of the Revolution, and those beheaded included several prominent early leaders of the rebellion. During the crisis, a strong man arose and captured the Revolution, eventually naming himself emperor of France in 1804. Now everyone is back where they started minus thousands of dead and a swarm of wars stemming from the Revolution. It did not really end until **1815**, after the strong man was defeated at **Waterloo** and the Congress of Vienna convened to stop the wars and achieve a political balance in Europe. The strong man was **Napoleon**, and his ideas on war and government came to dominate the age. The French Revolution set off numerous new political, social, and cultural ideas, but in the final event the "old order" prevailed, suppressing many of the innovative ideas. Still, such ideas did not die, and a permanent structural change took place in the culture and the societies of Europe touched by this inferno.

It all started in the late seventeen hundreds when France was a prosperous state, and one of the most powerful nations in the world. **Louis XIV** (1661 to 1715), the Sun King, pushed the boundaries of France to the Rhine River, and the luxury of his court was unmatched in Europe. However, novel ideas were starting to challenge monarchies. The **Enlightenment** was taking hold of the intellectual minds in Europe, and they questioned everything. **Reason** was their god, and they knew no other. To these intellectuals, "reason" consisted of applying empirical methods to all matters (some said apply the "methods of Newton," but that was the scientific method), and under this analysis the "divine right of kings" was suspect.[108]

The expansion of France under Louis XIV, plus his extravagant lifestyle, drained the state treasury. As time went on, French kings refused to reduce

---

108 The "*Divine Right of Kings*" is a philosophy that holds the king is appointed by god; thus, he/she can do no wrong, and they rule by Divine Right. Only god can replace the king. Europe's intellectuals were starting to think this kind of belief was pure hogwash and had to be reevaluated.

their lifestyles. The French court and nobility were well-known for beauty and pageantry—all very expensive. Unfortunately, the **tax situation** was mediocre due to several exclusions from the tax rolls, the Catholic Church being the largest, followed by exclusions for the nobility. As **Louis XVI** ascended to kingship, the financial situation was atrocious. Making a bad situation worse, the 1780s had seen a series of meager harvests, and the poor were doing without food. Additional tax money is hard to find amongst the starving. Casting about for a way to get taxes from Church holdings (which were extensive in both land and buildings[109]) and the wealthy nobility, Louis XVI decided to call together the **Estates-General** in May of 1789 (the same year the USA adopted its Constitution). The Estates-General was a gathering of the three classes of society in a national assembly, and in theory it possessed the power to impose taxes where the king could not. Unfortunately, for Louis XVI and his queen **Marie Antoinette** he had called together a group of men who would lop their heads off.

After the Estates-General assembled an impasse soon arose. The First and Second Estates were comprised of the clergy and the nobility, and they refused to allow any kind of tax change, especially in exemptions, because their taxes would increase from zero to something, and that something might be a lot. The clergy also feared the seizure of Church land. The Third Estate was comprised of everyone not in the First and Second estates and represented ninety plus percent of the population. The Third Estate stormed out of[110] the Estates-General in an unhappy mood, and formed the **National Assembly**. Shortly thereafter unrest increased and a Paris mob stormed an old jail called the **Bastille** on ***July 14, 1789***, and released its prisoners—all six of them. During the storming of the ancient jail the army was mustered to suppress the rioters, but the military refused to fire on the starving public and joined the revolt. That was the end for the monarch of France. This event is often used to mark the start of the Revolution. The National Assembly decided to transform France into a constitutional monarchy. They promptly freed the peasants by abolishing serfdom, confiscated all the lands, buildings and money of the Catholic Church in France, and acted as if King Louis XVI was a criminal. The pope rejected the idea that a government could seize Church property, thereby

[109] Land and buildings are good things to tax because they are very hard to hide, and their ownership is normally very clear. The Catholic Church had been immune to taxation all over Europe for centuries, and a lot of the new leaders were fed up with that arrangement. Obviously, the Church had decreased in power.

[110] The First Estate was the **clergy,** the Second Estate was the **nobility,** and the Third Estate was the **commoners**—the ones that were starving.

raising the issue of *authority*. Who owned the land, the French National Assembly or the Church? The fellows with an army easily answered that issue, and the Church lands were lost. The word flew across Europe about the new government in France, the *Declaration of the Rights of Man*, and other pronouncements indicating the age of monarchs and popes was over and the age of the people was dawning. Unfortunately, it was a red dawn.

We should pause to note that the French Revolution differed extensively from the American Revolution even though tax policies started the trouble both times. The American Revolution started because England was pushing Americans around, and they objected with gunfire. The settlers wanted Parliament to leave them alone. It was a war of independence from Great Britain more than a revolution. A revolution aims at the ruling government and its desire is to replace that government with another. In America's case the revolutionaries wanted to keep their local government and get rid of the overseeing government in England. In France, the Revolution was started by bad economic times and starving peasants, then expanded to answer the question "who had the ultimate right to rule?" The people won, and the assembly of the people took over from the king—for awhile. The goal of the uprising was to oust King Louis XVI and replace him with a different kind of government. They did not want a new king, they wanted a new state. And that the French revolutionaries both compelled and received . . . in spades.

Intellectuals across Europe saw the French Revolution as a wake-up call for the monarchs who continued to rule most of Europe, and not benevolently. The peasants everywhere wanted a change, and the French model seemed a good place to start. This alarmed every government in Europe. The radical ideas of the French Revolution might overthrow the conservative governments. As the danger was amplified through increasingly radical words and actions from Paris, the governments of Europe began preparations for the coming storms. The popularity of the French Revolution with the peasants and intellectuals of many nations, and growing threats against the Revolution from neighboring realms, triggered the French decision to export the Revolution. This in turn led to the pitiless wars of the 1800s often called the **Napoleonic Wars**.

In Paris, the National Assembly beheaded the king and his family[111] after an escape attempt. It was probably a sad sight watching the royal family,

---

111 King Louis XVI was put to death on January 21, 1793, and his queen on October 16, 1793.

surrounded by cheering crowds and dressed in peasants' clothes, put to death because they were of royal blood. There was no other crime except their status. That was enough for the Revolution and the **Committee of Public Safety** as they began killing anyone of royal blood or royal connection. With France fighting to maintain its national sovereignty, radical elements of the Revolution gained more power, soon beginning the **Reign of Terror** (1793 to 1794) which took the lives of several extremist leaders of the Revolution. At the height of the terror, **George Danton** and **Maximilien Robespierre** led the Committee of Public Safety, supervising a killing machine sweeping through France murdering over 18,000 in Paris alone. Both these men's heads would roll by the very method, the guillotine, they had used to slay so many others. The extremist journalist and publisher **Jean Paul Marat** got a killing knife stuck in him by the counter-revolutionary **Charlotte Corday** on July 13, 1793, leading to increasingly harsh measures by the Committee. Marat was demanding the execution of nearly everyone, and the publisher could rouse the mobs of Paris to zealous action at his whim. Charlotte said she killed one man to save one hundred thousand, and was much later viewed as a hero. Scorned at the time, Charlotte was executed four days after she stabbed Marat. In Paris the government devolved into chaos, while outside Paris European states invaded France trying to bring the Revolution to a halt.

War now seemed to be the only way to protect and spread the Revolution. The National Assembly began drafting citizens of the French Republic (the Revolution's new name) *in mass* to fight for the "new" nation. An army made up of *large numbers of draftees,* rather than small numbers of professional soldiers, was an original concept in the Europe of 1800. Once this large army took the field smaller opposing armies endured defeat after defeat. Under Napoleon Bonaparte with his innovative ideas, the combination of massed armies and inspired leadership proved almost unstoppable.

Napoleon Bonaparte was a low ranking artillery officer in the French Army prior to 1789. Born in Corsica, a French island off the Mediterranean coast, his chances in the old aristocratic French army were nil, but revolutionary France opened the door for the rough but able Corsican. Proving himself on the battlefield, he quickly achieved the rank of general and soon held sway over all the armies of France. By 1799, he established a military dictatorship over France and its (his) conquests. The dictatorship was cleverly masquerading as a continuation of the Revolution and the French Republic. Napoleon had conquered nearly all before him, and he expanded the French Republic (later the French Empire) over the face of Europe.[112] On May 18, 1804, while declaring the French Empire, *he crowned himself* **Emperor Napoleon I**. It is important to note that he crowned himself; no priest or government official put the crown on his head. As such, he claimed no right flowing from god, the church, or anybody else (such as the people of France). By crowning himself he was showing that his person alone was the cause for his becoming emperor. This is very much in line with the Age of Reason. Once more, as in Rome, we go from a Republic to an Empire through the actions of a great general—only very much faster.

The ascension of Napoleon to the crown ended the French Revolution; although, it really ended in 1799 after Napoleon took over as a dictator in everything except name. The French Revolution rocked Europe to its foundations. All the fundamental truths accepted without question for hundreds of years were gone. Critical to European culture was the decreed demise of the Church and the rise of the nation state. After Napoleon, the Church was irrelevant to underwriting a king or queen's power. The emperor or king or parliament held power because they could and did as they pleased with state power. They determined good and evil by their will alone. The Church lost its lands, and its monastic orders underwent dissolution. God was nothing to the revolutionaries of France.[113]

In May of 1794, the Revolution abolished the Christian Religion. Reason was to control the minds of men, but "reason" led to the Reign of Terror, the murder of the king and queen, and wars that were brutal beyond measure. The new killing fever was not because one god fought another, but because one man fought another over differing views on government. Gods could not stop men from killing, but now that man claimed to be free from gods, he managed to come up with other reasons to kill every bit as motivating as any god had been. Worse yet, as the government of France existed without the sanction of any god, and as it admitted to no god beyond reason, it was freed from all restrictions as long as "reason" justified the actions. Had the revolutionaries acknowledged the existence of God and the relevance of the Bible, Christian moral restrictions would apply; however, with Christian moral restraints removed and replaced by reason *it was found that "reason" could justify any action* including the Reign

---

112 For all his victories on land, Napoleon failed to win at sea; and this isolated him on the European landmass. Several key English naval victories by Admiral Nelson—Trafalgar in 1805 being the most famous—sealed Napoleon's fate.

113 Of course, it is hard to kill religion by decree. The Catholic Church survived the decree, although its political power was much reduced.

of Terror (remember the Sophist?). Reason, it seemed, recognized no absolutes.

France decided all things must be questioned by the light of reason. The French decided history itself must center on their Revolution; thus, they created a new calendar to reflect its central importance. The metric system of weights and measures was adopted, new fashions were invented, and the Napoleonic Code was published just to name a very few of the concepts arising from the French Revolution; on the other hand, for all their thoughts about being the center of the world and their Revolution the focus of history, *not much changed.* In the end, Napoleon destroyed himself in a series of military blunders rivaling Hitler's some 124 years later. After a massive attack on Russia and the total loss of his frozen army, Napoleon was sent to the island of Elba and exile. His final gasp was his return from exile followed by France restoring him as emperor (how dumb can people get), the declaration of war on Napoleon by England, Prussia and nearly everyone else in Europe, and the final battle at **Waterloo** in **1815** where a combination of English and Prussian forces crushed the French. This time Napoleon ended up on a drab Pacific island where he died in 1821, probably from poison slipped into his food by a servant working on the island who hated him.

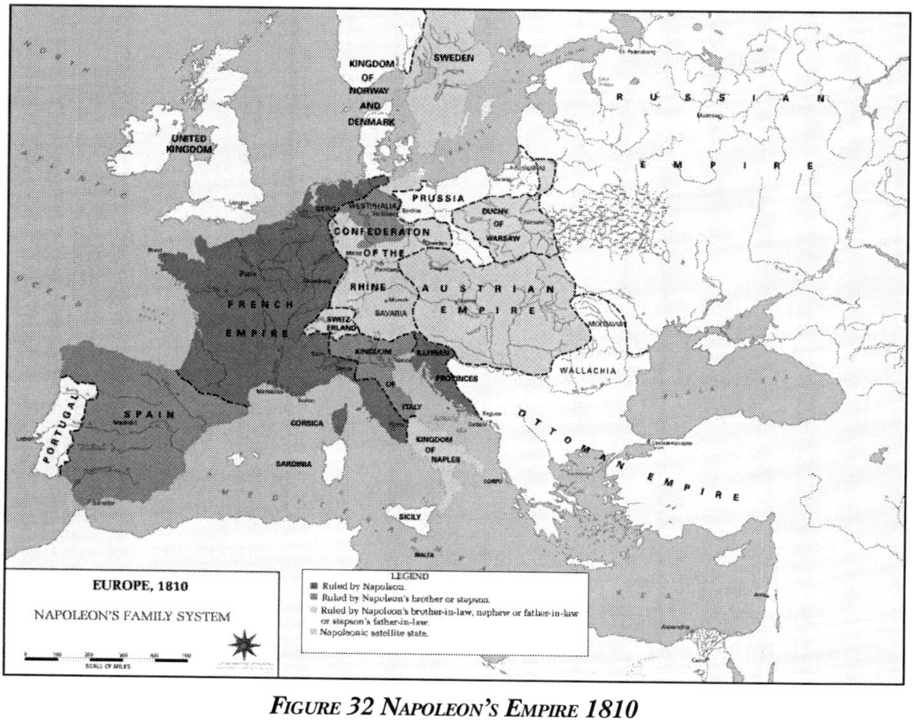

FIGURE 32 NAPOLEON'S EMPIRE 1810

After Napoleon's fall, the nations of Europe assembled in the **Congress of Vienna** which sorted out all the trouble caused by the French, re-established the "old regimes" in Europe, and set the foundations for modern Europe. *This peace would hold from 1815 to 1914,* ninety-nine years in all, and resulted in remarkable prosperity and success for Europe. The Congress of Vienna was historic, and even though small wars occurred during the ninety-nine years, the great powers remained generally at peace saving the world from untold suffering.

THE IMPACT OF EMPIRES

1650 to 1950

Empires held by Western European nations had an unqualified impact on world history. The British, French, Portuguese, Spanish, Belgium, and the Netherlands's empires gobbled up much of the world's surface outside of Europe and the United States, and these empires lasted a very long time.

From about *1650 to 1950* is a general period for the existence of European Empires; thus, *Europe had control of most of the world for three hundred years.* The growth of these empires was especially rapid. In 1815, about 35 percent of the earth's habitable area was controlled by Europe, but by 1914, this percentage was at 85 percent. The only non-European nation establishing a modern empire was Japan whose empire was Asian. These empires, especially the English, brought Europe's technological advancements to all parts of the globe. This in turn brought goods and raw materials from the world to Europe, leading to a general prosperity having a worldwide positive impact. The citizens of the mother countries did not run the empires as a whole. A few government administrators in powerful positions made decisions affecting the daily lives of millions of common folks across the planet. In general, a handful of men positioned at the top of their nation's officialdom governed the colonies of each imperial power. One order could send out lesser administrators to alter lives across the globe.

One must comprehend the worldwide reach of the empires to understand the world of 1700 and beyond. These empires made England, France, Holland, Portugal, and other European states the *center of the world* in financial, military, political, and cultural power for more than three hundred years. As such, the political machinations of Europe hit the entire globe. The boundaries of the empires really displayed political considerations in Europe, and they were placed to assist Europeans in governing their empires. As such, the lines drawn by the European Empires were not a fit solution for the situation existing on the ground. Nonetheless, as the empires toppled, the lines established in Europe became the boundaries of modern-day states. The inappropriateness of these boundaries is obvious as vicious wars over the frontiers continue even today.

As the empires flourished, so did the world. Extensive trade, the adoption of the gold standard to ease the payment problems between nations, and increasing prosperity led to more inventions and more infrastructure development in Europe and their empires. England ruled the world because of her powerful navy and extensive empire. Raw materials from the world over hurried to England's factories for transformation into finished goods ranging from ships to tea. With Britain's extensive coalfields, energy to fuel its expansion into an industrial giant was easy to find. The United Kingdom became the world's richest nation, and its wealth was growing constantly during the Age of Empires. The rest of Europe was doing fine as well, and after the Napoleonic Wars and the Congress of Vienna, growth and prosperity were commonplace in the Western world.

(See Figures 19, 20 and 43 for maps of the colonial empires)

The Industrial Revolution

1750 (approximate beginning)

Before the French Revolution, another revolution had started which would have considerably more impact on the world. The **Industrial Revolution** started **about 1750**, when water was first used to power new mills for cutting wood, weaving cloth on new kinds of looms, and otherwise putting something other than human or horse muscle to work making products for growing worldwide commercial markets.[114] Since the end of the fourteenth century the population of Europe had been growing, increasing the demand for goods and services.[115]

---

114 Rome had industrial-level factories using waterwheels to grind flower and do other chores. These overshot waterwheel-driven factories turned out impressive amounts of grain for the vast empire. When the Dark Ages arrived, this Roman technology was lost.

115 By 1399, the effects of the Black Plague were over; and the population was expanding again.

Numerous inventions marked the new age. The flying shuttle loom was invented in 1733, improving the production of finished cloth goods; by 1740, the processing of cast iron and steel progressed markedly; 1779 saw the first iron bridge constructed in Britain; in1782, **James Watt** developed the double-acting steam engine; in 1785, the power loom was invented in Britain, and in 1793, **Whitney** invented the cotton gin in the United States. By 1807 the first commercial steam boat was operating in America; by 1814, the first steam locomotive was running in Britain and by 1825, Britain opened its first railroad. 1837 saw the invention of the steel plow in the US, while in 1839 France photography developed with the daguerreotype. **Goodyear** vulcanized rubber in America that same year. Moreover, these are only *a few* of the achievements that occurred during the eighteenth and nineteenth centuries.

Something invented in England during the Age of Discovery would have an unprecedented impact on the Industrial Revolution—the **corporate form of enterprise**. Originally, these were companies formed by individuals with the approval of the crown and were given an exclusive area of trade such as the East India Company. These were very successful, and soon private stock corporations began to show they too could achieve success. A corporation normally consists of owners (stockholders) who hire people to oversee the corporation (the board of directors). The board of directors hires the corporation executives (president or chief operating officer, treasurer, sales manager and so forth), and the corporate executives are responsible for making money for the shareholders. If they fail to do so, the board of directors can, and will, replace them with other executives. If the board fails to act rationally, the stockholders can fire the board and hire other people to insure the enterprise makes money. The corporate form of enterprise has shown itself to be a most powerful organizational tool. Repeatedly, corporations outperformed individuals competing against it. One example was Henry Ford. He built the most powerful automotive company on earth which he operated as the sole owner. An upstart company combined many small automotive companies together and adopted the name General Motors, but they also adopted the corporate form of enterprise under the leadership of Alfred P. Sloan. Within a few years the men at General Motors had nearly driven Ford Motor Company out of business.

Of course, corporations fail all the time, but the power of the corporate form of enterprise is easily proven in modern business life. The top companies in the world are corporations. Year after year, corporations dominate Fortune Magazine's list of the top 500 companies. This ability to combine management talent was one reason the Industrial Revolution made such good progress. Once more, we should notice this new organizational tool was perfected in the Western world.

These advances brought a new kind of life to the world, an urbanized life in cities that would be larger than ever before but also connected to the countryside and other cities as never before. As railroads grew, connecting cities across various nations, the ability to transport raw materials increased as well. Factories, such as iron works or textiles, were constructed near the people needed to operate them and close to the populace that would buy the finished goods. The new urban centers brought together the railroads, the workers, the shoppers, and the sellers all in one relatively small area. With demand for labor growing wages were good, and the new machines coupled with cheaper delivery of raw materials allowed the prices of manufactured goods to fall. People financing these new ventures, bankers and stockbrokers for example, made enormous amounts of money as did the new manufacturers themselves.

The urban environment included some very rich folks, many of them new to such wealth. In the urban centers entertainment, housing, food delivery, and many other comforts grew to serve the new wealthy citizens flowing into the cities. For many, the new urban centers were shining examples of a new world where people could live in safety and contentment making a good living and building a sound future. Throughout Europe after 1815, economies grew at an unprecedented pace. Prices were falling and wages were rising all over Europe. Things were looking up for the common person as well. Peasants were turning into factory workers, food production was going up (new growing and harvesting techniques), and new inventions were making work simpler and easier all the time. The confluence of science, inventions, and work were changing the world in dramatic ways.

Naturally, not all of this was good. As the peasants moved to the cities, many found themselves crowded into small and unsanitary living areas (*slums*). The new factories polluted the rivers, air, and ground. The factory workers were expected to work extremely long hours under strenuous conditions. As long as there was a labor shortage the wages kept rising, but as the new machines became more efficient the need for labor fell. This created a labor glut that drove wages down. There was also the new *boom and bust cycles* created by the new economies. Market crashes affected more people, and downturns became a problem for the rich and poor alike. Governments themselves became concerned with these cycles, as market troubles put people out of work and increased stress on societies and their ability to address the problems created by hunger and homelessness. Some of the panics were long and harsh. Luckily, most of these panic cycles were short, lasting only 1 to 2 years, and the cities and governments endured without much change. However, far-reaching new philosophies came forth dealing with these new environments created by cities and the working class poor. In **1848, Marx and Engels** published the *Communist Manifesto* that decried the conditions of the working classes and predicted a revolution would overthrow the capitalist system. Other reformers working to change the lives of the poor, such as the Women's Christian Temperance Union (WCTU), thought alcohol was the root cause of urban evils and lobbied to ban liquor sales.

As the new cities continued to grow, the new underclass also grew. The problems of the urban poor would not abate in spite of the actions of social welfare agencies and special interests groups such as the WCTU. Crime was rampant in the crumbling areas of the cities where poverty reigned supreme. Theft, molestation, rape, prostitution, murder, beatings, and gang activity were ordinary events. Whores were everywhere in these areas, drunkenness was common, drug abuse relentless, and all manner of low behavior was ensconced in these eroding neighborhoods of the new urban scene. None of this was new; nevertheless, the scale of the problems had expanded greatly (except perhaps in ancient Rome). Ancient civilizations could not solve the problems, and the new urban centered civilizations likewise found no solutions.

ART AND THE FUTURE OF EUROPE

1874

Art was taking a new turn as the **French Impressionist** began exhibiting in **1874** (**Monet, Manet, Renoir** et al). These artists refused to paint glorious scenes from the past; rather, they painted scenes from the glorious, and not so glorious, present. Prior to the Impressionist, painting in France was confined to scenes from antiquity showing great moments in history such as the birth of Venus or a celebrated battle scene. The Impressionist broke this pattern by painting everyday scenes such as railway stations, a person sitting at a bar, or a crowded city street scene complete with balloon vendors. No longer did a painting have to show something noteworthy. The common person was now a good subject for immortality in paint. The Impressionist changed the methods of painting. The Impressionist avoided the insides of studios where a painting's completion took weeks or months; instead, they went outside, and by using modern tube paints and canvas painted scenes rather quickly. Light was their subject, and the play of light across the scene was all important. Catching the fleeting light was hard; consequently, the faster one painted the better one could seize the ever-changing rays and convert them into a picture. The application of paint to the canvas was unlike the smooth style employed by accomplished French salon painters. Impressionist applied paint in dips and dabs that, if looked at closely, appeared to be a mess of colors; yet, upon standing back the colors, dips, and dabs fused to form a brilliant and glimmering recital of light and substance. In precise hands the effect was light and life dancing on the canvas.

FIGURE 33 MONET, HOTEL DE ROCHES NOIRES, TROUVILLE, 1870.

The Impressionist displayed a new world of speed and commotion which was chaos up close, but from a distance became beautiful and seductive. As art "progressed," this beauty fell into a deep ugliness without form or reason. The "splatter paintings" of the 1950s by Jason Pollock were foretold by **Van Gogh** (usually considered Impressionist), **Gauguin, Seurat, Matisse** (Fauvism 1909), **Max Ernst** (1923 early surrealism), **Picasso and Braque** (Cubism 1910), and **Salvador Dali** (Surrealism 1931). **J. Pollock** represents Abstract Expressionism of the 1950s.

Artists' predicted where the world was heading from 1870 through 1914, and the destination was not the gleaming cities of sanity and serenity envisioned by the common person in 1800.[116] According to the artists of the late 1800s, the world was plummeting into insanity and darkness where life would make no sense, and the world of reason would melt away. According to the art of the 1950s, life had no meaning and the future was chaos or worse. The decline of the world, according to the artists, began about the time of the Industrial Revolution and the rise of science. Art foretold of a world without sense, purpose, God, or reason to guide mankind. A world ruled by machines doesn't need a God. The purpose for existence was gone according to the painters, writers, and composers.

The visual arts lost their way after Impressionism. The world, while bad in many ways, is not awful everywhere. People do live for more than death. Science does not tell us the world has no God. Impressionism still observed the confused world as a good place where each person and event had a purpose. [117] To make this statement, they did something new and broke all the old traditions. As art went onward, it seems "new" was all that mattered. If it had not been done before, then it was genius. As a result, Picasso "sculpted" using an old bike seat with bike handlebars attached, called it "*bull,*" and won acclaim. Pollock threw paint at a canvas, a huge canvas, and became the greatest artist since Rembrandt. The same elitist trends go on today. This is not art. Art without skill, real and abiding skill with attention to detail, is nothing.

The Industrial Revolution never ended. Machines continue to improve, and new inventions are coming all the time. In the year 2010, machines and computers have long since been married and the result is very smart machines. People may be the same murdering, cheating, conniving slime

---

116 Literature, music, and other artistic forms were expressing the same themes.

117 In spite of the splotchy, close-up look, each stroke had a purpose, each color was exactly placed; and even when standing far away from the painting, the subject could still be discerned. When a person gets too far away from a painting by the old masters, the subject becomes indistinct. The Impressionists were showing the world that even though confusion seemed to be the scheme of life, in fact that confusion was organized into a solid, coherent whole when looked at in concert.

we have always been; nevertheless, we have nice stuff. From the end of the Napoleonic Wars to 1914, Europe generally enjoyed prosperity and peace. There were wars in faraway places as colonial powers fought to keep their conquests, and short wars erupted between Austria, and later France against Germany; however, to most people in England and Europe things looked good. Great advances were being made everywhere. One of the greatest was made by Frenchman L. **Pasteur** in 1864 with his germ theory. After Pasteur's discovery, medical science began an unprecedented advance to the modern age and its fantastic medical miracles. Most of this was due to the Industrial Revolution. Our modern world enjoys industrial progress because of the foundations laid down from 1750 onward, and that prosperity still looks good.[118]

RISE OF NEW NATIONS IN CENTRAL EUROPE

After 1700, both Italy and Germany (Prussia) began to coalesce as nation states. By the peace of 1815 and the defeat of Napoleon, both Prussia and Italy gained territory and more independence. In 1848, there was a general revolt in the German and Italian principalities, but the armies remained loyal to the central governments, and in the aftermath these governments grew stronger. The sovereigns liberalized their policies by abolishing serfdom and adding power to representative assemblies. The **Kingdom of Italy**, proclaimed in 1861, grew to include Rome and Venice by 1870. Italy was at last united, but still struggling with industrialization and modernization. **Otto Von Bismarck** proclaimed the **German Empire** in 1871 after conducting wars to consolidate areas around Prussia forcing them under Prussian control. Bismarck was the political giant of the age, as his practical but cold-blooded politics united Germany, defeated Austria and France in war, and resulted in a German Constitution and Empire. Conflicts with Austria stopped its interfering with Prussian affairs, leading to reform in the Austrian monarchy and the establishment of Austria-Hungary in 1867. A final war of German consolidation took place between Prussia and France in 1871 (the Franco-Prussian War) which was sharp but short, resulting in Alsace-Lorraine being taken by the German Empire while France's Second Republic was toppled and replaced by the Third Republic. Now Germany and Austria-Hungary were established as nation states in Central Europe, with Germany being the foremost of these nations. Bismarck then set out to prevent wars involving Germany from

---

[118] As Will Rogers said during the Great Depression, "We (the US) will be the first nation to drive to the poor house."

occurring. He had what he wanted, a united Germany, and he desired to maintain the status quo while Germany consolidated its industrial power. The advent of a new Kaiser, Wilhelm II, ended Bismarck's foreign policies designed to keep Europe at peace.

The newly formed Germany wanted recognition and respect. Its problem, its new Kaiser thought, was Germany had an insufficient navy and no colonies. This was a very poor analysis. The Kaiser set out to get both, thereby putting Germany on a collision course with England and France. The competition for prestige and influence resulted in an all-out arms race. Germany's main goal in the arms race was a powerful navy because she already possessed a powerful army. Germany managed to acquire colonies in Africa and the Pacific, but they never got to the point of satisfaction. Trying to be on a par with England and France, who pursued colonies for over a century before Germany's founding, was insane. Why Germany thought it must be like England or France to achieve greatness is hard to understand. Germany's obvious path was that of a great Central European *land* power, not a world sea power. Seeking sea power made it necessary to challenge England and upset the apple cart holding Europe's balance of power. Dumb German decisions would trigger arms races and other tensions, thereby fostering the policies and decisions that led to a general European war in 1914.

The new nation states were stirring things up. The old pot of Europe began boiling over as the emerging nation states tried to push aside older nation states that disliked the unhappy interlopers for many reasons. Economic competition was unwelcome in 1900s Europe as nations looked upon economics as a win-lose game. In fact, when trade increases everyone benefits—even if some benefit more than others do. Thus, competition in Europe heated up, and centuries old hatreds refused to die. Mistrust piled upon tensions dating back to Charlemagne causing the European world to become a heavily armed and nervous camp.

Let Us Learn

History teaches us through the Armada to plan well, communicate well, and train people for the task. Spain's leaders planned poorly, in that the Armada's ships and crews were unfit for the task. Better training for the crews, better ships for the job of defending the Armada, and better communication to the troops in Holland might have altered history. Also, never assume God is on your side as King Philip assumed. From England's response, we learn to be prepared, be ready to do the unusual to grasp the goal, and be flexible enough to act in accordance with the changing situation. And just because one is small, defeat does not follow by that fact alone.

The Protestant Reformation shows the dangers of corruption. The Catholic Church forfeited the right to lead by engaging in corrupt practices for centuries. It finally caught up with them. In addition, part of the corruption involved persecuting individuals calling for righteous change. Best listen to those asking for honest corrections to shady activities, even if they are your own. This revolt tells us the power of an idea. One man, after several suffered death before him, spoke of salvation by faith alone. Anyone reading the Bible could reach the same conclusion. That idea started the Protestant Reformation, a world changing series of events. People respond to ideas with fervor; recall this when watching political rallies or reading about revolutions. Rejoice in the power of ideas and understand their full power and potential.

Nations chasing England's path to world power illustrate the idiocy of assuming what worked before will work now. Each nation's or individual's situation is distinct. Unclear, stilted thinking threw away chances for positive progress by Germany and other countries trying for "greatness" through military power and colonial acquisitions. Mapping out the best course of action requires knowing your unique situation, the situation of others involved, and knowing your own strengths and weaknesses. If you are five foot nine and weigh 165 pounds your chances of playing linebacker in the NFL are nil. Learn to live with that. If you excel at math attend college and major in engineering. Germany blew it big time by poorly analyzing their fundamental situation and its advantages and disadvantages. Rather, they dreamed of achievements not fitting their situation, angered everyone with their activities, and then ignored the anger and the danger. Don't do that. Learn to be realistic and take things one step at a time. If your actions bring trouble coupled with active confrontation immediately change course so your actions bring positive results. Flexibility, clear analysis, and superior research bring positive rewards while avoiding dreadful pitfalls.

The French Revolution teaches us moderation. Radicals seizing the Revolution destroyed its ideals achieving worse than nothing. Practice moderation and notice where your actions are taking you. If your path is laced with strife, alter the path. Concentrate on small (moderate) thoughtful changes and notice the results. The big changes in France shook up the neighborhood turning all governments against them. The French Republic needed to alter course. Instead, they kept the same course and eradicated themselves. Avoid that error.

CHAPTER 11

AMERICA AND THE AMERICAS

LATIN AMERICA

In the late 1700's historic events were taking place in Latin America because of events in Europe. After Napoleon conquered Western Europe (Spain included) he placed his brother Joseph on the throne of Spain. The Spanish people abhorred Napoleon and started a long gruesome guerrilla war against the French; plus, in Latin America the Spanish colonies likewise rejected French tyranny. **Simon Bolivar** (1783 to 1830), a Creole (colonist of Spanish descent), rose up against the French. His army won battle after battle against forces loyal to the Spanish throne, even though it was occupied by a Frenchman. He and other freedom fighters such as **Jose San Martin** (1778 to 1850), set an entire continent free. From the tip of Tierra del Fuego to Mexico, Spanish and Portuguese rule was ripped away allowing the formation of free and independent states.

Looking back on what Simon Bolivar accomplished it seems a miracle. In spite of his numerous victories Simon Bolivar's name is not a household word, and yet he was as accomplished as George Washington in setting men free. Of course, that is the best thing about General Bolivar; he conquered to spread freedom.

President James Monroe announced the **Monroe Doctrine** in 1823, warning Europe that the United States would not tolerate interference in Latin American affairs. The United States could not enforce this doctrine, but England could because she controlled the seas, and the doctrine fit with her policies since Britain wanted European powers to stay away from South America. Because of the American doctrine and its enforcement by Great Britain, Latin America was able to develop without unnecessary interference from Europe.

UNITED STATES OF AMERICA

In 1791, Congress established the first Bank of the United States (a central bank), and stockbrokers began meeting under a tree on Wall Street in 1792. The brilliant Secretary of the Treasury Alexander Hamilton was cleaning up the financial mess the United States had gotten itself into, and George Washington was unanimously elected to a second term as president. George Washington quit after his second term saying two terms was enough, and this precedent held until Franklin Roosevelt won election four times after declining to adhere to President Washington's example. Now the US Constitution limits the president to two terms.

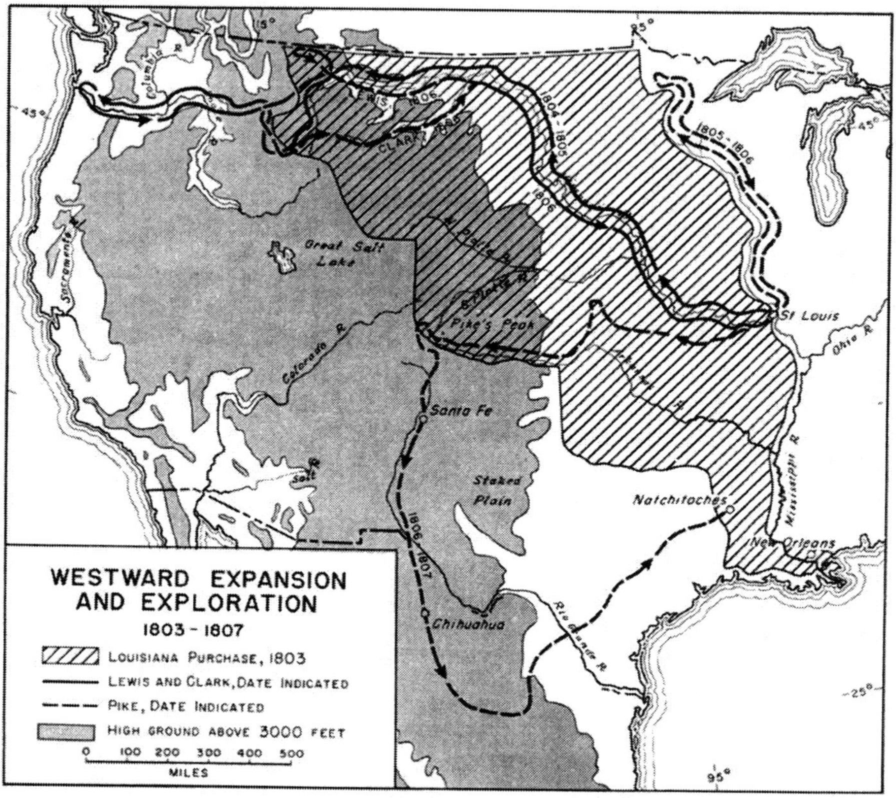

FIGURE 34 WESTWARD AMERICAN EXPANSION—EARLY 1800

After winning the war for independence and the battle for the adoption of a new Constitution America set out to move west. Moving very far west was going to be a problem because France claimed the Louisiana Territory which was the drainage basin of the Mississippi River. This would effectively block westward expansion unless the United States was willing to fight for the area. This time America was lucky. France wanted to get rid of its American holdings and offered Louisiana to the **Jefferson** administration at a low price.[119] The third US president had a problem. The Constitution failed to say whether or not the president's powers included making such a deal. Jefferson believed in limiting federal (central government) power, by confining it to powers that were specifically named, but went ahead with the **Louisiana Purchase** in April of 1803 anyway because it was good for the country. Jefferson had no idea how good it would be for the nation. His use of an unstated power did expand the power of the president, but his decision was one of the most important ever made for the country. No one knew the size of the land area purchased so the government set out to find out. The Lewis and Clark expedition was sent to discover what the Federal Government bought. It turned out the acquisition more than doubled the size of the United States.

George Washington, in his farewell address as president, told America to stay away from foreign entanglements. Good advice, but in spite of its best efforts the United States was drawn into international affairs because of its widespread trading with Europe and the Caribbean. The small US Navy successfully fought the Barbary Coast pirates off North Africa after the US refused tribute to them in 1805; however, about the same time Britain was seizing sailors and US merchant ships during yet another war the United Kingdom was conducting against Napoleon. The United States became angry when the British ignored several warnings to cease. Talk of war increased the distress of New England area traders who realized their international trade connections might be cut by the United Kingdom in a war. Words soon turned to bullets as the United States declared war on England in 1812. As their ports fell under a blockade, New England merchants began talking about leaving the Union. The key reason for the war? The USA did not like the bully Great Britain pushing it around. The Americans were a feisty bunch.

---

[119] Jefferson, the third US president, was elected in 1801, and this was the first power transfer between political parties. And yes, this is the same Thomas Jefferson that penned the Declaration of Independence. Note that political parties were not anticipated by the drafters of the US Constitution. Jefferson wanted Congress and the president to stay within the **specific** powers given them in the US Constitution, and since the ability to buy land was not specifically given to the president he worried that he was, by his actions, going to expand the power of the executive. Of course, he did expand the power of the executive, but it would make little difference given the massive expansion of power that would come later.

THE WAR OF 1812

Wars of pride often go badly, and the War of 1812 went badly for the small USA against the mighty British Empire. The British seized Detroit at the outset of hostilities and repelled an American attack on Canada. As the war went on, Captain Oliver Perry won control of the Great Lakes for the United States in a stunning fresh-water naval victory over the British. The British landed and defeated an American militia force guarding Washington DC in the Battle of Bladensburg on August 24, 1814, then marched to and *burned Washington DC.* The British next advanced on Maryland and planned to seize the city of Baltimore. **Fort McHenry** was the main barrier standing between the British and Baltimore. The British bombarded the fort all night in an attempt to breach its defenses, but the fort held so the British advance came to an end. During the action at Fort McHenry the United States of America gained the words to its national anthem. **Francis Scott Key**, held on a British ship in the harbor as the bombardment took place, wrote the "Star Spangled Banner" as he anxiously awaited the battle's outcome. (He wrote the words that were later set to music.)

In the West, the British encouraged Native Americans to attack the advancing American colonists, making alliances with them during the war against the United States. In fighting along the western frontier and northern frontier with Canada the Americans faced combined British and Native American units in many hard-fought actions. The Native Americans and British allies often got the best of the Americans in these battles; however, the Native American chief **Tecumseh** caught a bullet in the Battle of the Thames and died on October 5, 1813. Tecumseh's death effectively ended Native American support for the British and eased the pressure on the Americans. The British conquered a portion of Maine, but this was relinquished back to the US in the treaty ending the war.

At sea, the British maintained a blockade of the American coast severely hurting trade, nonetheless, in several single-ship duels on the high seas American frigates defeated larger British ships. Perhaps the best known was the *USS. Constitution's* [120] victory over the larger and better armed HMS *Guerriere.* Even though the Americans won several single-ship battles, the British blockade was effective and significantly impaired US commerce.[121]

---

[120] Old Iron Sides was her nickname because metal sheeting placed over the hull caused enemy cannonballs to ricochet off.

[121] It was in one of these engagements that John Paul Jones, aboard the Bonhomme Richard, was asked to surrender by the British commander. Jones replied "I have

The last battle of the war took place when the British assaulted the city of New Orleans at the mouth of the Mississippi River on January 8, 1815. Unfortunately, the war was *already over* when the battle took place, but the forces were unaware of this fact because word of the treaty's signing was slow to reach the British or American armies. The British forces drew up on a flat area near the town and launched an all-out attack but **General Andrew Jackson** had expertly fortified the area the British had to assault. The battle was fierce, nevertheless, well-protected defenders shot down the British as they attacked across open ground. Over two thousand English troops were lost to approximately one hundred Americans killed in the action. Word of this unnecessary victory reached Washington DC about the same time as the news of the signing of the treaty. The result was a huge celebration and the illusion of a war won against the British.

The Treaty of Ghent, signed on December 24, 1814, ended the war. Not much was gained by either side. The impressments issue went away because the English stopped impressments after the war with Napoleon ended. England gave back the portion of Maine they conquered. The one real gain was on the frontier where the American settlers would no longer face Native Americans allied with and supported by the British. After several defeats and the near secession of New England from the Union over trade issues, perhaps the American leadership learned a lesson. This was the last war between the United States and the United Kingdom.

AMERICAN GROWTH AND PROBLEMS

By **1815, the population** of the United States and its western areas (not actually a part of the nation) was about *10 million.* In Europe (including western Russia), the population was over *200 million.* In India, the population was estimated at *190 million,* and in China about *320 million.* Japan stood at approximately *20 million.* Thus, the United States enjoyed a small population compared to the industrialized nations of Europe, the colony of India, or the Far East. In trade, however, America was doing very well. The American method of manufacture was starting to spread throughout the United States. In this method machines produced parts so well that no additional human handiwork was necessary before assembly. In one showing of how this worked, an American firearms manufacturer put new parts from several rifles right off the machining process into a box and shook it. After he shook

---

not yet begun to fight," and then went on to win the battle. His ship sunk after the battle, but he captured the still afloat British ship and continued on his way.

them up, he took them out and assembled the rifles that functioned properly without any additional work. In Europe the manufactures were still using gunsmiths for the final assembly because the parts did not come out of the machines ready to install. Tweaking was required before the parts would fit. Thus, each rifle ended up as a semi-custom gun with the parts individually fitted. Such innovative techniques made American goods cheaper and the parts were easier to replace.

As time advanced, things were not all sweetness and light in the new republic of the United States of America. In *1838*, Joshua Giddings from Ohio became the first representative elected to Congress on a platform of ending slavery (**abolitionist**). As the abolitionist made progress in Congress the southerners began to worry about their economic future. In 1841, the first wagon train arrived in California implying that many new territories east of California were ripe for admission to the Union. The year 1845 brought the Irish potato famine to Ireland, and many Irish families immigrated to the New World to escape starvation in the old. The immigrants came to the great manufacturing centers rising in the northeastern areas, adding significantly to their population. This combination of a growing population in the north plus new territories wanting admission to the Union spelled big trouble for the slave-owning south. Nevertheless, it was about to get much worse because of a brilliant American success in a war with its Spanish speaking neighbor.

MEXICAN-AMERICAN WAR

1846 to 1848

1846 brought another war. It all started with **Texas** revolting and separating from Mexico in 1836. A small army of Texans led by Sam Huston defeated a large invading Mexican army under General Santa Anna.[122] Texas then applied to join the United States, and the application was accepted which admitted Texas as a territory in 1845. The United States attempted to purchase Texas and other areas of the southwest, including California, but the Mexican government was in no mood to bargain. Mexico warned that accepting Texas into the Union would mean war. Mexico also claimed the territorial boundary between itself and Texas was150 miles north of the

---

[122] It was in this war that the famous stand at the **Alamo** took place in San Antonio, Texas. Davy Crocket and several other well-known American frontiersmen died fighting for Texas and freedom.

Rio Grande River. Texas and the United States said the boundary was the Rio Grande. After the annexation of Texas, Mexico sent troops to enforce its boundary line; hence, the United States sent troops to establish the Rio Grande as the boundary and to protect Texas. After a small clash between the two armies, Congress declared war on Mexico on May 13, 1846. The US president, **James K. Polk,** was a driven personality wanting to acquire territories claimed by Mexico. Polk was preparing for, and fomenting, the Mexican conflict to achieve his purpose. Polk was a one term president, but his impact on American history is considerable.

Polk wanted Mexico to relinquish claims to the southwest and California, but so far the Mexicans refused to bargain. Early fighting in California and New Mexico was indecisive, so President Polk decided to invade Mexico by sea. General Scott would land at Vera Cruz, defeat the Mexican forces there, and then move to attack Mexico City if necessary. Under the leadership of General Zachary Taylor (a future president), a small US blocking expedition moved to northern Mexico. General Santa Ana, in charge of the Mexican forces, knew an American sea expedition under General Scott was on its way to Vera Cruz. The Mexican general moved north planning to defeat Taylor's small force first then hurry south and defeat Scott. This was a good plan, but Santa Anna's troops executed it poorly. Taylor advanced into Northern Mexico and occupied a defending position in the mountain pass of Buena Vista when General Santa Ana, with an army of about 15,000 men, assaulted the Americans on February 22, 1847. The Americans held, although only after a timely artillery bombardment by Captain Braxton Bragg and a desperate charge by Mississippi riflemen, led by Jefferson Davis, drove off the nearly victorious Mexicans. That was about it for the northern Mexico campaign. Santa Ana broke contact to hurry south as Scott's force of 8,500 men was landing at Vera Cruz.

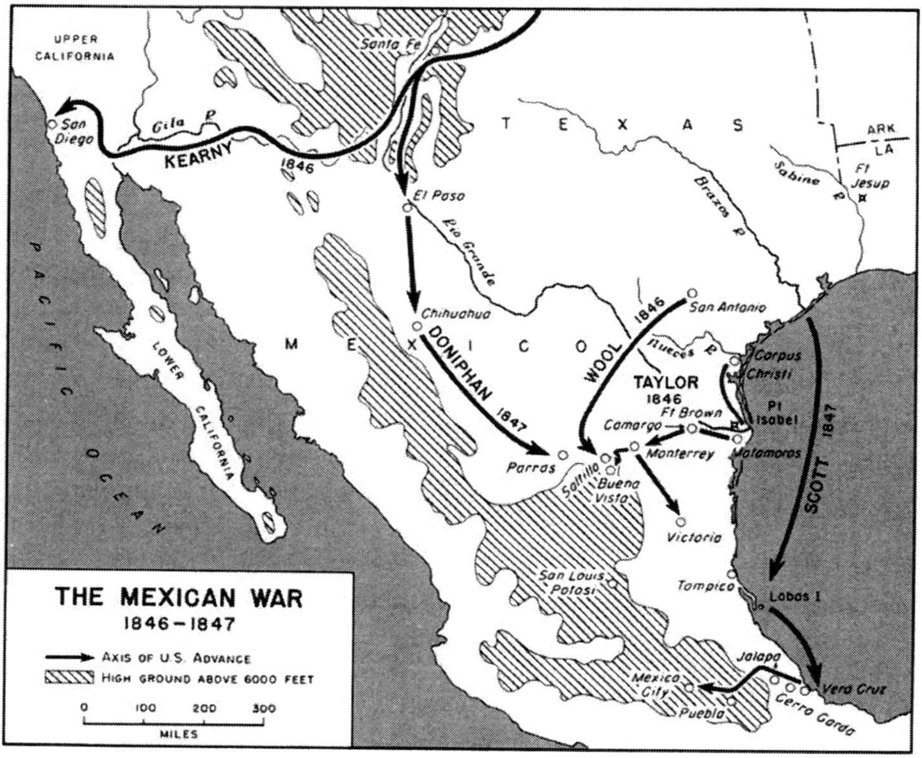

FIGURE 35 THE MEXICAN AMERICAN WAR

General Winfield Scott conducted a brilliant campaign, defeating the larger Mexican Army and capturing Mexico City. The march on Mexico City took place after an amphibious landing at the city of Vera Cruz. This was the first amphibious landing in US history. After a twelve-day siege the coastal city fell. Scott then marched toward the Mexican capitol. In all, Scott would win seven battles on his way to Mexico City. In one of the larger confrontations General Santa Ana, with over 12,000 men, entrenched in a good defensive location near the town of Cerro Gordo and attempted an ambush; however, poor discipline among Mexican troops gave away their positions. Even so, the Mexican positions were formidable. Scott skillfully flanked General Santa Ana thus defeating Mexico's forces. The Mexican Army fell back on Mexico City and the protection of its bastion at Chapultepec. A determined assault by US Army and US Marine forces captured the protective citadel and Mexico City fell immediately thereafter. In US Marine tradition, the Corps captures Chapultepec after the US Army failed in two assaults. The Marines discovered and stormed a lightly guarded gate, captured the fort, and then advanced to Mexico City ahead of the US Army. Thus, the

US Marine Corps hymn contains the following words, "*From the Halls of Montezuma* to the shores of Tripoli . . ."[123]

The Treaty of Guadalupe-Hidalgo ended the war in 1848 and ceded the southwest and California to the United States for a payment of 15 million dollars and the assumption of over 3 million in claims. *The extensive territorial gain led to the controversy over extending slavery to the new territories, and then the US Civil War.* At least a few commentators say *if* the Mexican-American War never occurred avoiding the Civil War would have been much easier. Some of the lower-ranking American officers who contributed to this campaign became well known later: Robert E. Lee, US Grant, Stonewall Jackson (not known as Stonewall then), and George Meade were just a few.

In 1853, the United States finished out its southwest boundaries with the Gadsden Purchase of the Gila River Valley from Mexico. Americans rejoiced over the victories of the war with Mexico, but the next American war would spill only American blood on American land.

THE AMERICAN CIVIL WAR 1861 TO 1865

(The First Modern War)

This may be the saddest time in the history of the United States of America. The emotions stirred by the Civil War remain with America today. It was the bloodiest and hardest war the nation ever fought. **All** the dead were Americans, and every bit of land and property devastated was American.

Before Vietnam, many said America never lost a war. This is not true. The **Confederate States of America** (CSA) fielded an American army, and they fought for their view of freedom with a fury and determination seldom seen in the history of the world. Nevertheless, the South lost; therefore, the first war lost by Americans was the Confederate States of America in the Civil War.[124] Southerners always contended they were fighting another American Revolution, claiming they only wanted the powerful North to

---

[123] Ok . . . Ok. I did not tell you Montezuma was the Aztec emperor Cortez captured and defeated. Come on . . . it is the SUPER summary after all. The Halls of Montezuma is a reference to the Aztec ruler and his capitol of Mexico City. The "Halls of Montezuma" = Mexico City. Get it??

[124] Many would point out the Seminoles were never defeated by the United States, and the War of 1812 was probably a tie at best, so things are not clear-cut in the

leave them alone. The North astutely claimed it was fighting a continuation of the American Revolution, saying they were fighting to set men free from slavery and oppression. Either way, the problems of the United States came down to a clash of arms. Legislation and compromise failed, only death and destruction would answer the issue.

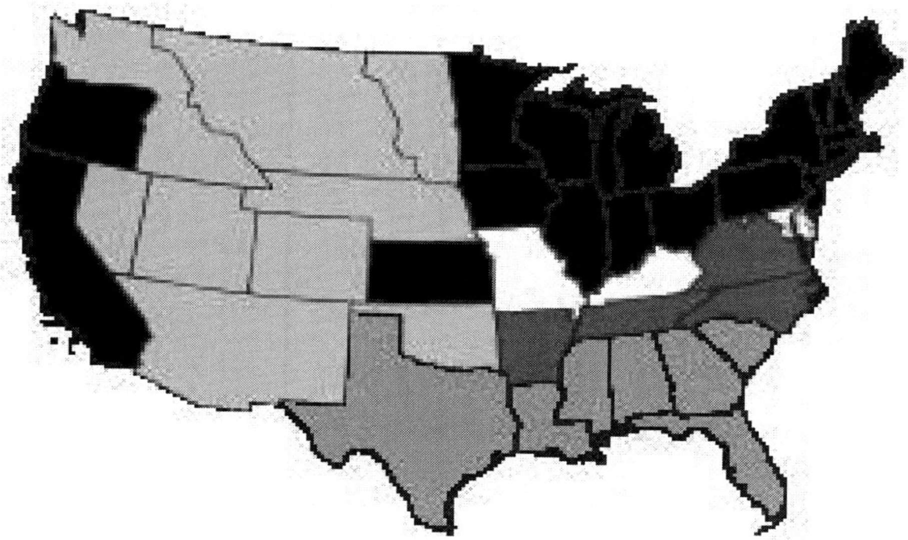

FIGURE 36 AMERICAN CIVIL WAR
BLACK—UNION STATE (NO SLAVERY)
LIGHT GREY—DEEP SOUTH, LEFT UNION BEFORE 4/15/1861
DARK GREY—STATES THAT LEFT UNION SOON AFTER 4/15/1861
WHITE—UNION STATES PERMITTING SLAVERY

CAUSES

The causes of the Civil War are legion. Most try to boil it down to slavery, but that generalization avoids a lot of history and a lot of thinking. By 1860, there were deep cultural, economic, and political differences between the North and the South. Fundamentally, the North was a highly urbanized industrial manufacturing powerhouse, and the South was a rural patriarchal agricultural region. Trade, for example, became a considerable unresolved issue between the industrial North and the agricultural South. The North wanted tariffs to protect its industries, but the South wanted zero tariffs so

---

won-loss department of US history. In addition, the US did not lose the Vietnam War. South Vietnam lost the war. See the Chp on Vietnam.

it could sell its cash crops of cotton and tobacco to Europe without facing retaliatory foreign tariffs.[125] The South actually exported much more, in terms of monetary value, than the North; thus, any tariff would harm the South greatly even while it protected the North's industries. Because the economic interests of the North and South were so divergent, continuing clashes were predestined over a wide range of economic and social issues. In fact, these two regions are still clashing over economic and social issues.

Perhaps the greatest divide between the North and South was cultural. The North was an urban society attracting the wealthy, inventive, and liberal social thinkers of the era. In urban societies social movement, from poor to middle class or uneducated to educated, was common and somewhat easily done. There was far more opportunity for advancement on merit in metropolitan areas where race, class, ethnicity, and the like did not totally determine one's place in the world. The South's rural society determined status by birth, and change over the course of one's lifetime was unlikely. Landowners controlled the wealth, with a few exceptions, and the middle class was small. This was a stratified rural society, much like the society of the Dark Ages, divided chiefly into the wealthy and the poor.[126] The South was populated mostly by poor white farmers who were either sharecroppers or held small farms on poor ground. The rich folk's families had arrived first, acquiring the best land and building large plantations. These extraordinarily wealthy landowners became the slaveholders. Owing to their menial economic situation, Southern hardscrabble farmers could not own slaves. Thus, the solid majority of southerners were NOT slave owners.

The stratified society of the South broke along more than racial lines. Whites were not to mix with blacks; the poor did not mix with the rich; the educated avoided the uneducated; men and women were highly regulated in their conduct with one another, and one always held their "place." This kind of separation is common in agricultural societies because large landowners are set apart from common soil tillers by a large economic gap. The dirt poor vastly outnumbered the superbly rich; thus, keeping the poor in their place, both black and white, was critical for elite landowners.

---

125 The US would place tariffs on incoming goods, then the foreign nations would place tariffs on US goods coming to them. Result: cotton and tobacco sales would suffer.

126 Like the Dark Ages, there were the very rich and the very poor. The middle-class merchants were a small part of society in the Dark Ages and in the pre-Civil War South. Typical in an agricultural society.

These two societies, Northern urban and Southern rural, could not live in harmony unless they left one another alone. If each side ran separate societies, without the federal overlap, peace might prevail. For example, the South could have abolished tariffs while the North kept them; however, the nature of federalism demanded one must destroy the other unless each ignored the other. But interference happened. The radicals of the North roared that slavery, this outrage to humanity, deserved destruction no matter what the cost. As the furor of the language increased, trust decreased. The South distrusted the North on regional issues. If the North gained control of the Senate, by even one vote, they would use it to pass legislation harming southern regional interests, including the abolition of slavery and raising tariffs.

Because the landed elites ran the South (as usual—money talks), slavery was a major factor in every regional dispute in Congress. The northern states banned slavery by 1860. There was a virtual tie in the Senate between slave states and free states, and the South recognized maintaining the balance as new states came into the Union was vital, otherwise, they could not protect their regional interests. The Mexican-American War and the following land acquisitions made the problem acute. The timing and method of allowing states into the Union created a "perfect storm" where compromise broke down.

Another problem was the *emotional nature* of the slavery issue. Southerners wanted the North to go away and leave them alone. Why should northerners be able to order them around? Why were the northerners so adamant about ending an institution not in their area and causing them no harm? Northern propaganda concerning mistreatment of slaves galled the South. Why would slave owners mistreat their property? Would they mistreat their horses? Northerners must know slaves were valuable, and mistreatment caused their value to decrease. The southerners believed that just because families might endure separation at slave sales or some slaves required physical punishment to keep them in line was no cause for concern on behalf of those not owing slaves. In the North, abolitionists were crying out for justice. In newspapers and speeches across the North, the abolitionists' cause drew ever more attention to ending slavery.[127]

---

[127] *Uncle Tom's Cabin* by Harriet Beecher Stowe published in 1852 was *the bestselling novel of the nineteenth century* and was a significant piece of northern propaganda that incensed people of the North **and** the South.

Southerners argued northerners should *pay* slave owners to set the slaves free. Emancipation by purchase was a practical idea, but the abolitionists refused to pay because they thought the institution was ungodly, cruel, and immoral. And there was another rub; the Constitution, as we have discussed, told the government to pay for property it took and southerners said slaves were property. The southerners thought the Constitution was clear—the North must pay for any slaves it forced them to free. The abolitionist also thought morality was clear—no man had the callous right to own another. Because the two societies existed side by side, and the one would not leave the other alone, the problems failed to subside.

The ultimate problem: the Constitution stood *silent* on a state departing the Union. Many in the South thought, as a legal matter, that if a state could vote to join the Union it could vote to leave the Union. In the North many feared a Union split up would significantly impair the nation and argued no state could leave without the consent of Congress. As southern congressional power declined, they considered the ultimate solution: ***leave the Union.***

The stage was set for an armed conflict to decide ***if a state had the right to leave the Union.*** *This was the true issue of the war.* Slavery along with vast cultural, economic, and emotional issues may have caused secession; however, none of that was directly at issue. The one issue to be decided as the war began was whether a state could separate from the Union without Congressional approval. **Abraham Lincoln** refused to debate the issue. After the South seceded, he called up the troops and immediately moved to force the secessionists' states back into the Union. Blood spilling over countless battlefields would now answer the political question.

The **Republican Party,** founded in 1854, was a reaction to the Kansas-Nebraska Act expanding slavery to the new territories. The new party opposed any expansion of slavery to the territories; however, many thought it also stood for abolishing slavery, but this was not an immediate goal. In 1860 its candidate for president of the United States, Abraham Lincoln, won the election because he received the most electoral votes. The fact that the southern vote was split actually gave the Republicans the white house. Worst of all, the vote was split along northern and southern lines. The election displayed the extent of the national split. Even though Lincoln was *not* going to abolish slavery, he would stop its expansion to the territories. The South knew they would soon be a minority in the Senate. Lincoln's election triggered the immediate secession of seven Deep South states followed later by the relatively moderate Border States. As Lincoln entered office the secession was underway. From his first moments as president he faced the crisis of the Civil War.

THE TIME LINE TO WAR:

Dec 20, 1860: South Carolina secedes

Jan 1861: Mississippi, Georgia, Alabama, Louisiana, and Florida secede; Texas secedes Feb 1, 1861

Feb 4: The seven seceding states meet in Montgomery, Alabama to draft a Confederate Constitution

March 4: Lincoln's inaugural address. Lincoln states *he will not end slavery* in states where it already existed; however, seven (7) states had by now seceded from the Union. The ones that will later secede (Virginia, North Carolina, Tennessee, and Arkansas) would be some of the most powerful in the Confederacy, but they were still with the Union after Lincoln spoke. Some would, in fact, vote to stay prior to April 15.

April 12: Ft Sumter shelled (April 14, surrenders).

April 15: ***Lincoln calls up 75,000 troops—each state to contribute troops.*** This move outrages Virginia and the other southern states still with the Union.

Apr 17: ***Virginia secedes*** (8th state) on a vote of 88 to 55. Prior to the assault on Ft Sumter, secession was voted down 89 to 45 (April 4). *Virginia was the key state.*

May 6: Arkansas secedes.

May 7: Tennessee secedes.

May 20: North Carolina secedes.

Border States: Missouri, Kentucky, Maryland, Delaware do *not* secede. This was crucial to an eventual Union victory. In1863, W. Virginia was made a Union state by splitting it away from Virginia.

It is arguable that the Southern States seceding *after* April 15 left for reasons other than slavery. In their **Declarations of Disunion,** some say oppression by the Federal Government caused the disunion. Historians ignore these declarations since it is felt they covered up the real cause of secession (slavery); yet, at that moment there was no reason to cover up anything. In fact, Virginia's secession motion was soundly defeated in their legislature just prior to Lincoln calling for troops. Virginia left *after* the call for troops saying they feared Federal oppression. It seems they were telling the truth about their reasons for secession.

Why rush to call up troops when the South harbored no intentions of invading the North? It appears Lincoln hurried into the war. Some Northerners thought that mustering the troops for action alone would end the rebellion. Others thought winning a battle or two might be necessary; nevertheless, they believed a short war was certain. Therefore, most northerners thought calling up the troops was necessary and good at this point. Both Sherman and Grant (famous generals for the North) knew the war would be difficult and long, as did Winfield Scott, the Union's commanding general in 1861. One would hope Lincoln knew the South would fight relentlessly, but why move so quickly to build a Union army and prod it into action? Lincoln must have thought as other northerners did, that the South could be quickly defeated.

Why fight for Fort Sumter when its strategic value was minimal and resupplying it could be very difficult? The reasons for trying to resupply Fort Sumter were probably political. If the South fired the first shots of the conflict they would take on the role of the aggressor. Southern aggression would rally the North to support the war and might keep the South from gaining overseas support.

Lincoln asked *each state* to provide men for the war against the secessionist states; however, such a move would infuriate Virginia as well as other slave holding states. *This action would surely result in Virginia, and others, joining the rebellion thereby increasing the combat and economic power of the Confederacy exponentially.* Almost any move keeping Virginia and other non-secessionist states in the Union was better than driving them out. Why not negotiate with the individual secessionist states in a bid to split a few off and weaken the remainder? The defection of any of the original seven states would cripple the ability of the rest to survive. If political moves could mortally wound the session why not try them? How to lure at least one back? Find a state whose leadership was interested in projects that might buy them off, such as: bringing the transcontinental railroad through their state, building harbor facilities, new roads, or perhaps guarantees on the tariff issue.[128] Lincoln decided to call on the military right away and either ignored the certain results of the move or thought the remaining slave holding states would stay with the Union. However, Virginia had sent unequivocal warnings about the results of using military force against the secession. Lincoln could not have missed those danger signs. Going ahead in the firm knowledge that Virginia, along with other powerful slave holding states, would join the Confederacy was pure insanity. Nonetheless, that was the president's action. Lincoln's claim to greatness comes from his absolute determination to save the Union; however, this inability to handle the secession with anything other than immediate war reflects badly upon him. His moves immediately before and after the inauguration in response to the secession crisis were abysmal.

CASUALTIES

The American Civil War cost the North about six hundred thousand casualties (about 360,000 dead) and the South about four hundred thousand casualties (about 258,000 dead) out of a population of perhaps 32 million for the entire nation (all these are estimates). This puts the military casualty total at about 1 million out of 30 million; thus, a 3 percent casualty rate.[129] The total number of men who were under arms was over 2.2 million in the North and just over 1 million in the South; thus, over 3 million men were under arms, which was 10 percent of the population at the time. Most nations in critical wars manage to field about 10 to 20 percent of their population, and thereafter, they are scrapping the bottom of the manpower[130] barrel. This was the bloodiest war in US history as of 2010 because all the dead and wounded were American.

---

[128] Louisiana was one southern state that was not rabid about leaving the Union and perhaps could have been brought back. If Louisiana stayed Union, the Mississippi would be under Union control, and Texas split off from the rest. This might be a death blow to the Confederacy.

[129] Literally the ***man*** power barrel because women did not fight in this era. During World War II, the Soviets made extensive use of female units; however, the Western Allies did not send women into combat. They were used extensively in noncombat roles.

[130] Casualties include both the dead and the wounded.

STRATEGY—THE NORTH

General Winfield Scott designed the North's war strategy. Scott's plan was to established a **naval blockade** and then **split the South into sectors** which could be defeated one by one if necessary. The first thrust went down the Mississippi to New Orleans. Once the Mississippi River was under Union control Texas would be isolated and could not give aid to the east. The second splitting thrust started in Tennessee and drove to the coast of Georgia, thereby breaking off the resources and men of the Deep South from states farther north. This was termed the *anaconda strategy* after the boa constrictor snake because it squeezed the South into submission; however, except for the naval blockade this was anything but a strangulation strategy. This was an aggressive plan that required extensive offensive action.

General Scott's strategy required extensive sets of armies and a large navy. Southern coastlines were long and peppered with small bays and harbors. A blockade of such a coastline required a substantial navy. The South gained an army and good military leadership upon secession as many excellent officers moved south to support their states. The strategy of General Winfield Scott recognized the need to conquer a map. To split the South into parts required at least two armies, both very large. The same applied to the naval blockade. The North had neither a large army nor navy, but it soon would have. The Federal navy expanded rapidly, and the *blockade was one of the most important parts of winning the war. The blockade destroyed the South's economy* which was just as important as other strategic moves since it substantially weakened the ability of the South to fight. The other naval contribution was the riverboats that successfully bombarded the southern troops and forts in the west as the Union moved down the massive river systems into the South.[131]

Throughout the war Lincoln ran an efficient and focused government. Immediately seeing the strategic weakness of the South, Lincoln knew victory would be his if he just kept fighting. Even after disasters such as Fredericksburg, he knew losses the Union sustained could be replaced, but Southern losses could not. Lincoln also recognized the importance of the blockade. Lincoln threatened war when Great Britain neared the completion of two powerful commerce raiders for the South. England wisely refused delivery. Lincoln became a good military strategist, and

---

[131] The rivers of the west moved *into* the south, thus providing highways to penetrate the defenses. Rivers running *across* the line of advance would have helped the South immensely.

decision makers in the Union government were clear on their goals from the moment the war began.[132] All Lincoln needed was a set of generals equal to his resolve to win. It took time to find them, but after he appointed Grant and Sherman to assault the South the war was won.

STRATEGY—THE SOUTH

The South decided on the classic *cordon defense strategy*, wherein their armies protected invasion routes around the Confederate perimeter and awaited attacks from the North. This strategy is teeming with problems because the defender cannot quickly mass forces against the enemy. When the blow falls the defender is weak at the point of attack and must rally troops to stop the advance. The power of the North also enabled it to invade simultaneously from several directions requiring the South to spread its forces thin. When reading about Hitler's Europe in WWII, we will see the Nazis faced the same problem and adopted the same solution—with the same results.

Early in the war, during the Peninsula Campaign by the Union, **Stonewall Jackson** attempted in vain to convince **Robert E. Lee** and Confederate President **Jefferson Davis** to invade the North. The Union Army of the Potomac was fighting east of Richmond, Virginia, leaving the way north lightly guarded. Jackson advocated an invasion driving for Baltimore, Maryland or Pittsburg, Pennsylvania, and destroying the rail lines and factories located in these regions. Such a strategy would also force the abandonment of the Richmond campaign. If this worked and resulted in an early southern victory, the South could remain intact. Only in this condition would the Confederacy have a chance of surviving as a nation. By waiting for the Union invasion it was bound to lose territory, thereby minimizing its chances of success even if it "won" the war.

With few exceptions the South fought the war with fewer men and on its own soil. It is also estimated as many as 300,000 white male southerners fought for the Union Army, and another 200,000 mostly southern blacks joined the Union as well. A loss of nearly 500,000 men to the North was a telling

---

[132] Some of the Union generals may not have been so clear on the goals. McClellan was accused of wanting the South to suffer as little as possible. McClellan's actions were so incompetent he brought these rumors upon himself. How else could his actions be explained, except by treachery, many thought. Of course, it is always possible he was incompetent in battle. Several Union generals proved to be his equal in this department.

blow to the South. If an infantry division in1860 was about 10,000 men, the defection equals the loss of between 30 to 50 divisions! Some northerners fought for the South, but the numbers are few and speculative.

As their economy fell apart, the southern armies were reduced to rags and very little food (fried corn was a staple). Northern determination to continue the war and its nearly unlimited supply of men and materials crushed the South. As long as the North held its determination and focused its power on achieving victory the South was doomed. Only if the North quit could the war end with a southern victory; however, if we examine this "victory by the South" scenario we might notice a few problems. Assume the North ran out of steam in 1863 after capturing New Orleans, Kentucky, Missouri, and a lot of Tennessee. The remaining South would be in extremely poor shape, and the North would never give back the area it bled to win. The results of such a "victory" are impossible to discern, nevertheless, with its lack of resources, damaged economy, and weak central government the smart money would bet on a quick economic and political failure followed by a request to re-enter the Union.[133] The Confederate states were small in number and resources, hence, a "victory" that lost large tracts of territory to the Union guaranteed the non-viability of the remaining states. Why the South fought on after 1863 and the loss of the Mississippi River is a mystery; although, most pin it on pride (I pin it on stupidity).[134]

The South's political leadership and its governmental system started disjointed and uncoordinated, and then never changed. Many southern state governments held back men and resources to protect their own state, and constantly argued with their central government about recruitment and supplies as the war went on. As a result, the Confederacy failed to maintain its economy, muster troops, or feed and clothe its troops. In a very short time the roads, railroads, economy, and small industrial base were in shambles. The Union blockade stopped the export of cotton and tobacco devastating the Confederate economy. The southern nation only maintained itself through the superhuman exertions of its excellent armies. The Confederate troops held on through hell itself and then some. How

---

[133] Of course, other possibilities abound. The South may have requested to join England or Mexico; but in either event, they would have to abandon slavery. If they had to end slavery why not ban it and then try to rejoin the Union? The scenarios are endless.

[134] You will hear more about this later, but **logistics** are the key to victory in a long modern war. When the South lost its ability to trade by sea, it lost its ability to supply itself. Thus, no supplies and no victory.

these men kept fighting with such astounding bravery and endurance while starving and freezing is remarkable. It is clear from the economic situation of the Confederacy they had lost the war economically before the Battle of Antietam in September of 1862. Yet they fought on, winning victory after victory; nevertheless, the end was not in doubt as long as the Union kept fighting. Lincoln recognized this fact from the first.

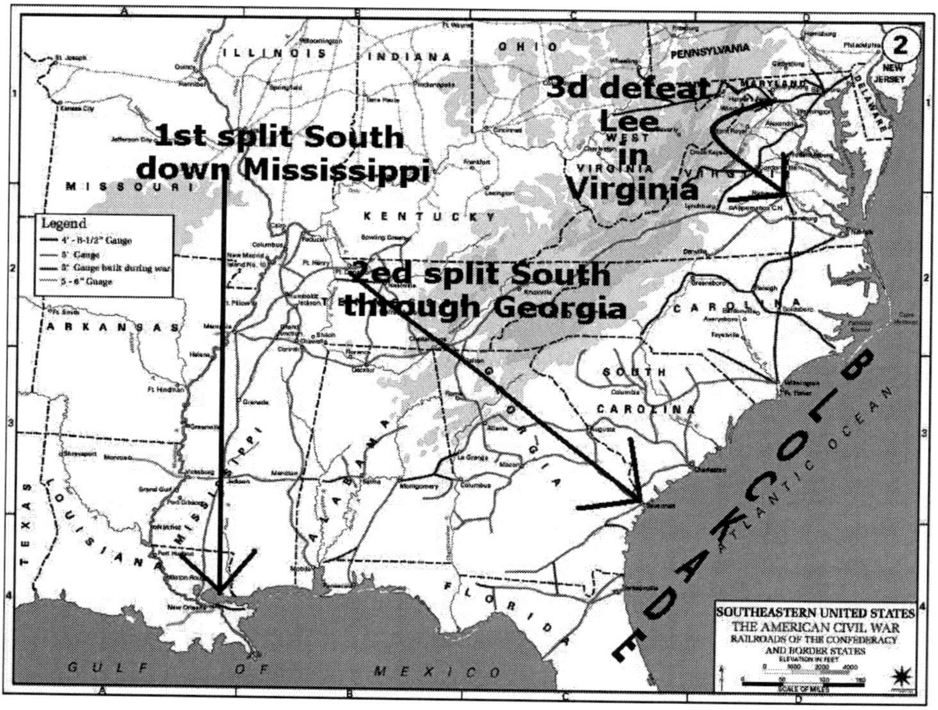

FIGURE 37 PRINCIPLE CAMPAIGNS OF THE CIVIL WAR—
1: SPLIT THE SOUTH DOWN THE MISSISSIPPI,
2: SPLIT THE SOUTH ACROSS GEORGIA,
3: DEFEAT LEE IN VIRGINIA,
4: MAINTAIN A TIGHT NAVAL BLOCKADE

THE WAR BEGINS

There are so many excellent books on the Civil War and its battles there is no need to recount the battles here (a few of the best books are listed at the end of the section); however, a couple of campaigns will be covered along with my opinions on what was going on in the war.

From the outset, Lincoln was determined to keep the South in the Union. After Lincoln's inaugural address, where he said slavery could continue to exist where it was then legal, Virginia voted to stay in the Union. The key Border States were Virginia, Tennessee, and North Carolina. Each of these Border States allowed slavery but did not want a war with the North. After the South fired on the **Fort Sumter**, a federal military post in Charleston Harbor in South Carolina, Lincoln used the event to call up troops to invade the South, thus making a tragic political blunder. He required each state to send men to put down the rebellion. Lincoln told Fort Sumter to fight, and he tried to resupply the fort, thereby guaranteeing the South would fire the first shots of the war. Then Lincoln used the fall of the fort as the reason to call up the troops. Thus, the South firing on Fort Sumter was not a surprise, and calling up troops was planned *before* the Confederates fired on the fort. All this makes it impossible to believe Lincoln tried to avoid the war. It is obvious he decided negations would serve no purpose, and went forward with a plan to start the war on his terms. Unfortunately, his moves pushed the states of Virginia, Tennessee, and North Carolina to join the Confederacy. Not smart. After the second wave of secession, Lincoln negotiated with Maryland, Kentucky, Missouri, and Delaware to keep them in the Union, and they stayed. At least he was a fast learner.

That was it; the Border States seceded because they refused to send their troops against the secessionist states, and because they thought the Federal Government was becoming an oppressor. These Border States, especially Virginia, were the key to maintaining a viable South. When the key Border States joined the secession the power of the rebellion grew dreadfully. After Virginia joined the Confederacy the capital of the rebellion moved to Richmond, Virginia, only a few miles from Washington DC. This small area between the two cities saw a Noah's flood of blood spilled out between the two armies.

FIGURE 38 FT SUMTER BOMBARDMENT—1861

The first battle was at **Bull Run** in Virginia in July 1861. It was a Union defeat, and it gave General Jackson his famous name "Stonewall." As southern troops were about to break during a Union assault on vital Confederate positions, a Confederate officer among them pointed to Jackson and his men saying, "There stands Jackson like a stone wall . . ." Responding gallantly, Confederate troops rallied and drove back the Union attackers. The blow to the Union at Bull Run was significant and led to a new general taking over with orders to get the Union Army of the Potomac ready to fight.

The new general, **George McClellan**, took over on July 26, 1861 and immediately set about creating a good army. In this he was a total success; however, being a good organizer and trainer of men does not make one a good battlefield general. McClellan decided to march on the Confederate capital of Richmond, Virginia, by coming down the peninsula to the east of the city. By coming from the Atlantic Ocean side he achieved surprise, and he outnumbered the Confederate troops significantly; nonetheless, George McClellan was a timid leader. He threw away his chance at an early capture of the Confederate capital via hesitation and fear. As the Union Army inched its way toward Richmond, General Joseph Johnson, commander of the Army of Northern Virginia, fell wounded. This wound changed history. General Robert E. Lee, arguably one of the best military commanders of all time,[135] replaced him. Lee soon put McClellan on the run causing the Union Army to retreat to the Washington DC area. Many Union generals were so dismayed by General McClellan's conduct they called him a traitor. At one point General Lee was attacking the Union positions and gaining little except exorbitant casualties. Worse, the position abandoned to retreat to Washington, DC was the best defensive position of all. If McClellan had dug in and repelled several more Confederate assaults, he may have damaged Lee's Army of Northern Virginia beyond repair. Instead, he fled. Lee had lost so many troops because he was trying desperately to completely destroy the Union army, but the terrain and his subordinates worked against his plans.

Even after several Confederate victories Lee worried about the situation. Following consultations with Jefferson Davis, Lee's army planned to invade Maryland because the state's many southern sympathizers might be persuaded to join the South if an army arrived to assist them. If Maryland joined the rebellion it would be a immense blow to the Union. Lee marched off to Maryland, however, one of Lee's lieutenants lost the entire invasion plan which was soon found by Union forces under McClellan. Someone wrapped the plans in a bunch of cigars and promptly lost the cigars along with the plans. After the plans came to light, McClellan bragged he could crush Lee because under the attack plan Lee divided his already limited forces; therefore, if McClellan attacked a portion of Lee's divided army with his entire Union army he could destroy it before other Confederate units could help. McClellan could then turn and destroy the reduced Rebel army before it retreated to Virginia. Given the larger size of the Union Army, the task should have been within easy reach of even the bungling McClellan; even so, McClellan outdid himself in his search for defeat. The lost plans led to the great battle at Antietam, where McClellan assaulted a portion of Lee's army trapped with its back against the Potomac River.

---

135 Many historians disagree. The brilliant Bevin Alexander in *How Great Generals Win,* thinks Lee was mediocre. I will disagree based on Chancellorsville, and his ability to defend the South for years against an army that outnumbered his, had more and better equipment, and was well fed if not well led. It is true that Lee did not see the early potential of a northern invasion, as suggested by Stonewall Jackson, and he may not have had the vision of Sherman, but he did accomplish a lot with very little and for that he should be remembered as an excellent commander. By the way, *very* few generals have had the vision of Sherman or Jackson.

ANTIETAM AND EMANCIPATION

The great battle at **Antietam** (Sharpsburg) came to pass on September 17, 1862. As usual, McClellan squandered many chances to destroy Lee's trapped army, or at least cause it irreparable harm. After many hours of fruitless frontal assaults against well established Confederate defensive positions the Union attack stalled. At the last moment Lee managed to recombine his divided army, defeat another Union attack, and retreat back from whence he came across the Potomac. McClellan remained frozen in position, thus allowing the battered men in grey to escape. Lincoln was livid and moved to find a new general. Meanwhile, a Maryland woman witnessed the southern troops passing by her home and in her diary wondered if these were the men who had defeated " . . . our gleaming legions." She described the southern soldiers as men in rags, no shoes, and so hungry their ribs were showing. She reported their battle standards were the only non-ragged thing about them. Anyone reading the diary would know the South had already lost in September of 1862.

In spite of the poor outcome at Antietam, Lincoln declared a Union victory and issued the **Emancipation Proclamation** *freeing the slaves held in the southern states still in rebellion.* Note it did *not* free the slaves in states that were not in rebellion such as Kentucky and Maryland. The issue of what to do with these slaves remained until after the war.[136]

Lincoln issued the Emancipation Proclamation as a political move to assure nations overseas, such as England and France, that the North was against slavery. This put the southern cause in a bad light overseas since England and Europe banned slavery years before and did not want to hint at any kind of support for the institution. Now the South could never convince any powerful European nation to sustain it in the war. Gaining European support was a key reason Lee invaded the North. Southern victories in the North might convince some European nations to recognize the Confederacy as a viable state; hence, gaining support for independence. By issuing this proclamation, Lincoln put a major political and strategic dent in southern hopes.

The Proclamation also helped the Union cause within the United States. It gave the Union something more to fight for, because "maintaining the Union" could not carry the weight of the war much longer. The body count

---

[136] The Thirteenth Amendment to the US Constitution ended slavery, and the Fourteenth and Fifteenth protected the civil rights of the former slaves.

required to maintain the Union was already too high for some. However, the proclamation *changed the war aims of the Union.* Now the *federal forces were fighting to set men free* and the South to enslave men. This allowed the Union to withstand much higher casualties and keep fighting. In this Emancipation Proclamation stratagem, Lincoln showed himself to be a masterful politician achieving several significant goals at one stroke.

In the west, Union forces were attacking down the Mississippi River, and the Union Navy seized New Orleans cutting off a major supply route for the South. **Ulysses S. Grant,** placed in charge of the Western Theater of War, took the vital Mississippi River link of **Vicksburg** on July *4, 1863* in what was probably Grant's best campaign. Now the Mississippi River was totally Union, and Texas, Arkansas, and nearly all of Louisiana were cut off from the rest of the South. The Union blockade was stopping all supplies flowing to the Confederate states from overseas. The South was finished, but its leaders demanded it fight on, ignoring the fact there was nothing left to win.

GETTYSBURG

The day before the capture of Vicksburg the Battle of **Gettysburg** ended in the north. Gettysburg's took place from *July 1 to July 3, 1863,* and the cost in men and material was enormous. The South lost *twenty-eight thousand men (28,000)* in the confrontation and the North *twenty-three thousand (23,000).* The North could afford to lose men at this rate, but not the South. Those twenty-eight thousand southerners were veterans of many battles and impossible to replace.

Gettysburg represents General Robert E. Lee's second and last invasion of the North, and perhaps the last chance for victory by the battered South. Lee's men were starving. The entire South was starving, and supplies of clothing, shoes, blankets, food, and other essentials (except gunpowder and bullets) were very low. By invading the North in July, he could forage off Union land rich with crops. In addition, he might be able to draw the Union Army of the Potomac into a decisive battle. Lee realized an overwhelming victory was necessary, one totally overthrowing the Army of the Potomac. Perhaps such a victory would gain foreign support and a peace deal from the Union. If he failed, the South faced grounding down like corn in a mill. After full considerations of the options, the invasion seemed the only reasonable course of action. By just waiting, the Union would come after them again; and Lee's men and horses would have less food than before. By moving north Lee's army could at least eat.

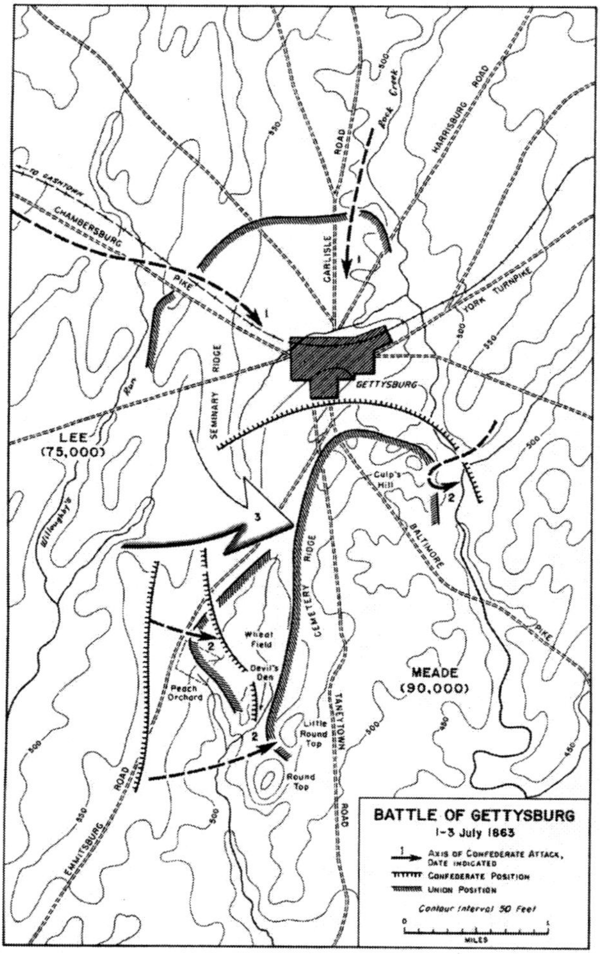

FIGURE 39 GETTYSBURG,—PICKETT'S CHARGE—ARROW LABELED 3

Gettysburg was what military men call a meeting engagement; that is, an unplanned encounter where two armies just run into one another. This was the worst kind of battle for the Confederates to fight. Lee faced a much larger army led by **George Meade**, who was cautious but determined. If nothing else, Meade knew good defensive ground when he saw it, and by taking up positions on Cemetery Ridge and Big and Little Round top he established an impressive defensive situation. At nearly any point before General Pickett's famous charge Lee could have disengaged and looked for another battlefield. Lee needed to plan what to do before the engagement rather than making quick decisions during the engagement. Lee, however, decided to fight at Gettysburg. Why is not clear.

After a series of poor performances by his junior commanders on the flanks of the Union lines, he made a disastrous decision to attack the center of the enemy line on the high ground at Cemetery Ridge. Robert E. Lee had observed the results of mass assaults on prepared positions throughout the war. *This decision to assault a dug in position on high ground defies comprehension.*

Lee seldom made mediocre decisions.[137] Now he made a move that put an end to any hope of the northern invasion working at any level. The battle had been going on for two days when Lee looked to the high ground at the Union center as the place to strike. Not only that, his artillery was short of ammunition and federal cannons were in place opposite him that enjoyed a range and accuracy advantage.[138] Lee was therefore attacking a prepared position covered with artillery. The commander of Lee's artillery told him he could not quiet the federal guns on the ridge before Pickett's assault. One of Lee's senior commanders (Longstreet) objected to the idea from the start, nevertheless, in his most injudicious move of the war, Lee ordered Pickett's Charge.[139]

Pickett's men were a tough bunch. Through accurate rifle fire, grapeshot, and cannon shells pouring in on them from Union positions Pickett's hardened veterans kept going. Somehow, they reached the ridge top achieving a small breakthrough, but Union reinforcements put an end to that and drove Pickett's remnant down the ridge. After the failed attack, Lee feared a Union counterattack that might destroy his army. However, the cautious Meade remained cautious, and once more General Robert E. Lee escaped to continue the war. Meade's caution allowed Lee's escape, but it was that same caution that won the greatest battle to ever take place on American soil. Lincoln's ire was up once more as he learned of Lee's escape. He knew he still needed a fighting general, all the same, fate was turning his way.

---

137 For reasons unknown, Robert E. Lee never wrote a book about the war; thus, many of his decisions go unexplained. This is a great loss to history. Grant's memoirs are highly useful because we get to look into the mind of the man making the decisions.

138 The Union cannons had rifling, and the Confederate cannons did not. Rifling makes a projectile fly straighter.

139 Compare this to George Washington at Boston. He had wanted to assault the city but listened to his fellow commanders when they told him they were against it, which was excellent advice. Lee did not listen to his fellow senior commanders and his men, and his cause, paid dearly.

Grant and Sherman Destroy the South

General **Ulysses S. Grant** had been winning battles in the west for years. From Shiloh to Chattanooga he was unbeaten, and he was aggressive. Lincoln had found his fighting general. On March 12, 1864 Lincoln appointed General U S Grant general of the entire Union army, and Grant immediately appointed General William Tecumseh **Sherman** to command the west. Together they would form an unstoppable juggernaut devastating the South. Grant decided on coordinated assaults; thus, as he started toward Richmond, Sherman started toward Atlanta. Grant began his advance in May of 1864. Now called the **Overland Campaign**, Grant was grabbing Robert E. Lee by the lapels and never letting go. Grant was determined to pummel Lee until his army was destroyed. US Grant was smart enough to know he could not outmaneuver Lee; nevertheless, his men could fight as well as the southerners, and Grant had a lot more of them. Grant knew he would take large casualties, but he never imagined how large they would be as he battered his way toward Richmond.

Grant

Grant first challenged Lee in the **Battle of the Wilderness,** but when victory proved elusive he pulled out of the forested area and then *turned south* toward Richmond. In fact, Lee had won a significant victory, but Grant refused to be beaten. This was a telling move. When the Army of the Potomac lost to the Army of Northern Virginia in previous campaigns the Union generals turned the troops back to Washington DC to lick their wounds and prepare for another try months down the line. Not so this time. When Grant ordered the troops to continue south a cheer went up. The troops (and Lincoln) knew what was necessary all along, now they had the man who would do it.

Lee perceived Grant was moving toward Richmond rather than retreating (proof of an excellent general), so he pulled out of his positions in the Wilderness and got ahead of Grant's army to block him at Spotsylvania where Grant's men again failed to break the southern line. Nevertheless, Grant did not stop. He ordered another flanking movement toward Richmond, and Lee to pulled out to meet the Union movement once more. This pattern continued as Grant moved south consistently. Lee's army never broke, but Grant never quit. At Cold Harbor, Grant made the classic error of attacking a well-prepared fixed position across open ground, and the results were bloodcurdling. Grant ordered the attack hoping to catch the Rebels before they could prepare their defenses. In ***eight minutes*** the Union lost ***8,000*** men—one thousand per minute! Grant swiftly ended the assault. Still, Grant did not stop. The Union casualties were piling up, but Grant moved ever forward to Richmond.

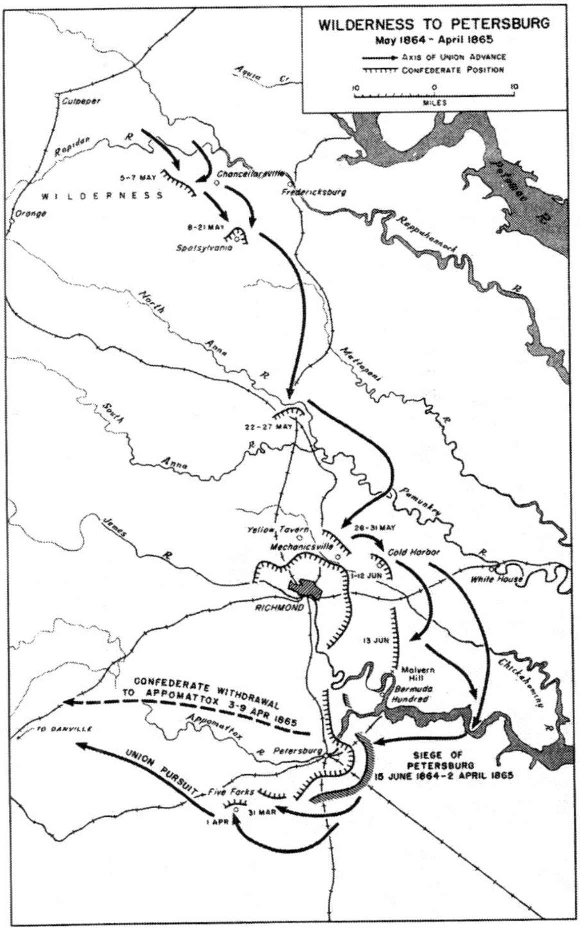

FIGURE 40 GRANT'S OVERLAND CAMPAIGN

In the course of *seven weeks,* Grant lost *sixty-five thousand men.140* As Grant moved to the east and south of Richmond to **Petersburg,** Lee's men dug

---

[140] At Waterloo, the total losses were about *fort-seven thousand* men killed and wounded between all three armies (English, Prussian, and French). After more than 3 *years* fighting in Iraq the US lost about 5,000 men and the public wanted an end to it. Time does change things.

in, and the two armies became locked in trench warfare for nine months in a bloody and terrible prelude to World War I. The main difference between this trench warfare and World War I was equipment, such as the lack of machine guns, heavy howitzers, sophisticated artillery shells, and quick-firing bolt-action rifles. Even under conditions where the defense was muzzle-loaded rifles and cannons, the Union could not break through because of the intense defensive fire.

Think how much harder it would be against machine guns and modern rifles. The American Civil War was the first modern war, but the Europeans avoided studying the American Civil War calling it a fight between two armed mobs. The world missed what was going on. *This was modern war, and it would only get worse.*

A lesser president may have given up after seeing the casualties and the stalemate; however, Lincoln never faltered. Winning the war was all.

With Lee's men in trenches to the front, Grant decided to extend his trenches causing the Confederates to do the same to protect their flanks. However, Grant was not flanking Lee, he was trying to thin out the Confederate line by making them cover additional ground. It worked, and in a surprise attack at **Five Forks** on April 1, 1864, the Confederate line broke. Grant's men flooded into Richmond, raising the stars and stripes over the Confederate capitol.

SHERMAN

To the west, as Grant began the Overland Campaign, **Sherman** started his attack to reach Atlanta, Georgia, and then the sea. No southern army could stop Sherman. General **Joseph Johnson** commanded the Army of Tennessee and, conservative by nature, he avoided risking the loss of too many men in action. If Sherman were to destroy his army the South had nothing left. General Johnson attempted to force Sherman to attack prepared defenses, but Sherman avoided such attacks. Knowing assaults on prepared defenses was suicide, Sherman kept finding ways to circumvent Johnson's defensive lines forcing the Rebels back toward Atlanta. In one instance, Sherman almost got a blocking force positioned to trap Johnson's entire army, but a subordinate moved to an inappropriate location losing the chance to destroy the Army of Tennessee. Time after time, Sherman consistently forced Confederate retreats out of well prepared defensive lines, thereby winning battles without heavy fighting. Sherman's campaign to win Atlanta was brilliant in all respects as he accomplished the goal of the campaign with few Union losses. No other civil war general did as much with so few losses, with the possible exception of Bedford Forrest, the commander of various Confederate cavalry units.

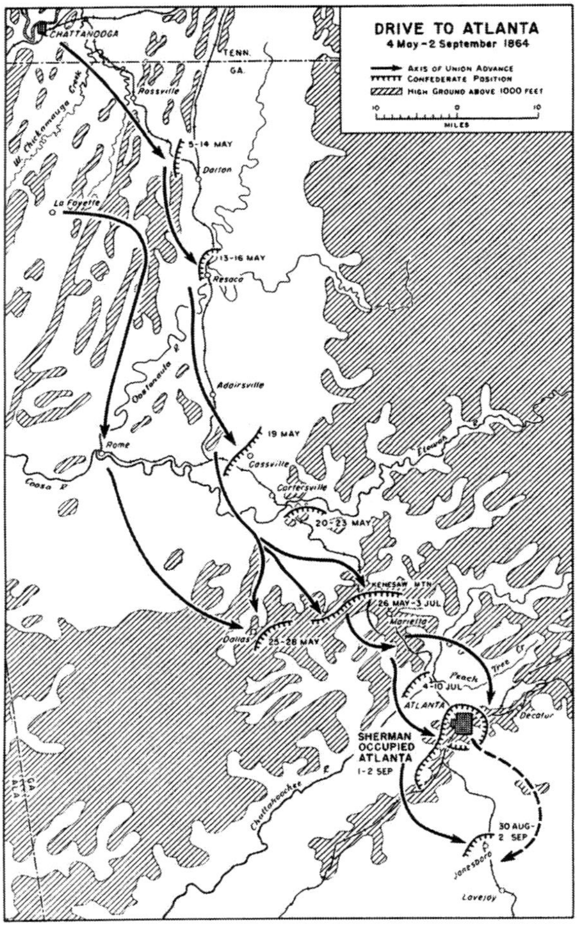

FIGURE 41 SHERMAN TAKES ATLANTA—1864

By conserving his men, Johnson at least put Sherman at constant risk. The Army of Tennessee was a tough veteran unit not to be underestimated. Johnson's strategy infuriated the political leaders of the South who demanded an all out assault to defeat Sherman.[141] Johnson dared not take such a risk so they replaced him with General **John Bell Hood.** Hood was

[141] More proof of how incompetent they were.

reckless—at times to the extreme. He was a poor choice to lead the Army of Tennessee, the last army between Sherman and the deep south. Hood assumed command as Sherman's forces moved on Atlanta, Georgia.

At the Battle of Atlanta on July 20, 1864, Hood attacked Sherman's army. He set up a plan to roll up Sherman's flank and deliver a blow to his rear-supply areas. By attacking Sherman's supply line Hood hoped to damage the Union army's logistic situation enough to stop the advance. At least focusing on logistics was the correct strategy. The Confederates needed to get at the Union's supply and communication line (there was only one rail line) and block it to stop the advance.[142] Johnson missed his chance to accomplish the same thing earlier in the campaign. In the event, Hood miscalculated the time and distances involved, and Union troops held on to vital areas, destroying the Confederate plan. Hood lost a large number of men and achieved nothing.

After a series of excellent moves to confound Hood and cut *his* supply lines, *Sherman took Atlanta on September 2, 1864,* thereby sealing a military victory and an electoral victory. Seizing Atlanta virtually guaranteed Lincoln's re-election to a second term. For unclear reasons, the city of Atlanta burned to the ground. Perhaps the fire was started by Hood's retreating army blowing up stores or by Sherman's army deciding to torch it, no one really knows. The results were clear; Atlanta all but ceased to exist. Sherman took Atlanta's population south by train and then made them debark for the countryside. In doing this, Sherman released thousands of starving, homeless southerners onto their neighbors who could ill afford to take care of them.

After the fall of Atlanta, Hood's army mustered thirty thousand troops to oppose Sherman's eighty thousand plus men, so Hood decided to march north toward Nashville and the Union's railroad and supply centers at that location. Hood's attack came to naught, except for the complete destruction of his army, thereby allowing Sherman a free hand for the rest of his campaign. For the rest of his operation, Sherman's army faced little to no organized southern opposition. Sherman marched from Atlanta to Savannah, Georgia, and burned and destroyed everything along the way.[143]

---

[142] This would have forced Sherman to attack well-prepared Confederate positions blocking his supply lines, thereby costing him dearly in men.

[143] *Sherman's march to the sea.* This was truly modern war. The target was the civilian population of the South. After this operation, there would be no such thing as civilians in war. Everyone was now a target. In spite of treaties and other documents

By the time Sherman reached the Atlantic Coast at Savannah his reputation as a destroyer of life and property was well secured. Sherman's aim was to completely demolish the economy of the South and thereby end the war as soon as possible. "War is hell," he would famously say, and few in Georgia would argue the point. After Savannah was reached, Sherman turned north to ravage South Carolina and trap Lee between his army and Grant's.

Even after the fall of Richmond, the burning of Atlanta, the devastation of Georgia, and the annihilation of their every army, the southern political leaders tried to fight on. They thought by reaching Texas the rebellion might survive under their continued encouragement. Lee saw no way out. As the Union army was pursuing his army from Richmond, he stopped at **Appomattox Court House** and requested an audience with General US Grant. It was there Lee surrendered the Army of Northern Virginia on *April 9, 1865.* Other ragged, starving Confederate armies surrendered soon thereafter, and the political leaders of the South fell into captivity before they got very far (some dressed as women). Lee showed himself to be the consummate American when he ordered his army home. He could have told his army to fight on in guerrilla style in the hills and mountains of the land, but he did not, even though many counseled him to do so. Lee decided it should be totally over. An extended guerrilla war, deepening the burning hatred of each side, might destroy what was left of the nation. Certainly, the North's response to such southern actions could have been repressive in the extreme.

Lincoln was prepared to admit the South back into the Union without punishment. During the war the Union's war aims expanded as the number of dead alone demanded more than just saving the Union. The Union agenda soon included abolishing slavery as a key war aim. President Lincoln was shot dead by John Wilkes Booth on *April 15, 1865,* just a few days after Lee's surrender at Appomattox Court House. His death removed the main obstacle to the Radical Republican agenda of punishing the South for its rebellion. At this point, a surprising split developed between the new

---

trying to say otherwise, the fact is that every member of the opposing state is now a valid target for death and destruction. The bombing of civilians in WWII by both the Axis and the Allies, the atrocities of the Japanese, Germans, Soviets involving not only soldiers in uniform but civilians as well, and the latest terrorists attacks of the 21st Century, clearly show there are no civilians. The slaughter of Christians by Muslims, the slaughter of everything and everyone by the Mongols, the complete destruction of ancient cities by the Assyrians, show that this has long been the case, but somehow people cannot accept this blatant fact.

president, Andrew Johnson, and Congress. President Andrew Johnson was a Democratic senator from Tennessee when that state seceded from the Union; however, Johnson stayed on in the Senate, as he was pro-Union. The other southern senators resigned as their states joined the rebellion. Lincoln chose Johnson as a running mate to widen the appeal of the Lincoln ticket to pro-Union Democrats. The Radical Republicans had decided the ideology fomenting the war was to be crushed out of the South. President Johnson tried to put Lincoln's ideas into action, but this entailed opposing the Radical Republicans in Congress who believed they alone possessed the legal right to structure and run the Reconstruction of the South. Johnson, as Lincoln before him, thought Southern Reconstruction flowed from the executive branch as part of the war powers. Incensed by Johnson's opposition, the House of Representatives **impeached** him, and failed by only *one vote* to remove him from office. Nonetheless, the Radicals marginalized President Johnson by enacting their program of southern "reform" over his objections.

RECONSTRUCTION OF THE SOUTH

1865 to 1877

Funny Name, Bad Results? What'd you mean you can't tell?

The war of shot and shell had ended, but the war of words and legislation, ideas and ideologies, continued. The period of **Reconstruction** was a legislative and cultural war that went on for twelve years, or more, and cleaved profound divides into the "restored" Union. This is one of the most controversial periods in US history, as some view the era as one of great social experimentation with significant successes, and others think it was an outright occupation of American territory and the denial of Constitutional rights to ex-Confederates. If a better peace is the purpose of war (remember Scipio at Carthage?), then the North certainly failed to achieve the objective. Certain events, such as the destruction of the agriculturally rich Shenandoah Valley, Sherman's devastating march to the sea, the Union blockade starving women and children in the South, and other northern war activities, although no doubt shortening the war, caused southerners to believe the North treated them as savages. Southerners thought they fought against oppression, but the Union treated them all like slave holders. The hatred engendered by the war failed to dissolve. Reconstruction fell far short of helping the traumatized nation recover, as once again the South bowed to overwhelming northern force.

The Radical Republicans under their leaders Representative **Thaddeus Stevens** and Senator **Charles Sumner**, considered the South conquered territory and totally under federal control. In addition, they thought Congress controlled Reconstruction issues, not the president. Issues such as who should be allowed to vote (ex-Confederates, blacks, etc.), how the rebel states should be allowed back into the Union, how the residents should be taxed, whether blacks should be allowed to hold public office, and many others were decided along ideological lines drawn hard between the radicals and the moderates in Congress. In the election of 1866, Radical Republicans gained enough congressional seats to override presidential vetoes; thus, the South was controlled by Radical Republicans in Congress, the Carpetbaggers,[144] Freedmen (free blacks), and US Army. Congress decided that readmission to the Union required a state's voters to swear allegiance to the US Constitution and ratify recent Constitutional amendments, among several other actions. Northern states, logically concerned about the old southern leadership resuming its role and putting former slaves into economic bondage in place of legal bondage, began searching for ways to keep the Negros free and the old south suppressed. Former southern slave owners must not be allowed to resume their pre-war society. Congress, under Republican radical leadership, passed civil rights acts guaranteeing blacks the right to vote and preventing actions to restrict that right. Congress also passed numerous government service laws requiring southern states to provide education and care for orphans and the insane among other social endeavors long available only in the North.[145]

Southerners thought the Union was destroying their culture and taking away their constitutional rights. Even after their loss, southerners were proud of their "cause" and still believed they were right to leave the Union. Union actions proved to most southerners that oppression was the ultimate northern goal. Some southerners fought back violently in the form of mystic groups such as the Ku Klux Klan, but most just wanted to get back to work and restore their economy. Union troops stationed in the South were an occupying army for more than a decade as southern

---

144 The Carpetbaggers were northerners who moved south during Reconstruction for economic and political advantage. They bought plantations, became wealthy landowners, and managed, with the help of Freedmen in the state legislatures, to buy up southern railroads. By 1870, the Carpetbaggers controlled 21 percent of southern RR by mileage. By 1890, they controlled 88 percent of the RR by mileage and held an average of 47 percent on the boards of directors for the southern RR.

145 P. 184 et seq, *The Stakes of Power, 18945-1877,* Nichols & Berwanger, 1982

states gradually regained admission to the Union. The last state to regain statehood was Georgia in 1870.

An economic downturn called the **Panic of 1873** caused the Republican Party to lose seats in the House and Senate reducing the Radical Republican's strength. Political events in 1876 finally ended Reconstruction. In the presidential election of 1876 a dispute arose over who won, Rutherford Hayes (R) or Samuel Tilden (D). Tilden, the Democrat, won the popular vote, but because of a third party candidate neither Hays nor Tilden gained enough electoral votes to win the presidency; however, the Democrat needed only one electoral vote to take the presidency. This deadlock threw the election into the Congress. What happened is a mystery; however, most say a deal ended the deadlock, and Republican Rutherford B. Hays became president after winning all the disputed electoral votes. The deal seemed to be that Union troops would leave the South. The Union troops marched out in 1877. Soon thereafter the white southern culture rebounded, finding ways to limit black voting by restrictions not openly based on race. The methods successfully ended black suffrage in the South for about 100 years.

The Reconstruction era added *three Constitutional Amendments*: the **Thirteenth Amendment** abolished slavery; the **Fourteenth Amendment** gave citizenship to all persons born in the United States or naturalized and established civil rights for all citizens; the **Fifteenth Amendment** secured the right to vote no matter what a person's race, color, or previous condition of servitude. These amendments did not pass easily, and their provisions raise serious questions today because the southern states, not yet back in the Union, did not vote on the Amendments. *Please note that the Fifteenth Amendment failed to give women the right to vote.* Odd as it may seem, men of all races would have the right to vote but no woman could vote.[146]

As President Grant assumed his second term scandals and corruption were rife. Newspapers found immense corruption in the Federal government and the Reconstruction governments in the South causing Republicans to lose political power. With western farmers asking for cheap money (greenbacks—paper money not backed by gold or silver) and no tariffs,

---

146 Women are not a "minority" because they outnumber men; however, the US Supreme Court classified them as a minority (granting them the status of a protected class) because they have traditionally been treated as a minority. Once again, we have a court imposing a total fiction on the people through the use of its power to tell the nation what the Constitution means.

and the eastern businesses battling for tight money (money backed by gold or silver) and high tariffs, the Republicans lost voters in the west. As the South came back into the Union all the previously Confederate states voted universally for Democrats; thus, Republicans started losing governorships, senatorial seats, and soon would lose the House of Representatives altogether. As the blacks came under increasing pressure in the South, Republicans balked at responding fearing the loss of even more political power. When the Republican Party restrained its Congressional actions the states stepped in and started handling previously federal issues as local matters. The South refused to obey Federal laws on voting, and eventually the Supreme Court struck down the Reconstruction civil rights laws Republicans had pushed through during Reconstruction.

The Civil War era had ended at last, or so it seemed in 1877. However, it had not. In the 1960s, under the leadership of Martin Luther King and others, blacks in the South again attempted to gain the civil and voting rights enjoyed by white citizens of the United States. The civil rights movement once again caused the North to attack the South, only this time legislatively through its majorities in Congress. Northern institutions began to pound southern culture using the federal courts and federal law enforcement. Northern newspapers and TV reporters characterized southerners as Neolithic in customs and culture; therefore, the South fully deserved harsh punitive measures for their treatment of blacks. This propaganda was like that used by the abolitionists in 1860 to stir emotions in the North against the South. It worked in 1860, and it worked in 1960. Eventually, large numbers of laws passed giving additional protection to minorities. The power of the courts would grow immensely during this legislative, legal, and media onslaught against southerners.

In 1960, Southern States subtlety and openly discriminated against blacks. During the WWI era, President Woodrow Wilson's Administration ignored discriminatory laws passed in the South. Over time these *Jim Crow laws* became more separatist in nature. The US Supreme Court upheld this societal and legal separatism declaring "separate but equal" was Constitutional. In fact, the facilities were unequal. Many white southerners disliked these laws; however, nothing changed until black activists began to demonstrate, risking arrest for defying discriminatory statutes. Once the nation became aware of the plight of the southern blacks millions rallied to their cause. In Congress, especially the US Senate, the South held powerful committee chairmanships and were the senior members of the ruling Democratic party in 1965. The southern Congressmen voted as a block, so the remaining northern Democrats could not gain a majority on discrimination issues. Only by joining with the Republican Party could northern Democrats overcome the southerners voting power. Over the objections and obstructions of southern Congressmen, Congress pushed through civil rights legislation to protect minorities. The president, Texas southerner and liberal Lyndon B. Johnson, signed these bills into law. It was perhaps Johnson's greatest achievement.

The press, especially the electronic media (TV, radio), played a major role in bringing the nation's attention to the quandary of the blacks. The press, however, went overboard in condemning southern culture and laws. Not every southern white in 1960 supported discrimination; however, the northern press painted the South with a broad brush making it sound as if every white southerner was racist by birth.

What occurred as a result of this pressure was a change in the law for the better, but it also resulted in a tremendous growth of power in the federal governments—especially the Federal Courts, and the US Supreme Court. By using racial discrimination as its platform federal courts expanded their power to rule exponentially. For example, courts forced busing on local jurisdictions causing local governments to expend large amounts of money by order of the court. In effect, the courts were telling legislatures how to spend money when the US Constitution, and all state constitutions, clearly set forth only the House of Representatives, or its state equivalent, has the power and legal right to spend money. The courts took on the role of unelected legislators not subject to any oversight by the people. When the US Supreme Court held state legislatures must be based on population alone, it was a direct blow at the peoples' right to choose how they were governed. The courts interfered with law enforcement, schools, local employment, and other facets of local governance and private life. Courts added to the powers of the federal government and truncated the powers of state governments immensely as a direct result of the crusade against racism. Many commentators opined race was a ruse to increase central government power, including the power of the federal courts; and, in fact, much less intervention was necessary to solve the legal and cultural problems of racism.

AFTERMATH—THE IMPACTS OF THE CIVIL WAR

The greatest impact of the Civil War was the saving of the Union. The second greatest impact was the considerable growth in power of the federal government. The power of the presidency grew enormously, as did the powers of Congress.

By extension, the power of the states significantly decreased. Today, few think anything about federal government involvement in local schools, local government, prescription drugs, medical care, vehicle safety, and on and on. Before the Civil War this would have been an outrage. Today, the federal government directly takes huge amounts of people's salaried earnings—considerably more than the local government takes; however, before the Civil War the federal government did not tax individuals directly, and it controlled far less money than the states. After the Civil War everything changed. Another enormous change was in the economy. The Civil War expanded the industrial economy of the North and helped to make the United States a world power of industrial production.

Let Us Learn

What can the Civil War have to say to us? How about *moderation* and understanding are all important in human relations, and impatience leads to trouble. The South went off half cocked and destroyed themselves. The Union sought to pressure people harshly, and almost destroyed themselves. Keep cool, be ready to bargain, know the other side, understand what they hold dear, and realize that half a loaf is better than none.

Another important historical lesson involves learning where things are going, and adjusting to the direction. After 1862, and the loss at Antietam, the South needed to get real and just settle with the Union. At that point Lincoln might have accepted a deal freeing the slaves and in return give the South monetary help to rebuild their shattered economy. This deal would leave the South unoccupied, its economy still half-way intact, and could reduce the punishment the Radicals were ready to bestow. *Learn to cut your losses.* If things are going bad, get out. Take the hit and keep the ability to control your destiny to some extent. With the war going against them, but still not real badly, the South kept fighting. Don't do that. Life is not a football game where there is always next season. Life often hands us situation in which there really is no tomorrow. The best time for the South to approach the Union for a settlement was after a significant Southern victory like Chancellorsville (April 30, 1863). With a proper calculation of where the war was going the South could have chosen a good moment to approach Lincoln, thus bettering its chances of getting a decent deal. However, even if the deal was unconditional surrender the South should have taken it early on. Cut your losses, take what you can salvage, and build up for the next project. That is how to survive and prosper.

BOOKS AND RESOURCES:

Great Books on the American Civil War (There are hundreds of books on the Civil War; a few are great, and a few of the great ones are listed below).

Bruce Catton: his writings include many wonderful books on the Civil War (*Mr. Lincoln's Army, Glory Road, A Stillness at Appomattox, The Coming Fury, The Terrible Swift Sword, Never Call Retreat, Grant Moves South, Grant Takes Command,* and others).

James M. McPherson: *The Battle Cry of Freedom* (my favorite one-volume work on the Civil War), *Ordeal by Fire: the Civil War and Reconstruction.* **I highly recommend** *The Battle Cry of Freedom.*

Shelby Foote: *The American Civil War, a Narrative History*. Excellent set of books.

A Battlefield Atlas of the Civil War, Symonds, the Nautical and Aviation Publishing Company, 1994.

The American Civil War (West Point Military History Series), Editor T. Griess, Square One Publishing, 2002. The West Point publications are always superb.

The Stakes of Power 1845-1877, Nichols, and Berwanger, Hill and Wang, 1982

FROM THE CIVIL WAR TO 1900

INDUSTRIAL EXPANSION

From the end of the Civil War until 1900 was a period of relative peace and prosperity in the United States.[147] The power of America's industrial base continued to grow. During this time Rockefeller, Carnegie, and other industrialists consolidated economic might into monopolies or trusts; and financial wizards like **J.P. Morgan** built financial empires spanning the globe. To demonstrate the power of these men we note that J. P. Morgan bailed out the US Treasury after the financial panic of 1893-1895 when a gold drain threatened the nation's money value. Think about that for a moment, *one man* possessed the financial power to save the US Treasury. In 1869, the transcontinental railroad linked the US east to west with the driving of the golden spike in Utah, and the Panama Canal opened, linking the Atlantic and Pacific Oceans through the small isthmus connecting North and South America. This canal was vital to US military and economic interests because it allowed linking the East and West Coasts of the United States by sea, avoiding the extremely long sea route around Cape Horn at the tip of South America. In **1876, Alexander Graham Bell** invented the telephone and revolutionized communication.

---

[147] "Only" one war, the Spanish American War in 1898 . . . oh . . . and a small invasion of Mexico when Pershing was chasing Poncho Villa.

Other occurrences were starting to influence the nation. Western farmers since the end of the Civil War were under great economic pressure because of the government's refusal to sponsor cheap money; that is, go off the gold standard and print money thereby causing inflation. To overcome some of the problems of the era farmers formed the Grange, an organization helping farmers modernize farming methods, and increasing their political power. The Democrats soon learned to harness the votes of these folks by appealing to their special needs. In the industrial areas of the nation workers began forming unions. One of the first large unions, the National Labor Union, had a real influence on the election of 1872. The membership and power of these early labor unions grew until the Panic of 1873, after which the number of unemployed swelled substantially; thus, shrinking union power. Nonetheless, the power of reform movements to stop government corruption, and help the workers and farmers, advanced during the late 1800s. The resurgent Democrats were the main beneficiaries of these movements. Liberal Republicans wanted similar reforms but failed to gain control of their party. This philosophical split reduced the power of the Republican party.

The Panic of 1873 was severe. In 1866 and 1870, Europe suffered through two wars of limited extent; still, these wars brought on recessions and numerous European business failures. Europeans sold their American securities driving down the price, and reducing their value as collateral held on loans. This in turn affected American banks holding these securities as collateral making their financial positions weaker (for more information on depressions and the accompanying financial mumbo jumbo see our discussion of the Great Depression). In the USA there was no central bank, leading to an inability to transfer funds from bank to bank. For example, a bank failing in Kansas would need money to stay open; however, it would have a hard time getting additional funds from New York banks that held all the cash. Worse, if the New York banks began to fail they could literally make it impossible to for other banks to get money (capital) to continue business operations (remember, they held almost all the money), leading to a chain of failures.

Then the next blow fell. The railroads needed money because shipping was down and the investment houses put money into them thus draining the New York banks of their financial reserves (now no bank had money). When major bank drafts (checks) began showing up New York banks held no money to meet the demand—so they shut their doors (wow, sounds like 1929, 2008 etc). Of course, this caused a wave of bank failures followed by businesses bankruptcies. Between 1873 and 1878, business failures went from 500 per year to *10,000 per year*, and about *40 percent* of the nation's factory workers lost their jobs. The price farmers received for their products fell dramatically. This caused a demand for relief, mainly through cheap money polices, such as the unlimited coinage of silver. Farmers, among others, wanted inflation. Inflation would allow the sale of crops for more than they paid to grow them. Tight money policies forced farmers to sell crops at about the same price it cost to grow them, leaving farmers no profit. As tight money policies continued states passed legislation bringing some railroad cheats under control.[148] At least the legislation against railroad discrimination provided the farmers some relief from overly expensive transportation costs.

The Panic of 1873 did not end until 1879, and unemployment hit 14 percent by 1876. The economic problems led to railroad strikes and violence when President R. B. Hayes called in Federal troops to end the strikes. All of this led to political problems for the Republicans. As a result of the long depression the Democrats won the House of Representatives in 1874. Similar events were taking place in Europe, but Europe recovered faster.

Much of the progress from 1864 to 1900 was wonderful for the common person. The average American (or European) gained the ability to travel from coast to coast, talk to friends over the telephone, and buy goods from all over the world. However, like all changes, it also brought undesirable results. The urban world brought urban squalor and intense poverty. It seems as people advance technologically they stayed the same emotionally and intellectually. Reformers arose and challenged society to fix these problems, but they were never fixed; however, it was not from lack of trying. Recall these reformers came forward and demanded society "do something" about the plight of the underclass during an age of progress when society thought any problem could be solved. Unfortunately, nothing any government tried since 1750 solved the problem of urban poverty and the disassociation from society caused by world modernization. The new, larger, and more powerful cities created new, larger, and relatively powerless groups of people struggling along on next to nothing while living hungry

[148] For example, the Illinois legislature passed laws controlling railroad rate setting because railroads favored large terminals over smaller ones, and either would not service small terminals or would charge a lot more to service them. These kinds of practices favored larger shippers over small ones, and effectively gave the large city merchants a decided advantage over the small merchants due to the price of transporting goods to market. See p. 210-226 et seq, *The Stakes of Power 1845-1877*, Nichols & Berwanger, 1982.

and often immoral lives. In turn, this group gave birth to children who fared no better, so the cycle of poverty, immorality, crime, drug use, filthy living conditions, and exploitation continued unabated.

The new cities were (and are) massive, and the problems of this struggling class are unsolvable (so far). Urban reformers always wailed for more money to give these careworn folks, but giving them money failed. Feeding and clothing them at public expense, and trying to train them for productive work, among other efforts, failed consistently. The problem with urban reforms, stopping drug addition, preventing alcohol abuse, limiting crime, feeding the poor, and helping the underprivileged, all turn on the one invariable of history—human nature. Reforms will fail as long as human nature remains the same. How can we know that? History tells us so. From ancient Rome to modern New York the results of these programs are always the same, total failure. Why? Because human nature stays the same. For unknown reasons, human nature does not allow anything, including better living conditions, extra money, gifts, training, or education, to change its basic character. Criminals stay criminals, prostitutes stay prostitutes, lazy folks remain lazy; thus, all the reforms tried by all the societies that ever existed failed to change these facts. Somehow, this lesson of history remains unlearned. New theories of social reform, new psychology, and new government programs consistently came forth with ever increasing financial demands on the average person to pay up and pull these people out of poverty and squalor. However, nothing ever worked. Rome, Great Britain, America, and an endless parade of other societies tried numerous solutions; still, the urban underclass and their problems remained.

It seems strange to mention that as all this urbanization and modernization was going on one Colonel George Armstrong **Custer**, along with 265 of his men, underwent a butchering by Sioux warriors at the Little Bighorn River in 1876. This displays the many contrasts on the American scene. "Wild Indians" were attacking cavalry units in the west while people were planning to string telephone lines over paved city streets in the East.

In 1850, most Americans wanted to stay out of world affairs. The same was true in 1900 because the nation was fundamentally isolationist. However, powerful men wanted the United States in the world arena, and to that end they would build up the American military and project the nation onto the world stage. In 1885, Josiah Strong published *Our Country*, which argued for American Imperialism. How could a nation that rebelled against British Imperialism now want to embrace the very thing it fought so hard to jettison? Under Secretary of the Navy **Theodore Roosevelt** the US

Navy expanded and modernized its fleet. It seems politicians always want more power both at home and on the world scene. So it was that in 1898, Cuba became the center of US attention, mostly through US newspapers demanding war with Spain.

AMERICA BECOMES AN IMPERIAL POWER—1898

On February 15, 1898, an explosion aboard the USS *Maine* anchored in Cuba's Havana Harbor sunk the ship, killing and injuring many men. An ammunition accident in the battleship's forward main battery probably caused the enormous explosion.[149] American newsmen, blaming the Spanish government for placing a mine, shrieked for war against Spain. Much to the joy of the Hurst newspaper chain Spain's diplomatic overtures fell on deaf ears. The United States declared war on April 21, 1898. **The Spanish-American War** was a short, sharp conflict where the US Navy under Commodore George Dewey managed to defeat the Spanish fleet at Manila Bay in the Philippines on May 1, 1898, and the US Army defeated the Spanish in a series of battles in Cuba centered on the city of Santiago. Theodore Roosevelt was in Cuba leading the charge of the Rough Riders (who were foot soldiers) up the critical position of San Juan Hill. After several battles the Spanish defenders of Cuba surrendered at Santiago on July 17, 1898. Defeats in Cuba and the Philippines convinced Spain to throw in the towel. The Americans acquired significant Spanish possessions in the Caribbean and the Pacific. Thus, America became an imperial power gaining the Philippines, Cuba, Guam, Wake Island, and Puerto Rico from Spain. Cuba gained independence rather soon in comparison to the Philippines that remained a virtual colony for decades. The people in the Philippines did not like US imperial rule any better than Spanish imperial rule and revolted against the United States in 1899. This blood-spattered guerrilla insurrection went on for years, ending in 1902 with the United States declaring the Philippines unorganized territory whose people were not US citizens.

So now the United States fought rebellions in its imperial territory much like England in 1776. A weird circumstance brought about by leaders in the US Government, and the US news media, desiring world power for the United States. As such, they copied England, as Germany and the rest of Europe did, and created an overseas empire. The United States could not compete with the British, a major trading and financial partner, but some

---

[149] US battleships were named after states.

leaders in America wanted their share of the international spotlight; so, they created an empire, small as it was. As time marched on Cuba became a thorn in the side of the US Government for decades (after Castro), and the Philippines required an immense sum of money and lives to free it from Japan's conquest in World War II. After WWII the US quickly got rid of its colonial "empire." Overall, this imperial adventure proved costly in the extreme for the United States of America.

Copying Britain

Throughout the 1800s, nations desiring world power copied the greatest of world powers at the time, the United Kingdom, by seeking colonies and empires. It seems a bit odd trying to gain a world empire in 1900, because England, Holland, and France already controlled most of the world, so little remained for the Johnny-come-lately. Nations like Germany and the United States needed to follow a different path to greatness, but no one had any ideas on how else to do it. And, naturally, just as everyone began wanting an empire the Imperial Age became an anachronism, ending because colonies were hard to keep. Between putting money into them for development, other financial outlays became constant and necessary to protect the original investment. The overall costs were more than the benefits derived, but few noticed at the time. England's imperial system created a preferred trade zone where exchanges within the British Empire were duty free. Britain protected the sea-lanes, built railroads to bring goods to market, and otherwise expended effort to gain more benefit from its colonies. To make this work Britain needed several colonies with a wide variety of raw materials and locally manufactured goods. Unless another nation could recreate this variety of resources *and* pour a lot of money into infrastructure development the payoff was not there for gaining colonies. The English put the infrastructure in place over many decades; thus, the funds were sunk costs, and maintenance alone could hold the infrastructure together. New nations on the colonial scene had a lot of expensive catching up to do, as the USA, Germany, Italy and others were to find out. Smart political leadership looks for new ways to achieve goals, but smart political leadership is a rare commodity; thus, new nations chased England and France to become world powers. Not smart. At least the US kept it small and did not get upset when more could not be acquired. Germany would react differently.

From 1800 to 1900, industrial and technological development around the world continued. Especially important was the development of ***electricity***.

From about 1800, when Alessandra **Volta** invented the battery, to 1886 when **Nikola Tesla** invented alternating current, the new phenomenon of electricity was showing what the future could look like. **Michael Faraday** invented the electric motor in 1821 and this allowed the use of electricity for an ever-increasing number of applications. The invention of alternating current propelled the world forward into a new age of power some have termed the *second industrial revolution.* Tesla invented so many modern concepts he is called the *Father of the Modern World.* Some of his accomplishments include alternating current, the induction motor, the rotating magnetic field, wireless technology, and the US Supreme Court deemed Tesla the true inventor of the radio. In 1884 in Britain, **Parson**'s steam turbine was unveiled. In 1885, **Daimler** of Germany created the internal combustion engine.[150] In 1895, the first public cinema opened in France. In 1901, J.P. Morgan created US Steel, the first billion-dollar corporation. America cheered its first Rose Bowl game in 1902.[151] On December 17, *1903,* the **Wright brothers** became the first to manage powered flight at Kitty Hawk, North Carolina.[152] In *1908,* **Henry Ford** opened the first assembly line for vehicles.

---

[150] Note that the internal combustion engine is still the mainstay of automobile transportation in the twenty-first century (2010), and it was invented in the eighteenth century. It seems that we managed to perfect the mechanical dinosaur.

[151] Notice that the Rose Bowl was being played before the invention of powered flight!

[152] In 1903 the first powered aircraft flight took place, and in 1969 men landed on the moon; thus, in 66 years people went from a flying a few seconds to a space flight of incredible complexity and distance. This kind of progress is commonplace in the world today. In fact, it may be the most significant thing in the 21st Century.

FIGURE 42 TESLA, FATHER OF THE MODERN WORLD

However, something patented in 1883 by **Hiram Maxim** would change the face of the world by blowing it off with great efficiency—the machine gun. The name itself tells the story, a gun of the machine age. It fired large amounts of ammunition automatically, that is, without a person reloading it one round at a time. By just pulling the trigger it fired until the ammunition ran out. The main financier of the factory needed to construct these guns was Vickers (an English firm), and they were constructed in large numbers by England in the late 1800s. Their use in colonial warfare was decisive, allowing advancing technology to keep the Europeans in control of their far-flung empires with fewer men. Their use in the Great War of 1914 to 1918 caused paralysis on the Western Front and millions of deaths.

The world is now at **1900**, a watershed in history. The world changed dramatically since 1800. The twentieth century saw unmitigated change, social disorder, ideological upheaval, and endless butchery. It is to that story we now proceed.

Books and Resources

Dreadnought, Robert K. Massie, 1992, Ballantine Books. Massie reviews the entire era leading up to WWI in grand style. He gives fairly complete biographies on each major personage of the times from Cecil Rhodes to Queen Victoria.

Wizard: The Life and Times of Nikola Tesla : Biography of a Genius, Marc Seifer, 2001, Citadel Press Books

CHAPTER 12

1900: THE DIVIDING LINE TO THE MODERN WORLD

Since a new era is dawning, we need to **review** what was going on around 1900.

INDUSTRIALISM AND THE MACHINE AGE

The years between 1880 and 1900 were an era of great prosperity and a belief in a glorious future. **Progress** was everywhere. Trains were moving people and goods faster than ever and at reduced prices. Transportation influenced prices on all kinds of goods and services so as transportation prices fell prices on nearly everything fell. Mass production became common, and this made textiles and a wide array of manufactured goods available at lower prices. At sea, fast ships traveling around the world brought goods to Europe and America from across the globe. As Europe thrived, the third world prospered by supplying the Europeans with their needs and wants which consistently grew. New factories were constructed, and new factories meant better machines and more competition, driving prices down. It also upped employment numbers. International trade was booming, and the future looked brilliant. Machines seemed to be the key to the future. They made everything better.

In terms of warfare, the last ninety years were good because very few large wars between major powers occurred. Since Napoleon's defeat in 1815, European nations cooperated as never before in preventing war. If events in Europe appeared to be moving toward an armed clash, the ambassadors gathered and started working out terms to prevent a conflict.[153]

---

[153] Through the so-called **Concert of Europe**.

Overall, the world seemed to work well; however, underneath it all a growing angst presided. Philosophy started predicting an irrational world, one ruled by harsh reality, power, and greed. Art was coming undone. Reality evaporated, and modern painting started taking over wherein the minds of artists turned to images of wilting watches and fantastic scenes never glimpsed before. Even this degenerated into darker paintings of worlds without recognizable features. Literature followed suit with stories of meaningless existence overlain by horror. Music also echoed the tune of no rhyme or theme and began to declare there was no unity in music or in life. It all came together in **science,** where the world people thought they knew melted away with incomprehensible theories that failed to fit everyday experience. The theory of relativity (Einstein) told the world that the universe was a strange place where the speed of light never changed, and events changed depending on a person's viewpoint in space. Plank's quantum theory postulated a world of atoms where "certainty" was a calculation which stated only the possibilities—NOTHING was certain here. Freud displayed the power of hidden areas of the human mind and proved rational decisions were anything but rational. Decisions and ideas were not based on systematic thought (logic and reason), but on the emotional, and very irrational, part of the mind he called the subconscious. Freud made the mind irrational and thus the world irrational. Where could this be leading?

Little did anyone realize how close this placid Victorian world was to the ultimate irrationality; *World War I.*

Machines

By 1900, machines ran the modern Western world. Machines took jobs and created jobs. Machines ruled nearly every aspect of work and life. From the factories to the fields, machines performed more and more work under the oversight of humans. **Trains** made hauling people and possessions faster and cheaper. Railroads were crisscrossing continents other than Europe by 1900. From England to India, trains were the center of modern urban life and the center of economic life everywhere in Europe, America, and the colonial empires. **Ships** began running on coal-fired engines, and a new product—the **automobile**—ran on gasoline (mostly). The automobile became the foundation of the machine age when **Henry Ford** (1863-1947) introduced the Model T Ford October 1, 1908. Using assembly line methods he cut the cost of production making the vehicle affordable. The price was $825 when it rolled off the assembly line in 1908, and the price fell as Ford improved his manufacturing methods. The first **airplane** flew in 1903 when, at Kitty Hawk, the **Wright brothers** made the world's first powered flight using a gasoline engine. The need to fuel the machines began dominating business and governmental decisions worldwide. Oil was the key to both fueling and maintaining the new mechanical world. Without a large supply of oil the machines would die. As electricity became more useful, ways to generate electricity became more valuable. Falling water runs electric generators, but not everyone lives near a big river. Once more, power from burning coal or oil became the answer. As machines came of age, **coal** and then **oil** became the gold of the machine era.

POLITICS

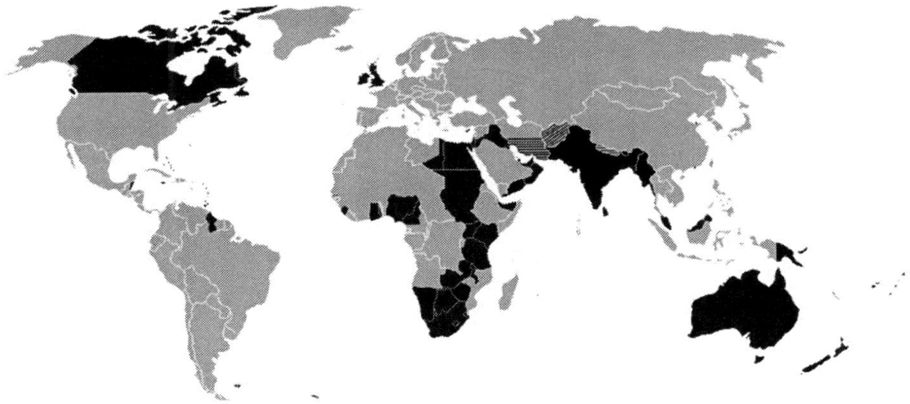

FIGURE 43 THE BRITISH EMPIRE IN 1923

Britain ruled the sea and an exceptionally large part of the world. She was the most powerful and prosperous nation in the world long before 1800, and her position seemed unassailable. Britain desired free trade and, as a nation, committed herself to keeping the oceans open to shipping, and keeping trade barriers low. All in accordance with **Adam Smith**'s ideas as set forth in his book, *The Wealth of Nations,* published in 1776. Britain believed the goods and raw materials flowing to England strengthened her as a nation, and strengthened the colonies producing the goods and raw materials. As a whole, Britain ran her colonies well and relatively free of corruption. India, the crown jewel of Britain's colonial empire, attracted many English citizens to live in the comforts of the imperial possession.

England also advanced on the social front. Under **Queen Victoria (1819 to 1901)**, the second and third **Reform Acts** passed giving more classes of people the vote, and better labor laws passed to protect working people. In the United States, amendments to the Constitution passed ensuring voting rights and citizenship for blacks and minorities, and social welfare programs expanded to help the poor, the uneducated, and the insane. Powerful business interests operating to the detriment of small enterprise, such as railroads, at last began to face serious regulatory threats from state governments.

France also possessed a great worldwide colonial empire, but it did not add as much to the economy of France as English colonies did for Britain. The French empire was rife with corruption and incompetence. France and England viewed their empires differently. England built schools, hospitals, railroads, and the like for its colonies. Overall, the English colonies received much from the mother country. France did build railroads and generally improved its colonies, but the British did more. France viewed the colonies as benefiting France and little else. Britain viewed the colonies as a two-way exchange where the mother country owed the colonies, and both benefited from the colonial system. While the French did not acutely oppress people in their colonies, they let them know about French superiority in all things.[154] Holland, Portugal, and Germany held colonial empires, but they were a shadow of the English empire. Germany was especially desirous of obtaining more colonies to equal England, its rival for world power. Germany's numerous problems included coming very late to the colonial game, and being a land power in Central Europe—not a sea power. Sea power brought colonies, and Germany was nowhere near the equal of Britain at sea.

Germany's ship building program pushed Britain's policy of having a fleet twice the size of any other nation to the limit. Germany was making headway by building more ships than England. Nevertheless, England's outstanding naval architects pulled a rabbit out of the hat, outperforming Germany in innovation. Britain's navy under the First Sea Lord, Fisher, invented a new kind of battleship,[155] the **HMS *Dreadnought*** (1906). This revolutionary ship

---

154 A holdover from King Louis XIV, the French Revolution, and Napoleon.

155 The term "battleship" means the largest fighting ship afloat carrying the most guns. In 1900, naval war planners envisioned battleships as the key to gaining and maintaining naval superiority at sea. Because these ships had the largest caliber guns that could fire further than the guns on lesser ships they would rule any sea battle. The battleship could start firing sooner, and even one battleship shell could devastate an enemy vessel. It was thought columns of these huge ships would line up and fire away at each other thus determining who would rule the oceans. The

made all other battleships obsolete the instant it hit the waves, because it had more large guns and greater speed than anything else afloat. The Dreadnought's new turbine engines made the ship amazingly quick. All those many ships Germany constructed to catch up with England became useless. As England constructed more *Dreadnought* type battleships Germany retreated into the doldrums of naval power, but Germany strained every muscle to keep up. The very costly *Dreadnoughts* resulted in England and Germany spending piles of money on an arms race that increased world tensions and damaged their economies in the process. By World War I Britain had 21 Dreadnoughts and Germany 13.

Large standing armies impoverish the people.—Sun Tzu, *The Art of War*

At a fundamental level, Germany was a land power. She beat France in the Franco-Prussian War of 1870 to 1871 rather easily and obtained Alsace Loraine from France as a result. Germany's population was outpacing the population of France, and Germany's industry out produced France in key economic areas. France recognized these facts, which were terrifying the French government and people.

Germany needed to rethink copying Great Britain as its strategy for gaining world power. Enjoying a central position so as to benefit from trade with France, England, Russia, Central Europe, and others, Germany could grow her economy without preparing for war at sea or an aggressive war on land. Germany could position herself to gain allies rather than cause others to seek treaties to isolate her. Germany's aggressive Prussian military heritage impaired her in the international arena since Prussia's renown was its formidable army.[156] Had Germany chosen to spend money on industrial infrastructure rather than warships it would end Britain's worries about German sea power. Britain would have no pressing reason to ally with France. If Germany constructed defensive lines and reduced the size of her army France could have relaxed, and alliances with Russia would be unnecessary. By befriending the nations around her Germany's economic power could grow immeasurably, and Europe—and the world—would

---

importance of better cannons had been recognized since the invention of artillery and its placement on ships. King Henry VIII of England invested in developing the best cannons in the world, and the best ships to carry them; thus, putting England ahead in the early naval race. Until WWII, England held that lead. During WWII it became evident that the time of the battleship was passed.

156 The joke was that Prussia was an army with a state, rather than a state with an army.

benefit owing to no arms race and the positive influence of a good trading partner. All this is speculation, because Germany would challenge France and Britain for world power and prestige with appalling results for Western Europe and the world.

France decided its best protection against Germany was alliances, especially with England and Russia. Once France secured the alliance with Russia, Germany was facing a two-front war. **Otto von Bismarck**, Germany's leader for years, made it a point to keep his nation from encirclement by co-joined enemies; however, by early 1900 Bismarck was gone, and the new German leader, **Kaiser Wilhelm**, was irresponsible in foreign policy. By allowing Bismarck's alliances to ebb away he gave France the opening it needed to gain an alliance with Russia, proving again that heredity and competence are not synonymous.

England also became an informal ally of France. This was most unusual, in that Britain and France were consistently at war with one another for over four hundred years. From before Agincourt (1415) to Waterloo (1812), England and France fought over ownership of Europe and the world. Even in the late 1800s, the antagonism remained strong, particularly over colonial issues. Nonetheless, in 1900 French policy changed, as did English policy, and the two became informal allies. The man behind this change, and probably the man who saved France from conquest in WW I, was the Minister of Foreign Affairs for France, **Theophile Déclassé.** For years Lord Salisbury, Prime Minister of England, had been trying to hammer out an alliance with the Germans to forward England's policy of containing Russia. Failing at that endeavor, he managed to gain an alliance with Japan to limit Russian expansion in the far east. Déclassé saw his chance after Salisbury finally soured on his chances with Germany. The French Foreign Minister knew the major difficulty with an alliance was the colonial competition with the British, however, he saw that the real issue was the fate of only two areas, Morocco and Egypt. Déclassé negotiated a deal where Egypt went to England and Morocco went to France. The deal was cut and finalized on April 7, 1904. Germany objected because she had an interest in Morocco, and under pressure Déclassé resigned; nevertheless, Germany was not satisfied and called for a large conference of the major powers to work out the fate of Morocco. The conference did not go well for the Germans and their constant threats of war disturbed England and France. The net result was a stronger relationship between Britain and France, just the opposite of what the Germans wanted. The fear of Germany drove England and France to partnership. As the ancient enemies came together as friends, it was certain the world was a much-altered place in the era of 1900.

The European arms race not only produced new ships, it also produced new weapons of land warfare, terrible in their portent but untried on the battlefield. Machine guns, fast-firing breach loading cannons, howitzers (high-firing long-range cannons), fast-firing rifles (breech-loading bolt actions with magazines holding several rounds), and other innovations made the prospect of war chilling. Some even said the new weapons of mass destruction made war impossible or unthinkable (compare to the atomic bomb). However, thinking and planning future wars went on as if the new weapons might shorten the war. Worse, these new weapons had unknown effects. Some generals maintained that machine guns could not kill enough men to stop a determined assault. The French generals in particular decided men had to have a real spirit of the offensive (*élan*) to overcome machine guns and massed artillery fire, and with that spirit they would prevail. This kind of thinking did not bode well for French privates.

Russia was improving its military. Stung by the defeat at the hands of the Japanese in 1904, Russia made great strides in training and equipping its military. Still, Russia lagged well behind England, Germany, and France in military firepower. The Russian army's size, along with the ability of its troops to withstand hardships without complaint, frightened potential opponents. Germany watched the Russians closely since they were the major threat from the east and now allied with France. Economically, Russia was far behind Western Europe in both methods of farming and manufacture. Russian Tsarist traditions also failed to help its society to develop a proper concern for the individual. The result was appalling oppression of the peasant population.

Japan continued growing in power. After adopting Western ways and technology, Japan advanced as the only real industrial power in the Far East. Japan defeated Russia, a major Western military power, in 1904, and now believed she deserved honorable treatment as a world power. However, European powers still viewed Japan with condescension, angering Japan's people and inadvertently handing power to the militarists who were demanding the forcible expansion of Japanese territory into Korea, Manchuria, China, and the Pacific.

On the fringes of Europe, the Ottoman Empire was imploding. Once stretching from Morocco to India's borders it had steadily shrank to encompass what is now modern Turkey, Palestine, Iraq, Iran, Lebanon, Syria, and parts of Greece. Contracting since 1800, the Ottoman Empire devolved into a threat to peace. Because of colonial competition each

European colonial nation, including Russia, became highly interested in the Ottoman's fate. While Britain and France gave aid to Greece in its revolt against the Ottoman Empire, they sent aid to the Ottomans to forestall their loss of Egypt. Eventually, the major powers of Europe decided to support the continuation of the Ottoman Empire because it helped maintain the balance of power in Europe. An Ottoman breakup could cause a scramble for colonies and confrontations leading to war. This shows the ticklish nature of the European situation. A weak nation on the fringe of Europe was warily dealt with to avoid a general war involving the great world powers of Europe.

America

The United States of America was a growing economic power by 1900, but its diminutive army and midsized navy were no threat to Europe.[157] Oil became a major industry in America after 1864, fitting right into the dawning machine age and giving its promoters excellent profits from the very first. Americans were strongly isolationist even though some elements of society wanted America to join the great powers, acquire colonies, and help rule the world. Most Americans wanted nothing to do with world power. The Spanish-American War was fomented by the press (Hurst mainly) allegedly to sell more newspapers. Hurst's papers printed outright lies to whip up public opinion for war, and a strange explosion that sank the USS *Maine* in Havana harbor was enough to tip the Congress for war. For the average American, the purpose of the war involved revenge against Spain for dishonoring the USA. Americans on the street never expected colonies from the war with Spain. However, Spain lost, and America gained the Philippines, Cuba, and other small-island possessions formerly belonging to Spain. The United States gave Cuba its independence but kept Puerto Rico in the Caribbean and the Philippines in the Far East as virtual colonies. Many in America detested owning colonies because it was antagonistic to American principles of national sovereignty and individual liberty. To some extent, the split over world involvement revolved around an urban versus rural viewpoint. The urban dwellers often wanted the United States to become more involved in world events, while the rural citizen wanted to stay away from the world. In 1900, the United States

[157] Immediately after the Civil War the North had a massive army and navy, among the largest in the world. This was quickly reduced in size because of American isolationist policies.

was more rural than urban, so the rural ideology favoring isolation still ruled nationwide.

Since America was a democracy the Congress reflected the split mood of the nation, but overall, the nation was still isolationist, wanted to stay out of European affairs, and did not want to be like Europe—at least politically. The warnings of George Washington, American's first president, to stay out of foreign entanglements still rang true with a majority of voters. Thus, while some leaders, such as President Theodore Roosevelt, loved to send the Great White Fleet (the American navy) around the world to show off American power, most Americans just wanted out of world politics.

From the end of Reconstruction in 1877 to 1933 and Roosevelt's New Deal, neither Republicans nor Democrats had unfettered control of the Federal government. Even when one party controlled in name, divergent forces within the parties tended to reduce their power. Liberal and Conservative were often better labels to describe a politician's position than Republican or Democrat. Meanwhile, blacks sunk into oblivion as the US courts helped the "Redeemers" [158] in the South recover the old southern political culture. In 1896, the US Supreme Court in *Plessey vs. Ferguson* upheld "separate but equal." This allowed the South to segregate its society and relegate blacks to second-class status (again). In Washington, DC, Corruption ruled as men of money bought Congressmen and judges as easily as flapjacks. Reform movements, such as the Progressives, called for fundamental changes in government. The civil service system, introduced by the Progressive movement, required testing for government positions and prohibited firings for political reasons. Several states allowed proposed laws onto the ballot so the public could pass legislation, and state constitutional amendments, by popular vote. This cut into the ability of corrupt political bosses to prevent reform legislation from passing. All this was trying to end government corruption and influence peddling which deeply damaged the American political system. The results of their efforts were uneven.

---

158 The Redeemers were southern whites who wanted to end Reconstruction and take over the reins of power in the Old South. The goal was to put the future of the South back into southern hands and get the North out of southern affairs. As the Redeemers took over southern governments, they attempted to re-establish the culture of the pre-civil war South where the rich ruled and the poor did what they were told. The only substantial differences were the rich now constituted more than the planter classes as new industrialists were prominent in the social order, and they were careful not to openly offend the powerful North for fear of the legislative consequences.

Power of Women

In 1900, the role of women in the world was up for debate—at least in the Western Democracies. Women wanted to vote, become professionals (doctors, lawyers, university professors, etc.), and to work at the same jobs as men for the same pay.[159] For centuries, women were relegated to the home and rearing children, stuck with only household employment. Some exceptions were around, like textile manufacturing where women made up 50 percent of the workforce in 1870. Of course, there already were women doctors, architects, university graduates, and the like; however, women wanted this to be commonplace rather than unusual. In 1893, New Zealand gave women the vote. By 1920, women in the United States obtained the right to vote. Britain, Germany, Austria and Poland gave the vote to women in 1918. France waited until 1944 to extend the vote to women, and Switzerland stalled until 1971. When women obtained the vote the size of the electorate effectively doubled.

Women prevailed, obtaining all of these things much faster than supposed in 1900. The Great War and World War II propelled women to equality with men in voting, the workplace, professional life, and a host of other realms; but in 1900 these changes were over the horizon. Women started exercising their feminine muscle and, as they gained the vote, began to win elections, work in factories, and do the things men alone used to do; they gained stature. Women balked at being the chattels of men as they began shaking off history's cobwebs.

In the 1900s this movement confined itself to Europe, its colonies, and America. For much of the world, even in 2010, women do not have equality with men. Many religions require women to be inferior, and many traditions do the same. Women won in the Western Democracies and expanded the economic and intellectual power of those nations. In places where women are excluded from the benefits of society, society itself suffers. This is one seldom discussed reason the West dominated the world for so long. By opening its societies to women, they freed about one-half of their population to contribute to the growth and power of their nations. Other societies forfeited this intellectual and economic dynamic by suppressing women and radically limiting their role in society.

---

[159] Oddly enough, the terrible Civil War in America had given black men the vote, but not women of any race.

POWER OF THE PRESS

In 1900, the press (newspapers) was *the* source of news. Radio was not up and running and TV was only a dream in some visionaries' head. As such, the print press wielded enormous power and influence over public opinion. As demonstrated by the Spanish-American War, the press could bend public opinion to their view, thereby influencing the actions of parliaments and legislative bodies in democratic societies. Because Europe and America enjoyed freedom of the press, these newspapers shaped elections, and they enjoyed the power to make or break many a politician—or even governments. The problem with the press was its ability to lie and get away with it. If they lied about an individual a libel suit was possible, but if they lied about events, such as the sinking of the battleship USS *Maine,* there was no one to call them on it. On their opinion pages they could really let go and castigate anyone they wished, and this brought the fear of the newspaper gods upon the politicians of the era. In other nations the press was not free, often becoming the mouthpiece of the government for political and social manipulation.

In 2010, the press, including the print and broadcast press, still tells lies in order to advance their political or philosophic agenda.[160] Just by arranging which stories appear on the front page or in the first minute of a TV broadcast the press can influence a nation's agenda. More disturbing, the news media universally think the same stories are important. Why do newspapers, magazines, and broadcast news repeatedly carry the identical story as the headline? Do they all think alike? (Yes) This was a problem in 1900 and it remains a problem in 2010. If all the major news outlets say the same thing, they can shape public opinion without the competition of ideas. So it was in 1900, and so it is now. The mass media was so important by 1900 that it guided the destiny of nations.

---

160 In the United States, the press may outright lie and not be in violation of liable laws. The US Supreme Court has set an "absence of malice" standard; that is, the press may lie about a public figure if they do not act with malice—knowing the story is false and publishing it with the expressed purpose of harming the individual. Under this standard, the press may print almost anything about a person as long as they qualify as a public figure.

POWER OF RELIGION

God was not dead in 1900, although several philosophers said so. Religion in Europe, the colonial empires, and America played a key role in governance and in everyday life. Almost everyone believed in a god of some type, most attended church, and most would agree on the basics of morality. Using the Christian Bible as the foundation of law Europe, its colonial empires, and America agreed on fundamental issues, such as, monogamy was good, divorce was bad, children were good, stealing was bad, being clean was good, adultery was bad, hard work was good, murder was bad, abstinence from alcohol was good, etc. From the family to the courtroom there was general agreement on good and evil. This general agreement on the common good versus evil formula reflected Christian ideology. Catholics or Protestants might disagree on the role of the church, the power of the priesthood, the role of ancient rituals and language, but they would agree the Bible was God's word and the dos and don'ts therein were from God himself.

Because of this religious influence, there was universal condemnation of lying, pornography, cheating, stealing, and a host of other ills; thus, controlling much of what the media dared publish for viewing in the newspapers, magazines, and books of the era. These publications were part of the age, and they displayed the general tenor of the 1900s where reputation and status were very important. One did not disgrace the family or themselves. This kind of self-control went a long way to assuring at least some order without the necessity of having a policeman on every corner. We would be amazed at what a person could buy in 1900 that is forbidden today. Explosives, drugs such as cocaine and arsenic, and all kinds of items strictly controlled in 2010 were purchased without question in 1900. A lack of governmental bureaucracy and trust in the individual helped. People in the USA felt what they did was none of the government's business. The stamp of government control was not yet firmly impressed upon their minds. Controls we accept today with little argument would have caused outrage in 1900.

Not everyone was Christian or agreed on Christian principles. Uprisings were common and keeping control of an empire was a considerable and constant problem. In China, the Westerners made many Chinese angry as they practiced their new religion and displayed arrogant ways. Warlords and rebels often attacked the Europeans on religious grounds, but the Europeans and their superior technology held on inflicting sizeable losses on the attackers. In spite of sustained efforts by Christian churches, the Christian religion converted relatively few within the colonial empires.

In spite of these exceptions, the world united behind a Christian viewpoint and Christian principles. From the press to the role of government in society this Christian viewpoint, and the supporting principles, influenced society in countless ways.

POWER OF SCIENCE

Science grew in importance rapidly by 1900. Through the scientific (empirical) method, mankind made broad advances in understanding and controlling the world. Medicine uncovered new ways to fight disease; engineering invented new ways to build everything from trains and ships to houses and skyscrapers. Myth was out; proof was in—scientific proof. The scientific method requires *repeatable experiments* that yield repeatable results. Because of this repeatability people worldwide could conduct the same experiment (test) and know the results would be the same. As new empirical knowledge emerged mankind advanced to new plateaus of provable knowledge.

There was a problem. Science was discovering a world beyond what a person's senses reported as fact. Einstein's theory of relativity replaced Newton's mechanical universe *in 1905*. Max Plank's quantum theory, published in *1900*, and Freud's theories on the subconscious mind (*The Interpretation of Dreams, 1900*) all pointed to a world of seeming irrationality.

Plank's theories of quantum mechanics concerned subatomic particles (smaller than atoms), and that world was without absolute certainty. The position of an electron is stated in terms of probability, particles and waves exhibit similar behavior, and particles "communicate" with one another over large distances faster than the speed of light. Einstein's theories described the large-scale universe. In Einstein's world, distances were vast and nothing traveled faster than the speed of light which was always constant. In relativity, a person's observational position determines what is observed; thus, "truth" varies with the observer's position. In Newton's world, truth was absolute (laws); but in Einstein's world, truth did not exist as an absolute—except for light . . . maybe . . .

The discovery that the world is made of atoms was critical to science, and it had a profound impact on the intellectual world as well. Atoms, the building blocks of everything, are mostly nothing. Between the center of the atom (the nucleus) and the electrons flying around the nucleus is . . . nothing. If a nucleus of an atom was the size of a basketball and placed in downtown Los Angeles, the nearest electron would be located (if it could be located) somewhere around San Diego or Bakersfield, some 200 plus miles away. The point here is the distances on a quantum scale are actually huge, and the space in between contains zero. It would seem impossible for this to be a fact because how can nothing become a solid something? The answer is the strong and weak electromagnetic forces existing between the atoms. These strong and weak electromagnetic forces actually hold individual solids apart so solids "appear" solid. However, as the reader can easily ascertain, this is not the world of our human senses. Thus, science told the world that what you see, taste, or feel is not reality. Reality was far deeper and more mysterious than anyone could have dreamed.

Physicists understand another problem separates the theory of relativity and quantum theory. One (relativity) described the macro; the other (quantum) described the micro, and *they do not agree.* How could it be that the tiny "universe" of atoms, electrons, and quanta acted and reacted in a very different way than the huge universe of planets, solar systems, and galaxies? Could the universes, large and small, be so different that the fundamental principles of one do *not* apply in the other? The answer in 1900 was *yes*, and the answer is the same today. So far, science agrees that the two "universes" exist and they do *not* operate by the same basic principles.

Worse yet, Freud probed the human mind and theorized the subconscious portion of the mind, unknown and uncontrolled by the conscience mind, actually controls actions and decisions at the conscience level. For illustration, people choose everything from clothes to mates based on signals from this subconscious area of the mind to the conscience area; however, these signals are unknown to the person making the decision. Thus, decisions are fundamentally irrational because the subconscious mind is not a rational thinking part of the mind; rather, it is an area of wild emotions and unconnected deep experiences normally suppressed below the conscience surface. Freud tried to reach this area of the mind through dream analysis (one method) and psychotherapy which caused the patient to reveal the meaning of symbols appearing in dreams. These symbols contained keys to conflicts in the mind patients must resolve to rid themselves of various mental illnesses caused by these conflicts. Thus, at a fundamental level, Freud proved humans were not rational (any historian could have told him that).

Another "science" came onto the scene before 1900, but it was gaining more steam by the turn of the century. **Darwin** wrote *On the Origin of Species* in 1859 putting forth the theory of evolution saying species found on the earth had long ago been simple one-celled creatures and slowly developed to the complex organisms of 1859 through a series of small steps. Which creatures take the next step was the product of evolution determining what type of organism best suited the environment. Those most fit survived to have more offspring which then became dominant and competed with others to see which ones would be most fit to advance again. In theory, each advance was to a more complex organism better able to fit into a niche in the environment.[161] The organism should not become too specialized, that is, fit for only one unique kind of environment, because a change in environment would destroy the species. Some generalization is good in that it increases the chance of survival if the environment changed.

One can see there is little room for a god in this theory. The natural forces of the earth drive everything, and as the environment of the earth changed so did the organisms dependent on that environment. Knowledgeable people in 1900 realized this theory applied to people as well as animals. After 1900, a secularized scientific world-view dominated the West, and evolution fit nicely into this view. In education, the secularized *naturalist* worldview became dominate under the guidance of men like Dewey.

The science of **geology** came of age at the same time the theory of evolution came into vogue. Lyle, an attorney, is the father of modern geology. He studied the landscapes very closely, deciding the processes at work on the environment in 1859 were the same forces at work in 500,000 BC or earlier. He stated, *"As things are now, they have always been."* This was the *uniformitarnism* theory that was directly at odds with the catastrophic theory of earth's history which had been the accepted idea. The catastrophic theory held cataclysmic events formed the earth causing massive geologic changes over short periods of time.

For Darwin's theory to be accurate the uniformitarnism theory had to win acceptance as the foundation for geologic theory. If the earth were formed by cataclysmic events the species would not have time to evolve between the obliterations. The numbers of species on earth is great, and to reach this kind of diversity took long spans of *uninterrupted time.* Thus, the two theories of evolution and uniformitarnism managed to complete

---

161 Why the change was always for additional complexity is hard to explain.

one another, bound together as a package. This fact is seldom part of an analysis of the theory of evolution.

Darwin's theory challenged religious beliefs about the nature of man. If man was not created by God (or gods), then he was just an animal. The problem here was the lack of purpose and a lack of foundation for evaluating human behavior. Without God, where would morality come from? Who could then say what was right and wrong? Philosophy battled this problem since the ancient Greeks and never reached an agreed conclusion. Thus, science added to the stripping away of rationality from the world; and the world became a place without meaning, purpose, rationality, or god(s).

ART AND LITERATURE

Including music, philosophy, economics, and more

In the era of 1900, the artistic world experienced the death of rationality. Realism turned up dead, cause and effect dead, humanity dead, purpose of life . . . dead. Most ordinary people overlooked this in 1900, but it became evident soon enough.

As usual, artists led the way in predicting this new "reality." Painters moved beyond Impressionism to Modernism. In this new way of painting, reality was unimportant. Van Gogh painted his famous *Sunflowers* in 1888, and this was already a great departure from Realism. Monet's *Water Lilies* exhibited in 1916, and it is a stretch to call this Impressionism. Other paintings were coming, paintings of a dark and sordid world where shadow and form merged and made the subject hard to discern. In some paintings, clocks melted and landscapes became unrecognizable, or surrealistic, as we say today. Paintings contained no recognizable theme and often no recognizable center of attention. Most of the rules were gone. Cubism allowed the viewer to see the subject from many different perspectives; other paintings seemed formless, and without the title could not be recognized (*Nude Descending a Staircase,* Marcel Duchamp, 1912), and in others (*The Scream,* Edward Munch, 1893), the subject itself melts into a controlling title. In *The Scream,* the subject is the scream even though a scream is a noise. The artist made the person screaming appear as noise as much as a human (barely recognizable as human).

FIGURE 44 DUCHAMP, NUDE DESCENDING A STAIRCASE, 1912

How artists can know the future before it arrives is an interesting issue; but in the era of 1900 the predictions of a dark and sinister future world were there for anyone to see.

In literature the same theme emerged. Nietzsche's ***Thus Spake Zarathustra***, 1883, and Marx's ***Das Kapital***, 1867, predicted the coming of new worlds. Nietzsche foretold of a world without a god, a world ruled by the supermen of the epoch who were without mercy or rationality. In 1848 Karl Marx (1818 to 1883), in his *Communist Manifesto,* wrote of a utopian world without government, ruled by workers who overthrew their capitalist masters and replaced them with workers (without a government) who gave and received as needed.

Figure 45 Munch, The Scream, 1893

Marx wrote as a revolutionary. He lived in a class-conscious England and wrote of a revolt by the oppressed working poor. Workers were cheated out of the increased value they added to raw materials, which the capitalist turned into profits; thus, the workers must seize the factories (means of production) and obtain the increased value for themselves. He called his system communism, and envisioned a utopia where governments evaporated as men lived honestly with one another without hostility because everyone was equal in his classless society. Marx thought the new world was inevitable, and close. Marx said the communist revolution was the last stage in history, and the workers' revolution was already upon the industrial societies of the West. As a predictor of the future he was perfectly wrong. Communism did arise in Russia, China, and elsewhere; but it was not through a revolution of the workers. Rather, it was through the leadership of radicals who were often intellectuals leading peasants fired by the thought of creating a new social order by changing the economic and political system. After these revolutions the government, rather than melting away, became stronger and more oppressive than ever. By totally controlling everything in society through an increase in autocratic oversight, the radicals were the opposite of anything envisioned by Marx. Karl Marx fundamentally misunderstood economics and human nature. Ruthless men twisted his noble thoughts and words to gain the support of peasants and workers who could never dream what they were really supporting. Only after the dictators took power and began killing on a scale unheard of in human history did their true nature become known to the mostly illiterates they had duped. Marx viewed the poor of modern urban societies as a product of the capitalist system; however, they were actually the product of human nature and not the capitalist system. The urban poor had been around since cities began, and communism would not solve their problems.

If Marx was a fool dreaming of a world that could never be, then **Nietzsche** (1844 to 1900) was a clairvoyant foretelling of a world no one in their right mind would want—but received anyway. Nietzsche was predicting the world of the future would be harsh, but that is the way of the world (he might say), so get used to it. He was right. The world to come would be very harsh, and his ideas predicted super dictators doing as they willed with millions and caring not one whit for the lives of those they controlled. Just as the "overman" or superman in Nietzsche's philosophy, the dictators did what they willed because they were superior to others; thus, others meant nothing. Only the overman ruled by right, and only the overman decided good and evil. In fact, good or evil did not exist; there was only the will of the overman.[162]

Nietzsche's world recognizes no god; thus, the overman becomes a god on earth, and his will alone decides good or evil. This was the ultimate world without a god. Unfortunately, Hitler, Stalin, and Mao fit Nietzsche's overman idea all too well. Complete dictators in control of the apparatus of state which could, and did, watch and order nearly every aspect of human existence.

George Orwell, in his book ***1984***, published in 1949, wrote of a fictional society watched over by the seemingly benevolent "Big Brother" which was

---

162 If this sounds like god, you are right. The government was god on earth (Thomas Hobbes, The Leviathan, 1651) and the overman was the natural outcome of that fact. To Nietzsche, god did not exist; only the human existed, and the superior human's will was everything. Note how "the will" has replaced rationally, morality, and logic. All that is irrelevant, only the overman is relevant. Sounds like Hitler, Stalin, Mao, Ho Chi Minh, etc etc

in fact part of a ruthless dictatorial society in which uncontrolled human thought and emotion had no place. However, Hitler, Stalin, and Mao made the world of ***1984*** look good. These dictators murdered millions upon millions because they simply wanted to kill. No reason, no rationality, no purpose—just killing for killing's sake. Just as Nietzsche predicted.

An event of total irrationality occurred in 1914, confirming the use of science and industry for death and chaos. An old invention, propaganda, using new moving pictures and clever words was convincing people to endure what they would never dream of in another place or time. Murder on a mass scale, war on an industrial scale, and irrationality on a titanic scale became everyday facts in World War I. Even the nickname shows the irrationality of it all: "The war to end all wars." Not only would wars go on, they would grow in violence and senselessness.

Music was also predicting the chaos to come. In music, the Renaissance period gave way to the **Baroque** era followed by the **Classical** era of music that lasted from about 1730 to 1820. **Romantic** followed classical music, in vogue from approximately 1815 to 1910. The composers from the Classical and the Romantic periods of music are literally household names: **Haydn, Mozart, Beethoven, Chopin, Tchaikovsky,** and others. During the Classical age the symphonies became ever more complex and the musical instruments available to the composers expanded. The symphony's complexities are astounding. The composers coordinated every aspect of dozens to perhaps a hundred instruments, which would all be playing at once, to create just the right sound. So many aspects of the music were involved it is difficult to understand how one person could have written a major symphony.

These symphonies enclosed literally hundreds of thousands of notes, and each nuance of each note was vitally important to the overall composition. An accomplished listener would instantly know something was wrong if even one note was left out or significantly changed. As time went forward, much of this complex harmony started to fade. When Stravinsky performed the "*Rite of Spring*" in 1913 in Paris, this idea of deep complex harmony was broken. Note the date, one year before the Great War when all harmony in the Western World would cease. The "*Rite of Spring*" is a brutal and disjointed work. At its first performance the complex and violent music, depicting a pagan fertility rite, drew boos because of the harmonic discord. Arguments followed and then a riot requiring the intervention of the Paris police to restore order.

Whether Stravinsky knew he was predicting the future or not he managed the feat with astounding accuracy. The classical world of music where each note enjoyed a distinct place was withering, eventually to be replaced by a world where no one note meant anything in relation to the other notes. People would soon fall into the category of meaningless, just as the notes in Stravinsky's work became; however, at least the notes were there and recognizable. If a note were left out it might be hard to discern at certain points in the work, but a close listener would still know something changed and the piece was somehow out of sorts; accordingly, the notes still mattered, but they were not part of some grand harmonious universe where all fit together so nicely. One note might be moved or removed and not affect the whole as much as such a similar move or removal would influence a symphony of the classical age. If the analogy applies to the worth of the individual, the implication is clear: the individual was a part of the whole, but how important to the whole was open to interpretation. One person would not have a massive impact on the whole just as one note would not have a great impact on the whole of Stravinsky's "Rite of Spring." In the late twentieth century even that would be lost, and the individual note in a musical piece would disappear in importance just as the individual's importance would disappear in a meaningless universe. In music, art, and literature chaos replaced harmony, disunity replaced unity, meaninglessness replaced meaning, and ugliness replaced beauty. Just like the world to come in 1914, it was harsh and irrational.

Philosophy has a way of moving slowly, so theories that come forth take years to bear fruit. Nietzsche wrote in 1883 and sold perhaps one book. He died insane and unknown. Nevertheless, by 1900, people began to notice his ideas and the brutal future of which he wrote. Mill's ***Utilitarianism***, published in 1863, espoused the "greatest happiness to the greatest number" as the definition of morality, but it too foresaw a world where decisions had to be based on something other than religious grounds. By 1900, this philosophy was also gaining adherents.[163]

Another art was coming of age, and it combined art and science; it was **photography**. I can hear what you are thinking now . . . so what? Why does photography matter? If you have never seen a Mathew Brady photograph of an American Civil War battlefield you have not fully experienced the impact of photography. These photographs are simply statements of what

---

163 This morality changes with the whims of the majority; thus, no truth. The Christian religion holds there is one truth, that truth which is revealed by God in the Bible. By definition, for Christians, man cannot know truth—it must come from God.

was in front of the lens at the time of exposure. *It is art by a machine.* The man places the camera (that is the art part), but the scene is the scene and cannot be altered from its basic truth (at least in 1864); and that is the science part.[164] The photos of the battlefields of the 1860s are a blunt statement of death or life. They are stark and plain, almost without a soul. I will name this "*harsh truth.*"

Compare these photos with the many drawings or paintings of the age. Battlefield artists painted and drew much of the Civil War action. In comparison with the photographs the drawings, even those made on the scene, depict a different nuance or feel even though very accurate. Comparing the drawings to the photographs, rather than paintings, is interesting because both creations took place on the spot during the event. Paintings were finished back at a studio far away from the event. The drawings (or paintings) show what I will name "*heroic truth.*"

FIGURE 46 DRAWING OF PICKETT'S CHARGE, GETTYSBURG

Note that both are "truth," but truth seen through the eyes of science and truth seen through the eyes of a human are different. The photographs

164 Yes, it can be manipulated, even in 1864, by moving things in the scene; however, even in 1864 this was discouraged.

have no "heroic" sense about them. Men are lying dead in the fields or roads with little around them except more dead. The men seem part of the landscape. The figures are unmoving, unknown, and without a higher purpose. That is the view of science, rather harsh but blunt, plain and very straightforward. The drawings have a heroic sense to them. Men seem to move, waving hats and sabers, falling in battle while smoke fills the air, and horses thunder toward waiting masses of men. A higher purpose screams from the artist's paper. These men have purpose, because they are defending the rights of other men or their homeland, and showing courage in fierce combat. It is humanity at its highest, sacrificing for God and country, family and friend, wife and child.

FIGURE 47 PHOTOGRAPH OF CONFEDERATE DEAD AT ANTIETAM

War is much more like the harsh photograph than the heroic drawing. Therefore, here is the contradiction; the photograph is as real as it can be given the state of science at the time, but it adds to the philosophy of chaos and meaninglessness because it displays the human being in a mechanical way. Nothing is special about the humans in the photographs because they end up as objects, like all other objects in the photograph. Nothing moves, even the men lay still, their color and the color (shade is more like it) of the surrounding objects nearly the same (1864, all black and white). Of course, in 1864 photographs remained silent again reducing the humanity.

Nonetheless, the photographs were striking. They brought the war home to the civilians left behind with a gruesome truthfulness. Photographs were nothing like the heroic battle drawings of men pushing forward for the cause. Photographs of dead men refuse to look like much, but they reveal a startling fact; these men were once alive. Now they lay lifeless in a mechanical picture. The impact of photography on life was an important part of the New Age.[165] In many ways, photography became the most powerful art form of all time.

THE POWER OF CHANGE

Before 1900, big change was rather unusual. People lived out their lives often never leaving the small villages in which they were born. After 1900 in the West change came so fast people struggled to adjust. From 1900 to 1970, one lifetime, history saw WWI, WWII, Korea, and part of the Vietnam War. A person would have seen soldiers marching off to war in 1914 with bolt-action rifles and horse drawn carts. By 1970, that same person would have seen men marching off to war with automatic rifles, tanks, trucks, jet aircraft, and huge cargo aircraft to carry them across the seas. In 1914, our viewer of history could have seen a small bi-wing airplane putting along overhead, but by 1969, that same person could have witnessed, as it happened, men walking on the moon. In 1900, no radio, but by 1970, TV broadcast from around the world and even from the surface of the moon. Of course, outside of Europe and the United States of America many people did not experience any change in their way of life. Worldviews also changed, and that was the hardest fact of all to adjust to. What was accepted as absolute truth in 1900 was openly questioned by 1960.

This pace of change influenced the early 1900s, as people thought change was endless. The world was advancing, they thought, and people should welcome change. World War I smashed those illusions. Still, the idea that changes represent progress hung on and it is still with us today. Not as much as in 1900, but to this day in the year 2010, people think the world can get better, and change is thought to be positive for the most part.

---

[165] In 1895, France Lumiere opened the first public cinema.

The concept that change is expected and is good goes a long way toward explaining how the West accelerated ahead of the rest of the world and stayed there so long. Many regions of the world view change with skepticism, impeding progress. The acceptance of change is a powerful agency forming one of the many foundations for vigorous progress by the Western world.

Let Us Learn

Citizens of this new world of the 1900s had to adapt to its manifest traits of turmoil, uncertainty, exploding knowledge, and apparent meaninglessness. But **is our world meaningless**? **Are we, as individuals, meaningless**? Recall that the universe is marvelously well ordered, as is life here on earth. Is it possible that such a harmony forms the underpinnings of chaos? If the universe is well ordered, and if life on earth is exactly harmonized, can it also be meaningless? From the moment of the Big Bang, the universe seems to have been designed for life by the very nature of the universal elements, and the exact timing of events (inflation). Can such fine tuning set the foundations of chaos for the individual life? Since *everything* in the universe is ordered to an exactness beyond imagination, can the individual exist for nothing? Isn't it possible that every life has an precise place in the universal order? The symphony writers thought so. Each note was supremely important. Isn't it possible that you have that same significance in the symphony of the universe?

CHAPTER 13

THE FIRST WORLD WAR 1914 TO 1918

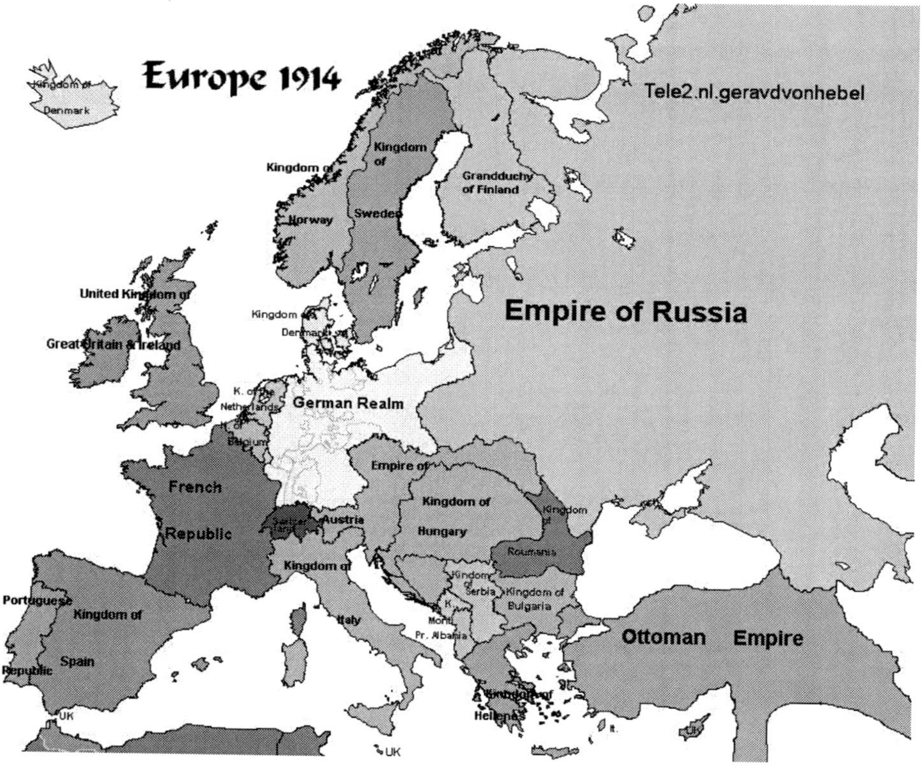

FIGURE 48 EUROPE 1914

This is THE war, in that it set the foundations of the twentieth century; a century of war, murder, and devastation beyond anything seen before. If we take the position, as many do, the First World War caused the Second World War then the First World War is the most important conflict in history. However one desires to look at it, World War I changed everything. We must recognize that World War I set the foundations for the 20th *and* the 21st centuries, and shattered the idealism of the 19th Century. It was a momentous turning point.

In theory, if WWI never occurred, World War II, the Depression, the Cold War, communism, and a host of other ills evaporate from history's pages. Prior to WWI, the world experienced a long peace in the sense that no general war had broken out between great powers since the Congress of Vienna in 1815. In 1913 a person traveling around the world using the English pound as currency and speaking the English language encountered very few problems. European empires controlled colonies the world over generally uniting the world in a Western European ideology. A monetary system based on precious metals kept the world markets relatively stable, and international trade grew steadily. The world experienced peace and prosperity across the globe. Europe ruled most of the world creating a trading bonanza because business found predictable governmental systems, many uniform laws, safe trade routes, stable currencies, and access to huge markets. Rising wages with falling prices enabled consumer purchasing. Scientific and industrial advances transpired consistently, and people of the era came to suppose the future held wonderful promise.

World War I smashed the illusion of a good and predictable world. WWI was brutal beyond all explanation. Artillery, machine guns, bombs, and repeating rifles destroyed life in mass. Men marched into hopeless battles facing certain failure and all but certain death. It was war outside comprehension and beyond reason. All sides fought claiming virtue and honor belonged to them alone. **Propaganda** played a large role by deifying one government while demonizing the opposition, and it encouraged the opposing populations to endure monstrous hardships. Propaganda also played into the unrealistic and harsh **war aims** adopted by the two warring sides and guaranteed prolonging the war to the bitter end.

CASUALTIES

"The war to end all wars," referring to World War I, began in August 1914 and ended in November 1918. The Allies (England, France, Russia, and later Italy, and even later joined by the United States)—also known as the **Triple Entente**),[166] and the **Central Powers** (Germany, Austria-Hungary, and

---

[166] The Triple Entente because the original parties were England, France, and Russia

Turkey)[167] together lost approximately **8 million** dead and over 20 million wounded. On the Western Front alone, casualties on both sides *averaged 2,250 dead* and approximately 5,000 wounded every day. In England, three men were killed in WWI for every one man killed in WWII. In 1921 England there were 55 women to every 45 men in the most marriageable age group of twenty to thirty-nine years of age. During the *first **two months*** of the Great War (August and September 1914), France lost about *360,000* men, Germany *241,000*, England *30,000*, Austria-Hungary *230,000*, Serbia *170,000*, and Russia about *50,000*. In spite of these losses early in the war, the most deadly year was 1918. The British lost more men in 1918 than they lost in all of WW II.

After the war, a great influenza epidemic hit the world causing *50 to 100 million* deaths worldwide. Most researchers think men coming home from the Western Front spread the influenza. Coupled with WWI, this was a human disaster of incalculable proportions. Pile this on top of WWII casualties and you know why the 20th Century earned its name as the century of slaughter.

FINANCIAL COSTS

All the warring nations spent vast sums financing the conflict. The major European warring nations alone spent over ***200 trillion dollars***, and after the war large repatriations were required from Germany to pay back the winning sides' expenses to the tune of *thirty-two billion dollars*. Few recognized it at the time, but these war expenses shattered the world economic system. World War I strained the monetary system beyond its capacity. The world trade system began to collapse after the war, then tariffs were passed by the major economic powers to protect their internal markets causing retaliatory tariffs by other nations. International trade dried up as a direct result of these tariffs. After the stock market crash in 1929, US banks began calling war loans to Europe rather than extending them. The world economic system imploded, and an unremitting depression swept the world. Because of governments' mismanagement after the crisis hit, the Great Depression lingered on unlike past depressions. This depression began in 1929 and lasted past the start of World War II in 1939 until 1941 or later.[168]

---

[167] Many smaller nations were involved.

[168] Except for the Panic of 1873 previous depressions or recessions had lasted one to two years on average. The Great Depression lasted about ten years and was worse in the United States of America than other Western countries. Some claim the US

OTHER COSTS

World War I gave birth to a new world menace: **communism.** In 1918, Russia's monarchy suffered a revolution and overthrow directly related to its grave mishandling of the war. A rather-small group of communist fanatics eventually took over the nation. Russia left the war in 1918, withdrawing into itself in an orgy of murder and destruction so vast the nation remained wounded until WWII. Russia took itself out of the world's markets after the Communist Revolution causing additional European economic disruption. Communism spread after World War II and remained a direct challenge to the Western Democracies for decades (China is still communist in 2010). *The number of people killed in the name of communism runs well over 94 million.* Absent World War I, the world may have dodged this worldwide scourge.

Now the worst part. The great powers as a group desired peace, the war began for stupid reasons, and the war continued for the worst of reasons; both sides demanded total "victory."[169] The ultimate cost was the destruction of a world without equal in history which, like Rome, plunged into that dark abyss of the uncaring past.

CAUSES OF THE GREAT WAR

World War I resulted from many *indirect* causes, and among the most important (*in no particular order*) were:

1) An **arms race** between Germany, France, and England raising world tensions. The main arms race was between England and Germany over sea power. For years the great problem standing in the way of peace was Germany's insistence on constructing a fleet that would equal England's. Every attempt to reach a compromise on the issue of fleet size failed, and this failure can be traced directly to German Admiral Tirpitz and the Germany's Kaiser. Dreadnaughts were terribly expensive, so the arms race was consuming enormous amounts of money resulting in higher taxes as well as higher tensions

---

did not recover from the Great Depression until the 1950s (it depends on how war production is calculated).

169 How warring parties define victory can control how the war and its aftermath are handled. Remember Carthage? And when we get to WWII think about how "unconditional surrender" effected the Allied war effort. Same for Vietnam and Korea.

2) Germany, **encircled by the Allies**, faced a losing two-front war unless it took desperate measures such as the Schlieffen Plan. Those plans meant Germany must move at the first sign of trouble. Under these circumstances any general mobilization by Russia or France would mean war.
3) The various **interlocking European alliances** were complex and often secret causing widespread mistrust. England struggled to keep the balance of power in Europe which entailed supporting weaker European nations against any nation becoming so strong it could rule Europe. England wanted to avoid another problem like Napoleon. In 1914, Germany was the nation with the ability to rule Europe as it could defeat France even if France were united with Russia; however, England supporting France increased the power of the anti-German alliance significantly. The problem: a wrong move by any nation could draw all the Great Powers into war.
4) The **failure of diplomacy** for many reasons including a lack of time, and German resolve to allow the Austrian attack on Serbia. After the assassination and Austria's announced its move against Serbia, the mobilizations began so quickly that there was no time to react with diplomacy. Another problem was Russia's pride. Russia was recently forced to back down in a confrontation with Germany and Austria, and the Tsar decided any challenge from Austria, backed by Germany or not, would be immediately accepted. The Kaiser's diplomacy had also failed to prevent Russia and France combining in a military alliance against Germany. The Kaiser was very inept at handling foreign affairs and allowed the combinations arranged by the brilliant Bismarck to expire while failing to prevent the formation of deadly alliances against Germany. Worst of all, a few German leaders had decided on war in 1914 and conspired with Austria to allow Austria to crush Serbia.
5) The emergence of super nationalist **terror organizations** sponsored by desperate nations such as Serbia. The Serbs possessed extensive desires with few resources. Thus, they turned to terrorist activities, such as assassinations, to create chaotic circumstances possibly benefitting Serbia—which in fact happened. It was one of these Serb backed terrorist organizations, the Black Hand, that killed Archduke Ferdinand.
6) A dramatic change in German political philosophy took place in 1897 after **Kaiser Wilhelm II** took power and decided to expand German military power on land and *at sea*, plus acquire additional colonies, thus upsetting the balance of power in Europe.

The *direct cause* of the Great War was the murder of **Archduke Ferdinand,** next in line to the crown of Austria, and his wife Sophie by **the Black Hand**, a terrorist organization sponsored by Serbia. After the assassination and the discovery that Serbia sponsored the student murderer Gavrilo Princip, Austria sent Serbia several written absolute demands; however, Serbia rejected a few. Austria gave the Serbs 48 hours to respond, and the pressure of time limited the diplomat's ability to gather the parties for talks. Serbia asked and received from Russia assurances saying if Austria attacked Serbia, Russian mobilization and war on Austria would follow.[170] Austria, meanwhile, contacted Germany and the Kaiser responded he would support Austria if Russia declared war. Russia contacted France and France told Russia they could count on the alliance (again unconditioned), and France promised to declare war on Germany if Germany mobilized against Russia.[171]

Encased in all this maneuvering were several unseen problems. Austria asked Germany to support their position against Serbia. Diplomats always condition responses to achieve flexibility; however, the German Kaiser's response was ***yes**, and without conditions.* Being no diplomat, the Kaiser's response put Germany in a poor position, forfeiting all ability to leverage its uninhibited partner toward moderation. Moreover, the Kaiser answered *before* knowing the demands Austria sent to Serbia. A most unwise move since the Austrian demands were quite harsh. Serbia must reject the worst demands or forfeit national honor (a big no no in 1914). The unlimited German promise freed Austria to declare war if any demand suffered rejection. The 48-hour Austrian time limit for Serbia's response denied the Great Powers time to arrange negotiations to avert war. In addition, several heads of state were absent from their capitols and were hard to reach. Worse, the underlings left in charge apparently desired war. Russia's

---

170 Russia apparently made this promise to support its Slavic "neighbor," as Russia was also a Slavic nation; however, it makes little sense. Russia was not in a geographic position to render sufficient aid to Serbia before it was overrun. The only reason to support Serbia was to *prevent* a war, and this Russia could not do if Germany was in the picture. The smart move was to threaten mobilization and then do nothing. If Serbia was crushed so be it, but somehow the Czar thought a war with Austria-Hungary AND Germany was OK. Could it be the alliance with France gave him false hope? Anyway, his actions were stupid. So were the Kaiser's, the British, and later the USA. With so many dumb guys ruling major powers maybe the war *was* inevitable.

171 *World War I,* Keegan, 2000, Vintage Press. Keegan, excellent, as always, on WWI and its causes, and the importance of time.

growing strength convinced the German military to recommend war before Russia grew any stronger. We now know the Germans and Austrians were working together to start a war against Serbia, so diplomatic actions that would stop the march to war were rebuffed by Germany. Austria's foreign minister, **Leopold von Berchtold**, despised Serbia, and he pressed for war to end Serbian expansionist policies. With Germany's backing he hoped to demolish the Serbs, but Russia had to stay out for Austria to win. Russia had backed down before when faced with a joint Austrian—German front and Berchtold hoped for a repeat, but this time it was different. Russia's military told the Tsar that a limited mobilization was impossible and unwise, plus the Tsar wanted to avoid another humiliation at the hands of the Germans, so he ordered a full mobilization. France failed to encourage Russia to moderate its actions. For example, if Russia had initiated a *limited* mobilization the nervous German plans would not require action. Finally, there was the **Schlieffen Plan**.

THE VON SCHLIEFFEN PLAN

Germany's major problem involved a threatened two-front war against France in the west and Russia in the east. The alliance of France with Russia specifically sought to keep Germany under control; unfortunately, the desired cautious mindset failed to appear. Instead, desperate plans became a necessity in the German mind because of the dual alliance. The German General Staff came under immense pressure to find a way to win a two-front war rather than avoid it at all costs. The result of German thinking became the famous **von Schlieffen Plan**. The plan required Germany to attack France at the *very outset* of war with a colossal assault while a few troops moved east to hold back the Russian tidal wave until France capitulated. Thereafter, Germany's focus could shift to Russia. The built-in predicament entailed *the need for an instant attack in the West.* Everything depended on knocking France out of the war before Russia mobilized and moved its considerable numbers of troops to the front. Realizing England might join France, the plan's need for speed increased exponentially. France must be defeated within six weeks, before significant help arrived from England or Russia. Germany's plan confirmed its desperation, as well as carrying numerous grave risks and false assumptions.

The plan required an attack through *neutral* Belgium followed by an encirclement of French forces near Paris. The great wheeling movement required enough force and coordination to smash French forces manning the north of France, then charge south toward Paris, and finally rotating east to capture France's military in a pocket. What a tall order! The plan also called for allowing French forces attacking Germany at the frontier to advance during the first few days of the war, thus pulling them away from the main attack and deeper into the German pocket. Oddly, French Plan 17 called for this very attack into German territory. Imprudently, the German military staff took no notice that attacking neutral Belgium guaranteed England would declare war, as England ensured Belgium's neutrality. This is another indication of how desperate von Schlieffen perceived Germany's situation.

The German plan did not address failure. There was no plan B. *Everything* depended on defeating France within six weeks.[172] For a general staff to shun planning for possible failure is inexcusable. If the plan failed, as everyone knew it might because it required a number of great gambles, Germany's future depended on improvisation rather than a well researched backup plan. Because of this lack of foresight Germany went forward under a gross assumption that the plan must succeed. A close examination of the failure alternative might have convinced even the most hardened general that peace trumped war in this instance. Failure predestined Germany to fight on two-fronts against the massive Russian army to the east and a very good set of armies to the west. The consequences of a British naval blockade and the resulting lack of supplies and food was obvious. Peace was by far the best course of action; nevertheless, peace failed to pass muster. Worse yet for Germany, a new set of German generals significantly changed the Schlieffen Plan.

MOBILIZATION

Austria resolved on war with Serbia and mobilized, declaring war on July 28, 1914; then Serbia called on Russian support, and Russia mobilized. Germany then mobilized, thus leading to a French mobilization. England stayed out at this point. If England had continued to stay out, history might have changed course dramatically. As France mobilized Germany struck immediately because of the von Schlieffen plan's speed requirements. Germany crashed through neutral Belgium and England immediately entered the war. England sent its army to France very quickly, and gave significant aid to France at the key moment of the German assault.

---

[172] "Everything" meaning the survival of the German nation.

Due to the reasons listed above, the great powers of the day stumbled into an all out war no one wanted. *None of the great powers would survive intact.* Austria-Hungary ended up broken up; the Turkish Empire ceased to exist; Germany lost territory, economic power, and prestige;[173] England gained colonies but lost a generation of young men and its financial underpinnings; Russia lost its government and its national soul to an evil beyond all calculation; and France lost a generation in the trenches as well as its financial foundations. Serbia suffered assault and defeat. Serbia lost the least and gained the most considering its culpability in inaugurating the avalanche of doom. The Black Hand murderers achieved their goal of an independent Slav state (Yugoslavia). The assassin Princip is still considered a hero in Serbia. In short, the terrorists won and everyone else lost.

A *short* summary of events: Serbia murders Archduke Ferdinand of Austria, Austria makes demands on Serbia, Russia backs Serbia, Germany backs Austria, France backs Russia, Austria attacks Serbia, Russia mobilizes, Germany attacks France through Belgium, England enters war. Even this sounds complicated.

DECIDING FACTORS (IN ORDER OF IMPORTANCE):

1. **The British Blockade of Germany and its allies**. This devastating blockade prevented any kind of material, including food, from reaching Germany or its allies. Even the Ottoman Empire suffered. Syria claimed the loss of one-half million people due to starvation from the blockade. Cut off from its traditional food sources in Russia, Austria-Hungary's agricultural system began to collapse in 1917 increasing starvation in their nation. In the end, England starved the Germans and their allies into submission. Even after Germany agreed to the armistice, Britain continued the blockade while thousands of civilians starved to death needlessly (and people wonder why the Germans started WWII).
2. **The Failure of the Schlieffen Plan**. Germany staked everything on the Schlieffen Plan. After it failed, Germany fought a war on two fronts, eventually proving the pre-war prediction of certain defeat. After the failure of the Schlieffen Plan, Germany needed to consider offering peace even if the terms were unfavorable. Years of slaughter followed but still failed to change the course of the German nation.

---

[173] The all-important factor to the involved nations, it seems.

3. **The Entry of the United States into the War** on the Allied Side. Once again, like Britain, if the USA had remained neutral, the world's future might have transformed. With no intervention by the USA, WWI might have continue stalemated; thus, requiring all sides to consider some kind of negotiated peace where everyone "lost." Senator Warren Harding, a future US president, led the Republicans in arguing against entering the war but failed to convince the public or the Democrats who controlled Congress.
4. **The Code Breakers**. England was reading Germany's codes consistently, leading directly to the deciphering of the Zimmerman Telegram bringing the United States into the war. The code breakers knew beforehand everything the German High Seas Fleet was doing, enabling them to block any move to destroy or significantly damage the English fleet. The code breakers also warned the Allied generals of coming German offensives. Overall, the Allied code breakers were a key war-winning factor (just like WWII).
5. **Allied Technological and Tactical Developments**. The invention of the **tank** and **combined arms warfare** (tanks, aircraft, artillery, and infantry all working together as a team) broke open the Western Front leading directly to the defeat of Germany. In addition, the invention of the convoy system and new detection devices destroyed Germany's undersea offensive, which was their last chance to break England. Allied aircraft became much better as the war progressed giving the Allies control of the air, another key component in winning on the Western Front.

THE WAR BEGINS

The war began with Germany executing its Schlieffen Plan, which violated the neutrality of Belgium. The English then entered the war because of this neutrality violation and straight away landed troops in France. Meanwhile, the French were positioning their troops improperly. Under the **French Plan 17** they planned an immediate attack on the German frontier, thus, inadvertently putting themselves into the German sack. Germany's generals had *changed* the Schlieffen Plan by positioning more units on the German frontier where the French attack took place. The French attack suffered heavy losses followed by a retreat. *This was not what Schlieffen had wanted.* Von Schlieffen placed only a few German troops on the frontier because he *wanted them driven back.* The French drive would continue if they thought they were winning, making it impossible to reposition their troops fast enough to prevent their encirclement. Critically, since the French attack experienced a bloody repulse, the French units were in position to move swiftly by rail to meet the German advance on Paris. *This rapid repositioning of their forces saved France.* Quickly retreating Allied units from the Belgian frontier caused confusion near Paris, allowing the German advance to nearly reach the city. But, similar confusion in the German forces resulted in a wide gap between units at a key location on the German front. Allied reconnaissance aircraft spotted the gap near the River Marne, and the British launched an attack into this gap threatening the entire German advance. In a series of engagements on the River Marne the combined French and English forces defeated the Germans and "saved" France in the **Miracle of the Marne**.

The word "saved" is in quotes because "salvation" meant a long cruel war for France. Millions of additional Frenchmen died due to the Miracle of the Marne. If the German plan had achieved success the war could have been mercifully short thereby saving millions of lives. Until the next war anyway.

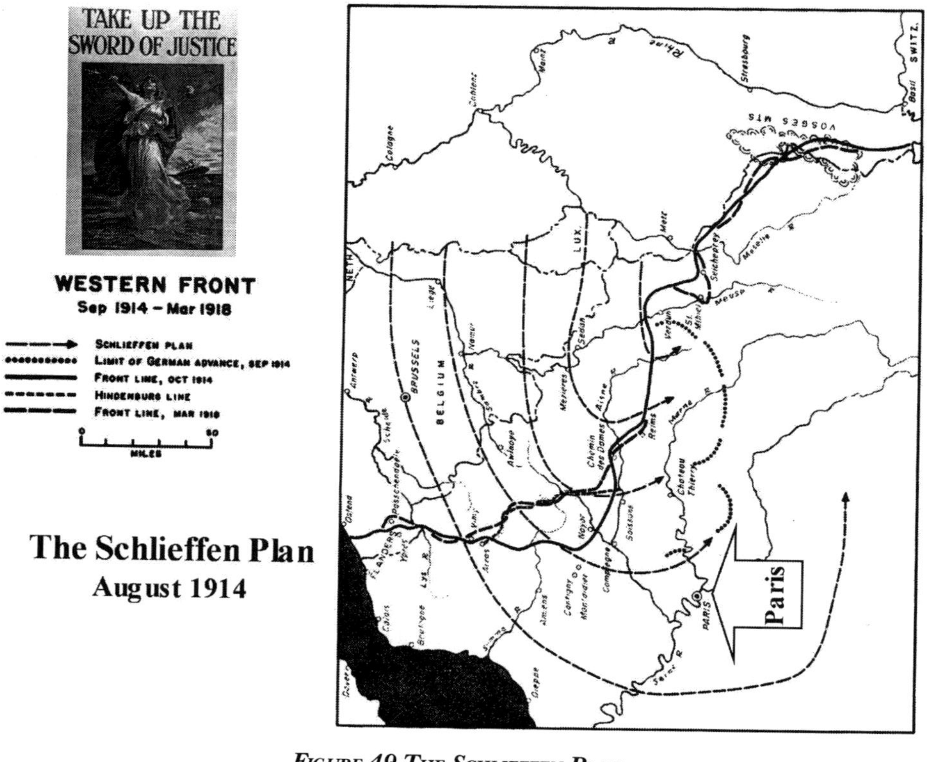

FIGURE 49 THE SCHLIEFFEN PLAN

The German plan failed for many *tactical* reasons, including: lack of coordination between advancing German armies; stiff resistance by the small, but extremely professional, British Army; too few German troops on the critical right wing; too many German troops at their frontier; the swift repositioning of French frontier forces; the German High Command stripping troops from the right wing for the Eastern Front before concluding the critical encirclement of French forces; the Allied decision to immediately abort French Plan 17 and reposition the troops; the German field commanders allowing a gap to develop between their divisions; the Allies quickly locating the gap with air reconnaissance and immediately attacking into the gap.

The *strategic* cause of failure: the plan's timetable proved far too ambitious. The timetable was the plan's key feature, and if the timetable failed the plan failed. Foot soldiers could not hope to keep the plan's timetable. After the Germans left their jump-off points they advanced on foot. Marching men trying to cover the given distances faced an impossible task. The heat of summer, the lack of supply transport, stiff resistance by British and French troops, and a lack of coordination made victory, for mere mortals, unattainable. The lack of radio communications made the problem of coordinating movement overwhelming. The plan could solve these concerns only by striking with such crushing force that all problems of coordination, timing, and distance fell before the sheer weight of the assault. If enough troops were available to stop counterattacks, keeping the momentum on the attacker's side, it might have worked, although it would have taken more than the planned six weeks. Von Schlieffen designed in this extra strength; however, less skillful generals changed the equation by decreasing strength in the attacking armies while increasing defensive strength in the wrong places.[174] After the Germans faltered, the French and English forces counterattacked effectively causing the Germans to withdraw. The Germans entrenched in defensive positions, blocking Allied counterattacks. The entrenchments then lengthened, soon extending from the English Channel to Switzerland, creating the ultimate front without a flank.

Momentarily think on this: if WWI caused WWII, then WWI becomes history's most important war. Thus, the Schlieffen Plan is history's most important plan, and the Battle of the Marne the most important battle. The reasoning is flawed due to numerous disconnects, but it is easy to argue

---

174 See: John Keegan, *The First World War,* 2000 Vintage Press.

the position.[175] By arguing against or for such propositions we gain a better understanding of history. Comparisons deepen understanding.

STALEMATE IN THE WEST

The Germans failed to destroy France and possessed no plans for this result in the west. The Allied problem was that Germany held a large part of France containing quality resources and many French citizens. The Western Allies reasoned that the Germans could just sit where they were. France could not allow such an outcome, so frontal attacks against well-fortified positions seemed to be a necessity (recall there was no flank). The Germans assumed the same and took pains to deepen and strengthen their positions. For three years, the power of these defenses proved impossible to overcome. [176]

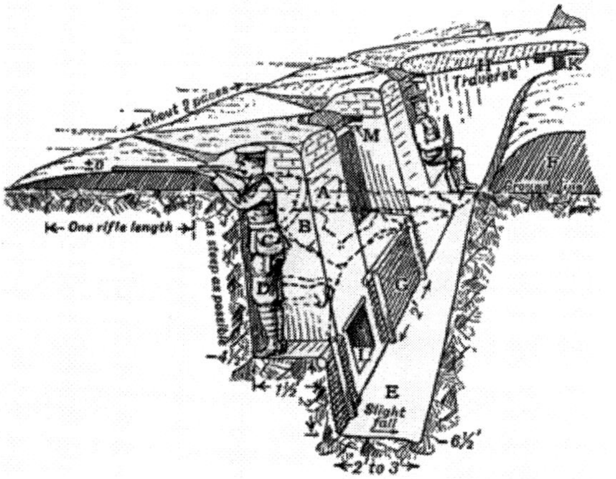

FIGURE 50 TRENCH SYSTEM, FROM ENGLISH ARMY MANUAL 1914

---

[175] The disconnects are many: the jump from the German plan to the battle of the Marne is too attenuated—who knew a gap would open up? Also, push the argument to the extreme; if the Marne was most important battle, then the gap was the most important gap, and the aircraft flight spotting the gap the most important airplane and flight in history, and the pilot the most important pilot, and the gas in the tank the most important gas, and the truck that delivered the gas the most important truck, and the truck driver the most important driver, and his mom the most important mom, etc It get ridiculous very quickly.

[176] The same thing happened in the American Civil War around Petersburg—and they were using rifled muskets.

The Maxim gun, the first reliable machine gun, was a main instrument for trench defense. The machine guns of World War I, invented by H. Maxim (thus the name) in 1884, fired about six hundred rounds per minute (ten rounds per second), and were so heavy it took several men to move, maintain, and shoot them; however, they also decimated attacking troops. The Germans protected their machine guns until the Allied artillery stopped firing, then set up the guns to drench the advancing troops with bullets. The howitzer artillery piece, a defensive and offensive machine, fired a projectile at high angles while out of sight (behind a hill for example) for a long distance. New shells exploded in the air scattering great quantities of fast flying, hot, steel fragments (shrapnel) capable of killing numerous men in an instant. These new machines of war erased men's lives by the millions as they advanced across the open, muddy, barbed wire covered ground of No Man's Land.[177]

Following 1914, the Western Front settled into doomed and nightmarish Allied attacks against excellent defensive fortifications held by the Germans. During the next three years, the front hardly moved in spite of countless sacrifices by hundreds of thousands of troops. The **Battle of the Somme,** a combined British and French attack on German trenches in July 1916, lasted four and one-half months. When the ordeal ended, British casualties totaled approximately *420,000*, French *205,000*, and German *500,000*; and, *the attack failed to reach objectives set for the first day.* At **Verdun**, a million men died, while positions hardly changed.[178] These battles were typical for the Western Front.

THE WESTERN FRONT

The French and British generals, such as Nivelle for France and Haig for Britain, kept frontally attacking the perfectly dug-in Germans. After achieving nothing, and scratching their heads for a moment or two, they demanded more men and attacked just as before, notwithstanding some minor adjustments (more men, more artillery). The next attack will do it, they promised their political overlords; nevertheless, the only difference was higher piles of dismembered dead. Alarmingly similar results hardly worried the military leaders. As shredded bodies and splintered bones piled up civilian governments in England and France began asking their

---

[177] "No man's land" was the area between the two opposing trench lines, so called because neither army controlled it.

[178] These figures are all approximate.

generals embarrassing questions. The responding generals said the Germans were suffering many more casualties than the attacking allies; thus, with each offensive victory grew closer. Liars. If insanity is doing the same thing over and over while expecting different results, these generals qualify as insane. And the political leaders were stupid and timid. Of course, the politicians were being lied to, but they needed to dig out the truth. Widespread incompetence is verified by the politicians accepting the general's statements without analysis while the grim reaper prospered.

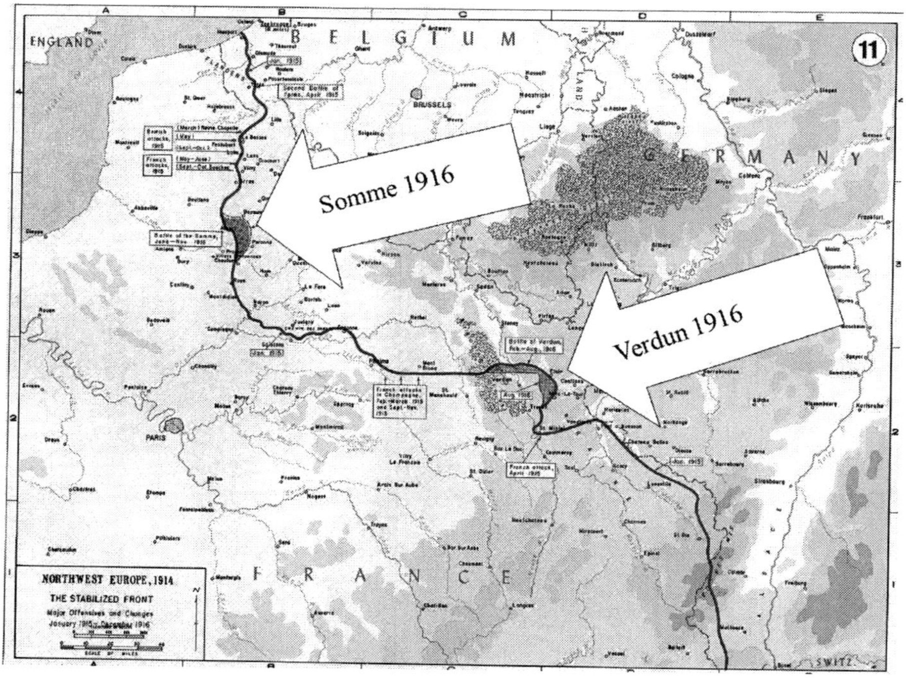

FIGURE 51 LACK OF MOVEMENT ON WESTERN FRONT
(SHADED AREAS WITH ARROWS SHOW CHANGES IN THE FRONT)

This view of the war is not universal. Numerous historians now take a new view, saying the Allied generals did a good job of trying to cope with a new military situation. They point out the generals changed tactics, increased the bombardment by artillery, fielded new weapons, and perfected new artillery techniques. One technique, the walking barrage, involves falling artillery shells creating a literal moving box of explosions around the advancing troops, protecting them all the way to the enemy trenches. New weapons, like aircraft, helped in observation to better assess enemy capabilities. The invention of tanks, pushed by Winston Churchill, tested by the Royal Navy's Landships Committee, and fielded in 1916 helped break the stalemate. Meanwhile, by 1918 the Germans invented a new assault technique called *infiltration,* which entailed the first attackers bypassing enemy strongholds for reduction by follow-on troops. In the last German offensives of the war these methods proved effective, but not war winning. By 1918, the British developed *combined arms tactics* which coordinated tanks, artillery, aircraft, and infantry into a team that crashed in unison through the defensive trench networks. Thereafter, they effectively followed up the assault with reserves, achieving deep penetrations into enemy territory. The British tactics were war winning. These combined arms assaults moved the front miles each day instead of yards. Unfortunately, the new techniques were discovered in 1918, which was far too late for most of the men.

There was a collective condemnation of the war at the time, even before the fighting ended. "We saved the world," proclaimed the Allied generals; however, the surviving troops and grieving families thought otherwise. WWI destroyed the world rather than saved it, and the public knew it. Civilian governments discovered the generals had lied about casualties and the effects of the Allied frontal assaults on Germany. When the war's trivial causes surfaced an antiwar movement arose condemning the diplomats, government leaders, and generals directing the Western Democracies into such a futile, murderous, and destructive war, and then refusing to end it.

This historical survey adopts the old view that Europe's leadership was hollow. In defense of this older view, please take note of **one fact**: *On the very last day of the war, after the armistice was signed, with fewer than three hours to go before the war's end, the Allied generals ordered an attack on German positions causing casualties in excess of ten thousand men.* The generals, and the men, knew the war was ending at eleven o'clock that day, but the Allied leaders ordered the assaults to begin at 9:00 AM. German positions scheduled for *surrender to the Allies the next day* were the targets. The men went forward, as ordered, dying for nothing. The explanation given? Germany's utter defeat must be proven to them; thus, the large scale assaults had to be made to prove to them they were totally defeated. This is irrational to say the least. The tired, battered, hungry Germans on the front lines needed no additional proof of defeat. Why attack them? Some Germans at home, far beyond the reach of Allied guns, thought defeat came through traitors at home. How was this attack going to convince those Germans of defeat? The fact that a general even contemplated such an assault, much less carried it out, is mind boggling. Of course, the generals safely relaxed miles away as bullets ruptured their soldier's bodies. This is the proof that the historians new view of the generals is mistaken in the extreme.

These incompetent generals were murderers. Each of these "hero" generals needed a swift hanging. Because such men go unpunished (except by historians) those following them often remain callous towards the lives of their troops. Until their last days on earth, these generals contended they saved the world for democracy, obviously believing their own vapid propaganda.

The Russian Front

In August 1914, the Germans on the Eastern Front faced the realization that the Russians were able to mobilize faster than anyone thought possible. Two massive Russian armies advanced to the frontier while thin lines of Germans maneuvered to stop them. In carrying out the terms of the alliance with France, the Tsar launched an instant offensive against Germany and her partner Austria–Hungary. The German staff received nervous calls for help and, anxious about the unexpected swiftness of the Russian attack, pulled units from the west, consequently reducing German combat power in the advance on Paris. The Germans experienced serious problems in the east for a while, but a new set of German generals arrived and turned the tide. **Generals Hindenburg and Ludendorff** became the team eventually giving the Germans victory over Russia. The costly conquest came with new infiltration methods of assaulting the enemy and a brilliant performance by German troops and their leaders in the field. Hindenburg and Ludendorff's triumphs earned them promotions, and they eventually earned the command leadership of all Germany's armies.

The Eastern and Western Fronts are dissimilar because in the east flanks existed. Trenches did not extend continuously across the landscape. This war required maneuvers over huge expanses of land, often in subzero weather. On this front, Austria-Hungary (Austria) engaged Russia along with their German ally; however, the Austrians failed miserably in every endeavor. The Austrians found themselves quickly defeated by Russia in the early battles, and soon threatened with complete defeat. Germany sent troops to their aid. Stretched thin by failure in France, pressure from Russia, and now the need to help Austria, Germany began to falter.

The German problems in the east included the landscape and immense numbers of Russian troops. Russian troops, mostly ill-trained peasants, were tough beyond all imagination. The Czar's troops withstood endless hardships and continued fighting. Russia's main problems revolved around leadership and logistics. Russian officers displayed ineptitude of the first order (with some notable exceptions), often throwing soldier's lives away for little gain. For example, at the start of the war, in battles around Tannenberg, two Russian armies made good ground, threatening to defeat the outnumbered Germans. Unfortunately, the two Russian commanders despised one another and refused to cooperate in their individual advances. Excellent German leadership prevailed, after a narrow escape or two, and defeated each large Russian army separately.

Russia's poor leadership displayed itself in several ways. Their equipment and supply system often did not hold up when it counted (logistics). The Russians could build up for an offensive well enough, but after the attack started supplies always dwindled quickly. Nonetheless, Russia played a key role in the Alliance, pulling numerous German units away from the Western Front, and often mauling them in the process. Russia wrecked the Austria-Hungarian armed forces causing Germany to expend critical resources in efforts to prop up their faltering ally.

THE WAR AT SEA

The war on land and the fight at sea turned against Germany by 1917. At sea, the German East Asian Cruiser Squadron under Admiral Spee won victories in the east and off the coast of South America in 1914 against superior English sea forces, but England swiftly hunted down the German cruisers and hammered them under the waves. Britain immediately initiated a total blockade of Germany, and soon nothing entered the nation, causing German civilians and troops to starve. The British blockade, as invoked, violated international law; nonetheless, this was total war making everything cricket according to the English Navy. At the **Battle of Jutland,** fought on May 31 to June 1, 1916, the German surface fleet tried to ambush a smaller British force, but ended up being ambushed themselves and nearly destroyed. The British broke the German codes early on and knew of German plans before their execution. Only excellent maneuvering saved the German High Seas Fleet. Since Britain lost more ships than Germany the Kaiser proclaimed victory. Such a claim was pure propaganda. The German fleet never again put to sea in force. All that manpower and firepower sat idle for the rest of the war.

The Germans, in desperation, then turned to submarines, and for a few months huge numbers of English merchant ships plunged to the ocean floor. Over 860,000 tons sank due to enemy action in April of 1917. The

German submarine threat virtually ended after England countered with convoys and better underwater detection. Germany's surface navy failed; thus, Germany would starve. Germany's undersea navy failed; thus, Britain would not starve. Britain's propaganda made every German sinking of a neutral ship an act of piracy and a slaughter of innocents by the demon Huns; however, while Britain broadcast German evils thousands of German civilians, including children, died of hunger because of the British blockade. The inability of Germany to make effective use of propaganda overseas hurt its cause immensely. *At sea, and in propaganda, the English victory was total.*

NEW TECHNOLOGY

World War I became increasingly vicious. The use of technology for killing saw manifold increases. Germany introduced poison gas to the battlefield (which availed them nothing), being immediately matched by Allied use of poison gas (who likewise achieved nothing). Air power became important for observing and bombing the enemy. Allied troops dug tunnels under the German lines and exploded large mines (which also achieved nothing). At sea, the Germans began unrestricted submarine warfare, often destroying neutral shipping bound for England thus angering the world (not good). Germany used large airships and Gotha bombers to bomb London and Paris (no real impact). Flamethrowers, hand grenades, smaller machine guns, and new artillery shells invented by the warring parties to win the war, only increased the slaughter. Each side hoped to slaughter the other with new technology, but their adversaries quickly picked up the new instruments of war and threw them back into the inventor's face. All this became increasingly deadly and *very* expensive. In the final analysis, Allied technology won the war with tanks and airplanes superior to the Central Powers' and produced in much larger quantities. **Tanks** were the major land innovation. The Allies thought them up, learned how to best use them, and then produced them in large enough numbers to smash German trench lines. Early on the Germans produced outstanding aircraft, but over time, the Allies produced more and better aircraft, wrestling the skies from the Kaiser. As a result the Allies had better reconnaissance information, and continually harassed the German troops and supply lines bombing and strafing everything that moved. The Allies won with war winning technology combined with new tactics.

FIGURE 52 TANKS ON THE WESTERN FRONT, VIMY 1917

THE EASTERN FRONT AND REVOLUTION

On the Eastern Front, Russian problems amplified. Inept Russian leadership regularly turned victory into defeat. Russian troops fought with outdated weapons and seldom received supplies of clothing or food needed to keep going. During 1915, Russia suffered 3.8 million casualties, and by 1917 they lost 2.3 million dead and 5 million injured. The government came under intense pressure to do quit, and when they refused the **Bolshevik Revolution** started in October 1917 overthrowing the Russian Czar, murdering the royal family, and starting a bloody civil war leading to a communist government controlled by **Vladimir Lenin** (1870 to 1924). The communists sued for peace with Germany. Germany extracted a harsh settlement from Lenin, but he needed Russia out of the war. The Treaty of Brest-Litovsk, signed on March 3, 1918, took Russia out of the war and massively increased the power and strategic advantages of the Central Powers.

OTHER FRONTS

Prior to the Russia defeat in 1917, the Allies in the west tried a few adventures to get around the stalemated Western Front by achieving victories elsewhere. **Winston Churchill** convinced the British government to attack Ottoman Turkey, who joined the Central Powers in November of 1914, to knock the Ottomans out of the war and open a warm-water supply line to Russia through the Bosporus. After a naval expedition failed to breach the straights using ships alone, Churchill decided on an amphibious assault to clear the Turkish forts guarding the passageway. This transpired in 1915 at **Gallipoli** with Australian and New Zealand troops achieving surprise landings near the Dardanelles; however, lack of aggressive exploitation resulted in a costly stalemate as bad as the Western Front. It became a disaster for the Allies and Churchill. Following a year of suffering, the British withdrew from Turkey after experiencing serious losses in men and ships. Gallipoli cost Britain's colonials, Australia and New Zealand, 250,000 casualties. Elsewhere, Italian attacks on Austria–Hungary through mountainous terrain failed with terrible losses, and an Allied landing in the Balkans went literally nowhere. The Western Allies then paused. They were at their breaking point. *The French Army mutinied in 1917* by refusing to leave their trenches for offensives. They were tired of donkey generals slaughtering them for no purpose. By putting down the mutiny and restoring the French Army General Petain of France saved the Allied cause; nonetheless, Allied troops were exhausted. When Russia quit the war immediate German exploitation might have put France and England on the ropes, but a dreadful German diplomatic move changed everything.

Over in the Middle East, then part of the Turkish Empire (Ottoman Empire), the English **General Allenby** began changing the world. With Arab help, he marched from Egypt across the Sinai Desert to Jerusalem, defeating the Turks everywhere along the way. Simultaneously, another British army attacked up the Tigris-Euphrates river valley for the second time in the war and finally seized Baghdad. General Allenby then prepared to invade Turkey itself, and the Turks were none too happy about these developments. Earlier in the war, they defeated a British expedition marching up the Tigris-Euphrates river valley and an English incursion launched out of Egypt. Those early victories were long past now, and the Turks worried about the English driving into Istanbul, so they sued for peace. WWI ended shortly after the Turks capitulated; thus, Allenby's efforts went mostly unrecognized, but he had altered the world dramatically. At Versailles the Ottoman Empire would fade into history as Britain and France divided the old empire between themselves. To this day, the division of the Ottoman Empire made at the Versailles peace talks haunts the world.

Turning Point: The United States of America Enters the War

The United States stayed out of the war, even though the sinking of US ships angered Americans and turned public opinion against Germany. English propaganda played its part by depicting the Germans as beasts murdering innocents.[179] So far, this had failed to persuade the United States to join the fight. Then Germany's foreign minister, Mr. Zimmerman, committed the ultimate act of idiocy by sending a telegram to Mexico requesting it join the war on the German side by attacking the United States.[180] In return, Mexico would regain areas lost in the Mexican-American war. Naturally, the telegram was in code, but English code breakers had been reading Germany's code since the war broke out. Now the code breakers gave England the hammer it needed to break American reluctance to enter the war. And, once again, proving the importance of codes. Britain broke the German codes in WWII with similar outstanding results.

When the American public learned of the **Zimmerman Telegram** they demanded war. America's president, Woodrow Wilson, campaigned for his second term on a peace platform; however, after the Zimmerman telegram Congress quickly declared war against Germany. Secretly, Wilson wanted to enter the war against the Germans, but American public opinion prevented the move until this moment. The United States of America entered the Great War in **April 1917**. *This was the turning point.* Germany faced her doom unless, by some strategy, she could defeat France and England before the Americans managed to arrive in force. With troops from the Russian front, new training in improved infiltration assault techniques, and new leadership at the top of the army (Hindenburg and Ludendorff),[181] and high hopes, the Germans began their last great offensive. The large German assault (series of assaults actually) initially made good headway, but then faltered without achieving even one key aim. The assaults failed because Germany lacked troops and because Ludendorff failed to focus his plan. The Americans soon arrived, turning the tide against Germany for the last time. Interestingly, Ludendorff had failed to establish a plan for what to do if the offensive failed. Just like they had in 1914 the Germans went forward assuming the plan would work even though it was a big gamble.

---

179 Literally. British posters depicted gorillas wearing German helmets grasping fainting women while their teeth dripped blood.

180 This was conditioned upon US entry into the war on the English and French side.

181 The two German generals had been promoted to head the entire German war effort because of impressive successes against Russia.

Ludendorff pushed the attacks too far, and scarified too many men in the assaults, probably because the attack had to work. Without an alternate plan he had no other choice.

As Germany starved and scraped the bottom of the manpower barrel it also stumbled in the technological war. The Allies produced tanks (a lot of them), better tactics (combined arms assaults), better aircraft (a lot more of these too), better technology for warfare at sea, more equipment, more spare parts, and better code-breaking methods—just to name a few Allied advantages.

After the last German assault bled to a halt, the Allies took the offensive all along the Western Front. For years, the Germans successfully moved troops from one location to another as each Allied campaign began. [182] Now the Allies attacked everywhere at once, and Germany's dwindling reserves could not plug every hole. As the German Army retreated, Ludendorff lost his nerve abruptly announcing to the Kaiser that Germany must surrender at once. At the same time, mutinies were taking place in the German Navy and spreading to the populace. The news stunned the Kaiser and German civilian leadership, remembering that only a few weeks ago they were told Germany was opening a war winning offensive. Violent questioning changed nothing, as German military leadership continued to insist on capitulation. The public knew nothing of these behind the scene military and political maneuvers. As the mutinies spread, Wilhelm II abdicated and the armistice was signed; nonetheless, the English blockade continued for months, starving women and children from Germany to Syria for reasons unclear to this day. With each innocent's death, German hatred grew because of the shortsighted English policy.

The German Army forced the nation's capitulation, but the Allies failed to enter Germany proper. Later, *the myth* arose that the German Army was "stabbed in the back" by enemies at home rather than suffering defeat in the field. This myth ballooned to a widespread belief and helped Adolph Hitler rise to power in Germany. Hitler, the man who started World War II, fought bravely in the Great War winning the Iron Cross—very hard for an enlisted man in the Kaiser's army. His hatred of the French, his condemnation of Germany's defeat, and the armistice terms of Versailles drove him to start a war to salvage German honor. Some Allied generals,

---

[182] The previous Allied attacks had been on relatively narrow fronts; this allowed the Germans to shift reserves to the endangered area without having to worry about assaults elsewhere.

Pershing among them, predicted that unless the Allies marched into Berlin the Germans would not admit defeat and the war would renew itself after a few years. The war did renew itself after a few years, and the new war proved worse than the old; however, the origins of WWII go far beyond an Allied failure to march on Berlin. While the myth dovetailed into post war evils, far greater issues pivoted on an international economic collapse, German economic problems, poor leadership in the West, and poor leadership in Germany that allowed **Adolf Hitler** to worm his way into power.

AFTERMATH

(And you thought the war was bad . . .)

The Germans cringed when they received the peace terms, but the Allies ripped at their throat. Germany must sign or be utterly destroyed. Germany was not allowed to enter the peace conference until told, as only the winning nations were allowed to attend. There were no negotiations. Over German protest, especially the clause saying Germany started the war (the War Guilt clause), the French and English battered Germany into signing the **1919 Treaty of Versailles**. The negotiations between the winning parties over the contents of the treaty were probably the most important in history. Many modern worldwide problems started with the Treaty of Versailles. World War II grew from this document, as well as numerous civil wars. World War I was a grave error for the West, but the Treaty of Versailles compounded and extended the error to future generations. The American Senate, to President Wilson's dismay, decided *against* the treaty and the US later signed a separate peace treaty with Germany.

As the Kaiser fled and the German parliament sued for peace, Germany itself faced a left-wing revolution. Communist cells, established all over Europe by the USSR and competing socialists movements, now attempted to take full advantage of the upheaval to gain control of governments in Germany and other troubled European nations, such as the new nations forming from the crumbling Austria-Hungarian Empire. As the German government tottered the streets became scenes of chaos. The starving populace began rioting, and the police strained to maintain order. In the short term, at least a semblance of order paved over smoldering difficulties; however, the future shown none too brightly for Western Europe as the forces of radical change swept the continent. Germany became the **Weimar Republic**, a weak government struggling to survive after the Great War.

As the war concluded, a horrendous influenza pandemic swept the world in 1918 and 1919 killing about **50 to 100 million people**. [183] The influenza exterminating the world probably came from the trenches of World War I, when a normal strain of flu moving through millions of men radically changed in the process. Then infected men took the flu back to their home nations where it became an invisible hurricane killing anyone susceptible. Humanity found no cure, and the killing storm simply exhausted itself as survivors were apparently immune to its effects. The pandemic killed far more people than the war itself.

The Great War's victims were many. Millions were dead, and billions spent. The Ottoman Empire, destroyed; Austria-Hungary, dismembered; Germany's overseas colonies, and national territory stripped; German honor, shattered; the French and British populace, decimated; the world's economy, in torment. The great world of 1900, murdered. European wealth and society was destroyed by stupidity beyond imagination.

Versailles' Treaty stripped Germany of its army and navy, forced the nation to admit responsibility for the war, and forced its citizens to pay *thirty-two billion* (in 1919 dollars, much more today) in repatriations to the Allies.[184] The United States refused to ratify the treaty. **Woodrow Wilson**, the American president negotiating the treaty, sold out everything for his concept of a new organization joining the leading nations of the world in a setting where diplomacy substituted for wars—the **League of Nations**. Wilson, an idealist, dreamed of the League forming the centerpiece of a world without war. However, the US Senate must ratify US treaties, and the Senate rejected the treaty and the League of Nations. The United States signed a separate peace with Germany, bitterly disappointing the Europeans. The world's nations went ahead with the League, but America never joined, and the USSR (Russia renamed by the communists)[185] stayed

---

[183] Some call this the **Spanish flu**. Earlier estimates of deaths were in the 50 million range, but newer estimates raise the total to 100 million.

[184] If we multiply the 1919 dollar amount by forty to try and adjust for inflation since that year we get: (32 x 40 = **1,280 billion dollars**. You can see the amount is gargantuan, especially when we recall Germany spent herself into bankruptcy during the war just like the Allies. Where was Germany going to get that amount of money? Why the multiple of 40? A new car in the 1920 era was about $500, and a new car today is about $20,000. 20,000 divided by 500 = 40. A very rough estimate and filled with assumptions . . . I know. It is just a way to get an idea of how much money we are really talking about.

[185] USSR = the Union of Soviet Socialist Republics.

away until 1934. As organized, the League possessed little ability to enforce any rules it might pass, and passing rules was nearly impossible because taking action required a unanimous vote. It became mostly a talking club, and when talking failed the League failed. The Concert of Europe depended on balance of power politics to maintain the peace, and that produced arms races and the Great War. The League would not rely on balance of power politics that it thought caused the great conflagration, and the ideal of a mutual defense against aggression failed to prevent a swift march to a new murderous conflict.

Economic calamity overtook Germany and Europe immediately after the war, with only England and the United States seeming to emerge from the firestorm with something like their old economies intact. An illusion, at best. England spent its national treasure on the war, and it borrowed heavily to sustain itself during the fighting. The German economy launched into hyperinflation where a thousand marks could not buy a loaf of bread. At one point, *a million German marks* equaled about *one US dollar.* The United States also spent deeply to enter the war and sustain the fight. Little did the "winning" nations recognize the world economic system sustained enormous strain, and even one misstep by the economic ministers could cause the international system to fail. In fact, several missteps came in the form of higher tariffs, tightening national money supplies, increasing taxation, and more government control over economies (socialism—which resulted in even higher taxes). The world economic system crumbled and the world's worse depression hit—**The Great Depression**. With millions out of work; banks failing and taking people's savings; industry shrinking; production falling; and international trade dying the government bureaucracies choked. Around the world finance ministers seemed unable to deal with the emergency, and the steps governments did take made the Depression worse. From 1929 to 1939, the Depression gripped the world, but the Depression hit hardest in the world's most industrialized nation—the United States.[186]

In the United States, President **Hoover**, who took office in 1929, tried to keep wages high, and he approved of recent congressional moves to increase tariff rates substantially. Hoover adopted high government spending to solve the crisis, and he tried many economic moves never tried before. By keeping wages artificially high Hoover caused layoffs

---

186 Europe was showing signs of recovery by 1932, and some recovery was underway in 1933. In the USA these years were among the worst of the depression era. See: p. 332 et seq, *The Third Reich in Power*, Evans, R., Penguin, 2005

in major industries, keeping high tariffs shrank international trade, and high government spending created high taxes taking money away from consumers. President **Roosevelt**, elected into office in 1933,[187] also desired high wages, did nothing to reduce the towering tariffs, and his administration spent far more than Hoover's. Roosevelt tried to raise the price of farm products and manufactured goods, he created extensive government works programs, and he *raised taxes.* This caused fewer goods to be available for purchase and took more money away from private enterprise inhibiting new hiring. Roosevelt's "**New Deal**" programs did much more harm than good. Recovery from the Great Depression began only after World War II took men out of the workforce as soldiers, and started massive production to fight the war. In fact, some economists claim the recovery did not happen until the 1950s. (See our section on the Great Depression).

As the worldwide economic disaster started, dictators began taking over major nations in Europe and Asia. It seemed capitalism and democracy failed, as shown by the Great War and now the Great Depression. Italy moved to **Mussolini** as its leader (a dictator) in 1922; Russia came under a brutal dictatorship by 1928 (**Stalin**); Germany elected **Hitler** (another dictator) as its leader in 1933, and in Spain **Franco** became dictator in 1934. The economic tragedy of the Great Depression, caused in large part by WWI, led to a political catastrophe where powerful modern nations fell to cold-blooded dictators. In this fashion, World War I led to World War II. The Great War had changed everything, and everything collapsed quickly.

Some Thoughts on the Great War and the Aftermath

The great problems of the First World War stemmed from the Treaty of Versailles, the enormous debt incurred fighting the war, the massive death toll, the social dislocation, damage to political and economic structures, and the humiliation of the German nation. At the conclusion of any war, especially a momentous war such as WWI, the winning nation(s) must strive to create a peace stabilizing the situation in a fashion that prevents another war. This is ***winning the peace***. The Roman general Scipio Africanus understood the principle of winning the peace, and this was why he made a generous peace with Carthage. Scipio ended the very long and brutal Second Punic War where Hannibal spent sixteen years destroying

---

[187] The same year Hitler came to power in Germany.

Italy as well as butchering several Roman legions. Scipio had won a total victory, and burning Carthage to the ground posed no problem—as was later accomplished in the Third Punic War after inferior leaders in Rome destroyed Scipio's diplomatic triumph. Scipio knew Carthage could become a trading partner and assist Rome in controlling Africa; thus, Scipio designed a peace to avoid further war and bring additional prosperity to Rome *and* its ancient enemy Carthage.

The drafters of the Versailles Treaty failed to follow Scipio's example, creating a treaty calculated to crush and humiliate Germany. France intended to stop another war by being so harsh with Germany she could never threaten Europe again; however, by making the Versailles treaty so ruthless the leaders all but guaranteed the next war. The axiom is simple enough to understand: it is not wise to humiliate a great people.[188] By destroying Germany's wealth through huge repatriations they guaranteed the world additional financial tribulations.[189] The great debt incurred by the warring nations hurt their economies and international trade, but no one saw that by harming Germany's economy they wounded every economy worldwide. These problems, plus feeble financial decisions by key economic powers in Europe and America, resulted in an economic collapse of epic proportions.

Economically, the world was in a fairly good place in 1900 and the future seemed bright. Democracies or paternal monarchies ruled most of Europe and by extension most of the world. Industrialism brought benefits in new and better products at lower prices while workers earned higher wages. Science helped to advance industry bringing ever improving manufactured goods. (These thoughts are my opinions. Many historians disagree.)

---

188 Or anyone for that matter. In our world humiliation of nations doesn't seem to matter so much; however, in 1919 Europe it mattered a lot. The war guilt clause in the Versailles Treaty infuriated the Germans. A popular song in Germany was Deutschland uber Allies (Germany over the Allies); now, that thinking comes from people seeking revenge. Be smart reader, do not humiliate anyone and your life will be much easier. And you were told history couldn't teach you anything . . .

189 The Germans did not actually pay the repatriations. Loans from the US and England allowed the Germans to pay with the loans rather than their gross national product. The Germans received more in loans than they were required to repay. The amount of repatriations was also adjusted down several times.

Many observers see things another way. They view the pre-World War I era as one of oppression and imperialism. These people see a world filled with inequality and the desperation of people downtrodden by the Western World and its monopoly on modern weapons. Such spectators perceive the West dissipating wonderful cultures by imposing Western ideas and ideals upon an unwilling populace while using the oppressed people's natural resources and labor to further enrich super wealthy imperialist capitalists. Imperialism is still a pejorative term today. In fact, imperialism brought a modern way of life to countless people, including medical care, sanitation, increased crop production, increased equality for many (women for example), education, improving economies, and other unqualified enhancements to areas in India, Indochina, China, Africa, and others. It would have taken decades or centuries to achieve this progress without the "curse" of imperialism.

The Western World's leadership failed miserably after 1900 in numerous clumsy and dim-witted ways. The major failures include: the failure to stop WWI; the failure to end the war once it started; the fundamental failures in drafting the Treaty of Versailles; the destruction of Austria-Hungary; the imposition of huge repatriations on Germany; the imposition of high tariffs that killed international trade; the utter failure to mitigate the Great Depression; the failure to stop Germany's rearming; and the failure to stop WWII long before it began. The cause of each failure: poor decisions by governments and military leaders. Any of the above occurrences cried out for avoidance. Utter, complete, and total leadership incompetence underpinned these events.

Let Us Learn

The lessons of the First World War are many and complex. For our daily lives we can learn to slow down when making significant decisions, avoid letting pride fog clear thinking about ultimate consequences, think out the "end game" of any significant decision before taking action, and, when involved in a losing situation, cut your losses by getting out immediately. You must also watch for desperate acts by weak people that can cause unusual disruptions and poor decisions.

Tally up what you have and learn how to keep it. One of the first rules of life is avoid destroying what you have in the search for more. Europe in 1914 enjoyed the fruits of hundreds of years of progress. Why they tossed it out is a multifaceted question; nevertheless, we must note the fact that it was thrown away for no reason beyond human pride and stupidity. In your life, keep track of your positives, and remember they entail more than money. Good health is an asset of invaluable worth; thus, keep it safe. Loyal friends are another asset with value beyond measure, learn how to nurture those relationships. A sense of humor holds the key to a happier life. Respect for others should be recognized, acknowledged, and encouraged. Financial security must be planned and then carefully sought after. If financial security is finally achieved, protect and enjoy it.

Europe's financial bounty in 1912 was beyond compare. Its social interactions were world renowned. The arts, theater, literature, painting, engineering, philosophy, and so much more were at their zenith prior to WWI. All this was destroyed by avarice, fear, distrust, and hatred among world leaders. Leaders must keep what their nations' have intact and risk its loss only in the most dire circumstances. If Germany backed away from its commitment to Austria-Hungary, would it have been cowardly? Even if it was, would a bad reputation destroy her? Could Russia swallow its pride and allow Serbia to go under? After all, Serbia caused the death of the Archduke. Decisions made in anger or pride are poor decisions. Respond to situations with cold logic. Give yourself time to think before acting. Do not make decisions based on pride as Serbia, Austria, Russia, Germany, France, and perhaps even England did in starting the First World War. Remember what you have and ask if you want to lose it. Even WWI "winners" lost heavily. Keep in mind that winning can include keeping what you have intact. Destroying an enemy while destroying yourself is not winning at all.

Books and Resources on the Great War:

World War I, Keegan, 2000, Vintage Press. Must reading for understanding the great war.

The 11th Month, the 11th day, the 11th Hour, Persico, 2004, Random House. Lets the reader understand the horror of the war as few other books can. It tells the story of the last attacks by the Allies just hours before the war was to end.

World War I, SLA Marshall, is excellent reading.

The First World War, A Complete History, Martin Gilbert,1994, Owl Books.

The Great War (West Point Military History), by W. Griffits, Square One Publishers, 2003.

Cataclysm, The First World War As Political Tragedy, Stevenson, 2004, David, Basic Books, Perseus Book Group.

The Third Reich in Power, Evans, R., Penguin, 2005

Dreadnought, Massy, 1992, Ballantine Books
The World Crisis, 1911-1918, Churchill, 1931, Free Press
Fighting the Great War, a Global History, Neiberg, Michael, Harvard University Press, 2005.

Chapter 14

The Interwar Years 1919 to 1939

The "war to end all wars" was finally over in 1919 with the execution of the Treaty of Versailles. Europe was at peace. It would remain at peace for twenty years. It turned out the "war to end all wars" only set up Europe for the next conflict which was even greater. World War II would officially start in 1939 with Germany, led by Adolph Hitler, invading Poland. **Winston Churchill**, Britain's lord of the admiralty in WWI[190]and its Prime Minister in WWII, stated the Second World War should have been easy to prevent because the Western Democracies only needed to enforce the Treaty of Versailles to stop Germany from rearming. Along with economic errors and the Great Depression, these flawed decisions paved the way to World War II.

After the Great War of 1914 to 1918, with its attendant slaughter of at least 8 million soldiers, the people of the United Kingdom, France, and the United States tried fixing the world in an attempt to prevent a repeat of WWI. To that end, the governments of the great powers including Great Britain, France, Germany, Japan, and the United States entered into arms limitations treaties to prevent arms races. Under these various agreements, the major world powers agreed to limit the tonnage of warships constructed, among other items. The **League of Nations** involved itself in keeping the peace through diplomatic efforts. Large peace organizations formed in America, England, and France to keep their countries out of wars. "Peace at any price" was their motto.

---

190 Churchill was lord of the admiralty until the disaster at Gallipoli, which he had underwritten, and was then fired; later, rehired (appointed) head of munitions. As one can see, in 1900's England the same leaders just stayed on in new roles. Recall the Versailles treaty said Germany could not have an army, an air force, or a navy of any size. IF the Allies would have prevented Germany from re-arming, no WWII. How hard would that have been? Once the Allies became aware that Germany was acquiring arms just go in and take over. After all, what would they stop them with?

As it happened, the great powers would not have the money to engage in arms races. The **Great Depression** deprived the nations of funds needed to construct and field large armies or invest in extremely expensive weapons systems. No money equals no arms races. Peace seems to require the bankruptcy of all.

After the Great War, America, England, and France disarmed to a large degree and went back to civilian budgets. In America the US Army shrank dramatically, but the navy did somewhat better because nations usually avoided scrapping battleships like beer cans. Germany was stripped of its army and Austria-Hungary ceased to exist. Turkey also faced financial problems that limited its ability to rearm. In the USSR under Stalin, the Soviets began a massive rearming and rebuilding of its army. Its secret arms buildup included development of the excellent T-34 tank. During this period between 1919 and 1929 an economic boom of sorts was underway, and the nations of the world prospered. Europe could trade once more, even though Germany was on the ropes, and the USSR took itself out of international trade under their communist regime. Money was available for investing, and companies expanded to meet growing consumer demand.

From 1919 to 1933, the United States tried another experiment in abolishing evil. Just as the nation abolished slavery it would now abolish drunkenness by making sales of liquor illegal.[191] The **Eighteenth Amendment** to the US Constitution, approved on January 29, 1919, prohibited the sale of alcohol in America. This forced many distilleries, bars, and transportation companies out of business or into other businesses. The law made some very expensive property valueless. Legally owned property became contraband overnight. Once again, the government did not pay for the property it made worthless. After all, the property was not seized by the government for public use. Washington DC just said it was illegal to use any property for the now illegal production of alcohol.[192] The great experiment of taming drunkenness fell flat, and in 1932 Roosevelt and the Democrats ran on a platform of overturning the Eighteenth Amendment. Roosevelt was elected in a landslide in 1932 because of the Depression, but one might wonder how many voted Democrat because it would bring back booze (Even I may have voted for that. How dumb are these Republicans anyway?).

---

[191] After 1919, a fellow could be out of work AND sober. What could be worse?

[192] Remember the abolition of slavery? This is the same concept.

THE GREAT DEPRESSION 1929-1942?

BACKGROUND

From 1919 to about 1929, the world economic situation seemed okay. England and France were recovering from the war, supplies of food and manufactured products were plentiful, and living standards were going up. In the USA, President Calvin Coolidge's administration was running a financial surplus, cutting taxes dramatically, and experiencing a growth in real income *per person* of 2.1 percent.[193] Underneath however, things were not so rosy. The world's economic system developed dynamic cracks that were growing and endangering the *global* economic system.

The Great War devastated France, destroying large swathes of land requiring millions of francs to restore. France had taken on massive war debts with England and the United States which had to be repaid, but these large debts caused devaluation of the franc making repayment difficult.[194] France was counting on Germany to pay for everything through repatriations ("Germany will pay all" the French government proclaimed); however, the expected repatriations did not show up. Germany was broke. Payments were much lower than agreed and slow in coming. The problem of German repatriations dogged the European powers throughout the 1920s. Germany could not repay England and France, and America would not cancel Allied war debts. Several conferences were held, but no real solutions to the financial problems were ever found. The 1932 Lausanne Conference, held in the middle of the Great Depression, terminated the wrangling over German repatriations by requiring one final payment from Germany. Today it is clear that Germany received more in American loans than she paid in repatriations. Never trust accountants mixing with politicians.

Britain experienced critical economic problems as well. In 1922 the Conservatives called for protective tariffs, a move which would surely damage international trade. This was contrary to England's traditional free trade policy. At the urging of Winston Churchill, Chancellor of the Exchequer, Britain went back onto the Gold Standard in 1925, but this also failed to re-establish stability in the world's money markets. As trade

---

[193] For statistics on the 1920s through the Great Depression see http://www2.census.gov/; however, this site is hard to use as the data is simply in a list by year, and it is difficult to tell what you are calling up until it is on the screen. Typical government operation.

[194] Devaluation means their money was worth less than it was before the change.

began to shrink more nations enacted protective tariffs further damaging international trade.

On the financial front, credit markets were getting tight because the money supply was lessening as the decade wore on, businesses were worried about getting loans, and the supply of investment capital was drying up. This was taking place worldwide, and some of the problems included the debts being carried from WWI. In Germany, super inflation was threatening European economic stability. When the economic future turns bleak people with investment money pull back; thus, investment capital was vanishing. Except for Germany's inflation, most of the problems were sub-rosa and not a concern for the public—at least, that is what the elite leaders of the world believed.

Britain's Empire also proceeded to give Britain trouble. Former colonies now wanted independence and nationhood. England responded by giving many colonies more independence, including a parliament and independence in foreign policy, while still maintaining a close relationship to the mother country. Those former colonies included Canada, Australia, New Zealand, and the Union of South Africa. Most notable in *not* gaining additional independence was India. The new nations often refused to follow Britain's foreign policy, thus complicating matters for Britain in the 1930s.

Political problems erupted all over Europe because of growing radical leftist and rightist movements in several European nations. Adolf Hitler, a Germany radical rightist who led the **Nazi party**, languished in prison in 1925 after a failed coup d'état. While there he wrote *Mien Kampf* (*My Battle*) detailing his thoughts about the future of Germany.[195] Hitler's radical ideas would eventually lead his Nazi party to winning elections in Germany, eventually gaining control of the nation itself. In his book he set out his future plans for conquest, however, few read the tome. Unfortunate, because Hitler adhered to this published plan after he assumed the office of Chancellor of Germany. Due to a good world economy during the early to mid-1920s neither the rightist nor the leftist movements made headway in Europe or Asia, but as the economic situation grew dire things changed. Communist movements gained ground with the result that rightist also attracted followers concerned about the Reds taking over. It was during the crisis of the Great Depression that men like Hitler gained power through

---

[195] This screed remains popular today (2010) in Muslim nations, probably because of its anti-Jewish statements.

the support of the common person who wanted a return to stability. The Great Depression brought on worldwide radical political changes, so please understand this unprecedented economic collapse was a globe changing event and a major reason for WWII.

In the 1920s, England and France were having money problems and sought loans from the United States, or loan extensions, to cover war debts and other matters. American bankers extended the loan payments and gave new loans to Europe keeping the nations economies afloat. It seemed to most these loans were good business because the future looked bright and money was being made everywhere. The banks thought that as the world economy continued improving the money would come flowing in. These assumptions of a bright future proved false.

CAUSES

We will now start an analysis of the Great Depression's causes; however, they are still widely debated and unresolved. Many economists argue the 1920's era displayed real growth, while others think it was an era of false prosperity—profitless prosperity—because business profits were weak even though the economy was booming. Raw data from the 1920's indicate real profits and real growth, as manufacturing output rose over *23 percent*, but underneath it all something else was eating at the foundations. That something else was the money supply. The **Federal Reserve** (Central Bank or Fed) was making money easy to get in the mid-1920s by increasing the money supply, and the Fed injected money into the credit markets. This, some say, created a boom economy based on money supply growth and easy loans, not business growth in real terms (whatever "real" means).

Economist **Milton Friedman** says the Fed *reduced* the money supply and raised interest rates after the 1929 crash, thus making the downturn worse; other economists say the Fed *increased* in money supply after the crash and propped up failing businesses, thus increasing the severity of the debacle. The cold facts: Between 1921 and 1927, the money supply *increased 60 percent.* That is a lot by historical standards, and made loans easy to obtain. Starting in 1928, the Fed began *tightening the money supply* by raising the discount rate (the rate paid to borrow money) from 3.5 percent to 5 percent, thus making loans harder to get. Then came the 1929 stock market crash. In 1931 the money supply was *decreased 30 percent* or more, and in 1936 the central bank doubled the reserve requirements (the amount of money a bank has to keep on deposit as a safety net against failure);

thus, taking more money *out* of the financial system. Those differentials represent a large swing in the supply of money between 1927 and 1936. Note that the Fed *decreased* the money supply *after* the crash. Private business capital investment also fell to zero, creating a situation where money was almost impossible to obtain. Everyone was living hand to mouth. Sounds like Milton Friedman was right. The Federal Reserve took money out of the system before and after the crash, just when it needed money the most, thereby increasing the severity of the Great Depression. The problem in studying the Great Depression revolves around the chosen economic theory, because that determines which statistics are the most important, and how they are interpreted. One thing is certain, the crash of 1929 became a worldwide disaster throwing people out of work in great numbers and causing starvation and fear on a world wide scale.

We must now look at a few economic concepts that are central to understanding the Great Depression.

Money Supply—Money Value

Money supply and money value are esoteric economic and banking concepts of major importance to the modern world, and understanding how the Great Depression is analyzed. A nation's MONEY SUPPLY is the amount of money in circulation in the nation's economy. This is important because it determines the amount of money available for bank loans. A nation's **central bank** tries to control the nation's money supply, among other things. If money is easily available to banks they will try and loan it out by dropping interest rates, because loans are how banks make money. When there is less money available banks reduce lending and borrower's interest rates rise.

Another key factor is the VALUE OF MONEY. Strange as it may seem, money does vary in value *in relation to other currencies*, especially if they are "floated" (not backed by gold or silver) which allows money to rise or fall in value with the strength of a nation's economy. If one nation's economy is strong its money will have more value than an economically weak nation. Note what happens during value changes. As the value of a nation's money increases, its merchants can buy more goods from other nations because the outside products cost relatively less, however, it makes it harder to sell goods because the cost of its products rise with the value of its money. When the value of money shifts then buying power shifts. When a nation just prints money without backing it up with gold the value of its money *decreases* because there is more of it. If the supply of money decreases, the value of money will normally *increase* because there is less of it.[196] All this can be very obscure, as everything from cash flow to emotion impacts the increase or decrease in the value of money, and often in ways not fully agreed upon by economists.

In general, the central bankers would rather that the value of money remains stable, but many elements of a society push and pull on the government to favor their position. Debtors, like farmers, want "easy money" so they can borrow dollars and then watch their value fall because of inflation, thus paying back their debt in cheaper dollars than they borrowed. Creditors, such as people selling farm equipment, want "tight money" so the value of the money stays the same allowing them to receive full value for their loans even if they are paid off over time. In any event, numerous factors influence the value of money, so its value changes a lot. For example, I once purchased a German Olympic air rifle at what I thought was a high price. Checking the price of the air rifle one year later it had jumped over 30 percent. The product was no different, but the value of the Euro (a European currency) increased relative to the US dollar; thus, increasing the price in US dollars. However, the price of US made air rifles stayed the same thereby making them more competitive. If a US merchant imported those German air guns, he would pay 30 percent more than a person selling the same air gun in Germany. However, a German air gun merchant could import US made units for 30 percent less because of the growth in value of his nation's money. *In theory*, when a country's money increases in value the money begins to leave the country because its citizens can buy items abroad cheaper.

In 2010, a controversy continues between the US and China because China keeps the value of its currency artificially low compared to US dollars; thus, keeping the prices of their goods low. This value differential angers US merchants who say China is cheating in trade competition and driving US manufactures out of business. Now the US central bank is lowering the value of the dollar causing more turmoil in the world money markets. As one can see, monetary value and supply is serious stuff in international relations.

Money supply and money value tie to another economic idea, the GOLD STANDARD. This simply means that when a nation is on the gold standard

---

196 When the United States buys foreign goods money leaves the US system, thus lowering the money supply. It is the same when immigrants send money out of the United States back to the home country.

that nation's paper money can be traded for gold bullion (you know, the *real* stuff). Many economists claim the 1800s and early 1900s were prosperous because most nations adhered to the gold standard. In America, for example, the government promised its paper money was redeemable for gold at a rate of $20.67 per ounce.[197] Having a currency on the gold standard helps stabilize its value, stabilizes the money supply, contains inflation, and makes international trade easier. Using the gold standard, a nation can only print money up to the value of the amount of gold it holds. Since the amount of gold and the amount of paper money must be equal, excess money cannot be printed and this controls inflation. Since a nation on the gold standard cannot just print money the belligerents in WWI went off the gold standard, allowing them to print more money to pay for the war. This, of course, led to economic problems in the 1920s and 1930s as nations tried to readjust by going back on the gold standard. During WWI, nations incurred big debts with devalued money (money printed without backing by gold) and were paying the debts back after the war in high value money (money backed by gold). This split in money value contributed to instability in the financial markets in the 1920s. Few nations today are on the gold standard.

Instability in the value of money greatly affects international trade. What many overlooked in 1929 was the interconnected nature of the world economy. No nation stood alone any longer in the economic world. Events in one nation often had worldwide ramifications. As events would soon show, the interconnectedness ran deep.

Interest Rates

INTEREST RATES are another economic concept we should try to understand. Once again, interest rates influence business and personal loans. Private banks borrow funds from the central bank at set interest rates and then loan the money to their customers. The banks then add

---

[197] p.127 *The Politically Incorrect Guide to the Great Depression and the New Deal,* Murphy, Regnery, 2009. Note: if a nation sets its price on gold redemption at 20 dollars per ounce, then the amount of money it can print is limited by its supply of gold. If a nation has 1 ounce of gold, it can print twenty dollars worth of paper money. With no gold standard (or silver or other precious metal that holds a stable value) a nation can print all the money it wants, and the money's value with rise and fall with the amount printed and the strength of the nation's economy. How the money men figure a nation's economic strength vs the amount of money in circulation is beyond me, and, naturally, there are other factors.

a few percentage points to the federal loan percentage and then loan the money to the private sector. Thus, as the central bank increases their interest rates to banks, the banks have to increase their interest rates to their customers, and it becomes harder for businesses and individuals to obtain a loan.

This is important to the national economy because, like the money supply, it affects a bank's willingness and ability to loan. As loan funds dry up businesses find it harder to expand, hire new workers, or buy better equipment. On the other hand, if too much money is available and being loaned out below market rates this causes an economy to "heat up" or begin expanding faster than it should, resulting in inflation hampering the economy and destroying its ability to function if the malady gets bad enough.[198] A nation's central bank tries to ensure that enough money is available for loans, at reasonable rates, so the economy grows at a steady but sustainable rate, without much inflation, and no hefty contractions (depressions and deep recessions). This is difficult, because economies respond slowly to changes in the money supply, interest rates, and changes in monetary valuation. Months can pass before economic changes become evident, and by then some other change may be necessary to keep the economy on track (steady but reasonable expansion without much inflation and reasonable contractions or corrections). [199]

When the money supply gets tight and loans are hard to obtain businesses stagnate and often stop hiring or start laying workers off to save money. Fewer employed people results in other businesses selling fewer items and they start to lay off workers. This cycle, if continued, can trigger a depression and destroy an economy. When the money supply is easy and loans are easy to obtain businesses may borrow to expand and hire more workers.

---

198 During the 1930's in Germany, inflation became so bad that a wheelbarrow full of money would not buy a loaf of bread. This happened because the German government printed too much money. When there is a lot of something, like air in an open field, it has little value. When you have very little of something, like air in a collapsed mineshaft, its value rises dramatically. Of course, the item must be wanted or needed. Who cares about an abundance of cockroaches?

199 This is an often misunderstood point about capitalist economies. Corrections must take place if the capitalist system is to work. Irregularities are shaken out by periodic corrections so the economy can continue to expand. If the irregularities are allowed to go on, they can cause depressions and a lot of economic hardships. Andrew Mellon, secretary of the Treasury under Coolidge, believed this and adjusted his economic program accordingly with excellent results.

More employed people means more goods are sold. If many people try to buy the same items the prices will increase under the rules of supply and demand. If these prices continue to rise they can cause runaway inflation which can also destroy an economy. It is a tricky balancing act to keep economies on track.

Prior to the advent of the central bank concept, financial markets set the interest rates banks could charge for loans without government interference. Coupled with the gold standard, the market handled the variables of money supply, monetary value, and the interest rates charged for loans very well before the depression. During the Great Depression, nations went off the gold standard and began economic manipulation, eliminating the free market financial mechanisms setting interest rates and other monetary variables. This was a major and permanent change in the financial world.

Tariffs

Tariffs are critical to international trade. TARIFFS are a financial charge placed on goods coming in from foreign nations, thus making foreign-made goods more expensive. The international community knows that if one nation raises tariffs the nations negatively impacted will also raise tariffs. In practice, England might raise tariffs 10 percent on cars from the United States, and in response the United States will raise tariffs on English tea by 15 percent. Then England will retaliate for that US move, and back and forth it goes until both nations price themselves out of the markets for tea and cars. In **1930**, the Congress of the United States passed very high tariffs on goods from other nations in the **Smoot Hawley Tariff Act**. This could not have come at a worse time. The world's nations responded by rising their tariffs and international trade began to implode, especially for exports from the United States. Fewer export goods sold because the overseas price took buyers out of the market. This tariff act, along with retaliatory acts passed by other nations, prolonged and increased the severity of the depression and made the disaster truly global.

THE CONTRACTION STARTS

By 1929 in the United States businesses faced new problems getting loans because the money supply was shrinking. Tariffs were going up and decreasing trade. The same was happening around the world. In essence, business was shutting down, markets were contracting, the economies of the world were starting to collapse, and business investment was falling precipitously. Somehow, this economic earthquake remained silent until *October 25, 1929.*

In **October of 1929,** all illusions came to an abrupt end. The **US Stock Market crashed**. Billions were lost on the New York Stock Exchange in just one day. Industrial stocks peaked at a high of 452 in 1929, but by 1932 industrial stocks were at 58. By 1932 in the US 23 million were out of work. The 1929 crash started a panic and millions of institutions and individuals began selling stock causing a continuing and precipitous market decline. Many paper millionaires, because of their extensive stock holdings, found themselves paupers within a few days. Some large banks failed because they held substantial stock investments. The panic spread to the middle class who owned few stocks but kept savings accounts in local banks. A bank does not keep enough money on hand to pay all its depositors their money at the same time. Banks loan out the deposited money, retaining only a small amount in demand deposits to pay the few customers coming into the bank on a normal day wanting cash. Because of the stock market crash thousands of depositors descended on banks demanding their money. The banks could not pay; consequently, *banks began to fail by the hundreds all over the nation.* When the local banks failed *they took the depositor's money with them into default* causing people all over the United States to lose their life's savings. As a result, fewer people put money into banks resulting in more money going out of circulation (and under mattresses) further decreasing the money supply and making money harder to obtain. As **fear** of the economic future took hold fewer people purchased items not absolutely needed, the business community suffered a greater slowdown, and more people experienced layoffs. Therefore, the descending economic spiral began and would not stop.

The economic crash became worldwide. American loans to Europe, previously easily extended, were now called. The American banks needed that money, but the European nations could not pay. The chaos in the world economy caused even more trouble, and as manufacturing declined more people were laid off, and with more layoffs fewer goods were bought (people without work stop buying) causing more layoffs. Things began to look very bleak. *This was a downward spiral that fed on itself.* Stopping this cycle became the major focus of economists all over the planet, but classical economic theories of the 1920s seemed unable to explain it. Unfortunately, governments were already trying to "solve" the crisis.

HOOVER AND ROOSEVELT—THE TWINS OF ECONOMIC FAILURE

Governments around the world responded poorly to the crisis. In America, President **Herbert Hoover** began lobbying businesses to *maintain high wages.* He was certain if wages remained high people would keep buying, the national economy would right itself, and things would be fine. As the downward trend continued Hoover instituted government work programs and *raised taxes* to pay for them. President Hoover tried many things to overcome the Depression that no president before him dared attempt. In fact, his intervention into the economic system was unmatched until his successor took office. When Hoover lost the presidency to Franklin D. Roosevelt the new administration went far beyond what Hoover tried, but the focus of the effort was fundamentally the same. Under Roosevelt the Congress instituted massive work programs, tried to control wages and prices, tried to prop up farm-produce prices, supported union organization of labor in large industries, and *raised taxes* far more than Hoover's administration to support new and larger government programs. Roosevelt created regulatory programs stifling competition in an attempt to raise prices because competition kept them down. The National Recovery Act, a centerpiece of Roosevelt's economic plan, created business cartels with fixed prices and criminal prosecution for anyone trying to undercut the set price. The US Supreme Court ruled the act unconstitutional. An enraged Roosevelt moved to "pack" the Supreme Court with additional justices favoring his programs.[200] The Court converted under this pressure, approving New Deal legislation even if it breached Constitutional standards.

Roosevelt fought to end the Depression and tried everything his economic advisors—mostly university professors—could think up. Experimentation with everything became acceptable because of the national emergency. If a program failed they would try something else, but everything they

[200] The US Constitution does not say how many justices are on the Supreme Court. It just establishes the court. Roosevelt was threatening to add enough justices to the court to overcome the rather conservative majority that was striking down his New Deal programs.

tried involved deep government interference with the capitalist market economy. Most of the interference came under the philosophic heading of **corporatism**, or **tripartite** control. Corporatism means government combined with big business to create cartel like situations limiting competition and imposing price controls. Under a typical tripartite scheme government, big business, and big unions join together to decide production levels, wages, prices, and regulatory oversight routines. With both corporatism and tripartite concepts the government has the ultimate say so, and it can enforce the decisions of the group with government power. These concepts were implemented in the Great Depression, WWI and WWII, although less effectively in the US than in the nations of Europe. Both ideas, like socialism, destroy the free market.

Strangely, if Hoover and Roosevelt had *done nothing* the Depression in the United States may have ended in a year to perhaps three years. Today there is little doubt that government interference with the market economy prolonged and deepened the Great Depression.[201] Sharp downturns occurred in previous years under various presidents, but the government sat still allowing the recessions to run their course. Usually, they cut taxes and just rode out the problem for a few months. From 1854 to 1919, the **average downturn was over in *17 to 24 months*** (see stlouisfed.org). From 1873 to 1879 a severe panic hit the nation; however, the government allowed the economy to punish marginal businesses, and the recovery, although delayed, was very robust. In 1920 through 1921 another panic hit and unemployment reached a high of 11.7 percent, but the government, under President Coolidge and Treasury Secretary Mellon, remained aloof and the adjustment was swift. Unemployment fell to 2.4 percent in 1923. After World War I bigger government was the rule, and some intellectuals (university professors) thought the government could solve the economic hardships, overturn the rules of classical economics, and build a bright tomorrow. They were very wrong. Nearly everything the government did under Hoover and Roosevelt was wrongheaded and backfired in ways beyond imagination. Huge voting majorities continued to back Roosevelt and the Democrats because they were "doing something" about the Depression. Roosevelt's propaganda was excellent, and the public failed to understand the harm done by its well-meaning, but economically ignorant, government leaders.

---

201 P. 187, *Against Leviathan, Government Power and a Free Society*, Higgs, Robert, 2004, The Independent Institute.

By the mid to late1920s America increased production by 24 percent and real income grew by 2.1 percent; that is real prosperity. The next ten years stood in stark contrast to the prosperous 1920s. Even after the 1930s and 1940s America's problems continued, and the nation's return to true prosperity occurred in the 1950s.[202]

A few statistics should help focus the issue:

1929	Unemployment	**3.3%**
1930	"	8.9
1933	"	**24.9** (Roosevelt takes office in March)
1935	Unemployment	20.1%
1937	"	**14.3**
1938	"	**19.0** (5 years in office)
1941	"	9.9 (8 years in office)[203]

Clearly, the chart shows FDR's New Deal did not solve America's economic problems until after 1941.

By interfering with the economy, the government destroyed the economy's ability to adjust. Wages, for example, must be allowed to *fall* along with prices in economic downturns (classical economics—see Economic Theory below). This allows businesses to maintain their employment levels even though their goods are selling for less, otherwise (if wages stay artificially high) employers must lay off employees as earnings fall. The result of Hoover's high wage policies was more jobless people. Raising taxes took money away from consumers who would normally spend the funds for goods, and businesses who could have maintained higher employment levels. The drop in consumer spending, in part because of high taxes, severely affected the business community. High taxes rob funds from private enterprise normally used to create jobs and additional goods. Lowering taxes during economic downturns increases funds available for consumers and businesses. Raising taxes as Hoover and Roosevelt did was the worst possible economic move.

---

[202] War economies are hard to judge because the employment and production are skewed; however, when the production is being blown apart in some far away land it cannot really add to the domestic product. How to measure a war economy is still up for debate, but many economists say WWII was not a period of economic recovery.

[203] *The Forgotten Man, A New History of the Great Depression,* Shlaes, Amity, 2007, Harper Perennial.

Roosevelt's interventionist policies created substantial monetary, regulatory, and economic chaos. This led to ***increasing uncertainty in the business world*** and accordingly prolonged and deepened the depression. No one knew what was coming next, and new programs constantly came out of Washington that reduced profits and destroyed business flexibility. All these programs imposed massive additional administrative and legal requirements on business; consequently, predicting the future business environment became impossible. Those borrowing or investing large amounts of money need reliable business projections. If tomorrow brings more chaos, higher taxes, fewer markets, more regulation, and the like businesses cannot make reliable projections and avoid investing money or otherwise accepting risks. Fear of unexpected government moves can shut down business as effectively as enormous taxes.[204] As a result, **private investment in industry** fell to *zero* percent (that's right—0%) through most of the depression, and in 1938 it was actually 800 billion *less* than zero. Investment from private sources went very negative after the crash.[205]

Liberal economist and politicians roundly reject the classical economic theories supported above. They endorse Keynesian economics or outright socialism. (See: *FDR's Folly*, Powell, Jim, 2003, Three Rivers Press). Under their analysis of the Great Depression Hoover failed because he refused to do enough, but Roosevelt's programs succeeded; however, they also contend Roosevelt's success was tempered by a *lack* of spending. Keynesians argue that if Roosevelt had spent much more much sooner, like the government did in WWII, the Depression would have ended in two or three years (by 1936).

At least one factor going unanalyzed in the Great Depression is the impact of the great 1919 influenza pandemic. Falling populations can cause economic downturns, and the deaths of 100 million people worldwide could have contributed to the Great Depression. Over 500,000 may have died in the United States, 250,000 in Britain, 400,000 in France, and over 17 million in India. This all took place between 1918 and 1920, and the Great Depression arrived in 1929; thus, most will automatically believe there was no correlation. Still, the deaths of *100 million people* (probably 5 percent of the world's population) should have an economic impact. I know of no studies on this issue.

---

204 *The Forgotten Man,* Shlaes, Amity.

205 p. 110, 111, *The Politically Incorrect Guide to the Great Depression and the New Deal,* Murphy, Regnery, 2009. Fun book to read, easy for the non-economist.

ECONOMIC THEORIES

There are at least six major economic theories floating around, and each made a difference in how governments approached the crisis.[206] Here is a quick survey of the basic positions:

1. **Capitalism**: is a system of private ownership of property, including the means of production, coupled with a small amount of government intervention in the economy. Capitalism does not aim for social justice. Unlike other economic ideas, capitalism's aim has nothing to do with concepts of justice or equality. Capitalism recognizes human selfishness and claims it is good when harnessed correctly. It is a *classless* theory, where people make money by competing and not by government action. Economic control is by *private market competition,* where individuals or corporations compete against others to bring goods and services to the market desired by private citizens (they hope). This is a decentralized economic system where central planning is minimal. The markets are thought to regulate themselves. Regulation of business is the key form of government control under capitalism, but this regulation is to insure a "level playing field" and to protect the public against crime, but little else. This system was in use in America since its inception as a nation and was only de-railed by the Great Depression and the New Deal era. During the Great Depression, the USA passed many laws governing the economic life of the nation, but left the basic concepts of capitalism in place. In modern capitalist societies "welfare capitalism" has evolved, wherein the government provides safety nets for people who are out of work or otherwise unable to support themselves. Prior to the Great Depression the USA was, for decades, the world's fastest growing and strongest economy.
2. **Socialism**: is a system of government ownership of most businesses and central planning of the economy. It is also a system of social justice. Under socialist thinking, equal property distribution is justice which will uplift the lower classes and bring universal peace accompanied by the reconciliation of all peoples (no joke). In this summary we will only deal with the economics of socialism. Socialist

[206] We are all captives of our theories. Theories set the framework for analysis of various problems, and a lack of theories—or faulty theories—can hamper the ability to respond to events effectively. When Keynes came up with his monetary theories about how to end the depression they presented the decision makers with a new way of looking at events, and new ways of solving the crisis.

think the community as a whole should own the means of production; however, as applied in Europe in the 1930s, it generally meant the government nominally controlled the largest businesses but required very high taxes and the redistribution of wealth through social welfare programs. Governments embracing socialism guarantee free or low cost medical care, housing, food and other essentials to the populous. England, France, and other European economies began turning to socialism after World War I. Modern socialism continues to stress the importance of full employment, generous benefits to laborers, and high taxes to support the educational, medical, and welfare aspects of society. Central planning forces the production of products the government deems desirable, or prevents the manufacture of products deemed undesirable. This utopian dream of universal peace is yet to be achieved.

3. **Marxism**: was developed by Karl Marx and Friedrich Engels. Its aims include the liberation of workers from exploitation, coercion, and misery. The theory opines societies' fundamental elements are determined by their methods of production. The method of production eventually decides the property relationships of society, and these property relationships determine everything else—including religion, politics, and classes of persons in that society, et al. In modern capitalist societies of the late 1800s, Marx and Engels believed history was reaching its climactic moment, as these societies would soon succumb to violent overthrow by the working classes. The proletariat (working classes) would establish the final society—one without classes—where each person worked and gave to others freely as their needs dictated. In this final classless society, ownership does not exist. Marx and Engels theorized the proletariat revolution was inevitable. This theory of an ultimate unavoidable utopian society eventually developed into Soviet style communism unlike anything envisioned by Marx. No nation has installed a utopian Marxist government, and no society ever managed anything like the utopia Marx and Engels imagined.

4. **Communism**: is a philosophy flowing from Marxism requiring the vesting of *all* property and authority in the community at large (the state). Its aims are justice, freedom, and humanity. In pure Marxism, each gave according to his ability, while the wealth of

society was given according to ones needs, and without intervention by state authority (it did not exist); however, all communist states allow government acquisition of all property and all authority (power), making the state all powerful. This results in an autocratic centrally planned society. The government controls all aspects of life (for the good of all—of course). Prior to Stalin, the political bureau of the communist party was the sole determiner of the "will of the people" according to the Constitution of the USSR. In the Stalinist USSR of the 1930s and to Stalin's death in the 1950s, only Stalin determined the will of the people in spite of the USSR's Constitution (what document ever stopped a murderer?). After Stalin, the Soviet leaders partially melted into the political bureau for collectivist decision making, but the real and final power always rested with the leader of the party. As an economic system it has failed many tests, including the Soviet Union, Red China, and North Korea.

5. **Mercantilism**: an economic theory developed in the 1600s stressing the importance of international trade to acquire gold or silver; hence, shoring up a nation's currency and economy. The ideal economy required importing raw materials at low prices and exporting finished goods at high prices, thereby attracting money (read, precious metals) into that nation's economy. By maintaining a favorable balance of trade (exporting far more than importing), a nation would remain economically strong. Huge theoretical problems surfaced in the 1750s, because the Mercantilist theory assumed a fixed amount of trade; thus, attaining more trade for your nation required taking it from others. Later economists argued the size and strength of a nation's economy determined its "wealth" not the amount of gold in its vaults. Economists also determined the amount of international trade was not fixed; thus, killing mercantilism as a theory. However, the reader should note that many nations in 2010 still operate on a quasi mercantilist theory by stressing the development of heavy industry, and adopting policies that make exports more important than imports (in the 1930s many nations were doing the same). Japan and China are the key modern examples—although they would deny using this theory. Both China and Japan stress the development of heavy manufacturing for export, and the import of low cost raw materials for manufacturing purposes.
6. **Fascism:** is a political philosophy requiring individuals be subservient to the state, and controlling the state was a strong leader executing the desires of the people (Stalin took a shortcut,

he just executed the people). Social justice is feigned by fascists, but it is not a central concern. It is highly nationalistic and glorifies war. This becomes an economic philosophy because heavy industry is subject to state control, and getting everyone to work is a major goal of this political ideology. The Fascist would not care about a bicycle shop, but they became very concerned about what the nation's major industries were producing, and they would order the major industries to produce what was good for the expansionist Fascist state. Under the Italian form of fascism industries were organized by type, and a committee of government and industrial bosses ran each economic sector through these committees—although the government had the ultimate say. Modern corporatism is said to be a form of fascism. Germany was the premier Fascist state in the 1930s; however, Benito Mussolini had introduced fascism into Italy years before Hitler initiated it in Germany. It totally failed as an economic and political philosophy; however, it is not dead. Many nations actually practice fascism while calling it something else. Cuba under Castro is an example of a fascist state calling itself communist.

Note the key distinctions between capitalism and, as a group, socialism, communism, and Marxism: Every one of capitalisms' competitors stress social and economic justice. These philosophies stress the harm capitalism brings to workers through exploitation, economic oppression, and misery. To gain "justice" property owners in non-capitalist systems are separated from their money and property by the state. As a necessity, the three counter-capitalist philosophies emphasize the group is superior to the individual, otherwise the government cannot justify seizure of the capitalist's property. Somehow, they think that once capitalism is dead something beautiful automatically takes its place. Once capitalism is gone human nature will change, all evil will be wrung out of the world, and a society without problems will bloom. In stressing the communal over the individual, the groups' power increases to totally submerge individuals. The Greeks who faced down the Oriental tyrants of Persia would not have agreed with the communal standard. They argued, with word and sword, that the individual is superior to the group. Capitalism agrees with the ancient Greeks. So does Ayn Rand and others.

In **capitalist** societies several theories exist concerning the interface between the economy and government. One is minimal government interference or *laissez faire* economics—sometimes called classical economics. This was advocated by **Adam Smith** in *The Wealth of Nations*, published in 1776, and was the dominate capitalist economic theory until the 1850's, after which governments took more economic control. Classical economic theory held that an economy would recover from downturns automatically. During the Great Depression the theory came under attack. **John Maynard Keynes** submitted another theoretical approach to capitalism in 1936. Keynes argued classical *laissez faire* economics failed in situations like the Great Depression. His theory explained that an economy would not correct itself automatically and could spiral down indefinitely if not stopped. The economy needed a kick, and that kick was to increase *aggregate demand* by *increasing government spending* (or by lowering taxes). Keynes felt the *potential* total economic output could be measured against the *actual* output, and if there was a significant gap that gap could be bridged by government spending. Thus, like Hoover and Roosevelt, the theory tells the government to spend its way out of economic problems. In 2009 the United States under President Obama spent money in the trillions to escape an economic recession. Obama spent more in 2009 than all the previous administrations combined, building the national debt to 12.4 trillion. In 2010 it is obvious the strategy failed. A society cannot spend its way out of economic trouble.

Capitalism started yet another economic theory that gained popularity in the 1980s under President **Ronald Reagan**—supply side economics. Under **supply side** economics, high taxes and government spending are economic negatives because they destroy incentives that encourage work and savings. Supply side economists think governments must scale back significantly, thereby allowing investments, savings, and innovation to pull the economy along or out of a depression. This theory wants the government to encourage high production, savings, and productivity through low taxes, few regulatory restrictions, and an improved infrastructure. It differs from *laissez faire* economics because it believes government must work toward encouraging high production and productivity with proper taxing and regulatory policies. *Laissez faire* economics wanted a super small government doing nothing to encourage or discourage economic outcomes. Supply side ideas seem to originate with theories advanced by Ludwig von Mises and Friedrich Hayek in 1974, then termed the **business cycle theory.** Business cycle theory claims action by a central bank harms the economy, and interest rates are better set by free markets. Only free markets can truly determine the rates of saving and borrowing that can safely take place. Mises and Hayek thought central banks commonly set interests rates improperly, usually causing quick economic upturns (bubbles) that eventually collapse. By allowing the markets to take care of themselves they can better regulate the credit markets and prevent the cycles of boom and bust.[207]

One great difference between classical and Keynesian economics revolves around the **theory of wages**. Should government allow wages to fall during an economic downturn? Classical economist argue wages must drop to keep people employed; conversely, Keynes argued that if wages drop it decreases incomes followed by in a drop in demand, which in turn decreases production further dropping income and demand in a never-ending downward spiral. Keynes theorized the way forward was to stop the downward cycle by a jolt of government intervention, translation—the government should spend a lot of money. Keynes' theory, for the first time in economic history, attempted to show why classical economics could not reverse a depression cycle. Classical economists claim both Hoover and Roosevelt tried Keynes' methods, to different extents, and they flopped. Keynesian economists argue his ideas were not properly implemented by either administration, and they say Roosevelt's actions did work to relieve the depression.

Modern liberal economists argue that classical economics failed in the Great Depression, and that Keynes' methods were not really tried as the government did not spend enough money. The student of history should note that *classical economics were not tried at all.* Hoover did not decrease taxes, lower regulations, lower tariffs, or otherwise get the government out of the economy as recommended by classical economics. In fact, Hoover *and* Roosevelt raised taxes, increased tariffs, increased regulatory intervention, increased uncertainty in the business world and did everything the classical economists said NOT to do. Even today, governments the world over do not respond to economic trouble by getting out of the way and decreasing taxes and regulations. Some of this stems from the Great Depression and the concept that classical economics failed. If they knew history they would know otherwise. *This false concept still influences government economic decisions.* History, and a real understanding of what actually happened, is critical for decision making.

---

207 p. 166, *The Politically Incorrect Guide to the Great Depression and the New Deal,* R. Murphy, Regnery, 2009.

EUROPEAN GOVERNMENT'S UNDER STRESS: FASCIST AND COMMUNIST

The economic chaos of the Great Depression led to disillusionment with democratic governments in Europe, and radical governments began to replace democracies. Pushing this change was a new ideology supported by a major world power, the USSR. The communists in Moscow formed revolutionary cells in nations throughout Europe and the world. These cells agitated for the overthrow of capitalist governments and their replacement with communist regimes. Communists preached that capitalism had led to World War I and the economic disaster that engulfed the world following the Great War. People seemed ripe for a change.

In response, radical movements grew up to oppose communism. Fascist parties appeared with the idea that government should control major industries and insure full employment, but the fascist rejected revolutionary change pushed by the communists. Owners of industries feared a workers revolution seizing their property. The fascists made headway, in part, because propertied people feared communism. They had good reason to, because in the USSR millions of murders followed the implementation of communist ideology. Fascists came to power in Italy (1922—Mussolini), Germany (1933—Hitler), and Spain (1934—Franco). How could the people of Europe know they were opting for one group of dictators and murderers, the fascists, over another group of dictators and murderers, the communists?

The Western Democracies: England, Canada, France, and the United States being the major ones, faced a frightening future. In a very few years, the world changed spectacularly with new untried economic and social philosophies being implemented, and murdering dictators running major world powers. England was frightened of Communist Russia (the USSR) and wanted a strong power in Central Europe to offset growing Soviet power. Since WWI dismembered Austria-Hungary into a hive of competing small nations, only Germany remained to potentially offset the USSR. Hitler assumed power in 1933, and immediately began rebuilding Germany's military; nonetheless, Britain and France restrained their objections hoping Germany could counterbalance Soviet power. And so Germany could have if someone other than a demented dictator had assumed the helm.

Hammered in WWI, France wanted to avoid another war, especially against Germany. They wanted to stop Hitler's rebuilding Germany, but they could not muster backing from their voters, or England, to oppose Hitler's violations of the Versailles Treaty. Without England, France could not move. Hitler's words were soothing, praising peace, but his actions threatened war. Hitler was rebuilding his army along with developing a large, modern air force and navy. The world's newest weapon, the airplane, became war's focal point. Germany could not rival England's massive navy; however, airplanes could render the Royal Navy irrelevant. For the first time in history England's navy could be leapfrogged by a major weapon system—the airplane. France expended vast sums on defense by constructing the Maginot Line, leaving little for aircraft and tanks.

Hitler then started making unreasonable territorial demands on neighboring nations. This went unchecked by the Western Democracies because their voters and intellectuals opposed arms races, increases in military spending, or standing up to Hitler. Virulent antiwar movements preached "Peace at any price" because of the sacrifices of the First World War. *"How horrible, fantastic, incredible it is that we should be digging trenches and trying on gas masks here because of a quarrel in a faraway country between people of whom we know nothing,"* stated England's Prime Minister, **Neville Chamberlain**, on September 27, 1938. This sums up the feeling of the antiwar groups. Nothing was worth another conflict. Unfortunately, these attitudes threw away the sacrifices of WWI.

Meanwhile, Axis nations (the Axis: Germany, Italy, Japan) cheated on arms limitations agreements while the Western Democracies disarmed beyond the treaty requirements. Germany developed aircraft, submarines, and tanks in secret. Japan constructed super battleships in violation of the treaties. Unknown to the rest of the world, the Soviet Union was also preparing for war. In total secrecy the USSR developed the world's best tank (the T-34) and a massive army. Stalin then decided to shoot the army's officers, and for no reason.

The world stage began grimly drawing back the curtain on a catastrophe surpassing WWI. Once again, the world's leading nations utterly mishandled the growing crisis, missing several chances to avoid war. Since 1900 Europe's great powers, and the United States, had failed to stop WWI, the Great Depression, the ascension of brutal dictators, or the invasions of Ethiopia, Korea, and Manchuria. A decade long string of deadly decisions by European leaders triggered WWI, and similar decisions made it impossible to halt. Economic mismanagement produced the Great Depression, and it deepened because of governmental malfeasance. Now the Western Democracies chose to appease Hitler and ignore Japan. The West hoped Hitler and the Japanese warlords were rational, desiring peace, but diplomatic solutions meant nothing to the hungry dictators. Poor decisions by the major democratic powers led the world into a war in which the stakes were far higher than WWI.

English propaganda during the Great War portrayed German and its allies as an utter scourge; however, the Central Powers were more like their opponents than unlike them. Germany was no more a world scourge than England. No matter who prevailed in WWI, the world was safe from murdering, depraved dictators.

The enemies faced by the Western Allies in WWII *were* a scourge. The leaders of Germany, Italy, and Japan despised democracy. Hitler believed world conquest was his destiny, and Japan's militarists thought Asia should be theirs. Mussolini was visualizing a new Roman Empire for himself around the Mediterranean. The Axis and Soviet dictators murdered massive numbers of people. Mild jokes about the Nazi regime often led to arrests and most unpleasant prison terms. To Hitler, Stalin, and militarist Japan, human life was meaningless. To these godless dictators every aspect of life was a part of the state while the individual was nothing. Life's sole purpose was to serve the state, because an individual's life belonged to the state. The modern dictators enjoyed new faces, new technology, new methods, new ideologies, but the same ancient goals of ultimate personal power over vast empires. This danger was very real and far worse than anything faced in WWI.

World War I destroyed the old order, and the new order was frightening beyond all measure. The Soviets, Nazis, and Japanese, using the machinery of the modern state (the bureaucracy), began controlling populations to a degree never before imagined. Their complete ruthlessness eliminated millions with assembly line efficiency. Thus, populations of entire world regions bowed to the whims of one man (or in Japan's case one group of men—the militarists). Nearly everything done by these dictatorships was racist in nature. In Japan and Germany, the racist populations viewed themselves as deserving an exceptional place in the world. In both nations, those not of a certain assumed superior race were considered much lower forms of life and therefore could be brutally treated. The results included Japanese bayoneting babies in the Philippines, torching American prisoners of war just prior to liberation, and subjecting girls to vile sexual mistreatment. In Europe it meant the destruction of the Jews, gypsies, Slaves, and many more.

In the Soviet Union, the target was control rather than race. The Soviets shot anyone having a capitalist thought. Under the paranoid Stalin each budding rival faced quick eradication. At a party congress with 1,010 members attending, a secret ballot vote resulted in about one hundred (100) delegates voting no confidence in Stalin. Stalin had *all* 1,010 delegates murdered. Stalin routinely shot generals for losing a battle. Most consider Hitler the worst dictator of the era, but Stalin easily murdered many more and was more brutal and paranoid. Stalin is the most destructive and evil man who ever walked the face of the earth, especially if we credit the millions of deaths caused by the spread of communism to him.[208]

The Western Democracies in the 1930s were in real peril. Their economic decline resulted in decreased spending on military training and equipment, and reduced the size of their armed forces. The democratic nations were not keeping pace with technological advances or new combat methods. Many of these new combat methods originally came from the British and French military; however, the Nazis adopted these formally theoretical methods and actually put them to use. Germany rearmed and planned to use aircraft, tanks, artillery, and infantry together on the battlefield in a new kind of lightening war (Blitzkrieg).[209]

Japan developed a modern aircraft carrier force with some of the best fighters (the Zero), dive-bombers, and torpedo planes in the world. Japan developed the best torpedo used in WWII. Germany developed new methods of submarine warfare (the wolf pack). The West played catch-up from 1936 on. The dictators had no worries about popular opinion and began spending on military expansion as soon as they came to power.

JAPAN TAKEN OVER BY MILITARISTS

Japan's power expanded during World War I. By astute diplomacy Japan joined the victor's side early on, and by rendering a minor amount of assistance managed to gain a bonanza of territory from Germany and China. Japan's economy prospered during the war and during the 1920s. Japan

---

208 Stalin supported the spread of communism to China and planned and supplied the North Korean invasion of South Korea, among other violent acts perpetrated throughout the world. We are talking total deaths, not percentages. Mao might be able to claim more murders, but it is hard to tell. The current count is Hitler killed 21 million, Mao killed 34 million, and Stalin killed 62 million. These numbers are from a study by the University of Hawaii in 2008.

209 This was the **combined arms doctrines** developed by the British on the Western Front in WWI.

had tried a parliamentary-style government with a Diet (the legislature) and a prime minister; however, all was not well with the government as the military continued exerting more control over decisions than desired by the civilian authorities. Radical elements in the military murdered two prime ministers who attempted to stop the war in China, but the civilian government held on tenaciously in an unsuccessful attempt to limit military influence.

As Japan prospered the military's control waned; however, after the stock market crash of 1929 Japan's prosperity vanished. Japan depended on external trade, and as the world markets failed so did Japan's economy. As in Europe, this economic downturn helped radical elements expand their influence in the government. Eventually, the army and navy took complete control of the civilian politicians. The prime minister found his appointments subject to approval by the army, as the army controlled the cabinet. Japanese parliamentary government was a dead, rotting corpse by May of 1932. The militarists expanded the war in China and decided Japan must attack the Western Allies blocking Japan's control of resources in the South Pacific. After France fell, believing the West remained focused on Hitler, Japan moved to improve her economic and military position by seizing key territory in Indo-China and the Pacific.

Japan's desire to conquer China put her on a collision course with the United States of America. Japan attacked the United States mainly because it refused to acknowledge Japan's claims to China,[210] continually demanded Japan stop murdering the Chinese, and wanted Japan to surrender Chinese territory won since 1937.[211]

The Future Goes Dark

Popular opinion about the future of the West soured in the 1930s. The Great Depression continued and memories of the Great War haunted everyone. In 1900 the future appeared brilliant, now it emerged dark and menacing.

The Impressionist art movement started bringing new vigor to the art world. The normally bright and colorful paintings of the Impressionist, made outdoors when possible, emphasized the immediate and the present.

---

210 Japan was fighting in China right up until the end of World War II in 1945, because that was a major focus of the military government—winning in China.

211 *Japan's War: The Great Pacific Conflict,* by Edwin Hoyt.

Previous art emphasized the classical world and great moments in history and not the actions of everyday folks. The pre-Impressionist painters normally worked in a studio, spending long hours perfecting the paintings so everything looked very lifelike. The Impressionist changed everything by recording seemingly unimportant events going on around them, working outside, and making paintings look like a bunch of paint splotches close up; however, when the viewer stood back, the paint splotches blended together by the eye transformed the painting into a glorious burst of originality, color, and substance.

After WWI art trends began to change, and a world of disjointed darkness, often with unrecognizable features, started to flow from the painter's brush. Painting no longer bound itself to realism. Abstract painting started before WWI (about 1910) and foresaw the disruption of the modern world long before it happened. After WWI, life's lack of meaning became a major theme in art. Another art form became important in the pre-WWI years—the motion picture. The stars of the silver screen became worldwide icons making enough money to qualify as royalty. The movies set forth popular themes such as romance, comedy, the futility of war, or living in the modern world. The dictators used the new art form for propaganda to keep the populace believing the party line. Governments used this instrument of the modern world for the modern purposes of suppression and mind control. Worst of all, it worked.

Science, so obvious in motion pictures, became more evident in everyday life. Overnight, it seemed, the world invented skyscrapers, electricity, hot water heaters, cars, inside plumbing, better medical care, wonder drugs, flushing toilets, vacuum cleaners, and a host of other modern tools and conveniences. During the Great Depression many great public works projects started construction, such as the Hoover Dam in the United States, and the autobahn in Germany.

The world was a strange mix of worry and wonder. The stress on society by the new fast-changing world, the frightening nature of world politics, the wonder of science and its fantastic accomplishments, the warnings coming from artists and writers of pending chaos, and the seemingly unending economic misery all swirled together creating a disconcerting world. *Predictability was gone.* Recall the world of ancient Egypt, the steadfastness of it all with the unchanging centuries slipping easily into history's vastness. The ability to adapt may be humanity's best trait, but that adaptation was accomplished over long spans of time. Now humans were adapting in months to titanic changes.

From **1850 to 1950**, the changes were staggering. From fire light to light bulbs, horses to cars, balloons to jet aircraft, muskets to machine guns, dirt roads to paved roads, stage plays to movies and then television, brooms to vacuums, wash boards to washing machines, and much more. A person born in 1850 and living to the age of one hundred would see all these changes if they lived in the United States or Europe. A person living in Egypt in 2000 BC could live to the age of five hundred and never see any change (except a Pharaoh or two).

This review only scratches the surface of the changes going on after 1919, but this is the Super Summary so we cannot go too far. The tenor of the age was one of change and great improvement; but the long shadow of WWI, the Great Depression, and the darkening clouds of WWII put the stamp of uncertainty on the era. Once the dictators were in power, the world became ever more frightening and ever more deadly.

Let Us Learn

The Great Depression teaches us economies fail, often very fast. Even a stable economy can collapse with blinding speed. It also taught us the financial world is very complex and very important. Have some money in a safe place in case of economic decline. Trying to spend your way out of debt, or into prosperity, is folly. Two American presidents and their super educated advisors made that mistake. Learn from their errors. If hard times hit, cut spending. Do not follow the government's example; they never get it right anyway.

The depression era shows we are all captives of our theories. Recall that the economists of the 1930s analyzed the crisis through the prism of their assumptions (theories). Many people never try to figure out what theories (assumptions) they use for analysis. For example, what is your theory of human nature? Are people fundamentally good or evil? Does life operate on cause and effect relationships; that is, if one is good to someone will they be good back? If we work hard, will rewards follow? Each of these questions, among others, discloses theories concerning life. Be aware of the theories binding your thought processes.

Watch events in other countries, because even small far away occurrences can affect the entire globe. The murder of one man plunged the world into the hell of World War I. Hitler came to power after winning one

German election and torched the world. Stay alert to world events and unusual trends.

Watch for big trends and try to analyze them. A trend to worldwide dictatorship is not good. A trend toward bank failures should raise your concern. Very large trends usually have large impacts. Population trends within various nations, and the world, often foretell of critical changes.

Finally, the interwar era teaches that aggressors *must be immediately confronted,* and if war is necessary to prevent their exploitation, then war it must be. **If one wants peace prepare for war**. What seems like an ideological oxymoron is actually a primer on human nature. The strong will take advantage of the weak. The prepared will crush the unprepared. So it has been, so it is now, and so it will always be. To forget these facts is folly.

BOOKS AND RESOURCES ON THE GREAT DEPRESSION AND THE RISE OF THE THIRD REICH:

See *http://www.euronet.nl/users/wilfried/ww2/1939.htm* for excellent information on the state of European affairs just before WWII.

See *http://history1900s.about.com/library/photos/blygd24.htm* for excellent history and photographs of the Great Depression

Books on the Great Depression and the Rise of the Third Reich:

The Rise and Fall of the Third Reich, William L. Shirer. The classic, but not so easy to read.

The Coming of the Third Reich, Richard J. Evans, 2005, Penguin.

The Third Reich in Power, Richard J. Evans, 2006, Penguin. I like this book. It records many laws that were on the books under Hitler's murderous regime. It records the nightmarish existence under the Nazi regime.

The Gathering Storm, Winston Churchill. Churchill is always easy to read, but beware of some of his concepts. Churchill was very English and very supportive of the concept of the English Empire.

FDR's Folly, How Roosevelt and His New Deal Prolonged the Great Depression, Powell, J., 2003, Three Rivers Press. I actually enjoyed this book more than *The Forgotten Man* by Shlaes. *FDR's Folly* gives more economic background.

The Forgotten Man, Shlaes, Amity, 2008, Harper. Excellent, but concentrates on personalities in the place of more economic facts.

The Politically Incorrect Guide to the Great Depression and the New Deal, R. Murphy, Regnery, 2009. Like all PIG books this one will raise your consciousness about the Great Depression, and may raise the hair on the back of your neck as well.

Against Leviathan, Government Power and a Free Society, Higgs, Robert, 2004, The Independent Institute. Wonderful book. A must read.

Churchill, Hitler, and The Unnecessary War: How Britain Lost Its Empire and the West Lost The World, Buchanan, P., Three Rivers Press, 2009. For a completely different take on the run up to WWII.

Chapter 15

World War II 1939 to 1945

The Second World War shattered the world. After the war Europe was spent, its power and glory evaporated in an orgy of violence created by technological advances and new ideologies of hate and murder harnessed by cruel dictators. After the Second World War, new nations took the world's center stage, and these nations' ideology and governmental forms were diametrically opposed. The "Cold War" started immediately after WWII, involving new nations in a new kind of war and competitive diplomacy.

How Many Dead?

Estimates of the number of dead vary greatly, but deaths from battles (military) were **at least 65 million** between the USSR, Germany, United States of America, United Kingdom, Italy, and Japan. Estimated civilian deaths not associated with battles are **over 35 million**. The number killed in China is unknown, but it would be millions. In Japan, the total dead are unknown although there are good estimates. In my opinion, the Soviet Union understated its death toll by at least one-half to hide their casualties from the West. After the fall of the Soviet Union scholars examined the archives to try to determine the total number of Soviet deaths in WWII. Most think fifty million (50,000,000) citizens of the USSR were killed (*At the Abyss*, T.C. Reed, Ballantine Books, 2004, p 296). If this number is accepted then the death toll from WWII exceeds 100 million.

In addition, wars in Ethiopia, Spain, Korea, Manchuria, and China prior to the "official" start of WWII add hundreds of thousands to the count. China suffered immeasurably during the war. The Japanese launched yearly "rice offensives" at harvest time, stealing the rice crop for shipment to Japan. The number of Chinese dying from starvation because of Japanese actions would be hundreds of thousands at least. The numbers who starved or died of neglect in Eastern Europe after WWII are not included in the official count in spite of dying as a direct result of the war. Although reasonable estimates put the total dead at about 65 million, this number is probably low. In my opinion, WWII destroyed well over 100 million lives worldwide, especially if fatalities in conflicts like Korea, China, Spain, and Finland before the war are counted, and deaths from noncombat causes suffered immediately after World War II from starvation, disease, and wounds are included (for example, radiation sickness).

Compare 1914 and 1939

At this point, we should analyze the major similarities and differences between 1914 and 1939:

In both cases, horrible wars exploded from Central Europe and engulfed the world. In both wars, the major players were practically the same. Germany was the centerpiece in Western and Eastern Europe in both wars. England, France, and Russia fought in 1914 for the Allies, but in 1939 the USSR signed a peace treaty with Hitler leaving France and England alone to face Germany until June 1941. In 1914, Japan was with the Allies; however, in 1941 they were with the Axis. In both wars the United States of America attempted to remain neutral, eventually entering the wars with decisive consequences.

Prior to World War I, the "Concert of Europe," an informal system of conflict resolution, encouraged great powers to work out disagreements through diplomatic exchanges thus resolving threats of war. This was a balance of power system. In 1914 the system of diplomacy utterly failed after the assassination of Archduke Ferdinand, and nations moved on impulse rather than rationality.[212] From 1919 to 1939, the League of Nations failed to act in several cases of aggression by Japan, Italy, and Germany, consistently losing credibility. Compounding the League's inaction was the policy of **appeasement** adopted by England and France in the hope of avoiding war; however, this lack of resolve led the Axis partners to increasingly belligerent actions.

World War II was the *direct result* of Hitler's appointment to German Chancellor in 1933. Excluding the USSR, nations fighting for the West in the Second World War opposed the governmental philosophy of the Nazis

---

[212] See: John Keegan, *The First World War*, 2000, Vintage Press.

in every possible way.[213] Totalitarian dictatorships of the Axis fought to rule the world against democracies fighting to shield their way of life. Japan's policies mimicked Hitler's with Japan openly stating that totalitarianism was superior to democracy. It was a winner-takes-all contest. As such, the worldwide battles determined if democracy and individual freedom would survive. Never was the purpose for war clearer.[214]

In 1900, the world was a relatively stable place; however, in 1939, the world faced turmoil from China to Europe due to revolutionary ideologies and power-hungry dictators. The "old order" was still in place prior to WWI and it tended toward conservative and practical government. The Great War of 1914-1918 shattered European societies and revolutionary leftist movements, such as communism, gained substantial popular support. The backlash from anti-revolutionaries supported rightist movements like the fascist[215] trying to block the march of the communists to power. The problem with the revolutionary movements of the 1930s (communist, socialist) was their adoption of violence to achieve their ends. With labor strikes and armed force, the revolutionaries threatened governments and industry alike. The response of the right wing anti-revolutionary parties (fascist) was to adopt force to restrain the left. Undeclared civil wars broke out in many European nations, and governments were not stable enough or strong enough to control the situation. In Japan, the violent nature of militarism resulted in the assassination of two prime ministers and the endless war in China. Pre-World War I this was not taking place, as internal or external forces struggling for primacy could not easily challenge the established governments.

Japan had strove for recognition as a major world power since 1900. By skillfully playing her position Japan gained colonies from World War I, but

---

213 There are large problems defining fascism. Most of their economic programs were socialist as the government controlled industry and tried to ensure the populace made a decent living; however, the fascists were militarists and ardent nationalists advocating expansionist policies. Fascism in Italy was much different than Germany where racism was a key element of the mix. Socialism is not automatically expansionist; however, Communism is expansive in nature. All these interlacing ideas make fascism difficult to pin down

214 In Eastern Europe, two similar dictatorships struggled for triumph. Ironically, this totalitarian clash determined if democracy would survive in Western Europe. The purpose for war was clear in the **Persian Wars** also. Maybe I should say the modern purpose for war was never clearer.

215 See: Winston Churchill, *The Gathering Storm.*

not the recognition she craved. Before World War II, Japan defined itself as a "have not" nation believing America and Britain remained wedded to the status quo to maintain their imperial power. Japan decided to act with naked force to establish itself as a "have" nation. It would do so to shatter the status quo and the imperial powers; hence, avoiding being forever blocked by the old order. The same reasoning held true in Germany and Italy. All the Axis powers believed *they had to challenge the status quo* to gain economic power, resources, and respect. To the Axis, the Western nations supported the status quo and argued for peace, morality, and humanity only because it maintained their power. Axis leaders believed without a change in the power structure, through war if necessary, they would always be second tier nations.

Prior to World War I, European great powers aimed at peace. No major nation in World War I supported violence as a key component of national policy. Prior to World War II the fascists and communists proclaimed violence was well within the purview of their philosophies. The communist, socialist, fascist, and militarist claimed democracy was failing and caused exploitive imperialism, the Great Depression, the Great War, and created vastly unequal classes. The radicals said democracy had the working poor dying and starving while war profiteers grew rich on the peoples' blood. These claims found ready support among the dispossessed of Europe and within the "have not" nations of the Axis. Communists leftist established violent revolutionary cells all over Europe trained in pushing an international revolution, and they struggled to seize governments by subversive means. Meanwhile, the fascists won elections, took control of entire nations, and used national power to smash the leftist. The fascist tactics established repression and violence as suitable policies for national control. Most Europeans welcomed the end of chaos, even by an oppressive government. Oppression of the people was a given under the radical left or right. The communist, fascist, or militarist nations all embraced violence to control their dominions.[216] Post 1919, the Soviets, Germans, Italians, and Japanese abandoned all philosophical niceties and just conquered whom they wished. Power alone was lord.

---

216 When I say violence as a part of government control, I do not mean some police officer kicking a rioter. The kind of violence adopted included executing or forever imprisoning people who were opposed to the government. If a person even talked about disliking an official in the regime they could be, and often were, executed.

In World War I, the Russian Empire helped the Allies from the first and played a critical role in staving off Allied defeats in 1914. Prior to Hitler's invasion of Poland in 1939, Stalin signed a peace treaty with Hitler allowing the Nazis to strike west without the threat of a two-front war. In 1914-1918 France held the line against Germany at tremendous cost. In 1940, France fell six weeks after the German assault began. The fall of France had major repercussions, as Japan decided to assail Allied interests in the Pacific, and England was left fighting alone until the Nazis invaded the USSR in the summer of 1941.

Comparing 1914 and 1939: in ***1914, war was outright foolish. In 1939, it was a necessity***. By avoiding a European war in 1914 the world could have progressed along paths of democracy and steady increases in personal liberty and wealth. If democracy continued sidestepping war with Hitler in 1939, the Axis may have created a world hell itself would envy.

DECIDING FACTORS

Some of the deciding factors of the war in ***order of importance*** were:

1) ***Poor decisions by Hitler***, the leader of Nazi Germany,
2) ***The breaking of the German and Japanese codes*** by English and US code breakers,
3) The amazing **performance of the Soviet Union** against the German Army in 1941,
4) The considerable **industrial might of the United States,**
5) The **unbreakable will** of the English people,
6) The **quality of Allied leadership**—they made good decisions,
7) The **fall of France**, and
8) The ***good luck*** of the Allies.

Some of this will need explaining.

1) ***Better decisions by Adolph Hitler*** *would have changed everything.* One example should suffice for now. If Hitler had followed his general staff's war plan for the invasion of the Soviet Union, he may have been able to knock the USSR out of the war (obtain a favorable peace) by 1942, thereby releasing enormous numbers of veteran troops and their equipment to defend his Western European empire.

2) ***The code breakers were critical.*** Assume for one moment that Hitler broke the Allies' codes, and the Allies did not break the Nazi codes. One can see German submarines accurately directed to Allied convoys, Allied bombing raids consistently intercepted, massed Axis units throwing the D-Day invasion into the sea, the Battle of Stalingrad stalemated, and Rommel stopping Montgomery at El Alamein. Just defeating the D-Day invasion would have changed the war and the world immensely. Had Japan broken the American codes, she could have annihilated the US carriers at Midway and intercepted the US invasion force steaming for Guadalcanal. *Outside of Hitler's incredibly poor decisions, breaking the Axis codes was the most important event of the war.*[217]
3) ***The USSR's miraculous performance saved the West.*** The USSR suffered horrifically in 1941 when the Germans invaded. German generals were right to be happy with the way the war was going; after all, they destroyed an army at least their size and seized enormous amounts of territory. How could anyone believe a nation could take that kind of punishment and survive—much less turn and destroy the invader? Nevertheless, the Soviets did just that. In 1941 the USSR absorbed the loss of over 2 million troops, nearly all of its air force, huge numbers of tanks plus other military equipment, and moved its heavy industry east so the Germans could not capture it (this alone was a miracle). The Soviets lost vast amounts of farmland, resources and numerous cities. By winter the Germans reached Moscow, but were too exhausted to storm the city. The Russians held on and successfully counterattacked the Germans pushing them back from Moscow. They later amassed new armies with better equipment, aircraft, and artillery to smash the Nazis. Had the USSR quit in 1941 or 1942, a considerable number of German troops would be released (1 to 2 million) to Western Europe. These veteran German troops could have prevented any successful invasion of Western Europe. Hitler would own Europe, and the United States and England could not have taken it away. The Wehrmacht was

---

[217] *Ultra*: the British broke the German *Enigma* code, a machine code which the Germans believed unbreakable; thus, seldom changed. *Magic*: the United States broke the main Japanese code, a traditional "book" code that was often changed, thus destroying the US ability to read the code until new keys were found. One might say the invasion of the USSR was the most important event of the war, but that was a decision by Hitler and thus absorbed into the first reason given in the list.

never the same after 1941, because their best men perished in the Soviet maw.

4) ***The industrial might of the United States of America*** supplied war production in enormous amounts to all Allied forces. The United States fought a two-front war, in the Pacific and Europe, and supplied them both. In addition, America imagined a wealth of new designs, then produced them in great quantities with superb quality. Without the influx of US equipment, the Soviet war against Hitler might have faltered; the English may have lost at El Alamein (they used huge numbers of US tanks and artillery); the postponement of D-Day was certain; and every sinking of an Allied supply ship would increase in importance. Everything changes without abundant supplies from the United States of America.
5) ***If England*** had given up the war and made peace with Germany in 1940, after the fall of France, Hitler could turn on the USSR with all his forces, including an undamaged air force, and may have prevailed. England's defiance was critical for the West's eventual victory. Without England, an invasion of Europe would be almost impossible. England held on with no allies while Hitler bombed them and sank large numbers of their merchant ships. The will of the English people, fighting on against the odds in 1940, doomed the Nazis.
6) ***Allied leadership made good decisions*** throughout the war. World War II was a technological war, and the Allies recognized this and began developing the winning technology right away (Hitler had ordered long-term research stopped). The Allies ordered a total war status when the war started (Hitler did not), and Allied leaders usually refrained from interference with the professionals in waging war. Hitler interfered with his generals constantly. Eventually, Hitler began running the war in detail ignoring the expertise and the decades of experience possessed by his professional warriors (another very bad decision by Hitler). Overall, Allied decision making was excellent. The Axis decision making was deeply flawed.
7) ***The Fall of France*** in 1940 was a key moment in the war. The reasons for France's defeat are complex; however, *when France fell everything changed.* The French had enough men and high-quality tanks, but they did not have Germany's new methods of war. If attacking through Belgium (like WWI) as originally planned, the Germans would run head-on into the best troops of France and England, and even the excellent German warfare methods might not have broken the Allies easily. In computer war games with the best French and

British divisions in head-on conflict with the best German divisions, a steady, but not disastrous, Allied retreat results. Germany wins the war game after much destructive fighting. Germany's real world victory resulted from a brilliant and well-executed plan developed by General Von Manstein and forced on the German generals by Hitler (this was *a great decision* by Hitler).[218] The quick fall of France negated the need for large formations of German troops in Western Europe. *Japan's thinking* about their plans changed with the fall of France. England was battered and Japan correctly thought this weakened Britain's Far East forces. Hitler's later attack on the Soviet Union took a major antagonist off Japan's northern frontier and opened the way for the Japanese attack on Pearl Harbor. Hitler invaded the USSR because only a weakened England remained in the west. All of this happened because France crumbled before the German onslaught.

8) ***Good luck*** is often the key to victory in war, and the Allies enjoyed exceptional luck. At Pearl Harbor the Japanese managed a surprise attack of the first order; however, the main targets, the US aircraft carriers, were all at sea. By pure luck the US Navy retained its foremost assets intact. At Midway the Americans miraculously surprised and sunk four Japanese carriers. The United States possessed only one modern carrier airplane at the time, the Dauntless dive-bomber. This solitary up-to-date weapon arrived over the Japanese carriers at the moment they were devoid of air cover and had numerous bombs and torpedoes improperly stowed around their decks. The American bombs hit the Japanese carriers at their most vulnerable minute with devastating results. In 1939 brilliant *Polish code breakers* were deciphering the German codes and had obtained a German **Enigma** machine. The Polish code breakers luckily escaped after the Nazi invasion and gave everything to England. The war could have changed dramatically if the Polish code breakers had fallen into Nazi hands.

---

[218] We must acknowledge Adolf Hitler's brilliance as a politician. He went from a corporal in the army, to the leadership of a penniless Nazi Party, to ruler of all of Germany, and then ruler of Europe in a very short time. One must also acknowledge it was Hitler's support for the new tactics of Blitzkrieg—the use of tanks and aircraft in massed formations—and the development of the tanks and aircraft themselves, that allowed this to happen. Hitler's ready acceptance of the new ideas changed warfare.

World War II Begins

1939

After appeasing Hitler for months, and having him break his word and his treaties, England and France faced down the Nazis over Poland in September of 1939. It had been a sinuous road to this point. March of 1936 saw Hitler abolish the Treaty of Versailles by his reoccupation of the Rhineland. France wanted to move, but England did not, and France would not challenge Hitler alone. Hitler's seizure of Austria (Anschluss—reunification) took place in 1938, followed by the 1938 Munich conference where England and France gave Germany a large part of Czechoslovakia rather than risk war. The worst part of the Munich capitulation only surfaced since the 1970s. Newly released British Cabinet notes reveal Chamberlin made a deal to dismember Czechoslovakia with the Nazi dictator *long before* the conference. The USSR had promised support to France and England if they stood up to the Nazis at Munich. As Stalin watched the Allies cave he decided Hitler was a more reliable partner than the cowardly West. Hitler promised peace and stability (again), and then he completely subjugated the rump state of Czechoslovakia in March 1939. This move stunned Neville Chamberlin who overnight saw the light and turned on the Axis like an angry mongoose. Hitler quickly followed up his Czechoslovakian conquest with territorial demands on Poland, but this time the Western Allies guaranteed Poland's territorial integrity.

Some say this was an abrupt about-face by England and France, confusing Hitler and not allowing him time to readjust to the new Allied policy. After all, he watched them run yellow so many times before, how could he reasonably expect firmness this time? However, after the Fuehrer "annexed" Czechoslovakia, trashing his promises to England's Neville Chamberlin that his territorial ambitions were over, Hitler received confirmation that England and France would stand no more. Chamberlin made several speeches in the House of Commons saying conclusively that appeasement was at an end, and promising Britain and France would block Hitler's next move. By scuttling the Munich agreement Hitler convinced the Western Allies his word was worthless and force alone would deter the deceiver. Any rational man would have known that invading Poland assured war with Britain and France.

Poland, probably unwisely, rejected Hitler's threats. The Fuehrer was poised to invade, but word reached the dictator that both England and France promised a declaration of war if Germany invaded Poland. For a moment Hitler hesitated; however, he had seen England and France back down many times, so he hypothesized there would be no war over Poland of all places. After all, the Allies could do nothing to help Poland directly. Moreover, there was Stalin to consider. The entire world knew the USSR and Germany signed an alliance guaranteeing the Nazis safety in the East. Poland could not win, and the Allies could not help. Hitler threw the dice once more gambling England and France would fold. Dreadfully miscalculating, Hitler invaded Poland on **September 1, 1939**. England and France declared war; nevertheless, the Poles were isolated and, unknown to them, trapped in a massive vice.

Hitler possessed largely mechanized armies and modern air forces, and Poland did not. In the first hours of combat the Polish air force succumbed to heavy damage, and its poorly placed troops quickly found themselves surrounded and crushed by armored double envelopments. The remaining Polish troops fell back toward their capital of Warsaw, all the while radioing France and England to help. The Allies could do little to assist the Poles. One possible move involved launching a significant offensive in the west, forcing the Germans to pull troops away from Poland to protect their western frontier. The French and English failed to launch any major offensives in the West. According to Winston Churchill in his book *The Gathering Storm*, France lacked the ability to launch an offensive so soon after the war began. This lack of boldness doomed Poland, but the Poles bravely fought on. Then an unexpected blow fell from the East. *The USSR had made a secret deal with Hitler* to split Poland, and after the German attack was underway the USSR invaded, overwhelming the scant Polish resistance. England and France did nothing. (No declaration of war against the Soviets.) Stalin engaged in the same actions as Hitler, but England and France feared expanding the war, and as a result Stalin got away with assassinating Poland. After Poland fell the Russians and Germans exterminated millions of Poles, subjecting them to shocking atrocities that were discovered long after WWII.[219]

After Poland fell a period of non-action ensued (the "phony war.") During this time the Germans adjusted their Blitzkrieg tactics by adopting the lessons learned in Poland. During the lull, the German general staff approached Hitler with a bold plan to capture Norway. In April 1940 Hitler launched the plan, and using a combined naval and air assault overran the nation. Hitler approved the plan because he needed the raw materials

---

219 The USSR occupied Poland after WWII and covered up their murders of the Poles until the fall of the USSR in 1989-1991.

Norway could supply, and it would protect his vital steel ore supply from Sweden. The invasion's success thwarted an English plan to violate Norway's neutrality by mining their coastal waters[220] to stop the flow of raw materials to Germany. The German U-boats discovered, to their dismay, that their torpedoes were defective. Germany returned to WWI torpedoes, but at least they discovered the problem. Norway remained in Nazi hands for the remainder of the war.

THE BATTLE OF FRANCE

May and June 1940

France and England now stood against Germany in the West. The capture of Norway, the quick defeat of Poland and the assistance of the USSR in its slaughter, traumatized the Allies. The Germans had unleashed a new kind of warfare. Their mechanized units sped across Poland disrupting the Poles' attempts to form defensive lines. Their use of aircraft to bomb ahead of advancing German tanks disheartened the Polish troops at the key points of attack, and allowed German breakouts when and where desired. The French and English realized this, but they neglected altering anything at this stage because extensive retraining and reorganization of their armies was required, and they thought they knew where the Germans would strike; thus, negating the German mobility advantage. While it is not wise for comprehensively trained modern armies to improvise on the eve of battle, one must adjust to circumstances. Surely some essential changes could be made while keeping the troops within their training. In this task of adjustment the Allies failed. They also failed in an essential element of defensive planning; hold something back for the unexpected (*the reserves*).

In spite of Hitler's demands, bad weather allowed his generals to postpone the attack on France. For months the front remained static in what was termed the **Phony War**, but events brought on by the delay were not transpiring in the Allies favor. Germany studied its invasion of Poland and determined a lot had gone wrong. During the pause, the Wehrmacht made critical modifications to its armored tactics helping immensely in the coming battles. The Germans originally planned an attack through Belgium, and the English and French guessed as much. The Belgians

[220] By mining the coastal waters, the English would force ships out of neutral waters into the North Sea where the Royal Navy could intercept them.

should have cooperated with the Allies, but they stubbornly stuck with their suicidal policy of neutrality. (Just like WWI). As a result, the Allies had to wait until the Germans entered Belgium before they could advance to defensive positions within that country. The French and English were certain the German attack could not fall further south because of a massive French defensive system of guns and forts named the **Maginot Line,** after its creator. However, the line did not extend all the way to Belgium. Between the end of the defensive line and Belgium grew a dense forest which French planners thought was too difficult for mechanized forces to cross; thus, the Maginot Line stopped at the forest. Even worse, the defense of the forested area depended on second-class troops comprised of older conscripts with few modern weapons. Of course, this was the fatal disposition because it was through this forest the German mechanized armored forces struck.

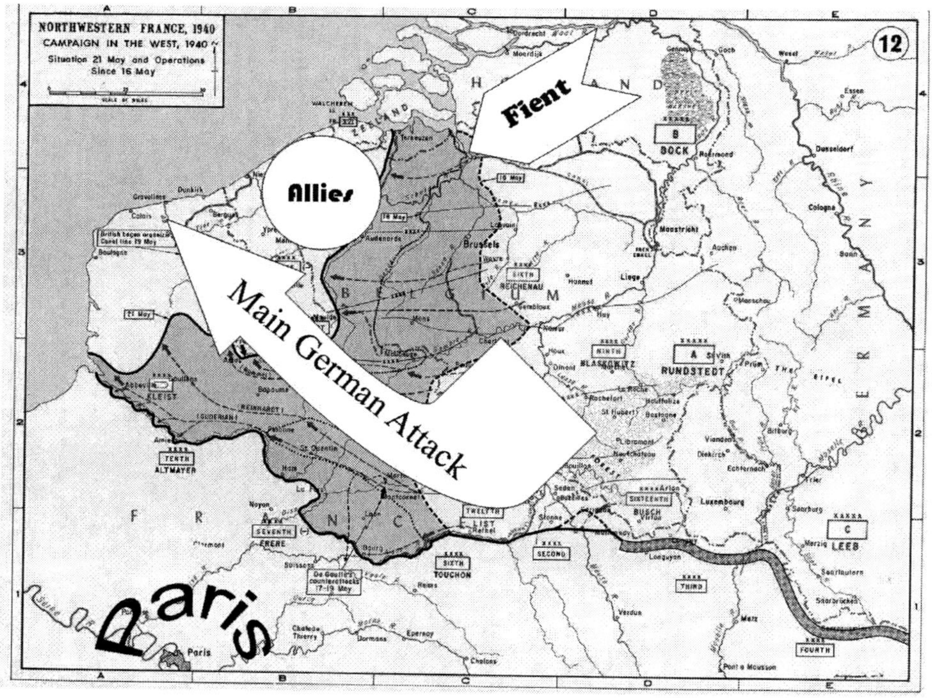

FIGURE 53 THE FALL OF FRANCE 1940

Strangely, the German plan changed only after an aircraft accident where a German officer, ineptly carrying the plans of attack, crashed in Belgium. The plans were recovered from the wreck and confirmed Allied speculation about the German assault in the West. Back in Germany Hitler remained calm because he never liked the plan anyway and wanted his generals to create a better one. One German general, **Eric Von Manstein**, did have another plan, but his superiors on the general staff had dismissed it. Von Manstein had worked up an idea to attack with mechanized units through the forested area (the Ardennes) ignored by the Allies. The plan called for a feint (false attack) into Belgium which would draw the Allied units north. This would be followed by the Wehrmacht's main attack coming from east to west toward the sea from the Ardennes Forest, thereby trapping numerous Allied units in Belgium. Once cut off from supplies and reinforcements destruction of the Allied armies could proceed. Thereafter, the Germans would turn on the remainder of France. Once briefed, Hitler instantly adopted this audacious idea. The plan went forward over the strong objections of his staff officers who had the plan jammed down their throats by the Fuehrer. It was perhaps Hitler's best military decision (One of the few good military decisions).

When the German blow fell on May 10, 1940, the French and English troops hurried into Belgium anticipating the German main attack. The Germans moved units into Belgium to draw the Allies in, and the Allies took the bait. The Germans began assaults on the Belgian forts around their main cities. These forts fell at once as brilliant German planning overcame the defenders. As the Belgian Army disintegrated, the Allies prepared their positions well inside Belgium for the expected German onslaught. Then disturbing reports filtered in of heavy fighting near the Ardennes forest, soon followed by the bad news of a German breakthrough at Sudan. The Allies began to realize they were in the wrong place.

The reports of strong German breakthroughs were correct. German armored units struck through the forest sweeping past the surprised and ill-prepared defenders. The German spearheads crossed the Muse River and turned west moving quickly toward the English Channel. German aircraft dominated the sky, bombing Allied columns moving south and disorganizing units in front of the German onslaught. Allied air attacks on German bridges constructed on the Muse River failed, resulting in heavy aircraft losses. French tanks supported their infantry; thus, only small groups of tanks were operating within the infantry units. The Germans assembled their tanks into large dominant armored strike forces comprised of many tanks using combined arms warfare. They overwhelmed the small confused tank units comprising French and British armored opposition. The German armored units hit like a wrecking ball, demolishing all before them.

As German mechanized units pushed forward against panicked opposition the far away French High Command lost touch with the front, mainly because modern communication equipment was lacking (such as telephones or radios).[221] French lack of mechanization prevented rapid movement, and inadequate French communication prevented rapid reorganization; consequently, they failed to stop the fast moving Germans.

Soon the Germans reached the sea trapping a number of Allied divisions. The British Army retreated to the port of **Dunkirk** on the orders of Lord Gort, the commander of the British Expeditionary Force. Lord Gort gave the command without London's authorization but saved the British Army by the decisive decision. For unknown reasons, Hitler stopped the Axis advance on the port. [222] During the delay, the English army managed to escape by sea through the efforts of the British Navy and hundreds of civilian boats sailing into action to save the troops trapped at the seaside. When the Germans resumed their advance the rescue of three hundred and forty thousand troops from Dunkirk was complete (about one hundred thousand were French). After a pause to refit, the Wehrmacht carried out the second phase of their plan storming past Paris into the remainder of France. The French reorganized into hedgehog redoubts, but they lost so many units in previous combat they stood no chance. After Dunkirk the British withdrew all RAF[223] aircraft to defend their island home. France objected, but England could not afford to lose its air force fighting in France. France had no strategic reserve (why is obscure), and the nation's fighting spirit was gone.

The campaign in France ended on June 25, 1940. The Germans allowed the French to keep a small part of their nation in the south of France,[224] but the Germans governed the rest. Hitler wanted the French Atlantic ports for his submarines. France's empire still existed, but France elected to surrender without moving the fight to their empire. The French Empire became a German puppet, although the Free French under General Charles de Gaulle continued to fight the Germans from England. The French suffered another indignity, although the British administered this

---

221 They were using motorcycle messengers, just as they did in World War I.

222 Just another very bad decision by the Fuehrer. Why he gave the order is unknown. Lots of speculation, but no one knows because he did not write it down or tell anyone that a historian could trust. He left a will and *Mien Kampf* but no diary as such.

223 Royal Air Force

224 Vichy France named for its capital city.

blow when Churchill, Britain's new Prime Minister, ordered the French fleet sunk to prevent its use by the Nazis. France was furious.

With France defeated Hitler may have assumed England would desire peace. Churchill, Britain's Prime Minister, emphatically said no. Many speculated about Germany invading England, even though it was autumn and only a few weeks of good weather (if it could be called that) remained. No invasion could be mounted without air superiority. Accordingly, Hitler launched coordinated air attacks on England's RAF that entailed bombing airfields and aircraft industries. This air action was the **Battle of Britain**.

BATTLE OF BRITAIN

August to October 1940

Starting in August 1940, the German Luftwaffe began concentrated daylight attacks on English airbases and its aircraft industry. Hitler's goal was to destroy the RAF and then stage an invasion of England. Well . . . maybe. From the start the Germans were at a disadvantage. *As designed, the only use of the Luftwaffe was to support the German Army; thus, close air support was their mission, not bombing an enemy nation into submission.* German aircraft were short ranged, the bombers were two-engine affairs with almost nonexistent defensive firepower, and they carried light bomb loads. Up against modern fighters such as the Spitfire or Hurricane they were absolutely inadequate. **General Kesselring** knew the weaknesses of the equipment, and, as one of the architects of the air assault, limited their key operations to southern England. Royal Air Force production areas were bombed, but this was more difficult than getting at the airfields. Air warfare against cities was not new as WWI saw numerous long-range bombing raids; nonetheless, air attacks on a world power to attain air superiority was new. Kesselring understood and followed Clausewitz's principles (defeat the enemy's army in the field).[225] He wanted to defeat the Royal Air Force by destroying its bases of operation, pilots, aircraft, and ability to construct aircraft.

Radar was England's technological ace in the hole. Although primitive, the English radar stations detected incoming flights of bombers, supplying

---

225 *ON WAR*, 1833. Clausewitz's book was the primer on war and its execution—at least prior to 1970. Some today argue it is out of date, others think it is still relevant and anyone ignoring its precepts is going to face hardships or outright defeat. I think it is still THE primer on war.

information on course and speed. Britain's Fighter Command, under Air Chief Marshal Hugh Dowding, then launched the intercepting fighters. The ME-109s sent to protect the bombers could not stay long over the target, thus, protecting the bombers was problematic. Furthermore, each German pilot shot down was lost to death or captivity, whereas the English pilots shot down could be recovered to fight again (unless KIA).[226] From the start the Luftwaffe took a beating. Nonetheless, the experienced Nazi pilots shot down numerous RAF aircraft, and the bombers damaged the airfields significantly. Dowding worried he might lose the fight allowing Germany to gain air superiority over Southern England.

However, fate intervened, and Hitler ordered the bombing switched to London thereby wrecking the German staff's planning at the moment victory winged into view. This violated Clausewitz's principle of defeating the enemy's army (air force in this case) before doing anything else. London was further away from Luftwaffe air bases resulting in more time over enemy territory, with its flack and fighters, and less time over the target. The new raids caused extensive damage to London and the Luftwaffe, in addition to allowing the RAF to recover their losses then attack with renewed vigor. As winter approached and losses worsened, the Luftwaffe suffered defeat by Hitler's decision, radar, and English determination. The fact that British bombing raids heavily damaged the Nazi invasion barges is another seldom-discussed key factor. Fighter Command won the battle by just surviving.

INVASION?

Watching documentaries on the Battle of Britain, we hear the narrator deeply intone that should Britain lose the crucial air battle a Nazi invasion would surely follow. This idea is pure propagandistic humbug. The RAF was hard pressed, but it retained valuable options beyond total destruction. Germany lacked the resources to invade England even if it won the air battle by a wide margin. Plus, the battle started in August, far too late to seriously contemplate an invasion because of the approach of winter and bad weather.

If Fighter Command was being destroyed, it could pull its aircraft out German range and await the invasion while rebuilding its strength. Also waiting out of range would be the English Navy with its aircraft carriers,

[226] Killed in Action

battleships, cruisers, destroyers, and more. Upon sighting a German invasion armada, it would sail into action with all available land, sea, and air support.[227] Even with total air superiority, Germany could not have overcome such an onslaught of British ships and aircraft.[228] The Battle of Britain was history's first struggle to gain air superiority over another nation's territory. The Germans failed while significantly damaging their air force. This hampered Luftwaffe operations in Russia the following summer. Hitler may have been trying to get England to quit the war through this air effort; however, who can know the mind of Adolf Hitler?

THE BATTLE OF THE ATLANTIC

September 1939 to May 1943

As the Luftwaffe suffered defeat over Britain, the war's longest campaign started in the Atlantic.[229] However, Germany lost the **Battle of the Atlantic** before it started. This was a *technological fight* from the first, and at the start of the campaign the Germans held several advantages. **Admiral Karl Donitz** (also Doenitz), the German U-boat commander, devised a new way of waging war with submarines. Donitz recognized the two highest hurdles for submarine warfare were spotting a convoy and then successfully attacking it. Believe it or not, finding the convoy was the hardest part, but once found the submarines needed to sink several ships to gain victory. First, a line of scout submarines (sub) was deployed to spot convoys. After a sub acquired a convoy they radioed the position, speed, and direction of the ships to U-boat headquarters in France. Second, German HQ radioed a number of subs and ordered their convergence on the convoy for a large coordinated attack designed to inflict maximum damage while overwhelming the convoy escort. Donitz's **WOLF PACK** concept gave the Germans a critical advantage during the first months of the war. The problem in modern war is technological and tactical advantages disappear fast.

---

[227] In fact, they would have sailed in without any air support if necessary (my opinion)

[228] I know others, even German generals, have said otherwise; but I still hold my opinion. Also, remember logistics. How could the Nazis get supplies to their troops once they were on the beach? The British navy could easily have cut the sea supply line through night actions alone.

[229] Most of the material in this section comes from: *Hitler's U-boat War: The Hunters, 1939-1942*, by Clay Blair, Modern Library, 2000; **and** *Memoirs*, **by Carl Doenitz**, Da Capo Press, 1997 . . . note the author of this book.

The Germans lost before they started because they *produced so few modern oceangoing submarines prior to September 1939.* The majority of their subs were coastal types, designed for shallow water and not cruising on open seas. In the critical prewar years Germany produced few oceangoing subs, and one year they produced just ONE U-boat. During the essential months of 1939, Germany had ***twelve*** oceangoing subs, and struggled to keep *four* U-boats on the western approaches to England.[230] Even with so few U-boats, ace German captains sank numerous British merchant ships. The Royal Navy swiftly took countermeasures to avoid the wolf packs through the code breakers by just routing the convoys around the subs with known locations. With so few subs an effective picket line was impossible. The few U-boats available at war's outbreak doomed the Nazi effort. Donitz needed *three hundred* oceangoing U-boats for his campaign. The admiral possessed *twelve,* about 4 percent of his needs.

Documentaries on the Battle of the Atlantic show German U-boats attacking from under water in daylight. In fact, few attacks occurred this way. Underwater, a U-boat was very slow and could not keep up with a convoy; therefore, Germans carried out their attacks at night on the surface. U-boats stayed on the surface when searching for convoys and, once the quarry was spotted, tracked it at a safe distance while surfaced. Underwater, the U-boats found it impossible to spot or track convoys; thus, surface operations were imperative. After a Wolf Pack assembled, the German U-boat captains awaited darkness then skillfully approached the convoy, on the surface, avoiding the escorts. Once in close, the subs, gliding low in the sea, either fired their torpedoes outside the convoy perimeter, or—if expert and fearless—sailed into the convoy itself, *between the lines of ships,* and commenced their attack from point blank range.

For the first few months of the war an extremely small set of brilliant U-boat commanders accounted for the majority of English shipping losses. As these superb captains and their crews were destroyed Britain's shipping losses declined, illustrating the impact of a few extraordinary men.

By 1943, the technological advantage lay completely with the Allies as new submarine detection and fighting methods forever shifted the tide. The increasing Allied ability to place aircraft above the convoys ended the U-boats' operational effectiveness, and Allied shipping losses fell significantly. To illustrate: in 1942 Allied shipping losses were 8,245,000

---

[230] One-third at sea, one-third in transit, and one-third in for repair and resupply. *SEE DONITZ, Memoirs.*

tons, for the loss of 85 U-boats; in 1943 Allied shipping losses were 3,611,000 tons for the loss of 287 U-boats. The tide turned dramatically in May of 1943 and Germany lost the undersea struggle.

All this Allied technological innovation and its rapid deployment was assisted by decisions at the **Casablanca Conference** in January 1943, where Roosevelt and Churchill met to co-ordinate strategy. The leaders *agreed the U-boat was the number one menace* to the Allied cause and directed extra resources to defeat the German undersea navy. Interestingly, their second priority was defeating the Luftwaffe, hence showing the technological orientation of the Allies. Meanwhile, Hitler's U-boats lacked resources until it was far too late in the battle because Hitler put other priorities ahead of the Atlantic struggle. In fact, *98 percent* of Allied shipping crossed the Atlantic without incident. This victory is directly attributable to the Allied emphasis on defeating the U-boat threat as their *first* priority. Nonetheless, from 1939 and up through May 1943, the Germans were causing major concerns with their U-boat offensives. During the Battle of the Atlantic, the Germans sank 2,603 Allied ships for the loss of over seven hundred submarines. In Operation Drumbeat alone the United States lost three hundred and ninety seven ships between January and June of 1942.

The Battle of the Atlantic, and the entire war, completely depended on another factor: industrial production.

INDUSTRIAL PRODUCTION

(Entire war) 1939 to 1945

Most students of war like concentrating on battles won and lost, great personalities dominating the era, or the machines of war; however, the available resources properly committed to numerous battles habitually decide wars between great powers. As such, the ability *to harness and properly direct these resources* is vital to the outcome of war. The nations marshaling their resources most effectively, turning those resources into what is most necessary for success, and then efficiently delivering the end product, all but assures ultimate victory. Resources include more than weapons, because properly trained men, new methods of war, and new methods of production are critical to victory. This study of stuff is termed **logistics**.

During the war, Hitler made many errors (to say the least), but perhaps his most important blunder was not ordering total war production prior to 1943 (or prior to 1939 for that matter). Haunted by WWI's citizen depravations the Fuehrer wanted Germans to enjoy some consumer goods, and he hoped the war would be short. Another major error was stopping development of weapons systems (aircraft for example) taking longer than a year to move to production. Both of these decisions were directly responsible for Germany's destruction by 1945. If Hitler had made the opposite decisions and allowed continued research on all weapons systems, and went to full production by 1940, then the delivery of jet aircraft, new tanks, new submarines, and a lot more would have taken place years sooner than actually delivered. For example, if Germany had developed and produced in quantity the ME-262 jet aircraft eighteen months sooner, the Allies may have lost air superiority over Europe thus delaying the D-Day invasion (I know . . . a *lot* of very big ifs).

The Allies went to total war production immediately. In the United States the huge supply of idle machinery from the Depression went back into use, out of work men got work, and a host of other economic changes took place after 1941. The Great Depression was no more, and all that pent-up potential exploded in a torrent of production and innovation stunning the Allies of the United States as well as its enemies. It took more than idle production availability to cause this industrial flood of supplies and equipment. The organization of industry, the ability to control *quality* as well as turn out large *quantities* of materials, and the ability to develop new methods of war and new methods of war production were as necessary as the machines and men of war. Immediately after Pearl Harbor **General George Marshal** reorganized the war department to reflect the new realities and methods of war. Even considering this change on the eve of war would chill most leaders, much less after the war had started and things were going badly. The same reorganization was happening in American industry. This was one of the secrets of success for the United States in WWII. The Americans were willing to reorganize, reshuffle, and reinvent almost everything if it would better serve the war effort. Flexibility of this nature allowed innovation on a grand scale. Often the innovation was stunning. For illustration, reflect on the Kaiser Company's construction of transport ships in weeks using prefabrication methods rather than months by normal shipyard methods.[231]

The US Armed Forces ensured their fighting men received excellent weapons. The Americans quickly designed, tested, and put into production new aircraft that easily out performed aircraft developed before 1940.

---

[231] Similar ship construction was accomplished in WWI as well.

The M-1 semiautomatic rifle, designed just before the war, was rushed into production, and in months all the soldiers, airmen, and marines of the United States carried this excellent rifle. The M-1 displays the skill of the United States in focusing its efforts on where they would do the most good. The United States and the British developed new methods of anti-submarine warfare, crushing the Nazi's undersea threat by May of 1943. In the Pacific War, the US Marines militarized a civilian amphibious tracked vehicle (LVT—landing vehicle tracked), for scaling coral reefs. First used at Tarawa, it saved the invasion. Large landings, such as D-Day, required large transports, but the Allies went further developing huge transports capable of unloading directly onto enemy beaches. This was the **LST** (landing ship tank). This one craft made large amphibious assault less complicated and more successful. It was one of hundreds of Allied innovations focusing on the best use of available resources.

Coupling new industrial innovations with new methods of war greatly facilitated crushing the Axis. As an example, the US Navy invented the "**seatrain**" concept. With seatrain the US Pacific Fleet resupplied at sea eliminating steaming back to port for supplies and refueling. This idea, and the construction of cargo ships and oilers to realize the concept, allowed the US Fleet to strike suddenly anywhere in the Pacific. Admiral Nimitz rapidly crossed Pacific, stunning the Japanese Navy and ruining its capacity to adapt. It was a major reason for Japan's defeat by 1945. This again displays the Allied aptitude for focusing resources on ideas yielding remarkable results once implemented.

The Axis failed miserably in the realms of production and focusing the use of resources. In Germany the prime cause was Hitler. His poor decisions in military and industrial matters doomed his nation. One decision was right. He appointed **Albert Speer** as armaments minister in 1942. Speer displayed outstanding organizational genius. Under his oversight, the Third Reich increased armament production during the height of Allied bomber offensives against its industries. Over thirty months (1942 to 1944) he increased production fourfold. Speer receives little credit for his feat, possibly because his genius prolonged the war; yet, there is no denying he accomplished miracles of production.

For instance, Speer joined, for the first time in the Reich, minds in German universities with the need for faster construction of better submarines. Germany soon developed a superior submarine drive system that pushed the submarine's underwater speeds beyond their surface speeds.[232] Speer adopted new prefabrication construction methods, significantly decreasing submarine construction time. It all came too late for the Reich. Allied bombing destroyed the new submarines in dry dock. If such submarines had been put to sea one year earlier, the Battle of the Atlantic could have gotten extremely dangerous for the Allies.

Germany brought its war experience to the industrial front on a few occasions. Panther tank development, although flawed, came from hard experience fighting the Soviet T-34 (the best tank of the war). An entirely new weaponry concept, the assault rifle, flowed from exceptional German field research. Their original German assault weapon, Sturmgewehr 44, became the prototype for the famous Russian AK-47.[233] The Sturmgewehr was arguably the best rifle of the war. Once more, the German idea failed to influence the war, but it exhibited German talent in conceiving an idea from combat experience then bringing it to fruition even as its industrial base was being devastated. The Sherman tank shows the Allies occasionally failed at marrying combat experience with equipment.[234] Somehow, the news that the Sherman was outclassed by German tanks in 1944 failed to reach Allied decision makers in Washington.

Hitler simultaneously maintained numerous overlapping projects, some of them outrageous, thereby squandering valuable resources of every nature. Hitler should have ordered production one very good but easy-to-construct and maintain tank, rather than several excellent but hard-to-build tanks.

---

232 Seventeen knots underwater speed which was faster than the Type VII surface speed.

233 The designer of the AK-47(Kalashnikov) denies he took the design from the German model; however, he does admit the idea came from the German gun. In my opinion, looking at both weapons, they are very similar. The Panzerfast was another German weapon, and was developed into the RPG (rocket propelled grenade) that is widely used and extremely deadly.

234 The Sherman does get an undeserved bad reputation because people do not understand it was **not** supposed to fight other tanks. The **tank destroyer** was designed for that task. In pre-war doctrine, the Sherman would punch a hole into the enemy infantry line (trenches and the like), the Germans would then counterattack with tanks. The tank destroyer was to move in and deal with the counterattack. After the tank destroyer defeated the counterattack, then the Sherman would be on its way once more and exploit the breakthrough. These pre-war ideas were brought into Europe in 1944, and, unfortunately for the US and UK, the Sherman was often forced into tank to tank combat with superior German tanks.

Germany needed to focus their limited resources on practical projects that could be in the field in a reasonable time. Case in point, the ME 262 jet fighter. Hitler demanded a combination fighter and bomber, thereby delaying production and squandering resources. To really impact the war an early unleashing of the ME 262 in quantity was necessary. Hitler also expended a tidal wave of human effort and hard-to-get materials on vengeance weapons such as the V-1 and V-2 rockets. The V-1 was a simple piece of equipment, easy to produce, modest in cost, and effective in reaching London. Increasing its effectiveness only required a little more effort on improving the guidance system and speed. Hitler instead opted to expend valuable resources on the V-2. Directing these men and materials to speed production of the ME 262 would have increased their impact exponentially.

One set of wasted Nazi resources is difficult to discuss. Hitler ordered the destruction of the Jews, Gypsies, Slavs, Poles, mentally retarded, mentally ill, the old, the sick, the infirm, and more under the "**final solution**" for his Jewish problem. Millions went to the Nazi industrial killing centers. In purely economic terms this was a massive waste of resources. The use of the trains and trucks to transport these millions of victims misdirected vital transportation units to tasks unrelated to winning the war. In addition, troops were guarding the camps, workers constructing and then maintaining the facilities, and resources were also expended destroying evidence of the evil acts. Many of the murdered were loyal Germans who would have fought for their country. The thousands of men used in this killing effort were sorely needed to fight or work in factories. Some of the murdered were experts in vital fields or highly trained workers, impossible to replace. On the Eastern Front, groups of SS troops (Einsatzgruppen) roamed about killing Slavs by the hundreds of thousands, thereby misusing those resources and turning the entire population against Germany. Recognizing that the minds directing this industrialized murder were twisted, I know I am attempting logic where no logic can apply. Still, we must recognize the massive expenditure and wastage of resources extensively degraded the Nazi war effort. It also proved the true depths of evil confronted by the Western Democracies. The death camps forever answered the question, why did we fight?

Italy's industrial base was unprepared for war because of outdated methods and machinery. Italian industry had no capacity to produce the quantity of military equipment needed, and it struggled with changes to new manufacturing methods. Thus, Italian troops fought with outdated and difficult to fix equipment. In the North African campaign photos of Italian tanks often show sandbags piled all over them. This was necessary because Allied projectiles easily penetrated the armor. Men saddled with outdated poor quality weapons are seldom highly motivated warriors.

Japan adopted modern industrial methods of design and production before 1910; thus, Japan began the war with excellent weapons of their type. The Japanese "long lance" torpedo (twenty-one inch, oxygen propelled) was the war's best, and Zero fighters excelled in 1941 (note these are naval developments). A few powerful families (the zaibatsu), following Japanese military directions, operated the Japanese industrial base; however, the Imperial Army was slow to innovate. During the war, Japan failed to develop new weapons or new methods of production. The **Kamikaze** concept [235] grew out of desperation to make do with out-of-date aircraft that were good for nothing except ramming American ships. Why the Japanese failed to develop newer aircraft, rifles, machine guns, and tanks is difficult to understand. Japan's industrial giants had two or more years to design and deploy newer weapons before the US bombing campaign became a factor.

The Japanese built excellent ships throughout the war. What the Japanese needed to do was build sufficient *merchant shipping* to supply their war needs. All of their important raw materials and much of their food came from the south by ship. When American subs began sinking large numbers of cargo vessels Japanese shipbuilders failed to replace the losses. Prewar Japanese planning ignored protection for merchant shipping. For the first six months of the war, because of defective American torpedoes, little damage was done to Japan's merchant marine; however, after correcting the malfunctions, US submarines extensively damaged the Japan's cargo fleet. As this disaster unfolded Japan's leaders ignored the problem. They delayed using the convoy system, failed to develop adequate anti-submarine warfare methods, and did not commit enough ships to protect their vital merchant fleet.

We should note here that industrial and military cooperation between the Axis partners was nil. If Japanese plans for the Long Lance torpedo had made it to Germany before the war the course of the conflict could have changed dramatically. If Japan had adopted German anti-shipping submarine warfare methods the Pacific War would have grown much harder for the Allies.

---

235 Suicide attacks in which the pilot stays with the aircraft and rams it into the target. In essence, this is a (man) guided missile.

England's industry performed well, especially its aircraft industry. England produced the Lancaster, one of the best bombers of WWII, as well as many other superb aircraft. The LST, conceived and designed in England, was built in the United States, showing the knack of the two allies to work closely together toward common goals. The P-51 Mustang was an aircraft that both the United States and England contributed to designing and constructing. Cooperation among allies at this level within the industrial base is phenomenal, and a key reason the Allies won the war. English industry turned out enough freighters, rifles, aircraft, and the like to keep them in the war. The US could, and did, produce these items in such superabundance it became a war-winning factor all by itself.

The Crucial Years

1939 to 1942

The early days of the war were critical because decisions made then caused nearly irreversible impacts on future events and operations. We have discussed many critical decisions above, but note how many were made early in the conflict. Once in place, decisions can take on a life of their own becoming impossible to reverse. I like to think of these as *foundational decisions*. Allied victory was constructed on excellent foundational decisions early in the war. By contrast, the Germans and Japanese made especially poor foundational decisions. Hitler's decision to start the war was partially based on an economic problem. His mishandling of the Germany economy placed it on bankruptcy's edge, and only a conquest with the attendant plunder of raw materials, slave labor, and perhaps precious metals could save it and him. That was a foundational decision of the first order, and very stupid.[236]

North Africa

1940 to 1943

The tank battles in North Africa's deserts became the stuff of legend. Tanks in the desert are somewhat like ships at sea. Aircraft rule the sea, and the same is true in the desert. The side with air superiority held an unbeatable

---

[236] *The Third Reich in Power*, Evans, 2005, Penguin Books. Section 4: pages 352-454, esp pages 410-411.

advantage. Early on the air forces were near equals, but once the Allies gained air superiority it was over.

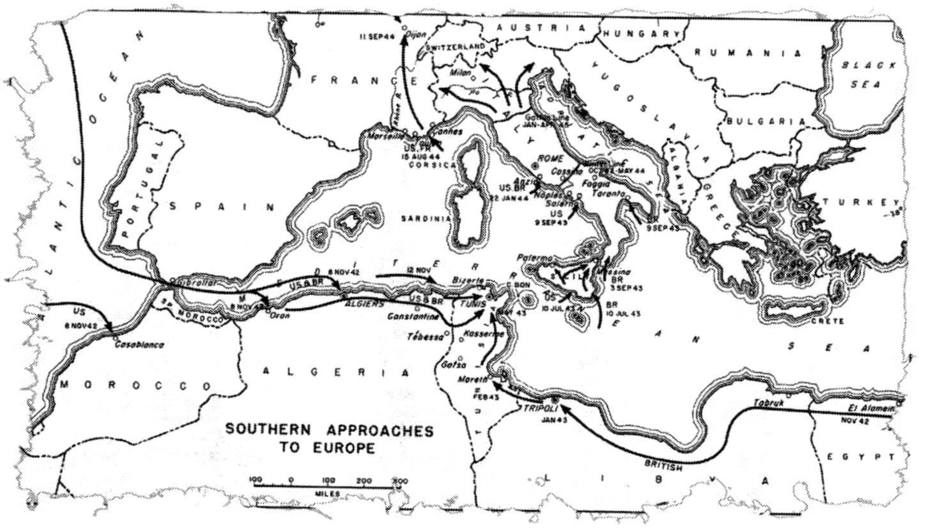

FIGURE 54 SOUTHERN APPROACHES TO EUROPE

Mussolini declared war on the Allies hoping to gain a Mediterranean empire. By attacking Egypt from Italy's Libyan bases on June 10, 1940, and invading Greece through Albania on October 28, 1940, Mussolini fumbled the ball in the end zone. As both invasions turned disastrous, Hitler bailed Mussolini out by directing German units into the Balkans and North Africa. At Greece's request, the British sent an expeditionary force; but, the Germans quickly rolled up another victory conquering Greece and Crete in the bargain (at a high cost). Hitler also delayed the invasion of the USSR by a few weeks. Whether or not this influenced the war is still debated (more on this later).

After the initial Italian assault in North Africa, British forces drove the Italians back through Libya and captured large numbers of troops and equipment. Mussolini was embarrassed, and it looked as if Britain would soon own North Africa from Egypt to Tunis. Unable to suffer this, Hitler sent a small force to help the Italians in 1940. From this decision the legendary ***Afrika Korps*** was born. Their leader, the intrepid **General Erwin Rommel**, went on the offensive right away. The Germans and their Italian partners soon pushed the English back into Libya, threatening their port redoubt at Tobruk. Back in London Churchill fumed while sending reinforcements, along with demands for new offensive efforts.

Rommel, one of the war's great generals, consistently bewildered the British in North Africa. He commanded a small military force having so few good tanks it seems miraculous he won at all, much less for so long. The key was his tactical ability. Rommel attacked using combined arms methods mixed with surprise and just enough audacity. He positioned his antitank guns and artillery to support armored assaults. His anti-tank guns included the fearsome 88mm antiaircraft gun adapted to an antitank role. The 88mm could rapidly chew up any group of tanks, thus giving the Afrika Korps an edge in all engagements. On defense, he made the English run a gauntlet of antitank fire before engaging his armor. The English, never absorbing the gist of this, continually attacked without proper artillery or antitank support. Eventually, British General Montgomery used combined arms methods to beat Rommel, but the real key to Montgomery's victories was overwhelming force. Hitler missed his chance to capture the Suez Canal by failing to reinforce Rommel long before El Alamein, but Hitler consistently refused to reinforce success and just as consistently reinforced failure.

The British took the offensive again in 1942, driving Rommel back toward his start points; but, even though outnumbered he was not to be out-generaled. He struck back at the first opportunity and drove the English east once again, this time conquering Tobruk in 1942. With the fall of Tobruk, Rommel captured some thirty-five thousand enemy troops and a first-rate port. Rommel was eager to press on to Cairo. Nevertheless, there was a rub—***supplies.***

Rommel's superior was General Kesselring,[237] in charge of the entire Mediterranean theater of war, and he wanted to halt Rommel's advance near Tobruk. Kesselring needed all available resources to assault **Malta,** a small island in the middle of the Mediterranean Sea, controlled by the British, and lying directly across *Afrika Korps* supply lines. This tiny island caused the Axis enormous problems because English subs and aircraft operating from there ravaged Rommel's supply lines, often sinking *one-half* of the shipping bound for North Africa. The Italians worried about shipping losses and the Germans worried about the loss of supplies—especially fuel. The hardworking Allied code breakers knew the sailing time and course of Axis convoys traveling from Italy to North Africa, and this information allowed the despoiling of Italian shipping. (Think on what could happen

---

237 Remember Kesselring from the Battle of Britain? He was one of the Luftwaffe team who designed the assault on RAF airfields that nearly succeeded.

if the Germans intercepted this much information about Allied convoys! Could one-half of the ships bound for Britain have been lost?)[238]

Rommel wanted Cairo, the key to Egypt, Suez, and perhaps the entire near east. Rommel's reasoning was straightforward. The English were defeated and were on the run. A tight pursuit, pushing them hard, could result in breaking their army, thereby allowing German forces to win Cairo and the **Suez Canal**.[239]

Kesselring analyzed the issues differently. He knew Axis **logistics** (supply) problems were severe in the Mediterranean, and he deeply understood supplies were fundamental to winning any war, especially a war so heavily dependent on tanks and aircraft (both gas hogs).[240] Kesselring recognized the extended supply lines of the *Afrika Korps* could be their undoing. The British fell back on shorter supply lines, while the German supply lines stretched ever longer. English air power consistently increased, threatening to gain air superiority, and opening the lengthy German supply lines to air attack. Malta must be taken or the Axis faced disaster on the deserts of North Africa. A stop at Tobruk, permitting resource diversions for Malta's conquest, was critical for supply line protection. Once the supply lines were secure, Rommel could advance on Cairo or defend Tobruk. Hitler decided it was "on to Cairo," so Rommel kept his meager resources, and Britain kept Malta. German supplies were interdicted at ever-increasing rates even as Hitler refused critical reinforcements for Rommel. This was *the key decision in North Africa.* On such decisions, the fate of the world often turns.

El Alamein

June to October 1942

Rommel drove eastward until he confronted a new English line north of the Qattara Depression near the tiny railroad stop of El Alamein. The British

---

[238] For a while, the Germans did have critical information on convoy sailings through insurance companies in Switzerland that kept records of the sailings

[239] The Suez Canal allowed the transport of oil, men, and material to and from India (the key British colony), Iran, and Australia. Closing it would mean the ships carrying these key supplies would have to round Africa to reach England. This voyage would be longer, use more fuel, and expose the ships to German attacks for a longer time.

[240] Kesselring knew of the supply problems all over the Axis theaters of war, and he knew logistics would be a key factor in victory or defeat everywhere.

general Auchinleck decided to forego other defensive positions and retreat to El Alamein, thereby gaining time for preparing a decisive defensive line. The depression, a sinkhole in the desert impassable by tanks or mechanized units, caused a shrinking of the battlefield to a narrow strip of land between the depression and the coast. Up until this point, the armies fought on an open desert without a southern flank. Anchoring defensive positions on the coast protected the northern flank, but the southern part of any position was just hanging in the air. Rommel made good use of this, and his panzers liked rounding the exposed flank to smash it in thus causing many British retreats. Anchoring both the northern and southern flanks ended the dashing war of maneuver Rommel used so well. Instead, Rommel faced a position requiring frontal assaults and static fighting, much like World War I, wholly favoring the English.

Upon arriving at El Alamein, Rommel realized that giving the English preparation time was not a good idea; so he launched a strong frontal attack on General Auchinleck's forces with his combined German and Italian army in June of 1942. This was the *First Battle of El Alamein,* and it was **the deciding battle in North Africa**. It was now, before the arrival of massive British reinforcements, the *Afrika Korps* enjoyed its best chance of breaking through the tired and demoralized British.

Rommel's major problem was the disparity in forces. He controlled eight infantry divisions and four armored consisting of 96,000 men including 56,000 Italians; however, only two of the armored divisions were German panzers. The other two were Italian units with outdated tanks. On paper, Rommel could muster 582 tanks, but *only two hundred* of them were reliable panzers. To make matters worse, the Axis air forces possessed less than five hundred aircraft. The British Eighth Army fielded 150,000 troops in seven divisions, three armored divisions of *1,114 tanks,* 1,000 artillery pieces, supported by *1,500 aircraft,* and they had dug-in positions to defend along with ***exact intelligence*** on Rommel and his army. A simple review of the forces makes one wonder how the Germans could succeed under any scenario. To win when the forces are lopsided, maneuver is essential; and at El Alamein maneuver was subtracted from victory's equation. Rommel nearly succeeded anyway. In his estimation, one ridge stood between him and knocking the British out of this ideal defensive area, but that one ridge held against Rommel's exhausted men and dwindling supplies of fuel and ammunition. The defenders of Ruweisat Ridge, a medium rise of land in the middle of the battlefield, stopped the Third Reich and one of its best generals. Not for the last time, lack of supplies played a key role in the defeat.

For less than appropriate reasons, Churchill replaced Auchinleck with General Montgomery.[241] As fall arrived in the desert, Rommel grew seriously ill and left for hospitalization in Europe.[242] Meanwhile, Montgomery had assembled 220,000 troops, 1,351 tanks, 1,500 aircraft, and over 900 artillery pieces. In tanks and aircraft, the English had a 3 to 1 or better advantage.[243] Montgomery was finally ready, Rommel was hospitalized, and the Germans were unaware the assault was about to begin. Montgomery's timing was perfect (The code breakers again? Absolutely). Montgomery timed his attack to coincide with Allied landings in French North Africa—far behind Rommel. No matter what occurred at El Alamein, the Germans were in a vise and retreat would be compulsory after the North African landings.[244] El Alamein was a total English victory and a debacle for the *Afrika Korps.* It's back broken, it retreated across 1,500 miles of harsh desert with the British Desert Air Force pounding them every step of the way. North Africa fell to the Allies in **May 1943**. German and Italian prisoners of war exceeded *275,000*, and over one-half were German. These veteran troops were irreplaceable.

General Kesselring knew the ultimate question of victory or defeat for Germany would not be answered in North Africa; however, total defeat in North Africa could unduly influence the true arena of decision—the USSR. Delay would equal success, but it required a well-thought-out defense in the rugged mountains of Tunis, Malta being in Axis hands, and more air power and sea support. An expensive undertaking, but such a strategy might have added a year to the Allied efforts in North Africa. It is entirely plausible that Kesselring, a master of defensive warfare, could have achieved this goal; nevertheless, he would not get the cooperation of the Fuehrer.

---

241 Montgomery had fought in WWI, and this is definitely a WWI attitude. Plus, such overwhelming force is difficult to come by since most nations cannot field that kind of army.

242 The German general staff had sent General **Von Paulus** to Africa, and he recommend an immediate withdrawal. Rommel decided against this, but it was one of his worst decisions. Von Paulus would surrender the German Sixth Army at Stalingrad.

243 Three hundred of these tanks were American Sherman's with its new 75mm gun that outclassed most of the German tanks available to Rommel's men and all the Italian tanks

244 So why attack? Politics mostly. This was the last pure English victory of the war. Well . . . kind of pure. They used American equipment.

THE USSR

June 1944 to August 1945

BARBAROSSA

Hitler invades the USSR on the same month and day Napoleon invaded Russia, **June 22,** 1812. This time it was 1941. The result was the same; the destruction of the invading army and its delusional leader, but how it came about was much different. The scale of conflict in the USSR was so immense that anything coming before it, or after, simply fades away in comparison. Millions of men were fighting across thousands of miles of terrain with every device of war available to them. Innumerable numbers of men, aircraft, tanks, trucks, horses, wagons, artillery, and a profusion of other equipment pushed the campaigns forward. Moreover, this war was personal. Hitler and Stalin despised one another and the governmental systems each man controlled. Murder and torture were commonplace. This was industrialized war set to the tune of uncompromising ideologies. Chaos was upon the world, and chaos had a name—**Operation Barbarossa.**

Hitler doomed his armies before his invasion was underway. Dread gripped the German generals upon Hitler's announcement that an invasion of the USSR was set for launch in April or May of 1941. Britain remained unconquered, their navy and nation still intact, and her forces were trying to capture North Africa. How could Hitler even contemplate such a move since it would result in a two-front war?[245] Ever since Chancellor Bismarck's time, Germany knew it was trapped between the power of Russia in the east, and France and England in the west. Because Germany was a central European land power, the generals understood war with the USSR and England would force expenditures of men and materials on two fronts simultaneously, thereby fatally diluting Germany's combat power.

---

245 Some argue there was no two-front war since Britain had no forces on the continent; however, Hitler had troops in France, the United Kingdom was bombing the continent, the war at sea required a large number of resources (submarines), and North Africa was an active front; thus, many resources were committed to the contest with Britain.

Orders being what they are, the German general staff dutifully drew up plans for the invasion and used war games to study them.[246] The plans were revised until they satisfied the general staff. In these initial plans, the German staff officers made *Moscow* the principal objective of the invasion. Taking Moscow would disrupt Russian command and control systems, because Moscow was the transportation and communication hub of the nation, and taking Moscow would make troop movements from one battlefield to another difficult.

The original OKH (German army headquarters) plans called for a drive on Moscow with large forces. Plan 1 used army group center to push to Moscow with smaller but ample forces moving to take Leningrad. In OKH plan 2, the drive to Leningrad employed fewer units, and the campaign for Moscow was even larger. Adolf Hitler dismissed both plans and *made up his own plan*—which was not war gamed or deeply scrutinized by knowledgeable military men. The Fuehrer's plan targeted Leningrad by removing large numbers of troops from the critical Moscow drive; thus, vital disconnects began between Hitler and his Wehrmacht army headquarters over the grand strategy. By the way, Hitler's planning headquarters was OKW. Yep, there were two planning organizations, and Hitler disliked OKH because they had the temerity to argue with him.

Hitler made these demands late in time, and the generals could not dissuade him from this unstudied course of action. Why he demanded these changes is unknown, but Hitler often thought in economic terms rather than military terms. Gaining valuable raw materials such as oil, or cutting off others from the same, often weighed on his mind. The generals concerned themselves with demolishing the enemy's army as quickly and efficiently as possible. OKH (army headquarters) detested Hitler's plan, and, when time came to order the armies forward, they often shunned Hitler's wishes and surreptitiously kept Moscow as the prime objective. Later in the campaign, Hitler completely absorbed the general's functions and began moving forces himself, and in detail, confusing the goals of the invasion. The lethal decision changing the carefully planned offensive was another dreadful foundational decision which was irreversible.

---

[246] This is an important process whereby the generals set up their cardboard units and the supposed enemy units to fight one another over the same terrain the battle (s) will be fought on. Generals take sides and then fight it out with referees watching the game. In this way, armies are able to discover flaws in their plans before implementation. Interestingly, German **logistic experts** predicted the limits of the invasion with good accuracy before it was launched.

General Guenther Blumentritt stated that Heinrich von Brauchitsch, Franz Halder, and Gerd von Rundstedt were all against the plan to invade the Soviet Union in June 1941. According to General Blumentritt:

> *All three realized the difficulties presented by the nature of the country from their experiences in the 1914-1918 war—above all, the difficulties of movement, reinforcement, and supply. Field Marshal von Rundstedt asked Hitler bluntly, "Have you weighed up what you are undertaking in an attack on Russia?"*

The original date for the invasion was May 15, 1941, but bad weather and Italy's Balkans problem postponed the date. Mussolini decided to invade Greece, for prestige mostly, and purposefully failed to inform Hitler of his plan. Italy's invasion ran into trouble right away, its troops fell back, and Greek forces were soon poised to invade Italian territory. Then the English landed troops in Greece. Unable to stand idly by while his weak ally (dumb too) was invaded and his oil supplies threatened, Hitler sent his panzers into Yugoslavia and Greece. The action ended quickly as Britain fled before the Wehrmacht. Greece surrendered after German troops neared Athens. This operation was an additional example of the Wehrmacht's superb fighting ability in 1941. On the heels of this victory, Hitler allowed a German parachute army to invade **Crete**. The Germans won a close fight, but the losses were heavy.[247]

Did this diversion cost precious time? The invasion date for Barbarossa moved to June 22; accordingly, about a month was lost on top of wear and tear on equipment, loss of men, fuel, and other resources. However, the German generals said *bad weather delayed the invasion date,* and weather histories confirm their claim.

The battles in the USSR determined the outcome of WWII. Germany was tackling a giant. It needed an excellent plan of attack, outstanding leadership, and good luck at every turn. They received none of the above. The German leadership in the field was extraordinary, and the German generals and their troops performed skillfully; but, Hitler created a shoddy plan, made farcical decisions during the struggle, and the Soviets received the luck—like the worst winter in decades.

---

[247] Hitler did not realize the code breakers read the German codes and warned the defenders of the impending attack; thus, surprise, a key element in any airborne assault, was totally lost. Was this the reason Hitler did not want to attack Malta? No one knows.

Barbarossa's scale was unimaginable. Barbarossa easily overshadows the D-Day invasion, Battle of the Bulge, or the entire Pacific campaign. The Germans attacked the USSR with *3.5 million men,* 3,400 tanks, and 1,945 aircraft. The Soviet forces comprised *2.5 to 4.7* million men, 20,000 tanks, and 7,700 aircraft. The Germans caught the USSR by surprise, which is astonishing in itself because Stalin received numerous warnings of the coming assault; however, great spies are one thing, believing their information is another. Whatever the cause, the Russian Army suffered shocking losses because Stalin lacked good sense. The USSR lost 1,200 aircraft the first day, and subsequent Luftwaffe operations continued to destroy numerous outdated Soviet aircraft. As the offensive went forward German close air support of their troops was the difference between victory and defeat in numerous battles. Entire armies of Soviet troops were surrounded by the Germans and forced to surrender (six hundred thousand plus at Kiev alone); however, the German encirclements never managed to bag enough Russian troops to shatter their ability to resist. Many Russians avoided capture because of porous Wehrmacht lines. The Soviet losses of men and equipment became staggering. Stalin's orders to shoot any man falling back helped the Germans bag a lot more men.

In spite of these majestic German victories, the Russians continued to counterattack consistently. The Russian's secret tank, the T-34, surprised and astounded the German troops. Initially, nothing stopped the clanking monster. After discovering the awe-inspiring 88 mm flack cannon could demolish the Soviet T-34, morale improved; nonetheless, meeting a squadron of T-34s set German commanders on edge. The well-developed combined arms doctrine, and the Wehrmacht's superb leadership, carried the offensive forward.

At first, the German invasion went well, killing or capturing millions in Soviet troops and spectacular amounts of equipment. As the drive proceeded the generals became more optimistic, and they made statements that they won the war in the first six weeks. An impartial observer can understand why. The Germans killed, captured, or wounded perhaps ***six million*** Russians and destroyed over one year's worth of equipment production, enough to man and equip an army almost twice as large as the German invasion force. The estimates of USSR losses: 802,000 killed; 3,000,000 wounded; 3,300,000 captured; 21,200 aircraft destroyed; and 20,500 tanks destroyed. Major cities and industrial areas rich with raw materials fell to the invaders as well as thousands of square miles of farmland. This kind of damage would destroy any nation, right?

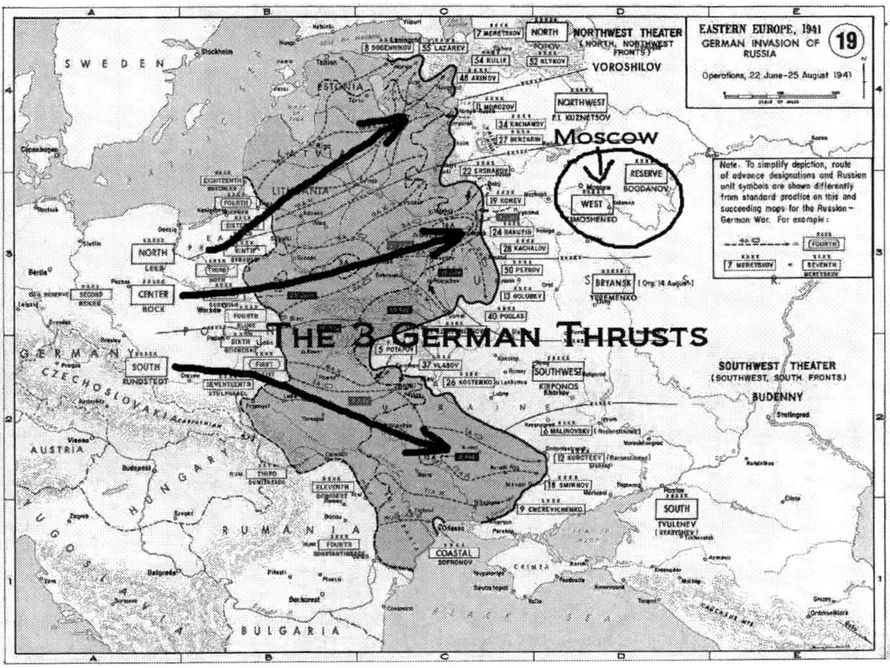

FIGURE 55 OPERATION BARBAROSSA 1941

After the war, Gerd von Rundstedt explained why the German Army failed to conquer the Soviet Union in 1941:

> *"Long before winter came the chances had been diminished owing to the repeated delays in the advance that were caused by bad roads, and mud. The 'black earth' of the Ukraine could be turned into mud by ten minutes rain—stopping all movement until it dried. That was a heavy handicap in a race with time. It was increased by a lack of railways in Russia—for bringing up supplies to our advancing troops. Another adverse factor was the way the Russians received continual reinforcements from their back areas, as they fell back. It seemed to us that as soon as one force was wiped out, the path was blocked by the arrival of a fresh force."*

In spite of terrible losses the USSR continued to counterattack Nazi units, and Soviet troops defended mother Russia fanatically, but the diverging three German drives continued. Then Hitler ordered a halt to Army Group Center's advance in October of 1941. For two months that summer, General Bock's troops sat at the Desna river. Worse, Hitler ordered huge numbers of troops redirected away from the advance on Moscow to battles of encirclement far to the south. Hitler failed to understand how difficult it was to move thousands upon thousands of men and their equipment in a new direction over land with very poor roads. The encirclements worked and bagged large numbers of Soviet troops, but *the drive to Moscow stalled.*

Leningrad was within the reach of the northern German thrust, but *Hitler ordered a stop* and that gave the Russians time to reinforce the city. When the German drive resumed they failed to make good headway. Hitler then ordered a siege, because fighting in a city was not his army's prowess (he said in 1941—how soon he would forget). Leningrad would hold, although Soviet soldiers and civilians endured a 900 day siege producing inestimable famine and suffering. Hitler again, for reason unknown, threw away a key opportunity for victory.

General Guenther Blumentritt was convinced that the German Army could have taken Leningrad in 1941. He stated,

> *"Leningrad could have been taken, probably with little difficulty. But after his experience at Warsaw in 1939 Hitler was always nervous about taking big cities, because of the losses he had suffered there. The tanks had already started on the last lap of the advance when Hitler ordered them to stop—as he had done at Dunkirk in 1940. So no genuine attack on Leningrad was attempted in 1941, contrary to appearances—although all preparations had been completed, including the mounting of long-range artillery that had been brought from France."*

As the Wehrmacht advanced, special killing squads (Einsatzgruppen) advanced behind the front killing Jews, Gypsies, and Slavs just for breathing. These roaming death squads murdered perhaps hundreds of thousands of civilians, but the numbers are uncertain. People initially welcoming the Germans as liberators, and eager to help overthrow Stalin, turned against the invaders and began resisting in every way possible. War is brutal in any event, but this war became more brutal by the hour. This was modern total war, a war of annihilation, devoid of mercy. No civilians and no soldiers, in the classical sense, existed any longer—only the living and the dead. And the living were in the business of creating many more dead.

Stalin allowed 2 million people to leave Moscow as the Germans drew close, but he stayed. Everyone who could walk assisted in building defenses for the communist capital. The world held its breath as the fascist slogged toward victory . . . *then it began to snow.* The temperature dropped like a stone, and the German advance froze—literally. With few winter clothes (poor logistical planning again), little shelter, and the wrong oil for their vehicles and guns, German troops froze to death as their equipment failed. Tank engines refused to run, machine guns jammed, and freezing, dog-tired men huddled in trenches trying to survive. Horses, the mainstay of the German supply system, died by the thousands. ***The Wehrmacht was finished.*** Not even Hitler's towering rage could get freezing, worn out men to move in these conditions, especially after months of constant warfare.

German **logistics** experts predicted the greatest extent of the German advance. Before the invasion started, and not knowing the specifics of the various plans, they accurately predicted how far the Wehrmacht could progress before a long halt would be necessary.[248] Calculating the Russian railroads were a different gauge than Western European railroads (necessitating building new railroads from the Russian border on), the supplies available, fuel resources, amount of fodder required for the horses, the number of tires, the maintenance requirements, and so on, the logistic experts got it right. It was predictable. Hitler's plan should have considered these estimates, but it did not. Modern military leaders know that **amateurs study strategy and tactics, professionals study logistics**. Hitler was an obvious amateur, and he made the fundamental error of downplaying logistics and ignoring the professionals. As in World War I, Germany now faced a long two-front war without sufficient resources, and military experts knew it. Hitler directed Germany to its doom, but it would take time for the ax to fall. Nonetheless, it was falling. Hitler had lost.[249]

As if to put an exclamation point on the fact, the Soviets launched an offensive in December of 1941 with fresh armies of Siberian troops who were quite used to winter conditions. Hitler issued his customary "no retreat!" order. The German forces fell back two hundred miles in spite of the order, but the Soviet offensive finally stalled. German losses were great, but they had held. The great professionalism of the German Army came through during the Siberian offensive. Freezing, starving men, operating

---

248 Page 138, *The Great Crusade,* Willmott, 2008, Potomac Books

249 "Lost" in the sense that the USSR would not be conquered. Many German generals thought the Soviets could still be fought to a standstill, and Germany could achieve a stalemate and a truce which would release German units to fight in the west.

near frozen equipment, shot the Soviet Siberian armies to pieces. Superior German tactics and field leadership accomplished a miracle. However, the German Army was clearly diminished by the ordeal. *Never again would the German Army be the force it was in June of 1941.* Its equipment improved, but the men were gone. Irreplaceable men, who successfully fought from Poland to Norway, France to the Balkans, and then to Moscow's gates were gone forever, and with them the unbeatable Wehrmacht.

No Retreat

A controversy has arisen over Hitler's "no retreat" order given as the Siberian Army's offensive began. Many great historians (Shier, *The Rise and Fall of the Third Reich,* for one) argue this order saved the German Army. They believe that without this order the German Army would have disintegrated and suffered a butchering, just as Napoleon's army retreating from Moscow had in 1812. I do not agree. The German Army of 1941 was not Napoleon's army. The Wehrmacht would have prevailed because of its impressive leadership and discipline. In fact, a general retreat might have saved more men and equipment. [250] We can never know what may have occurred without the order. Hitler did give the order, and no rout occurred; that much we know. Nevertheless, why did no rout occur? Was it the order, or was it the men carrying it out? The men were the key, not the order.

Thus, the German Army faltered against terrific odds and it lost significant combat power. The Wehrmacht captured a large part of the Soviet Union in 1941, and should have gone over to the defense. Most postwar generals, and the German generals in 1941, think that would have been the wise move. Germany's Army would be on the defense, and using its superior mobility with reserves still available could have imposed significant additional casualties on the attacking Soviets. It could take years, but a moderately successful defense might have pried peace overtures out of the Soviet Union. Hitler—ever the blockhead—demanded the outright conquest of the USSR and threw away this defensive advantage.

Moving Soviet Factories to the Urals

The Soviets accomplished numerous miracles in WWII; however, the movement of their heavy industry to the Ural Mountains stands out.

---

[250] After the advance on Moscow failed, German generals wanted to retreat to better defensive positions and prepare for possible counterattacks; but Hitler refused to give up any ground even for tactical advantages.

When it became apparent the Germans would overrun large parts of the western USSR, the Soviets dismantled their heavy factories and moved them east, well past Moscow, to the Ural Mountains. The Soviets accomplished this feat of innovation in record time, quickly putting the factories back in production. The loss of these manufacturing facilities would have extensively harmed Soviet logistics capabilities. While moving their aircraft factories, they retooled them to produce up-to-date aircraft superior to their Nazi counterparts. This was another foundational decision extensively contributing to the Soviet victory over Germany.

Meanwhile, on the other side of the world, WWII was taking another turn for the worst against the Axis, but for over a year it did not look that way.

JAPAN ENTERS THE WAR DECEMBER 7, 1941

BACKGROUND

Japan had planned for a war against the United States since at least 1905[251] (the date of the Russo-Japanese War), and by 1930 America was the inevitable enemy. After 1930, militarist factions took over Japan's government and began urging the conquest of the Far East. Even when the civilian government in Tokyo firmly opposed expansion the military did what it wanted. With Tokyo's blessing, Korea was "annexed" as the diplomats would say at the League of Nations, and operated as a fiefdom of what was now Imperial Japan.

In *September 1931, the Japanese military invaded Manchuria,* winning control in six months. Many date this invasion as the true start of the Second World War because it was brutal fascist aggression that set the stage for future events. The Japanese formed a puppet state and requested its recognition by the League of Nations. The League refused, and Japan walked out. Japanese overseas troops were staging "incidents" to incite short but victorious conflicts with China, which Japan would settle after China granted Japan's territorial demands. After conquering Manchuria, the Japanese triggered another "incident" at the Marco Polo Bridge which lead to another armed conflict with China. This time China refused Japan's demands for territory and repatriations. By August of 1937 an all-out war raged in northern China, and the war was spreading. In November of 1937, Japanese troops

[251] *Japan's War: the Great Pacific Conflict,* Edwin Hoyt.

occupied **Nanking**[252] and began a remorseless orgy of murder, rape, and plunder. Reports of these savage acts went by without real protest, and no action from the League of Nations and the Western Democracies.

In December of 1934 Japan allowed the Washington Naval Treaty (an arms limitation agreement) to expire. September of 1940 saw the Japanese government sign the **Tripartite Pact** with Hitler. It was a protective treaty with each guaranteeing to support the other in case of war. For Japan, the treaty's main purpose was threatening the Soviet Union with a two front war if it attacked Japan. It was not a real military alliance in the normal sense of the word, but it took America by surprise and heightened the sense of confrontation with Japan.

A significant but little discussed event took place on the northern border of **Manchuria in July 1938** when the Soviets and Japanese clashed at the **Battle of Lake Hassan.** The USSR, under **Zhukov**, beat the Japanese easily, and inflicted high casualties. In 1905, during the Russo-Japanese War, Japan had quickly defeated Russia (pre-communist) on land and sea causing a stir in Europe. Thirty-three years later the Soviets handed the Japanese their heads in this one-sided land engagement. The Soviets expertly used numerous tanks and stunning new combined arms tactics, easily outclassing the Japanese in every phase of the battle. Soviet tanks made the Japanese equipment look like junk. Japanese antitank weapons proved useless against Soviet armor (wonder how the Germans missed this?).

Studying this battle extensively, the stunned Japanese determined that competing against the Soviets required a complete reworking of their armed forces, its equipment, battle tactics, and strategy. Japanese generals calculated it might take five years plus millions of dollars to remake its army. This was too much time and far too much money. Thus, Japan decided it must *avoid attacking the Soviet Union.* The push into China would continue, but to attack north was simply out of the question. The Japanese looked south after this battle for conquests. *This decision held great consequences* for the Western Democracies, especially the United States of America.

Japan's military believed the war with China would be over within a few months after the Marco Polo Bridge incident, but China snubbed surrender and territorial concessions. Chiang Kai-Shek, the Nationalist Chinese leader,

---

[252] Some think 260,000 civilians died in Nanking. Estimates at the time put the death toll at 50,000.

retreated into China's hinterland, fought delaying battles, and allowed China to swallow the Japanese. Chinese Nationalist troops were poorly armed and led, and were often loyal to the local warlord rather than the central government. However, Chiang realized he did not have to defeat the Japanese. He only had to avoid a total defeat himself. The Chinese Communists were also present in force; nonetheless, they chose to sit out the war in their strongholds in the Northern provinces while allowing their Nationalist opponents and the Japanese to destroy one another. Later, they could step in, destroy the "winners," and claim China as a communist state (it worked). The communists and the Nationalist had been fighting a brutal civil war for years before the Japanese invasion, which is one reason China was so weak.

The United States, concerned about Japanese aggression against China, put continual diplomatic pressure on Tokyo to end the war. Tokyo refused. As tensions grew Japan gained permission (through German persuasion) from the Vichy French to occupy French Indochina. Japan had also signed the Tripartite Pact in September 1940. America was incensed at these moves, and in August of 1941 put an **embargo on oil** shipments to Japan.[253] This was a disaster for the Japanese because they obtained about 80 percent of their oil from the United States.[254]

Japan decided war with the west was the only course open to them, and they began meticulous preparations for attacking the United States, British, Dutch, and Australian military units in the Pacific. The plan was to damage the US Fleet at Pearl Harbor then systematically move south, capturing the oil and resource-rich areas of the South Pacific and Southeast Asia. Realizing the impossibility of successfully invading Australia or America, the plan required seizing large regions of the Pacific around their main objectives (Java, Singapore, Malaya, Borneo), thereby forcing the Americans and their allies to attack through the perimeter and march island by island to the Japanese homeland. Japan beleived Americans ought to tire of the war quickly, especially with defeats at sea and bloody island invasions sapping their morale, causing them to seek a negotiated peace. Japan would retain China plus whatever remained of her island empire. Many Japanese leaders realized a long war doomed Japan, but they hoped their

---

253 Poor planning and thinking on Japan's part. Japan signed the Tripartite Pact to keep the United States from interfering with Japan, but in fact it convinced the Americans that Japan had to be stopped. *This was a major foreign policy blunder.*

254 *Japan's War: the Great Pacific Conflict,* Edwin Hoyt

calculations were correct and the United States and its Allies would quit after a short but bloody war.

Some historians argue the United States forced the Japanese into war with its oil embargo. These historians think the US left the Japanese no choice; therefore, the United States brought the war on itself with short sighted polices leaving the Japanese without options.

This position is brainless. *All the United States was asking of Japan was to stop slaughtering the Chinese.* Is that so hard? The Japanese simply desired war, even though many other options were open to them. If Japan pulled back from Indochina and stopped attacking in mainland China, the United States probably would have kept the oil flowing. America was deeply isolationist, and President Franklin Roosevelt wanted to avoid a war with Japan. Of the many courses of action open to Japan she decided only one was valid; thus, by absolutely rejecting all US demands she left war as the only option. *National honor* and the transition from a "have not" to a "have" nation all played key roles in Japanese thinking, but no matter how one slices it America was not threatening Japan or trying to expand American territory in the east. Expansion and war were Japanese national policies long before 1941, and China was the main target. It is interesting to note the USA had no plans to attack Japan over China. Because of isolationist sentiments, if Japan did nothing the USA's only recourse was to economic sanctions.

The decision for war in 1941 may have revolved around intelligence gained from the German seizure of a British ship carrying memos from a British war cabinet meeting. In the memos Britain stated it had no resources for defending its Asian Empire. Japan may have acted because this allowed them to capture Britain's Imperial holdings and limited them to one bona fide adversary, the US Navy.

Japan's history included conducting surprise attacks before declaring war. Historically, these surprise attacks, such as Port Arthur before the Russo-Japanese War, heavily damaged the enemy's naval capabilities giving Japan the edge. In 1905, Russia's fleet had to sail long distances from the Black Sea to Japanese home waters and only then was able to engage Japan's fleet. The Japanese were waiting, and they sallied forth at the best moment for THE DECISIVE BATTLE with a tired and demoralized Russian enemy. After one splendid victory, shattering the enemy's fleet, Russia requested terms. Knowing this, the US prepared for a surprise attack . . . right?

DECIDING FACTORS IN THE PACIFIC

The Japanese would lose the war based on some of the factors ***listed below in no particular order:***

1. ***Japan's false assumptions*** were the foundations of defeat. For example, Japan believed its fighting spirit was superior to the West. Japan viewed war as a spiritual fight most of all, and only Japan possessed the necessary spirit to win. Japan, limited by its prewar assumptions, stuck with their original war plan; however, the US Navy came up with stunning new ways of advancing across the Pacific which the Japanese failed to match. *All their major prewar assumptions proved false.*
2. ***The Americans broke the Japanese codes*** which led to American victories at Midway, the Battle of the Philippine Sea, and other critical engagements. *Assume* Japan broke the American codes while the Japanese codes remained secure and the importance of code breaking becomes clear. Japan would know the US Fleet's location, thus giving Japan a major advantage in each battle. Midway would turn into a terrible American loss, as would Guadalcanal and other crucial engagements.
3. ***Lack of Japanese war-production capability***. The island nation of Japan had a good ability to turn out war materials; however, that capacity was far below that of the United States alone. Add in the production of Britain and Japan was completely outclassed. For example, this chart is the merchant ship tonnage produced during the war:

USA	33,993,230 tons
Japan	4,152,361
UK	6,378,899
Italy	469,606

4. ***Lack of production flexibility*** in developing better aircraft types, ships, or even small arms during the war. Japan could not effectively bring its war experience to its production lines, and failed to design newer and better weapons to place in the field.
5. ***Lack of doctrinal flexibility***. Once the Japanese decided how to fight the war they stuck with those ideas. Meanwhile, the Allies changed war itself. Island hopping was one innovation destroying

the Japanese assumption that each occupied island must fall for the Allies to reach their homeland. Japan's planners also failed to account for the effect of submarine warfare on their merchant fleet. Japan's merchant fleet incurred heavy damaged before the Japanese responded, and even the late response remained insufficient.

6. ***Staying with traditions too long***. Because of the Japanese traditional belief in the decisive battle (one all or nothing battle), it became axiomatic to think about naval warfare those terms. The idea became an **unstated assumption**—which is the worst kind of supposition. This tradition (unstated assumption) remained unexamined and therefore unchallenged. Recognizing such an assumption is necessary for unclouded thinking. In fact, in a modern naval war the size of World War II many battles would take place and no one of them would be completely decisive. Another unstated, but natural, assumption was Japan would *win* the decisive battle. Even after several losses Japanese admirals kept saying that if they could bring the Americans into *the* decisive battle Japan could win the war. Japan's leaders needed to recognize there were "decisive" battles, but Japan had lost them. In the Japanese mind this failed to compute, as Japan *must* win *the* decisive battle.

The Japanese assumptions about America refusing to fight long wars were closer to reality in 1940 than one might think. In **War Plan Orange**, the battle plan for war with Japan, US Naval planners assumed a war must be won quickly or US citizens would revolt. Even in 1919, Orange planners assumed the war must be won in less than two years or voters would tire of the effort and make the political decision to quit. The redoubtable Admiral Mahan concluded the American public could not even tolerate a two year conflict. He believed, as did the Japanese, that American society was fickle and had no stomach for hardships. Naval planners predicted that Orange (Japan) would wage a war of endurance trying to outlast the US. It is plain that the original Japanese assumptions were near the mark. It was the sneak attack at Pearl Harbor, Japanese brutality, and effective propaganda management that allowed the US to fight on past two years. (P. 26-30, *War Plan Orange,* Miller, 1991, US Naval Institute).

The stage was set for the largest naval war in world history, and it started with the United States, Britain, Holland, and Australia being frequently humiliated at the hands of the experienced and well prepared Japanese.

PEARL HARBOR AND THE JAPANESE CENTRIFICAL OFFENSIVE

1941 & 1942

In my opinion, war is the art of ambush, and Admiral Yamamoto's attack on **Pearl Harbor** was an excellent ambush.[255] Redact out Japanese bad luck at Pearl Harbor and the war's history is different. Most documentaries covering the Japanese attack detail US errors, bad luck, and missed clues to the coming surprise attack. Seldom do such programs point out the Japanese errors or their extremely poor luck.[256] The key Japanese error was *failing to launch a planned third wave* attack against oil and dry dock installations at Pearl Harbor. Their bad luck included *not finding the American carriers in port and not getting the declaration of war delivered on time.* Japanese errors and bad luck actually exceeded the bad luck and errors of the Americans.

Overwhelming US errors are well summarized in congressional investigations concluding there was a lack of "air mindedness" among American commanders. Also, while many calculated Japan would strike they assumed the strike location was the Philippines. Because of this false assumption when information came in suggesting an air attack on American units people were thinking Manila (in the Philippines) rather than Pearl Harbor. As a result surprise was total. The United States paid a heavy price for this surprise in men and material at Pearl Harbor.

The Western Democracies were unprepared for modern war. They were lacking the men, equipment, training, and the hard attitudes necessary for victory. Peace movements following World War I are partly to blame. Peace movements argued anything was better than war. The US only slowly awoke to the fact that some things are worse than war. Slavery and murder at the hands of power-mad dictators for example, but it took time for the average person to see the truth. War or slavery was the choice. War it would be, but a war the Western Democracies were ill prepared to fight.

Pearl Harbor was *not* the main objective of the overall Japanese offensive. Japan's main goal was capturing the oil and resource-rich areas to the south of the Philippines, including Dutch Borneo, Sumatra, and Malaya.

---

[255] Yamamoto was the commander of Japan's Combined Fleet.

[256] The movie *Tora, Tora, Tora* does this, but the viewer must have enough knowledge to appreciate the magnitude of the Japanese errors.

The attack on Pearl Harbor was aimed at crippling the striking power of the US Fleet long enough for the Japanese to seize their new empire and establish a defensive parameter. Japan needed to take key South and Central Pacific islands, build airfields, and fortify their positions against the eventual assault by the United States Navy.

Pearl Harbor

On Sunday morning, **December 7, 1941**, at about 7:50 AM, 353 Japanese aircraft, flying in two waves, struck the US Pacific Fleet at Pearl Harbor, Hawaii.[257] The US Pacific Fleet was smashed in one of the most successful attacks in history. The United States was at peace when the attack struck. Japanese diplomats in Washington DC were required to deliver a declaration cutting off all negotiations about thirty minutes before the attack. This message substituted for a formal declaration of war; however, Japan's Washington Embassy did not have a good typist that day (it was Sunday and the secretaries were gone) so translating and typing the document took too much time. The result was the critical message telling America that Japan was breaking off diplomatic relations (going to war) arrived over an *hour late*. By then Pearl Harbor blazed with the wreckage of the US Fleet, and over 2,400 Americans lay dead from the assault.

The late delivery of this crucial message was a political blunder of the highest order—right up there with the Zimmerman Telegram of WWI. This was now a sneak attack. Admiral Yamamoto himself stated, *"I can think of nothing that would infuriate the Americans more . . ."* He knew America well, and realized a sneak attack would drive the United States to crush Japan. After Pearl Harbor no terms were possible. Another result of Pearl Harbor was unintended; the sneak attack completely united the heretofore deeply divided nation. Prior to the raid, the United States was split between the isolationist and those wanting to enter the European war. Roosevelt promised in a speech for his unprecedented third term that he would not send US troops into a European war. Now that Hitler was conquering Europe the promise looked increasingly dumb; however, the Japanese attack coupled with *Hitler's declaration of war* on the USA freed Roosevelt and Congress from any restraints.

---

[257] At Dawn 'We Slept: the Untold Story of Pearl Harbor, Prange, Gordon., 1981, McGraw-Hill, The Pearl Harbor Papers: Inside the Japanese Plans, Prange, Gordon W. (1999), Brassey's, ISBN 1574882228

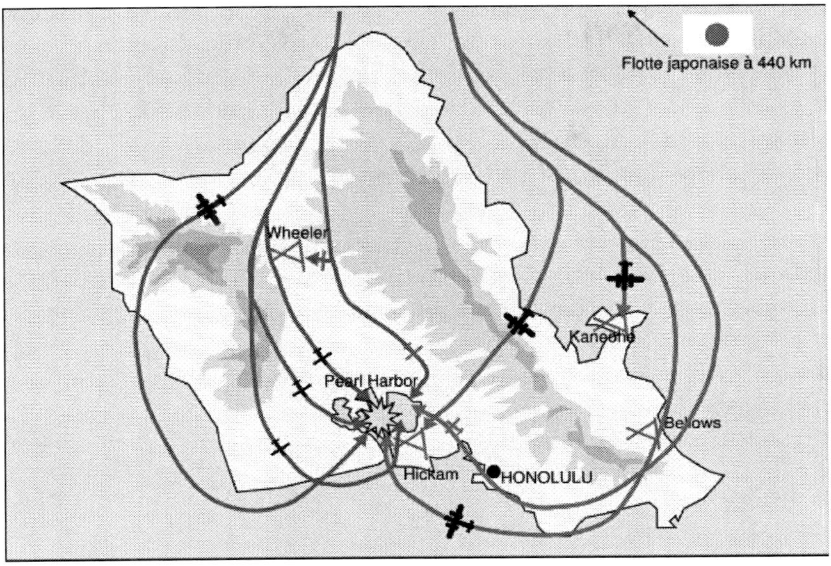

FIGURE 56 PEARL HARBOR AIR RAID, DECEMBER 7, 1941

The Pearl Harbor raid destroyed the mighty US battleships, but ships at sea dodged destruction and three US aircraft carriers, the raid's main target, were at sea. *This was blind luck and nothing else.* Japan's bad luck should include the fact that the Japanese took several precautions to ensure the carriers were at Pearl before the attack, but every one of the precautions failed. Providence dispensed two vital breaks to the United States of America: the first was an attack coupled with a political blunder that united the nation as nothing else could, and second was the miraculous deliverance of *all* its most vital aircraft carriers.

Admiral Nagumo, the leader of the strike force hitting Pearl Harbor, decided to forgo the third wave attack on Pearl Harbor aimed at the construction yards, dry docks, and oil facilities. Because of this decision, made over the objections of the officers on his bridge, the United States was to have critical dry dock and oil facilities throughout the coming months when the Japanese had the edge in the Pacific. It was a poor decision, but Nagumo's reasoning contained a bit of logic. He knew his force of six aircraft carriers were essential for the main thrust into the Southern Pacific. Nagumo also realized his main targets were not at Pearl Harbor, and he did not know where they were. If a US carrier surprised him he might have one or more of his carriers lost or heavily damaged. Nagumo stated it was going to be a long war (a different attitude from some of his superiors) and the aircraft, pilots, and ships would be needed. He did not want to lose them on a mission to tidy up the attack on Pearl Harbor. Nagumo's first wave had lost 9 aircraft, but his second wave lost 20. A third wave assault might cost a lot more. In addition, waiting around for a third wave to return would take hours, and every hour exposed his fleet to assault by US submarines or carriers. His objective, crippling the US Fleet, was attained, so why incur additional risks?

Looking back over sixty years Nagumo's error appears appalling; however, we should try to put ourselves into the situation at the time of the attack and realize Nagumo focused on a broader picture that included the South Pacific. What really hurts Nagumo, from a historian's point of view, is all his fellow officers were in favor of the third wave assault. None-the-less, Nagumo's strike force sunk the US Fleet at a cost of 29 aircraft lost. A cheap victory.

Japans' Southern Offensive

1941 & 1942

Japan's southern offensive was superlative. The closely planned attacks went off precisely and professionally with spectacular results. Everywhere Japan was ascendant. On most islands, such as Dutch Borneo, there was virtually no resistance, although Dutch engineers set the oil fields on fire, and the Japanese beheaded them for their trouble. Hong Kong, after light resistance, surrendered on Christmas Day 1941. There were two keys to the region: Singapore at the end of the Malay Peninsula (British), and Manila Bay in the Philippines (American). In both cases troops were available in sufficient numbers to put up a good fight, but in both cases, Japanese commanders utterly out generaled the Allied commanders, while inflicting appalling troop losses on the ill prepared Dutch, British, and US forces.[258]

Singapore

From Singapore the British could control the oil rich areas of the South Pacific. If this bastion held the Japanese would have trouble getting their

[258] Some OF the trouble stemmed from lack of preparation because of the impact of the peace movements, but poor leadership was the main cause of the Allied debacles.

merchant shipping back to Japan. When analyzing the defensive position at Singapore the English calculated an assault would most likely come from the sea. Of course, the British knew an assault could come down the Malaya Peninsula, but they assumed any such attack through the dense jungle would take months, giving them time to react. Unfortunately for the British the key to the area was no longer Singapore harbor, it was air power. The British long ago pulled most of their first line aircraft out of Malaya, and the remaining planes needed maintenance. The Japanese spotted the few completed air bases and quickly destroyed the sparse numbers of English aircraft. Japan easily gained total air supremacy.[259]

Even though resources were scarce, Churchill sent two of Britain's most powerful ships to defend the Asian fortress: the *Prince of Whales* (a battleship) and the *Repulse* (a battle cruiser) along with four destroyers. When Admiral Sir Tom Phillips, commander of this striking force, gained intelligence of Japanese landings underway on the Malaya Peninsula he was determined to strike. He called for air cover from land-based aircraft, and he counted on darkness and poor weather to keep his ships invisible until he was on the Japanese transports, but luck had abandoned the striking force. On December 10, 1941, the weather cleared, no air cover appeared, and a Japanese submarine found the two large ships and reported their position. An all-out air attack sunk both ships in *minutes.*

The sinking of these two capital ships was an important moment in history. Never before had capital ships under power at sea and ready for battle been destroyed by aircraft. For a decade, the battleship admirals had claimed aircraft could not sink a battleship underway and ready for action—at least not easily. Aircraft had easily sunk battleships moored in port with surprise attacks, but this time fully manned and ready battleships swiftly slid beneath the waves after an air attack at sea. About 300 years of history also slid beneath the waves as aircraft now ruled the seas, and ships carrying those aircraft became the capital ships of the fleet.[260]

The British in Singapore were now without air cover or naval assets. Still, it seemed they should be able to significantly delay or stop a Japanese attack down the peninsula. In this they failed. British troops were not

---

259 Note the Japanese landed on an undefended beach. They landed far from Singapore to avoid British resistance during the landing.

260 Aircraft carriers. It should be noted the aircraft that sank the two British ships were land based. Since the 1600s battleships or ships of the line had ruled the waves. The attack off Singapore changed all that forever.

sufficiently trained in jungle warfare, did not possess the right equipment, and their commanders were unable to get a handle on how to stop the rapid Japanese advance. The Japanese were experienced jungle fighters and quickly outflanked defensive lines placed by the British. Consistently forced back, the British set up one defensive position after another, but flanking attacks, infiltration or landings from the sea jeopardized each site. Simple equipment, like the bicycle, hastened the Japanese advance leaving the British defenders reeling. Moreover, the Japanese brought tanks. British commanders thought the jungle was much too dense for tanks; nevertheless, like the Ardennes forest in Belgium, the Allies were mistaken once again. With tanks and bicycles the Japanese advanced rapidly keeping the English defenders off balance and preventing the construction of adequate lines of defense. By January 1942, the Japanese stood at the northern gates of Singapore.

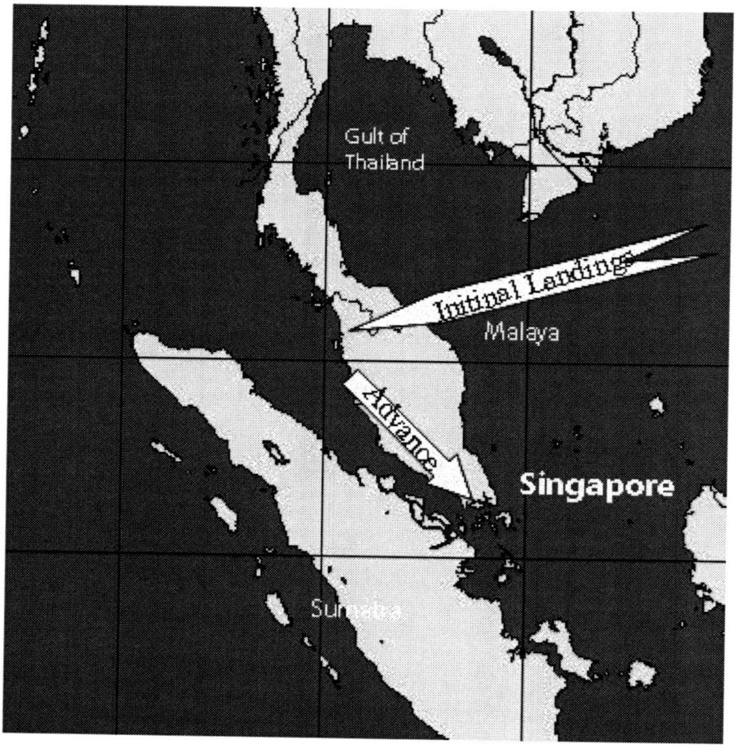

FIGURE 57 JAPANESE ADVANCE ON SINGAPORE

Singapore is an island, and the recently reinforced British forces should have held out against the exhausted Japanese force for months. Instead, Singapore was immediately subjected to artillery bombardment and aircraft attacks. The Japanese rapidly crossed to the island and captured the fortress in February of 1942. Approximately *130,000 men surrendered.* It was a great defeat and the largest surrender in English history. Very few of these men ever saw Britain again. They would die of starvation and physical abuse in Japanese slave labor camps. The privates paid a high price for the ineffectiveness of their generals, as usual.

This disaster falls completely upon the British commanders for failing to prepare the peninsula for defense through properly training and equipping their men, preparing dug in defensive positions well ahead of time, and properly positioning their lines. Another general was displaying similar incompetence in the Philippines, only this commander was American.

THE PHILIPPINES

General Douglas MacArthur (1880-1964), an American icon lionized by the nation during and after World War II, was the man in charge of defending the Philippines and the vital harbor at Manila Bay. In this he utterly failed, causing thousands of men to die needlessly or suffer horribly at the hands of the merciless Japanese.

Prior to World War II the United States, as nations always do, planned for a war with Japan.[261] The planners assumed Japan would invade the Philippines at the outset of war. **War Plan Orange** (the code name for the plan; orange being the code word for Japan) called for a retreat to the Bataan Peninsula and the small island of Corregidor guarding the entrance to Manila Bay, the best harbor in the region.[262] The Japanese would have to take Bataan to control the Philippines. MacArthur was to fall back to fully *prepared* positions on Bataan and Corregidor then hold out until the United States could send help. In fact, Washington knew help was impossible to send in a timely manner; as a result, the men on Bataan and Corregidor were doomed in all but the most favorable circumstances. The point of the defense was to prolong the conquest and remain a thorn in Japan's side for as long as possible.

---

261 Nations prepare for war against all other nations of any consequence by war gaming the conflict and then drafting plans based on those war games. These plans are updated constantly.

262 War Plan Orange was updated to the Rainbow Plan that assumed a war with Germany and Japan, but still called for the defense of Bataan in the Philippines. *War Plan Orange*, by Edward S. Miller,1991, US Naval Institute.

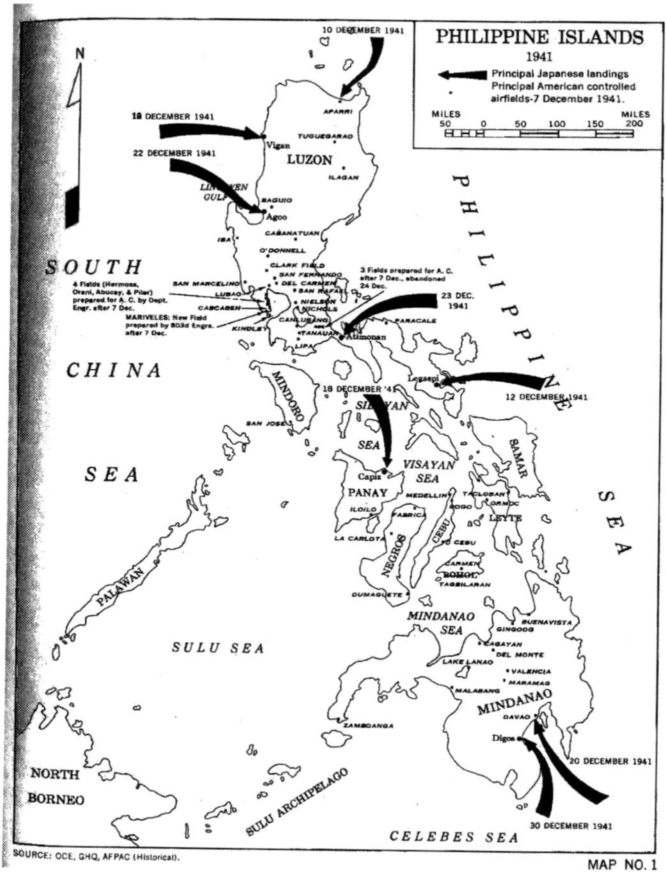

FIGURE 58 JAPANESE CONQUEST OF THE PHILIPPINES 1942

MacArthur rejected this "defeatist" attitude and decided to defend the Philippines at the landing beaches and expel the invader. This was an unwise decision. The war planners in Washington knew the striking power Japan could bring against the isolated and distant islands and they knew the Japanese would have the initiative.[263] MacArthur decided on a defense requiring the American and Philippine forces to attack and repel the invader upon his landing. If the enemy took the beaches he would fight them all the way to Manila. Unfortunately, the Philippine forces were far from first line troops, and the American forces were few and without

---

[263] The "initiative" is a term that means the power to determine what to do next. The attacker decides when, where, how, and with what forces to attack. The defense then responds. Thus, the attacker has the initiative. Note there is both a strategic and tactical initiative.

adequate equipment for such an adventure. In addition, MacArthur had no idea where the Japanese would land.

It gets worse. MacArthur *utterly failed to prepare a defense on Bataan. Moreover,* ***no food or medical supplies*** *were stored on the peninsula.* MacArthur failed to follow orders, and he failed to develop a backup plan in case his new plan collapsed. American troops would pay the price in blood for MacArthur's incompetence in this critical matter.

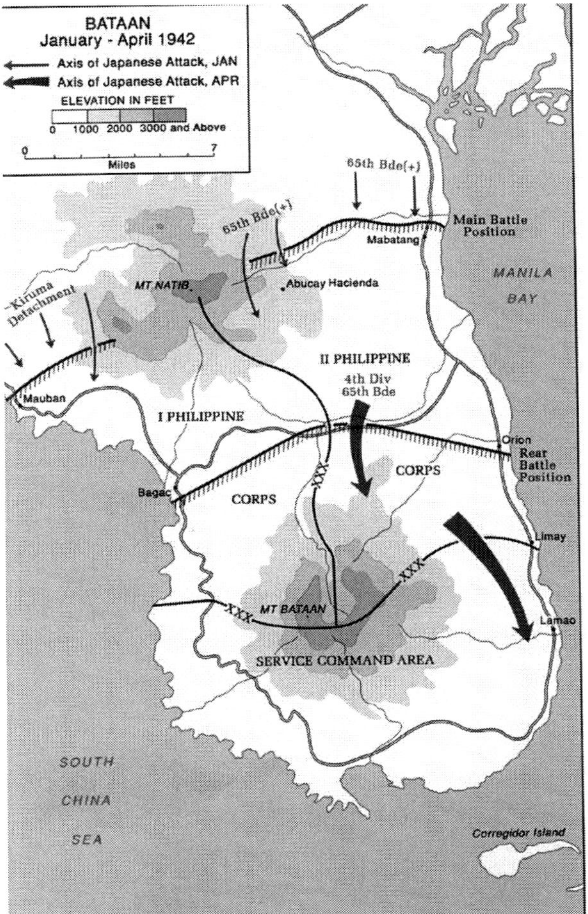

FIGURE 59 JAPANESE ASSAULTS ON BATAAN 1942

The Japanese landings took place in the northern areas of Luzon on December 10, 1942, and then quickly moved south toward Manila. Regretfully, for the Americans, the critical battle had already taken place.

After warnings that Pearl Harbor had been bombed, and pleas from his air commanders to allow them to strike Formosa where the Japanese air forces were concentrated, MacArthur did nothing. Soon thereafter, *MacArthur's entire air force was destroyed on the ground* by Japanese air raids. Without air cover the navy was forced to leave stripping the islands of everything except infantry forces. Japan moved forward with complete air and naval superiority. There was no hope now.

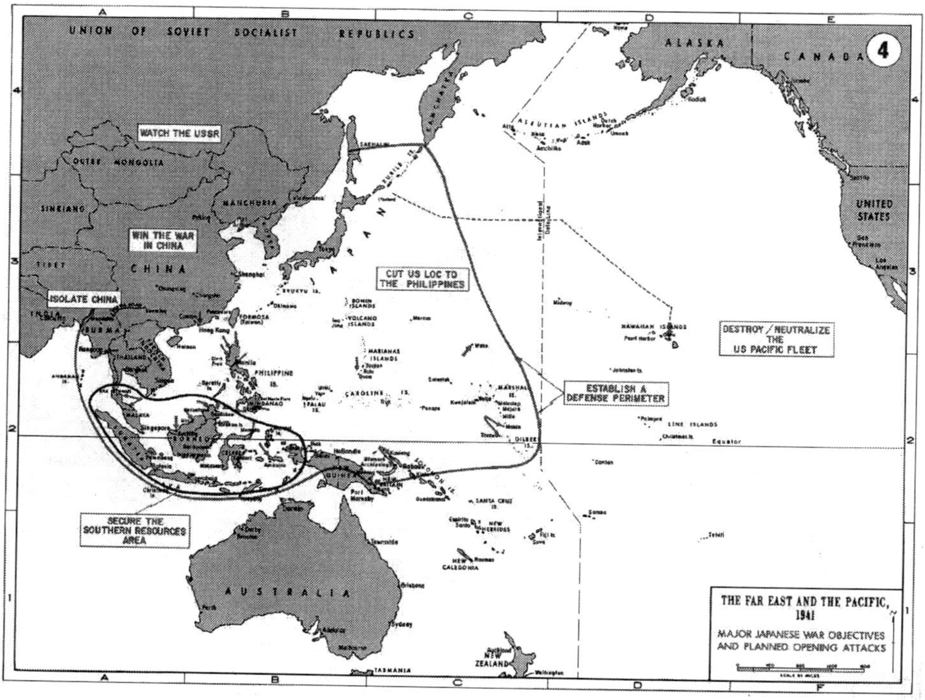

FIGURE 60 JAPANESE CONQUEST 1942

In spite of the loss of his air force and his naval support, MacArthur insanely went forward with his plan to meet the invader north of Manila. Japan's excellent veteran troops with air and sea support routed the combined Filipino and American forces. The Japanese then began maneuvering to surround Manila where the Japanese assumed the Americans would make their last stand. This assumption helped with the withdrawal to Bataan. As a complete military disaster stalked the defenders, **General Wainwright** (MacArthur's second in command) managed to reposition key units allowing the army to reach Bataan. However, MacArthur failed to prepare Bataan for a siege and the hastily retreating army took little food or medical supplies with them. Wounds, disease, and hunger proved to be an enemy every bit as strong and effective as the Japanese at eliminating the defenders.

Bataan's American and Filipino troops threw back Japanese attacks, including amphibious assaults on the western beaches; however, they continued falling back. Starving and ragged men fought while suffering from malaria and constant gnawing hunger. Food rations diminished to one thousand calories per day. Japanese artillery pounded the men, enemy aircraft bombed and strafed their positions, and to all this Allied soldiers possessed no effective answer. MacArthur kept demanding help from Washington, but after the defeat at Pearl Harbor no help was possible. The US Navy was just holding on around Australia, and the destruction of MacArthur's air force doomed ships trying to gain access to Bataan, except occasional submarines and PT boats. The defenders fought on until May 8, 1942 when Wainwright surrendered the last of his emaciated command on Corregidor. The Philippines had fallen.

MacArthur missed the surrender because he was in Australia demanding that Wainwright fight on. Escaping by PT boat on February 22, 1942, along with the president of the Philippines, he then went by aircraft to the comforts of Australia. After Wainwright surrendered MacArthur demanded he be court-martialed. President Franklin Roosevelt had appointed MacArthur as the US Army's commander for the Pacific Theater of War. The starving dying men he left behind would never understand Roosevelt's decision.[264]

After the surrender of the Filipino and American forces the Japanese subjected the men to the vilest murder and torture. Japanese soldiers thought surrender was dishonorable, and quitting proved you were not a soldier. Few of the more than eighty thousand American and Filipino prisoners of war would return. Over *twelve thousand died in the Bataan Death March* alone. Meanwhile, from Australia, MacArthur avowed to the press corps, "I shall return . . ."[265]

While the conquest of Bataan and Singapore continued, Japan also pushed a rapid advance through the South Pacific. Sea control was critical, thus, a combined Allied force of American, British, Dutch, and Australian (ABDA) ships under Admiral Doorman (Dutch navy) attacked the Japanese at the

---

264 He also received a huge sum of money from the Philippine government . . . for some undisclosed reason (want to make a guess?).

265 US Army thought he should have said, "WE shall return . . ."

Battle of the Java Sea on February 27, 1942. The small fleet was making a last gasp attempt to slow the Japanese juggernaut. Due to poor coordination among the Allied ships, and excellent tactical control by the Japanese commanders, a smaller Japanese force annihilated the ABDA force.[266] ABDA lost *5 cruisers, 5 destroyers, and 2,300 sailors.* The disaster is right up there with Pearl Harbor. Japan lost four loaded transports. By May 1942, the Japanese fleet of eleven battleships, ten aircraft carriers, eighteen heavy cruisers, and twenty-eight light cruisers plus numerous destroyers had campaigned from Pearl Harbor to the Indian Ocean without the loss of a single major ship. Along the way they destroyed or damaged every battleship in the US Pacific fleet, damaged the US Far East squadron at the Philippians, annihilated the ABDA naval force, chased the Royal Navy from the southern seas, and forced the Australian navy back to its home waters. Total victory sailed with Japan. The only forces left in the Pacific that threatened them were the three US aircraft carriers that Japan missed at Pearl Harbor.

Admiral Yamamoto, Japan's chief of naval operations, was lobbying for an effort in the Central Pacific to lure the US carrier fleet out to its destruction in a decisive action. He knew the United States would out produce Japan in a long war so he thought it a necessity to destroy the US aircraft carriers now, before the US Fleet recovered from its defeats. The Japanese high command wanted to continue the push to the south and draw the US Fleet into an action there. Yamamoto argued the US Navy must believe a vital asset was in jeopardy before they would choose to do battle with the more powerful Japanese Combined Fleet. He believed actions in the south would not draw the US Navy into battle. By attacking and seizing Midway Island he threatened Pearl Harbor by putting it in bomber range. The Doolittle raid on Tokyo (April 18, 1942) decided the matter.[267] If a US carrier task force could threaten the emperor[268] that threat must be eliminated; thus, the high command agreed to Yamamoto's plan but with substantial changes.

---

[266] The Japanese had aircraft spotters to help direct their shell fire and they had the **Long Lance torpedo**. The Japanese Long Lance torpedo had a twenty-mile range, one thousand pounds of explosives, was very accurate, and always worked, which made this the best torpedo of the war by far. Four Japanese destroyers defeated a larger Allied force in an action at Badung Strait with these superior torpedoes.

[267] This was a daring raid by B-25 aircraft flown off of the carrier USS Hornet. The air crews successfully bombed Tokyo and flew on to China.

[268] The emperor was a god on earth to the Japanese, and he had to be protected.

Admiral Yamamoto's plan was overly complex. It divided his forces in the face of the enemy, and it assumed the Americans would not fight unless forced to by dire circumstances.[269] Most military types will tell anyone who will listen that if you have the larger force use it all at one point of assault and gain absolute superiority over the foe. The Japanese plan put four carriers away from the main action at Midway. Two large carriers sailing with an invasion fleet to Port Moresby planned to return in time for the Midway action, but why take them so far away, and put them at risk, so near the date of the big show? These carriers failed to join the action at Midway, and this reduction of striking power haunted the Japanese fleet at the battle.

Yamamoto's plans began to go wrong quickly. At the **Battle of the Coral Sea** on May 4 through 8, 1942, only pilots from the aircraft carriers saw the other fleet. For the first time in history two fleets fought it out never coming in sight of one another. When it was over, the US Navy lost the heavy fleet carrier *Lexington* and the Japanese lost a light carrier (*Soho*). In addition, the US Fleet carrier *Yorktown* suffered extensive damage. The loss of the Lexington was a hefty blow to the US Navy. On the surface, it seemed the Japanese won another victory; however, two Japanese fleet carriers Shôkaku and Zuikaku lost a large number of aircraft and pilots, plus they suffered battle damage and returned to Japan for repair and replenishment of pilots and aircraft. Thus, two fleet carriers were lost to the Midway operation and the Japanese invasion fleet turned back, thereby failing to invade Port Moresby. The Battle of the Coral Sea was the first strategic defeat for the Japanese navy.

The Japanese may have wondered why two US aircraft carriers happened to be hanging around the Coral Sea at that particular moment in time. It was not bad luck. The code breakers at Pearl Harbor's station Hypo deciphered parts of a key Japanese code and through brilliant analysis unscrambled Yamamoto's plan. Admiral Nimitz, now in charge of the US Pacific Fleet, had trusted his code breaking genius, **Commander Rochqfort**, and sent his carriers to intercept the Port Moresby invasion fleet. He would trust this same man and his team's analysis again when they declared that Japan's next objective was the tiny island of Midway. Nimitz sent ALL three of his available carriers to fight the Japanese fleet at Midway. By holding zero back Nimitz took a huge risk with his last and best naval units. Literally everything would ride on their performance and luck.

---

[269] See, *The Shattered Sword, the Untold Story of the Battle of Midway*, by J. Parshall and A. Tully.

THE BATTLE OF MIDWAY

June 4 to June 6, 1942

Many historians consider the Battle of Midway as the turning point of the Pacific War, and one of the most important naval battles of all time. It is a complex battle where decisions by Nagumo (same admiral who led the Pearl Harbor attack), and persistent bad luck doomed all four fleet carriers of the Japanese strike force. Instead of ambushing the Americans and sinking their carrier fleet, the opposite occurred. For the US Navy and its three available carriers the Battle of Midway was an immense gamble. Battle damage to the **USS *Yorktown*** at the Battle of the Coral Sea, and six month repair estimates, only added to the risk. Nimitz ordered the repairs done in *three days.* American construction crews accomplished this marvel, and the *Yorktown* was off to the battle.[270]

We cannot go into all the details of the battle here, but the results were four Japanese fleet carriers burned and sunk, and one American fleet carrier (the damaged Yorktown) was lost to Japanese submarine action after being badly damaged by air attacks. Japanese personnel losses were high as well (over 2,000), and all of those lost were highly trained and experienced flight crew members. Some blame Admiral Nagumo for the loss, complaining he lacked aggressiveness; nevertheless, the planners were actually responsible for the loss, because they cut the striking power of the Japanese carrier fleet by one-half in side show actions at the Coral Sea and the Aleutian Islands. Better luck would have helped the Japanese. One of their critical search planes launched behind schedule and spotted the US fleet much too late. In carrier battles, the first carrier to spot the other fleet and launch its aircraft has an immense advantage. The Japanese

---

[270] Admiral Halsey's place at Midway in command of the USS *Enterprise* was taken by Admiral Spruance due to Halsey's being ill. USS *Yorktown,* in a different task force, was commanded by Admiral Fletcher.

search pattern was not as concentrated as it could have been because the Japanese were operating on the assumption the US Navy would be absent.[271] In the matter of searching for the other fleet the Americans enjoyed a large edge in its very-long-range Catalina seaplanes operating out of Midway, and American intelligence reports predicting the enemy fleet's approach headings.

American luck, determination, and bravery played a large role in the battle. Commander Wade McClusky Jr, leader of a flight of ***USS Enterprise*** Dauntless dive bombers (SBD) running low on fuel, spotted a lone Japanese destroyer traveling at high speed and changed course to mimic the destroyer's heading.[272] He found the Japanese carrier fleet and, unplanned, arrived over the enemy carriers concurrently with a flight of *Yorktown's* SBDs led by Commander Maxwell Leslie.[273] Both attacked simultaneously without coordinating the attack. Japanese air cover was missing in action. The Zero fighters were landing to refuel after annihilating two flights of outdated American torpedo planes. Up until this moment in the battle numerous American attacks had scored no hits while suffering large losses.

During this instant America's only good weapon, the Dauntless dive-bomber, appeared above the Japanese carriers. Three Japanese fleet carriers became sinking infernos, helped along to their doom by their ordinance crews leaving bombs and torpedoes improperly stowed, adding to the damage when they detonated.[274] The remaining Japanese carrier, the *Hiryu,* struck back heavily damaging *Yorktown,* but *Hiryu* was sunk in turn by Dauntless

---

271 There is some dispute about this: see, *The Shattered Sword: the Untold Story of the Battle of Midway* by Parshall and Tully; *Midway, the Battle That Doomed Japan,* by M. Fuchida, M. Okumiya, R. Spruance and C. Kawakmi; *Miracle at Midway,* by Gordon Prange*; Incredible Victory,* by Walter Lord, among others.

272 This destroyer had been depth charging the US submarine *Nautilus* that was trying to get in on the battle. The Japanese destroyer was heading back to the main fleet.

273 **SBD** was the Dauntless designation meaning Scout, Bomber, Dive (or, slow but deadly).

274 Nagumo was badly served by his staff during these critical moments in the battle. Constantly changing orders caused the ordinance crews to rush, leaving bombs and torpedoes just lying on the deck. When the fire reached the ordinance it exploded helping to sink the carriers. One bomb was enough to sink one of the Japanese carriers.

strikes from the USS *Enterprise*.[275] The damaged Yorktown was later sunk by a Japanese submarine.

Losing four first class carriers and their crews was a massive blow to the Japanese navy.

In several books on the battle, the titles sum up most people's views on the action: *Miracle at Midway*, by Gordon Prange, and *Incredible Victory*, by W. Lord. Nimitz risked it all and won. After Midway, Yamamoto realized it was necessary to go over to the defensive and await the US Navy's assault on the Empire's vast new perimeter.

The South Pacific and Indochina

As all this transpired, the Japanese army was trying to conquer the rest of Indochina and New Guinea. The Japanese army and navy were also pushing south down the Solomon island chain toward Fiji and New Caledonia to establish air bases and make supplying Australia problematical for the Americans.

Since Japan was having trouble conquering China they decided to isolate the country by cutting off all outside help. To this end, they captured all of China's major coastal harbors and towns by 1940. Japan attacked and gained control of Burma, cutting the **Burma Road** that was bringing supplies to the Nationalist Chinese. The United States flew supplies over the Himalayan mountains to China month after month in an effort to keep China in the war. *Keeping China fighting* and tying down Japanese resources there was a major US war aim.

In Burma, the Japanese administered a resounding defeat upon the English. Now the Japanese controlled all of Indochina and its vital natural resources. Burma was lost because of superior Japanese jungle fighting methods, Japan's complete control of the air, superior numbers where it counted, and the toughness of the Japanese soldiers.[276] Japan was now on the border of India, but with long supply lines. Many feared Japan would go forward and conquer at least part of India; however, Japan's resources were stretched

---

275 Because of outstanding damage control efforts, it took two Japanese air strikes hitting the *Yorktown* with four bombs and two torpedoes, plus torpedoes from a Japanese submarine, to put the *Yorktown* under.

276 Sounds like the battle for Malaya and Singapore.

to the limit. In fact, she had overextended herself dramatically. This error would compound other Japanese mistakes, thus making the defense of her newly won empire much harder.

In New Guinea, the Japanese again proved their robust nature. Since the invasion convoy bound for Port Moresby turned back after the Battle of the Coral Sea, the Japanese decided to assault the port by crossing the Owen Stanly Mountains dominating the center of the island. The Allies, as usual, thought this mountain range was impassable because of height (over 6,000 feet high), extremely rugged terrain, and the uniquely hostile jungle. The Japanese thought otherwise, and attacked over the **Kokoda Track** in July of 1942. The Australians fought all the way but fell back just the same. The Australians and Americans dug in just outside of Port Moresby, determined to make a last stand.[277] In January 1943, thirty two miles from Port Moresby, the Japanese force received orders to turn back because of events on Guadalcanal. Reluctantly, the Japanese began their retreat. Nonetheless, the accomplishment of crossing the Owen Stanly range against stiff Australian resistance was a remarkable military accomplishment. The retreat also showed the psychological effects of war, as the same Japanese soldiers who went forward eating grass while shrugging off disease and the effects of battle while they were winning, lay down and died after they started losing. Victory gives men hope and purpose while defeat saps them of life itself.

Port Moresby remained under Allied control. Later, after a fierce set of battles on the border between India and Burma, the British forces successfully blocked the threat to India. In the Solomon Islands the Japanese were still advancing south down the island chain, building airbases as they went and putting garrisons on each island. The code breakers found clues the Japanese were building an airbase on the island of **Guadalcanal.** Another chapter in the Pacific War was about to open.

GUADALCANAL

August 7, 1942 to February 9, 1943

This was the campaign *(note: not a battle, a campaign or series of battles)* that broke the back of Japan's offensive power.*278* Midway certainly took the

[277] The Japanese force was starving as it advanced up the Kokoda Track because of inferior logistic support. Still, they went forward.

[278] See: *Guadalcanal: the Definitive Account of the Landmark Battle,* by Richard B. Frank

initiative away from the Japanese Empire, but Guadalcanal damaged their military nearly beyond repair. The Japanese losses in merchant shipping during the campaign were high, and this was one of the weakest areas of Japanese war preparation and production. Japanese and American losses in the campaign were steep. The difference was the Japanese faced a much harder task making up their losses in men (especially aircrew) and materials.

Ground Losses:

US—1,768 dead
Japan—25,600 plus another 9,000 dead of disease (estimates)

Naval Personnel Losses:

US and Allies—4,911
Japan—3,543

Ship Losses:

Allied—29 (does not include merchant shipping)
Japanese—38 (does not include merchant shipping)

Aircrew Losses:

US—420
Japan—1,200 (estimates)

Aircraft Losses:

US—615
Japan—880 (estimates)

The campaign for Guadalcanal centered on Henderson Field and air control. The US Marines landed on the island of Guadalcanal **August 7, 1942** at the behest of **Admiral King**, the US Chief of Naval Operations. Admiral King realized a Japanese airfield at Guadalcanal was a threat to Australian supply lines; conversely, the US lacked the resources for such an early offensive move. Accepting the risk of defeat, King ordered a US Marine assault. (Like all leaders, he accepted the risk of getting a lot of other people killed) After an unopposed landing the marines successfully captured the nearly completed Japanese airfield. Completion of the airfield by the troops and engineers was urgent because Japan was moving swiftly to annihilate the US effort.

On the night of 8 August 1942, the US Navy and its Allies suffered a signal defeat at the hands of a Japanese cruiser force commanded by Vice-Admiral Mikawa off **Savo Island**. The Japanese skillfully avoided two Allied picket destroyers, completely surprising several Allied cruisers. Four Allied cruisers were sunk (one Australian, three American), plus one cruiser and two destroyers were damaged. 1,270 Allied sailors died, and 790 wounded.[279] The Japanese suffered light damage on three of its cruisers and about fifty killed. The Japanese force was set to destroy the still loaded transports and the supplies stacked high on the beach when, mysteriously, Vice Admiral Mikawa withdrew as he was on the verge of total victory. Why he failed to bombard the unprotected transports is a hard question. Admiral Mikawa stated aircraft could attack his ships at first light unless he got out of flight range. The decision was a tide-turning event. If he sank the supply transports and bombarded the supply stacked beaches a swift withdrawal would have been the only choice for the Americans. To protect seven cruisers Vice-Admiral Mikawa sacrificed an early and decisive win at Guadalcanal.

Some people reading about naval warfare erroneously think warships are the key to victory. The king of the seas is the transport—the lowly supply ship—that trundles along without glory or much of anything else. The carrier may be the queen of the seas and all the other warships the royal entourage; however, *they all exist to get the cargo ship to its destination* quickly and safely. That is why the Germans knew they could win the war with England if they could sink enough transports. All the battleships, cruisers, destroyers, and carriers in the English naval inventory would mean nothing if the transports were sunk. Who can eat a battleship? Do the soldiers, no matter how brave and resourceful, stand a chance without bullets? As Japan found out on Guadalcanal, troops who are starving to the point of death seldom attack enemy positions acceptably.

Recall that the US code breakers were unable to read Japan's codes for months because of cipher changes after Midway; however, the United States did have a unique source of intelligence during the Solomon campaign, the *Australian Coast Watchers*. Hiding in the jungle with radios they transmitted vital information to the Americans on Guadalcanal. To illustrate; if US Marine pilots knew early enough Japanese air attacks were on the way

---

279 See p.977 *The Oxford Companion to World War II,* editors Dear, & Foot, Oxford University Press, 1995.

they could scramble their Wildcat fighters and climb above the incoming raiders, then dive down on them as they approached the island. This tactic inflicted additional Japanese losses because the Wildcat performed best in a dive. Failure to warn the Wildcats soon enough would mean much higher US losses. Without the Coast Watchers every Japanese raid would be a near surprise.

The numbers of naval and air assets favored Japan at the start. Because of the threat of continued Japanese assaults on the transports, Admiral Turner, in overall charge of the Guadalcanal operation, decided to withdraw the navy along with the precious transports that were still partially loaded. His decision left the marines in the lurch without sufficient supplies, ammunition, or equipment. For months the US Navy opted for small convoys delivering just enough ammunition and food to Guadalcanal for the troops and airmen to carry on.[280] Somehow, with a minimum of supplies and support, the US Marines and US Army held on halting several Japanese assaults on Henderson Field's perimeter. If Japan's troops broke through and took the airfield it would be over for the invaders. Henderson Field was the key to the campaign.

Both navies began to understand that controlling the Slot was vital to winning the island contest. As a result, a number of naval battles took place around the Solomon Islands deciding the fate of the marines and army troops on Guadalcanal every bit as much as the ground fighting. Some of the sea battles were: the Battle of Savo Island, Battle of the Eastern Solomon's, Battle of Cape Esperance, Naval Battles of Guadalcanal, the Battle of Tassafaronga, and the Battle of Santa Cruz Islands. In these exchanges both navies suffered high losses. More than once the US Navy was down to one operational carrier (the *Enterprise* once, and the *Hornet* once). In this naval war of attrition Japan could only lose. American production and training capability were coming on line and with it a massive outpouring of new and better equipment with torrents of well-trained men to accompany that equipment. Japan boasted an excellent navy at the war's beginning, the equal of any in the world with its high training standards, fine ships, and aircraft. With this kind of force there is a need to strike swiftly and withdraw. In a war of attrition, the side with the largest army (or navy) and the best production ability wins.

---

[280] As the battle went on, the Japanese became much worse off. Even with fast destroyers as the delivery method, little food got through. Japanese troops were literally starving to death and eating grass trying to stay alive. Again, we see the importance of logistics in warfare.

While Japan's generals were planning another large offensive to throw the Americans off Guadalcanal, the Japanese merchant marine reported they lacked the shipping to support an attack. Japan needed all its transport capability to keep shipping war materials to the home islands; thus, no transports could be spared for Guadalcanal. Japan decided to leave the island. The Japanese evacuation of Guadalcanal was a perfect operation. The Americans discovered the retreat after an unopposed offensive found a few starving, sick, and abandoned Japanese troops.

Midpoint in the Second World War Europe: Key Decisions

July 1942 - June 1944

By mid-1942, important milestones approached the warring parties. In the East, Russia held on at enormous cost, saving Moscow, but the Germans retained the initiative. In the West, France was conquered, but England fought on while Spain stayed out.[281] In the Atlantic, German submarines won some significant victories, but Allied losses remained low enough to sustain the war effort. On the Pacific front, Japan swept all before it until the Coral Sea and Midway where she suffered strategic defeats.

Each warring power now faced a few **critical** decisions:

1) The Allies knew they must *stay on the offensive* and keep the Axis on their heels. In war conferences between the British and Americans prior to December 1941, they agreed Germany must be defeated first. The Allies continually held conferences during the war to decide what course of action was best for all concerned. This kept the Allies on the same page allowing a coordinated response to disorderly events. Good planning was a hallmark of the Allied powers.
2) Japan's Pacific defeats made the decisions for them. Japan's reverses put it on the defensive. She was smarter than Hitler in this respect because Japan at least recognized the changing situation. The empire could attempt to make headway against China, but even this would be difficult. Japan decided to defend its gains with fierce efforts aimed at causing her antagonists unacceptable

---

281 Hitler wanted fascist Spain to join the Axis, but Franco (Spain's leader) wanted no part of another war. Sub-rosa, Spain did aid the Axis, but stayed neutral. Spain joining the Axis would increase the Axis power base substantially.

losses. In retrospect, this was an appropriate decision because Japan was overextended and probably should have made this decision sooner.

3) The best German generals knew they had lost the war. However, Hitler demanded offensives in the East with the aim of destroying the USSR. This was another bad *foundational decision* by the Fuehrer. Germany's best move was to adopt the strategic defensive, retreat to better lines of defense, and use its still ample mobile reserves to demolish Soviet advances.[282] The Germans would hope to bleed the Soviets until they decided to quit, and then attack in the west. However, Hitler demanded new offensive victories. This decision was opposed by the German general staff, and held extraordinary risks.

AXIS (MIS) MANAGEMENT

Both Germany and Japan conquered huge resource-rich areas with large numbers of people that, if used correctly, would add immeasurably to their industrial and military power. If Hitler had convinced people in the conquered areas of Russia and Eastern Europe to work and fight for him millions of additional men would be available to supplement his industrial and armed forces. If the Japanese had worked at creating a true cooperative effort within their conquered territories they too might have enjoyed additional war making potential. Fortunately for the Allies, the Axis utterly squandered these potential assets.

By mismanagement on a scale beyond comprehension Japan and Germany turned conquered peoples against them, failing to obtain a good return on the raw materials and physical assets they captured. The Axis planned for wars of conquest, but they failed to effectively plan for the well-organized use of their conquered resources during the war. They assumed that once these assets were seized they would simply do what they wanted with them (including the people). To their consternation people resisted murderous oppression and raw materials failed to simply up and move themselves to factories in the homeland. The skilled workers who knew how to extract the raw materials often ran away to avoid the oppressors. Those staying were enslaved, so they worked slow and made many "mistakes."

---

[282] Reserves were available on the Eastern Front in early 1942 **IF** no further offensives were undertaken.

A key element in this lack of resource management was failing to convince conquered peoples to join the fight against the Allies (especially the Russians). There were exceptions, but as a rule, people "liberated" by the Japanese and Germans found them harsh taskmasters. As a result, they came to resent their Axis overseers and refused to serve as their soldiers. Compare this result to the communist Chinese who recruited the central government's own people to fight for them in China's civil war. Had the Axis consistently convinced even a small percentage to join their camp a lot could have changed. This failure by the Axis to show proper concern for people falling under their sway was *central to their loss of WWII.* It seems no single decision drove this course of action. This was just collective stupidity on an extraordinary scale.

HITLER ATTACKS IN THE EAST

1942

(. . . or What's in a name?)

In the summer of 1942 Hitler began operations to capture large amounts of land and resources south of Moscow. In this region there were ample supplies of *oil,* grain, and raw materials that could help the Nazi war machine. The attack's direction surprised the Soviets and initially allowed the Germans to make good ground. Note that Stalingrad was NOT originally a major target of the advance.

As the German offensive wore on the front expanded. It was like going up a funnel rather than down; thus, German units became widely separated. Non-German units began to move into the line to fill the voids left by the expansion of the front. German units were superior to Italian, Romanian, and other friendly Axis forces in the quality of their equipment and training. Even in static defense non-German units could not repel a strong Soviet attack. As the Germans moved into **Stalingrad** the Soviets began reinforcing the city. If the Germans had moved swiftly the city would have fallen early, but hesitation resulted in disaster. As at Leningrad, the failure to take Stalingrad in a timely manner had dire unforeseen consequences. At Leningrad the result was a long siege where the Soviets retained the city. At Stalingrad the results were crippling German losses of men and material.

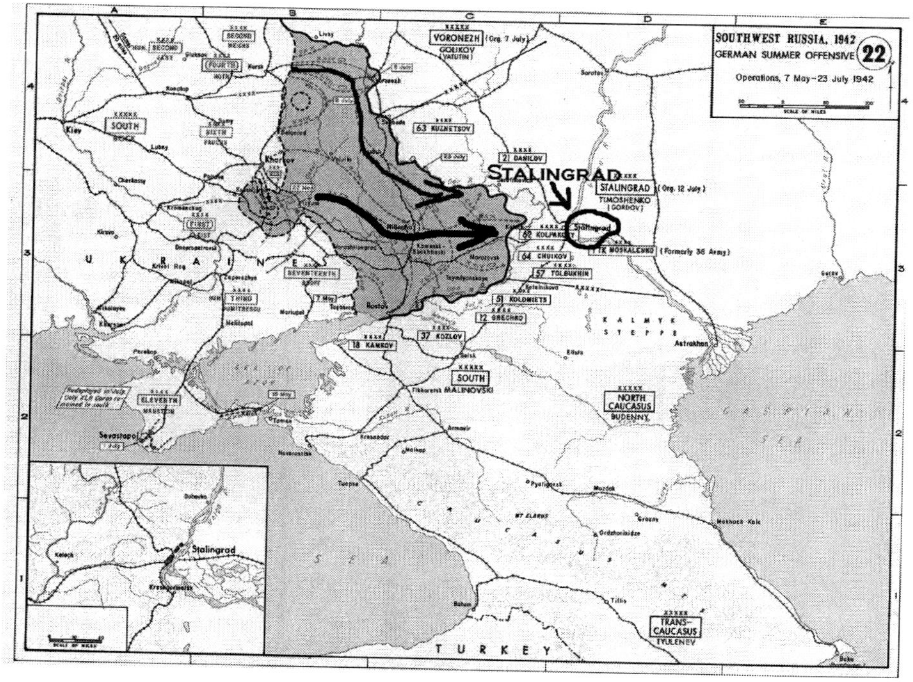

FIGURE 61 GERMAN SUMMER OFFENSIVE 1942

Before the battle at Stalingrad began the German general staff recommended bypassing the city, but Hitler thought he must conquer the city named after his archenemy. In making this irrational decision, Hitler condemned his forces to the type of battle every German general wanted to avoid. The entire point of the German Blitzkrieg was maneuver, that is, avoid the WWI style clash of attrition. Fighting in Stalingrad was committing the German Army to the wrong type of fight. Moreover, Hitler ordered his Sixth Army into a head-on clash against a Soviet army *outnumbering* his troops and fighting on *smashed city terrain ideal for defense.* Worse, the Soviets were receiving ample supplies and reinforcements. Worse yet, on the flanks of Stalingrad non-German units were in place because of a lack of Nazi units, and these flanking forces were not positioned for in-depth defense. The German line was therefore very weak at vital points on the flanks of the city.[283]

After a colossal struggle the Sixth Army reached the Volga (the river running on the eastern side of Stalingrad) leaving only a few Soviet pockets of resistance. At Stalingrad it was said even the rats fled the city, only men

283 General Von Paulus commanded the German Sixth Army fighting at Stalingrad.

remained. *Homo sapiens* alone could inflict or withstand such slaughter. The battle's descriptions are unbelievable. During the horror of the fight inside the city, Soviet General Zhukov was assembling forces outside the city on the German flanks. After months of building up, he was ready to spring his great trap. It was winter, and the freezing conditions impeded movement by the mixed Axis forces; conversely, these same conditions were ideal for the Soviet counterstrike designed to break through positions held by non-German troops and encircle the German Sixth Army in Stalingrad.

It was November of 1942 when massive Soviet attacks surprised and scattered Romanian units guarding Stalingrad's flanks. A shallow Soviet double envelopment surrounded von Paulus' army in the city. General von Manstein, leading a counterattack by the redoubtable Forth Panzer Army, tried to reach the trapped men but fell a few miles short. Von Manstein ordered Von Paulus to attack toward him to complete the breakout. Von Paulus refused saying it was impossible; however, the trapped general previously radioed Hitler requesting permission to break out, *but Hitler refused* (There's a surprise). Hitler's "not one step backward" order condemned the German Sixth Army and the foolishly loyal von Paulus to a sub-zero deathtrap.

After withstanding weeks of Soviet bombardment, little food, dwindling ammunition, and no heat Von Paulus surrendered his army in January of 1943. Over *330,000* German soldiers were killed or captured in the pocket, and probably a year's worth of production from German factories vanished. Total losses for the Wehrmacht in the fight for Stalingrad were approximately *750,000.* This was a grave defeat for the Wehrmacht and Germany, and they never recovered. Remember, the USSR suffered worse defeats in 1941 and not only survived but also regrouped, launching large counterattacks before Moscow. The fact that this defeat could finish Germany shows how thin their prospects of victory were in June of 1941. Stalingrad, with its constant attrition of German forces followed by the death of an entire German Army, wrecked all chances for success. The Soviets were on the offensive and receiving massive amounts of supplies from the USA and the United Kingdom. After Stalingrad, the power-hungry Stalin would strike until he possessed Hitler's head and Germany's homeland.

Hitler fought on, ordering one more offensive (limited—at Kursk), but the war in the East was impossibly lost. As usual, Adolf Hitler continued issuing "stand fast" orders only to witness his men's extinction in the thunder and fire of massive Soviet mechanized assaults. Operation Bagration's annihilation of Army Group Center[284] in June of 1944, blew open the door to Germany by virtually eradicating the Wehrmacht's ability to defend the fatherland. Hitler's unmitigated incompetence lost Germany's best troops in the snow and mud of the USSR. He was next.

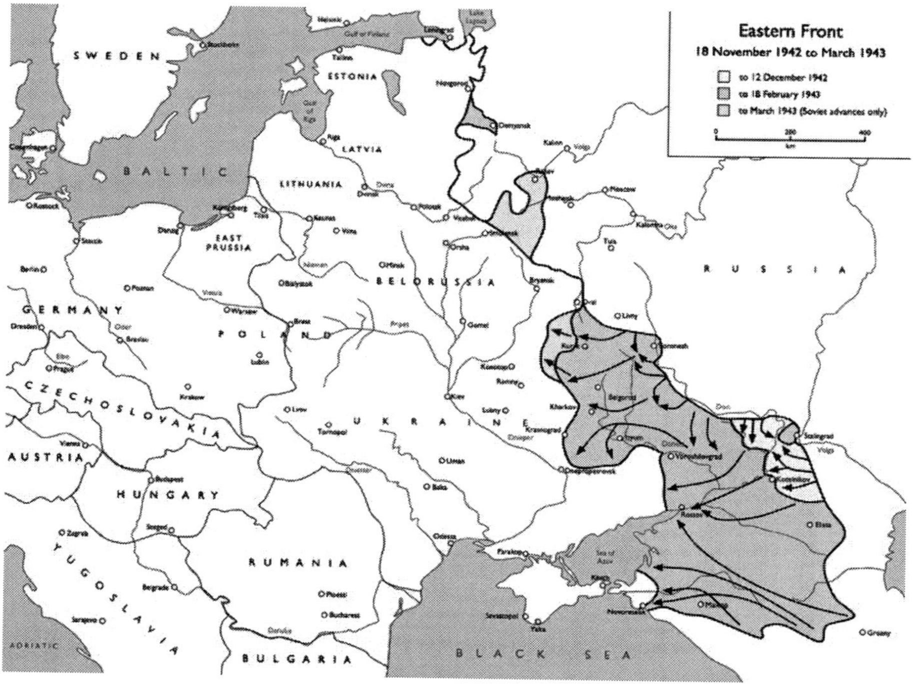

EASTERN FRONT 1942 AND 1943—ADVANCE TO THE BLACK SEA FROM STALINGRAD

WAR IN THE ATLANTIC

January 1942 and beyond

In January 1942, Admiral Donitz sent his U-boats west to attack shipping along the Atlantic seaboard of the wholly unprepared United States. Only a few submarines were available for this task, and the long voyage was a difficult mission for the Germans. The German submariners packed every inch of their undersea boats with food and supplies. To assist the assault,

---

284 After the attack, Germany's Army Group Center ceased to exist. It was wiped from the German order of battle as completely as the Sixth Army had been after Stalingrad. And this was an ***ARMY GROUP*** of twenty-five divisions or more, not just one army.

the Germans thought up special types of submarines called *Mulch Cows* that carried supplies to the central Atlantic and resupplied the submarines on station, thereby allowing them to remain in the critical war zone much longer.[285]

This assault on US shipping in American home waters was a phenomenal success. US merchant ships sailed alone, *no convoys,* and often sailed at night while US cities continued to burn their lights, creating perfect silhouette targets for the Germans. Often, the subs attacked at night on the surface using deck guns rather than the more valuable and limited torpedoes.[286] The British hounded the United States to adopt the convoy system, which Admiral King, commander of the US Navy, refused to do in spite of the fact the US Navy knew from WWI that convoys worked. *Three hundred and ninety-seven (397)* cargo ships hit the ocean bottom between January and June of 1942. This was a naval and logistics disaster. **Admiral Earnest King** was the man ***solely responsible*** for the failure to adopt convoys, a *known remedy* for submarine attacks. As merchant ships sailing along the US Atlantic coast plunged to the ocean floor, King steadfastly maintained that he did not have enough escorts for convoy protection and stated that a weakly protected convoy was worse than no convoy.[287]

---

285 Operation Drumbeat.

286 German Type VII submarines carried twelve torpedoes

287 In fact, there were barely any escorts for convoy duty. The United States failed to construct or even design ships suitable for convoy duty or fighting submarines. Convoy escorts are normally smaller ships with a large carrying capacity so they can haul a lot of fuel and depth charges and stay on station for long periods of time. The larger and faster destroyers are not well suited for that kind of duty, but they

King's argument was pure rubbish. The English and the US had the experience and proof that *convoys alone (without escorts) cut shipping losses tremendously.* Every naval officer in WWI, in both the Royal and the US Navy, knew these facts. This is so because the submarine has problems locating ships. Locating one ship is about as hard as locating an entire convoy, because the convoy does not take up much more sea space. By sending ships out singly, it gives the submarine many targets. By sending out convoys the submarine has fewer targets because they are all concentrated in one relatively small area. After adopting convoys enemy submarines look at a lot of empty sea. Admiral King had to know this, but *why did he block effective action while this Atlantic slaughter was going on?* There is no answer to this question. There is no excuse for failing and refusing to adopt convoys immediately to prevent the loss of so many vital cargo ships and their crews. This situation grew so critical that General Marshall, the general in charge of the entire war effort, asked President Roosevelt to order Admiral King to start using convoys. Apparently, it never came to that because a strongly worded letter from Marshall to King turned the tide. King adopted convoys. Nonetheless, King's actions cost the Allies dearly in lives and material.

All this causes one to wonder, how many men does a leader get to needlessly slaughter before being relieved of command? Admiral King slaughtered many, Generals MacArthur and Clark many more, and the Generals of World War I on the Allied side hundreds of thousands more. Somehow, these "leaders" literally get away with murder. It is easy to understand how ruthless dictators such as Hitler and Stalin can throw away lives, but how can military leaders of democracies get away with such dim-witted brutality?

As 1943 began the Battle of the Atlantic came to a head. Admiral **Max Horton** determined he could protect the convoys from German wolf packs, and he was ready to prove it.[288] The turning point came in April and May of 1943 with convoy ONS-5 that was made up of forty-three merchant ships. ONS-5 was attacked by thirty U-boats in a coordinated wolf pack assault. After the battle's end thirteen merchant ships were gone, but six U-boats were lost. Such losses were unacceptable to Donitz, but it would get even worse for the U-boats. In May of 1943 these Allied efforts paid off with the sinking of thirty German submarines in one month with the

---

could have been used for convoy protection given the state of the emergency in 1942.

288 Horton was one of the most important and least known men of WWII. He was the key man in the defeat of the German U-boat menace. He was in charge of the Western Approaches to England.

corresponding loss of only a few Allied cargo ships. Admiral Donitz would continue to send his submarines out to fight, but these would increasingly become suicide missions. The German submarine branch suffered a higher percentage loss rate than any branch of any other service of any warring nation (over 70 percent).

Some argue the German submarines failed as a strategic threat because the vast majority of supplies and troops crossed the Atlantic without a problem (about 98 percent), and the Germans never came close to sinking even the tonnage they calculated in 1939 as necessary to win the war at sea. However, this overlooks one important point: the *Allies themselves at the Casablanca Conference designated the defeat of the German submarines as the number 1 priority.* Thus, the submarines were a strategic threat because the leaders of the Allied nations thought so. The U-boat defeat in 1943 is traceable to the Allied decision assigning the Atlantic victory top priority, followed by the dedication of vast resources to achieve the goal. Germany's top priorities vacillated with Hitler's whim, and he failed to assign a high priority to the submarine fleet and its Atlantic struggle. Because the Allies decided to defeat the submarines first and the Germans adopted dissimilar priorities, there were far different end results. These decisions, one to give the fight top priority and the other to give the fight a much lower priority, shows what a difference alternate decisions can make. Germany's submarines failed in 1943 because of the different priorities set by the two warring sides.

The Allied commanders foresaw the potential for the submarines to restrict the flow of supplies to England. They realized the submarine threat could prevent the assets of the United States from reaching Europe in quantity. *The projection of US power across the Atlantic was the most important* ***logistic*** *factor for winning the war in Western Europe.* Knowing the submarines could impair this essential effort, their defeat won top priority.[289]

NORTH AFRICA

Allied Victory—1943

As Rommel retreated toward Tunisia after El Alamein, American and English landed on the west coast of Africa in Morocco, and began moving east, along with French forces that joined the Allies. The German and Italian formations were soon crushed, and in **May of 1943** the Axis force

---

289 This shows how essential supply is to war. **Logistics are THE first priority.**

in Africa capitulated. The conquest of North Africa was an epic victory. The scale of the conquest was beyond all expectations. Along with the capture of approximately *275,000* Axis soldiers, one-half of which were German, (equal to10 divisions or more, which is on a par with the debacle at Stalingrad in January 1943) the Western Allies had captured the initiative in the Mediterranean. Once the Axis lost the strategic initiative in the West their lack of manpower began to damage their ability to resist the next Allied moves. Everything was turning in favor of the Allies.[290]

Sicily and Italy

The Western Allies decided Sicily, a large island near the boot of Italy, was their next Mediterranean objective. It was an unpopular decision in the American military. The British, at the Casablanca Conference, convinced President Roosevelt that action was required in the Mediterranean; however, American military commanders wanted to invade the continent (France) at once. The English successfully argued that American strategy was much too ambitious; moreover, while the Allies built up their forces they could move against what Churchill called the "soft underbelly of Europe." Good sounding phrase, but a total misconception. Anyone looking at a map could easily tell the soft underbelly was really a tough old gut. Finding good ground for defense is not always easy, but here in Southern Europe the ground was tailor made for defensive fighting. Why Churchill failed

---

[290] Well . . . not everything. In the category of armor missteps occurred. *Fast Tanks and Heavy Bombers: Innovation in the US Army, 1917-1945 (Cornell Studies in Security Affairs)* by David E. Johnson (Paperback—Mar 2003). The Germans had better tanks, and both the British and American troops knew this by 1943. Somehow, the Allied generals did not get the message until late 1944. Better Allied steel, slopping the armor, better ammunition, and a high-velocity 75mm gun could have made a substantial difference for the main Allied battle tank, the M-4 Sherman. The Sherman was inferior to the German tanks but was not upgraded until sometime in late 1944 (Battle of the Bulge saw some improved Shermans). Some of this was due to Allied battle doctrine wherein the *Tank Destroyer* was to fight other tanks; however, anyone should have seen, as the Allied troops did, that the Sherman was totally outclassed at D-Day and needed immediate improvement or replacement. The tank crews were simply riding in their coffins as they faced German Tiger and Panther tanks. On the plus side, the Sherman was fast and reliable, and once up gunned it did a little better against the German tanks. The German Panther was an excellent tank, but it too had problems stemming mostly from design flaws that were caused by Nazi infighting during the production process.

to recognize this is often debated, and it is another reason the Americans thought he was more interested in protecting the British Empire than winning the war quickly.

FIGURE 62 INVASION OF ITALY 1943

The American military voiced at least two objections to invading Sicily: First, Sicily and Italy's terrain were ideal for defense. There were rugged mountains throughout, the river valleys were steep, the rivers were fast flowing, and they cut across the line of advance. Second, such an undertaking was secondary to the goal of destroying the German Army. Americans believed, as US Grant demonstrated against Lee in the American Civil War, the key to victory was the destruction of the enemy army (Clausewitz would have agreed). Britain wanted to whittle down the Nazi army before an all or nothing confrontation.

US military experts distrusted Churchill, whom they thought might be more interested in protecting the English empire than in defeating Germany. Churchill, for his part, was already worrying about the postwar world and the escalating power of the USSR. He was trying to convince the Americans that a move through the Balkans (the area north of Greece) might cut off the Soviet advance in that area preserving more free territory in Europe.

The Americans refused to wait around worrying about postwar Europe. They wanted to engage the Nazis, defeat them as soon as possible, and then go home. In the event, the Americans folded at Casablanca because Roosevelt insisted the United States immediately get into the ground action and stay in it. Waiting around to build up forces in England for six months to a year, while doing little else, was political suicide. Thus, the United States and England invaded Sicily after the conquest of North Africa and then moved on to Italy. Originally, the invasion agreement only included Sicily with the decision on Italy coming later. However, the conquest of Sicily went faster than expected making the invasion of Italy automatic.

The invasion of Sicily went well considering how new everyone was at massive amphibious operations. The true problem with the capture of Sicily was the *escape of the Axis divisions* across the strait to Italy with their supplies and equipment. With the Allies having local air control and total control of the sea allowing the Axis escape was a paramount blunder. To this day it is unclear how the Allies allowed this to happen. It was crucial to trap and destroy the Axis armies on Sicily. *Apparently, the capture of the German and Italian armies on Sicily was not foreseen or planned.* The Germans who escaped from Sicily played key roles in holding up the Allied advance up the Italian boot.[291]

With Sicily seized, the Allies quickly invaded Italy at the bottom of the boot and at the beaches of **Salerno** just south of Naples on the west coast. (See Figure 62) Montgomery proceeded to land at the toe of Italy's boot and at the east near the top of the heel, while the Americans went ashore at Salerno. At Salerno, Kesselring's troops put up a stiff defense from the heights overlooking the beaches. Following up with effective counterattacks, Kesselring nearly drove the Americans into the sea. Luftwaffe attacks on the fleet damaged several ships while German tanks drove within shouting range of the beach; nevertheless, naval gunfire broke the Nazi offensives, and Allied air power soon captured the sky over the beaches. After securing the beaches, the Americans struggled to expand the pocket and requested Montgomery hurry his advance;

---

[291] In later years, Montgomery said the invasion of Italy was planned in the men's room at Allied HQ. The results certainly make it look like the plan was drawn up in the men's room.

however, Montgomery did no such thing. When Montgomery did arrive the Germans were already pulling back to new and very well prepared lines of defense south of Rome—**the Gustov line**.

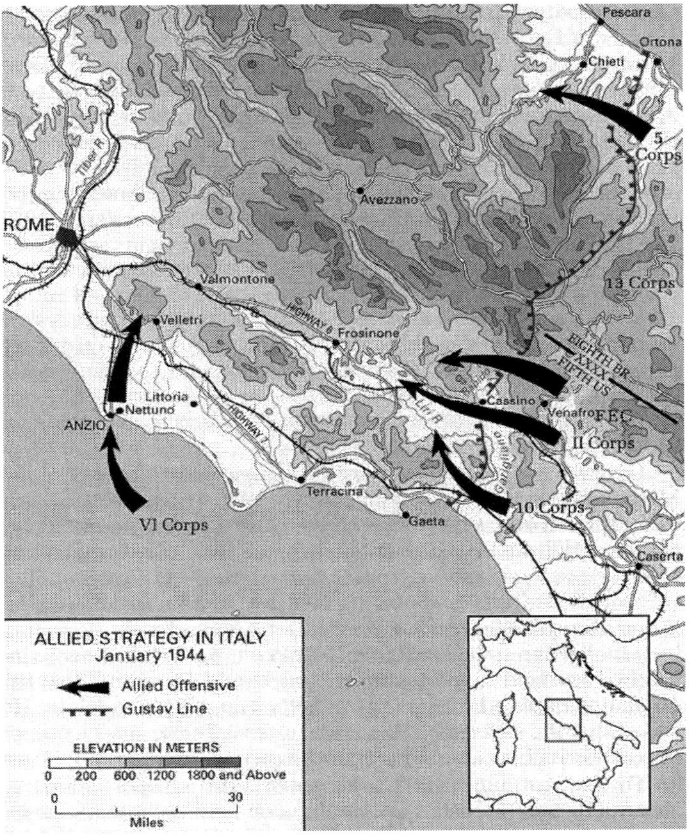

FIGURE 63 ITALY—ALLIED ASSAULTS ON GUSTOV LINE AND ANZIO 1943-4

Advancing past Salerno, the Allies ran into exceptionally well-chosen and prepared German positions on the Gustov line south of Rome. Kesselring and his German engineers chose this mountainous area because of its ideal defensive terrain features. After numerous bloody attempts to breach the line had failed, the Allies mounted an amphibious assault behind the Gustov line at **Anzio** on the western side of Italy just north of the Gustov Line and south of Rome. (See Figure 63) Unfortunately, the invasion's commander was under specific orders from General Clark to attain the beach and then *dig in.* Following these orders doomed the Allied invasion to bloody stagnation. If the troops had moved inland at once, behind the Gustov line, a forced German retreat was axiomatic. This is one of the best ways to wage war, force your enemy out of superb positions without an assault as Sherman consistently accomplished on his march to Atlanta (see the US Civil War). Kesselring responded to Allied sluggishness by swiftly placing his men on the invaluable high ground above the beaches; thus, preventing a breakout and subjecting the trapped troops to monumental artillery poundings. It became clear that to get off those beaches help was necessary from the Allied troops along the Gustov line. The tables were turned, and the men originally assigned to get the help now had to give help if the Allies were going to hang on at Anzio.

The breakthrough came when the overall commander in Italy, British **General Alexander**, rejected General Mark Clark's ideas, adopted his own direction, and mounted an offensive all along the Gustov line. The French colonial forces found that the Germans had severely thinned out of the center of their line to reinforce the troops fighting at Monty Casino itself. The Nazi line was quickly breached and the advance northward began. Then Mark Clark threw another monkey wrench into the gears. Alexander ordered Clark to take his forces, which were on the left flank of the advance, and turn right (east) to cut off the German retreat. Clark *disobeyed these orders* and instead made north for Rome and the glory of "liberating" the city. Rome fell on June 4, 1944, but the battle for Italy continued. The German forces escaped AGAIN to delay the Allied advance for additional months.

The problems in Italy were multiple, but poor leadership for the Allies is at the top of the list. Only after Alexander began to exercise more control over his subordinates did matters improve somewhat. General Clark disobeyed orders and moved on Rome rather than blocking the German retreat to a new defensive zone, but nothing was done to Clark. The fact that his actions would cost the lives of Allied troops assaulting yet another of Kesselring's defensive lines to the north of Rome seems to have counted for little. All these years later it seems the original US thoughts were correct. The Italian campaign would continue until the end of the war with little to show for all the sacrifices of the troops involved on both sides.

PLANNING D-DAY

With the Allies advancing up the Italian boot the Western Mediterranean was firmly in Allied hands, and planning for the invasion of Nazi occupied France could begin in earnest. **General Eisenhower** was appointed as overall commander, and Ike appointed British General Montgomery as ground unit commander. This was a massive undertaking and the largest amphibious assault ever mounted.[292]

The planning for Operation **Overlord**, as it would be termed, started long before the appointment of General Eisenhower. The pre-Eisenhower planners chose **Normandy** as the best area for invasion. They decided on May for the invasion because of the moon, tides, weather, and other considerations, and they called for three divisions to cross the channel supported by a large naval armada. Although the plan would undergo considerable change, the foundations were poured. The moment Eisenhower and Montgomery examined the plan they expanded the landing force to *five divisions* landing from the sea and *three more airborne divisions* airdropped behind the beaches on the first day. This expansion to well over one hundred thousand men increased the need for shipping, equipment, aircraft, and everything else by more than double. While it increased the chances for success it also increased the risk, because information leaks, increases in errors, and a host of other "friction of war" problems would naturally proliferate. The need for secrecy increased exponentially. If the Germans figured out the time and place of the landings the resulting slaughter would be indescribable. The raid on **Dieppe** was well remembered, and if the Germans could repeat that Allied disaster the consequences would be immense.[293] Allied failure at Normandy would mean, under reasonable presumptions, the Soviets would seek a separate peace with Hitler, which they had already tried. (Yes, we know about the A-bomb, but that discussion is too long and speculative for The Super Summary).

MIDPOINT IN THE SECOND WORLD WAR—PACIFIC:

1943 & 1944

After the victory at Guadalcanal in 1943, US forces began to move up the Solomon island chain. In a series of bloody encounters the US Navy, Marines, and Army pushed north against fanatic Japanese resistance. On

---

[292] The landings in Sicily were about as large in terms of men committed to the initial assault; but at D-Day, the follow-on forces were much larger and the stakes far higher.

[293] Large British raid of 18 to 19 August, 1942 on the German-held French coast at the town of Dieppe involving some five thousand Canadian troops. The raid was a colossal failure resulting in the loss of two-thirds of the invasion force.

New Guinea, Australian forces pushed the Japanese back over the rugged Owen Stanley mountains in one of the most difficult campaigns of the war. American and Australian forces then began leapfrogging up the eastern coast, landing where the Japanese were not present, thus cutting off the Japanese garrisons they bypassed.[294]

At sea, Japan started feeling the full weight of American air power and innovation. In the **Battle of the Bismarck Sea** in **March 1943**, a Japanese troop convoy sailing to New Guinea from Rabaul harbor on New Britain was located at sea and totally destroyed by air attacks. B-25 aircraft (same type that bombed Tokyo) with six .50-caliber machine guns mounted to the nose for strafing ships, tackled the convoy. The pilots also used new skip-bombing methods to slam the bombs into the sides of the transports. The attackers sank all the transport ships and most of the escorts. The US Army Air Force under General McKinney developed these new techniques.**295**

"Island hopping" was the key to US strategy in the Pacific. The idea was simple. The Allies did not have to conquer every island held by the Japanese. By taking only a few vital islands, and cutting off support for the rest, the Americans smashed the original Japanese assumptions about fighting the war. With each passing month the speed of the American advance increased. Japan faced an enemy with techniques of war undreamed of in 1941. Knocked off balance by Allied methods and technology Japan's leadership never regained its footing.

By November of 1943 the US Navy was prepared to start an advance across the **Central Pacific**. This line of attack was *in addition* to MacArthur's line of advance in the South Pacific. The first target was the Gilbert Islands, and the key to this group of island atolls was **Tarawa** (Betio). The island's importance came from its air base. The Japanese anticipated an attack and studded the island with defensive fortifications, including a tremendous number of protected machine gun emplacements (pillboxes), large caliber cannons, huge bunkers, and barbed-wire entanglements defending every approach to the island.

---

[294] In one location, the Americans found a buried chest full of Japanese code books enabling US code breakers to read Japanese transmissions more extensively, thus giving US commanders better intelligence on Japan's actions.

[295] General McKinney is largely unknown because he served under MacArthur, who was a fanatic about keeping his name ALONE in the news. It was "MacArthur's air force sinks convoy." McKinney was never mentioned. Most military men didn't care. They were fighting to win the war, not gain accolades from the press

Throughout the Pacific campaign, the islands seized had enemy air bases or land areas where the Americans could build air bases. Tactically, the Pacific War was fought over who held what air base. *The airplane was the centerpiece of the Pacific War.* The goal of the Central Pacific advance was winning islands within air range of Japan, and starting a bombing campaign to destroy Japan's infrastructure. The goal of the South Pacific advance was winning back the Philippines, and cutting Japanese supply lines to the home islands.

We must talk about storming a defended beach for a moment. Before World War II, invaders avoided going ashore at a defended beach. From the Trojan War through the first part of World War II, the way one combatant invaded another's territory from the sea entailed going ashore on an undefended beach away from the target and then advancing on the objective overland. In World War I, the British invasion of Turkey at Gallipoli proved the point that an amphibious operation against defended shores was suicide. The Japanese commanders knew the history of offensive actions against defended beaches, and they knew the assaults were usually failures. They noted that *many small islands in the Central Pacific had no place for an unopposed landing.* In addition, airstrips could be placed on the islands with ample aircraft to defend them. The Japanese believed an island was an unsinkable aircraft carrier endangering any fleet sailing within range of its aircraft. At first the US thought the same thing.

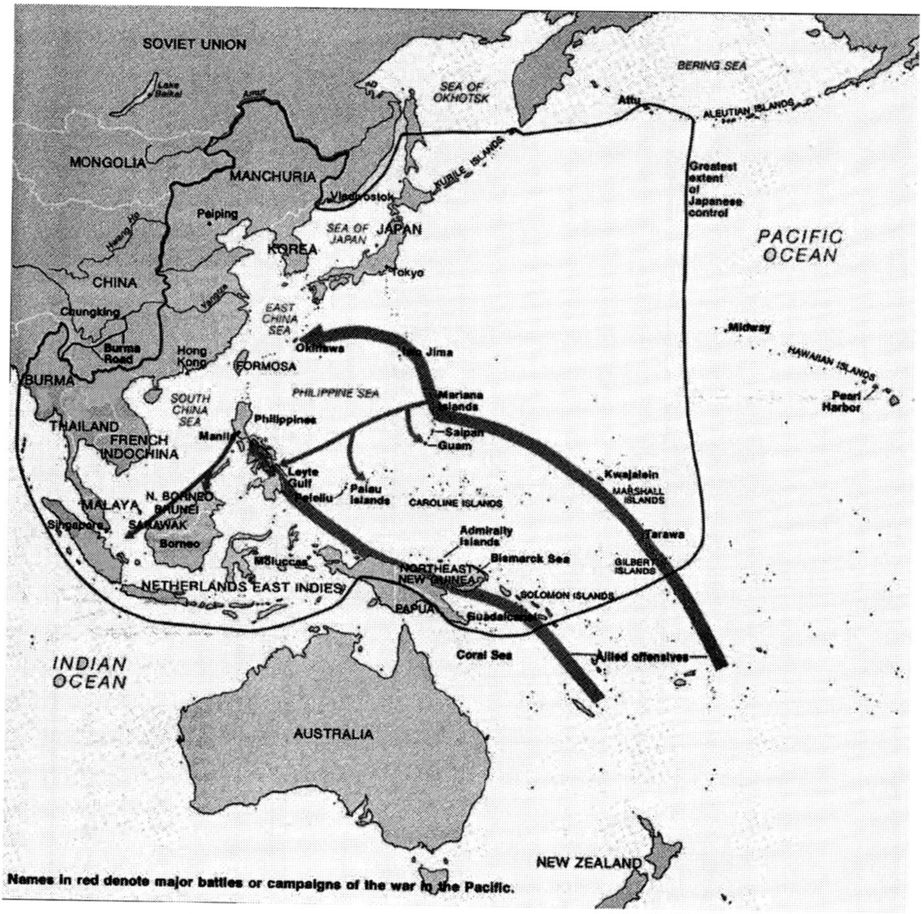

FIGURE 64 AMERICAN DUAL OFFENSIVES AGAINST JAPAN

By 1943 US Navy carrier forces had combined their air units for overwhelming aerial assaults razing Japanese air power on the island fortresses. Then the fleet sailed up and disgorged the troops who took the island. These actions punctured Japanese assumptions about defending their empire. The fact that the Americans quickly took heavily defended Pacific islands shocked Japan's high command. Japan confronted an enemy doing the impossible, and doing it very well. The Japanese commander at Tarawa had stated that, "A million men could not take this island in a thousand years" (or something close to that), but the US Marine Second Division took it in *three days.* To be fair, the Japanese commander never heard of Amtracs (boats with tank treads). If he had known his confidence might have ebbed.

TARAWA

We will use Tarawa as an example of Pacific island assaults. For adequate reconnaissance of the Marshall Islands, the next target, Tarawa's airfield was necessary. Weeks before the US Marines landed on Tarawa long-range B-24 Liberator bombers cratered the island and its runways. This bombing effectively ended air threats to the US Navy.

The Japanese possessed a critical terrain advantage—*a coral reef* surrounded the island about eight hundred yards from the beach that could stop the Higgins[296] boats. To overcome this defensive advantage the marines decided to employ tracked landing vehicles (LVT-1: Landing Vehicle Tracked), which could climb over the reef and continue to the shore. The marines discovered one hundred new LVT-2s in San Diego that were larger, faster, and carried a heaver payload than the LVT-1s. An all-out effort was undertaken to get these boats to Tarawa before the landing. They made it in the early morning hours on the day of the invasion. One hundred twenty-five LVTs assaulted Tarawa of which ninety were lost (72% casualty rate), but without them the invasion would have failed.

The Japanese planned a fleet counterattack (*Hei* Operation 3) once they determined the US Navy's next objective, but the Japanese high command was guessing where the blow would fall. They failed to envision the United States mounting two simultaneous offensives, one already underway in the South Pacific, and another through the Central Pacific. To prepare for the expected offensive, Admiral Koga, Japan's chief of naval operations since Yamamoto's death, concluded the Central Pacific activity was a feint, and moved 173 carrier aircraft and several cruisers to Rabaul in the South Pacific. On November 5 and 11, US Carriers launched two large raids on Rabaul, shooting down about *100 Japanese aircraft* and damaging several cruisers. The loss of so many carrier pilots ended all counterattack plans. At the time, no American knew the impact of these raids, but they were critical to the success of the Gilbert's (Tarawa) operation.

[296] The Higgins boat was a landing craft with a flat bottom, a shallow draft, and a bow ramp that dropped to let the troops rush ashore, but it needed **four feet** of water to float and the reef was **three feet** below the surface on invasion day.

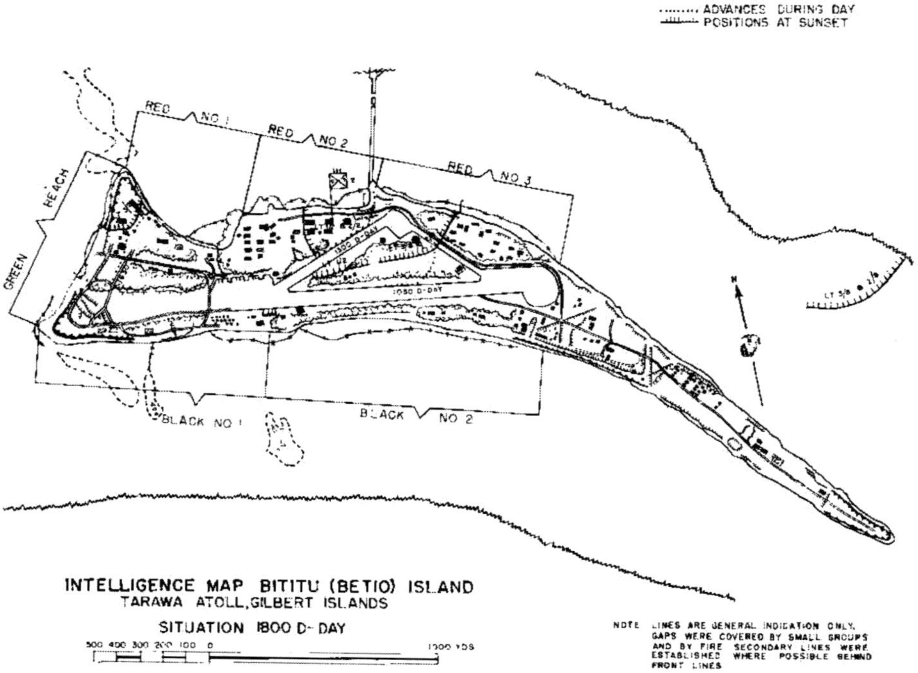

FIGURE 65 BETIO (TARAWA) MAP

A surfeit of errors plagued the Tarawa assault. Some of the important failings were: the naval command ships were too far away and unable to receive needed information or see the action; the fleet's big guns were fired at a low angle and failed to demolish enemy pill boxes or bunkers which required plunging fire to destroy; marine radios were not waterproof causing nearly all to fail; and there was *insufficient firepower at the squad level* (flamethrowers and machine guns). A lot more went wrong, but this list is a sample of the problems.

The first two waves in Amtracs got ashore with acceptable losses; however, the low tide stopped the Higgins boats at the reef. The marines who were stuck at the reef had to either wait there under scalding enemy fire for an Amtrac to take them in, or attempt to wade ashore in chest deep water while receiving fearsome enemy fire. The Japanese 75mm dual-gun anti-boat cannons, along with the heavy 13mm machine guns, fired accurately and with devastating effects on the LVTs and the Higgins boats. Marine unit cohesion disappeared as men struggled ashore separated from their squads or companies without officers, radios, heavy weapons, or the ability to communicate with other units. Small packets of men under continuous fire huddled against a log seawall that was sticking up along the landing beaches a few feet from the ocean. LVTs burned all along the beach, splintered Higgins boats wallowed at the reef, and Japanese gunners scythed men down trying to wade ashore from the reef.

All the planning had gone wrong. The Japanese survived the naval and air bombardment; their guns were intact and firing accurately; hundreds of Japanese machine guns and cannons hammered at the marines; and the command structure ashore was disorganized. The commanders offshore lacked information. There was little or no communication even among the men who had reached the island, so assaults were uncoordinated. The Japanese suffered as well since the naval bombardment cut their communications, destroyed several key emplacements, and stunned the defenders; nevertheless, they successfully rallied and were directing enormous volumes of heavy and accurate fire onto the landing forces. The US Marines were in big trouble. The plans were useless now. In war, plans often fall apart leaving the troops alone to gain victory by their sacrifice. The marines on Tarawa, as individuals, determined to press forward into hell itself in search of triumph.

Slowly, with gallantry and fearlessness beyond comprehension, the US Marines inched forward. Marines by the hundreds died trying to reach that beach, but the United States Marine Corps kept coming. Once at the seawall, surviving men found enemy fire raining down, death everywhere, blinding smoke, confusion, and a lack of control. A couple of privates were all that remained of platoons. Corporals were in charge of the remains of companies. None of this mattered; the US Marines continued exchanging blows with the enemy. Tiny groups of men facing a torrent of enemy fire were scaling the sea wall and fighting inland. At Green Beach, the single remaining Sherman tank, name Colorado in marine scrawl, moved forward clearing a path for men to move inland. As the day wore on a recipe for catastrophe was cooking up. Disjointed units pinned on the beach without sufficient cover, stripped of heavy weapons, without communications between themselves or their ships, and lacking supporting fire, were facing their doom if the enemy counterattacked.

Then, a miracle. Before the first day was over, a group of Japanese standing atop a bunker was vaporized by naval gunfire. That group included the commander of the island, Rear Admiral Shibasaki and his staff. The Japanese were now without their top officers. This event was critical to the outcome of the battle.

As night descended the disorganized marines prepared for a counterattack aimed at driving them into the nauseating blood stained sea only a boot's length away in places. Over one thousand Japanese and several tanks were available for the counterattack. A determined Japanese effort that first night, supported by tanks, could have destroyed the marines. The attack never came. Killing the Japanese commanders prevented the order from being given and probably saved the invasion. Over the next two days the marines completed the bloody capture of the island, enduring a well-planned counterattack during the night of the second day. When it was over, *997 marines and 30 navy corpsmen died taking the island, and 4,183 Japanese died in its defense.* On this tiny rock in the vast Pacific, over five thousand men died battling for an airstrip.

This was a foretaste of the storm battles to come as the United States crossed the Central Pacific. Studies by the US Navy concerning errors at Tarawa changed future operations, lowering casualties in upcoming battles; yet, the cost was persistently high as each island invasion relentlessly devoured lives. Stunned by the swiftness of the American victory at Tarawa, the Japanese high command failed to effectively respond. By island hopping and a coordinated dual advance across the Pacific the United States kept the Japanese high command wondering where to commit their resources; and the Imperial Navy often guessed wrong. The Japanese expanded their defense zone too far, and being overstretched damaged their ability to respond to US initiatives.

After the seizure of the Gilbert Islands the United States used the bases to reconnoiter the islands in the Marshalls. **Kwajalein** was the next target of the Central Pacific campaign. Prior to the fleet move to the **Marshalls,** US Army, Air Force, and Navy carrier aircraft swept the islands free of Japanese air power, destroying 92 of 110 Japanese aircraft in the area. Using new firing methods, including plunging fire from battleships, the US Navy bombardment devastated Kwajalein. After Kwajalein, the Japanese abandoned the doctrine of a shoreline defense and opted for in-depth defenses in future battles.

FIGURE 66 MARINES AT TARAWA

MARIANAS AND NEW GUINEA

In May of 1944 the United States attacked the **Marianas** which included the islands of **Saipan, Guam, and Tinian**. These were large islands with tough in-depth defenses, but the speed of the US advance precluded the proper and complete preparation Japan desired. At Saipan, fighting through difficult landings and rugged terrain, the US Army and Marine Corps pushed Saipan's desperate defenders back. The Saipan struggle ended with a Bonsai attack by 3,000 Japanese troops that initially overwhelmed American lines and resulted in 650 US Marine dead. The fatal charge ended Japanese resistance on the island by July 9, 1944. On Guam, the Japanese chose to assault US lines repeatedly, thereby destroying their units. Japanese Imperial forces finally retreated into the jungle interior to continue their resistance. After intense jungle fighting, Guam was secured by August 8, 1944.

As US amphibious forces fought for the Central Pacific, Australian and US Army troops were conquering **New Guinea**. Using code decrypts, MacArthur avoided Japanese strong points and landed in areas where US forces could set up a defense and cut off the isolated Japanese units. The campaign in New Guinea went on from 1942 through 1945, much of it fought by Australian troops under the worst possible conditions. The fighting was intense, bloody, and merciless. Japanese forces fought determined battles even when outnumbered and in poor tactical positions. General MacArthur never gave the tough Australians their due, mainly because he would not get all the credit for their accomplishments. Nonetheless, they were vital to Allied victory in the Pacific.

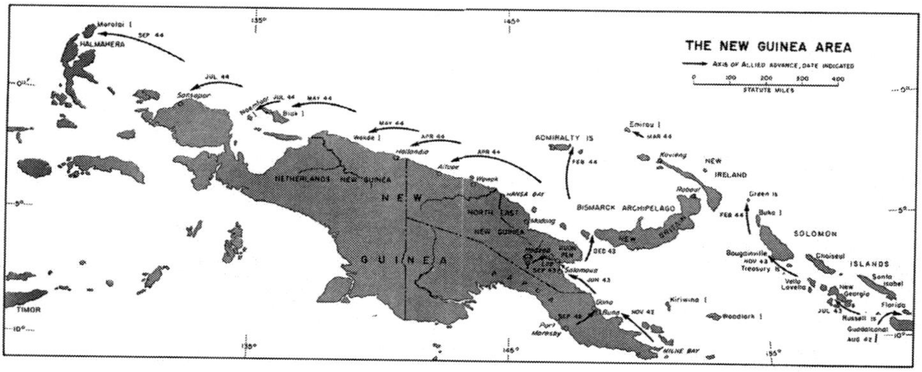

FIGURE 67 NEW GUINEA & RABAUL OFFENSIVES

Storming the well-defended Central Pacific islands was costly for the marines and the army, but the advance was swift. The navy-marine-army team moved from Tarawa to Saipan in the Marianas in about *eight months* against stiff enemy opposition. In just a few months, between November of 1943 and July of 1944, Japan lost vast amounts of its empire, and the Philippines were now ripe for invasion. The losses of Guam, Tinian, and Saipan in the Marianas were demoralizing blows to the Japanese empire. Admiral Nagumo[297] was in charge of Saipan's defense. After the US Marines gained the shore he radioed Tokyo, saying, "*Hell is upon us,*" and he did not mean his troops on Saipan. Nagumo knew that **B-29** aircraft would start bombing the home islands as soon as airfields were constructed in the Marianas. And the American Seabees worked fast.

---

297 The admiral led at Pearl Harbor and Midway, but had been demoted after Midway. He died on Saipan.

Japan knew the Marianas must be held or disaster would ensue. Their fall would cut off oil, rubber, and other war supplies to the homeland from the conquered Southern Pacific areas. Capturing those resource rich regions was the reason Japan started the war. Japan's Imperial Navy planned an all out air attack on the US fleet to protect the islands. On June 19 and 20, 1944, Japanese Combined Fleet attacked the US fleet, fighting the **Battle of the Philippine Sea**. During the engagement the *US Navy lost 123 aircraft* (80 percent of the crews were recovered), and the Japanese lost approximately *600 aircraft and 3 fleet carriers.* Japan's losses were heavy due to a poor plan and green pilots. After the battle, only thirty-five Japanese aircraft were fit for action. The losses Japan suffered at the Battle of the Philippine Sea were irreplaceable. It was over for the Japanese Imperial Navy. At **Leyte Gulf** the Japanese navy would sortie out once more, but the carriers were bait, and the surface ships were on a suicide mission.

THE PHILIPPINES—The Return of the USA

On 15 September 1944, just prior to the invasion of Leyte in the Philippines, the marines and army landed on the islands of **Peleliu** and Angour respectively. The battle for Peleliu and Angour lasted two months and cost an inordinate number of American lives. This landing was a Philippine invasion covering operation to secure the Allied flank from attack. Admiral Halsey thought the Japanese were too weak for offensive action from this quarter and recommended cancellation; unfortunately, the Joint Chiefs allowed the operation to continue. On Peleliu, the Japanese implemented a *new plan for defense* they would adhere to for the remainder of the war. The Japanese defenders settled into well prepared deep-cave positions and awaited the attackers. No suicide attacks, counterattacks, or aggressive maneuvers to hurl the enemy into the sea. Winning entailed killing the maximum number of Americans and nothing else. The best way to accomplish this goal was to avoid exposure to massive American firepower by digging in and forcing the enemy to assault well prepared positions. Fighting on Peleliu decimated the First Marine Division. The battles before Peleliu were bad, but every battle after Peleliu became horrific. Japan's new tactic significantly drove up the cost of war.

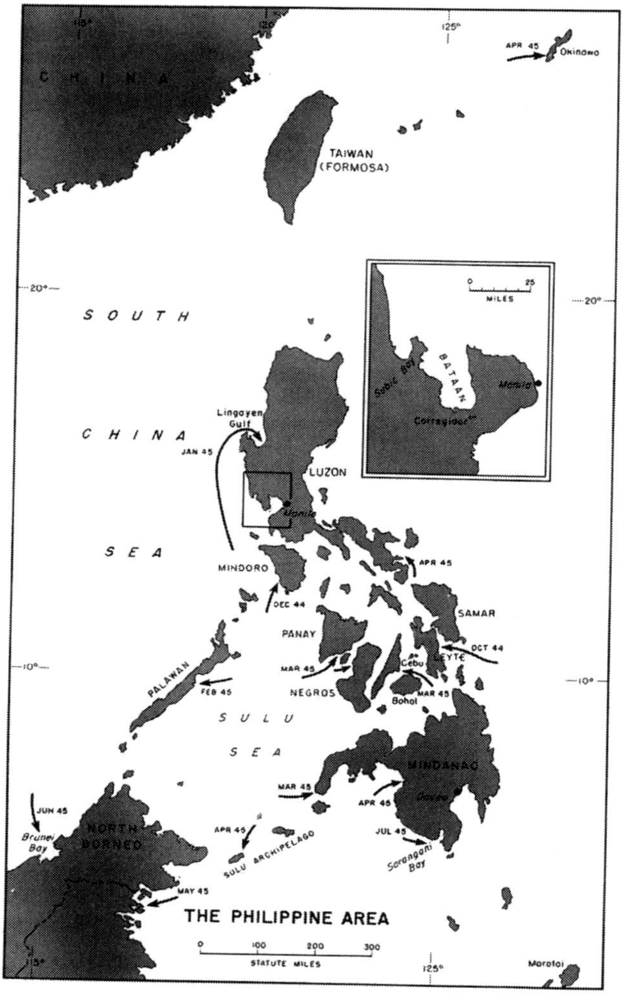

FIGURE 68 US ASSAULT ON THE PHILIPPINES 1944

American forces under General Douglas MacArthur began operations to retake the Philippines by landing at Leyte Island at the midpoint of the island group on **October 20, 1944.** This landing precipitated the **Battle of Leyte Gulf** (see below). Japan was well aware that holding the Philippines was essential, and months of hard fighting were required to secure the central Philippines. In January of 1945, the US Army landed on the main island of **Luzon** and advanced to the capital, Manila, which was recaptured in March after a cruel struggle. Fighting in the mountains of Luzon north of Manila went on until the end of the war, but the harbor and capital were in US hands again after protracted difficulties with Manila's defenders.

HAMMERING TOWARD VICTORY—THE PACIFIC

The Pacific: 1944 to 1945

By the end of 1944 in the Pacific, America was winning in the Philippines and threatening to cut the supply line of oil and other war making materials back to Japan. The capture of Saipan put the home islands within reach of America's mighty B-29 bombers. Japan had lost the war;[298] however, the Japanese Military held a different view. The military believed Japan might be saved from invasion; therefore, they would continue fighting. The Americans and British had demanded unconditional surrender for all Axis forces since the Casablanca Conference. To the Japanese this meant America would *depose their emperor*, which was wholly unacceptable. They would die to the last man, woman, and child to preserve the emperor, their god on earth. The unconditional surrender pledge by Roosevelt at Casablanca, made to reassure the Soviets that the West would not make a separate peace with Hitler, backfired when considered against the backdrop of Japanese history and culture. Nothing would make Japan fight on more assuredly than a threat to remove their emperor.

Because of the importance of the Philippines, and the Allied threat to Japan's supply lines if captured, the Japanese fleet made one more attempt to strike at American naval supremacy. On October 23 to 26, the Japanese launched the last of their sea power toward the American landings at **Leyte Gulf.**

The Japanese plan was complex, but it wisely took into account the aggressiveness of the US Navy.

BATTLE OF LEYTE GULF—THE PHILIPPINES

The key element of the Japanese plan was for its carriers, devoid of aircraft, to sail in from north of the Philippines as bait for the US Carrier fleet. (The Japanese Northern Force) The hope was that the US Navy, and its powerful carrier task force, would sail north to battle the carriers. Then two powerful surface forces would converge on the landing areas. Coming from the south, through the Surigao Strait, was a Japanese force of two

---

[298] Lost in the sense they could not achieve their war aims; however, they might prevent an invasion of their homeland. Thus, they would lose the war but "save" Japan, if not successfully invaded.

large battleships, a cruiser, and four destroyers. (The Southern Force) From the north, through the San Bernardino Strait, came Japan's force of five battleships, twelve cruisers, and thirteen destroyers. (The Central Force) The Central and Southern Forces were to converge on Leyte Gulf where the US Transports were located and blast them to bits. Attacking transports was a new tactic for the Japanese. They began to see the importance of supplies and, at last, focused their energy on destroying those vital elements of American power.

The plan went better than expected for the Japanese. The Americans, under Admiral Halsey, did chase the Japanese carriers, the San Bernardino Strait was left open, and the powerful Japanese Central Force sailed through and made for the landing zone at Leyte. Everything was set for a total Japanese victory, in that the cargo ships at the beach were unprotected. But, along the way to the landing zone, the Japanese encountered a diminutive force of small jeep carriers and destroyer escorts off **Samar** that was supplying close air and sea support for the troops ashore. The sudden appearance of Japanese cruisers and battleships caused great alarm among the little ships.

Commander of the central force, **Admiral Kurita**, then blew it by ordering a general attack. He had mistaken the escorts for the larger fleet carriers. In a display of courage beyond belief, the US destroyers counterattacked the Japanese fleet with their tiny five-inch guns and deadly torpedoes. Aircraft from the escort carriers attacked the Japanese ships with machine guns and antipersonnel bombs. During the fight, three US destroyers and three of the escort carriers were sunk. The much larger and stronger Japanese fleet lost three heavy cruisers. The remaining US vessels were escaping when they noticed the Japanese had turned north, *away from the landing zone.* What happened? Admiral Kurita had ordered his force north to regroup. After gathering his ships, he made a stunning decision. Kurita, concerned about the US Fleet's return from their wild goose chase, *decided to retreat* through the San Bernardino Strait![299] This decision defies all reason. Kurita knew his ships would be of no use later. His ONLY viable course of action was to continue and destroy the American transports and supplies at Leyte.

---

[299] Kurita HAD to know the plan was to draw the US fleet away from where he was, so why was he surprised to be told the US fleet was elsewhere? It was supposed to be elsewhere. Even if it was not, his mission was to destroy the supplies, not to attack carriers.

Meanwhile, the Japanese Southern Force approached Surigao Strait. The Americans were forewarned[300] and awaited the Japanese in the darkness at Surigao. US Admiral **Oldendorf** laid the perfect trap. As the trap was sprung the Japanese ships were wrecked by concentrated fire from numerous destroyers, cruisers, and the old battleships of Oldendorf's line.[301] Meanwhile, the decoy Japanese carrier force lost two carriers from American aircraft attacks. Looking at what was accomplished by the successful deception of the Northern Carrier Force, the Japanese plan should have succeeded. If Kurita had destroyed the transports and the supplies it would have spoiled the US capacity to remain on Leyte.

Yet another missed opportunity for Japan. Remember *Savo Island*? The Japanese cruiser force battered the Allied cruisers guarding Guadalcanal's supply ships. The transports were dead ahead and unprotected when the Japanese admiral failed to advance and destroy the cargo ships. The reader may recall that at *Pearl Harbor* Nagumo failed to launch a third strike, fearful of being detected by the missing US aircraft carriers. Another missed opportunity was the *Battle of the Coral Sea.* The Japanese invasion force turned back after the encounter with American carriers, an encounter the Japanese had not lost. Admiral Yamamoto wanted the fleet to continue on and invade Port Moresby. Had they done so, the Japanese stood an excellent chance of capturing the last Allied bastion on New Guinea. Then, Kurita's Leyte retreat. At three key moments a major tactical victory was within the grasp of Japanese admirals, and they missed each one (the Coral Sea, Savo, Leyte). What caused the lapses of judgment on the part of these men? In each case the missed opportunity was substantial, and nothing stood between them and victory. Couple the destruction of fuel and harbor facilities at Pearl, the capture of New Guinea, winning at Guadalcanal, plus winning at Leyte, and Allied plans could have been significantly delayed.

The individual decisions of four admirals dramatically hurt Japan's cause. History illustrates that *often a few people control the hinge point of events.* Different decisions by these four men, while not winning the war, would hand their leaders a better chance at controlling later events. The strategic decision for or against war is the most critical because it is foundational; however, numerous poorly made decisions at the decisive point of battle can doom any nation. The Allies made good decisions throughout the war

---

300 US submarines had seen and reported the Japanese ships.

301 Some, like the California, had been raised from the mud of Pearl Harbor to rejoin the fleet.

at the strategic level,[302] and the Allied fighting men made good decisions at the tactical level. Given the totality of decisions made by the Allies and the Axis, the Allies did far better.

SUBMARINE EFFORTS—AXIS AND THE ALLIES

Any discussion of the Pacific and Atlantic wars must refer to the US Submarine efforts against Japan and German efforts in the Atlantic against Britain. At the start of the war, US Navy torpedoes were defective. Reports of their defectiveness reached ranking admirals in the navy, but they were ignored. Only after the admiral of the submarine forces threatened to resign were tests run on the torpedoes, and they *were* defective. The problem was the magnetic detectors on the warhead that were supposed to recognize when the torpedo was directly under a ship failed. In WWI the torpedoes had mechanical detonators. The torpedo hit the side of a ship, the mechanical detonator fired, and a hole was blown in the ships' side. Between WWI and II, torpedoes were improved and a magnetic detonator was invented which detected when the torpedo was beneath the keel of the ship causing the torpedo to explode. This difference was critical because when the torpedo exploded under the keel of a ship it broke the ship's back (so to speak), the ship would sink faster, and it would take fewer torpedoes to sink a ship—usually only one (for a merchant ship).

The Germans encountered the same problems with their torpedoes; thus, they switched to WWI mechanical detonators and the German submarines had to fire more torpedoes to sink a ship when one should have sufficed. German Type VII subs only carried twelve torpedoes. A German investigation discovered the officers in charge of testing the torpedoes in the Kregsmarine were the same people that investigated any later-alleged flaws. The quality control testers covered up the fact that the detonators were malfunctioning. In Germany, these men were quickly put to death (after a trial, of course). In the US, Navy investigators determined the men originally in charge of testing the torpedoes were the same men looking for later problems with those torpedoes. If these men disclosed the flaws in their original testing they could get into trouble, so they kept quite. Do

---

302 Defeat Germany first then Japan, defeat submarines first then the Luftwaffe second, keep China and USSR in the war, take North Africa, invade Europe in 1944, put massive emphasis on technology, keep full war production from the outset of the war, listen to the generals not the politicians about how to wage the war, etc.

the facts ring a bell? Only here, the US Navy failed to outwardly punish the men. They just fixed the problem and moved on.

The US Submarine service was terribly hampered by these malfunctioning torpedoes. Submariners risked their lives in the Philippines, for example, to get shots at Japanese ships landing troops on Luzon only to have the torpedoes breakdown. At Guadalcanal, US Coastal submarines operating in The Slot recorded several kills. This got the US Navy wondering why the coastal submarines were having so much more luck than the fleet submarines. No one thought to look at the torpedoes, although suspicions were growing. The small coastal subs were using World War I torpedoes because they were second class fighting machines, so they got the old stuff. The old stuff worked and gave the Japanese a lot of headaches. The new stuff did not work and gave the United States a lot of headaches. Fixing the torpedoes led to spectacular kill rates for US Submarines after 1943. The Japanese failed to concentrate on protecting their merchant shipping, and US Submarines began slaughtering their transports. By the end of the war, US Submarines effectively cut off ocean transportation to Japan.

Germany fared poorly in spite of great efforts. Effective code breaking, anti-submarine technology, convoys, and new fighting methods ended Germany's chance of an undersea victory in 1943. Ultra and the defective German torpedoes were key elements in their downfall, along with the Allied decision at Casablanca to defeat the U-boat threat first.[303] The Japanese constructed excellent long-range submarines and possessed the best torpedo of any combatant. In spite of these wonderful weapons, Japanese tactical doctrine on how to use submarines failed them. Based on their ancient warrior's code, enemy soldiers were the main targets of attack, not supply lines. As such, the Japanese totally misused their submarines by confining them to attacking warships instead of cargo ships. If the Japanese had placed a number of submarines between Hawaii and the US West Coast and attacked Allied cargo ships, they could have significantly hampered Allied operations in the Pacific.

---

303 *Memoirs*, by Carl Doenitz, Da Capo Press, 1997.

HAMMERING TOWARD VICTORY—EUROPE

1944-1945

D-DAY AND BEYOND

> *Never, never, never believe any war will be smooth and easy, or that anyone who embarks on the strange voyage can measure the tides and hurricanes he will encounter. The statesman who yields to war fever must realize that once the signal is given, he is no longer the master of policy but the slave of unforeseeable and uncontrollable events.*
>
> **—Sir Winston Churchill**

BACKGROUND TO D-DAY

Stalin kept pressing the Allies for a second front. Easy for Stalin to demand, but an invasion of Nazi occupied Europe was going to be a huge, costly, and risky undertaking. Yet it had to be done. A failure to invade France had the potential of leaving all of Europe in Soviet hands after the war. England and America realized the Soviets were gaining strength and would defeat Hitler. The only issue was the cost of victory. On the other hand, if the D-Day invasion were a failure, or if the Allies refused to invade, Stalin might choose to quit if Hitler offered a good-enough deal. If that were to occur, two mass murderers could rule Europe for decades.

The English, led by Churchill, wanted to put off the invasion until 1945 and continue to raid the periphery of the Third Reich. This strategy of waiting and raiding served the British well for hundreds of years. It worked against Napoleon of France, Philip of Spain, and others. In World War I, the British committed their army to the continent, and the cost was horrendous. The British now returned to the ancient formula and thought by using their control of the sea and raiding ability they could hurt Hitler's forces and save their own for the final blow—when the "right" time arrived. The Soviets saw this as stalling, and constituted attempts by capitalist powers to bleed both Hitler and the Soviets white, then step in and claim all of Europe for their spoils.[304]

---

[304] Insightfully, this was exactly what Stalin had planned when France, England, and Germany went to war. Stalin was going to wait until the Western powers were exhausted

America had a different history and experience with war. The American Civil War formulated the ideas of war in the American military mind. Like Grant during the Civil War, the United States wanted to go straight at the enemy and destroy him as quickly as possible. US Generals disliked the periphery strategy of hitting the enemy here and there while waiting for the decisive moment to engage. The United States wanted to go ashore in France and have it out with the Nazis. They did not care to let the Nazis and Soviets kill each other off for a year or two before proceeding into France. In essence, the US wanted to win and go home.

Churchill could not fathom the American interest in an immediate sea assault on Nazi-occupied France. He knew casualties would be high, and the risk of a total defeat on the beaches was ever present. American generals could not understand England's reluctance to hit the Nazis and drive them into oblivion. America had great confidence in its ability to destroy the Nazi army, but the British were more cautious. England was driven to near defeat in 1918, chased off the continent in 1940, and mauled in a large raid on the French port of Dieppe in 1942. The Americans had initially taken a beating in North Africa, but they looked at the experience differently. In American eyes they had learned, then turned, and destroyed the Nazis in Tunisia. Note how a different history results in different decisions and outlooks.

In a series of Allied conferences, the Soviets demanded, and then received, a guarantee from the Western Democracies to invade Nazi-occupied France in 1944. The British loathed the decision; but as Roosevelt and Stalin reached an agreement they went along. It was a good decision for the future of the world. The invasion of France freed Western Europe, saving it from occupation by the Soviets. As the aftermath of the war would demonstrate, this was vitally important.

General **Dwight D. Eisenhower** led the largest amphibious operation the world had ever seen (and is still the largest to this day). The planning for the assault was intensive. Just getting the troops to the beaches was a monumental undertaking. The Allies needed a new kind of ship for that job, one that could disgorge huge amounts of supplies as well as vehicles, artillery, and even tanks directly onto the beach. The ship was designed by

---

in a World War I kind of confrontation, and then he would invade from the east and conquer all. But France buckled, and everything changed.

the English and constructed in America—the LST (landing ship tank).[305] This ship became so important that the invasion itself came to depend on the numbers available. Operation Neptune was the code name for the task of getting the assault troops across the channel to France and bringing on the follow-up forces and supplies for the many divisions ashore in France. Neptune was an unqualified success. Not one ship was lost to enemy action crossing the channel.

Once the Allies were ashore they had to build up their forces more rapidly than the Germans. If the Germans could bring more troops to the invasion zone than the Allies, they could overwhelm them. Allied air power could close off the invasion beaches from German reinforcements by destroying all the rail lines, bridges, and roads leading to the invasion area. The problem was the air commanders did not want to give up their heavy bombers for this task. **Author Harris**, chief of Bomber Command for the British, steadfastly contended his air raids would win the war, and to divert his heavy bombers for even a few days—much less the weeks needed by Eisenhower—would hurt the war effort immeasurably. Harris argued, but Ike (Eisenhower) won and the bombers bombarded the area behind the landing area (as well as other areas to throw the Germans off). This air campaign was one of the most successful of the war. After the raids were over, the bridges were down, the railroads mangled, and roads destroyed over a vast area of France near the invasion point of Normandy.

Normandy was not a perfect spot; overall however, Normandy was the best beach area the Allies could find. Other beaches had heavier defenses, lacked sufficient beach exits, and were beyond the reach of air cover, among other evils.[306]

Generals Eisenhower and Montgomery decided a minimum of *five divisions* would go ashore on D-Day with more to follow as soon as possible. Prior to these men touching the shore, *three airborne divisions* would jump into France behind the beachheads to secure vital bridges, causeways, and road crossings (eight divisions total in the first wave of assaults—over one hundred thousand men). They would slow or stop advancing German units

---

305 Several ships and men were lost to a surprise German e-boat attack while they were practicing for the invasion. The loss of several LST's worried the generals as they were low on landing ships.

306 See: ***Cross Channel Attack,*** by Gordon Harrision for detailed review. This is the **best book** on the D-Day invasion. Lots of maps and detailed background information—it's all there.

trying to reach the beachhead. It was a tall order for the paratroopers.[307] The paratroopers would go in at night, and the invasion would begin early that same morning. The ground troops had to reach the paratroopers before the Nazis could show up in force and demolish them.

The beaches were Utah, Omaha, Gold, Juno, and Sword. Utah and Omaha, on the right (if you are on a boat facing the land from the sea), were American sectors; Gold was British; Juno was Canadian, and Sword (the far left beach) was English. One division would go ashore at each beach with other divisions ready to follow on as combat allowed. The three paratroop divisions were the 101 (American), 82 (American), and the 6th (English). The airborne Americans would land behind Utah and Omaha while the English paratroopers would land on the left flank of Sword (looking from the sea) to secure vital crossing points over the Orne River and to stall Nazi attacks on the flanks of Sword.

In June of 1944, the Germans were in a poor position to defend the continent from invasion.[308] Allied aircraft ruled the skies and Allied ships ruled the sea. This prevented German reconnaissance flights or naval reconnaissance. Unknown to the Germans, all their agents in England were working for the Allies, and the Allies were reading the German codes in real time through the Ultra decrypt program. The French Resistance was feeding additional intelligence to the Allies and they performed key acts of sabotage. The Germans were blind and deaf while the Allies had eyes and ears everywhere.

German generals could guess where the Allies might strike. They knew the Allies demanded air cover, and that limited the places the Allies would land. Beach exits, tides, defenses, phases of the moon, weather etc., all played a role in the German analysis. However, weather was one part of the equation where they came up short. All the Nazi weather ships were destroyed by the English Navy. (The code breakers again) The Germans had problems knowing what the weather would be on any given day along

307 In making a WWII movie in England, a film company had to apply for a permit to tow the authentically constructed gliders behind aircraft. The permit was denied because the gliders were deemed not airworthy. Wonder if the guys knew that in 1944?

308 Note how difficult this invasion was and compare it to Germany's ability to cross the English Channel in 1940. The Allies had ten times the power of the Wehrmacht in 1944, and it would still be hard to accomplish. How could the German's have pulled it off in 1940 against a nation with a strong navy on top of everything else?

the French coast. The Allies would know because of extensive weather stations at sea and ashore.

The Germans guessed that either the Pas de Calais in the north of France near Belgium or Normandy near Cherbourg were the likely landing areas. The Germans heavily fortified the Pas de Calais beaches because they thought this was the most likely landing spot. They were "aided" in this analysis by an elaborate Allied deception plan designed to make the Germans believe Pas de Calais was the invasion beach. *General Patton* was put in charge of a large fake army with dummy tanks, trucks, and troops that were visible everywhere. This deception worked so well the Germans thought Normandy was a ruse for a number of days after the landings.

Germany's fundamental problem was how to defend the long coastline of Western Europe. One way is to keep a large *reserve* behind a weak outer line and counter attack wherever the invader strikes. Another is a *cordon* defense, where strong units are placed around the boundaries of the area to be defended with the goal of stopping the attacker at the boundary, then driving him back later with units assembled from other areas of the boundary defense. Two great German generals, Rommel and Von Rundstedt, disagreed on how to mount the defense of France. Rommel wanted a cordon defense because he believed Allied air power was so potent that it would shoot the German reserve troops to pieces before they arrived, and airpower would prevent the move from their reserve positions to the beachhead in a timely manner.[309] Von Rundstedt, very old school himself (anyone with "von" before his name was going to be old school), thought the large reserve was best. He disliked cordon defenses, as most modern military men do, because of its inherent inefficiency and lack of striking power on offense. Von Rundstedt thought the counterattack was the key. He did not want men all over the place knowing about 90 percent of them would be in the wrong spot when the attack came. Rommel insisted the battle must be won on the beaches on the first day of the invasion. Once the Allies were ashore in force, he thought, it was over because Allied air and sea power could continue to deliver troops to France without interruption, and Germany could not match the Allies' power. Because of the lack of German intelligence and reconnaissance capability, Rommel opted for the cordon defense as his only alternative if he was to stop the Allies on the beaches.

309 War gaming and the actual events show Rommel was correct about Allied airpower.

Want to guess who settled the argument? Adolf Hitler—who else? Hitler divided the strategic baby and allowed Rommel to reinforce some of the beach areas with a limited number of troops, but also allowed Rundstedt a reserve. The problem was *the reserve could not move unless Hitler himself gave the word.* It could not be any worse. The Germans had no coherent strategy for defense, and their main units assembled for counterattack were in the hands of a man hundreds of miles away (and not very rational . . . to say the least).

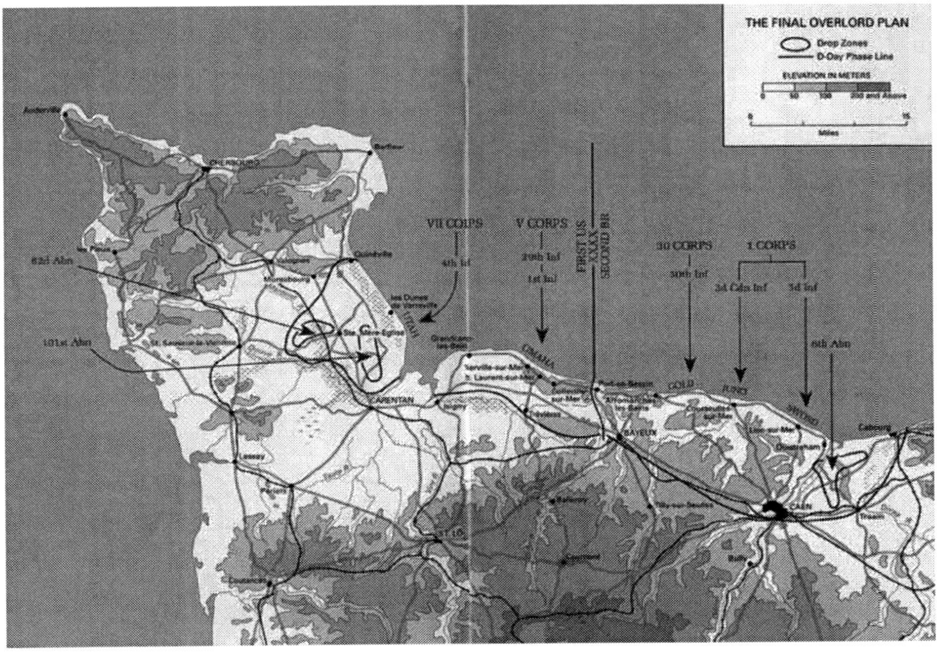

FIGURE 69 THE D-DAY PLAN

THE ATLANTIC WALL BREACHED

As the invasion loomed, two things happened that changed the course of the battle. First, the weather changed for the worse. A large storm hit the channel and made an invasion impossible. Then the Allied weather advantage came to fruition. Allied weathermen told Ike and his commanders a window of "good" (well, good enough) weather would appear on June 6, 1944 and last for a few days. Ike polled the commanders and then said, "Go". The room cleared and the invasion was on. The second thing that occurred was the veteran German 352ed division had moved into the Omaha Beach sector undetected by the Allies. On the German side, the bad weather gave them a break, or so they thought. Rommel went home for his wife's birthday, and a lot of other generals and their staffs took time off. Lack of weather information had changed the course of the war. ***Allied surprise would be total.***

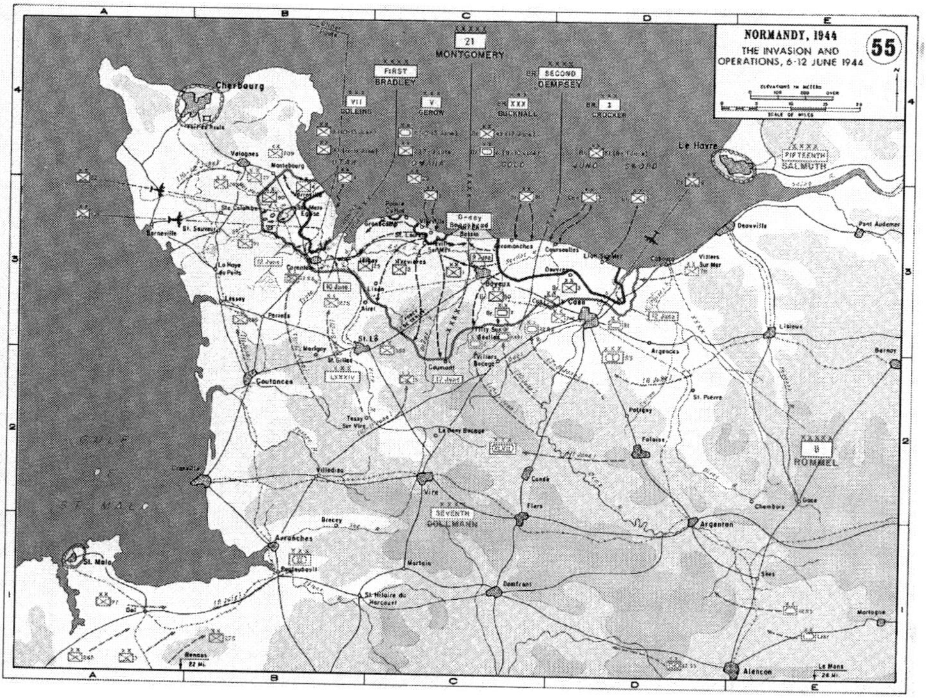

FIGURE 70 D-DAY PLUS SIX

The airdrop of troops into France did not go well. The pilots missed the drop zones, and some panicked in the flak and flew away from the drop zones before the men could jump. As a result, the paratroopers were scattered far away from their drop zones and objectives. The bridge crossing over the Orne River was the exception. The bridge fell to English glider and paratrooper units as the glider pilots put the aircraft down exactly where they should have, almost on top of the objective, totally surprising the guards. The rest of the paratroopers scattered behind the beaches began to mill around in the dark causing great confusion at German headquarters. Aggressive by training, the paratroopers joined themselves into ad hoc units and began attacking anywhere they could find the enemy. It was a mess, but it was confusing the Germans and causing delays—as planned.

As the fleet approached Normandy, Allied firepower pounded the beach areas in preparation for the landings. In the British sectors the naval gunfire was accurate, and overhead the bombers were on target. The British also developed a mass of special machines to help the troops get off the beach. They worked well.[310] British troop transports started closer to the beach than their American counterparts and reached the shore faster with fewer losses. On **Gold, Juno, and Sword**, the troops moved off the beaches rather quickly and established themselves inland. Unfortunately, they drove slowly inland, hence, failing to attain the first day's objectives. A key objective, the town of **Caen**, remained in German hands. **Utah** Beach was no picnic, but the units were ashore and able to traverse the marshes behind the beach because paratroopers had seized the vital causeway crossings.

Omaha beach was appallingly different. The bombardment aircraft dropped their ordinance far behind the beach, failing to destroy German positions overlooking the landing area. Naval gunfire overshot the defenses, thus German defenses remained intact and the beach was without craters, depriving the landing troops of cover. The veteran German 352nd infantry division defended Omaha. Unlike many other units on the Normandy beaches, this was no static unit. It was sent to Normandy for rest and refit after fighting on the eastern front. These men knew how to fight. At Omaha Beach a steep escarpment overlooked the landing zones giving the defenders a grand view of the area below. Men landing here had to cross 200 to 300 yards of flat sand to reach a place capable of obstructing the swarms of German bullets roaring down upon them. German gunners directed cannon fire onto landing craft from field guns just behind the beach untouched by air attacks or naval bombardment. These cannons were firing directly into the landing craft, blowing men to atoms.

As the ramps dropped, German machine guns opened fire with predictably bloody results. One man stated that his captain was "filled with bullets by the time he got to the bottom of the ramp." From undisturbed positions overlooking the beach, the veteran Germans fired down onto the men crawling or running for cover across the open landscape. American casualties on Omaha were terrible.

The so-called swimming tanks were sinking in the high waves on their way to Omaha Beach depriving the troops of needed armored support. Junior grade officers commanding a few LSTs laboring through high waves toward

---

310 Except for the wading tanks that had to get ashore on their own. Launched from LSTs, high seas sunk nearly all these specialized tanks, and many crews were lost.

Omaha beach decided to deliver the tanks by running their ships onto shore. By this expedient, some tanks got to the beach and began firing on the German positions. Heavy German concrete emplacements defied the fire of such small guns, but the Germans in the trenches overlooking the beach worried about the return fire. The men of the US 1st and 29th Divisions pinned on the beach rejoiced to see at least some armor driving out of the LSTs.

Observing the dilemma of the troops ashore moved another group of navy men to extraordinary action. American destroyers began sailing very close to shore (one thousand yards), firing their five-inch guns at the German pillboxes and trenches overlooking Omaha Beach. This naval gunfire devastated the defenders. Pillboxes and bunkers were destroyed, and the excoriating fire on the men below the cliff began to abate. Finally, small groups of men started fighting their way off the beach, up the draws and the escarpment, toward the German positions above the beach. As these draws were taken and the escarpment breached, the Americans could attack the Germans from the flanks and the pillboxes and bunkers from behind. The 352 division requested reinforcements from the German High Command, but none were sent. *This was a critical error.* Reinforced, the 352 might have driven the Americans off their tiny initial gains, thereby splitting the Allied forces. To the east, the British beaches could have held, but to the west Utah beach would have been isolated and difficult to hold. But, no German reinforcements arrived and the 352 lost men and material as the day marched on, which eventually caused them to buckle. This allowed the Americans to expand their beachhead, although not by much, on the first day.

Omaha beach survived and the Allies were ashore in force. However, the day went badly in one other crucial area. General Montgomery planned to capture the town of Caen on the first day. The British and Canadian troops moving inland from Gold, Juno, and Sword beaches were unhurried, and the Germans quickly reinforced the area around Caen. The Germans knew this route was the key to gaining the open plain to Paris. By denying the invasion forces the Caen area, the Germans pulled a major coup. By the time the Allies broke out of Normandy thousands of men had died trying to capture Caen's high ground.

The British and Americans were also starting to encounter the unanticipated Normandy hedgerow country. After the Allies were ashore they found the country behind the beaches arrayed with massive, deep, thick hedges. The roads were narrow and somewhat depressed below the bottom of the hedges. This was superb defensive terrain, and the Germans protected it with skill and courage. A war of attrition began that cost the Allies in casualties and time. As the Allies inched forward, the Germans moved more troops into the line, thereby preventing an Allied breakout. The next few days found the Americans fighting their way across the neck of land that held the city and port of Cherbourg. The goal was to close off the peninsula then attack north and seize the port. This effort was time-consuming, but the Americans moved relentlessly forward.

As the Americans captured the Cherbourg Peninsula, General Montgomery wanted to take Caen and the ridges beyond so he could break out into the plains behind Caen and strike for Paris. Monty mounted *seven* large attacks on the German positions, two of them quite large, and suffered heavy losses every time. Operations Perch, Epson, Windsor, Charnwood, Jupiter, Goodwood, and Spring were all costly failures. Operation Goodwood alone cost the Allies approximately *four thousand men and four hundred tanks*. Even though British troops took the town of Caen itself, the vital high ground remained in German hands. General Montgomery continued battering away at the entrenched Germans with high losses and few appreciable gains.

In the meantime, the Americans were making progress. The port of Cherbourg fell on June 26, but German engineers ruined the port and it remained unusable until August. At least the Allies had the Cherbourg Peninsula, a large area in which they massed troops, constructed airfields, and stationed aircraft for close air support.

Finally, the Americans decided they could break out in their sector near the town of St. Lo. After a massive air bombardment General Patton's Third Army broke through the German lines, and the Sherman tanks, fast and reliable, were now in their element. Hitler was advised to allow redeployment to the River Seine, but predictably refused to retreat. Soon the German Army defending Normandy was in a trap. As General Patton advanced in a sweeping movement south and then north, General Montgomery advanced south soon forming a pocket around the town of Falaise. Unfortunately for the Allies, General Montgomery failed to close the pocket and a large number of German troops escaped; however, they lost their equipment and had no ability to resist the Allies effectively until rearmed and reconstituted as a fighting force.

After the war, General Montgomery claimed it was always his plan to tie down the Germans around Caen and have the Americans break out from the west and trap the enemy. General Montgomery was covering his reputation. Pre-invasion plans clearly demonstrate Montgomery's desire to capture Caen for the expected breakthrough at that point. Montgomery formed no plans prior to the invasion for a breakout from the west by American forces. This possibility arose after the offensives mounted by General Montgomery failed at Caen. These offensives were massive in scale, and certainly not the kind of operation designed for tying down enemy troops. No mention of the American move to breakout came from Montgomery's headquarters. The idea was American; however, Montgomery did see the merit of the plan and immediately adopted it.[311]

Once the breakout was accomplished the Germans retreated with speed until they could regroup. The Allied advance across France was very rapid. One key to the quickness of the advance was the Sherman tank and the American two and one-half ton trucks (duce and a half). Both units were reliable, fast, and fairly easy to fix if they did break. For all the problems the Sherman had in tank-to-tank engagements it was wonderful in the pursuit across France.

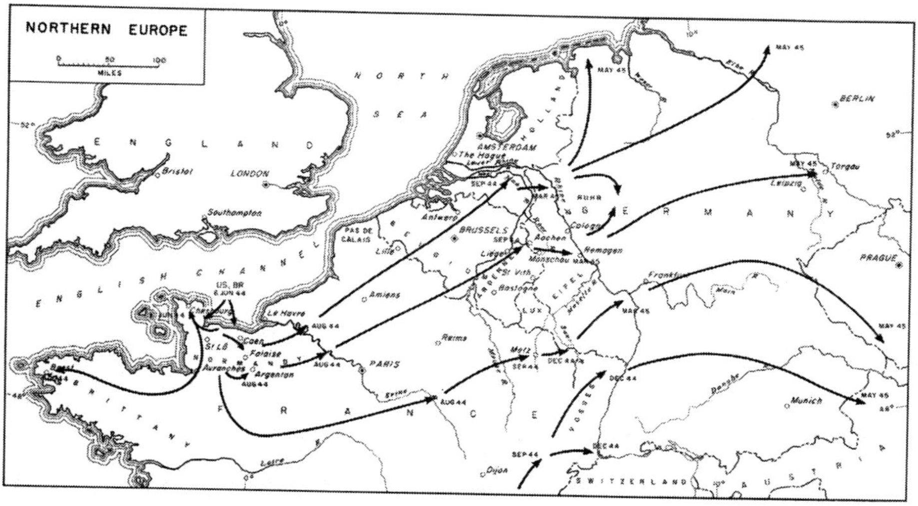

FIGURE 71 D-DAY AND BEYOND

---

311 Goodwood and Charnwood were the largest of these attacks and were complete Allied defeats. Charnwood did manage to take a portion of Caen; but as long as the Germans held the high ground above Caen, the town itself was nearly meaningless. See: *Decision in Normandy,* by Carlo D'Este, for a detailed look at the planning and fighting for Normandy.

The Allies were racing to the Rhine. Paris fell rather quickly after De Gaulle's French units disobeyed Eisenhower's orders and diverted to the city. Eisenhower was forced to redirect troops to Paris, squandering valuable time and fuel. At least the Germans disobeyed Hitler's orders to destroy the city. This diversion demonstrated the French war aims differed greatly from the English and Americans, and DeGaulle was going to pursue those aims no matter the cost to their fellow combatants. Because the Germans continued to hold the port cities on the Atlantic coast of France, and because a tremendous storm had wrecked one of the artificial harbors at Normandy, the Allies were having supply problems.[312] Moving fuel, ammunition, and all the rest from Normandy to the German border was expensive and time consuming (that troublesome word again, Logistics). Eisenhower wanted the port of **Antwerp** captured at once, but again General Montgomery dawdled, and the Germans reinforced the area thus causing the British troops delays and hard fighting after Montgomery finally directed his soldiers to take the area. Engineers worked on clearing mines and obstacles planted by the Germans to stop shipping from entering the port. All these problems caused a significant postponement in opening the vital harbor.

General Eisenhower followed a broad front strategy for the Allied advance where the entire front moved forward simultaneously, and all sectors enjoyed an equal call on supplies. General Montgomery wanted to limit the advance to a narrow area that would demand the lion's share of supplies. At first Ike refused the idea, but as the supply situation grew critical, he thought allowing the remaining supplies to be used for a narrow front attack could end the war sooner. Ike told General Montgomery to go ahead with **Operation Market Garden**, an assault with paratroopers and the British Thirty Corps designed to cross the Rhine from British positions near Antwerp. The assault was commenced on September 15, 1944.

Market Garden was a colossal Allied defeat. The plan itself was badly put together, and vital intelligence was ignored. Crack Nazi troops were in the region for rest and refitting, and the plans for Market Garden fell into German hands early in the operation. Thirty Corps' advance ran into deep trouble because the single road available for mechanized movement was easily defended. After days of pounding and no sign of Thirty Corps or

---

312 The British were on the left flank of the Allied advance across France where the port cities such as Dunkirk were located, but Montgomery failed to order their seizure thereby exacerbating the Allied supply problems.

communication from headquarters, the British paratroopers were done. Thousands of elite British paratroopers were killed or captured.[313]

On September 19, 1944, American units began assaulting **the Huertgen forest**. This assault was useless from a strategic point of view. The forest was classic defensive terrain, and German paratroopers were dug in there supported by heavy artillery. For some reason, American generals Bradley and Hodges thought the forest was vital, and threw nine divisions in all into the fight, battling for *three months* in an area where American firepower, air control, and ability to maneuver were useless. Huertgen was taken, but the cost was enormous for the advantage (if any) gained—*twenty-four thousand US soldiers dead!* US Generals Bradley and Hodges were responsible for this error in judgment and fully responsible for the lives of the men they sacrificed.

THE BATTLE OF THE BULGE

December 1944

On December 16, 1944, Hitler launched a massive offensive through the Ardennes forest. This assault caught the Allies completely by surprise. Allied units stationed at the point of attack had either been manhandled in the Huertgen forest, or were green units moved into a quiet sector. Given the condition of the US units opposing the Germans, they fought well and delayed the initial German advance appreciably; nevertheless, the German blow made good ground in the first few days. The **Battle of the Bulge** was on.

This attack was the brainchild of Adolf Hitler, forever the gambler, who staked his empire on one very risky roll of the dice. He managed to keep the assault a secret mainly because of radio silence. Allied intelligence was coming in through **Ultra** (the reading of Nazi radio transmissions) almost exclusively. Ultra intelligence reports were so unfailing Allied generals relied on little else. Furthermore, the Allies thought the Germans could

---

[313] Patton had argued he should get the supplies on his claim that he could reach Berlin if he got them. Typical of Patton; however, he may have had a better chance than Montgomery, given the speed with which he did cross the Rhine; and German forces to his front were not as accomplished as those Montgomery found on the way to Arnhem.

not mount such an offensive. The Allied generals believed the Germans were finished.

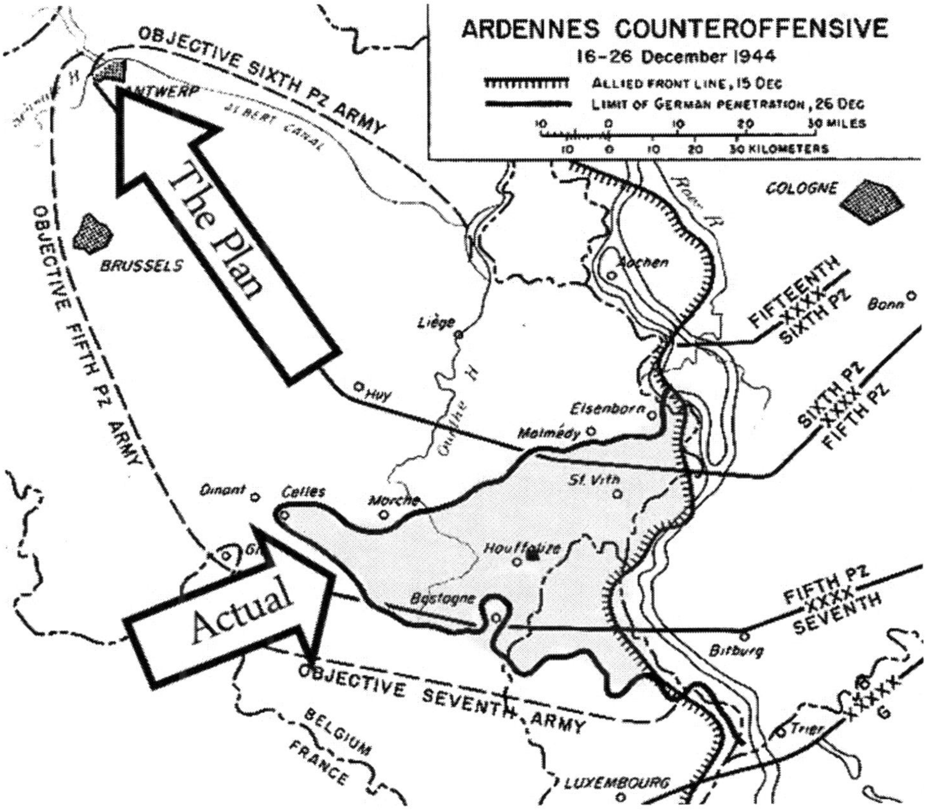

FIGURE 72 BATTLE OF THE BULGE, DEC 1944

Somehow, against all odds, Germany scraped together several divisions—armored included—and enough fuel to *open* a major offensive. Allied air operations failed to prevent this achievement, neither had enormous German losses in men and equipment over the past months in the USSR and on the Western Front. However, the men assembled for this undertaking were *not well trained.* The officers and most of the noncommissioned officers were veterans, but the troops were green. Moreover, the fuel supply was short. Capturing Allied fuel was necessary to keep the advance going.

Hitler's plan contained other flaws. The road grid his armored divisions moved over was awful. Small winding mountain roads, with small bridges, would be tough enough to attack over in good weather; however, for the assault to work the weather must be bad—very bad. Snow and overcast weather kept the Allied air forces on the ground, and this was essential for victory. German tanks traversed slick snow-covered roads surrounded by hills and trees that could, and did, hide defenders. Knocking out the lead German tank in these conditions stopped the entire column. Bad weather, large tanks,[314] small winding roads, not much fuel, and a movement schedule that would prove impossible to keep, all added up to failure before the attack started. [315]The experienced German generals knew the results before the attack started, the loss of Germany's reserves. Hitler had blundered again.

On the morning of the attack, the US Army troops under fire did not see Hitler's move as stupid. German tanks, artillery, and infantry were advancing everywhere, while American troops were falling back or fighting from encircled positions. Some German troops had a new assault rifle, the Sturmgewehr 44, developed from studies of how German troops actually fought in the field. American troops did not like this new development either. Valiant last stands seldom win wars, but American units fighting valiant, if small, last stands significantly hampered the German advance at key moments in the offensive. This proved critical as the battle developed. Hitler's goal was the port of Antwerp. He knew his forces must reach the River Meuse, cross it, and get on to Antwerp before the weather cleared.

The German assault soon began running out of steam. The 101st Airborne Division moved into a vital road junction at **Bastogne** and held on despite repeated German assaults. German units on the point of attack who were approaching the Meuse ran short of fuel and were beat up by American tanks and artillery. The flanks of the American line held at St.Vith, and American counterattacks began to threaten penetration near the base of the bulge. General Patton's Third Army made a ninety-degree turn north in record time and began assaulting the Germans holding the area between himself and Bastogne. As the weather cleared on Christmas Day, Allied air power began to pound German tanks and supply lines while Patton's army relieved the defenders at Bastogne. It was over. Hitler reluctantly ordered the retreat that spelled the end for Germany in the west. With his reserves destroyed, Hitler possessed nothing to hold back the Allied tide.

---

[314] German tanks in 1944 were MUCH larger than the German tanks of 1940 which had traversed this forest to attack France.

[315] I say this a lot, but good plans, without false assumptions attached, and good preparations are critical to achieving victory.

THE AIR WAR OVER EUROPE

1940 to 1945

Thus far, we have circumvented the air war over Europe. In fact, it was a massive undertaking involving resources on a vast scale for England, America, and the Nazis. The air war, from the outset, caused controversy. Bombing of civilians was a difficult thing to justify, but it was a requirement of total war. The Nazis started it, said Bomber Harris, and the Allies would finish it in spades. "They have sown the wind, and they shall reap the whirlwind," is a well-known quote from Air Marshall Harris (known as Bomber Harris).

> *"The pioneer in the air war against Germany was the RAF. The RAF experimented briefly in 1940 with daylight attacks on industrial targets in Germany but abandoned the effort when losses proved unbearably heavy. Thereafter, it attempted to find and attack such targets as oil, aluminum, and aircraft plants at night. This effort too was abandoned; with available techniques, it was not possible to locate the targets often enough. Then the RAF began its famous raids on German urban and industrial centers. On the night of May 30, 1942, it mounted its first 'thousand plane' raid against Cologne and two nights later struck Essen with almost equal force . . . the weight of the RAF effort, compared with tonnages later employed, was very small—sixteen thousand tons in 1940 and forty-six thousand tons in 1941 compared with 676,000 tons in 1944." (The US Strategic Bombing Survey)*

Thus started the night-area bombing of German cities. It was a practical matter. Daylight raids were too costly, and after dark it was impossibly difficult to locate a factory complex for pinpoint bombing.[316] Britain felt it had to use its only method of striking back, so it made the decision to "carpet" or area bomb the cities producing the machines of war, and if the "civilians" who worked and lived there were harmed, so be it.

When the Americans arrived with their B-17 "flying fortress," they were sure they could carry out daylight raids against German industrial targets. The American's thought by using the top-secret Norden bombsight the B-17s could put bombs right on the industrial target, thereby avoiding unnecessary civilian deaths and damaged homes. In fact, the B-17's bombs seldom fell on the target when dropped from high altitudes. In the

---

316 It was even hard to locate a city, much less a few factory buildings.

beginning, American losses were high but acceptable. The British raids were costing them far less in terms of crew and aircraft losses, but at times the raids missed entire towns. American airmen went forward with the daylight bombing, but the losses were climbing. Bomber Command kept trying to talk the Americans into joining the night raids, but American commanders thought they were on the right track. It went unsaid, but at first the US Airmen thought their approach avoided unnecessary civilian deaths and was therefore morally superior. This did not hold as the war progressed to firebombing entire cities, and any attempt to justify the bombing was summed up by "they started it."[317]

On August 28, 1943, and October 14, 1943, the USAAF staged daylight attacks on the **Schweinfurt** ball bearing plants. Allied analysis of the Nazi war machine had shown these ball bearing plants were critical. An all-out effort might destroy the Achilles heel of Nazi industrial power. However, the ball bearing plants were deep within the Reich, and the raids were disasters.

> *"In the famous and much-discussed second attack on October 14, 1943, when the plants were again severely damaged, one of the decisive air battles of the war took place. The 228 bombers participating were strongly attacked by German fighters when beyond the range of their fighter escort. Losses to fighters and to flak cost the United States forces 62 planes with another 138 damaged in varying degree, some beyond repair. Repeated losses of this magnitude could not be sustained; deep penetrations without escort, of which this was among the earliest, were suspended; and attacks on Schweinfurt were not renewed for four months." (US Strategic Bombing Survey)*

This report is an understatement. German radar detected the attack's approach, and the course taken by the bombers allowed the Germans to deduce the target. Additional fighters quickly arrived at key airfields along the route to intercept the B-17s both on their way to Schweinfurt and back. The raiders were butchered. Until long-range escorts could be developed, deep raids into Germany were cancelled. By December of 1943, the P-51 Mustang was reaching the end of its development and started becoming

---

[317] The reader may want to compare this logic to (1) The English blockade of Germany in WWI, the German U-boat campaigns in WWI and WWII, and the terrorist's attacks of the late twentieth century.

part of the Eighth Army Air Force.[318] In a few months, they would arrive in sufficient numbers to influence the air battles in early 1944.

The British were not deterred. Bomber Harris planned a prodigious series of night raids on Berlin to win the war outright through bombing the Nazi capital. Germany had been working on deterrent measures and put together both an improved radar system and a night interceptor network before the powerful British operation was underway. When the raids began on Berlin the British bomber force suffered high losses, and the losses increased as the size of the raids increased. During the three and one-half month battle of Berlin, the RAF lost over 1,000 bombers. Finally, even Harris had to admit the losses were too high, and the Berlin bomber offensive finally came to a halt.

As the escorts began to make their numbers felt, the long-range daylight raids could begin once more. A new general was at the head of the Eighth USAAF, **General Doolittle**, the same man who had led the daring raid on Tokyo, Japan, in 1942. General Doolittle saw at once that the use of US Air power was wrong. He changed the emphasis from attacking almost any German production facilities to attacking the German air force and its production facilities. General Doolittle sent the bombers up as bait to lure the German fighters into unequal contests with newer American and British fighters. The general also turned the Mustangs loose, in that he allowed some flights to fly apart from the bombers rather than close in to protect the larger aircraft. As a result, American and British pilots began to kill German aircraft at their airfields before they had even taken off. The resulting American air offensive against the German air force was a total success. Due largely to the genius of Doolittle, by June of 1944, the Luftwaffe was no longer a decisive factor in the war (recall this was the second objective of the Casablanca Conference).

After the defeat of the Luftwaffe, Allied bombers and fighters roamed the German skies at will, bombing and strafing everything. Doolittle had applied the precepts of the famous writer **Clausewitz** and his masterwork book *On War.* By defeating the enemy's army in the field first, the Luftwaffe being Germany's air army, so to speak, afterward he could do whatever he wanted. He wanted to bomb and machine gun Germany into submission, and his

---

318 The P-51 was a long-range fighter that could escort the bombers to the targets and back. Even targets deep in Germany could be reached by the P-51. In addition, even though it had tremendous long-range capability; it was also a superb combat aircraft.

pilots did their best to accomplish the objective. In the end, Germany did not fall because of the Allied air offensive. The German air force was destroyed, and that gave the Allies tactical air control over the battlefield—which made an enormous difference in the outcome of numerous battles. At the Battle of the Bulge, for example, Allied air power played a significant role in turning the tide against the German offensive. And without total control of the air, D-Day's amphibious assault may have been impossible.

When studying modern wars, think about how many battles were won when the winner on the ground controlled the air. It is quickly seen that the side ruling the sky has an enormous edge. If one cannot rule the skies, the airspace must at least be contested; otherwise the combatant controlling the air wins the ground battle.[319]

The problem with the bomber offensive was that the cost may not have justified the benefit gained. Of course, when people are saying the bomber will win the war there is a tendency to wonder if what was promised was delivered. In fact, it was not. The war in Europe was not won by air power. Troops still had to land and beat up the German Army to achieve victory. Air power severely damaged Germany's ability to wage war, but the ground pounders won the war one step at a time just as they have done since Sargon conquered Ur in 2371 BC.

The United States Strategic Bombing Survey tried to assess the impact of the huge, and extremely expensive, bombing effort. In essence, the survey concluded that the air war failed to deliver on its war-winning promises. Yes, it had contributed, but so had the ships and all the rest of the combat

---

319 I can hear you now . . ."What about Vietnam?" . . . well, what about it? The United States won virtually EVERY battle. Even after US forces were all but withdrawn, a major communist invasion from Cambodia employing many heavy tanks was turned back by a few US helicopters and the South Vietnamese Army. Also, the fall of Saigon may be traceable to the *withdrawal of US air power.*

arms support units. The USAAF and the Royal Air Force always considered themselves special, because they would do more to beat Germany than other Allied units. They were wrong. The fellow face down in the mud with bullets flying over his head was the ultimate key to victory. He always has been.

The result: the air war was important, but not of supreme importance. After the war, the major air forces of the world perked up because of the **atomic bomb**. Now they possessed a war-winning weapon, and air power was king. At least for a while. No doubt the bomb could destroy armies as well as civilization, but who would use it? In small wars, such as Korea (only a million or more killed there—very "small"), the Communist guessed the United States would not deploy the weapon, and they were correct. American scruples tied its hands and gave the communists an edge. The USSR stole the bomb quickly and cheaply through effective spying, and two (and later three, and then four, and so on) nations aimed nuclear warheads at one another. Meanwhile, wars continue to start, and many almost never end (Vietnam, etc.). What good was the bomb?

The air force never wanted to be "flying artillery," but that was why they were originally attached to the army. Reconnaissance and close air support WERE the missions of importance in the First World War, and it turned out they may have been the most important in the Second World War. Germany's entire air force was constructed around the tasks of reconnaissance and close air support.[320] Allied air forces wanted to be more. Because of theories put forth after the First World War by many air theorists, such as Italian General **Giulio Douhet321** and Sir Hugh Trenchard of England, aviators thought by bombing civilians the enemy nations would cave in. They thought the bomber would always get through. However, radar and other modern inventions soon showed the bomber would be detected and shot down unless it got some help. Moreover, bombing did not cause civilian populations to demand peace. And why anyone thought a totalitarian nation would listen to its people is another unanswered question.

Some have concluded that indiscriminate bombing, as well as using the atomic bomb, was a war crime. This is based on the idea that killing civilians is illegal and immoral; however, ever since Sherman's "March to the Sea" civilians have been fair game in modern war. The civilians support the war,

---

[320] Germany could have used a long-range bomber, especially for supply interdiction and reconnaissance.

[321] *Command of the Air* (1921) by Giulio Douhet

manufacture the machines of war, produce the food that keeps the army in the field, and provides the soldiers necessary to fight the war. Destroy the workers and the nation's ability to fight dissolves. Thus, *there are no civilians in modern war.* The Islamic terrorists know this, but many in the civilian world are loathe to admit this reality of our modern world.

Even with one thousand plane raids on Germany and around-the-clock bombing, air power did not work its predicted magic. It did kill many people and spread the misery of war far and wide. Now everyone suffered. Children and their mothers died right along with the soldiers. What a charming world we had invented.

THE EASTERN FRONT—AFTER STALINGRAD

The war in Europe was won for the Allies on the Eastern Front. The Soviets knew about the German offensive in the Ardennes through their excellent spy network in Nazi Germany (and everywhere else). Typical of the Soviets, they did not alert the Allies about the planned attack. Instead, they gathered their forces for another push at Hitler after his reserves were committed in the West. As the war in the East progressed, Soviet attacks were launched over a wide front with great effectiveness.[322] The ability to achieve deep armored penetration and encirclement destroyed German Army Group Center in Operation Bagration[323] and constituted the final extinction of any German hope of shielding the homeland from the rapacious swarms rushing from the east. Germany was unable to supply its troops with enough of anything, and the harsh Russian winters continued taking their toll. The basic Soviet attack consisted of enormous numbers of troops and tanks, supported by large numbers of aircraft and artillery, falling upon German positions in all-out attacks of the most violent nature. The USSR had complete control of the air. With new aircraft types produced in enormous numbers, the Luftwaffe was simply being swept aside. Stalin's orders included shooting commanders who failed, so Soviet commanders drove their troops inexorably forward while ignoring losses. Hitler's orders hindered the German commanders and prevented proper troop dispositions with the net result of defeat after defeat for the Nazis.

---

[322] See: p152 et seq, *Panzer Battles*, von Mellenthin, 1956, Konecky & Konecky

[323] This massive attack began on June 22, 1944, which was sixteen days after the Allies landed at Normandy. The pressure on the Wehrmacht was increasing beyond all imagination.

Spies were everywhere in the Nazi regime, and they were working for the Soviets. As a result, Stalin knew Hitler's every plan. Before the battle of **Kursk** on July 4 through 20, 1943, the last German offensive in the east, the Soviets knew about the attack through their Lucy Spy Ring, and constructed numerous and deep defensive lines in front of the German assault positions. The USSR assembled 1,300,000 men; 3,600 tanks; 20,000 artillery pieces; 2,400 aircraft; laid over 1 million mines; and had 23 antitank guns *per kilometer* in the Kursk salient. The Soviets even knew the time of the German attack, and opened an artillery barrage on German positions just prior to the German assault. At Kursk, the Wehrmacht threw nearly fifty German divisions into the strike, but it was a tragedy for the German Army. The Soviets possessed so many men and tanks that losing twice as many as the Germans meant nothing.[324] After the attack was underway, the Soviets hit the German flanks and drove through them to endanger the starting positions of the Nazi attack, causing Hitler to break off the offensive. Germany's losses were high, and they were losses the Reich could ill afford—in men or equipment.

After Kursk, the battles on the Eastern Front droned on like bitter winter storms. Well prepared and informed Soviet units attacked, supported by thousands of artillery pieces pouring tons of explosives down on German positions. Soviet troops in prodigious numbers moved forward with clouds of Soviet aircraft overhead bombing and strafing German lines as the Soviet infantry advanced. Waves of tanks moved with the Soviet troops, sloshing through mud and snow, firing cannons and spewing bullets. Overwhelmed, the Germans would fall back or were ordered to "stand fast" by the Fuehrer, in which case they were decimated or obliterated depending on the Fuehrer's next order and its timeliness. Even when the German troops could fall back, Soviet artillery and aircraft pummeled the withdrawing units. After retreating, the Germans would dig in again and await the next murderous Red Army assault. And so it would go, from 1943 until war's end.

---

[324] Soviet losses were underreported throughout the war. Even after the war, the true number of Soviet losses in men and equipment remained unknown. Most think it was double or triple what was reported after the war (triple is probably more accurate). It may be that Stalin simply did not have the resources to keep track; however, given Stalin's attitude toward people, it is likely he did not care.

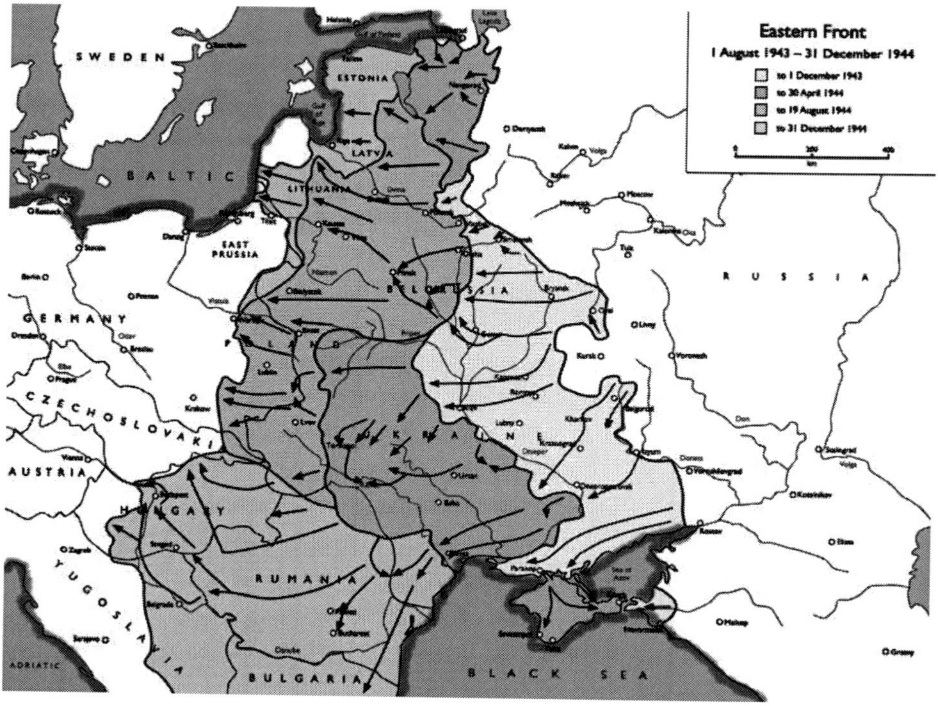

FIGURE 73 SOVIET OPERATIONS 1943-1944

As the Soviets rolled unremittingly forward, Hitler began ordering nonexistent units around. Hitler threw away the lives of his men as the troops of his most hated enemy, Stalin, entered Berlin and began the final slaying of the Nazi beast. Hitler married his long-time lover Eva Braun, and then, on April 30, 1945, they both killed themselves in his bunker deep below ground in the Nazi capital. Members of his entourage took the lifeless Fuehrer and his bride to the surface, placed them in a shell hole, poured gas over them, and set them ablaze while giving the Nazi salute. They only returned to the bunker after Soviet shells began falling all around them. Even in death, the Nazi leader commanded the unshakable loyalty of those few left around him.[325]

[325] Apparently, this was some kind of pseudo-Viking funeral for the Fuehrer and his bride.

THE END IN EUROPE

America, England, and the USSR made plans long before the capture of Berlin, and those plans allowed the Soviets the "honor" of conquering the Nazi capital. The Western Allies would halt at the River Elbe and await the Soviets. In spite of the agreement, Churchill wanted to continue on and capture Berlin before the Soviets; nonetheless, Eisenhower vetoed any such move. Eisenhower was not sacrificing even one soldier to gain Berlin and then hand it back to the Soviets. Churchill wanted to deny people and resources to the Soviets, and he wanted to keep people safe from slavery under Stalin. However, Eisenhower knew the Western Allies would keep their word and leave the area up to the Elbe River to the Soviets even if American and English troops crossed the line.

The last Fuehrer of the Third Reich was Grand Admiral Karl Donitz. Hitler appointed him in his will (yep, the murderer left a detailed last will and testament). The surrender of Nazi Germany took place on May 7, 1945. The Nazi leaders were rounded up, put on trial, and many were executed by the victorious Allied powers for their misdeeds. A new world organization was formed to try to prevent such terrible wars in the future. The **United Nations**, as it was termed, was the League of Nations reconstituted. It would have a major impact on the world, but not the one envisioned immediately after World War II.

THE END IN ASIA

Japan was determined to fight on to preserve their emperor and their honor. However, in every area of conflict, the Allies were winning big. In Burma, the English, under **General Slim,** defeated the Japanese and were pushing them back to Rangoon and beyond.[326] The Philippines were American again; Manila was recovered by the US Army, and the Japanese supply lines to the oil and resources of the South Pacific were cut. American submarines eradicated the Japanese merchant fleet, and American bombers burned the guts out of Japan's cities. The Japanese people were starving and dying by the thousands, but no thought of surrender was considered. Any burden was acceptable to the Japanese people when requested by the emperor.

---

326 Another outstanding general a few know about. He brilliantly reversed English misfortunes in the Southeast Asian Theater and completely defeated the Japanese.

Iwo Jima was invaded in February 1945. Once again, airfields were the target. American B-29 raids were flying around the island, adding many dangerous miles to the flights, and giving the Japanese early warning the bombers were inbound. By taking the island, the Americans would shorten the B-29 flights and use fighter aircraft based there to escort the huge bombers to Japan. The airfields could also be used to land damaged aircraft. Sulfur Island, Japan's name for Iwo, fell after thirty days of bloody fighting. Casualties on Iwo Jima stunned the US Navy and Marine Corps. Using the same tactics developed on Peleliu, the Japanese dug into the island and had to be blasted out one hole at a time. It was difficult work, and the United States Marines again paid a heavy price for a tiny Pacific rock.[327] About 1,000 damaged bombers used the island for emergency landings. In fact, damaged B-29 bombers started using the airfield for landings before the island was conquered. The number of aircrew saved probably exceeded the deaths the marines endured in taking the island.

President Nixon gave the island back to Japan in the 1970s. One surviving marine said that if Americans understood the sacrifices made to conquer the island, we would never give it back. Such is the way of the United States of America, always forward looking and forever forgiving the wrongs of the past. Perhaps it is best to forget at least some history. In the Middle East, memories are thousands of years long, and fathers long ago murdered must be avenged in our day. The carnage continues because of ancient never forgotten wrongs. Some things are best forgiven and forgotten.

Battle of Okinawa

April 1 to June 21, 1945

The invasion of **Okinawa,** a very large island just south of Japan, was the last major land battle of World War II. It was a joint army and marine operation, with the army in overall land control, which began on April 1 of 1945 and lasted some eighty-seven days. After the marines landed they proceeded north, and the US Army split away and attacked south. Attacked may be the wrong word, because initially the troops encountered no Japanese resistance. Only after the US troops reached the rugged mountains did the fighting begin. In a relatively short period, the marines captured the northern part of the island; meanwhile, the US Army ran into a masterfully prepared defensive network in the south. The Japanese

---

[327] 6,821 Marines dead, 494 missing (7,315 total), 20,703 Japanese dead.

thoroughly dug in, constructing an elaborate maze of tunnels and defensive positions in the mountains. These interlaced positions were mutually supporting with machine guns, mortars, and heavy artillery zeroed in on likely paths of attack. The Japanese fire was murderous, and the army took unusually heavy casualties during its assaults. After seizing the north, the marines joined the army units attacking to the south. **General Buckner**, in charge of land operations on the island, kept ordering frontal assaults on Japanese lines that gained ground, but at a high cost in lives. The marines suggested an amphibious assault to flank the main Japanese line, but Buckner rejected the concept. Slowly, very slowly, the US Army and Marines made headway against the superbly placed Japanese defensive positions.

Out at sea, a situation developed that bode ill for the US fleet. Waves of Japanese aircraft began ramming American warships. The pilots were committing suicide in an attempt to sweep the US Navy from the sea. This tactic was experienced earlier, but by only a few aircraft, during battles off the Philippines.

Kamikazes (Divine Wind) committed themselves to die trying to sink the US fleet now threatening their homeland.[328] Japan's outdated aircraft were unable to compete with newer American models. The Japanese pilots were unskilled, and the few remaining skilled pilots could make no difference against American strength. The idea of putting a person into an aircraft who was only trained to take off and crash into an American ship seems out of place to Westerners. It was the perfect solution for Japan, who could now put their out-of-date planes and untrained pilots to good use. Japan's tradition of sacrifice for honor and the emperor allowed their young men to commit suicide in return for having died for the emperor. Everything fit together very well from the Japanese point of view. The Kamikaze was a *guided missile.* Instead of a computer or mechanical device guiding the missile, a man would do the job. Loaded with fuel and bombs, these aircraft became lethal weapons against the fleet. Their effect was dreadful. American ships were knocked out of action at the highest rates of the war, and American sailors were killed in distressing numbers. The US Navy responded with increased combat air patrols and destroyer pickets to meet the raiders as far away from the fleet as possible. Kamikaze pilots were

---

328 Japan was saved from a Mongol invasion when a great storm blew up and sunk the Mongol fleet. The Japanese named the storm the Divine Wind because it had saved Japan from invasion. They now hoped the new mechanized Divine Wind would do the same.

poorly trained and often made the mistake of crashing into the destroyer pickets rather than going further to attack the carriers and battleships of the main fleet. Even so, the attacks were deadly.

Nimitz complained to the army about the slow pace of the land war as it was exposing his fleet to unnecessary hazards. In fact, about *five thousand* sailors died defending the fleet off Okinawa. Nimitz wanted to get the island conquered so his fleet could set sail to another location. General Buckner's cooperation failed to appear. He continued the slow grind of the campaign in spite of navy protest. The key problem was *differing doctrines of war.* Marine units were trained to assault relentlessly, moving forward at great costs if necessary to conquer the enemy ashore so the fleet could rapidly leave the area. Warships prefer non-stationary addresses, because the enemy can find them easily if they stay in one spot. The ocean's size is a major defensive weapon for a navy. Off the island of Okinawa, the ships were supplying the combat units and providing artillery support ashore. Japanese Kamikazes could find them without difficulty because of their fixed location.

US Army doctrine said nothing about moving quickly because of ships waiting offshore; thus, the army moved slower when attacking than the marines, taking fewer risks while advancing. The army refused to sacrifice its men for speed. In one instance off Makin in the Tarawa atoll, an escort carrier was sunk, and more lives were lost in that sinking than were lost taking the island of Makin. The navy thought the loss was due to the army's slow advance in taking the island, thus requiring the carrier to hang around longer than necessary and attracting unwanted attention.

Nimitz and the army remained at loggerheads because of doctrine. The speed required by the US Navy went unacknowledged by the US Army, who dared not change their basic combat doctrine in any event. Military units have to stay within their training to avoid even greater difficulties. However, the US Navy did have a point in that the advance was agonizingly slow. The landings requested by the marines could have broken one of the toughest Japanese lines and quickened the advance. Constant frontal assaults, like WWI, did nothing for the attacking forces. Buckner refused to change, and the frontal assaults went on. Bad weather helped the defenders in killing their American tormentors, but the outcome was never in doubt. American power simply hammered the Japanese to dust. General Buckner died before the end of the battle, killed by an artillery shell that left the many others near him unscathed.

At last Okinawa was captured on May 6, 1945.[329] For the Allies, it was a grim ordeal, and it gave America fair warning of how difficult it would be to invade Japan. In the battle for Okinawa, ***12,513*** Americans were dead or missing and nearly 39,000 wounded. The Japanese lost ***66,000*** dead, 17,000 wounded, and a very high 7,400 captured. At sea, the United States of America lost ***79*** *ships* sunk or scrapped, and 763 aircraft were destroyed. The Japanese lost *16* ships and over *3,000* aircraft. Approximately *150,000 civilians* on Okinawa were killed or missing. The Japanese flew over 1,900 Kamikaze missions, killing about *5,000* US sailors. The invasion of the home islands would be horrific if these numbers held true.[330]

Of course, the Japanese wanted the Americans to do something other than invade the home islands. A negotiated peace on almost any terms might be acceptable, but *the emperor must stay.* Japan tried to send peace feelers through the Soviets (they were not at war with Japan at this time) who conveniently failed to forward them to the United States. However, the Americans failed to understand the Japanese need to retain their god on earth, the emperor. Roosevelt died on April 12, 1945. President **Truman** (his successor) would honor the unconditional surrender demand, plus this concept was reaffirmed at the Potsdam Conference in 1945 (why it was affirmed is open to question).

Allied bombing raids on Japan were taking dire death tolls. The firebombing of Tokyo on February 23, 1945, killed an estimated *one hundred thousand* in the resulting firestorm. American submarines sunk Japanese shipping at a startling rate, thus causing starvation all over Japan. American aircraft mined critical straits and harbors, affecting large shipping losses and preventing the movement of food and supplies from one region to another

---

329 Nazi Germany surrendered on May 7, 1945.

330 Casualty ratios on Okinawa were about ninety to sixty or three to two; thus, for every two American casualties, there were three Japanese, NOT counting civilians. If civilians are included it is 4 to 1. An assault on mainland Japan, using the same ratios and assuming 3 million Japanese casualties, there would be 2 million American casualties (or 2 million Americans to 8 million Japanese if civilians are included). It is thought that 3 million Japanese casualties is a very low figure. In other Pacific island battles the US was killing its enemy at a 12 to 1 ratio in most battles. At Tarawa it was 1:5, and the ratio became more favorable for the US until the Japanese changed tactics in the Palau islands. (12,500 US soldiers dead, 40,000 US soldiers wounded, 5,000 US Navy dead = 57,000 rounded to 60,000; 66,000 Japanese dead, 17,000 wounded, 2,000 Kamikaze dead = 85,000 rounded to 90,000; thus a 2:3 casualty ratio.)

by sea. American submarines achieved in the war with Japan what the Nazis wanted to achieve in the Battle of the Atlantic; the devastation of an island nation's ability to wage war.

OPERATION OLYMPIC

In spite of the challenge, Japan's military rejected surrender. The Americans were putting together Operation Olympic (or Downfall), the invasion of the Japanese home islands, even as the Japanese readied themselves for the attack. The US assembled 14,000 aircraft and up to 100 aircraft carriers for the assault. However, Japan was producing suicide weapons in abundance. 10,500 aircraft were preserved for attacks on US invasion forces, hundreds of fast boats with high explosives inside were constructed for ramming American ships, and special long-lance torpedoes were prepared for carrying men who steered the torpedoes to their targets. Japan assembled and trained huge numbers of women and children to charge the Americans with sharpened sticks to cause a depletion of US ammunition before the following Japanese troops reached the American lines.[331]

Worse yet, and unknown to the Americans, with skilled radio traffic analysis and common sense the Japanese accurately deduced the landing area, the Southern part of Kyushu. Japan was quickly preparing hardened defensive positions in the escarpments overlooking the invasion beaches. The Japanese military finally decided that attacking warships was not the path to victory. All the suicide weapons would be directed at the transports, troopships, and landing craft. The LSTs were the highly prized targets instead of the battleships and carriers waiting further offshore (*The Pacific War Companion*, Editor, Daniel Marston, Osprey, 2005).

---

331 This is another battle I have war gamed. I landed where the Americans would have; and after a month of heavy fighting, I decided to abandon the invasion because of dramatically high losses of troops and ships. My biggest victory was just managing to evacuate my troops without further losses.

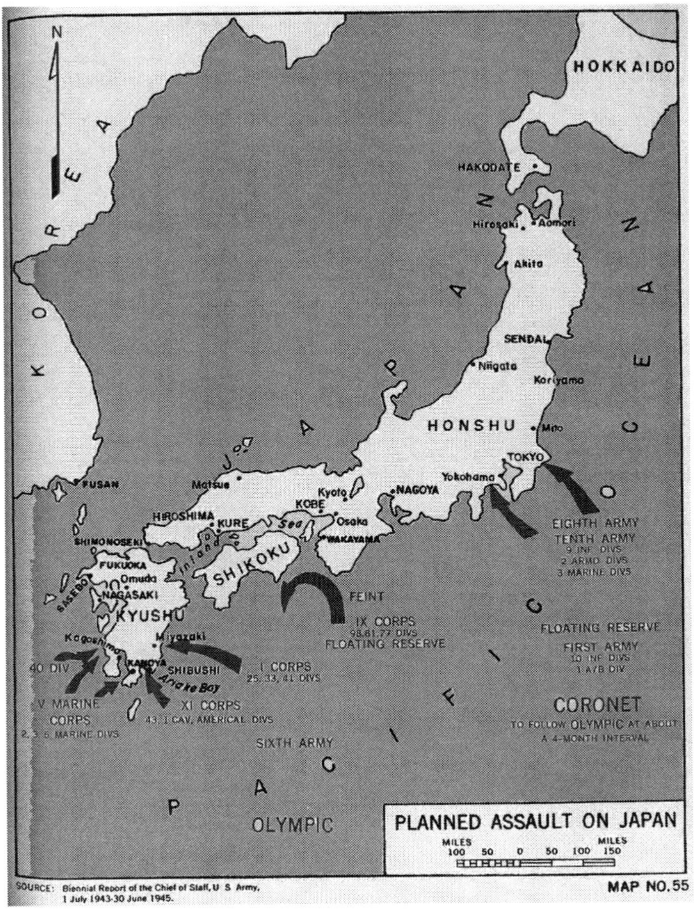

FIGURE 74 PLANNED ASSAULT ON JAPAN, OP OLYMPIC & CORONET

The tactical adjustment of the Kamikaze attacks was probably more important than discovering the landing area. With thousands of Kamikazes aimed at troop transports and landing craft, the carnage would grow immensely. The losses of men would occur before reaching the beach; decreasing unit combat power and increasing the confusion of the landing force (recall Tarawa). Once ashore, caves overlooking the beach would rain down heavy artillery on the invaders. Coupled with bunkers and pillboxes firing machine guns and mortars into the troop concentrations on the shore (as they did at Iwo Jima), the American soldiers and marines would be in a fix. The Japanese also assembled fourteen field divisions with 625,000 troops on Kyushu by August 1945, a truly prodigious number. The "charge of the innocents" (my phrase) would come next, with thousands of women and children storming the American lines. Could American troops shoot down women and children by the thousands? Even if they did, the follow-on assault by the remains of the Japanese army would press the invaders to the limit. Naval gunfire and close air support would probably provide the edge for victory, but imagine the slaughter. Many analysts calculated the probable death toll for the Japanese alone at two million if Japan was invaded—but they mean the entire campaign.[332] I doubt these analysts realized the Japanese had figured out the American landing area, or knew how many suicide planes, boats, and other specialized equipment the Japanese were preparing.

The US Fleet experienced problems with the Kamikazes flying from Japan to Okinawa. Defending the fleet would be much harder if the aircraft were coming in huge numbers and flying much shorter distances. In addition, the Kamikazes would be aiming at the LSTs and other thin-skinned landing ships. Such a mass killing zone would be beyond anything experienced in human history. Over a million people could have died in the landing areas alone. Assuming the Americans got ashore and moved inland, Japanese suicide attacks would certainly continue. As massive waves of humanity threw themselves against the US lines, American politicians might have rethought the conquest of Japan. At that point, a negotiated peace may have taken place with a few American concessions, one of which would have been retention of the emperor.

Truman Uses the A-Bomb

Thankfully, all this is speculation **because of the invention of the atomic bomb**. After a warning from the world-renowned physicist, Albert Einstein, that Germany was seeking an atomic bomb, President Roosevelt ordered the United States to begin development of its own bomb.[333] Unfortunately for the United States, the Soviets penetrated the small group of top scientists working on the bomb, and the secrets of the bomb were delivered to the USSR without cost or risk.

---

[332] Other calculations say 7 million Japanese would have died for 500,000Americans, but I don't know how they did the calculations. Note these totals are for deaths only, not casualties. The 2 million Japanese deaths were calculated by the American military **prior** to the planned invasion.

[333] Einstein emigrated from Germany to the United States of America before the war started. He was warned by physicist friends still in the Reich that Germany had started making heavy water, and Einstein then knew Germany was trying to manufacture an atomic bomb.

President Truman ordered the atomic bombs dropped on Japan based on his analysis of the various options available to America. Many options were considered; although, in reality, the options were seriously limited. America could try to starve everyone to death or use conventional bombardment to pound Japan into submission; however, surrender was not likely in either case because of the possible removal of the emperor and the anticipation of such conventional methods by Japan's leadership. Whether they were starved or bombed into submission, many months would pass causing perhaps millions of Japanese to suffer and die. Invasion was another course, and the one favored before the bomb emerged, except an invasion would result in innumerable deaths with both Americans and Japanese dying by the probable millions.

Truman's verdict to use the atomic bomb was the only rational course of action. The deaths of 180,000 (estimated) Japanese in the **two** atomic attacks were little compared to the slaughter required by an invasion or the suffering induced by an extended blockade starving millions. ***The atomic attacks saved millions of lives.*** Moreover, Roosevelt agreed with Stalin that the USSR would invade Japan within a few months of the German surrender. Stalin was good to his word (for once) and invaded Manchuria shortly before the United States of America used the atomic bomb on Japan. Battle wise Soviet forces rolled over the Japanese defenders with ease. They would have kept going to the coast of China, and into the Japanese home islands, if the war had not ended. After the surrender of Japan, the Soviet advance stopped leaving at least South Korea free and China still engaged in a brutal civil war, but not under Soviet control.

Some have said Truman used the bomb to demonstrate its destructive ability to Stalin. Truman clearly stated he used the bomb to end the war, and nothing else. If Truman was anything, he was a straight and plain speaker. If we take Truman at his word, we have the definitive statement from the one man who made the ultimate decision to use the bomb. Moreover, he was right to use it. It ended the most brutal war in human existence. Suppose there was an additional motive in using the bomb to show Stalin its power. If it prevented World War III, who cares? That alone would save the lives of untold millions. In my opinion, Stalin was ready to start another world war, but as long as America alone possessed the atomic bomb, he was afraid of losing. After the Soviets built their own atomic bomb, the United States responded by creating the hydrogen bomb (much larger blast), and the USSR hesitated once more. Some have opined, and it is possible knowing the history of Stalin, that Stalin planned a Third World War because he believed the United States was too weak. He further believed the USSR could take the human losses and the United States could not; however, (my opinion) those close to him learned of his idea and then poisoned him. The record of the last few hours of Stalin's life convinces me his associates did kill him, although the reasons are not clear. As history stands now, we will never know; but, *perhaps,* we should be thankful for a few men around Stalin who risked their own lives to save the world from the ultimate slaughter.

In the year 2010, so far removed from the realities of 1945, it is fashionable to fault President Truman's use of the atomic bomb. Critics' claim Japan's surrender was close, and by just waiting the United States could have saved many lives. Those making the claims are wrong. Postwar analyses of the Japanese plans disclosed there was no thought of surrender. Even after two atomic bombs were dropped, the Japanese military disavowed surrender. *Only the direct intervention of the emperor, with an unprecedented direct order by him to the heads of the military and the cabinet, ended the fighting.* The emperor was not, by tradition, to speak at cabinet meetings. He was only to attend and listen, nothing more. In the event, the emperor broke all tradition and arose, ordering the military to quit. It is doubtful the emperor could have made this move without the shock of the atomic bomb. The military men cried, and some went home and committed suicide. If the emperor had refrained from speaking, the war would have continued and untold millions would have died in China (remember the Soviet invasion), Japan, and in the American invasion forces.

The first atomic bomb was dropped on the city of **Hiroshima** on **August 6, 1945**. When no news came from Japan, Truman authorized the second bomb drop, and the city of Nagasaki was hit on August 9, 1945. Only after the detonation of the second bomb did word come from Japan that surrender was possible, but they still requested their emperor be allowed to hold his crown (it was not a condition). Truman relented and said the Japanese communication met the requirements of the Potsdam accords for unconditional surrender.

It was over. With the surrender of Japan, the fighting officially stopped, and the Second World War was at an end. A new world dawned, one much different than the last four hundred and fifty years. Europe was no longer the center of the world, and new powerful nations were emerging with weapons and methods of war changing the face of the future. The Allies celebrated as Europe and Japan smoldered, but a new war had already started. Former Allies soon confronted one another to decide what political philosophy would rule the world.

Let Us Learn

The best lesson from WWII? **Be prepared**. *If you desire peace, prepare for war.* The USA, the Great Britain, and France failed to prepare for war. Good men died in the Philippines, France, the USSR, Malaya, Pearl Harbor, and numerous other places because their nations failed to prepare for war. By wishing for the best, signing documents guaranteeing peace, and believing promises from men without morals the Western world's leadership came very close to losing everything to an evil beyond description. You cannot wish away bad people or bad situations, you must prepare for them.[334]

In your life, be prepared for the future. Keep food on hand, fire extinguishers, medical aid kits, and think over ways to survive in the event catastrophe visits you. Look to preventing the catastrophe in the first place. WWII was avoidable if France and England had enforced the Treaty of Versailles. Hitler's numerous violations allowed the Allies to intervene at many points, but they failed to interfere. If you look at what is going on around you many situations will cry out for early action, and postponement will result in much larger problems.

During your time on earth, you should compile ways of gathering good information. Discern what is happening, then react properly. Joseph Stalin rejected good information and nearly destroyed himself in the process. Don't pull a Stalin. Stalin also shot people bringing him bad news, thus, he was denied the truth when he needed it most. Encourage people to approach you with good or bad news. Reward them for accurate information. It is critical to success.

Another lesson from the Second World War; before taking action prepare thoroughly. Get all the information you can, act on the information, anticipate hardships then plan and equip for them, and keep an open mind to other possible reactions to the information. Set reasonable goals, making sure available resources can meet them. If resources are short then scale back the project, reset the goals, or assemble the necessary resources over time. Seek the right mind set for achieving your stated goals. Be consistent in your actions. If you change plans constantly, defeat will stalk you. Hitler hit the Soviets without proper planning, and he was not prepared for setbacks. He set impossible goals, and he changed the goals midstream. Hitler was guilty of false assumptions about the Soviets, and he rejected advice from highly experienced men. Hitler blew it.

---

334 See *The Gathering Storm*, Winston Churchill,1949, various publishers.

Finally, **luck** is necessary in huge undertakings. Yes, luck. It even makes a difference in small projects. Matters beyond your control must fall your way, or you will face trouble. If the Japanese had sunk the three US Pacific Fleet aircraft carriers at Pearl Harbor, as planned, the Pacific war would have changed dramatically. If the Japanese submarines or scout aircraft had spotted the US aircraft carriers earlier, Midway could have turned into a dire American defeat. If the Polish code breakers failed to escape Poland, the course of the war may have changed forever in Hitler's favor. There are numerous other examples. Luck is not something one controls (at least, that is what we hear—see Scott Adams and Dilbert for another theory), and normal mortals must sit, allowing the fates to decide. Nevertheless, it is a key factor in life. Recognize that failure is not always someone's fault. Realize events beyond the control of anyone might decide critical events and issues.

Remember, *winning is relative.* Setting proper end game goals enhance your chances of success. Good decisions, complete planning, and total commitment to reasonable goals can drive luck—at least partly—out of the equation.

You can do nothing about bad luck except struggle to rise above the circumstances. That is life. The USA was on the deck after Pearl Harbor, Bataan, Wake Island, and the Battle of the Java Sea, but America never gave up and came off the mat at the Coral Sea and Midway never to look back. Bad luck normally does not doom you; it only forces you to work harder to reach your goals.

Another great lesson is **Win the Peace**. After a conflict learn how to bring stability to the situation without embarrassing the vanquished. The best peace wins the conquered to your side, and makes them an asset.

Finally, the Second World War shows us how thin the veneer of civilization really is. The Nazi state quickly stripped away any semblance of being civilized. Normal everyday people adopted the Reich's cruelty without question or opposition. Starting with the persecutions of the Jews, gypsies, slaves, mentally ill, and many others, the German state turned its citizens into soulless barbarians, willing to murder without question. Germans accepted crushing the target groups like cockroaches. Hitler made it look easy, and that is the problem. It was easy, and if Hitler could accomplish it so can others. Humanity is only a short step away from barbarism.

BOOKS AND REFERENCES:

I have read hundreds of books on World War II. Here are a few of the best, in no particular order (* means superior):

**Cross Channel Attack,* Harrison, Gordon A., 1950, Konecky & Konecky. The best book on the D-Day landings at Normandy.

**History of the Second World War,* Hart, B.H. Liddell, 1970, Konecky & Konecky. One of the best books on WWII. Wonderful maps!

**Lost Victories: The War Memoirs of Hitler's Most Brilliant General,* von Manstein, Field Marshal Erich, 2004, Zenith Press. How the war in the east was lost, from the mouth of the man who was there.

**Miracle at Midway,* Prange, G., 1983, Penguin. A great account of the battle of Midway, easy to read, and authoritative. Considered a classic by most historians.

**The Oxford Companion to World War II,* Dear & Foot, 1995, Oxford Press. Huge reference book, probably the best general reference on WWII.

The Coming of the Third Reich, Evans, Penguin, 2005

The Third Reich in Power, Evans, Penguin, 2006

**The Two Ocean War,* Morison, Samuel Eliot, 1963, Back Bay Books. Morison can't be beat on the naval war. Please recall that Morison, like many of the early authors, did not know about Ultra, and Magic, the code breakers who did so much to win the war for the allies.

**There's A War to be Won,* Perret, Goeffrey, 1992, Ballantine books. I love this book. So much is explained so well that it is hard to overstate the importance of reading this author.

At Dawn We Slept: the Untold Story of Pearl Harbor, Prange & Goldstein, 1982, Penguin. Prange on Pearl Harbor, what more do you need to know? Gordon Prange also wrote Miracle at Midway.

Dirty Little Secrets of World War II, Dunnigan & Nofi, 1995, Morrow. Fun!

Eagle Against the Sun, Spector, Ronald H., 1985, Random House. Easy to read, and comprehensive when it comes to the Pacific War.

Guadalcanal, Frank, R.B., 1992, Penguin. This is a *must read* book if you want to understand the Pacific War, and why everything changed after this epic campaign.

How Great Generals Win, Alexander, Bevin, 1993, WW Norton & Co. Some coverage of WWII generals. Alexander's thoughts are always worth reading.

How Wars are Won, The 13 Rules of War from Ancient Greece to the War on Terror, Alexander, Bevin, 2002, Three Rivers Press.

Miracle at Midway, Prange,G., 1983, Penguin

Panzer Battles, von Mellenthin, FW, 1956, Konecky & Konecky

The Gathering Storm, Churchill, W., 1986, Mariner Books

The Pacific War Companion, From Pearl Harbor to Hiroshima, ed. Marston, D., 2005, Osprey Publishing

The Rise and Fall of the Third Reich, Shirer, William, 1990, Simon & Schuster. A classic, but somewhat difficult to read. None-the-less, there are few better books on the regime.

The Rommel Papers, Rommel, Erwin, 1982, Da Capo Press

The Second World War 1939-1945, Fuller, J.C.F., 1948, Da Capo Press. Yet another must read book on WWII by an outstanding English analyst.

The Shattered Sward, The Untold Story of the Battle of Midway, Pershall and Tully, 2005, Potomac Books. Excellent book, somewhat controversial.

The United States Strategic Bombing Survey, Greenwood, 1946 (also available on line). First hand information, great statics, well written.

The US Army in World War II, The Fall of the Philippines, The War in the Pacific, Roberts, Greenfield general editor, 1953, National Historical Society. This is a series of books on the US Army in the Pacific War. Excellent detailed analysis of each campaign, but detail on other services and their role is small, and the impact of Ultra and Magic is missing because of the date of publication.

The World At Arms, The Reader's Digest Illustrated History of World War II, Wright, Michael editor, 1989, The Reader's Digest Association Limited. Excellent and pithy account of the world wide struggle.

War Plan Orange, The US Strategy to Defeat Japan 1897-1945, Miller, Edward S., 1991, Naval Institute Press. Surprising analysis of the Pacific War, and how the US planned for the conflict.

Wikipedia, the on line encyclopedia. Look under World War II or the various subject headings, such as: Pearl Harbor, D-Day et al.

The Pearl Harbor Papers: Inside the Japanese Plans, Prange, Gordon W. (1999), Brassey's, ISBN 1574882228

Churchill, Hitler, and the Unnecessary War, Buchanan Crown Publisher, 2009.

Chapter 16

The Cold War 1945 to 1989

The Cold War dominated the time between the end of World War II and 1990. The USSR and the United States of America held the trump cards, nuclear bombs and missiles. The two nations controlled the fate of the world in the sense that they controlled whether the world would come to an abrupt end. While the Cold War progressed so did society which went on as if the threat of nuclear obliteration was just an apparition. The Space Race, computer development, superhighway construction, jet airliner development, the creation of an international phone system, the advent of television, enormous progress in medicine, and the creation of mass consumerism—among many other things—all played a part in the world that developed after World War II. However, much of the world progressed poorly compared to the Western Democracies. In Africa, India, Asia, and the Middle East, colonialism was in its last throws and transitioning to new ways of governance was rough. Hundreds of wars accompanied by mass killing marred the world emerging from eighteenth century colonialism. Nothing has been easy in this ongoing birth of a modern world.

The Cold War began immediately after World War II concluded, or perhaps even before, and ended when the Berlin Wall was torn down in 1989. There is little doubt that President Franklin D. Roosevelt wanted a world based on a sizeable level of trust between the United States and the Soviet Union. For reasons that are hard to determine, he trusted the dictator and murderer of millions, Joseph Stalin. Winston Churchill tried to warm up to Stalin, but quickly discerned Stalin was not trustworthy. He saw that Roosevelt was falling for the duplicitous Stalin's words of compromise and attempted to warn Roosevelt, but to no avail.

At war's end, Roosevelt was no longer the president of the United States, and Churchill was no longer the prime minister of Great Britain. Roosevelt died in the last months of the war and Churchill was voted out of office. The new men, Truman as president of the United States and Atlee as prime minister of Great Britain, took over where their predecessors left off. As for Truman, he was in the dark about everything. The atomic bomb was news to him. Roosevelt had told him nothing; as a result, Truman was on his own when confronting the problems of a new world filled with massive armies and atomic weapons.

One of Truman's first decisions was to drop the atomic bomb on Japan in an attempt to end the war. Some have said it was the first act of the Cold War, designed to show Stalin the power possessed by the United States, and to deter a Soviet attack on Western Europe. Truman, however, said he used the atomic bomb to end World War II.

The Cold War was going to be something entirely new for planet Earth. Actions in the international arena were not what they might seem to be. Some event may have a hundred starting points, no real end point, and what actually occurred might be foggy at best and denied by everyone in every government everywhere. It is very hard to tell the history of something so close in time when a lot of emotional baggage is still around and documents are all but impossible to come by in some cases. The Cold War was fought with technology, spies, and nerves. Clandestine operations were often the key to everything, and secret operations are not disclosed by most governments until many years have passed—if ever.

Economics played a large part in the Cold War. In Europe, with US help, a recovery without precedent took place between the end of the war and 1970. The recovery rate in the output of goods exceeded 200 percent. In 1957 France, Italy, and Germany led the way in starting a customs union, the European Economic Community. This union was the precursor of the European Union. In Asia, Japan's economy boomed with the Korean War era, and with American help Japan grew to a superpower, in economic terms anyway. The economic gap between the Soviet and American systems consistently widened during the entire Cold War period.

Soon after World War II, Winston Churchill, always good with a phrase, said that an **iron curtain** had fallen across Eastern Europe. He was more right than he may have imagined. Once the Soviets were in control of an area, no one and no information came out of that area again. Stalin, the so-called man of steel, had placed an iron curtain over his empire and that curtain would hang about until 1989.

Before and during World War II the Soviet Union developed clandestine cells and placed them throughout the world with the idea of spreading the communist revolution through subversion and violence. If these revolutions took control of many small nations, and perhaps a few large ones, the communists would control the world de facto if not directly. They also placed spies at the highest levels of governments all over the world. The Soviets were masters of the game and managed to insert spies into the uppermost levels of the Nazi, Japanese, British, and American governments. In the case of the American and British governments they penetrated to the heart of the espionage communities and even the counterespionage units of these democracies.

Communist spies in the American nuclear development program stole the secrets of the atomic bomb and the hydrogen bomb, and gave them to the Soviets. The Soviets recruited many spies from the ranks of Britain's top universities, mainly on ideological grounds, and simply waited until they entered the premier levels of government or technological work to extract secrets from them. The USSR placed spies at high levels of US Policy determination, in the US Treasury, and in many other important positions in the military and government bureaucracy. They even penetrated the American CIA and FBI, thereafter using these human resources to track what America knew about Soviet spies and to uncover American spies in the USSR. One spy was in the US Nuclear Submarine program and delivered to the Soviets complete details on how the US Navy was building super quiet submarines that were following the Soviet subs effectively. After these details were absorbed by the Soviets the United States could no longer track Soviet submarines, and many of these were nuclear missile submarines—also copied from American technological plans.

Throughout the Cold War the Americans were at a significant disadvantage in clandestine operations; and the Soviets easily matched the West's technological miracles by simply stealing the technology. This saved the Soviets billions of dollars in development costs. It also kept the Soviets at par with the West militarily. Not only did the Soviets steal plans, they stole many of the actual technological units. As the Cold War progressed into the 1980s, President Reagan used this Soviet ability against the USSR by allowing them to steal purposely planted defective parts and computer chips used for operating complex equipment. Because the parts were designed to be defective and for the defect to be nearly impossible to unearth, tremendous damage was done to critical Soviet operations, such as their Siberian oil pipeline, by component failures. It was one of the very few American espionage successes during the Cold War.

The Cold War brought the United States and the Soviet Union into a dangerous and deadly arms race. Each nation constructed more and larger nuclear warheads, better missile delivery systems, better jet bombers and fighters, and a lot more. Submarines showed dramatic improvements, which included the ability for one ship to launch up to *sixteen* nuclear-armed missiles while submerged. These missiles were intercontinental ballistic missiles (ICBM) carrying multiple independently targetable nuclear warheads. Each ICBM could carry up to ten warheads and each were capable of being sent to a different target. One missile could annihilate up to ten objectives. The Soviets constructed larger warheads, up to twenty megatons (twenty million tons of TNT), which was far more than the ten-kiloton bomb (ten thousand tons of TNT) that leveled Hiroshima. These multiple warhead ICBMs were installed on missile submarines thereby enabling one submarine to bring nuclear devastation to 160 targets.

As the Soviet warheads grew in power, the United States constructed hardened underground missile silos with the capability to withstand an atomic blast and still fire back. America maintained a number of B-52 bombers aloft at all times to enable them to attack the Soviet Union after an atomic attack on the United States and its airfields. The United States also placed missiles into mobile launchers and constantly drove them around the nation to make targeting them all but impossible. Another tool in the arsenal of second strike capability was the so-called doomsday tapes. It is said the hardened missile silos had computers which, once enabled, would fire their missiles at some predetermined future date even if everyone in the silo (or even the United States) was dead. As eerie as it may sound, everyone on earth could be dead from the nuclear war and months or years later the computers would still be launching continued atomic attacks on smoldering enemy landscapes.

The entire point to all of this military expenditure on the American side was to ensure the ability to strike back at the USSR after a surprise atomic attack on the United States. Much of this fear of a surprise attack was left over from Pearl Harbor and the resolve of the United States to never allow that kind of attack to happen again. In addition, the United States did not trust the Soviets or Stalin. They equated Stalin to Hitler, and the United States was determined to avoid any hint of appeasement. The name for this fantastic deterrent capability held by the Soviets and the United States was **Mutually Assured Destruction** (*MAD*). [335]A fitting name, but what was

[335] Older computers operated off magnetic tape systems. The large rolls of magnetic tape, such as seen on reel-to-reel tape recorders, held the data and the instructions for operating the computer. No floppy disks or CDs in 1955.

amazing about the entire philosophy is—it worked. War itself was not banned by the atomic bomb; however, no nuclear exchange has taken place (yet) so a crazy sounding policy has worked for sixty-five plus years.

From 1945 to 2010, the United States of America exercised a strong stabilizing force on the world. For over fifty years the USA held the line against communism, aggression, and instability. In 2010, forces within the nation are eroding its ability to stand firm against new threats. As the United States shrinks from its former position of insuring stability the world will go through many changes akin to the withdrawal of Great Britain from the world stage after 1945, but with no nation to step into the void as a replacement. Instability and chaos may well result from the resulting world realignment.

TRUMAN: NEOPHYTE COLD WARRIOR

1945 to 1952

Truman adopted a policy of *containment* regarding the Soviet Union and the communist threat. George Kennan, a State Department analyst, outlined this policy in 1947. Kennan assumed the Soviet Union would do everything in its power to spread communism. The purpose of the containment policy was to stop the USSR from spreading communism through invasion or subversion. To forward this policy, Truman gave aid to Greece in its war against communist insurgents, instituted the Marshall Plan to revitalize Western Europe, helped reconstruct West Germany to offset Soviet power, and fought the Korean War to repel a communist invasion. His problems included the loss of China to the Reds, large numbers of Soviet spies in the US Government and military, and his failure to remain ready to fight conventional wars.

During the Truman administration an American senator, Joe McCarthy, started a well publicized "commie hunt" within the US Government. Many of his accusations were challenged at the time, but a short window of opportunity opened for US intelligence when they broke the Soviet codes and began uncovering information about Soviet spies in the United States. The **Verona decrypts** proved many communist spies were operating at high levels of the US Government and intelligence services. This window was closed when a Soviet spy operating *within this most secret unit* discovered the decrypts and the Soviets changed their codes. The press and the liberal establishment vilified McCarthy, and his name is still used as a weapon against anyone wanting to throw a wide net in search of traitors or spies. For some reason he is often associated with the House Un-American Activities Committee, but McCarthy was a US Senator and was *not* part of the House committee.

In 1949, Truman failed to prevent the communist takeover of China. *One of the greatest political, diplomatic, military, and strategic failures in modern history was the loss of China to Mao Zedong and the communists.* The Kuomintang Army of General Chiang Kai-shek was corrupt to the core and a poor fighting unit by any measure; however, General Chiang Kai-shek was far better than any communist regime. At one point, the Kuomintang Army was about to crush Mao Zedong and his communists in spite of Soviet aid, but the United States stepped in and prevented what should have been the final assault on Mao. This American cease-fire let the communists regroup and then survive the attacks of Chiang. All of this was orchestrated by General George Marshall, famous for leading the US military throughout World War II, and the Marshall Plan that saved Europe from economic collapse after WWII. Somehow, his key role in the communist's victory in China is ignored by history. (*The Korean War is covered in another section.*)

The fall of China to communism produced the Korean War, the Vietnam War, and a lot of international tension over Taiwan. The communists also conquered Tibet, oppressing and slaughtering its people by claiming it was part of China, and thereafter moved Chinese settlers into the region. In fact, Tibet was not and had not been part of China for centuries. The invasion went unnoticed by the West as Western media and governments ignored what was happening. Even today communist China is a major threat to the West. Red China opened its economy to some capitalist ways and it has prospered beyond all expectation; however, Red China and its leaders are still communist dictators who have taken the lives of millions in their quest for power. They will stop at nothing to keep themselves in power. Human life is not now, nor has it ever been, something to worry about for the communists. Human beings are alive to serve the state and no other reason. *The sole purpose in life under a communist regime is service to the state.* These malefic dictators are no different than Stalin or Hitler, except for their extreme subtleness in presenting themselves to the world.

Truman did move dramatically in Europe in the aftermath of WWII. Europe was desolate, Germany was prostrate, and America was disarming rapidly. It was a recipe for disaster because the Soviet Union maintained its military power and Stalin awaited his chance to acquire the devastated area (he already had Eastern Europe). The communists could prevail by winning elections or subverting governments or waging guerrilla war. Stalin could "win" Western Europe without an invasion, and the attendant risk of a nuclear war, with subversive activities. Communist cells worked to convince the populace of Europe that capitalism had failed so they should turn to the East and communism to find a prosperous and peaceful future. The Americans sent General George Marshall to study the situation and he returned with a radical idea. The United States would have to rebuild Western Europe to save itself and democracy.

Before the war's end, America and England studied ways to de-industrialize Germany because it had started the two worst wars in history. They would turn the warlike nation into pastureland so it could never start another world conflagration.[336] After the war, both England and the United States realized that without West Germany the weakened states of Western Europe would crumble before a Soviet assault; thus, the decision was made to keep West Germany a strong industrialized nation to offset the impressive power of the USSR. If there was an invasion, fighting the Soviets from the moment they crossed the iron curtain was crucial; therefore, West Germany became the front line.[337]

The United States initiated the **Marshall Plan**, named for Secretary of State George Marshall (sec state 1947-1949; former general), giving Western Europe millions of US dollars to rebuild its infrastructure and military organizations. A similar effort was undertaken in Japan. This was an incredible break with history. Think of it, at the end of the Second World War, the worst war in human history, the United States of America rebuilt its friends *and its enemies* with millions of dollars that no one had to pay back. Never before in history had a nation fought a terrible war to a victorious end, rebuilt its enemies at its expense, and then left demanding nothing. The normal course of action was to conquer and stay or conquer and demand massive repatriations from the conquered people (WWI). The Marshall plan worked and Western Europe rose from the wreckage of war in a startling recovery that included West Germany becoming one of the world's economic leaders. The United States and Western Europe formed NATO (the North Atlantic Treaty Organization) which was a mutual

---

336 Remember, England and America believed the Germans had started World War I and World War II.

337 Given the size and combat power of the USSR, the only way to stop a Soviet advance was the atomic bomb.

defense alliance for protection against the Soviets and their eastern bloc allies. Recall the US tried to stay out of the last two wars so Europe had trust issues about American entry if the Soviets invaded. To convince Western Europe the United States would fight upon a Soviet invasion US troops were stationed there so Americans would be dying the instant a war began guaranteeing an immediate US entry into the conflict.

These plans worked and they worked very well. Truman and his administration performed admirably to secure the freedom of Western Europe won at such great cost during World War II. These administrative victories were critical in keeping Western Europe free from Soviet hegemony. Had even a few nations, such as Italy or Greece, gone communist and allied with the Soviets, the Cold War's difficulties would multiply making victory problematical. Western Europe remained in democracy's camp allowing the west to prevail in the Cold War.

In Japan, General MacArthur ran the nation as a virtual dictator (right up his ally). He was assigned to oversee the occupation and rebuilding of Japan after the war, and in this role he was masterful. With help from the Americans, and the Korean War, Japan rebuilt in record time to become the *second most prosperous nation on earth* by 1980 or so. Truman's policies helped immensely in rebuilding the Japanese nation. In drafting their postwar constitution the Japanese renounced war and decided to keep only a small national defense force for protection. Actually, the United States of America provided, and still provides, the military protection for Japan. This policy allowed Japan's economy to expand without the expensive burden of a large military force to slow it down (Remember Sun Tzu?). Instead, America adopted the burden of protecting Japan and Europe, as well as a number of other areas. Today, the nations of Europe and the Japanese can well afford to protect themselves, but as of 2010, the United States continues to supply military protection for Europe, Japan, and much of the world.

From 1945 to 1952, the Western Democracies made substantial economic progress. After WWII, the military downsized and the US economy began an expansion that was accompanied by low inflation and increasing trade with its old friends, England and its colonies, and its new friends, Germany and Japan. TV was just coming on the line and its impact would be massive. From the early start in black-and-white to the wide-screen color monsters of the 21st Century the influence of those blinking screens has been phenomenal.

The United States and its old allies (minus the USSR and China) tried to keep free trade alive, and tried to use the **United Nations** to advance a new view of the world which included collective security and a march toward the eradication of ignorance, discrimination, disease, and hunger. The UN was much like the post WWI League of Nations, but its charter gave it a bit more clout. Still, the Security Council was required to approve any action using force and one no vote could kill taking action. During the Truman and Eisenhower years the world acted as if it was on the side of the West, when in fact this was only a tactic to keep the might of the Western Democracies off the backs of the petty dictators and warlords who wanted the world to go on as it always had, leaving them with absolute power over their populations. As time moved forward, the petty nations of the world began to vote in favor of the communist super states turning the idea of an international organization for peace and progress on its head. The dream of world cooperation actually died with the League, but somehow its demanding corpse staggers on. Originally an American idea, it was an idealistic concept by President Wilson who failed in selling it to his own countrymen. Reviving it after WW II was probably a quixotic error, pushed by an optimistic concept that the world was becoming a new place. It did not become a new place after WWII, just a different place with the same problems of greed and desperation. Human nature remains forever the same.

EISENHOWER: CAREFUL COLD WARRIOR

1952 to 1960

Truman left office with the Cold War, the arms race, and the Korean War boiling on. Eisenhower, the general leading the Allied forces in Europe during WWII, became president of the United States in 1952. He inherited a nearly worthless, out-of-control intelligence community. Eisenhower thought his failure to reign in the CIA (Central Intelligence Agency) was one of his most significant defeats while in office. Under Eisenhower, the United States assured the world it would use the atomic bomb to deter aggression; however, this was a false promise and the communist world knew it. In many areas of the world the United States, through the CIA, supported petty murdering dictators for whom honest elections were an anathema. The CIA was afraid the communist, or at least left-wing radicals, would win an election and anything was better than an anti-USA communist government.

During the Cold War, the United States sent millions of dollars to support oppressive right-wing military dictatorships solely because they opposed communism.

The US commitment to Europe by Truman under the Marshall Plan prevented a potential communist takeover. Eisenhower continued all these policies and encouraged NATO to remain strong in its opposition to communism. The growth of European economies helped the US economy stay strong through the Eisenhower years. Eisenhower tried to reduce government spending, and he tried to reduce government's size. In this he was somewhat successful.

Nonetheless, the communists were very good at starting guerrilla wars and overthrowing governments, especially in nations made up of peasants. The communist promise of free land and a non-corrupt government struck a chord with many peasants throughout the world. Communist revolutionaries are generally fanatics, but have good rapport with villagers and rural groups supporting a revolutionary movement. As long as the population supported the communists no total victory was likely by the national government, and defeat was always a possibility as the insurgents gained backing and power. Where villages refused to support the revolution the village elders were murdered and replaced by communist revolutionaries. *It was a simple equation to the communist fanatics, join the revolution or die.* Most governments in rural farming nations had problems controlling outlying areas in the best of circumstances, and, as the villagers turned communist, control became impossible. The fact that America's CIA, usually without the knowledge of the State Department, paid off right-wing thugs to stave off communists was an evil necessity to the intelligence community trying to thwart world communism. Besides, the communists were murdering people and it was necessary to strike back.

Because of the deep penetration of US and British intelligence services by the Soviets (and probably others), using humans to spy for the US proved impossible. Accordingly, the Americans turned to their trump card: technology. By combining outstanding cameras with a high-flying aircraft the United States fabricated the U-2, one of the most successful spy aircraft in history. With this aircraft the United States could overfly the Soviet Union and photograph their military installations at will. Initially, the Soviets possessed no aircraft or missiles capable of reaching the high-flying U-2. These flights worked very well for a few years, but as time went on the missions became increasingly dangerous. In 1960, the Soviets shot down a

U-2 and captured its pilot Gary F. Powers. It was another costly defeat for US intelligence services.[338]

Technology continued to be the American's best option for intelligence, although it was poor second to human information gathering. The Americans developed spy satellites with cameras that had the phenomenal ability to see enemy activity in great detail from outer space. Eisenhower demanded that the United States develop spy satellites. Before he left office the first spy satellite was put into orbit, code named ***Corona***. The *Corona* spy satellite's first film drop gave the United States more intelligence on the Soviet Union than all the U-2 flights combined. The first satellites dropped film back to Earth to be developed; however, the Americans soon constructed satellites that would beam the information back to Earth in digital form with as much detail as before. It was a stupendous achievement, but it was top secret. Later, the United States developed the SR-71, another spy aircraft, that flew so fast and high the Soviets never found an effective countermeasure. America's undersea operations also produced wonderful results as US submarines managed to tap into Soviet undersea communication cables. As the United States could not break Soviet or Chinese codes they had to achieve a connection to a communication source thought to be safe by their antagonist so information would be transmitted in the clear (no code). The US submarine force's achievement was near unbelievable, and it gleaned information for years, but it was discovered by yet *another Soviet spy* in one of the most top-secret posts of the US Naval Service.

During the Eisenhower administration a new world threat was incubating. Radical Muslim groups committed to an ideology of hate developed by Parisian Muslims before World War II began attracting converts. These Muslims absorbed Hitler's ideas and fascism, especially his hatred of Jews. The fanatics thought a fascist style government operated to spread fundamentalist Islamic ideology was perfect for reuniting Muslims around the world and forming a caliphate to control the Middle East. All this Muslim fundamental philosophy and theology was given a big push with the creation of Israel in 1948. The Islamic world exploded, and war was immediately declared on the new Jewish state. Israel beat its Muslim

---

[338] Eisenhower was extremely worried about the last flight and reluctantly gave the OK after CIA assurances it was still relatively safe. The aircraft suffered an engine flame out causing Powers to descend to try a re-start, and the Soviets were able to reach him before he could adjust back to his safe altitude.

opponents rather soundly and established its new nation with additional territory won in wars against its aggressive neighbors. Many Palestinians left the state of Israel, becoming a homeless mob of seething hatred spreading throughout the adjoining states of Trans Jordan, Lebanon, and Syria.

This Palestinian question still haunts the world, and calls for an independent Palestinian state will continue; however, the Muslim nations surrounding Israel have never offered these refugees a national home. It appears they are political pawns in a much larger game being played out on the world stage. The Muslim elites seem to think this human vat of boiling revulsion for Israel is something to be used for political advantage rather than a group of human beings needing a place to live, a place easily provided by Saudi Arabia or Syria, but which has not and will not be offered. Having the international community in an uproar over the Palestinians helps with the condemnation of Israel, thus, the Palestinians stay homeless.

The establishment of Israel and the rise of fundamentalist Islam is a formula ensuring eternal religious conflict. When Muslim nations failed militarily against Israel, the fundamentalists Muslims argued that their god (Allah) was against them and only by following his express commands with fervor could the Muslims attain "victory." This fundamentalist thinking struck a chord with many Muslims, and a radical form of the Muslim religion was embraced. It would take a while, but the Islamic fundamentalist would eventually fly aircraft into the World Trade Center and the Pentagon on September 11, 2001. This thinking spawned **terrorism** and the immoral attacks on anyone not part of the terrorists' religious group, including other Muslims. The main target was Israel and its supporters, the United States and Britain. Hijacking cruise ships and airliners enabled the terrorists to achieve many of their goals: world recognition of their cause, release of captured comrades, and money. Since murder, bombings, kidnapping, and hijacking worked the terrorist kept using terrorism.

But in 1950, terrorism's irrational and asymmetrical threat was down the line, many years away. Until then, the main goal of the West in the Cold War was stopping the communists from conquering the world.

Eisenhower left office in 1960, warning about the military industrial complex, but his warning went unheeded. As the new president, **John F. Kennedy** came into office, new programs and weapons were coming off the assembly line of the military industrial complex that kept the United States militarily ahead of the communist nations. Kennedy won a critical

1960 debate with his opponent Richard Nixon, and one point concerned where the United States should fight for freedom. Kennedy stated that every inch of "free" soil must be defended. This led Kennedy into Vietnam and later—under his successor Lyndon Johnson—a complete commitment to Vietnam. History seems to say that the better argument was made by Nixon who had stated that the United States must choose its conflicts carefully, and not every inch of free soil needed defending (see the Vietnam War for more information). Nixon was giving the world a seasoned diplomat's view of foreign policy which focused on *vital national interests* and not on an ideology of defending everywhere all the time.

During the Truman and Eisenhower years the United States, Western Europe, and the Western Democracies had good economic times. After a slight recession in 1948, the advance to economic prosperity began. In the 1950's the GDP (Gross Domestic Product—the measure of a nation's economic vigor) doubled, and it doubled again in the 1960's. Eisenhower established NASA (National Aeronautical and Space Administration) and the Federal Housing Administration to help people purchase new homes. The US Military was guarding Europe and Japan, and the United States was developing the first ICBMs to guard the West from Soviet intimidation. With inflation rates of 2 or 3 percent, low oil prices, and a growing economy with Europe and Japan as major trading partners, and massive spending on improving the infrastructure of the nation, the US Economy continued to expand in spite of rather large military expenditures. It was during the 1950's that megacities began to form. The urban mass of New York, Boston, and Washington DC joined together to form one continuous city. Of course, no one joined the governments, which caused a lot of problems, but there was no doubt the phenomenon would be repeated in the US and throughout the world. As the megacities rose up so did the complexity of governing such a vast urban area that crossed jurisdictional lines. The problems created by this mass amalgamation have not yet been solved. Perhaps no solution exists.

While Eisenhower did try to reduce the size of the US government he was only partially successful. By the time Ike left office in 1960, TV was commonplace in the United States and Western European homes, the interstate highway system was being planned in the United States, and Europe itself was growing ever more economically and militarily powerful. France declared its independence from the United States and Britain by leaving NATO in 1966, developing its own atomic bomb and building up its military capabilities while struggling to maintain its old empire. Britain realized the days of empire were over and started a precipitous dismantling of its ancient empire, abandoning its control over millions of people worldwide.

The British decision to scuttle its empire was a bold one brought on by necessity. The people of England were morally opposed to the continuation of the old order and Britain was stumbling economically. Two world wars bankrupted the nation and it struggled to stay afloat. England would survive, however, it was not an easy transition from the world's greatest empire to just the United Kingdom. England's ability to influence world affairs was shrinking, and this required the United States of America to step in and take its place representing the Western Democracies around the world. For this to occur, America had to end its isolationist tendencies and enter into the unforgiving world of international relations where, as the leading nation, it would take endless flack for its decisions. The United States was not used to this role and the transition to a world leader was not easy for a nation wanting to being left alone.

Internally, America was going to face its own upheaval when the **civil rights** movements got underway in the late 1950s. The majority of white Americans disliked the way the southern states treated black Americans, but the issue was ignored for decades. Finally, blacks brought attention to their plight and America responded. This crusade against the bigots of the South was going to consume a large amount of time and energy. What no one could foresee was this struggle bringing as much bad as good. Victory over the discriminatory laws of several southern states should have brought harmony within the nation and a satisfaction in the expansion of liberty to minorities; however, the opposite occurred as black America decided the United States was a worthless country and not worth supporting. Violence did not decrease as the civil rights movement went on, it increased. Even after numerous laws and court decisions supported the black cause, blacks refused to rejoice in the progress made. Rather, they obsessed over getting more, or getting even, for past wrongs.

Meanwhile, the progress of technology continued apace. New smaller electronics were reaching consumers each year and progress in new kitchen and home devices of every type was commonplace. Everywhere in the West things were getting better—at least on the home front. Women were employed in increasing numbers and industrial expansion was accelerating. Even with the growing challenge from the East, the West was feeling it was superior.

KENNEDY: RISK-TAKING COLD WARRIOR

1960-November 1963

Kennedy addressed the Cold War in an aggressive way. He managed to get himself into the 1961 Bay of Pigs invasion of communist Cuba by former Cuban exiles(an absolute failure), and he allowed his brother, the attorney general Robert Kennedy, to run secret wars against Castro (the Cuban dictator) as well as other communists in Latin America. There were some successes; however, Kennedy soon came to realize the American intelligence services were hollow. Without good information making good decisions regarding the Soviet Union and other challenges abroad was difficult.

The CIA missed the Soviets' placing missiles into its client state of Cuba. The director of the CIA predicted, with no evidence, the USSR might try this gambit; however, such a move could start World War Three and no one thought the Soviets would risk it. However, the Soviets did make the move in 1962. Photos taken by a U-2 over flight and examined by a good analyst uncovered the evidence, but the missiles were already in the country by the time the CIA informed Kennedy of their presence. By careful analysis and more extremely dangerous over flights (one U-2 was shot down and its pilot lost) the United States ascertained that the missiles were armed with nuclear warheads. Messages to Moscow failed to elicit the desired response so Kennedy declared a blockade of Cuba and sent the US Navy to sea with orders to intercept Soviet ships sailing for Cuba with missiles for their Cuban arsenal.[339] As one might expect, the blockade triggered an international crisis while the United States and the Soviets sparred with one another behind the scenes.

Eventually, a deal was worked out whereby the United States would agree to never invade Cuba and to remove its nuclear missiles from Turkey. In exchange, the USSR would remove its missiles from Cuba. The communists won all around. John Kennedy and his brother Robert were adamant that no details about the removal of missiles from Turkey be leaked. As presented by the press the crisis was an American victory. The truth was unknown

---

339 The blockade did not get rid of the missiles that were already there, but at least he was "doing something." Americans like action. Sitting doesn't please Americans when problems arise.

for years. If it had leaked in 1962, Kennedy and the democrats might have lost the 1964 election.

The Cuban missile crisis was indirectly caused by the CIA's failure to discover the movement of Soviet nuclear-tipped missiles into Cuba. The direct cause was Kennedy himself. **Khrushchev**, the leader of the Soviet Union, had met Kennedy and decided he was not tough; that is, he could be bluffed if Khrushchev remained strong. It was a close call for the world because Khrushchev misread the American president, the US military, and the American people. The US military was lobbying for war after the missiles were discovered and Kennedy and his brother Robert had a hard time holding them in check. Because the two leaders of the USSR and the United States misread one another an atomic exchange leading to worldwide devastation became a real possibility.

This was always the ultimate danger in the Cold War, that someone would make an error, or a series of errors, leading to an unintended atomic war. Some experts worried about a diplomatic error, leading one superpower to think the other planned an attack or an error by one leader making a foolish read of the other's intentions and launching a pre-emptive atomic strike. Others worried about human error at the machines, because the missiles and aircraft armed with nuclear devices were ready to launch at a moment's notice. Both sides, America and the Soviets, were hit by surprise attacks in World War II that severely harmed their military capabilities. Both sides were determined not to let it happen again. This put the two sides on a nuclear hair trigger, and the trigger men on both sides were nervous. It might be a miracle the world came through this long period of threat unscathed by the nukes, but a lot of people in both governments put in many sleepless nights keeping the world safe from its ultimate destruction. Either side had the ability to destroy the entire world hundreds of times over; consequently, if either side launched the world was gone. It was a lot of people never taking their eyes off the ball that kept the Cold War from becoming World War III and both sides won on that score.

President Kennedy did not finish his term of office. He was murdered riding in a motorcade in Dallas, Texas, on November 22, 1963. The man who allegedly killed President Kennedy, Lee Harvey Oswald, was murdered in the Dallas police station on November 24, 1963, by strip club owner Jack Ruby. The Warren Commission, established by order of President Johnson (who was vice president when Kennedy was assassinated), investigated the assassination. Under the guidance of Chief Justice Earl Warren of the US Supreme Court the Commission concluded Oswald murdered the president as a lone gunman. They further concluded that Jack Ruby killed Oswald because he assassinated Kennedy.

The findings of the Commission were immediately challenged and numerous conspiracy theories continue to circulate even today (2010). Conspiracy theorists believe Oswald shot the president in the back and claim the bullet hitting President Kennedy in the head was fired from the front of the car rather than Oswald's position behind Kennedy. The Warren Commission found that Oswald fired the fatal shots from a third floor window in the Dallas book depository building. Amateur film taken of the assassination appears to show the president's head being pushed back and to his left (as viewed from the front of the car) when the bullet struck. The conspiracy theorists believe the government covered up the crime to protect someone or something of great importance.[340] It is certain that critical evidence was lost and suffered from tampering. Photographs of the Kennedy emergency room operation and autopsy are missing as are parts of his brain that were supposed to be retained. Stranger still, the missing photographs are said to be the very ones that could prove if the killing shot came from the front or the back of the president. The missing brain matter could also prove what kind of bullet hit the president. What really happened that day in Dallas may never be conclusively known,

---

340 Some interesting side notes: the day Kennedy was shot an investigator was briefing powerful republican lawmakers on financial misdeeds of Vice President Johnson, and a Mr. Baker, previously associated with Johnson's political team, was running a prostitution ring that included call girls that had "visited" President Kennedy, Vice-President Johnson, and many top democrat leaders in Washington DC. After Johnson became president, he killed the investigation through the committee the investigators were reporting to. On a straight party line vote the democrat lawmakers on the committee voted to stop the investigation—and they had the votes to make it stick. It is now clear that President Kennedy had been seeing prostitutes while he was president, and one of them was an east German spy. Also, Kennedy had let it be known that Johnson would not be on the ticket as vice-president in 1964. It is not a secret that Johnson despised the Kennedy clan, especially Robert Kennedy the attorney general. Johnson had been the most powerful man in Washington, and was still a tremendous force in Texas his home state. Many conspiracy buffs think it is compelling evidence that Kennedy was assassinated in Dallas, Texas, where Johnson was all but a king. Many of the conspiracy theories trace the murder back to Johnson, whose hatred for the Kennedy brothers was fierce, who did not want to be forced out of the government, who did not want to be exposed as a criminal or a user of call girls, and had powerful friends in Texas who wanted more business directed to the Lone Star State.

but the Warren Commission's investigation was sloppy and contained many unstated assumptions and flaws that caused people to conclude a government cover-up had occurred.

The Kennedy assassination was a blow to the upbeat nature of the nation. The 1950s was an era of growth and change, but the changes were moderate. The death of Kennedy threw a wet blanket on the times and the message was things were not as they once were. The newspapers were full of reports about the war in Vietnam, small as it was, and the continuing strife of the civil rights movement. The Space Race was proceeding and even there it seemed the communists were winning. Nonetheless, prosperity was evident, and the future seemed to promise more of the same. Europe started talking about a new organization, a kind of economic United States of Europe, where trade barriers would come down and laws could be homogenized. France was pushing the idea as they believed they would be the natural leader of any such organization, thus, enabling a further distancing from America and its inordinate influence on European affairs.

Most European states were unhappy with the US involvement in Vietnam, and they resisted pressure to fight the communist assault on the South. The world had larger problems, they thought, and a lot of those problems were just to the east of Europe as the Soviet Union gained economic and military power.

Lyndon B. Johnson: Worthless Cold Warrior

November 1963-1968

After Kennedy's assassination, Lyndon B. Johnson became president. Johnson, who had been a leader of Congress for years, had large plans. He launched the "War on Poverty," "War on Crime," and many other social wars for his "**Great Society**"; however, he did all this while engaging in and massively expanding a real shooting war in Vietnam. Johnson, who witnessed the importance of price controls during World War II, stated that the nation would enjoy both "**guns and butter**" with his administration. This statement illustrates an unrivaled irrationality. Wars bring inflation, normally on a massive scale; thus, governments move to inhibit inflation by imposing wage and price controls at the outset of a conflict. Discovered in World War I, this was not a secret and wage and price controls were immediately initiated in World

War II. Johnson knew all of this and chose to ignore it (he also ignored his economists).

The predictable result of this economic policy was massive inflation and economic stagnation. The impacts on the American economy were intensely negative which affected the Cold War. With America focused on Vietnam the troops and equipment in Europe, and other areas, languished. The Soviets upheld the peace, but if they had struck the US Army and its European Allies would have faced conquest from the east. All over the world communists were making progress in their insurgencies because the attention of the United States was on Vietnam. Johnson failed at fighting the Vietnam War and the Cold War. During his final years in office antiwar protests swept the nation. As the press turned against him Johnson watched his presidency implode.

We will handle Vietnam in a special section.

President Johnson began what he termed the Great Society which was a bundle of welfare programs designed to pull the poor out of poverty, decrease crime, improve education, and otherwise make the United States into the true workers' paradise he thought it could be. The megacities continued to grow and during the 1970's and the urban welfare programs did not alleviate the problems. All these Great Society programs were costly failures. His expensive programs, plus the Vietnam War, led to massive inflation coupled with an economic contraction. Presidents must make good decisions, and Johnson made some of the worst decisions in the history of the US presidency. He failed as few others have.[341]

---

341 In my opinion, he will end up as the worst US president in the 20th Century and perhaps the worst president in the history of the United States, at least up to 2010.

NIXON: WINNING COLD WARRIOR

1968 to August 1974

The antiwar movement, rallying around Robert F. Kennedy for president, drove Johnson from office; however, after winning the California primary in 1968, which all but guaranteed him the democratic presidential nomination, a Muslim terrorist murdered RFK.[342] In his place the Democratic Party nominated US Senator Hubert H. Humphrey. His opponent was Republican Richard Nixon, John Kennedy's opponent in 1960. The Republicans won the presidential race, but Congress remained strongly democratic and antiwar. Nixon extracted the United States from Vietnam by 1973; however, South Vietnam fell to an all-out communist invasion from the North in 1975.[343]

Nixon was the first US president to visit China in an attempt to bring about a new relationship between the two nations. China greeted Nixon warmly, but overtly little happened. The real "victory" was sub-rosa because just by visiting the communist nation he put pressure on North Vietnam. Nixon's visit was a key moment in opening up China to capitalism. Nixon also signed arms limitation treaties with the USSR; thus, lowering atomic war tensions. Nixon was attempting to limit the possibility of atomic war by allowing Red China, and the USSR, an equal place in the world which was the goal of every US president since Truman. What none of them seemed ready to acknowledge was the communist commitment to the destruction of the United States in particular and democracy in general. By following a course of live and let live they were giving the communist unlimited time to destroy the West.

Nixon inherited a contracting economy with enormous new government programs doling out billions of dollars to millions of people and institutions. Nixon, remembered as a conservative, *increased* these payments until they

---

342 This was another assassination with a lot of holes in the investigation. Once more, critical evidence was destroyed or lost by the LA Police Department (door jams and ceiling tiles) which may have shown there was a seconded shooter involved with the murder.

343 The term "invasion" is accurate. South Vietnam fell to a full-scale Korean-style invasion from North Vietnam. The communists had numerous tanks, large numbers of men, supporting artillery, and all the rest. Saigon's fall was not the result of a guerrilla action.

became the largest part of the federal budget. At the same time, he imposed wage and price controls to hold inflation in check because of the Vietnam War spending—but this came much too late to do any good. Government expansion continued under the Nixon administration. Nixon thought big and attempted significant changes to the world and the nation; however, Nixon could not overcome the hostility of Congress and the weak economy in his search for grand accomplishments. And his wage and price controls did nothing to improve the economic situation.

Nixon ordered the CIA to "spy" on US citizens which was against its charter, but they had previously engaged in many non-charter ventures. Nixon was convinced communist agents sponsored the antiwar movement; however, no proof was found. A break-in at Democratic Headquarters in the **Watergate** Building in Washington DC was traced back to the Committee To Re-elect the President, a Nixon campaign organization. A Congressional investigation accused Nixon of covering up for his White House staff and impeached him for obstruction of justice. Nixon resigned in 1973 to avoid, he said, putting the nation through an impeachment. The Watergate scandal drove Nixon from office. The new president, Gerald Ford, was not in office long enough to achieve any real change in economic or national policy.[344]

After Nixon left office **Gerald Ford**, the vice president appointed by Congress after the resignation of Vice President Spiro Agnew, assumed the presidency. After Ford came into office North Vietnam invaded South Vietnam in violation of the treaty signed with Nixon in 1973 and in violation of numerous UN Charter provisions. Ford did nothing because Congress had cut off all aid to the former ally. The United Nations also refused to act, in contradiction of its own charter. Ford, president for over two years, listened to Henry Kissinger on foreign policy matters and Kissinger advised doing nothing about the invasion of South Vietnam. Ford's biggest foreign policy decision was to forgo defending South Vietnam after the communist invasion. South Vietnam quickly fell to the North Vietnamese.

Europe was making progress toward joining into an economic union. This was tempered by the problems of socialism, because the new socialist world that Europe created after World War II was running into a funding problem. It was apparent that Europeans were not having enough children to replace themselves. One-child families were the norm, and this meant

344 He is the only president to hold office never being elected as president or vice president.

a shrinking young population would soon be supporting a fast growing retired population. The only way to handle the growing number of people, retired or otherwise, on the government dole was to raise Europe's already high taxes. High taxes were already hurting the European economy and increasing them would only do additional harm. The politicians in Europe had to keep increasing the dole to stay in office because powerful trade unions demanded increasing benefits; however, to do so was irresponsibly selling the future for the present. This demonstrates a significant problem in democracies adopting a Socialist or Wealth redistribution philosophy. When powerful groups gain control of the government they can force policies into law benefitting their groups at the expense of the nation as a whole.

The Muslim populations in Europe were growing. At first the Islamic people were an underclass who kept to themselves and seemed to bother no one; however, as their numbers increased so did their power. By the year 2000 they were a massive group demanding vast cultural changes in Europe to correspond to their view of religion and life. Using democratic processes these Muslim groups have demanded changes to Western law to meet their cultural views. From the first moment they began to establish themselves in Europe they refused to adopt Western ideas, dress, or culture. Now Europe faces a dynamic but growing minority that may soon be majorities in some nations. The failure to notice and deal with the non-assimilation of the Muslims now challenges Europe with massive change.

During the 1970's, satellite development made space a very important place. Telecommunications satellites began to tie the world together through television and radio signals sent to satellites in space that beamed them back to earth. This made it possible to televise events from anywhere in the world. As this theme progressed, it would lead to Global Positioning Systems (satellite tracking of positions on the earth's surface), cellular telephones enabling a phone the size of a deck of cards to communicate with anyone anywhere on earth, and a host of other wonders advancing our ability to tell each other "what's for dinner." It also enhanced the military's ability to put a bomb through a bathroom window from half way around the world. Now a guy's not safe anywhere.

Another innovation hit the streets in 1974, the **microprocessor**. This tiny, well . . . not so tiny at first . . . innovation allowed computers to be made a lot smaller—and cheaper. As the microprocessor improved, it helped telecommunications satellites, cellular telephones, cars, plus a lot more, to operate better. This was THE invention that put tabletop computing on the world scene. The invention of the microprocessor will probably rank with the printing press as one of the most important inventions in world history.

CARTER: INCOMPETENT COLD WARRIOR

1976 to 1980

Worldwide, the Western Democracies began losing the Cold War after the fall of South Vietnam in 1975. The United States was no longer viewed as an impeccable partner, and Soviet influence grew in Europe, Africa, and South America while Chinese influence expanded in Southeast Asia. Gerald Ford lost the next presidential election to **Jimmy Carter** in 1976, in part because he opposed a massive loan to New York when it was in financial difficulty. Mr. Carter was the former governor of Georgia, and before that he grew peanuts.

As Carter took office, the communists stepped up their march to world power and increasing the isolation of the United States. The Soviet Union invaded **Afghanistan,** turning the nation into a Soviet satellite. The Carter administration responded by canceling the US participation in the Moscow Olympics. To hardnosed Soviet and Chinese leaders this proved the United States was powerless against communist expansion. In Iran, radical fundamentalist Muslims overthrew the Shah and replaced him with a radical Muslim religious leader pulled home from exile. The Muslim radicals then seized the US Embassy, taking sixty-six Americans hostages and holding them until the end of Carter's term (444 days). This was additional proof the United States could be intimidated by bold actions.

During the Carter administration the US Congress, under the leadership of the Church Committee, discovered the CIA was spying on US citizens, and the committee discovered the intelligence agency paid off "immoral people" in its espionage operations. Congress banned the CIA from spying in the United States, employing "unsavory people" for intelligence operations, and prohibited the FBI and CIA from sharing information. These moves, among others by Carter and the US Congress, destroyed the intelligence-gathering capability the FBI, CIA, and other intelligence agencies possessed. These unrealistic laws stopped coordination in tracking foreign spies and terrorists. The Church Committee knew the problems this legislation would create, but Church and his colleagues chose to ignore pleas from the security agencies. The Church Committee truly eviscerated the ability of the US to gather intelligence in the Cold War, and this would continue during the War on Terror. As ragged as US intelligence was before, it shrank in value after Congress "reformed" the security agencies.

The communists made inroads in Africa and Latin America throughout the Carter years. The US lost control of the Panama Canal when the tiny nation of Panama seized the Canal Zone, Cuba sent troops to Africa and Latin America to fight for communism, Nicaragua went Communist, Iran went to the terrorists, Russia was threatening Iran and Turkey, and the United States was doing little to turn the tide. **OPEC**[345] doubled the price of oil in retaliation for President Carter freezing Iranian assets in the United States. The world over the United States was viewed with disdain as more nations fell into communism's sphere of influence.

The economy under Carter continued to stagger. Inflation accelerated along with government spending, meanwhile, the economy continued stagnating. With no economic growth and worsening world conditions, the future looked bleak. Some commentators were opining that the days of growth and prosperity were behind the Western world. The Western world's economies had wandered in the doldrums for years. Since the Lyndon Johnson era, it seemed nothing had gone right economically. The European Union was coming together, and it was clear the economic union would benefit Western Europe; nevertheless, that benefit seemed a long way off. Nixon's regulations failed to right the US economic ship, and even though these regulations were gone the economy meandered downward. The West, it seemed, was out of options. The Carter administration appeared unable to meet the challenge.

A nuclear accident at Three Mile Island, and the following media frenzy, destroyed the nuclear electric industry in the United States. France and other nations continued to build nuclear reactors for energy, but the United States would halt this construction, effectively removing this source of power as an alternative to oil or natural gas. The fuel crisis rippled through the United States and other Western economies, further crippling the already fragile system of economic interchange. Congress and several states passed bills protecting the environment that made building anything much more expensive and time consuming. Oil refineries, for example, were simply not constructed after the passage of the restrictive environmental measures (even in 2010, no oil refineries have been constructed in the US since the

---

[345] Organization of Petroleum Exporting Countries. This was (and is) a cartel controlling world oil supplies.

1970's). The price of everything was increasing while wages were flat which, in essence, shrank the economic power of the common person.

REAGAN: ULTIMATE COLD WARRIOR

1980 to 1988

(We win, they lose!)

FIGURE 75
PRESIDENT RONALD REAGAN

In 1980, **Ronald Reagan** was elected president of the United States. His first thought was to strengthen the US economy. Reagan cut taxes and decreased government regulation over many aspects of the economy. This was the magic bullet that no one else thought would work. Reagan decided *the government was the problem* with the US economy; thus, as he removed government restrictions and lowered taxes, the economy responded and began to grow rapidly. Inflation was tamed, wages began to increase as the economy expanded, and even tax revenues increased as the economy grew. Reagan proved the commentators wrong when they said the best days were behind the United States and the West. Reagan proved the best days were still ahead as long as the government gave the people the room to invent and the money (power) to do so. The US economy recovered from years of stagflation (a combination of inflation and stagnated growth) and began a more than decade's long expansion. Many future politicians would reap the benefits of Reagan's low tax and low regulation policies—without mentioning him of course.

Reagan armed the "freedom fighters" in Afghanistan (actually Muslim fundamentalists) and tried to arm Latin American guerrillas to fight communism. The efforts in Afghanistan tied down thousands of Soviet troops and allowed the United States to hurt the Soviets as they had hurt the United States in Vietnam. None of this was essential because everything was a sideshow compared to what Reagan was really planning, an all-out assault on the Soviet system itself.

After taking office Reagan told his staff he had a new idea for dealing with communism: "**We win, they lose,**" he said. This was a complete reversal of thirty-five years of US policy aimed at coexistence with the Soviets. Reagan wanted to destroy them, not live with them. To that end, he put his staff to work looking at what was weak in the Soviet system. The key flaw soon surfaced, their economy was on thin ice. To hurt the USSR's economy, Reagan began an arms race where American technology would outperform the Soviets and cause them to spend millions they could not afford in order to keep up. The plan worked. The Soviets were paranoid about keeping up with the United States in arms and arms production. As their spending for military and technological hardware increased it collapsed their economy. The Soviet Union began to do things no one ever thought they would witness. They allowed the reunification of Germany; Poland's independence; left Afghanistan, and they released their hold over Eastern Europe. By 1989 it was over, and ecstatic Germans, uniting their country after years of separation, tore down the Berlin Wall.

Eastern Europe was free, and many non-Russian areas of the Soviet Union declared independence. Belarus, the Ukraine, Moldova, Latvia, Lithuania, Estonia, Kazakhstan, and others fled the Soviet empire. The speed with which these formally subjugated regions left the Soviet Union was amazing. In spite of the fact the Russians controlled them for many decades, the moment a chance for freedom appeared they took it. The Communist Party no longer controlled Russia. This victory came suddenly and could hardly be fathomed until it was complete. Reagan left office in 1988 after two successful terms as president. He was a visionary who convinced the people of the United States to continue looking forward for the best days, because optimism was the tonic for the future.

George Bush number 41 (or Bush the "elder") was president of the United States when the Soviet Union collapsed, but *the policies of Ronald Reagan won the Cold War* for the Western Democracies. George Bush the elder worked his magic by helping the Soviets withdraw without bloodshed, which was common for such realignments in the past. Reagan viewed the Soviet Union as evil. Being evil, Reagan thought it could not last; therefore, if he concentrated on its weaknesses the USSR would fold. He was right, and he victoriously ended one of the longest, costliest, and most dangerous confrontations to threaten the world. President Ronald Reagan did what Hitler and Stalin could not, defeat Russia and cause the collapse of its empire. The cost of this Cold War contest cannot be calculated. Some estimates say the United States alone spent *8 trillion dollars* and sacrificed at least 100,000 US lives during the conflict.

As the US economy recovered under Reagan, the world economy began to pick up as well. In England, **Margaret Thatcher** managed to turn the tide against socialism for a while, and the British economy picked up after a period of rather tough government policies emphasizing growth rather than taxation and socialism. England was toying with the idea of becoming part of Europe, and the **Chunnel** (a tunnel between France and England) planning began. It would open in 1994.

By 1989, computers were being tied together forming the **World Wide Web**. This network grew to dominate the news and information sectors of the world. The Internet challenged governments' abilities to control the content and reach of this new communication method. Wireless telephones were also on the horizon, and the mobile phone would become as ubiquitous as leaves on the trees. The modern world soon filled with chitchat invisibly flowing over the airwaves.

The European Economic Community (EC) formed its **common market** in 1993, thereby expanding its trade and economic potential. The **Euro**, the EC's currency, was introduced in 1999, and by 2008 it grew to be worth almost twice the US dollar. It appears the economic power of the EC will grow to become a dominant force in the Western world. In 1995, the **World Trade Organization** was created with the idea of facilitating international free trade. This too became a formidable part of the world economy forming in the twenty-first century. As Asia (Japan, Korea, and China) increases in economic power along with the European common market, it is apparent a new world economic order is forming. The impact of the World Wide Web, instant communications, the World Trade Organization, the computerization of the world, communication satellites, spy satellites, and so many other world-changing technologies, coupled with the growth of markets, will influence the twenty-first century massively. Accelerating change is now the most apparent product of the new century. What must be acknowledged is that the pace of change is becoming incredibly quick. Also, we must also acknowledge a large part of the world is *not* changing. Africa and the Middle East are still in the 18th Century except for their plethora of full automatic weapons. Islam still embraces a medieval mind-set, rejecting the changes the world is undergoing, and wanting to raze what the West identifies as progress. As the West and parts of Asia hasten away from the stagnate regions of the world, turmoil is predictable; but how much? Will the moribund areas of the earth be willing to destroy the dynamic peoples of the globe with atomic weapons, biologic terror weapons, or other armaments of mass murder?

A new economic world order will most probably lead to a political world order challenging the individualism of the West. The United Nations is already showing how the non-Western world rejects the Western ideology of individual freedom and individual empowerment. The Western Democracies are isolated in the United Nations by the tribal and totalitarian societies that dominate the rest of humankind. As technology and economic interdependence increase in importance, will the world be able to incorporate its widely divergent views on how people should live? Such wide differences have led to conflict in the past, and if history is our teacher, it is warning we must be vigilant of these differences leading to momentous disarray in the future.

Books and Resources:

The Fifty-Year Wound: How America's Cold War Victory Has Shaped Our World by Derek Leebaert, probably the best book on the subject of the Cold War and its impacts.

Legacy of Ashes: the History of the CIA by Tim Weiner, probably the best book on the failures of the American intelligence services and its costs.

At the Abyss, An Insider's History of the Cold War, Thomas C. Reed, Ballantine Books, 2004.

http://en.wikipedia.org/wiki/Cold_War: excellent article and good overview of the Cold War.

Chapter 17

The Korean War

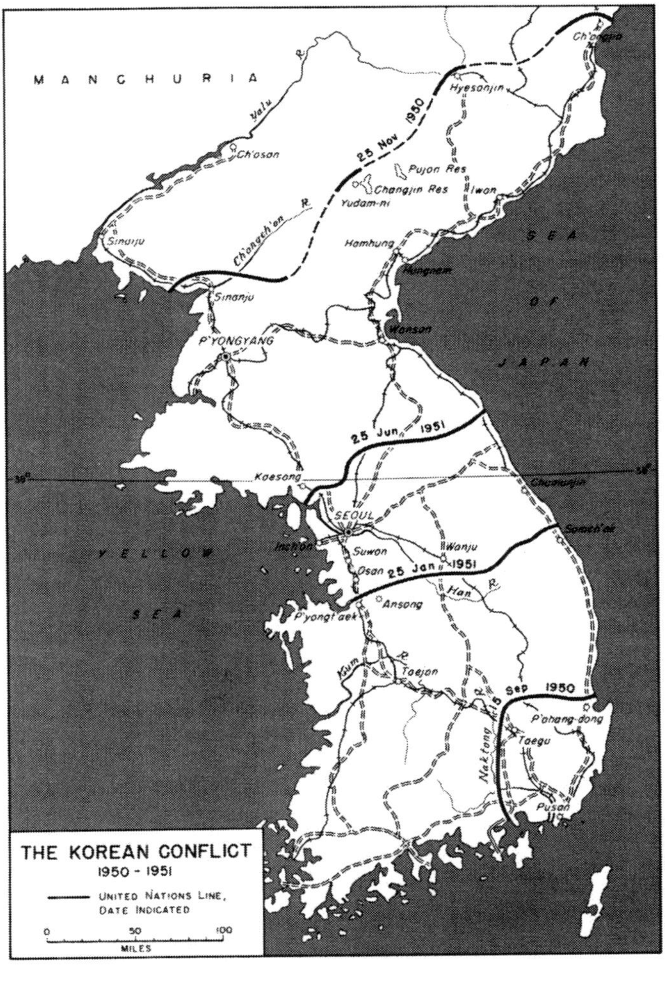

FIGURE 76 MAP OF KOREAN WAR

1950-1953

BACKGROUND TO INVASION

The Korean War is one of those almost-forgotten conflicts speckling the history of our planet. However, we need to remember Korea because it set the stage for the remainder of the twentieth century and established several foundational rules for the Cold War. America answered a direct challenge from the communist nations of China and the USSR while choosing to restrain the use of its available power. The Cold War had already started, tensions were soaring, and the stakes in Korea were high. The response of the United States of America, its allies, and the United Nations to this blunt challenge altered the course of history.

Before the invasion of South Korea, there were no negotiations, no demands, and no pre-war chest pounding—just pure aggression by way of an unannounced invasion. The United States could have ignored the plight of the small nation, but that would be an open invitation to more Hitler-like conquests. The experience of WWII filtered every decision of the Allies in the Korean conflict.

On June 25, 1950, the communist army of North Korea crossed the thirty-eighth parallel into South Korea beginning its bid to conquer the south. Stalin and Mao endorsed this move.[346] Stalin (leader of the USSR) and Mao (leader of Red China), both brutal murdering dictators, decided to *push Western ideas and control off mainland Asia.* The communist leader **Ho Chi Minh** would push the French out of Vietnam and then extend the assault to the rest of Indochina[347] thereby driving all Western control off the Asian mainland. In Korea, Soviet-trained troops and massive amounts of Soviet equipment would drive the South Korean army into the sea uniting Korea under communism. Both communist leaders thought America would not interfere in the puny peninsula's fall. Statements by the American Secretary of State **Dean Acheson** in 1950 may have led the communist to this conclusion about Korea.[348] Even if America wanted to defend, the assault would overrun the peninsula in thirty days, before the United States could

---

[346] The dictators of communist Russia (the USSR) and communist China (People's Republic of China) respectively.

[347] In 1950, both North and South Vietnam were controlled by the French as one colony.

[348] The Secretary of State, in a speech about US interests in the east, omitted mentioning South Korea. This may have led the communist dictators to conclude

respond. The communist dictators further calculated that America would not use the atomic bomb because of moral impediments. No such moral impediments existed in the communist dictatorships.

THE RED EMPIRES STRIKE!

June 25, 1950

The attack on South Korea on June 25, 1950, was an unqualified surprise to American intelligence which had received but ignored information from Taiwan. Some additional clues about a massive buildup of arms and men reached MacArthur's US Army staff, but it was thought to be unreliable. General **MacArthur**, who was running postwar Japan, did not even have his staff tell the South Koreans; thus, the Soviet buildup of North Korean forces went unnoticed. This kind of surprise would happen repeatedly over the years. The American intelligence services were nearly useless outside of aerial and satellite observation or electronic eavesdropping. Total defeats were imposed on the United States in the field of intelligence and counterintelligence decade after decade. For example, one man working for the US Navy in an extremely sensitive position was a Soviet spy, and he remained so for decades before his discovery. The amount of secret information delivered to the Soviets was beyond calculation, and it cost the lives of several Russians who were working with American intelligence. This disaster continues into 2010 and is a most important problem for the survival of America. Korea was a deep-seated failure for American intelligence organizations, and it should have been a wake-up call for improvement. Somehow, it was not.[349]

Communist success during the first days of the North Korean attack was so complete it appeared they would conquer the rocky peninsula in mere weeks. Truman moved at once and *without a declaration of war from Congress* to help the South Koreans. Untried American garrison units from Japan arrived to help stop the communist advance. Task Force Smith, one of the garrison units encountering the daunting communist attack, was shattered on first contact. Both American Army and South Korean infantry units were overwhelmed by North Korean human wave assaults supported by Russian T-34/84 style tanks that shrugged off American antitank weapons.

---

that South Korea was not a vital interest of the USA; thus, the US would not defend the little nation if it was invaded.

349 The terrorist attacks of 9/11/01 were another elephantine intelligence failure for the United States. No change from 1950 to 2001.

Massive barrages from Soviet-supplied artillery swept the battlefield as the North Koreans tore through Allied defense lines scattering the defenders to the four winds.

Exhausted and battered, South Korean and Allied forces were brushed back to their last stronghold at the port city of **Pusan**. Within the tight perimeter, South Korean and American forces rallied to withstand communist attacks. Amid the rain of artillery, thunder of tanks, and crashing waves of screaming communist troops ripping at the defenders of Pusan, there was hope. From the sea came US Navy aircraft smearing the attackers with napalm. Tons of exploding steel flung from the guns of US warships cleaved enemy attacks, and reinforcements moved in to stitch tears in the Allied line. Japan's airfields disgorged a mass of US Air Force bombers regurgitating death upon the brazen enemy. Far to the north, behind the Pusan perimeter, roads and bridges melted away under US bombardment, multiplying North Korean supply problems. The Soviet trained and supplied troops were not prepared for a US aerial armada projecting carnage and devastation deep behind their lines. Massive numbers of troops need massive amounts of supplies, and as the supplies dwindled so did the combat power of North Korea's army (logistics . . . *again*). The Soviet preparation of their partners failed to include the impact of naval gunfire which dismayed and splintered the communist troops. North Korea's leaders began to ponder the possible consequences of failure in the South.

The **United Nations** entered the war on a fluke. Normally, the **Security Council** of the United Nations must act before intervention in a war, and any member of the Security Council could veto such an intervention. The Soviet Union was a member of the Security Council and would have vetoed any action aimed at North Korea, but they were absent. The Soviets walked out of the United Nations in protest of another problem and were unavailable to file their veto when the war broke out. Thus, the United Nations could, and did, vote to intervene in Korea in accordance with the UN Charter to protect a nation from invasion. This was the first time the United Nations had acted with significant armed force to protect a nation invaded for the purpose of conquest. It was the best of "collective security" dreamed about by President Wilson after WWI. Unfortunately, it would also be the last until 1990.[350] For the most part, the responders were the Western Democracies. The United States of America, Australia, Canada, and the United Kingdom sent the most troops, but numerous other nations

[350] The United Nations would fail to act when North Vietnam invaded South Vietnam in 1975. It would act to repel the invasion of Kuwait by Iraq in 1990.

helped as well. Once again, even though it looked like the world was responding, it was the Western Democracies against the totalitarians of the East. So it had been since Marathon, so it was again.

The US Military was a shadow of its World War II self. The Truman administration had dismantled the world's best invasion forces after the war. Ships were decommissioned and entire units were disbanded as soon as the war ended. President Truman and his secretary of defense Louis Johnson tried to eliminate the US Marine Corps. After they were through, the US Marines had 27,000 men and a few World War II landing craft. The Marine Corps had to call up its veteran reserve units to build an amphibious force, but they responded at once. These men were experienced warriors and well able to fight and win land battles in Asia. After the problems at Tarawa, the US Marines put large amounts of firepower at the squad level to repel the Japanese human wave suicide assaults (Bonsai attacks) and dig them out of caves and other well placed defensive positions. This additional firepower at the squad level would be critical in the fight for Korea. In addition, naval gunfire and close air support were familiar additions to marine operations. The marines were the first units at Pusan to have extensive previous combat experience in Asia which served them well as they were shifted from one hot spot to another to repulse North Korean assaults on the fragile perimeter.

The US Army also dissipated after WWII, and the men who had destroyed Hitler and Tojo were in civilian jobs by 1950. Many who remained in the army were garrison troops without combat experience or training for a land war in Asia. US equipment was in storage, much of it out of date, and it would take time to assemble. Somehow, against all odds, the US Army managed to get good units to Korea in time to save Pusan. But it was close, and the communists were on the verge of overrunning Korea.

The problems with the US ground and amphibious forces could be traced to the development of the atomic bomb, coupled with the arrogance of the **US Air Force**, plus the folly of decision makers in Congress and the Truman administration. The Air Force had become a separate service in 1947, and they decided ground and sea forces were no longer necessary because the atomic bomb made them obsolete. They made this pitch to Congress and the Truman administration. They believed it; thus, non-Air Force budgets were gutted so the new US Air Force could have the needed aircraft and atomic bombs necessary for mid 20th century warfare.

Since late in World War I, the air forces of the world wanted a new strategic role not a tactical role. Airmen did not fancy being "flying artillery" under control of ground units. The air forces even chafed at the reconnaissance role which had proved vital in both World Wars because it entailed assignments from ground units. The attitude of the US Navy airmen was poles apart. They felt bombing a ship or enemy units ashore was vital to the fleet, and finding the enemy fleet was accepted as critical to victory. This difference in attitude is explained by the differing corporate cultures and equipment of the two services. The main difference was that naval aviation was small compared to the Air Force, and naval aviation did not stress large bombers because they could not take off from aircraft carriers. In the naval aviation services sinking ships, reconnaissance, and close air support for marines ashore were the primary roles; thus, they did not have the equipment or the numbers to be a decisive factor in crushing a nation from the air. The Air Force thought they did have the equipment and numbers to defeat an enemy from the air.

Using theories developed in the 1920s, air force proponents claimed air units could bomb an enemy nation into submission. This was attempted in World War II, first by the Germans, then by the English in partnership with the United States. Thousand plane raids against the Third Reich and the Japanese empire did not deliver victory. The *US Bombing Survey* conducted after the war admitted that the bombing raids did not have the desired impact of causing the enemy to quit the war. Before the war, air theorists had opined that civilian morale would collapse under bombing raids and they would demand their government to stop the war at any cost rather than suffer the bombings that would shatter their lives and cities.[351] In fact, civilian morale did not fail and often the bombings stiffened the resolve of the nation to fight on against the heartless villains who destroyed their lives from the sky. Then the atomic bomb was developed and used for the destruction of two Japanese cities. Japan surrendered and millions of lives were spared. Now the US Air Force had its war-winning combination. If wars could be won with the A-bomb, why fund the other services? The US ground and naval forces were dramatically cut. Saving money after the worst war in the history of the world was important to the Western Democracies.

History has a way of bringing irrational hopes to an end rather quickly. The A-bomb was not going to end wars where it was not used, and the A-bomb did not end the need for ground troops or naval units. After the

[351] I have always wondered why the air theorists thought bombing would work against a totalitarian government where the will of the people means nothing.

Soviets developed their own A-bomb, new worries about a nuclear war popped up to further dilute the concept that the atomic bomb had ended conventional wars. If no one could use the bomb then wars would go on. After all, who would risk the destruction of the world over a place like Korea? The Western Democracies had cut their militaries too much, and now their soldiers, sailors, and marines were going to pay the piper for the shortsighted decisions of their leaders (*again,* just like WWII).

General MacArthur had been put in charge of the UN forces after the invasion, and he hatched a brilliant but risky plan to change the course of the conflict.

The fighting around Pusan was as hard as any in history. General MacArthur realized trying to attack up the Korean peninsula from Pusan would be World War I all over again. A frontal assault on a numerically superior dug-in enemy in mountainous terrain would be costly, and winter was on the way. Take too much time moving north and the harsh Korean winter and rough terrain would make offensive action daunting. By using the amphibious ability of the US Navy and Marine Corps (or what was left of it), General MacArthur thought he could dramatically change the course of the war with a landing behind the enemy lines about half way up the west Korean coast near **Seoul,** the nation's capital. The US **Joint Chiefs of Staff** thought the plan too risky and wanted to land farther south; however, MacArthur pointed out such a landing would accomplish little. By landing at **Inchon** near Seoul the Allies could deal the invaders a lethal blow and force a North Korean retreat without attacking at Pusan. President Truman sided with MacArthur, and the invasion was on. Both the Joint Chiefs and the president had missed one critical point in MacArthur's plan. *He clearly said that after the capture of Seoul the troops would move north.* This aspect of his plan should have been thoroughly discussed, however, because of the focus on the risk of landing at Inchon the other major risk—moving north of the thirty-eighth parallel—was ignored.

INCHON THE UN ALLIES STRIKE BACK

September 15, 1950

Far up the west side of the mountainous Korean peninsula was a port just to the west of Seoul. The port was **Inchon**, a very unusual place. The harbor's tides were very high and mud flats appeared for hours every day when the tide went out, and these mud flats prevented ship movement. As the tide came back to cover the mud flats ships could once more move up Flying Fish Channel. MacArthur wanted to go ashore there and drive east to Seoul. Seoul was the road and rail junction for everything going south; thus, control of Seoul equaled control of *all supplies* trying to move south. Acute obstacles faced an amphibious assault at Inchon, and one severe problem was the condition of the once-mighty amphibious arm of the US Navy. Most of the assault craft and naval gunfire support ships were gone, and those that remained were in poor shape. Nonetheless, the navy and marines thought they could do it.

MacArthur's plan was brilliant. Risky as it was, if it worked the achievement would be colossal. The war could be won in a month rather than years. The communist army to the south would be cut off by the invasion and then destroyed by an attack out of Pusan that would push them against the waiting army at Seoul. It was a classic hammer and anvil move which could totally destroy the foe. The problem was winning on the beach and pushing quickly to Seoul. If the communists could thwart the amphibious landing, the UN forces would face a devolving military and political situation.[352]

The US Marines landed at Inchon at 6:30 a.m. on September 15, 1950. Wolmi-Do Island at the center beachhead had to be taken, and the marines took Wolmi-Do in less than two hours. The soldiers of the sea held on while the tide was out, and after it rose once again other US Marine units landed on beaches to either side of the island. The landings were a complete surprise and a complete success. The US Marines and army units moved inland toward Seoul. Far to the south, UN units at Pusan simultaneously attacked the communist lines and broke through. The resulting rout was one of the greatest military victories of modern times. The Inchon landings with the coinciding counterattacks at Pusan eradicated the North Korean army.

UN forces quickly drove to the thirty-eighth parallel *and then kept going.* If they would have stopped at or near the thirty-eighth parallel, the war may have ended right there and then; however, MacArthur pressed on with the idea of punishing the communist north for its invasion. The US Government and the UN approved the push north, but they did not fully consider the reaction of the Chinese communists who would not stand by and let a client state be conquered (especially when they had agreed to

352 Communist spies working on the docks in San Francisco and Japan had warned that something was up, but the North didn't listen.

the invasion), and the United States was devoid of accurate intelligence on the Chinese and their intentions.[353]

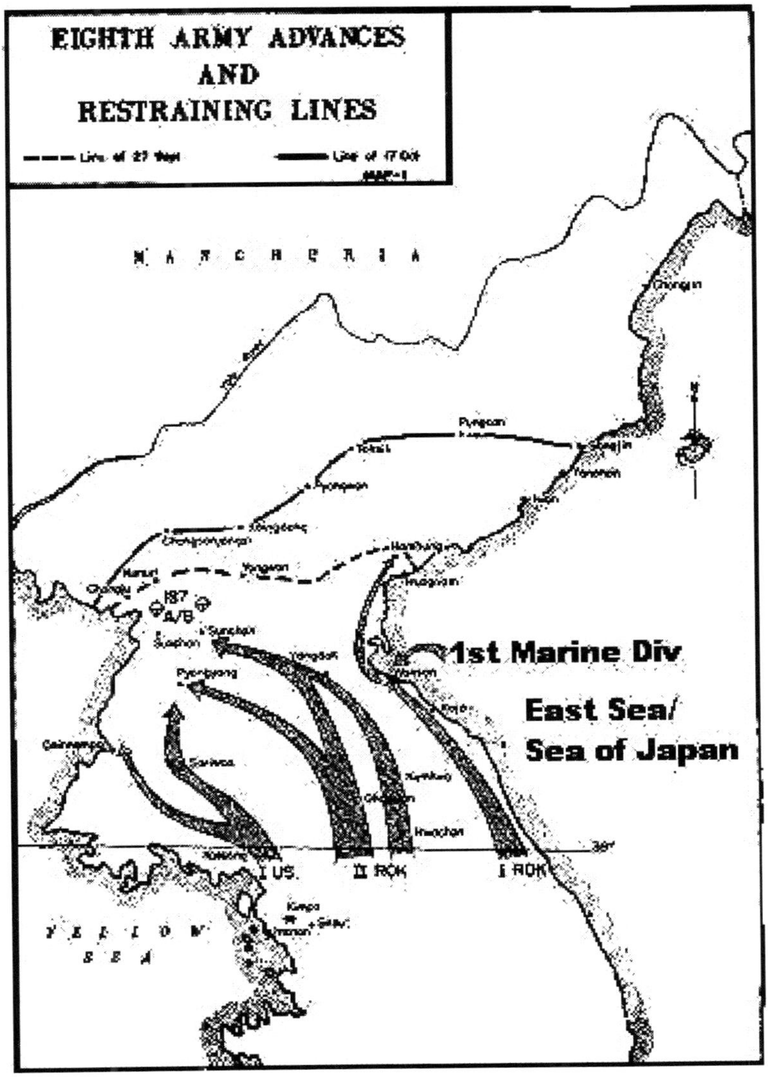

FIGURE 77 MACARTHUR'S ADVANCE NORTH

[353] Here is the rub of not fully discussing MacArthur's plan. The move north should have been considered *then*, not later after the landings and the move north had started.

CHINA ENTERS THE WAR

October 1950

Now MacArthur matched his horrific errors in defending the Philippines during World War II. The advance north was haphazard. His advance was in four widely separated columns with a lot of space for infiltration, plus the columns were not mutually supporting. In addition, he ignored the fact that the Chinese were in the war even after his troops had captured numerous Chinese communist troops as they approached the Yalu River which separated China from North Korea. Chairman Mao, the tyrant leader of communist China, warned the United States through neutral nations that he would intervene if the United Nations approached the Yalu River. The nationalist regime on Taiwan warned the United States of Chinese intervention. *All these warnings were ignored.*

US Intelligence failed to recognize the potential entry of the Red China into the war.[354] The massive Chinese assault caught MacArthur completely by surprise. MacArthur would go from genius to idiot overnight. The UN forces absorbed a massive blow as Chinese forces rolled back the defenders of democracy like waves running up a California beach (so much for MacArthur's concept of winter offensives being difficult). As the United Nations retreated below the thirty-eighth parallel, Seoul fell into communist hands again.[355]

Prior to the communist assault, the First Marine Division had landed near the Chosin Reservoir far above the thirty-eighth parallel, and when the Chinese offensive began they were trapped in the mountains by seven or more communist divisions intent on destroying them. In freezing weather, against thousands of fresh Chinese troops, the marines attacked toward the coastal port of Hungnam and deliverance.

---

[354] Satellite surveillance was not available in the 1950s.

[355] Seoul would change hands **four times** and be reduced to ruin by the time of the cease-fire in July of 1953.

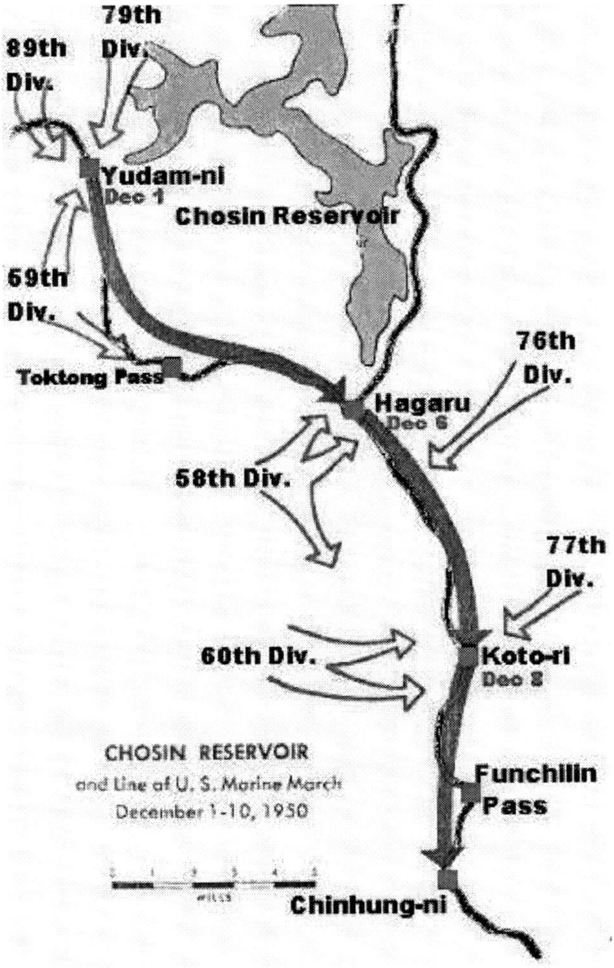

FIGURE 78 US MARINE MARCH FROM CHOSEN

Clear weather, at least clear enough at times, allowed US Navy and air force planes to bomb, napalm, and strafe communist belligerents attacking the marines. Air control and tough men were the key to getting the marines out. Chinese troops threw massed assaults at marine positions, but the extra firepower placed at the squad level by the marines paid off as Chinese attacks were repelled with staggering communist losses. The First Marine Division made it to Hungnam and embarked with their wounded, their KIAs, and their serviceable equipment. The Chinese communists subtracted nearly seven divisions from their order of battle because of casualties sustained trying to destroy the surrounded US Marines. For the rest of the war the Chinese would not frontally assault a US Marine position.

The UN line stabilized well south of the thirty-eighth parallel as the Chinese assault ran out of steam. It was impossible for the Chinese to keep their troops supplied since they were moving by foot and bicycle over mountainous terrain in the winter, mostly at night, and getting hit with constant air attacks. Nonetheless, they had recaptured the South Korean capitol and pushed the UN forces about two-thirds of the way down the snow-covered peninsula. The Chinese success centered on night assaults using infiltration tactics to disrupt the UN units' group cohesiveness. Using this method, large groups of Chinese soldiers would get past UN front lines and attack at night from the flanks using submachine guns with large capacity magazines to spray the UN positions with rounds[356] while other units assaulted the front of the UN positions with submachine guns, grenades, and mortars. The frontal attack held the defenders in place while the flank attacks surprised the defenders, forcing them to guard several axes of advance at once. These tactics confused the troops and small units lost cohesion, often scattering under fire or hunkering down lessening the defensive firepower of the unit. At the same time these attacks on the front lines were proceeding, other Chinese troops got past the UN lines and placed themselves on routes used by reinforcements; thus, as the reinforcements moved forward they would be ambushed and have to fight their way to the unit they were supposed to be saving. It took some time for the UN soldiers to adapt to these tactics; however, once they did the communists had a far harder time achieving success.

After the stunning defeat, MacArthur began publicly calling for bombing Manchuria and perhaps going to war with China. President Truman loathed this because he wanted to limit the war, and he did not want his military commander publicly demanding different strategies. Truman also thought MacArthur had sabotaged a possible peace deal presented by the Chinese. After some acrimonious exchanges Truman *fired MacArthur* and eventually appointed General Ridgeway as the overall commander of the UN forces in Korea. This turn of events caused a public outcry in America. MacArthur was a favorite general, and many in America thought he was correct to question Truman's strategy of limited war even if it did mean war with China.

---

[356] The Chinese and North Koreans did *not* use the AK-47 in Korea; they used the PPSh-41. This was a submachine gun with a 71-round drum magazine that fired a pistol round. It was very effective in spraying bullets all over the landscape, especially at night when they could get in close.

MacArthur had blundered intolerably in defending the Philippines, costing the lives of thousands of men. For his efforts, he was given command of the Army's Pacific Theater. He stumbled again in his defense and his original offensive actions in New Guinea, once more killing troops unnecessarily. Then he blundered in Korea by ignoring the warning of a Chinese offensive and failing to advance with mutually supporting formations, again costing thousands of lives. In spite of these egregious errors in judgment he remained in command. Only when he openly disagreed with the president was he dismissed. It would appear that slaughtering thousands of your troops isn't much of a problem, but disagreeing with a politician is a titanic problem.[357]

After General Ridgeway took command of the UN forces he investigated the disaster. General Ridgeway was disappointed in the performance of US Army troops during the Chinese communist offensive. After some study solutions surfaced. Communist tactics were dissected and ways were fashioned to counteract their effectiveness through new training. Once the troops were told what the Reds were doing, and how to thwart enemy efforts, UN combat capability increased dramatically. Another problem was firepower at the squad level, so firepower was improved for the US Army squads. Once these flaws were remedied, the US Army performed well against the experienced Chinese troops who were veterans of the wars with the Nationalist Chinese. Other adjustments in artillery and air support also enabled outnumbered UN units to survive the Chinese and North Korean assaults as well as advance against fanatic resistance.

THE NEW AIR WAR

For the last years of WWII, the Allies dominated the skies, but Allied air superiority was challenged in Korea. The United States was not prepared for another war just five years after the end of WWII, and its equipment illustrated that lack of readiness. In the skies over Korea, the United States was at first flying World War II aircraft like B-29 bombers and P-51 mustangs. Out of nowhere, the communists showed up with jet aircraft that blew the propeller aircraft and jets of the United States out of the sky. The MIG 15, which first appeared over Korea, was an excellent aircraft.[358] The United

---

357 For all my complaining about MacArthur, he was skillful in his management of Japan after World War II.

358 Which US intelligence did ***not*** know about (wow, that's news). The MIGs were a complete surprise.

States had jets (the F-80 Shooting Star, Panther, etc.), but they were no match for this communist jet. In addition, the MIGs were being flown by veteran Soviet pilots and well-trained Chinese pilots. The United States rushed to produce an aircraft to match the MIG 15 and quickly concocted the North American F-86 saber jet. This aircraft was a lucky combination of components that flew wonderfully and proved to be an excellent answer to the MIG 15. In the hands of US Air Force veterans it soon achieved a remarkable kill ratio (10:1 or better) against the MIGs. The challenge for control of the sky above Korea had been answered, and the US Air Force had won (on behalf of the United Nations, of course).

FIGURE 82 F-86 SABER

This marked the first time extensive air combat had occurred between jet aircraft. The new air war was like something out of a 1940s science fiction novel. Superfast swept-wing rocket-propelled aircraft streaked through the sky with their indomitable pilots wearing silver pressure suits, oxygen masks, heavy helmets with dark visors, and using advanced sighting systems to shoot at other aircraft. It was the start of a new age in aircraft design and production. The race for the air control fighter still goes on today between the world's major powers, because air superiority is so critical to success on the battlefield,[359] especially for the normally outnumbered troops fighting for the Western Democracies.

---

[359] It should be noted this is the WWII kind of set-piece battlefield, *not the "modern" battlefield* of indiscriminate murder by people with bombs strapped to themselves firing them off in a crowded marketplace.

UN Forces Move North—Again

With new firepower and offensive schemes, the UN forces soon retook Seoul and were near the thirty-eighth parallel. The communist Chinese decided they must achieve a decisive victory. To this end, they assembled a new army of impressive numbers and prepared to strike the American and British positions just north of Seoul at the Imjin River and east at Kapyong.

The communist spring offensive began on April 22, 1951 and involved well over 750,000 men. In a series of human wave assaults supported by artillery and tanks, they rammed the UN forces south from the Imjin River and Kapyong, thereby threatening to retake the still-smoldering city of Seoul. Even though UN forces were thrust out of their positions by swarming shadows in the night, this was no rout. While the United Nations gave back blood-soaked ground amid hails of lead and Red Army bugle calls, the new firepower and defensive doctrines were exacting an unexpected levy of death and dismemberment on the aggressors. The immense Red Army was suffering incredible casualties. American air power pulverized roads and bridges needed by the Chinese to bring supplies through the mountainous Korean terrain. US artillery and air power lay waste to attacking communist units. Remarkable stands at the Imjin River by British troops, and UN and American troops[360] at other locations, blunted Chinese attacks north of the capitol. The communist advance slowed and then stopped. The massive Chinese attack had literally bled to death.

Stalemate

July 1951 to July 1953

The United Nations started advancing again and retook the lost ground, finally stabilizing the front near the thirty-eighth parallel. Here a decision was made by the UN forces to stop the advance. The Chinese and Americans began frustrating peace talks at **Panmunjom** in 1951, lasting for years. Meanwhile, a brutal war of taking and losing hills along the thirty-eighth

360 As a side note, the US Marine 1st Division was in the line, yet no major communist assault was mounted against it. For the rest of the war, the communists would not frontally assault a US Marine position. When reviewing maps of this communist assault, look at the center of the UN line and look for the abbreviation 1st MarDiv (First Marine Division), and you will see the arrows of the communist advance hitting units on both sides of the division, but no attack on the position of the 1MarDiv.

parallel continued. Eisenhower was elected president of the United States in 1952, and he wanted to end the Korean War. The endless talks accomplished nothing, and the Chinese stalling tactics were unfathomable. What China gained from the prolonged twilight war can never be known, although they argued endlessly over the repatriation of prisoners. The Chinese wanted all prisoners of war returned to each side, but the Americans argued that only those who chose to go back should be returned. Had the Americans learned from their WWII experience (mistake) of returning Soviet prisoners of war knowing death awaited them? Why did the Chinese care if a few of their men did not want to return? Whatever the reasons, the talks went on from July 1951 to July 1953, and all the while men were dying along the thirty-eighth parallel for a few yards of well-shelled dirt.

The Korean War may have continued because Stalin wanted the fighting to go on. The murderer was losing nothing, except some equipment and a few pilots, and he probably counseled the Chinese to keep fighting. As long as they were taking the casualties what did he care? About four months after Stalin's death the cease-fire was signed.

Use the Bomb—or Not?

During the initial Chinese attack, as UN forces were overwhelmed, President Truman alluded to using the atomic bomb. It is questionable if he really considered its use, but a lot of preliminary moves were made that seemed to indicate its use was imminent.

The communist dictators had been correct in one assumption; the United States would not use the atomic bomb. Truman, the president in 1950, responded to the invasion with conventional forces thereby deciding the use of the A-bomb was inappropriate. Why Truman held back might be difficult to discover. An innocent nation was under attack and being overrun by a ruthless enemy. Thousands of innocent South Koreans were being murdered and the displacement of the South Korean population was an international tragedy. Why not use the A-bomb? Arguably, if Truman obliterated North Korea it might cause the USSR to obliterate South Korea, and who knew what would be obliterated next? Truman did not want this "small"[361] war to escalate into another world war. In addition, England and

---

361 In my opinion, the Chinese communists lost almost 1 million men in its attempts to push the United Nations off the Korean peninsula. Since WWII, most wars are categorized as "small" because by comparison they are small.

several other US Allies cautioned Truman against the use of the A-bomb, thus, the president's decision to forego using the A-bomb in Korea.

This decision became precedent, and the United States has not used the atomic or hydrogen bomb in any situation. It should be noted that the USSR under Stalin, or China under Mao, would have used the atomic bomb without hesitation if the roles had been reversed. Because the United States has not used its nuclear weapons, thousands of US soldiers have died in combat to preserve friendly regimes under communist or terrorist attack, and those struggles have not been universally successful. The notion that using the bomb increases the chance of a wider war should be balanced against the idea that abandoning the bomb encourages despots to start wars with the United States because of its refusal to use all its available combat power. The thought of a nation failing to use a decisive weapon because of unilateral moral reasons would have dumbfounded Clausewitz and other philosophers of war. Remember, the precedent for abandoning the A-bomb was set in Korea when Truman decided to forgo the use of America's most powerful instrument of war. This shows the importance of history on decision making. Decisions made long ago, and for different reasons, can impact the decisions of today.[362]

President Eisenhower, wanting to end the stalemate in Korea, decided to up the pressure on the Chinese and moved the bomber group armed with the atomic bomb to Okinawa which is near Korea. In addition, he leaked information to the Chinese that the atomic cannon would be sent to Korea. All this made it appear the Americans might launch offensives using nuclear weapons to blow holes in the Chinese lines or destroy vital rail lines and bridges over the Yalu River. Following these moves, the Chinese and North Koreans agreed to a cease-fire which stopped the fighting on **July 27, 1953**. A peace treaty was never signed, so from the original invasion in 1950 until today (2010) the two Koreas have technically been at war.[363]

---

362 Note the Soviets did not use nuclear weapons in Afghanistan. Were they somehow constrained by Truman's decision?

363 Technically, a cease fire just means the shooting has stopped for a time. N Korea repudiated the cease fire in June of 2009, but what this means is uncertain. N Korea has been developing nuclear arms. Pressure from the US to cease nuclear arms production has caused N Korea to lash back, and the repudiation of this agreement is part of the blowback.

Analysis

The political fallout from the Korean War was minimal considering its cost. About *33,746* Americans died or were missing in action during the conflict (The New York Times Almanac, 2008), and the United States still has troops there to protect the South from another attack. Communist losses are unknown; however, it is estimated that the Chinese lost almost *1 million* men in the war (official US estimate is over five hundred thousand), the North Koreans *215,000*, and the USSR *300* plus. The South Korean civilians suffered the most from the war in that millions were killed or wounded, and their homeland was destroyed.

America was glad to be out of the war, but the failure to win was hard on many in the United States. Fighting to a draw was not the kind of war Americans liked to fight. It was a good start for the United Nations as it had successfully intervened and saved a small nation from conquest; however, this was tempered with the realization that the USSR had allowed it to happen by being absent on the day of the critical vote. This must have been a blunder by the Soviets, but we may never know. Since the Soviets had calculated the United States would not react to the invasion militarily, they might have assumed that the United Nations would play no part in actively resisting the invasion.

Eisenhower's sub-rosa threat to use atomic bombs to defeat the Chinese, unknown for years, was one of the high points of his administration. At least he ended the fighting. A book entitled *This Kind of War* by Fehrenbach[364] warned America that Korea was the type of war it would face for the remainder of the twentieth century. The author meant amorphous and brutal wars seemingly without end and lacking traditional winners or losers. He was a prophet, correctly predicting the remainder of the twentieth century and the beginning of the twenty-first.

Americans cannot get used to the concept that they do not have to "win" these wars, they only have to "not lose." This is one lesson the United States needed to learn from Korea. Winning was going to be so costly in Korea the United States decided to leave it a stalemate and live with it. The US rejected this concept, however, if the United States can achieve a stalemate in a faraway nation and prevent totalitarians from taking over the government, America has achieved "victory." Not victory in a WWII sense,

---

364 *This Kind of War: the Classic Korean War History—Fiftieth Anniversary Edition* by T.R. Fehrenbach

but victory by keeping a friendly government in power without committing thousands of troops and millions of dollars for an indefinite time.

Korea has faded badly into history; nevertheless, it was a clash of giants in which the stage was set for the rest of the 50 year Cold War conflict. Millions died, but millions are now free because the United States, the United Nations, and freedom's allies acted. No Munich here. No appeasement. Korea was a victory in thwarting aggressors out to conquer the world one piece at a time. The lessons of World War II were learned . . . for awhile.

In 2010, the two Koreas are still a fact. The contrasts between the two should be studied. After the War, the South was devastated, but by 1965 the economy had recovered and the nation was thriving. *By the year 2008, South Korea was one of the top 15 economies of the world.* The North is a repressive, vacuous prison where people starve unless given international aid. It seems the only export of the North is terror. They have spent their tiny gross domestic product acquiring nuclear technology to build and sell atomic bombs to terrorists and rogue states. Red China keeps an army on its border with the North just to keep North Koreans out of China.

In South Korea, *democracy and capitalism* built a vibrant economy with a gross national product on a par with the most economically successful nations in the world just a few years after total devastation. In North Korea, *communism and dictatorship* imprisoned its people in a trash-filled wasteland with an economy that cannot feed its own population. Both these peoples were, and are, the same in every way except for their governments. *One side thrives, the other starves. This is the most realistic comparison of communism and capitalism ever devised.* The two Koreas are the ultimate experiment in the true outcomes of governmental choices. Few talk about it, but here is the reality of the choice between capitalism plus democracy plus freedom, and communism plus the inevitable communist dictatorship plus a controlled economy. For some unfathomable reason, many people in the United States and around the world still think the choice of communism and a controlled economy is best. All they have to do to learn the truth is look at the two Koreas.

Chapter 18

The Vietnam War

1945 to 1975 (United States involved 1964 to 1973)

After 30 years of war, Vietnam was conquered by the communists. Who were the winners? The communist leaders of North Vietnam were the clear winners. And who were the losers? The people of South Vietnam were the clear losers. Why did the South lose? The people of South Vietnam failed to find the fortitude to resist the invaders. South Korea won with American help because they were determined to maintain their freedom. South Vietnam lost because such determination went missing. How about the people of North Vietnam, did they win? No, they too lost. Only the leadership won. The millions of North Vietnamese bones littering Southeast Asia's landscape is proof enough the people of North Vietnam paid a horrible price for their leader's vision.

Background

After World War II, France re-established its control over Vietnam, its pre-World War II colony in Indochina. During the war the Japanese controlled the area using it as a base for attacking China and dominating the nearby sea lanes. After the Japanese surrender the Allies left the Japanese troops there to maintain order because communist guerillas were operating in Indochina, and without Japanese help they may have taken over before the French returned.

The French came back as the Japanese left. Japan believed the Vietnamese were racially inferior to them and had treated them harshly. The return of the French to their old colony might seem like a reprieve from oppression, but the French put their old administration back in place which favored the Catholic minority and generally continued to treat the Vietnamese as inferior.[365] Meanwhile, **Ho Chi Minh** had been leading a war against the Japanese. Now he would lead his troops against the French.

In Southeast Asia, Ho Chi Minh (Ho) would use Mao's guerilla war tactics to defeat the French in Vietnam and expand communist domination to the rest of Indochina. These plans were laid out in Moscow prior to the death of Stalin[366] and only came to light after the fall of the Soviet Union. Some Western scholars and politicians maintained the wars in Korea and Vietnam were civil wars having nothing to do with forces outside the divided nations.[367] Other academics had maintained the wars were part of a unified communist effort to push the West out of Asia. It turns out the wars were part of a unified plan to oust the West and its democratic ideology.

The communist dictators, Mao and Stalin, thought the West (mainly the United States) would not fight for Korea or Vietnam. In the actual event, the United States and United Nations intervened in Korea and fought the communists to a stalemate, but in Vietnam the French received less help and the United States found itself involved in Vietnam shortly after the French departed. How is it that the United States fell short in helping the French hold Vietnam but later on committed hundreds of thousands of its troops to continue the same war? This surrealistic chain of events must be examined to understand the Vietnam War.

Originally, the French were effectively fighting Ho Chi Minh's guerillas, although they were a growing threat. The 1949 fall of nationalist China to the communists changed the picture entirely. Now Ho received extensive aid that easily flowed from the USSR through communist China to Southeast Asia. The fall of China to the Reds (communists) was one of the most important events of the Cold War. The Korean War and the Vietnam War stemmed directly from that disaster caused by Truman's miserly assistance[368] to the nationalists, and huge blunders by General Marshall who advised the president on the situation. In addition, there were the usual failures of US intelligence.

---

365 The French have a way of dealing with others that seems to make everyone feel inferior, and this did not go over well after the Japanese had departed. The Japanese were far worse, but that did not mean the French were viewed as good.

366 Stalin died in 1953.

367 Many of them still maintain these were civil wars.

368 By miserly, I do not mean insubstantial. I simply mean not enough was given in military aid and support troops. US airpower alone may have given Chang enough of an edge to survive.

Once Ho was being well supplied he stepped up his campaign against the French. The strategy consisted of first gaining control of the countryside and its peasants by indoctrination of the villagers or by murdering the village leaders and replacing them with loyal communists. After the countryside was under control, larger attacks on the government would start with the goals of disrupting the economy and draining the resources and morale of the enemy. Meanwhile, additional emphasis would be placed on infiltration into the cities and establishing urban revolutionary cadres. In the final phase of the war, all-out assaults in World War II style would be launched against the French while communists revolutionaries in the cities would simultaneously rise up to overthrow the French supported government. After a series of major defeats the French would give up and leave.

The communists obtained help from the peasants through generous promises of more land and food. If cooperation from the peasants fell short, they would turn to indoctrination and then coercion. The communists counted on having excellent intelligence because they would infiltrate the government, both civilian and military, at every level. Even military secretaries were working for the Reds. The Reds would also take advantage of the corruption which riddled the society and the government in South Vietnam.

At first, the French won several bloody set piece battles[369] with the communists, but they were losing control of the countryside. After these losses Ho returned to guerrilla warfare forcing the French to spread their forces to protect many vital points of communication, command, and control. Communist ambushes of convoys became common. These ambushes cut French communications and causing numerous casualties. Because the French could not spread their units out and remain strong everywhere the insurgents struck where the French were weak causing French casualties and lowering morale. In the countryside the communists were stealing the crops from the villagers to feed their men, forcing young villagers to join their units, levying taxes on areas they controlled, and causing widespread discontent with the government.[370]

---

369 A set piece battle is a conventional battle. Two armies clash with lines of men, flanks, artillery and the rest. Guerrilla warfare entails avoiding set piece battles until the guerrilla units are strong enough for a set piece fight. The goal of turning to set piece battles is to finally destroy the government's army and take over.

370 *Street Without Joy*, Bernard B. Fall.

After years of conflict, the communist forces gained more control and built up their army to challenge the French to set piece battles once more. The war came to a strategic focal point at the battle for ***Dien Bien Phu** in 1954.* Dien Bien Phu was a large fortified French base with an airstrip in northern Vietnam near the Chinese border. The base was placed across a key enemy supply route to help stop infiltration of supplies and men into Vietnam from China. It was vital for the communists to remove this supply impediment. As the communists increased pressure on the base, the elite French Foreign Legion reinforced it. The engagement became one of prestige as much as military importance. Politically, it was a fight the French had to win.

Unfortunately, the French chose the battle site poorly. Their base was in a valley overlooked by rugged jungle-covered mountains which were perfect for concealment. In these mountains the communists dug in long-range artillery and antiaircraft guns. The French did not know the communists had these long range weapons. The French counted on their air force to resupply the base in case the roads were cut. The problem was the airstrip was under artillery fire from the moment the big guns were in place. The well sighted antiaircraft guns, concealed by the jungle, were able to ravage the French Air Force as their fighter-bombers descended to attack the hills crawling with hidden communist troops and long-range artillery.

The roads supplying the base were cut, trapping the French forces in Dien Bien Phu. Airdrops achieved some reinforcement and resupply to the trapped men, but the situation for the well-shelled troops inside the fragmenting underground citadel was anything but happy. As massive artillery barrages collapsed French positions, heavy infantry attacks engulfed their outlying strong points one by one. As always, the Foreign Legion fought bravely and savaged the Reds as they rushed forward. The communist casualties will never be known, but thousands upon thousands died in the assaults. Incredible Legion bravery and large enemy casualties made no difference as the fanatic Reds swarmed over shattered French bunkers.

Eisenhower Stays Out

The French had been asking for more American help all along, but now they increased their pleas. The French foreign minister flew to Washington to meet with President Eisenhower. The problem was that the French wanted massive American intervention, far more than an increase in the aid already being given. They needed American troops, materials, and anything and everything the United States could send in mass. To Eisenhower this sounded like another Korea, and he had just managed to end the fighting in that place. Plus, the French were asking the Americans to fight so France could keep a colony. Eisenhower thought Americans would balk at this idea.[371] Finally, the French asked the Americans to use the atomic bomb or give it to them so they could use it. Eisenhower once more demurred, and the French went home empty-handed. I think this decision hurt American relations with the French for decades to come. America had helped Korea why not help France, our old ally?

The real reason behind Eisenhower's refusal was his good sense for foreign affairs. Eisenhower did not want to commit America unless there was a **vital national interest**. This concept is critically important to understanding how a nation decides when and where to use its resources. A nation needs to closely define its VITAL national interests. Such vital interests may be military, economic, or whatever; but it must be agreed by the leadership and the people that these interests are so critical they are worth going to war over. Nations should commit their blood and treasure only on interests where national survival is at stake. At this point, we should note that totalitarian regimes do not have to consult the people on anything, so these kinds of definitions only apply to democracies (although dictatorships would be well served by following this rule).

Nations often fail to analyze their vital national interests properly. Note the problem with the Japanese analysis of their vital national interest prior to World War II. Japan decided China must be conquered as a vital national interest; therefore, the military must be supplied and oil and other resources must be obtained for military conquest. The US was standing in the way of Japan obtaining oil and other military supplies, and telling Japan to back off China; thus, America must be attacked as they were thwarting Japan's achieving a vital national interest. *Do you see the flaw*? The conquest of China, or not, would not affect the survival of Japan. Japan had decided the conquest of China was a vital national interest, but why? In fact, they just wanted to conquer China. Japan could have chosen to stop at taking Manchuria and Korea and they would have survived just fine. One might

[371] The United States believed the days of colonialism were over—and how right Washington was; however, the politicians did not see the end results of this quick collapse which brought turmoil and death on a grand scale as small nations went to war with one another over the unrealistic boundary lines drawn by the colonial empires.

decide to attack a nation that threatened them, but China was no threat to Japan in the 1930s. As such, war with the West was not justified in terms of Japan's vital national interest. The Japanese leadership determined Japan was a "have not" nation and must acquire territory to become a "have" nation. They further concluded Japan would always be under the thumb of America and Britain without the conquest of China. Oddly, after WWII, Japan was totally under control of the United State and it prospered as never before. It should have been clear in 1930 that Japan's move on China was unwise, and no challenge to America or the United Kingdom was necessary to remain a viable, prosperous country. Thus, the analysis of vital national interests *must be competent* if a nation is to expend its blood and treasure wisely.

Eisenhower clearly discerned that Vietnam was not a vital national interest of the United States. Protecting France from humiliation was not in that category either. Giving France the atomic bomb, or using it himself, could lead to worldwide complications—something Eisenhower wanted to avoid. The result was that France was getting no additional assistance from the United States.

Eisenhower had applied the correct formula for intervention abroad. The presidents that followed him would not be so wise because the philosophy changed when the men holding the top office changed. Eisenhower wanted to stay with the vital national interest analysis because it kept the United States out of foreign entanglements unless they had supreme importance. **Nixon**, Eisenhower's vice president who lost the race for the presidency in 1960, felt the same way. Presidents after Eisenhower decided when to send troops based on other concepts, and the results have been less than ideal as shown by public disenchantment with their policies.

The Fall of Dien Bien Phu

1954

With their backs to the wall, the French Foreign Legion at Dien Bien Phu fought on. Waves of artillery and enemy troops broke over the beleaguered fort and its exhausted defenders as French resistance bled away. Dien Bien Phu fell in 1954, and the communists captured about 16,500 tattered Frenchmen. The Reds paid a high price for the base (their casualties are unknown but thought to be thirty to fifty thousand), but they had it. They also had the French public. The people of France wanted out of the endless war in Southeast Asia.

At the peace talks the French gave the North to the communists while the South was to have elections to decide who would rule there. But the South did not hold elections, and a quasi-dictator, Diem, took the reins of power setting up the Republic of South Vietnam. The war was on again, but the nation of South Vietnam was weak and would fall quickly fighting against the experienced communist troops flooding down from the North.

AMERICA STEPS IN (IT)

1964

1962—Military Advisors

John F. Kennedy became president of the United States in 1960. Kennedy ran against Richard M. Nixon, the vice president under Eisenhower. As history weirdly turned out, Kennedy would start the American involvement in Vietnam and Nixon would end it many years later. In between these two men a series of incompetent decision makers created national angst over the involvement.

During the presidential race between Kennedy and Nixon they held, for the first time, a series of televised debates. These debates were critical in determining the winner of a very close contest between the two men. One significant issue was whether or not the United States should defend two small islands off the coast of Red China, Quemoy and Matsu, controlled by the Nationalist Chinese. These islands had been shelled by the communists, but no invasion had been attempted. If such an attempt did come, should the United States commit troops to defend these two small islands? Nixon, taking the approach of a seasoned diplomat's evaluation of vital national interest, said no. They were not a vital national interest because the survival of the US did not depend upon them, so no blood and treasure should be spent for the islands. Kennedy took the position that not one foot of free soil should be surrendered to the communists. Polls showed Kennedy had won on that issue. Somehow, the larger implications of this "fight for every foot of free soil" doctrine were not appreciated. This was an open commitment to fight communism anywhere and everywhere at any time. It constituted a total rejection of the vital national interest analysis. No one discerned that this idea could lead the United States into wearisome and unnecessary conflicts.

John F. Kennedy won a close election. After taking office, he began a new and far reaching foreign policy change which required a more active role for the United States in foreign affairs. The Cold War with the communists was running full blast, and Kennedy decided (along with his entire administration—including his brother Bobby Kennedy who was appointed the US Attorney General) that the United States would enact regime change if necessary to achieve victories over communism. An active role in the internal operations of foreign governments had rarely been tried before by American presidents,[372] but Kennedy wanted to do even more. It was a radical departure with the past, and it set an unfortunate precedent for the future.[373]

It was Kennedy who decided that the current president of South Vietnam (Diem) must go, and he helped coordinate a military coup that deposed and murdered Diem on November 1, 1963. It was also Kennedy who decided to commit American combat troops to Vietnam, although at the time they were called advisors and not many were sent. But the United States was in the war, and its involvement would intensify significantly.

In the United States another election was drawing near in 1964, and the debate over Vietnam had deepened. There were those in the US government who wanted a large commitment of US troops to Vietnam with the goal of achieving victory over the communists. Others were advising no increase in troops and perhaps a withdrawal of those who were there. Even the Joint Chiefs of Staffs for the US military were saying the war was unwinnable without a massive intervention, which no one wanted. According to some advisors close to President Kennedy at the time (1963), the president was planning a drawdown of troops to start right after the election in November of 1964 and a complete withdrawal was planned within a year or so thereafter. Was this true? It is very difficult to tell. The men close to Kennedy were loyalists and wanted to present him in a favorable light. The idea of an early withdrawal by Kennedy would add to his legend. The truth will never be known because the two men who knew what was next on the Kennedy agenda for Vietnam were both assassinated. The president was murdered on November 22, 1963, in Dallas, Texas, and

372 For example, T. Roosevelt had interfered in other government's internal affairs to get the Panama Canal constructed.

373 Vietnam, Kosovo, Iraq, and others.

his brother Bobby died by assassination on June 5, 1968, in Los Angeles, California. Robert F. Kennedy (Bobby) had campaigned on withdrawal from Vietnam, so there is no doubt what he was going to do if elected; however, this campaign was taking place for the election of 1968, and what changed in those intervening years was the mood of the American public. Support for the Vietnam War had badly waned, and the democrats were running on a platform of ending the war. What President Kennedy would have done after 1964, assuming he won the election, is unknown.

Johnson Commits US Troops—1964

Lyndon B. Johnson took over as president after President Kennedy's death, and won the presidency in his own right in 1964.[374] Immediately after assuming the presidency Johnson began to increase the troop levels in Vietnam. After the so-called Gulf of Tonkin incident, Johnson gained plenary power to commit troops to the war, and he did so in spades. Before Johnson left office he had placed *500,000* Americans into Vietnam. It is widely thought that Johnson lied about the attack in the Gulf of Tonkin to gain congressional authorization to widen the war.[375] By 1967, the war was not going well for the United States of America. Although American units were consistently defeating both North Vietnamese regular army units and the local Vietcong, nothing was resolved. In the few all-out battles against US troops, such as in the Ia Drang Valley in 1965, the communists learned US firepower was potent, and the US won total victories. With control of the air over South Vietnam, and lots of artillery, the US forces decimated the communists in anything like a set peace engagement. But the infiltration from North Vietnam, the ambushes, and the limited assaults went on; thus, control of the countryside and the road system was constantly in flux. Like the French, the United States and the South Vietnam military tried to protect all vital points and thereby spread their combat power. Without

---

[374] Johnson defeated Senator Goldwater by claiming Goldwater was a warmonger and implying he (Johnson) was a man of peace. It was Johnson that committed hundreds of thousands of US troops to Vietnam. Shows how much a person can trust the claims of a politician. LBJ also overcame Goldwater's charges of corruption, mainly because the press ignored them.

[375] Documents show that no attack took place on the night in question; but Johnson said otherwise, no doubt knowing the truth. Johnson was very used to lying to the public for his own gain. See: Means of Ascent (The Years of Lyndon Johnson, Volume 2) by Robert A. Caro, 1991, Vintage Press.

the support of the peasants the government of South Vietnam, even with massive American help, was not winning.

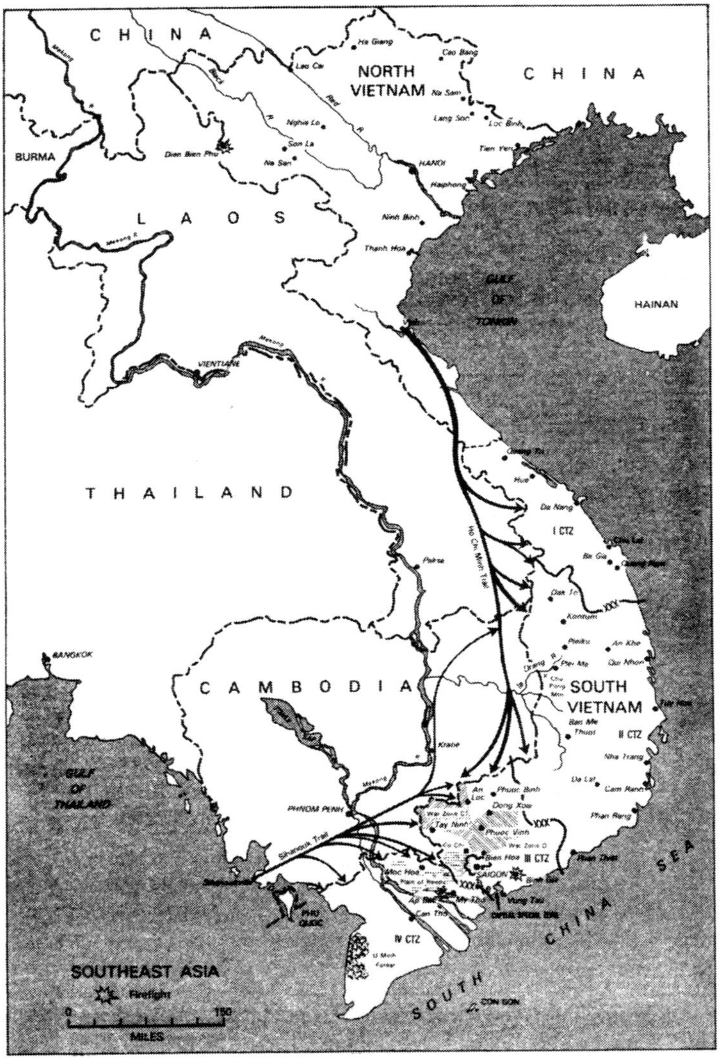

FIGURE 80 VIETNAM & HO CHI MINH TRAIL

General Westmoreland, commander of US forces in South Vietnam, was aggressive in his pursuit of the Red forces. He ordered "search and destroy" missions to sweep rural areas and keep the pressure on the communists. He rejected the strategy of establishing a line from DMZ across South Vietnam and Laos to stop enemy troops and supplies from moving south. Such aggressive search and destroy tactics put US troops at high risk because the communists knew, through spies ensconced in every corner of the South Vietnamese government, when the US patrols were going out and by what routes. The communist units could avoid the search and destroy operations whenever they wanted, but in many instances US troops were ambushed and had to fight against long odds to escape without being destroyed. US firepower, plus close air and artillery support, saved the day many times. The American problem was that no matter how many communists they managed to kill more would come down from the North. Casualties were meaningless to Ho (or his backers, China and the USSR). He had murdered hundreds of thousands after he came into power in the North, hence added deaths had no meaning to the communist leadership.

The real need was for a new kind of US strategy that would cut North Vietnam's ability to move troops and supplies south, thereby isolating the battlefield in South Vietnam. Cambodia and Laos were not neutral countries, and the US allowing this fiction to exist doomed all other efforts. South Vietnam was being invaded from North Vietnam, and the US needed to deploy its troops from the coast of South Vietnam along the DMZ through Laos to Thailand in order to cut the Ho Chie Minh trail. This would allow the ARVIN (South Vietnam's army) to pacify its own nation as the US had done in South Korea. During the Korean War, North Korea had tried to start problems in the south with guerrilla units, but the US let the South Korean Army handle that problem and concentrated on stopping the invasion from the North. At the outset of the conflict in Vietnam, President Kennedy had determined this was a new kind of war and must be fought on new terms; however, Clausewitz was not out of date and his precepts clearly told military commanders how to win this type of war (see: American Strategy in Vietnam, by H. G. Summers, Dover Publications, 2007). By isolating the battlefield in the south winning was at least possible. Without it the war would never end because North Vietnam would never stop sending troops south.

Robert McNamara, US Secretary of Defense during the Kennedy and Johnson administrations, played a key role in confusing US military goals. He implemented a complex budgeting and progress measurement system that completely disregarded the strategy and basic military principles of war (Clausewitz again) needed to focus US strategy and tactics on striking at the enemy's center of gravity, its movement of forces south.

FIGURE 81 US HELICOPTERS LIFT OFF

Another problem for the Americans was *corruption in the South Vietnamese government.376* The peasants did not want to fight for such a government making recruitment of good soldiers hard. In addition, the government was rife with communist spies. Every American operation had to be cleared through the South Vietnamese; thus, every operation was known to the Reds. In spite of these numerous disadvantages, the Americans were still "winning" in the traditional sense. More and more areas in South Vietnam were free of communist domination. The Americans also protected the harvest from communist theft and taxation, and this had impacts on the ability of the Reds to maintain control of the countryside. Nonetheless, the murders, ambushes, and coercion went on so the countryside was never secure.

American air power was having a negative impact on the communists. [377]From carriers offshore and airbases in Vietnam and Thailand, the United States could apply air power quickly and effectively at any point in the South. In addition, the United States used air power to try and cut the communist supply lines from North Vietnam to the South. The Ho

---

[376] The United States would face the same problem in the War in Iraq under President George W. Bush (Bush number 2).

[377] UH stood for Utility Helicopter. The troops nicknamed it the Huey. It was the "jeep" of modern warfare.

Chi Minh Trail traversed the area of Laos and Cambodia[378] all the way to the southern tip of South Vietnam. The United States tried to interdict this supply route with air power all through the war; however, even though tons of supplies were destroyed, the trail was never cut. In spite of the bombing attacks on the Ho Chi Minh Trail, and the other efforts to cut supply lines from North Vietnam, the communists in the South remained well supplied throughout the war. This again demonstrates the critical nature of the loss of China to the Reds. If the United States could have cut the supply lines to the battlefields in South Vietnam the communists may have lost. It was the endless movement of supplies from Russia through Red China to North Vietnam and then, after the addition of numerous men, to South Vietnam that determined the outcome of the war as much as any other factor.

President Johnson wanted the war to end, and after being rebuffed by the North in his call for negotiations he began bombing North Vietnam with the goal of forcing them to the negotiation table. Unfortunately for the United States, Johnson insisted on a list of politically correct targets that hamstrung the ability of the US Air Force and US Navy to successfully destroy the North's war-making ability. Their main harbor, Haiphong, was allowed to operate without any interference during the Johnson years. Russia, China, and other nations brought supplies openly to North Vietnam through this harbor, which made US Airmen furious. Because of US Bombing restrictions the communists soon developed, again without interference (American airmen could see the facilities being constructed), a sophisticated air-defense system in the North. The US attacks on ground targets became predictable (because of White House interference), so the communists had a simple time arranging their air defenses. Surface to air missiles (SAMs) and triple canopy flack brought down many US pilots. In addition, the North was flying excellent MIGs with good pilots against US airmen. The resulting air war over North Vietnam was intense. The United States was losing aircraft, and the results of the bombing were less than satisfactory. The Johnson White House restrictions allowed prime military targets to go untouched. Oil storage, hydroelectric power plants, harbor equipment (cranes, piers, etc.), and other vital installations were not bombed.

Not only was the United States not using the atomic bomb, it was not using its conventional war-making ability to its full potential. Somehow,

---

378 The neighboring nations to both Vietnams and controlled by the Communist along the area of the trail.

using all the military power available was unpopular in the Johnson administration. Even though the war was costing American lives at the rate of five hundred per month (at the peak), President Johnson seemed to believe world opinion would turn against him if he bombed the "off target" areas. In fact, all he did was drag out a brutal war. The air force wanted an early all-out bombing effort with no restraint, and they wanted the effort continued unabated until the North stopped sending troops and supplies south. Johnson's restrictions were a grave error, and it set another dreadful precedent for the future. When America later decided how to use its war-making potential the idea of a limited conventional response was adopted over and over again. It seems American military lives were less important than looking good to the international community.

The communists were ruthless in their suppression of villagers, and this was a key element in their maintaining control of the countryside. Murder, kidnapping, and theft were major components of communists' efforts to control the peasants of Vietnam. In 1961, before the US intervention, the communists killed *four thousand village officials in that year alone.* There was also the constant indoctrination of the young people and new recruits who were told they had to expel foreign invaders and tyrants from their land. Communist propaganda stressed how the kindly "Uncle Ho" would look after them as a grandfather might after the capitalist devils were driven off. All lies of course. After the communist takeover there was murder and imprisonment on a grand scale. Even though Ho Chi Minh died before South Vietnam fell, it is clear his followers did exactly what he would have done.

Tet Offensive

1968

In 1968, communist leaders Ho Chi Minh and General Giap[379] decided to launch a massive offensive with the goal of capturing the cities of South Vietnam and causing a popular uprising against the unpopular South Vietnamese government. The communists assembled their forces and managed to move them south without being detected by American intelligence. On January 30, 1968, Giap launched the **Tet Offensive** which managed to capture some cities in South Vietnam (most notably Hue), but no popular uprising resulted. In the end, Ho's offensive was

[379] Giap was the overall communist military commander for North Vietnam.

a decisive and multiphase *defeat.* The local Vietcong organizations were wiped out, effectively ceasing to exist, while the regular divisions sent from North Vietnam were extensively damaged. As a military operation the Tet Offensive was an unmitigated disaster for the communists.

But something else was in play during the Tet Offensive. The **American press corps** had decided the Vietnam War was wrongheaded, and their reporting became nothing more than communist propaganda. The TV networks (ABC, CBS, NBC), the major newspapers (*New York Times, LA Times, Washington Post, Chicago Tribune,* etc.), and liberal weekly news magazines (*Time, Newsweek*) all reported the Tet Offensive was a *comprehensive American defeat.* To do this, the reporters had to lie about what they saw all around them, and they had to disregard US Army reports about the extent of the enemy defeat. In essence, they denounced the reports from the US Army and State Department while publishing communist propaganda from North Vietnam as true.

FIGURE 82 MARINES IN VIETNAM

These press reports discouraged the American public. In any war, if the press tells of defeat the general population becomes demoralized. At the start of WWII the press reports were repeats of American propaganda, but as the war went on, with the cooperation of the US Military, the press reports became more realistic. The turning point was Guadalcanal where the navy decided to report just how things were really going there, and the possibility that the Americans might lose to the Japanese. The American public responded well to the truth, and it became common to report what was actually going on.

The activities and reporting of the mainstream news outlets about Vietnam unnerved the American military. Being negative was bad enough, but outright lying and repeating communist propaganda was outrageous. Mistrust began to grow between the military and the mainstream press organizations. The gap grew wider as the war went on, and at war's end the military abhorred the press and began systematically excluding the mainstream press from obtaining operational information. This mistrust continues to this day as US military leadership thinks the mainstream media is uniformly liberal, anti-military, and opposed to ideals the military reveres. History tells us that a lack belief in the nation results in defeat for the armed forces (Austria-Hungarian empire, Rome, France 1940). The media consistently leak secret or classified information to the world endangering military lives. The media also downplay military accomplishments. This current lack of trust between the military and the media started with how the War in Vietnam was reported.

President Johnson was toppled because his Vietnam War strategy failed. As major voices in the Democratic Party came forward and objected to the war, challengers appeared in 1968 to run against President Johnson for the nomination of the Democratic Party. Because of the pressure to step aside Johnson announced he would not seek another term as president. It is perhaps fitting that the man who committed the United States to the Vietnam War for foggy reasons at best, and fought the war demanding restraints impossible to understand, had to step aside. Johnson's unfathomable total political commitment to the war, his irresponsible constraints on the military, and the expansive social welfare programs enacted during the fighting, displayed incompetence in war, economics, and international affairs unparalleled in modern American history.

NIXON GETS THE UNITED STATES OUT

1973

The winner in 1968 for president of the United States was Republican **Richard Nixon,** an old name in politics and Kennedy's rival for the presidency in 1960. Nixon was back, and he was going to show the United States and the world his excellence in foreign affairs.

President Nixon clearly understood the American public wanted out of Vietnam, but a lot of them did not want to leave with a "loss." Through the process of "Vietnamization" he would turn the war over to the South

Vietnamese, and while doing so he would reduce the number of American units in Vietnam.[380] This was an obvious concept and should have been the policy from the inception. In fact, that was the role of the original US Advisors: show the South Vietnamese how to fight while the United States improved their equipment and training. The war should never have been a mainly US enterprise where the United States bore the brunt of the fighting. Clearly, if a nation cannot defend itself the United States cannot commit itself to eternal conflict on its behalf. Nixon simply implemented the simple solution, but he was restrained by time and a discontented democratic Congress. Somehow, he had to make progress immediately or he would fail in his endeavors to extract the United States while preserving South Vietnam's freedom (such as it was). Nixon wanted what he termed "Peace with honor." To this end, he wanted a peace treaty with the communist North which would guarantee the South's sovereignty.

To achieve these goals, Nixon allowed the military more latitude in prosecuting the war. Hanoi's Haiphong Harbor was mined which cut off supplies flowing to the communist capital by sea. He authorized bombing formerly off-limits military targets, and he authorized the carpet bombing of Hanoi by B-52 bombers. Diplomatically, he sent Henry Kissinger to Paris to talk with the North Vietnamese, and he began to open doors to normalization of relations with China. Nixon knew that between China and North Vietnam hostility was historically common, so his plans were to drive a wedge between them. Nixon realized China was not going to abandon the North in its war against America and the South; however, the mere threat of China *reducing* its aid would cause the North pause. Neither communist China nor the USSR had thriving economies, and the massive aid being sent to North Vietnam was a drag on their own economic positions; thus, a way out of the war would benefit them as well.

Nixon's moves were exceptional. By releasing the military to do their job he was able to inflict significant economic and military harm on North Vietnam. He allowed military raids into Cambodia to destroy communist

380 It should be well noted that other nations were in Vietnam. Australia, for example, perceived it was in their national interest to keep communism as far away from them as possible and so assisted in the war.

supply dumps, and his bombing of Hanoi inflicted significant and costly damage on its infrastructure. By allowing a quick increase in military pressure, while at the same time opening negotiations with China, he managed to get the North Vietnamese to sign a peace treaty agreeing to leave the South alone.

As the United States began its withdrawal from Vietnam Nixon got himself into the political tar pit of Watergate which ended his presidency. Nixon decided to resign from office in December of 1973, and the *unelected* vice president **Gerald Ford** took his place. At the same time, Congress, being controlled by huge democratic majorities that despised President Nixon, banned all US help to South Vietnam.

In 1972, before the last of the American units were removed from Vietnam, the North gathered together a large invasion force and attacked South Vietnam from Cambodia and Laos in a fierce Spring Offensive. This force included large numbers of tanks and armored vehicles. Some American troops and advisors were still in the country, along with helicopters and other aircraft. With help from these few Americans and their air power, the South Vietnamese drove the invading units back to their start points and inflicted heavy losses (over 100,000 dead) on the communists. At this point, many in the US military took heart. The partially trained South Vietnamese had done well. Maybe they could hold on after all.

THE SOUTH FALLS

1975

In 1975, after Nixon was out of office and Congress had cut off all aid, military and financial, to South Vietnam the communists invaded again. This time, they came from the north across the DMZ and from the west across the central highlands with an enormous force of more than 22 divisions. They began to attack down toward Saigon, the capital of South Vietnam. The invasion began in April of 1975, two years after the last US Units had been removed.[381] During those few years the South Vietnamese had not received military aid from America because of congressional legislation halting such aid. Now the aircraft and tanks the United States left in South Vietnam needed parts. When the South Vietnamese government

---

381 By 1972, only sixty-nine thousand US Troops were in Vietnam. South Vietnam held out longer than normally remembered.

approached the World Bank for a loan they had to deal with Robert McNamara[382] who was by then the head of the World Bank. They never had a chance with the ex-defense secretary. McNamara quickly refused their request. Another powerful American, in a new and important international role, turned his back on South Vietnam.

In spite of the odds against them in 1975, the South Vietnamese army initially fought well and held up the communist invasion. Then the president of South Vietnam issued a fateful order. He told some of the troops engaging the communists in the north to fall back to a predetermined line above the capital where a stronger defense could be mounted. Once the troops began to fall back the retreat turned into a rout, and the communists were in Saigon without delay (looks as if he should have issued a Hitler "no retreat" order). Pleas for help to American fell on deaf ears. The South fell to the Reds.

The United States had "lost" the Vietnam War, a war in which the it never lost a significant battle, and a war in which the Americans had inflicted untold casualties on its opponent.[383] About *48,000 Americans* had died fighting the communists. (*The New York Times Almanac*, 2008, reports US Vietnam War deaths at 47,355 from all causes, and including all services. Some of the differing figures result from different dates for the start and stop of US involvement) In my opinion, *at least 1 million communists* were killed by the US military during the period of US involvement. Additional losses were inflicted on the North by ARVIN units. The United States had lost in the sense that its former ally was destroyed. However, South Vietnam was not a US colony and US troops were sent there to preserve South Vietnam's freedom. The South Vietnamese were the losers, and the Americans were interested, if bloodied, participants. The major impact on the United States would be economic, psychological, and political.

The North Vietnamese had broken the treaty signed in 1973 and the United States did nothing. President Ford doubtless felt confined by the congressional acts preventing any kind of interference with events in Vietnam; however, Ford was still president and still in control of the military. He could have cited the breached treaty and easily justified bombing

---

382 The former secretary of defense who figured largely in starting and managing the war in Vietnam under Kennedy and Johnson. McNamara was one of the reasons the war was fought so poorly.

383 Proof that Clausewitz was right when he said war was political (a continuation of policy by other means).

the long columns of communist tanks and men moving south. At least it may have given the South Vietnamese a chance to hold on. As it was, the resignation of Nixon led directly to the fall of South Vietnam.

What is doubly strange about the events in Vietnam is that most people do not remember that Kennedy got the US into Vietnam, Johnson dramatically upped the commitment, and Nixon got America out of Vietnam. What the American media, and most people, want to remember is Kennedy was a hero and Nixon was a jerk. When discussing the presidents, Kennedy is normally credited with the desire to get us out while Nixon is smeared with the idea that he expanded the war. Love them or hate them, Kennedy got the United States in, and Nixon got the United States out. The old rivals of the 1960 debates bookended the war.[384] In the event, Nixon was right when he said the United States must closely evaluate its vital national interests, and Kennedy was wrong when he said we could not give up one foot of free ground. Vietnam was the test of the two theories—and Nixon was correct.

AFTER THE FALL

1975 to 1978

It was over. All of Vietnam came under communist rule at an extreme cost to the people of South and North Vietnam. The communists murdered thousands of people who had helped the Americans. Many boatloads of starving, half-dead South Vietnamese people, risking all to flee Vietnam, were picked up at sea. Some refugees made it all the way to Australia by boat. Horrifying stories of oppression and murder were recounted. The numbers who died trying to flee the "workers' paradise" of communist Vietnam are unknown, but it was clearly many thousands.

Worse was to come.

The communists took over the rest of Laos and Cambodia. Little is known about events in Laos, but in Cambodia the truth bled out. Literally. On April 17, 1975, the communists under Pol Pot captured Phnom Penh the capital of Cambodia. Immediately thereafter Pol Pot began systematically

---

[384] Kennedy and Nixon bookended another US endeavor, the race to the moon. Kennedy announced it was Americans' goal to reach the moon by the end of the decade. When the landing was made, Nixon was president.

killing millions of Cambodians—because they were city dwellers.[385] The communist Khmer Rouge marched millions of innocents into the countryside to "teach" them how to be peasants. In fact, no re-education occurred. It was simply a plot to kill everyone that lived in the cities. There was no reason to execute these people. This debauchery was a direct result of the communist takeover of Vietnam.

Why? The Analysis of the War and its Aftermath

The strange circle of history was complete. The United States turned down the French when they asked for aid against the communists, then the United States, under President Kennedy, committed troops to Vietnam. Following Kennedy's assassination, President Lyndon Johnson fully committed the United States to Vietnam and then refused to use the available power of the US Military to "win." Then President Nixon, Kennedy's rival in the 1960 election for president, took office and got America out of Vietnam with a treaty guaranteeing the North would respect the South's sovereignty. Nixon resigned under threat of impeachment, Congress forbade aid to South Vietnam, the communists invaded with a large army, and South Vietnam fell. Then, as predicted, Indochina began to fall to the communists, and slaughters of vast proportions took place in South Vietnam, Cambodia, and probably Laos.

Did all of Southeast Asia fall to the communists? No. Burma and Thailand remained non-communist without massive intervention of US Troops. Both nations were threatened with communist guerilla insurgents for a while, but those problems were held in check. What was the difference? The key difference concerned the governments and people of these nations. Both nations possessed marginally decent governments in 1975, in that, corruption levels were less than Vietnam. In both of these nations, the population remained at least somewhat loyal to the government. The terrain was similar, but the people and the governments vastly different. The communists failed to make inroads when the population remained loyal to the government and rejected communist intimidation tactics.

In addition, the lessons of Cambodia and Vietnam became well known throughout Southeast Asia. People could see what it meant to lose to the communists. The population began to reject the murderers' lies and

---

385 An estimated 1.7 million people were killed by Pol Pot and his Khmer Rouge. The estimate is probably low.

realized what they faced under communist rule. Understandably, the people of Thailand, Malaya, Burma, and Indonesia wanted nothing to do with the bloodthirsty murderers.

Another reason might have been in play, but one seldom discussed. The North Vietnamese admitted losing 1 million men in its war with South Vietnam; however, communism and lying go together. Reasonable estimates put communist losses at 2 million, and North Vietnam's infrastructure was badly damaged. After the United States departed Vietnam, China and the USSR ceased sending aid. Their goals were reached. The United States was humiliated, had lost a long and brutal war in Asia, and under President Carter became less involved with the world. The world became open to aggressive communist adventures designed to bring areas in the Middle East, Africa, and South America under communist control. Monetary debts owed by North Vietnam to China and the USSR for the massive amounts of arms, ammunition, rockets, cannons, and antiaircraft guns, must have been considerable, and that debt went unpaid—forever. Although default was probably expected, the communist giants had economic problems and the default no doubt caused tensions.

In my opinion, the rest of Indochina defeated communism because of losses the United States and its allies inflicted on North Vietnam, and because support from China and the Soviets ended. Looked at in this way, the Vietnam War probably prevented the subjugation of the rest of Indochina. Note that the economy of Vietnam is the worst in the region by far even thirty plus years after the end of the war.

Books and Resources:

This is a difficult subject to recommend books on because it is hard to get non-biased views of the war. Until everyone who fought and reported on the war is dead, emotions run too high for an unbiased view to emerge. I personally like books just recounting battles and their outcomes, while briefly listing political events in Washington DC. I recommend avoiding books listing only US casualties in the war, and *any* book by a journalist covering the war for major US news media outlets. **Nothing they say can be trusted**. The *Vietnam War for Dummies* is one of these books looking at the war from an antiwar perspective and is therefore *useless* for studying the events objectively. The vast majority of books on the war have an anti-war bias—*especially* books authored by journalists of the era.

Vietnam: the Necessary War: a Reinterpretation of America's Most Disastrous Military Conflict by Michael Lind, Free Press, 2002.

Unheralded Victory: the Defeat of the Viet Cong and the North Vietnamese Army, 1961-1973, by Mark Woodruff, Presidio Press, 2005.

Street Without Joy by Bernard B. Fall, 2005, Stackpole Books. Probably the best background book on the Vietnam War.

The Fifty Year Wound: How America's Cold War Victory Has Shaped Our World, by Derek Leebaert, Back Bay Books, 2003.

American Strategy in Vietnam, A Critical Analysis, by Colonel Harry G. Summers, Jr., Dover Publications, 2007. At 121 pages and a price of $8.95 this is probably *the best book* on the War in Vietnam that a student of history can acquire.

The Vietnam War, Bernard C. Natty, Barnes and Noble, 1998. A very factual record of the main events of the war and its aftermath. Very little bias displayed by this author.

CHAPTER 19

THE POSTMODERN WORLD . . . OR NOT?

What is a "postmodern" world? What is modern today will not be tomorrow. Many historians call the world we are in "postmodern," implying the modern world was yesterday. By definition that is unsound and confusing. *Modern is now.* The *Random House Dictionary* defines modern as "of or relating to the present . . . characterized by or using the most up-to-date techniques . . . from the Latin *modo* meaning just now." Thus, we should reject the term "postmodern" because it implies we have gone beyond now . . . which is impossible. However, the term "postmodern" has been widely applied to our time as describing a world of **relativity**. In the so-called postmodern world *all is relative and nothing has a permanent foundation because there is no clear central hierarchy or organizing mega-narratives*; thus, it embodies extreme complexity, contradiction, ambiguity, and diversity. This definition sets the world adrift with no moral, spiritual, or even realistic underpinnings. To understand even a smidgen of this we must consider modern philosophy and its impact on the world—the postmodern world. This we will handle below after a few words on other pertinent subjects.[386]

More than one author analyzing history has determined humankind is uncivilized. They opine that our civilization is a thin veneer hiding the barbarian right under the surface. Pointing to history they call out: The French Reign of Terror in the French Revolution, the Final Solution of Adolf Hitler, the murderers Stalin and Mao who massacred millions as proof modern people are not so modern, rather, we are similar to Mongols who slaughtered millions as they swept across central Asia and Eastern Europe.

---

386 For an excellent Post-modern view of history read *The Times History of the World*, by Richard Overy, 2008, Times Books. Especially interesting are pages xviii and xix where historical theory is discussed from the Greeks to the Post-modern era. Overy does not say his view is Post-modern; however, when he says there are no true turning points in history, and progress is a false concept, he is adopting the Post-modern view of no mega-narratives, or no overarching patterns.

Hitler, Stalin, and other modern dictatorships have shown ordinary people will willingly participate in such massacres. If these naysayers are correct, then our modern world is a façade that will quickly break down into vicious tribalism and ad hoc murder if unwatched for even one moment. This may tie into the postmodern world view of chaos and uncertainty.

The Long View of History

From a historical perspective, it is difficult to go beyond 1990 and call it history, since we are only in 2010 as I write. Eighteen years into the past is not really history. I remember Elvis Presley, and that was in the 1950s. ***When we get too close to the present we sacrifice the "long view" that tells us what is important and what is not.*** Moreover, the *emotions of the recent past* are still there. Vietnam still stirs up a lot of hate and discontent no matter what political side a person is on; thus, the long view is lost. The long view tells us that Impressionism was a very important art movement, but at the time most art critics and art buyers thought the paintings were junk. Nietzsche's philosophy books did not sell during his time, and most thought he was nuts (in fact he did go insane), but today we see Nietzsche as an accurate foreteller of the future. Without the long view we cannot know where history is really going or where it is now. If history had taken another course, Nietzsche could have been an unknown nut job and Impressionism relegated to the trash bin. From here on in, we must be very careful to note that we are dealing with events that are too close in time to judge effectively.

What About the West is Unique?

When we study the history of Western civilization we need to stop and ask ourselves what is unique about Western history and its inheritors: America, Canada, Australia, and New Zealand. In this we are mainly comparing the West (Western Europe, America, Canada, Australia, and New Zealand) to China, Siberia, Japan, Korea, Mongolia, Indochina, the Near East, Egypt, Turkey, the Middle East, India, Africa, Latin America, and Eastern Europe. Here is a list:

- *The individual is greater than the state* is the most important political idea in history, and the West acquired it from ancient Greece. The rest of the world rejects this notion.

- *The fall of the Western Roman Empire,* the subsequent colonization of Rome by barbarian tribes, and the loss of the Roman civilization is an event that is unique to Western Europe. The shattering of Rome was so complete it allowed a new civilization to grow up in its place; however, Roman law and literature survived to influence the new Western World that arose from Rome's ashes.

- The *Roman Catholic Church and Protestant Christianity* grew first from the ashes of the Roman Empire and much later the Protestant Reformation. These religions once dominated Europe because of the Renaissance, the Age of Discovery, and Imperialism. These ideals survive into the modern world as both a unifying and divisive force.

- *The Renaissance* was unique to Europe, and without this flowering of knowledge everything would be different. The Renaissance brought the scientific method, empiricism, modern philosophy, the concept of progress, and many other concepts to the West and the world. This event alone makes the Western World very different from the remaining world's cultures.

- The *scientific method* grew from the Renaissance and allowed Europe to advance far beyond the rest of the world in empirical knowledge, technology, medicine, and exploration.

- *The idea of progress* grew from the Renaissance, spreading to all of Europe and its offshoots in America and elsewhere.

- *World Wars I and II,* the most destructive in history, threw the Western World into chaos and made the dream of progress questionable.

- *WWI & WWII smashed Western Europe and Russia,* and this changed the outlook of Western Europe. America, Australia, New Zealand, Canada, and others maintained a more positive outlook; however, as time progressed, the gloom of the two World Wars, plus unsolvable new problems, overwhelmed even these areas. Victory in the Cold War did not eliminate the depressive effects of the 20th Century.

- *Capitalism, and economic freedom, including private property rights* are hallmarks of the Western world. They are major reasons behind the prosperity of the West because they open the door for vast rewards to the person who can innovate. Capitalism requires individual

> freedom and the protection of private property. Without political freedom capitalism cannot work. Whatever the problems, the economic and political freedoms granted by capitalism far outweigh any downside. Beyond the West, such economic and political freedoms are only dreams.

All these events make the Western world and anyone growing up in it unique. From this alone, we can see how history may determine mind-sets and thus decisions made by differing cultures. The West is unique, as each individual is unique, and the decisions by Western governments and individuals raised in the West show this difference.

MODERN PHILOSOPHY—OF THE WEST

Please understand that all the philosophies examined here are grossly oversimplified and do not in any way explain the true complexity of the ideas involved.—AD[2]

As stated in our chapters on ancient history, Greek philosophy covered all the basic ideas found in Western philosophy. As time marched on, Western philosophy began to get bogged down in definitional problems and finally came to rest on the jagged rocks of **epistemology**.[387] **David Hume** effectively argued that what we call knowledge is only a set of experiences which cannot be depended upon to be true. For example, just because one has been adequately sustained by eating bread does not mean that one will always be so sustained. He even went so far as to prove that just because we have watched the sun come up every morning for fifty years does not mean it will come up tomorrow; thus, there is no knowledge of any kind. Finally, Hume proposed that he did not exist and went on to prove it to his own satisfaction. Most philosophers wished Hume had not existed. His form of philosophy is termed ***skepticism***, and in Hume's case *extreme* skepticism.

British ***empiricism*** argued all knowledge came from *experience* alone. Empiricism was opposed to the philosophical position of ***rationalism***, which stressed *innate ideas*—ideas that come from the brain alone without sensory input—were all that was true. Since Hume destroyed the idea of knowledge coming from experience he put a hammerlock on *innate* ideas as well as *sensory* ideas. Oh well . . . since Hume proved he did not exist we can safely move on. By the way, empiricism and rationalism both survived Hume.

---

[387] The branch of philosophy studying the nature of knowledge and in particular its foundations, scope, and validity.

Compare empiricism to **Descartes (I think therefore I am)** who thought he was, and therefore he really was, and this means the brain can think without sensory input. Descartes' reasoning might be hard to follow, but at least he thought he existed, or because he thought he thought, thus he existed . . . or some such thing. Descartes declared, "I think, therefore I am." This was the classic statement allowing Descartes to prove his existence, and from that he built up his understanding of the world and all he experienced in it. The German ***idealist*** agreed with Descartes that the mind, its thoughts and ideas, was most important rather than the unreliable world of sensory perception. As the reader can ascertain, these arguments hearken back to the Greek philosophers Plato (forms or universals—the mind was most important) and Aristotle (the concrete world of sensory perception is most important).

Modern philosophy has tried to remove itself from this logical conundrum foisted upon it by skepticism, empiricism, and rationalism by avoiding definitional arguments. Many philosophies, such as **Ayn Rand's *objectivism*,** simply state as a given fact that the world does exist outside of our senses, and since we can measure this world we can depend upon its existence. Rand argued there was a "mind independent" reality, and individuals are in contact with that reality through their senses. By starting from this point, Rand avoided the problems of epistemology and its focus on how a person can know the world exists and whether their perceptions are accurately interpreting reality. Contrast objectivism with the ideas of **Descartes** who thought that sensory perceptions came to him involuntarily—that is without his having willed them to occur. From this, he concludes there is evidence of an external world which was something outside his mind; however, Descartes also thought that what existed in the mind was more important and more reliable than that which one "knew" through the senses. As one can see, both Descartes and Rand are arguing against skepticism because Hume had destroyed the ability of the human mind to prove anything existed. Rand puts the emphasis on the outside world of measurement, and Descartes puts the emphasis on the internal world of the mind (thought), but both agreed the world outside the mind did exist.

Kant, the great German idealist, tried a new way to break the deadlock by reasoning that rationalism (innate ideas in the mind) and empiricism (all knowledge is gained through sensory experience) could be reconciled. Kant decided there were two kinds of judgments: *analytic* where the truth is determined within itself, and *synthetic* where truth has to be determined by an investigation such as looking at a person to observe if they are present at a certain location. There was also *transcendental* knowledge (*a priori* or before observation or study—that which you know is true), and *empirical* knowledge (a posteriori or after) which one must study or experiment to find out if it is true. Kant thought a *synthetic a priori* concept could be a universal truth proven through experimentation. Thus, transcendental or prior knowledge which could be proven by experimentation could be the foundation for *discovering universal truths that all could agree on,* thereby putting philosophy on a firm footing and avoiding endless arguments about whether truth could ever be discovered or known. Using these methods, Kant decided the universe was chaotic, and man's mind imposed order onto what was actually chaos, and this perceived order becomes our reality. Nice try, but not everyone agreed. What else would one expect from men with sharp minds and strong opinions? Therefore, the arguments continue . . . Here are a few more variations on the theme:

Utilitarianism is a moral doctrine that states an action must be measured by its contribution to the good or "the greatest good for the greatest number." As we can see, this argument avoids the problem of epistemology by simply ignoring the discussion. It at least attempts to form a moral underpinning for a person's actions. Rather than engage in circular arguments about thoughts or senses, utilitarianism wants to discuss how to make moral decisions. The problem arises when people disagree what course of action will result in the greatest good for the greatest number, but even without philosophical agreement individuals will at least have an agreed upon common goal of attempting to reach "the good" ("The good" is me being rich and healthy . . .).

Positivism is another attempt to solve the problem of knowledge. This philosophy holds that the only authentic knowledge is scientific, that is, the only true "knowledge" is that obtained by using the scientific method. Of course, the skeptics simply said even this kind of knowledge comes from experience and is therefore no different from other knowledge gained from experience—unreliable. Positivism at least gives some basis for agreement on facts, in that the scientific method demanded repeatable experiments; thus, even though based on a belief in the reliability of sensory perceptions, at least it demands agreement on those perceptions. Simply saying one cannot depend on sensory perceptions is getting nowhere, so why not agree that if the same results can be obtained from experiments then the perception is valid enough to build on. Idealists and skeptics still want to argue the point, but the positivists ignore them (compare to objectivism). (Having performed numerous experiments, I am certain that happiness arrives when I have money, lots of money . . .).

Rationalism emphasizes the role of human reason in discovering reality.[388] The philosopher **John Locke** argued the mind is a blank slate and experience alone can leave a mark. This rejects the role of reason in discovering reality or truth. ***Realism*** is a philosophy that holds abstract objects corresponding to universal terms (chair for example) have a real existence (**Plato** argued this) much like rationalism. ***Idealism*** holds that nothing can be known outside of the human mind, and thus (in some idealist concepts) nothing exists apart from the mind (compare to Zen Buddhism).

Kant, who thought we could know more than just what is in our minds, developed ***transcendental idealism.*** Kant argued we could directly know the possibility of "things in themselves." This world of "things in themselves" might exist (a possibility), but actually knowing this world is impossible. Thus, when we experience something, a ball for example, we experience the object as it appears to us and not as the ball is "*in and of itself.*" (This kind of stuff drives me nuts). As we have pointed out above, Kant's efforts are exacting in that he was trying to establish a basis for agreements on universals, but this philosophy is hard to apply in the everyday world. For somewhat dull types such as me, Kant's arguments are mostly linguistic intrigues in which I quickly lose my way.

Existentialism argues life is meaningless, and people can decide for themselves their own meaning and essence of life and that determination is valid. An existentialist will focus on finding meaning in life through existence alone. Existentialism rejects any definition of humans as rational. Existence comes before, and is primary to, any human definition of reality. This avoids the problems of how we know the world exists, assumes it does, and argues one must find a meaning in life. Unfortunately, Existentialism says life is actually meaningless, but an individual must find meaning just from one's very existence. Worse, the individual must do this alone. When accomplished, the determination is valid for that individual.

Nietzsche made the famous statement "God is dead," meaning the secular, scientific world destroyed the concept of God. He thought the destruction of God must lead to the loss of an agreed upon universal perspective, and this would lead to the loss of the idea of truth as an objective concept (compare to post-modern). The result would be the death of morals and morality. All that remained to guide life was one's own internal perspective (compare to existentialism). Nietzsche was predicting a future world

388 Note that rationalism sounds a lot like Descartes, and empiricism sounds a lot like objectivism.

without morals in the traditional sense, which would also mean all the philosophers' arguments failed to produce anything except confusion and more arguments. Nietzsche's arguments were simple. The strong will rule and morality will not survive.

All this is contradictory and confusing. The ancient history section points out that as one philosopher came up with an idea another philosopher trashed it. There is a kind of time line to this, because the older the philosophy the more it is attacked. This is an endless progression of nothingness as no progress is ever made; however, another philosopher, **Hegel**, tried to overcome this problem with his philosophy (see, it never ends . . . never).

Hegel, who is nearly impossible to understand, wrote that progress is constant in nearly all fields of human endeavor (including philosophy). He believed that when any idea became generally accepted a contradictory idea must soon challenge it. These two opposing ideas would then battle it out, and eventually a change must occur that takes the best of *both* concepts and incorporates them into a third concept. The third combined concept then becomes the generally accepted idea, and we are back where we started. Following all this, the new generally accepted idea is challenged by a contrary idea hence starting the formula all over again. This process is termed ***the dialectic***. Through this progression constant improvement results in all fields of human endeavor. Hegel seems to be an optimistic fellow. This is summed up, incorrectly according to experts in Hegel's ideas, in this chain: ***thesis, antithesis, synthesis.*** Another way to put it might be old idea (thesis), contrary idea (antithesis), new idea that combines the old and the contrary ideas (synthesis, which transforms into the thesis) and then repeat the process again. The key here is the concept that the old and new ideas both contain truth that the synthesis will preserve. Hegel studied history and thought this is how history advanced.

I do not accept Hegel's concept as valid. For example, Christianity and Islam have been competing ideas for over one thousand years; however, there has been no synthesis between the two competing concepts. Two other competing concepts are democracy and dictatorship, and no synthesis has occurred between these two extremes. Where does one find a half of an election? Individualism and collectivism are also two conflicting ideas that have not found a synthesis because either the group (state) is more important or the individual is more important. These two ideas do not meld. Philosophy, modern or ancient, has not advanced because it cannot advance. People do not agree on ideas at a foundational level and never will as long as they think for themselves. Nevertheless, we do not want to underrate the impact of philosophy. It is of vital importance. For example, when the ancient Israelites invaded Canaan, God told them to annihilate the cities and people they found there. Seems strange, as people are a valuable asset; however, if a person thinks about the invasion from Hegel's philosophical point of view all of the people had to be killed because, if allowed to live, there would be a joining (synthesis) between the Israelite's ideas and the ideas of the conquered. Maintaining the purity of Israelite ideas required the death of all the opposing ideas. As ideas resided in the people's heads they had to be detached.

Philosophy deeply affects the actions of governments. For example, the Constitution of the United States embodies the concept of the individual being more important than the state as critical to governance. As a result, the first Ten Amendments to the Constitution set forth a series of individual rights, such as freedom of speech, that the government cannot violate ("Congress shall make no law . . ."). At one point, the US Supreme Court ruled nude dancing was freedom of speech (which I disagree with, but no one cares about my opinion), and as such, it took on the status of an individual right. Even though 99 percent of the nation might disagree with nude dancing, the individual can keep that right against the entire state because the individual is greater than the state. This is an expression of the ultimate power of the individual and is an open display of the power of the individual in the US Constitutional system. In other systems, the fact that 99 percent of the country would be against this "speech" would automatically end its existence. In a dictatorship, if the state (the dictator) decides nude dancing is wrong it remains wrong even if 99 percent of the people are for it, because the state is greater than the individual.

Be aware that these philosophic differences make a huge variation in the way people approach the world. If life has no meaning (***philosophical naturalism***) then why protect life? Abortion assumes that *certain* lives have no meaning. The Nazis applied the same concept when deciding to murder the Jews. They simply determined certain lives were without meaning or were outright evil. Once we determine that we can take certain lives, for whatever reason, the concept can expand to other lives branded as worthless by the state. The Nazis quickly expanded the "no purpose" rule to include the mentally ill, Gypsies, Slavs, and many others. We have already expanded the abortion rule (some lives have no value) to include those who are terminally ill and requesting death (euthanasia). Concepts of ***utilitarianism***, the greatest good for the greatest number, can easily justify abortion or euthanasia. A terminally ill person lingering on is a huge cost to our economy, society, and the family. The greatest good would be to kill the person and use the medical and economic resources elsewhere. ***Existentialism*** allows suicide or assisted suicide because the individual determines his own existence; thus, he can choose to end his existence. Compare this to the ***Jewish and Christian*** philosophies holding human life as sacred, and each life has specific purposes as determined by God. Christian and Jewish philosophy prohibits abortion, suicide, and euthanasia because God decides when a person's life must end. Why not prohibit capital punishment? Because God told people that certain acts are punished by death. There is another philosophical problem . . . .

This very long discussion points out the importance of philosophy in history and its failure to advance the human condition. Three thousand years of arguments concerning what is real, is there a god (or gods), the nature of humanity, the nature of god, and the rest have failed to produce a genuine agreement as to "truth" or anything else at a foundational level, thereby leaving the human condition where it was before the arguments began. Nonetheless, our philosophical beliefs guide our decisions, and decisions make history.

Propaganda

Propaganda has played a large role in human society from the inception of social interaction. The myth of the ruler being a god on earth is one kind of propaganda found in the ancient world. During the American Revolution the pamphlet *Common Sense* was a masterful piece of American propaganda, and probably saved the cause. The modern world, with the Internet, cell phones, television, radio, newspapers, and other information outlets is replete with propaganda; however, few recognize it as such. Modern Sophists, people interested in forwarding their agenda without regard for the truth, literally rule the media on political and social issues. During political campaigns their presence is especially noticeable, but most people are not used to discerning the difference between propaganda and the truth. As a result, "spin" (propaganda) is increasingly effective.

Another form of modern propaganda, originally honed by Adolf Hitler and his genius associate Dr. J. Gobbles, was the **big lie** technique. In this method, a very great lie is presented so it is easy to recall. Then the big lie is repeated endlessly and in scores of different ways. The goal is *not* for the entire lie to be accepted, but it aims for the acceptance of at least part of the lie. For example, during the Iraqi War protestors raised the chant (and also signage) that, "Bush lied, men died." Note the phrase was presented in an easy to recall fashion. President Bush did not lie about the war and men die every day for a variety of reasons; however, if the general public accepted that President Bush failed to say everything he could have, then the propaganda had achieved its purpose.

Modern propaganda turns to emotional responses to achieve its goals often without the recipient of the propaganda ever knowing what is happening to them. During the 1964 US Presidential election, President Johnson's team ran an ad showing a young girl picking flowers suddenly engulfed in an atomic explosion. This was followed by "Vote for Johnson" silently placed on the screen. The real impact was not logical, it was visceral. It implied his opponent was a war monger. This kind of emotional appeal is still present, but it is done in ways that are far more subtle. Today, propaganda artists make earlier work look amateurish, and this is a crucial problem for modern democratic societies.

Propaganda in all its subtle forms including sophistry, visceral methods, psychological methods, big lies and the rest is coupled with mass marketing through television, radio, the print media, and the Internet and now poses a real problem for the Western Democracies. If public opinion can be manipulated using the modern media, then elections and law making will warp to the side of those with the best, and maybe the most expensive, sophist and propaganda artists. This will make democracy something less than the will of the people and more of the will of the manipulators. If history is any guide, the ability to manipulate the masses will grow exponentially.

Beyond the Cold War

After the Cold War, the United States was the only "superpower" on the planet. Today, China is one of the foremost nations in the world, and its technological, economic, and military rise has been swift. China is a superpower by any standard, and many Asian nations are falling under the broadening Chinese sphere of influence. China became communist in 1949, and until the death of Mao it was fraught with political and economic repression. Mao's death on September 9, 1976 allowed Deng Xiaoping to take over. President Nixon's visit to China in 1972 started the process of opening the nation up to economic reform, and Deng Xiaoping acted to expand the economy through doses of capitalism. It worked. China is growing to be the most economically powerful nation on earth. Nonetheless, the political repression remains. The rise of China also threatens the survival of Taiwan. As China is communist and seeking more power and influence in the world, this will result in yet another challenge to the democracies. In the East, Japan remains the only indigenous power that can match the Chinese economically; however, it cannot match the Chinese militarily. The testing of medium-range missiles by North Korea in 2007, another communist power, threatens Japan as well.

The fall of the USSR led to a bad economic time in Russia. Criminal elements literally stole the Russian economy and destroyed it for their own gain. After the fall of the communists dictators, Russia turned to democracy as their plan for the future; however, as time has moved forward the forces of democracy began to lose out to the forces of totalitarianism in Russia, and the elections put men into power who were not going to leave when their terms of office expired. As former strong men in the old USSR began to move to the top of Russian politics, they promised a return to past glories by confronting America and building up the Russian military to match the West. It seems old ways die hard, and Russia is turning back to its past of individual oppression and state supremacy. It appears that the dictators are returning as men such as Putin find ways to stay in office, newspaper reporters are murdered, the Russian legislature has less and less power, and foreigners who report on the activities of the Kremlin die mysterious deaths by radiation poisoning—or they just disappear into the snows of Moscow. As Russia melts into its past and transforms itself back to its old monstrous self, the impact on the world will be profound; however, it is too early to say where this will go. All the observer can do is compare where Russia seems to be going with where they were in the past and report that the ground looks familiar.

Europe is also growing into an economic powerhouse through its uniting in any economic, and now political, union. After the EEC showed its promise in the 1960s, other European nations began to join. They formed into a single market and a free trade zone named the European Union in 1995. Then they moved to a single currency about 2002, the Euro. Since 1995 the number of nations in the EU has swollen dramatically. As economic freedom and prosperity has advanced, so has democracy. Several former semi-dictatorial states in the EU have moved to a democratic way of government. Overall, the EU has been a dramatic success.

As World War II ended, a new international organization was set up to help prevent new wars, the **United Nations**. The organization started with hope, but as the years went on it became a debating society much like the League of Nations. Without total support from the Security Council the United Nations cannot act. There is a clear division in the world between political philosophies, and each of those philosophies sit on the Security Council; thus, when one party wants to act at least one other does not resulting in constant deadlock. Even when outright slaughters are ongoing the United Nations does not move. In Rwanda, a devastating slaughter has been going on for years, and the United Nations either cannot or does not wish to stop the murder. Even though UN forces went to Rwanda they were inadequate in size, training, and motivation; thus, the mission failed and the slaughter continued. In other areas of Africa, such as the Sudan, Muslims massacre Christians and the United Nations does not act. Famines take place all over the globe, but unless nations such as the United States do something, the United Nations seldom moves. In the United Nations no criticism can be made of such goings-on because the body will not stand for such criticism. Religiously antagonistic and 'have not" states, whose agendas for the world are illiberal in the extreme, greatly outnumber the Western Democracies and consistently vote against the agendas of the West. Under these conditions the United Nations has devolved into stagnation.

Where the post-modern world will take humanity is difficult to say. Europe has shattered into a hive of small competing ethic regions. The same fracturing appears to be happening in Asia, Africa, and perhaps Latin America. Everyone wants to rule themselves. The shattering into small politically independent, but economically dependent, nations can hurt trade. Can these tiny areas really survive? The unifying force of religion is failing, as radical Islam stupidly adopts violence to unite people. Violence is the last method that works to unite people.

There are several trends influencing the modern world. Let's take a quick look:

TECHNOLOGY

Technology is alive and well in our modern world. It is intrusive, complex, and allows technocrats tremendous power over those who do not understand the machines that technocrats have mastered. Computers are now tied to every aspect of life in the modern Western world. Mobile telephones are everywhere, and the World Wide Web (the INTERNET) has proliferated beyond comprehension.

The start of much of this technological wizardry was the Space Race between the USSR and America. In 1961 when President Kennedy announced that America would reach the moon before the decade was out, computers were machines that filled entire rooms. The number of vacuum tubes in computing machines like Univac numbered in the thousands (and they burned out a lot). One of the major accomplishments of the space program was to shrink computing technology to diminutive scales so they could fit onto spacecraft and help navigate and otherwise assist the astronauts in the complex flying needed to reach and return from space.

When the United States landed on the surface of the moon on *July 20, 1969*, it was the result of fantastic progress in marrying machines with computers. Neil Armstrong (the first man on the moon's surface) and Buzz Aldrin (the second) were able to transmit from the moon to the Earth with radios that were minuscule compared to those available in 1960. When IBM launched its first personal computer it could address a maximum of 640 kilobytes of information at once. Now (2010) computers can address gigabytes of information with no problem. The growth of the power of the computer is one of the phenomena of the twentieth and twenty-first centuries that will reach far into the future. There is little doubt technology will continue to power the machines of the future, but the future itself may be dark or bright. The machines and computers will not decide that issue; *people* will decide.

In 1974, a group of computer geniuses invented the protocol that would lead to the **Internet.** In 1992, the number of Internet users was extremely small, but by 2006, the number had grown to 350 million with millions more being added each year. The worldwide acceptance of the Internet and computers displays the acceptance of change in the Western world. The Internet has had a dramatic impact on societies in the West, and its impact will only grow as computers and transmission techniques become better and faster.

Bureaucracy and technology nowadays unite in both wonderful and dangerous ways. We cover this topic in the section on Bureaucracy in the Modern World (below).

WAR

First the good news; since 1945 there have been no general wars between any of the great powers. The bad news is war is changing rather dramatically in the twenty-first century. The super weapons owned by the United States and other technologically advanced nation states are virtually useless against **insurgents** who are able to hide among the population and strike indiscriminately and without warning. This type of warfare is the most difficult for the Western Democracies to face because it is very different from previous conflicts, and it forces the West to get involved in cultures they do not understand. Winning the support of the populace is not an easy matter for political entities viewed as former imperial powers or, going even further back, crusaders.

The insurgents strike soft points for the purpose of inflicting casualties and gaining worldwide headlines. These tactics will be successful if the insurgents can carry them out consistently and wear down the forces of the West. The new form of warfare favors the enemies of the West because as long as they can keep or obtain the allegiance of the locals the Western powers cannot successfully prevail against them. The native factions making this kind of war often use terror tactics to gain and keep control of local populations. Thus, to "win" such a conflict the West must learn the ways of the locals and then attempt to convince them that democracy and moderation is the path to a better future. If for any reason the West fails in this endeavor, then the opposing combatants will continue to avoid capture and continue to inflict losses. The West should note that for hundreds of years the eastern cultures have been living next door and have not adopted Western ideas. Will they now choose to do so just because Western military units reside in or near their land? (See*: The Accidental Guerilla, by D.* Kilcullen, Oxford University Press, *2009)389*

Good intelligence is the key to victory in these new wars. What must happen for the West to succeed is that the locals must give away the positions of the insurgents and warn the Western Democracies fighting in the area of planned raids or the placement of bombs and other traps. A clear indication of nearing victory is an increase in accurate intelligence from locals wanting the insurgents out of their area. A clear indication of nearing defeat is zero intelligence tips, for whatever reasons. Thus far, the Western Democracies have not adapted well to this new form of warfare. Corruption in foreign governments presents a significant problem—if not the most significant. Budgets for the Western Democracies show the spending levels for massive new weapons systems to fight World War II type contests are either stable

---

389 Notice the West had not adopted eastern ideas of totalitarian governments and individual subservience to the state. If we do not adopt their ideas, why do we believe they will adopt ours?

or rising. To win the new wars the West must spend funds on additional intensive training and new specialized equipment for their foot soldiers and avoid spending excessive sums on super weapons capable of destroying entire regions in one blow.

Even as insurgent warfare is thrust on the West the old form of all-out war is still a threat. Red China still possesses a massive army, navy, and air force that threaten neighboring nations. The survival of Taiwan depends on US military protection. Russia is rebuilding its old nuclear arsenal and improving its military to enable it to challenge the West. These facts force the United States to maintain both a reasonably sized, technologically proficient conventional force, and, additional, highly trained and mobile forces to thwart insurgents that may gain control of vital raw materials or nuclear weapons. Maintaining these dual forces is expensive, and deploying to long wars without obvious endings will drain the financial resources and damage the political will of the United States and other Western Democracies.

In the war on terror, the atomic bomb changes everything. Now a small and otherwise inconsequential nation can literally destroy millions at one blow. If Iran or North Korea were unable to gain atomic weapons how much of a threat would they comprise? Without atomic weapons, the terrorist's threat is much less viable. With atomic weapons a terrorist state can shake the world to its foundations. All this puts the entire world on a razor's edge because there are so many nations controlled by leaders who would use atomic weapons without compunction.

Lack of political will to fight the long wars of insurgency is the most significant threat to the survival of the Western Democracies. As monolithic religious sects take over nation after nation in the Middle East, and elsewhere, the challenge to the West becomes ever greater. Meanwhile, the Western Democracies will debate the morality, cost, effectiveness, and sacrifice necessary to win these wars and will most often decide to pull out after a few years or high casualties—if history is any guide. The citizen of the Western Democracies hold their military to the highest standards of warfare, while their enemies of are held to no standard whatsoever. From a "political will" point of view the West is in trouble. Contrary to many views on the subject, the United States and the West ***can lose*** the war against terrorism, and the consequences would be devastating for the world.

US Civil Rights Movement

1955 to present day (2010)

The civil rights movement that began before the US Civil War, and ended with the nadir of Reconstruction, would return in the late 1950s and continue through the 1960s and beyond as the Reverend Martin Luther King and others began nonviolent opposition to laws in southern US states relegating blacks to inferior citizenship. A series of laws enacted by Congress, with substantial backing from people of all races in areas outside and inside the South, reinforced the political rights of blacks throughout the United States of America. The *Civil Rights Act of 1964*, the *Voting Rights Act of 1965* and the *Civil Rights Act of 1968* were just a few of the laws passed to insure civil rights for minorities. In addition, the blacks demanded social equality and equality in employment. Backed by the US Congress and the federal courts, the blacks managed to achieve substantial progress by the end of the 1970s. The civil rights movement continues in 2010, expanding to nonblack minorities, women, and homosexuals who now claim the US is an evil and unfair society.

For reasons difficult to comprehend, after the blacks had gained numerous laws protecting the civil rights of all minorities and numerous laws, regulations, and court decisions giving opportunities that even went so far as to discriminate against whites, the blacks still argued for more. Worse, the leaders of blacks and other minorities began contending that the United States was a fascist nation unworthy of their support. This contention of an evil United States spread and became a commonly held belief in many minority groups throughout the country. For example, black churches openly teach that the Federal Government invented the AIDS virus to kill black people, and under so called "Liberation Theology" black and minority churches openly call for violence against the white race and the overthrow of the US government.

What has been forgotten by a substantial number of blacks and other minorities (who by 2010 were majorities in many cities) is how the white race in America made sure minorities were protected and gained an equal place in society. In 1865, after suffering almost a million casualties in the Civil War, white northern soldiers and the US Congress freed the black slaves and passed Constitutional Amendments to protect their civil rights. In the 1960s, few blacks were in Congress when the civil rights acts were passed, and the judges from 1960 to 2010 making favorable decisions for minorities were white. Poor as this may sound, *white America freed the blacks who now seemingly hate them.* Somehow, freedoms won via the white majority caused blacks to believe they still suffer from oppression.

This mind-set is irrational. In one black rally in the 1990s, a sign held by a black protester read, "It takes a nation of millions to hold us back." The expression of this sentiment takes place after the Civil War and a million Union casualties, the passage of numerous civil rights laws by a white congress, plentiful federal and state court decisions favoring minorities by white judges, affirmative action (which is actually discrimination against whites), lowered entrance requirements for minorities in prestigious schools, and many other social and economic advantages bestowed in the name of race relations. On top of all this, blacks and other minorities received trillions of dollars over the years in financial aid from the federal and state governments, nearly all of which came from white America. How strange, that the groups most helped by America are the ones hating America so ferociously?

Blacks argue the white majority had to give them freedom; otherwise, the black race would rise up and destroy America. Obviously, the blacks and their leaders forget what Stalin, Hitler, Mao, and many other tyrants did to their populations without incurring any real problems. Do blacks believe their efforts could succeed under Adolf Hitler? Is there any doubt Stalin would take glee in murdering every single black he could reach? If the northern whites and southern liberals had withheld their support in the 1960s, blacks could not have gained government protection in the South. It takes only a few highly placed members of government with a few troops to oppress the population as shown by the Nazis in France after 1940. The Nazis kept control of France with very few troops because any transgression was punished with barbaric severity which discouraged most people from being brave. It would have been the same in the South of 1960 had the white race throughout the US decided to ignore the plight of the blacks. Only in the Western Democracies would such a small group have so much impact on the laws and culture of a nation. And yet, the very system allowing this adjustment to take place by increasing their freedoms generates hate from blacks and other minorities beyond all reason.

I know of no one who has studied this phenomenon and how it came about. This odd sequence of events needs study because it defies reason. Of course, as I have pointed out previously, irrationality is a hallmark of human existence.

Bureaucracy in the Modern World

A **bureaucracy** is a *group of officials who help leaders make and then carry out decisions.* Such groups are *extremely* important in the modern world and have been around since ancient times. The Egyptian and Mesopotamian empires had bureaucracies. Rome had outstanding administrators (another word for bureaucrat) running its empire. In China, their bureaucracy leapt ahead of others with the invention of civil service, wherein a person had to test and qualify to become part of the administration and remained in place even if the government changed (well, not always). At least they came up with the idea of a *professional group* of people to assist the leaders in making and carrying out decisions.

In the Dark Ages there was a widespread administrative breakdown. The notable exception was the Catholic Church which developed a very good set of administrators within a framework of hierarchical positions that still exists and functions well today. By the 1800s, with empires spanning the globe, good administrators were needed everywhere to keep faraway governments and government agencies running smoothly. England sent out its administrators with broad powers to deal with events in the colonies because these men could not wait for a reply from London before making a decision. One reason the English empire lasted so long was that its field administrators did a good job.

As the world moved into the twentieth century administrators everywhere gained power. Modern governments needed more control over people. Governments had to control who obtained drivers licenses, medical licenses, mail carriers needed to know where to deliver the mail, cars needed registration for tax purposes and to help prevent theft, censuses were required to find out how many people lived in the nation, the military wanted civilians registered so the government could know who to draft in case of war, and on and on. By 1914, governments intruded on the lives of individuals as never before, accomplishing the imposition with bureaucracies tracking and ordering numerous aspects of life for their political masters.

By the 1940s, these bureaucracies had developed to the point that dictators such as Hitler and Stalin could use them to control the population. The modern state with modern technology turned the bureaucracy deadly.

The administrators of the Third Reich and the USSR were unthinking, machine like people willing to grind citizens into rubble for the sake of the state, if so ordered by their murdering masters. Without this newer and more thorough bureaucracy, the dictators would have had a much harder time ruling, but with modern bureaucracy the modern state could control individuals very closely. We must remember that governments are things in and of themselves. Government will act in its own self interest as it is not a benign entity. As such, a government will use whatever powers can be acquired to control or suppress people that can harm it or dilute its power. Every government, democratic or autocratic, will do this just because it is the government. Modern machines will increase the power of the government dramatically and thus reduce the power of the individual dramatically.

The ability to categorize and track citizens has increased markedly with the expanding capability of the computer. This ever-multiplying capability to track every aspect of people's lives amplifies the power of these unseen and unknown administrators who eagerly carry out any command, no matter how evil, of their political rulers. Bureaucracies now hold tremendous power because of technology and its ability to identify and investigate individuals in the populace. As powerful computers begin to correlate the substantial number of individual records such as birth, medical, employment, military, tax, and many more such items, they will also electronically combine this data, thereby multiplying the authority of bureaucrats—and the government. Computers combined with satellites make tracking vehicles and people much easier, and this too will add to the capability of the bureaucracy to control individual lives. Dictators and quasi-authoritarians could make full use of this kind of capability, and the bureaucracy will fully cooperate because it is their job to obey the orders of the government.

This is a growing trend in the modern world. Without some supervision, the administrators can become dictators themselves. More administrative regulations are adopted in the United States than there are laws coming out of Congress. These regulations have large impacts on everyday people, their employment, and many facets of their daily life, but few recognize the administrative intrusion. In 2010, President Obama appointed over 100 Czars to oversee various aspects of his administration. To date, no one has reported the responsibilities of the Czars, what powers were conferred, and it is unknown to whom they report. The growth of a bureaucracy beyond legislative control is dangerous. Watching and controlling the bureaucracies is every bit as important as watching and controlling legislators, presidents, or the military because they can be freedom's greatest threat.

This growth of bureaucracy is an important part of world history. Without an improvement of the ability to carry out the demands of faraway governments empires could not have existed as they did in 1800. This same growth in administrative ability allowed modern states to evolve. We should note that if a needed bureaucracy does not operate well the public pays a high price. Bureaucrats handle emergency response, and deadly results are common where bureaucracies are nonexistent or poorly organized. The 2004 tsunamis hitting the South Pacific islands near Borneo devastated the area. Local bureaucracies failed to respond effectively; consequently, the number of deaths substantially increased.

In the United States, governmental educational institutions are failing as shown by falling scores on standardized tests and the graduation of students who cannot read their own diploma. Children graduate from high school unable to read or comprehend simple mathematical equations. This is a fundamental failure of the bureaucracy. Because education in the United States is a government bureaucracy it cannot be easily changed; thus, the children and the public continue to be the victims of this bureaucratic malfeasance.

Not all bureaucracies are controlled by the government. The East India Company, run by its private corporate board in England, had a great impact on world trade and government policy. Other large corporations with well functioning bureaucracies have also dominated the world scene from time to time. IBM certainly had a massive impact on the world with its computers, and automobile companies have made a monumental difference in the world as did railroad companies in the 1800s. Without able and well functioning bureaucracies none of these business enterprises could have accomplished much, but with such bureaucracies they had a worldwide influence. Thus, the contradiction of modern societies needing well-functioning bureaucracies, but these same instruments of the state can be turned against the people with stunning negative consequences.

The Future and our Ability to Discern the Future

Art can tell us about the future, or so it seems. Painting, music, and literature foretold a dark era of chaos before World War I descended upon the world. In the paintings of Leonardo da Vinci, the world is an orderly, unified, and beautiful place. In modern art, the world becomes unrecognizable, ugly, and chaotic. Classical music is a world of wonderful harmony, where everything fits together perfectly, and each note enjoys its exacting place. By the time of World War I music started showing the world as chaotic, disjointed, and ugly.

Examining the world of art and music as of 2010, we enter a dark and chaotic place where humanity is without meaning, and normality is nonexistent. In modern paintings, artists smear feces onto a canvas and win art competitions. The public coffers paid for a painting of Jesus upside down in a bucket of urine. In a painting entitled *A Bigger Splash,* no person is present, and only the aftermath of the action of diving into a pool is seen. People portrayed in film are often dirty, evil, tattoo covered, smoking, drinking, drug using, violent, and immoral scum without purpose or direction in life. In films, sex is no more than an animalistic act with no purpose beyond personal gratification. The big city environment is portrayed as a filthy, graffiti covered, trash filled, dangerous wasteland where anything resembling classical normalcy is a joke. Propaganda films are easily sold as fact (*Sicko, Bowling for Columbine, An Inconvenient Truth*). TV programs in the post-modern era often reflect the meaninglessness of human existence (*Sex in the City, Seinfeld*).

Music reflects the new worldview of nothingness and meaninglessness. In the classical era of symphonies, brilliant men were creating exceptionally complex musical compositions where every note was vital. Each note fit into its place with such precision that even the smallest nuance had meaning. If even one note was lost or out of place the overall harmony and perfection of the music was lost. In the 1940s, the music was also complex with many instruments playing together in a unified whole, and the accompaniment of the vocal artists joined with exactness into the whole (the Andrews Sisters, Benny Goodman, Glen Miller). These songs and musical numbers were a team effort where each person played an important part; accordingly, if someone were out of step or off-key, the entire piece suffered. In popular music of the 1950s through 1980s one could normally discern each note played and each word sung in a musical piece. In this era the music was simplistic with few people needed to perform the song or instrumental. Nonetheless, each note of the song was important, and leaving out a note or a word was noticeable, if not destructive, of the whole.

By 2010, music had devolved into stochastic sounds where volume is often more important than any other aspect of the music. So-called rap music had the simplest of beats, no musical accompaniment at all, and is reminiscent of the Gregorian chant of the Dark Ages. It is only lacking in the harmony found in the chant. In other modern music, individual instrumental notes are unrecognizable and the words of the performers blur into a haze of sound, usually covered by the almost-incomprehensible hammering of the instruments where individual notes do not exist. In modern music, individual notes or words have no importance. If a note or an entire range of notes disappeared few would notice. When words are noticeable, they are often vile in nature and espouse the worst of actions. Both the words and the music paint a dark and sinister world composed of little good and constant evil. Good is unrecognized in most post 1990s music as suicide, drug use, violence, and crime are extolled as desirable.

Since the individual notes have no meaning or importance, the message is that the individual has no meaning or importance. Life has no meaning, just as the music, the notes, the vocals, and the performers have no meaning. Finding unity, order, beauty, or harmony in this music is impossible; therefore, finding unity, order, beauty, or harmony in the world is impossible.

Post-modern music and painting depict a world without reason or meaning where the individual is without importance or value; in consequence, the arts say our world is dark, sinister, and filled with chaos. Note the painting "**Vine**" by Brice Marden (Figure 83). In this painting the world is without form or meaning, as the shadows and the substance merge into meaningless lines going nowhere and resulting in chaos. Note that a vine is a living growing entity, normally reaching for the sun and sprouting leaves, but in this painting even the vine cannot discern where the sun is and does not have leaves. The sun is out (note the shadows), but the vine is not reaching for the sun. It is lost and alone. Without leaves the vine is dead and without purpose like modern "life". (Fortunately, anyone looking at a real vine would see extreme order, beauty, and purposefulness.)

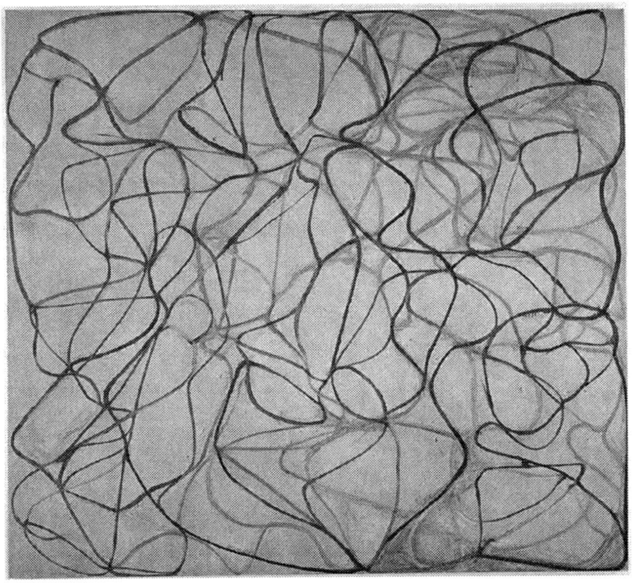

FIGURE 83 B. MARDEN, VINE, 1992-1993

This worldview of meaninglessness does have challengers. Classic music survives as the scores to popular films (*Star Wars, Superman, Raiders of the Lost Ark, The Chronicles of Narnia*), some of the best attended movies of all time set forth themes of good versus evil where evil is conquered (The *300, National Treasure, The War of the Worlds, the Star Wars Trilogy, the Passion of the Christ),* and religion has many followers. Still, one must admit the overwhelming popularity of modern music and art tell us that we are under the malevolent influence of World War I, the Depression, World War II, the cold war, and the ever-present danger of atomic annihilation. Cynicism, irrationality, and meaninglessness are the tattoos of modern life, but we also notice the marvels of technology are pointing to a brighter future if our world chooses to embrace it. If one thinks about it, the mere fact that our universe is highly ordered, from the galaxy to the atom, should confirm that life is not just chaos.

Can history tell us to what future the present is heading? Not specifically, but we can make some predictions based on the *assumption* that the *major trends of the past will continue.* By major trends, I do not mean events that have occurred in the past one hundred years, but events with the commonality of repetition that have been recurring for thousands of years.

If we can depend on anything, it will be that **people will keep killing one another**. There will be unremitting wars and slaughters of blameless people. Philosophers of hate will continue to attract adherents who will slaughter others who have the audacity to be different. This really is not a prediction; it is only holding up a mirror to the past, seeing what was, and extrapolating it into what will be.

If technological trends continue as they have since the Paleolithic, computers and **technology will have more and more control over our lives**, and every aspect of our existence may soon be in the hands of machines. Medicine is on the verge of defeating death. Is there any doubt that people start aging because something throws the DNA switches in our genes to command our cells to stop producing the stem cells needed to heal and correct deterioration in our bodies? According to *Science News,* scientists have discovered how to throw certain DNA switches. Once they discover which switches in the DNA code control aging they will be able to throw those switches and stop the aging process. In many ways the future looks bright, but there is always the cloud of human character hanging over humankind. Humans now have the power to destroy the entire planet overnight, and there is no doubt that some people are willing to destroy everything with a smile. Humanity may defeat death, disease, and other human problems with advancing technology, but human nature will remain the same. When it comes to inventing tools humans are unsurpassed. Avoiding our human characteristics for killing, conquest, and control is the problem.

The Hebrew prophets who wrote some three thousand years ago foretold of a future world governed by numbers and occupied by people who lived well past one hundred years of age.[390] These prophets predicted that everyone would have to have a number to buy or sell, and they predicted a one world government that would operate this system. Strangely, in the year 2010, we can see the outlines of this world forming. Prior to the advent of computers it was impossible to understand how everyone could be assigned a number and forced to use it to participate in the economy. With computer technology we can understand how easily the near future could contain such an economic system.

Today, it looks like the Hebrew prophets were right about the future world economy and the possibility of defeating death. These same prophets said the world would end in chaos, war, famine, pestilence, and plague. If this proves to be correct, then the world will end as it existed with the only difference being a much-increased degree of chaos, war, famine, pestilence, and plague. This prediction sounds reasonable given our increase in war-making capability. The world must also take note that our planet is a dynamic place where asteroid strikes, volcanic explosions, and changing weather all place humankind in constant jeopardy. There have been mass extinctions in the past, and we would be foolish to assume there will not be others. The Bible seems[391] to foretell of a combination of man-made and natural destructive events that will annihilate the world. As far as predictions about the future goes, this is about as good as it gets because it nicely covers what has happened in the past and simply brings the events of the past forward—with a twist thrown in of God's return to earth. It is interesting to note that many ancient cultures agree that the world will end in terrible violence.

The only way out of this evil termination of the world is to change human nature, and history says this will not happen. **The one commonality in all history is the unchanging qualities of human nature**. No matter where we

---

390 Isa 65:20. When it speaks of easily living past 100, the era spoken of is thought to be in the millennium, after the return of Christ.

391 I say "seems" because most of this is contained in the book of Revelations, and this last book of the Bible is exceedingly hard to decipher.

study the past, we can count on one never changing thread: human nature stays the same. We can read the writings of Marcus Aurelius (121-80 BC) and discover his thoughts were not so different from ours today, in spite of the gulf of two thousand years between his thoughts and ours. Cain killed Abel for no good reason according to the Bible, and everywhere we look people are still killing one another for no good reason. It seems people have been cheating, lying, seducing, raping, murdering, stealing, and conquering—among a host of other ills—since the human race started. If this does not change then the ancient Hebrew prophets will be correct, and we will end up the same way we started out, murdering one another.

Human nature is dogged by irrationality. People murder with increasing gusto, massive amounts of money are spent buying propaganda, pornography, illegal drugs, other fundamentally irrational things, more nations are acquiring nuclear weapons, and people ignore the plight of others. Meanwhile, science, empirical knowledge, new inventions, and new discoveries continue to accelerate and better the human condition. The dual nature of human beings is clear in this divergence. On the one hand, we enjoy magnificent rationality and progress while on the other hand we suffer irrationality striving to undo every advance. No human society has ever overcome the dual nature of humankind. The future may depend on our ability to meet this heretofore-impossible challenge.

A Final Thought

Look back over the history that we have covered. From the very start of history to the year 2010, at least one political division has been clear. Governments by dictators, kings, and tyrants who believed the state was everything and the individual was nothing, have been faced down by men who thought the individual was greater than the state, and only by respecting the individual did the government have any right to exist. From Marathon to Inchon and beyond, this has been true. It is still true today, and America is currently the only nation able to face down the tyrants and dictators of the world. America alone holds the future of freedom. If the United States of America fails, that dream of individual liberty fails. If radicals manage to change America by degrading its culture and its government America will fail, and with it individual liberty based on individual rights.

Observe closely what is happening around you. Read history and compare the events of the past to the events of today. Evaluate what the results of failure have been throughout time. Then look around and discern how today's decisions bring tomorrow's blessings or curses. *It is decisions that make history.* Make ***your*** decisions in favor of the bright line of liberty for the individual. Uphold the memory of Thermopylae and Trenton. A million ghosts of liberty are looking to you. Learn about the past and then, as you go into the future, *demand that the ancient dream of the individual being greater than the state remains alive and well.*

Your friend,

AD^2

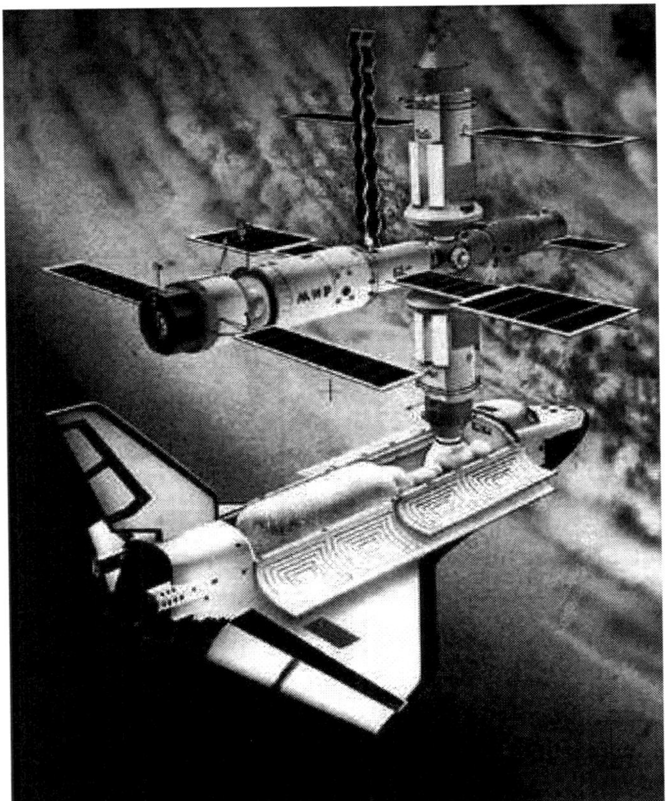

Online Sources

Many of our maps and information for commentary came from ***THE UNITED STATES MILITARY ACADEMY WEST POINT*** history site at:
http://www.dean.usma.edu/history/web03/atlases/AtlasesTable-fContents.html

West Point also publishes a wonderful set of books with attendant maps on World War II, Europe, and the Pacific in separate volumes (one book is text and another is a complete set of maps) and World War I. And the **UNIVERSITY OF TEXAS LIBRARY** Web site at:
http://www.lib.utexas.edu/maps/historical

Wikipedia can be a wonderful resource for information:
http://en.wikipedia.org/wiki/Battle_of_Kursk

will take you to the important WWII battle of Kursk. Type in World War II, and Wikipedia will take you through the entire conflict. The same is true for any era of history from prehistory to the cold war.

The **Hyperwar** site discusses the US Navy in World War II:
http://www.ibiblio.org/hyperwar/USN/USNatWar

US War Photos has an enormous number of excellent photos from WWII
http://www.uswarphotos.com/WWIIPhotos/index.html

The Library of Congress in online and has a vast number of resources
http://www.loc.gov/index.html

This is a link directly to the University of Texas maps of Europe by Perry
http://www.lib.utexas.edu/maps/europe.html

This is a link directly to the University of Texas maps of WWII by Perry
http://www.lib.utexas.edu/maps/historical/history_ww2.html

This is a link directly to the historical maps by William R. Shepherd
http://www.lib.utexas.edu/maps/historical/history_shepherd_1923. html

The *National Atlas* has good resources covering historical as well as modern maps
http://www.nationalatlas.gov/

Table of Figures

Index

A

D

I

J

O

P

Q

R

T

U

W

Edwards Brothers,Inc!
Thorofare, NJ 08086
14 June, 2010
BA2010165